KINO

KINO

A History of
the Russian
and Soviet Film

JAY LEYDA ˌ1910 –

COLLIER BOOKS
New York, New York

The Macmillan Company
866 Third Avenue, New York, N.Y. 10022

Kino *was originally published in Great Britain by George
Allen and Unwin Ltd. and is reprinted by agreement.*

LIBRARY OF CONGRESS CATALOG CARD NUMBER: *72-81661*

First Collier Books Edition 1973

PRINTED IN THE UNITED STATES OF AMERICA

This history is dedicated
to Iris Barry
who helped me begin it
and to Henri Langlois
who helped me complete it

CONTENTS

PLATES

Many of these photographs have been generously provided by
the Rosa Madell Memorial Collection, the Museum of Modern
Art, New York, and the Cinémathèque de Belgique, Brussels.

6 *Plates*

ILLUSTRATIONS IN THE TEXT

AN INTRODUCTION

I have not aimed, in this book, at a total history of a many-sided art and industry. Those who are chiefly interested in the economics of the film business, or in the sociology of the changing Soviet audience will find here only suggestions of those vital factors. Nor have I attempted to trace the influence abroad of the Soviet film, either in film-making or in the quickly responsive other arts; this is a matter that will certainly find elsewhere the ample attention it deserves. My chief aim has been to write a documented account of the artistic development of the Soviet cinema, and to trace the growth of its artists. It is possible that we are still too close to those lives, the recently dead as well as those who continue to make their country's films, to see outlines clearly. A consciousness of a common historical hazard (the too recent past) has prevailed to end my narrative proper with the death of Sergei Eisenstein in 1948. The ten years since then are treated, more generally, in the form of a postscript.

One reason that I undertook this problem in history, more than twenty years ago, was that I then saw an opportunity to throw light on certain evolutionary phases of Soviet cinema, an opportunity based on a familiarity with its films and on some years of personal experience as student and apprentice in the Soviet film industry. The great single works had not then been studied in a context of creative effort. Meanwhile, native historians of their phenomenal art have published surveys of this field, but there is a perspective in a viewpoint from outside. I am not certain that justice has yet been done, and I include this book in my uncertainty, to the extraordinary drama of the Soviet cinema's course. Today the excellent historical studies and detailed research of Soviet film historians show a greater willingness than previously to deal with awkward circumstances of the past, but there are still evasions and total omissions. No matter how plausible such omissions may be, they alter the reality of this history's greatest figures and accomplishments. Criticism of such lapses, as by Pudovkin of the first volume of Lebedev's history, or by Yutkevich of the group effort sponsored by the Academy of Sciences—also a first volume—should promote more historical courage in subsequent volumes. I still find the contemporary source more reliable and candid than historical accounts of the same period.

As in the history of any art, particularly one with such contradictory industrial aspects, the history of Soviet cinema has been an alternating succession of triumphant shocks and shocking (or standard) mistakes; the triumphs reach foreign screens, but we usually hear of the worst in over-eager correspondence, the mistaken films rarely leaving home. There was one period, from 1933 through 1936, when I saw all films released from Soviet studios (and a few unreleased). This was a valuable experience, for the only way to have seen *Salt for Svanetia* and *Snatchers* was to be there at the time, but exposure to the whole Soviet film product was, at first, a blow to my complacent generalizations about The Soviet Film. I grew to realize a deeper value in this, especially as it helped me to understand the struggle that every responsible film artist in any society must maintain against the easily accepted and the skilfully second-rate. That is why, when I read about the creation of any film masterpiece as of some natural fruit ripening in an idyllic atmosphere, I want to remind the people who love those films that masterpieces do not come into being without birthpangs.

I am often surprised to see how heavily the factor of chance weighed in this history, with the delicate balance held by a brave artist or a single far-sighted administrator. It is hard to imagine the world of films without *Potemkin* or *Mother*, but the first could not have been made if its production manager had not allowed Eisenstein to change his plans overnight (partly induced by a change of weather!), and the second might have been left unmade, except for the persistence of a studio official who believed so firmly in the Zarkhi-Pudovkin script that he challenged the powerful bookkeeping department. Dovzhenko, too, clashing with both small and large obstacles, usually won through, beyond the clashes, with a film.

Some less than happy episodes in Soviet film history are set down here. If their open discussion requires justification, this can be my belief that the 'idyllic' account does as little justice to issues as to individuals. And the fact that new thousands of film-makers, in China and Eastern Europe, not to mention new millions of film spectators, are influenced by the Soviet cinema, makes it imperative for any historical analysis of it to avoid concealment or distortion: an ignored mistake can be repeated. I am sure that there are errors of fact and of emphasis in my work, but they are not deliberate or tendentious. Whether true or false, single fragments of evidence are almost meaningless; I am interested in the relations between fragments.

Another matter that may be questioned is the volume of attention given to the supposedly negligible Russian cinema before the Bolshevik Revolution. Until recently Soviet and foreign historians made a total break between films produced in the Russian Empire and those produced under full Soviet authority. (Even now the least studied period is that from October 1917 to the end of NEP production, a period that reflected both past and future.) From the point of view of a young film-maker in 1924, bold with resolution and contemptuous of the past, such a distinction, though not Marxist, is understandable. An article written by Eisenstein shortly before his death describes that attitude:

'The new film specialists did not bring to the cinema a tradition, but a new artistic approach, an intense hatred of what was stale and discarded, an irreconcilable hostility to trash and sensationalism, a firm determination to keep out of the cinema the old and outworn practices entirely unsuited to the expression of the new thoughts, new ideas, new feelings and new words of a new era.'[1]*

This 'rejection' lasted for three decades, with few voices such as Venyamin Vishnevsky's to point to the positive qualities in pre-revolutionary films, and to their links with the present. Even so late as 1935, and in so well-tempered a book as Nilsen's *Cinema as a Graphic Art*, it was apparently difficult to examine these links. But since the last war, when tradition played an important propaganda and morale role, it has been easier to treat all Russian film production as a whole.

---

* Sources, in numbered footnotes, will be found at the end of the text; unless otherwise indicated, translations of citations from foreign-language sources are my own. Mr H. Silverman assisted with most of the citations from French texts.

When Vishnevsky's filmography of 2,000 pre-revolutionary fiction films was published in 1945, a reviewer could remark:

'For many years the history of pre-revolutionary Russian films was treated superficially and one-sidedly. All artistic value was denied films of this period, and hence the pseudo-scientific theory that Soviet film production started from scratch. This idea was entirely erroneous. By October 1917, Russian film producers had created a definite style and artistic school which were reflected in the best pictures of that period.' [2]

Film histories appearing in the Soviet Union since the war have adopted this attitude, trying to show the entire sequence of Russian and Soviet cinema. All such attempts, however, have had to depend more on published materials than on the films themselves, for most of the early works, especially of the war years when there was little distribution abroad *, disappeared (along with most of the films made during the Civil War) when the reconstructed industry was compelled to remove the emulsion from unwanted films in order to re-use the celluloid base. Copies of *The Death Ray* or *Strike* may have been printed on stock once used for the work of Bauer or Kholodnaya. In making any census of pre-1918 Russian films, the list of those preserved at Gosfilmofond, the Moscow archive, should be supplemented by single examples that chance has preserved in other archives, often due to the fact that Yermoliev brought his best productions abroad with his company. There is also a large collection of negatives, made by the Moscow studio of Pathé Frères between 1907 and 1915, stored at the Cinémathèque Française, where it is hoped prints will eventually be made for general examination.

In the appended list, selected from fifty years of Russian and Soviet films, there is no effort to show more than high-lights of these years. The chronological list omits some titles mentioned in the text, yet it covers significant films more systematically. As every film-goer seems to have elected a different film as the best ever made in the Soviet Union, I can only hope that most of these will be found in my selection. I should be glad to hear of unforgiveable omissions.

The individuals who have assisted this work with information and encouragement have grown so numerous in the many years since it was first outlined that I cannot trust my memory to do grateful justice to all. I am not sure that all would wish to be thanked. Many film-makers, from the earliest, Doublier and Drankov, have been most generous with their recollections, their documents and photographs. Of nearly equal usefulness to this study have been the memories of many members of the film audience. (For example: though Serge Soudeikine, the stage designer, did not work in Russian films, one of his contributions here is the detailed account of Meyerhold's lost film, *The Picture of Dorian Gray*.) Other Russian friends have kindly read my manuscript to point out its most

---

* Foreign distribution has often proved a boon to film historians; a Stiller film, not in the Swedish archive, has been found in London, and the only extant copy of an important early Chinese film has been returned to China from the Netherlands.

conspicuous errors. It could easily be claimed that a large number of people wrote this book.

Indeed, I doubt whether I would have attempted this particular historical task were it not for the exceptionally articulate habits of Soviet film-makers on every level of responsibility. This may derive from an established tradition among Russian artists of willingly talking about and discussing their work and problems. The historian who works on the United States cinema is not, in this respect, so fortunate.

In documenting the film past, Russian historians have done yeoman service. Among them my greatest debt is to Venyamin Vishnevsky whose death at the end of the war removed the most tireless of all film historians. The work of B. S. Likhachov, Nikolai Yezuitov, Wanda Rosolovskaya, Nikolai Lebedev, and Ilya Weisfeld has all been drawn on beyond the point of acknowledgement. The reader will also see how I have leaned on my English predecessors in this field, Bryher, Thorold Dickinson, Catherine de la Roche. Special thanks are due to Ivor Montagu and to Georges Sadoul for their unstinting help on every kind of problem presented to them.

The three specialised libraries in which most of this book's research was done were the libraries of the Museum of Modern Art in New York, of the British Film Institute, and the Fonds Rondel of the Bibliothèque de l'Arsenal. Other collections used were those of the New York Public Library, the British Museum, and the Library of the University of California at Los Angeles. The files of Soviet friendship societies in America and Britain have been open to me. To the historian who will some day prepare a less personal history, I should say that certain large research possibilities have not been explored. This history was prepared with only indirect aid from the basic archives at Moscow, nor did I have the opportunity to consult film materials in the Library of Congress, the Hoover War Library, and H. W. L. Dana's collection, recently deposited at Harvard University.

With a grant-in-aid from the Rockefeller Foundation this history was begun for the use of the Museum of Modern Art Film Library, and some of its material was first published as programme notes for their Russian Series. Other portions have previously appeared in *The Hollywood Quarterly, Sight and Sound, The Harvard Advocate, National Board of Review Magazine, Soviet Russia Today, Cinéma 58, Film Quarterly*, and *Understanding the Russians*, the last a collection edited by Bernhard J. Stern and Samuel Smith (Barnes & Noble, New York 1947).

J. L.

London, March 1959.

In the years since this history was published the Soviet cinema has gone through changes nearly as surprising as those between 1917 and 1927. The tinsel glories of Stalin's self-film-portraiture described in Khrushchov's 'secret' speech of February, 1956, were swept into the past, removing some films from distribution altogether; or the more extreme (and often laughable) measure was taken of snipping all the ex-Leader's appearances from such films as *Lenin in October* and the *Maxim* trilogy before re-issuing them. But the 'cult of personality' is too deep rooted an evil to be wholly eradicated. In the summer of 1964, only a few months before the retirement of Khrushchov from public life, I saw the great flapping banners of a central Moscow cinema advertising *Our Dear Nikita Sergeyevich*.

The change of policies announced in 1956 affected Soviet films in more fundamental ways than the disappearance of all the fictional Stalins. Stalinism, in its post-1956 manifestations, was a more real, live enemy to wrestle with. Now it was possible for the bravest people to reveal the true post-war problems of collective farms (*Chairman*, 1965) or administrative bureaucracy (*Your Contemporary*, 1968) or the other untouchable, thorny questions that young people were asking (*Could This Be Love?*, 1962; *I'm Twenty*, 1964), and once again we saw the talents of Soviet film-makers broadening their technical inventiveness with subjects that touched them deeply.

One injustice of the recent past was the subject of two important films. During and after the war any soldier who escaped from German imprisonment found, on his return to Soviet territory, that no honor or sympathy awaited him, only another prison and an accusation of treason. The least punishment he could expect was ostracism and exile. After Stalin's death the first to protest this personal ruling of Stalin was Mikhail Sholokhov, in a bare short story, 'The Fate of a Man.' At this time Sergei Bondarchuk was an established actor; he enrolled in an experimental school at the Mosfilm Studio, whose purpose was to train experienced film workers in other jobs within the profession, cameramen who wanted to try film-writing, actors and scenarists who longed to direct. Bondarchuk joined the course in film direction and chose Sholokhov's story for his test film. This was so good that it won him the chance to make his directorial début at Mosfilm; again he chose 'The Fate of a Man,' in which he also acted. *Fate of a Man* (1959) made such a deep impression on audiences at home and abroad that Bondarchuk soared to the highest level of Soviet film artists, and was assigned to the filming of *War and Peace*.

On his discharge from the army Grigori Chukhrai elected to attend the Film Institute, from which he graduated in 1953. The dramatic beauty of his *Forty-First* (1956) made it possible for him to choose his next subject from his own time and experience: this was *Ballad of a Soldier* (1959), enthusiastically received everywhere —except China. After several months of film work on the post-war life of a Soviet aviator, Chukhrai and the scenarist Khrabrovitsky were emboldened by *Fate of a Man* to concentrate on the more tragic aspect of a crashed, disfigured aviator's return home from a German prison. They junked all they had done and began work on *Clear Skies* (1961) with such passion and anger that it was completed in less time than the partial first version had taken. Since then Chukhrai has maintained a stubborn independence to the point of organizing a new studio for himself and any young film-makers who want to join him. But the might of the film distribution apparatus has stood in the way of this experiment, as it has for each film that is considered to have transgressed 'what Soviet films *should* be.'*

Neither does the film export office encourage artistic or political initiative. There is an enormous back-log of significant films made since 1956 that have never been offered to foreign buyers.† As with front offices everywhere, 'we know best' what foreigners should or want to see. The ignored accumulation contains comedies that we would never suspect were even being made in Soviet studios‡ ('not dignified'), powerful tragedies of the Civil War ('who wants to see a tragedy?!'), personal and pertinent dramas ('not typical')—size is one thing they feel safe about ('no trouble selling *War and Peace*'). In the case of 'controversial' films, the export situation seems hopeless and so it would be if it were not for the Union of Soviet Film-Makers. Fortunately for us it is this Union that chooses the films to be entered in foreign film festivals. The film-makers are genuinely concerned that the best of their work (regardless of 'controversy,' which is usually a domestic matter of no interest abroad) be seen and known by foreign audiences. Without this blessed regulation we might never have seen *Ballad of a Soldier* (Cannes, 1960), *Shadows of Our Forgotten Ancestors* (Mar del Plata, 1965), *The First Teacher* (Venice, 1966), *Andrei Rublyov* (Cannes, 1969), all work by young and determined writers and directors whom Sovexportfilm regards only as 'trouble.'

'Trouble,' otherwise known as creativeness, is springing up in many places and cannot be easily stamped out by narrowly equipped administrators. There is a tradition of surprise in Georgian films, so that the total originality of Ioseliani's *Falling Leaves* (1968) was a confirmation of my belief that it's nearly impossible

---

* Speaking of transgression, this office is also making its contribution to the destruction of the past. In the commercial re-issue of pre-war Soviet films some executive noticed that the original sound-tracks did not sound 'up to standard.' Whereupon a directive: replace these tracks with new ones. Not always consulting or notifying those connected with the original productions who were still alive and working, the distribution office proceeded to dub all voices, to commission new music and to record clean sounds, et voilà!—*these* are now worthy of the larger Soviet audience that wishes to experience our film classics. Strangely, no publicity was given to this cultural victory. The film-makers responsible for the integrity of *Road to Life, Chapayev*, the *Maxim* trilogy, *We from Kronstadt, The Last Night, Baltic Deputy, Lenin in October*, the trilogy of Gorky's childhood, etc. may be in for some shocks, with no stronger action possible than unanswered protests. If any of the world's film archives wish to acquire Soviet films from the first decade of sound-films, they should specify which sound-track version they wish, since it is possible (I hope) that Gosfilmofond, the Soviet film archive, has quietly preserved the originals.

† See Steven Hill's survey of Soviet films by young directors and scenarists in *Film Quarterly*, Summer 1967.

‡ Boris Barnet's lively comedy *The Girl with the Hat-Box* (1927) was recently commercially revived in New York (where it had been shown in 1928 as *Moscow That Laughs and Weeps*). A smiling lady leaving the theatre: 'What a pity they don't make comedies there anymore.'

for a Georgian to make an ordinary film. (I can find nothing in my memory to compare with the violent poetry of Abuladze's *Prayer* [1967].) The gentle, unforced humor and truth of *Falling Leaves*, a film about courage and youth and ideals, is a delight that I wish all could experience. Ioseliani's second film, *From Day to Day* (1971), is even less orthodox (no visible plot), with even more breath-stopping human surprises—perhaps a greater accomplishment than *Falling Leaves*. Mikhail Kobakhidze's graduation film at the Film Institute was *Marriage* (1965), a genuine film-joke of exactly the right proportions. Even the older writers and directors in Tbilisi have been infected by this wave of youthful spirits, and Georgian spectators (not all these films gain national permits) are getting good value for their ticket-money.

Next door is Armenia. Here Parajanov has made *Sayat-Nova*, an astonishing wordless successor to *Shadows of Our Forgotten Ancestors*, and young Armenian graduates of the Film Institute have taken courage from Ioseliani and Georgian originality (with an extra push from Olmi and his beloved *Il Posto*) to create their own film styles.

There are also promises of individual styles in the Moldavian and Uzbek studios, but the rush of first-class films from the Kirghiz Studio is too great an event to be left unnoticed. This quantity of exceptional films can be traced back to one exceptional person. He is Chingiz Aitmatov, to whom Russians refer proudly as the outstanding master of Russian prose today. Through the filming of his stories and his own excitement in the power of film he has developed the Kirghiz Film Studio into a cultural center for the entire Soviet Union—yet not one post-war Kirghiz film (either in Kirghiz or dubbed Russian) has reached a film-theatre in the United States. One film, *The First Teacher*, was included in the Museum of Modern Art's broad retrospective of Soviet cinema in 1969, but that was too limited an audience for such a significant film, and it was not the only Kirghiz production of quality that high—either by Russian or Kirghiz writers and directors. The almost-too-brilliant cameraman for Kalatozov, Sergei Urusevsky, decided that he wanted to direct at least one film (to prove something to himself); it was the Kirghiz Studio in 1969 that invited him to make a film entirely his own, *Beg inokhodtsa* (a particularly prized gait of a horse).* It is the grandson of the painter Konchalovsky who made *The First Teacher* (his first film) at the Kirghiz Studio, and who is now recognized (though not by front offices) as a major Russian film talent. His subsequent film, *Uncle Vanya*, made for Mosfilm, is the first filming of a serious Chekhov play that works as a film; its colour is bold but never intrusive—his grandfather's heritage? *Heat* (1963) was another Kirghiz film that began an important Russian career: Larisa Shepitko's next film, *Wings* (1966), worked with themes never before touched in Soviet films.† In mentioning *Wings* and Shepitko even so briefly, it is impossible to

---

* There is almost none of the display associated with his collaborations with Kalatozov. Kalatozov's *Red Tent* (1970), a reconstruction of the rescue of the Nobile expedition to the North Pole, is an improvement over the several unfortunate co-productions with foreign studios recently.

† Surprising little notice has been taken abroad of the many skilled Soviet women working as directors, writers, and cameramen.

ignore the wonderful and original film-trained actress Maya Bulgakova, who will take any rôle, of any age, and no matter how brief, if it looks difficult enough. As the protagonist of *Wings*, a middle-aged school teacher in a small town, suddenly disgusted with the increasingly narrowing limits of the woman she has become, she forces the spectator to enter her dilemma that is, amazingly for a Soviet film, left unresolved.

The studios of Moscow and Leningrad have by no means lost all their best talents, young or old, to the extraordinary Kirghiz Studio. At Lenfilm the tireless Grigori Kozintsev's *Hamlet* (1966) sharpened his appetite for the depths and heights of Shakespeare; his *King Lear* grew ever deeper and darker in the sad years of its production. Kozintsev is also the leading spirit of his studio's 'graduate class' for young film-makers who have completed their formal training and have studio jobs that they want advanced or changed. In this valuable enterprise there is a resemblance to the unique Balázs Béla Studio in Budapest, exclusively for the independence of the young.

After five years Soviet audiences are finally seeing *Andrei Rublyov*, and it may now go abroad freely. It is an amazing work, far beyond what I expected from the Tarkovsky who made *Ivan's Childhood*. Its plan and script can be considered a joint declaration of the two leading young film talents in Moscow, as Konchalovsky collaborated on the script. Together they made a relentlessly savage historical fable of the artist and society. In this now-past waiting period Tarkovsky began is new film, a science-fiction subject that is looked forward to by young people, in and out of the film industry.

In Moscow at the Gorky Studio (conveniently next door to the Film Institute) Marlen Khutsiyev began his career accompanied by the stormy objections of Khrushchov to his adventurous first film, finally released in 1965 (without much change) as *I'm Twenty*. Also at Gorky, Vasili Shukshin has made a series of realistic bitter-sweet comedies (very popular with Soviet audiences), beginning with *There's a Young Fellow* (1964), that tell more truth about modern Soviet life than the inflated, heroic dramas that seem to be a specialty of this studio. One conspicuous deflation: Mark Donskoy shows less of the intense belief in real characters that made his *Childhood of Maxim Gorky* (1938) internationally admired. But Nikolai Ekk is back at work again after too long and too painful a jobless interval (who denounced *him?*), and that's good news.

Mosfilm, the largest of Soviet film studios, maintains some of the firmest reputations in Soviet film history. I know that Abram Room's *Garnet Bracelet* (1965) had more high praise in its Swedish distribution than it found here. The campaign pursued by Dovzhenko's widow, Julia Solntseva, to film his stories and unrealized scenarios had its greatest success in *The Enchanted Desna* (1965), the film that Dovzhenko dearly wished to make about his own childhood. Working with a Polish team Sergei Yutkevich gambled on an experiment, making *Lenin in Poland* (1966) without any synchronized dialogue—technically a silent film!— and he won, supported by Maxim Strauch (then aged 66) playing a passionate, almost youthful Lenin. The other 1966 film from Mosfilm that will last a long time was at the other end of the age scale: Alexander Mitta's *Someone's Ringing— Open the Door*, a children's film that goes well beyond the traditional limits of such films. In 1967 Mosfilm finished *War and Peace*, to everyone's relief. Khut-siyev's *July Showers* continued this talented and uncurbed career and showed how much Antonioni's attitude influenced him; the result was a fusion of Anton Chekhov and Antonioni—a resemblance never before made so clear. When he's not earning production money, he makes television films or acts in his colleagues' films (all of the youngest directors do this, by the way). In 1968 there was the precise but chilled adaptation by Katanyan and Zarkhi of *Anna Karenina*. The most important film from Mosfilm in 1968 was *Your Contemporary*, directed by Yuli Raisman from a scenario by Yevgeni Gabrilovich.

Gabrilovich? Someone we should know about? Can he be an *auteur* if he 'only' writes films? Yes. In an exclusion of all but directors from a mechanical application of the *auteur* theory the work of Gabrilovich would be one of many stumbling blocks. In his long career of collaboration with Raisman (*The Last Night*, 1937; *Mashenka*, 1942; *Communist*, 1958), no division of responsibility could be fixed—they 'made' these films *together*. Any Soviet film director today knows that a Gabrilovich script guarantees a firm and filmic base. His post-war position closely resembles Pudovkin's pre-war achievement, but present-day international film criticism underestimates the one while over-rating the other. There is a similar historical problem in German film history: without directing a film, Carl Mayer's contribution is indisputable, even when his director was Murnau. And how Gabrilovich has joined another team whose first two films are magnificent: *No Ford Through the Flames* (1968) and *The Beginning* (1970). These are 'written' by Gabrilovich, 'directed' by Gleb Panfilov, and the chief rôle in both is played by the twenty-six-year-old Inna Churikova (now married to Panfilov), whose enormous talent and individual beauty had never before found anything but tiny roles where 'plain, average Russian faces' were needed. This perfect team plans to go on working together. It took forty years to bring Eisenstein's *Strike* to America. Will it take this long for us to be allowed to see the work of this new group? For Sovexportfilm to display its personal dislike for these films is a mistake that harms the image abroad of Soviet culture—these are the Soviet film masterpieces of today that would make us proud, again, that such films are made there. Only in 1971 did the Union find a festival abroad (the New York Film Festival) for *The Beginning*.

Some genres lag behind European accomplishments; Soviet cartoons (though the great talent of Tsekhanovsky was employed until his death in 1965) cannot be compared with the Bulgarian and Yugoslav inventions shown annually at Annecy, in the French Alps, and at Mamaia, on the Romanian coast. But in another genre, the compilation film, the people at both Mosfilm and the Documentary Studio have learned how to gather and manipulate archive footage for political and historical themes. We have lost Esther Schub but gained an experienced recruit from the fictional pavilions of Mosfilm: Mikhail Romm. And Romm did not intend *Ordinary Fascism* (1966) to be his last blow against the cult of personality, but his death left his next blow unfinished. So much buried and 'lost' newsreel footage has been unearthed (sometimes literally!) that Soviet film and television watchers are seeing their own history anew. A typically good new job of this sort is *Tunics and Tails*, on the first Soviet diplomats, written by

Novogrudsky and directed by Lisakovich. I am not very fond of the current 'musical films,' but in the touchier field of filmed opera there have been two victories almost unheard outside the Soviet Union—all the more needed, in that these two operas rarely find place in the repertoires of foreign opera houses: Stroyeva's rich filming of Musorgsky's unfinished *Khovanshchina* (1959, in Shostakovich's orchestration) and Shostakovich's own *Katerina Izmailova* (1967), filmed by Mikhail Shapiro.

The current of talent moving from the State Film Institute into the film crews of fictional and actuality films shows no sign of drying up, with or without the decisions of the domestic distribution system or Sovexportfilm. Kuleshov's death early in 1970 (soon after his seventieth birthday celebration that he was unable to attend) is a great loss; it was he who maintained the continuity of the bravest early Soviet films as inspirations for the youngest generation to invent, invent, invent—and to be honest. He was so proud that Parajanov was one of his students. As an Institute instructor Sergei Gerasimov offers greater freedoms and initiatives than he allows himself in his own films. His classes in acting and direction are now the best in the Institute. Another pioneer from the Kuleshov-Pudovkin tradition heads the camera faculty: Anatoli Golovnya. The most notable of today's and tomorrow's film-makers will point to their initiation at the State Film Institute.

New Haven, 1971　　　　　　　　　　　　　　　　　　　　J.L.

CHAPTER I

The Illusions

1896–1907

In Russia the government fears the current of fresh
air which comes eastwards, and would like to close
all the windows

NARODNAYA VOLYA

In May 1896, the most energetic pioneers of the cinema converged on a new
market, Russia. The coronation of Nikolai II had attracted crowds of visitors to
St Petersburg and Moscow. Among the hundreds of foreign merchants to take
advantage of this ready audience were representatives of the infant film industry,
from France, England, and the United States. It was, justly, the Lumière
Cinématographe that claimed Russia's first film spectators, during a performance
at the 'Aquarium', a St Petersburg summer theatre:

'The "hit" of the programme was of course the notorious cinématographe. It
was shown before the third act of *Alfred-Pasha in Petersburg* . . . and was certainly a novelty of unquestionably great interest. Especially effective were the
pictures of the train's arrival, the fight, the card-game, and the swimming. One
may say with assurance that the cinématographe will be a "magnet" for the
public. . . .'[1]

Two days later, on 19 (o.s.6) May 1896, the Lumière people opened the first
Russian film theatre at 46, Nevsky Prospect.

The English pioneer, Robert Paul, had announced the première of his 'Ani-
matograph' for May 4th, but the actual showing did not take place until May 26,
in the theatre at the Zoo. Also at the end of the month the Edison Kinetophone
was shown to audiences at a Moscow summer theatre, the 'Hermitage'. When
the Edison films were brought to St Petersburg one of their most enthusiastic
and vocal admirers was 73-year-old Vladimir Stasov, the critic who had played
so important a role in the lives of Musorgsky and Rimsky-Korsakov. He reported
his experience to his brother, Dmitri:

'What joy I had on Monday, seeing the *moving photographs*, that magnificent new
invention of the genius Edison. It was Glazunov who took me to see it. He had
been there earlier and his tremendous enthusiasm persuaded me to see it, too.
It is really extraordinary, resembling nothing previously known, and indeed it

could not have existed before our century. Glazunov and I were in such ecstasy
that at the end we applauded noisily and shouted, "Vivat Edison!" . . .

'The thing isn't perfect yet, of course, for the figures and objects and the background often blink and shake . . . but how can the idlers speak against this
magnificent achievement! When a whole train flies from the distance, tearing
aslant through the picture, what comes to mind in that very second is the same
image in *Anna Karenina*—it's almost unimaginable. And when all sorts of people
gaze about as others get off the train, with their bundles and all, and the train
goes on to the next station, and people move here and there in their daily routine
—you see a living crowd!

'Even more astounding is to watch a blacksmith at work, and see the whole
process of his work and the movement of his shoulders and arms . . . This is a
miraculous picture!

'And then to watch the sea moving just a few feet away from our chairs—
Mendelssohn's *Meerstille!*—yet this silvery movement produces a music of
its own. . . .'[2]

The first films to be made in Russia had actually preceded all these public
demonstrations.

After the attention given to the first public projection of the Lumière Cinématographe in the basement of the Grand Café, Paris, on December 28, 1895,
the two brothers made immediate plans to tour the invention throughout the
world, before its novelty wore off, or before rivals and imitators had a chance to
exploit a similar machine. During the single month of January 1896, Félicien
Trewey (a prestidigitator), Alexandre Promio (a booth showman), Francis
Doublier (a 17-year-old laboratory worker at the Lumière factory), and Félix
Mesguich, another *operateur-mécanicien*, were sent to four different corners of
France, Europe and the British Isles to make money with the apparatus in that
limited time that the Lumières imagined possible for their 'device'. The showman,
Promio, was to travel wherever he thought he could find distinguished audiences
to confer prestige on the invention. Young Doublier was given an itinerary that
was made up as fast as Cerf, of *Le Figaro*, could contact concessionaires.*
Louis Lumière placed in Doublier's hands one of the precious machines that
within its compact self and with the addition of simple attachments could be
alternately a camera, a printing machine and a projector, with the strict orders
never to let it out of his sight, and to let neither kings nor beautiful women
examine its mechanism. Setting up a show shop first in Amsterdam, Doublier
was sent a substitute to carry on, while he went on to Munich and Berlin. After
establishing shows there, he was ordered on to Warsaw and, in May, to St Petersburg and Moscow, to await Charles Moisson, chief engineer of the Lumière
plant, who was to film the coronation of Tsar Nikolai II. No one yet had bought
the demonstration concession for Russia.

Nikolai II had remained uncrowned for two years since the death of Alexander
III, but was finally to go through with the ceremony, not in St Petersburg, the
seat of government of the Russian Empire, but in Moscow, the capital of the

* It is through the courtesy and interest of Mr Doublier that the material on this first
step in the history of the Russian cinema has been collected.

ancient tsars. For months the date had been set—May 14th. Through the intercession of the French Embassy, who took all responsibility for the behaviour of the strange-looking machine that clicked as ominously as a time-bomb, the Lumière troupe was allowed to set up its apparatus on a specially built raised platform within the Kremlin courtyard, so as to view the entire movement of the royal procession. Everything passed off smoothly, both the coronation of the last Russian Tsar and the photographing of the first Russian films, consisting of little 60-foot rolls of celluloid to be taken back later to France for careful development*.

Two days after the coronation, another ceremony followed, that of the new Tsar's presentation to the Russian people and the distribution to each of 'a piece of cake, a bag of candy, a goblet bearing the Tsar's monogram, and a sausage, the total value of which was perhaps twenty-five cents,'[3] wrapped in a kerchief printed with portraits of the royal couple. For days people from all over the Empire had arrived at the Khodinka Plain outside of Moscow, where the ceremony was to take place, and by the morning of May 17th, it was estimated that half a million people were standing there, waiting to see their Tsar and receive their souvenirs. Naturally, Moisson and Doublier went out to Khodinka, and prepared to film the occasion from a vantage point on the roof of an unfinished building near the Tsar's stand. Doublier told me of the subsequent events:

'We arrived about eight o'clock in the morning because the ceremony was due to take most of the day, and the Tsar was to arrive early. When I saw some of the souvenirs being handed out ahead of time, I got down and pushed through the very dense crowd to the booths, about 150 feet away. On the way back, the crowd began to push, impatient with the delay and by the time I got within 25 feet of our camera, I heard shrieks behind me and panic spread through the people. I climbed onto a neighbour's shoulders and struggled across the top of the frightened mass. That 25 feet seemed like 25 miles, with the crowd underneath clutching desperately at my feet and biting my legs. When I finally reached the roof again, we were so nervous that we were neither able to guess the enormity of the tragedy nor to turn the camera crank. The light boarding over two large cisterns had given way, and into these and into the ditches near the booths hundreds had fallen, and in the panic thousands more had fallen and been trampled to death. When we came to our senses we began to film the horrible scene. We had brought only five or six of the 60-foot rolls, and we used up three of these on the shrieking, milling, dying mass around the Tsar's canopy where we had expected to film a very different scene. I saw the police charging the crowd in an effort to stop the tidal wave of human beings. We were completely surrounded and it was only two hours later that we were able to think about leaving the place strewn with mangled bodies. Before we could get away the police spotted us, and added us to the bands of arrested correspondents and witnesses. All our equipment was confiscated and we never saw our precious camera again. Because of the camera we were particularly suspect, and we were questioned and detained until the evening of the same day, when the Consul vouched for us.'

* These seven films, as listed in the Lumière catalogue, are included in the appendix of this book.

While the wagons, piled with more than 5,000 bodies, started toward a common grave, the Tsar danced all that night at a ball given by the French Ambassador. Not a word of the disaster reached the Russian press.

A week later the cameramen left Moscow, Moisson to Paris while Doublier, with his second apparatus which had escaped confiscation, went to Schwerin, Germany, to film and to project at the new beach there.

The Government paid particular attention to making the annual Fair at Nizhni-Novgorod attractive this coronation year, and the opening on June 22nd revealed, from the city on the bluff above, a many-coloured, bustling spectacle on the Fair site, down by the Volga. Among the visitors were Tartars, Turks, Georgians, Cossacks, as well as Russians and Europeans, well-to-do people in the majority, in contrast to the usual fair crowd, and all forgetting the Khodinka disaster or pretending that it had never happened. This was the audience that drifted past the Café-Concert of Charles Aumont and stopped before the announcement of 'Living Photography'. They paid 50 kopeks, came in and saw a programme similar to the one shown in the Grand Café basement and on the Nevsky Prospect. The first item was *Arrival of a Train at a Country Station*. This recorded in simplest possible fashion the following action; the train arrives, passing the camera as it slows to a stop, depositing on the platform of Villefranche-sur-Mer a number of passengers laden with bundles and baggage. The passengers, only mildly interested in what must have appeared a peculiar instrument to be found on their familiar railway platform, go home, leaving the screen empty, and that is the end of the film. The other items—cavalry, a falling wall, a beach, a baby being fed breakfast food, an army marching—never made more of an impression than that train. The entire programme lasted about fifteen minutes, but spectators refused to leave until they had seen the train steaming up towards them several times. As all over the world in that year—in London at the Royal Polytechnic Institute, in New York at Koster & Bial's Music Hall,[*] in Spain and in Sweden—Lumière's approaching train brought screams of terror from the more impressionable members of the audience.

There was one young man in the Russian audience who was moved to thoughtful speculation on the future and real meaning of this novelty. This was Maxim Gorky, then reporting the Fair for the Nizhni-Novgorod and Odessa newspapers.[4] He was deeply impressed by the invention, and devoted two articles especially to it, in one of which he says:

'Without fear of exaggeration, a wide use can be predicted for this invention, because of its tremendous novelty. But how great are its results, compared with the expenditure of nervous energy that it requires? Is it possible for it to be applied usefully enough to compensate for the nervous strain it produces in the spectator? A yet more important problem is that our nerves are getting weaker and less reliable, we are reacting less to natural sensations of our daily life, and thirst more eagerly for new strong sensations. The cinematograph gives you all these—cultivating the nerves on the one hand and dulling them on the other! The thirst for such strange, fantastic sensations as it gives will grow ever greater,

[*] Trewey arranged the showing in London, February 20, and Mesguich in New York, June 18.

and we will be increasingly less able and less willing to grasp the everyday impressions of ordinary life. This thirst for the strange and the new can lead us far, very far, and *The Salon of Death* may be brought from Paris of the end of the nineteenth century to Moscow at the beginning of the twentieth.'

Gorky was a truer prophet than he realized—a prophet writing from a city that was later to bear his name. He might have been writing a description of the development of the next sixty years of films, but his words were to apply even more accurately to the pre-revolutionary Russian film than to the films of any other time or place.

Meanwhile the roving demonstrator-publicist, Alexandre Promio, after dropping in on Mesguich in America, also reached Russia and aimed his campaign directly at the royal family. There is no record of his sales technique, but we know that he achieved his end by showing the Lumière programme to the Tsar, Tsaritsa, and entourage on July 7, 1896. Promio's exploits may have been excellent publicity, but they were also expensive, involving his staying at the best hotels all over the world, and an extravagant largess of bribes. His expense account ceased when he was recalled by his employers to Lyon.

But the Cinématographe's success at the Fair and in the Palace had done its work, and in Paris Cerf was approached by the two Grünwald brothers, Ivan and Arthur, who wished to buy the Russian concession. Two mechanics were sent from Lyon to open the Moscow shop, and when Doublier finished in Schwerin, he was sent back in September to take technical charge in the new establishment.

Thus the troupe of Doublier, his assistant Swatton, under the management of Ivan Grünwald, transformed a little store on Kuznetsky Most into the Moscow headquarters of the Cinématographe. There they operated their triple-purpose machine as a camera in the morning, filming Moscow sights and people, as a projector in the afternoon and evening, and as a printing machine, printing the day's newly developed films for the showing the following day. Much of their morning filming was only pretence, merely as ballyhoo for the performance. The store was roomy, and they cooked and slept there too.

The winter of 1896-7 was a disturbing one, both in the Kuznetsky Most store and in the Russian Empire. The great hopes the Russian people had had in their new Tsar were not materializing. A wave of strikes occurred throughout the Empire, mostly in Moscow. The Lumière troupe faced their own crisis when a half-dozen enterprises were set up in Moscow attempting to imitate the cinématographe and its success. But the Frenchmen weathered both winter and crisis by the superior performance of their machine. The over-cautious police made the usual trouble by withholding for two months permission to include in the programme the scenes of the Tsar's visit to Paris.

In March, Arthur Grünwald considered that they had milked dry the machine's Moscow audience, and set off on a grand tour to exploit the Russian Empire. This proved to be a lucky move because a catastrophe in France now seriously affected metropolitan cinema showings everywhere. In May, within a specially erected and flimsy wooden structure, the fashionable annual Charity Bazaar of Paris was taking place. The *beau monde* of Paris was watching an exhibition of the novel *cinématographe* when the pile of unprotected film caught fire, sending the building into a mass of flames in a few moments. The ashes yielded a total of 180 casualities, of whom 130 were notables of France. Hereafter every attempt to set up a cinematographic shop had to face the attacks of public opinion and the press. As the cinema became more and more familiar, it was driven out of town to the outskirts, to country fairs, to the countryside. Thus, through compulsion, the cinema acquired its natural audience—an audience with simple wants, who could not spend very much to satisfy them.

Cheap entertainment was a pressing Russian demand, either in the dust of summer or the mud of spring. Poor people in both town and village were usually reduced to self entertainment—group singing and dancing, but when a show they could afford came within their transportation radius they flocked to it. The theatre forms they saw were either primitive forms or extreme vulgarizations of the theatre as we think of it. The little films were manna from a French heaven. For two more years the wandering troupers were content to suffer Russian cold, some Russian hunger and the intrigues of Mr Grünwald, in order to scrape up all the kopeks as quickly as they could from the huge Russian audience.

By autumn, 1897, the Lumières were beginning to think that there might be more than a short career for their invention. The number of simultaneous and rival inventions was proof of this. Their Russian gold field was showing such nice results, that they encouraged further profits by sending Félix Mesguich to join Doublier and to bring the troupers an enlarged programme of recently filmed subjects to add to the old train, baby and army. Mesguich's first stunt was to show the new films to the Tsar in his southern palace at Livadia:

'I showed views of Russia: Moscow, the Kremlin, the coronation—and some scenes of France. The Tsar professed great interest and asked many questions concerning the mechanism. I explained, and offered him a fragment of film. He held it up to the light, looking through it, and passed the strip from hand to hand. He thanked me and wished me success with the Lumière invention in Russia.'[5]

The Tsar's career as a movie-fan was clearly under way.

Eighteen hundred and ninety-eight gave the Russian Lumières plenty to think about. At the Nizhni-Novgorod Fair of this year, a fire completely destroyed their exhibition booth, and another machine was lost. Mesguich ascribes this to superstitious incendiaries. But the incident made good publicity and the troupe was invited to give their films again at the Aquarium Theatre in St Petersburg on the same programme with Lina Cavalieri and La Belle Otéro, a strikingly vivid Spanish dancer. As a publicity stunt, Mesguich and Doublier filmed Otéro. A noble aide-de-camp assisted as foil and partner, with champagne and kisses. Two nights later the expectant audience, brilliant with grand dukes, ambassadors, and officers, was horrified to see the aide-de-camp so publicly humiliate himself on the screen, and Mesguich, in the booth at the time, was arrested for his 'offence to the Russian army' and taken across the border the same night, under police escort![6] Doublier's luck was holding out and he was not molested. However, just to be on the safe side, he persuaded Grünwald to start south on another tour.

In France the Dreyfus drama was reaching international dimensions. The case of Captain Dreyfus, imprisoned in 1894, was turned into a cause by Emile Zola in 1898, who in turn was tried and sentenced for his criticism of the War Office. In August, Colonel Henry of the French War Office shot himself after confessing his forgery of the Dreyfus documents. Bourgeois complacency was shaken to its foundations by the renewed scandal. Jews throughout the world were excited by this climax to a case which touched their personal and public life so closely. It was at this time that Doublier's tour reached the Jewish districts in South Russia.

During the two days spent in Kishinev, remarks were made about the absence from the programme of pictures of Dreyfus. This gave Doublier an idea that, in its circumstances and its realization, was a forecast of the ingenuity of film theories that were to arise in this same country twenty years later. By the time the show was set up in the next city, Zhitomir, the programme included a new item. Out of the three dozen film subjects they carried with them, Doublier put together a scene of a French army parade led by a captain, one of their street-scenes in Paris showing a large building, a shot of a Finnish tug going out to meet a barge, and a scene of the Delta of the Nile. In this sequence, with a little help from the commentator, and with a great deal of help from the audience's imagination, these scenes told the following story: Dreyfus before his arrest, the Palais de Justice where Dreyfus was court-martialled, Dreyfus being taken to the battleship, and Devil's Island where he was imprisoned, all supposedly taking place in 1894. The new subject was enthusiastically acclaimed, and their two-day stands were jammed as word got around. Doublier banked on an ignorance of dates and a swift departure from each success, before anyone had time to become suspicious. At that, there were occasional embarrassing questions about Dreyfus' height and the lack of foliage on Devil's Island, which the ingenious spiritual ancestor of the experimenting Kuleshov explained away. The trick had to be discarded when they arrived at more metropolitan centres.*

The troupers were not so easily finding cities where 'living photography' was still a novelty. The lode was becoming exhausted. In 1899 the company left Odessa for Constantinople on its way back home to Paris.

Copies and imitations of the Lumière apparatus were circulating through Europe, and the machines of other inventors made 'exclusive rights' an empty phrase. S. M. Nikolsky bought and demonstrated one of Robert Paul's projectors, and later R. I. Stremer brought a Pathé machine to Rostov. In Berlin, Messter sold one of his *Thaumatographs* to a Mr Rosenwald, who with it started his chain of Moscow theatres in 1904. The programmes for these machines came at first from Lumière, Pathé, and Gaumont in France, with a few strays from other countries. Fresh programmes of these 'illusions', as they became popularly known, were constantly being bought or stolen for Russian showing: all of them were attempts to duplicate the success of Lumière's frightening train and attractive box-receipts. After the departure of Doublier, the followers were forced to find greener fields than he had left behind him. They began to tour, not the

* Later, Méliès undisguisedly staged Dreyfus films which were swallowed whole by European audiences.

cities, but the towns, villages, and deeper into the countryside, carrying their own electric current along with them. Many Russians remember the apparatus being set up in the open, behind the rows of benches rented from the undertaker or the confectioner, waiting for the sun to go down, soon to amaze or frighten the audience with their black and white magic.

After the first free-for-all in the Russian country-fair and sideshow market, the French film-manufacturers took over the territory for themselves. The close Russo-French alliance, political and economic, was to be found in every cultural and industrial phase of Russian life. The French film-makers were not slow to take advantage of this and used every unfair and string-pulling method to force their non-French competitors out of the fertile field. The Russians were shown film programmes almost exclusively French in origin. The first film companies represented in Russia were Pathé Frères (in 1904) and Gaumont, and these pioneers held on to the entire market. If there were other film companies or countries other than France making films, Russian audiences were not aware of them. Pathé particularly occupied a strategic position through the entire period of the pre-revolutionary cinema, developing from the chief Russian distributor to one of the chief Russian producers. Both the Pathé and Gaumont companies organized their business on the sales of their respective projection machines, while the films at first were sold outright to the travelling showman; the idea of the rental office had not yet occurred to the industry.[7] The only distinction in price was that the first showman to buy and show a newly imported film paid 50 kopeks a metre, while others paid from 35 to 16 kopeks a metre for their prints.

The first Russian showman to realize the advantages of collecting and renting prints was a Mr Libken of Yaroslavl, who accumulated copies of every film he could afford to buy and rented them out to neighbouring towns and cities. His earnings led him to open several branches as well as to acquire the monopolies (for Siberia and Turkestan only) of the product of Danish 'Nordisk', American 'Vitagraph' and other companies that had not yet penetrated central Russia. One of his followers went so far as to borrow money to *produce* films, but went into bankruptcy in the process and was bought out by Alexander Khanzhonkov, later to assume a leading position among Russian producers.

The Russian cinema showmen preferred to tour. Although a few stationary film-theatres had been set up, these were merely converted shops opening right on the street, and the 'demonstrators', actually the owners of projection machines, found it more profitable to tour Russian centres, giving 'limited engagements'. But as the business became more organized and stable, and as a few of the braver showmen enlarged their repertoires with the help of the new rental agencies, with several programmes going on tour from a central base, it was not long before the most daring risked some of their surplus profits in the complete conversion and redecoration of buildings on the main thoroughfares of the larger cities.

The first showman to comprehend the future of the business that he had adopted as a temporary show idea, was I. A. Gutzman. In 1903 he opened two 'Electric Theatres' in the centre of Moscow, and so successful was the experiment that by 1905 he had a practical monopoly on the new territory of Latvia, a province of the Russian Empire.* He relinquished his hold on Moscow after Henzel and dozens of other brave new souls, moved in. Henzel's theatre, the 'Illusion', on Moscow's Broadway, Tverskaya, found a huge new eager audience, and no one doubted any longer that 'illusions' were a very profitable enterprise.

A thriving growth began in the innumerable renovated stores that posted up red and blue and green placards, as though 1904 had been a festival year, which it certainly was not. The 1904-6 period, a period of the first swift sweep of the film's popularity in pre-war Russia, was also one of the most critical periods in Russian history. In February 1904, the futile Russo-Japanese War began, 'through the greed of not more than half a dozen men who wished to secure in Manchuria vast concessions for their own benefit. This was opposed by the Japanese'[8] (who were after the same concessions), and war broke out. During 1904, the conflicts were between armies, fighting at a comfortable distance away. At home in Russia, the cinema acquired new audiences first from a joyous public sure that Russia would win in the East, then later from among those who wished to escape the horrible news from the Siberian and Manchurian fronts, or rather, as much of the horror in the news as the press censor allowed to be hinted at in the flag-waving editorials. Within this one year, the cinema business in Moscow had grown from such minor expressions as the tiny theatre run by the Belinskaya sisters, seating twenty-four, with standing room for thirty, to Abramovich's magnificent palace, seating 500. It was in this year that Rosenwald opened his 'Kinophone', in the Solodnikov arcade, advertised as 'Cinemo-theatre and display of post-cards, water-colour drawings and paintings', with the special added attraction of 'the greatest phenomenon in the world—an armless painter!— Señor Bartogi'. His was the first electro-theatre with a foyer, and a barker-doorman who drew in the public with shouts and leaflets. Once the public was in, they found a less desirable attraction—a strong smell of frying coming from the kitchen next door. This otherwise well-managed performance lasted for forty-five minutes. Rosenwald paid particular attention to drawing new audience-cadres from the school-children, whom he would approach at recess-time, offering his wares as of special interest to growing boys, with the added inducement of reduced rates. There was still, in 1904, enough confidence in the progress of the war for people to take real interest in the new entertainment. Rosenwald was approached by two visitors from the country whom his barker had lured into the theatre. 'We've been watching your show, and we realize that your method is to keep all those horses and men and equipment behind the screen, but what we want to know is—why do you drag them all here only to show a cannon being fired?' Country fairs had often included Chinese shadow plays, and it is easy to understand that the cinema process was bewildering. The cinema proved itself no ordinary toy by the fact that further knowledge of its tricks did not decrease its audience.

Nineteen hundred and five brought the fighting to the front door. From

* In Riga, Gutzman's two large theatres, the 'Crystal' and the 'Progress', were frequented by a little boy named Sergei Mikhailovich Eisenstein, accompanied not by his parents, but by his nurse because his nurse's dignity was not at stake. The boy was enchanted by the 'illusions' even though he had cried the first time.

January's bloody massacre in St Petersburg of the hundreds led by Father Gapon to ask work and bread of Nikolai II, to December's barricades in Moscow streets, it was a year of little encouragement to establishments for pleasure. The only foreign cameraman known to have been in Russia during this hectic period was Félix Mesguich, now on contract to the Warwick Trading Company. The world had its eyes on the Empire in its struggle with Japan and its threats of domestic trouble, and Mesguich was sent back to it to get pictures of the Tsar. Arriving in January, he found St Petersburg in an atmosphere of impending crisis. Three days after an attempt on the Tsar's life in front of his camera, Mesguich describes the subsequent events of 'Bloody Sunday', January 9th (o.s.):

'St Petersburg was gripped by the uprising. We lived in a state of daily terror and in an atmosphere of inquisition. Police arrested people at random. People on the street were searched, passports repeatedly verified. Day and night Cossack squads guarding Nevsky Prospekt made frequent use of their knouts. I stayed at the Hôtel de France near the Winter Palace. The hotel had been closed but the owners, Renault Frères, permitted a few correspondents to stay . . . The workers of the Putilov factory struck and began political action. On January 22nd, about noon, a crowd swept along the Morskaya right under the windows of the Hôtel de France. My camera was hidden behind a window on the first floor. Through the black curtain it could see without being seen. Suddenly the tide of demonstrators (I was told they were close to a hundred thousand) flowed into the Prospekt moving towards the Triumphal Arch, preceded by ikons and religious banners. They were headed towards the square in front of the Winter Palace where strong detachments of Cossacks and artillery had been posted. A bugle sounded. A squadron of cavalry, swords unsheathed, rode down on the crowd. I heard a terrible fusillade, then the screams of the crowd, trapped by the soldiers and trying to escape. It was a frightful débâcle. I heard the horses' hooves on the cobbles. Blood reddened the snow. Night fell; the strike of the electric workers threw the city into darkness; campfires were lit at the street corners. The wounded were removed in stretchers—hundreds had been killed. . . . ' [9]

Whether Mesguich safely got his film across the border when he left he does not say.

That night Isadora Duncan arrived in St Petersburg, and was astounded by the number of black coffins passing through the streets.[10] The following day she danced for a brilliant audience who obstinately refused to acknowledge, in their gaiety and display, that any tragedy had occurred. The only reflection of Russia's 1905 in the foreign newsreels is either new titles for old scenes, as in a subject entitled *Streets of St Petersburg Before the Revolution*, in which the renter is urged to exert his 'imagination as one views the scenes to picture a Father Gapon leading his hordes of irreconcilables', etc., or deliberately staged events posing as newsreels, such as were produced far from Russia in the Vincennes studios of Pathé Frères, by Ferdinand Zecca. He had discerned film material in newspaper reports of the revolution that alarmed all Europe, and staged a series of films listed in the Pathé catalogue under 'Historical, Political and Topical Events': *Assassination of Grand Duke Sergius, Riot in St Petersburg, Anti-Semitic Atrocities,*

Revolution in Russia, Mutiny in Odessa. This last, directed by Lucien Nonguet, was the first film treatment of the Potemkin mutiny which was to become so famous in film history.*

In Russia probably no one would have had the wish to go to a cinema-theatre, even if these 'documents' had been allowed on Russian screens, there was so much else to think about. One historian says of this period:

'The illusion of the military impregnability of the autocracy was dispelled in Manchuria, and the illusion of its benevolence was rudely shaken by the recollection of "Bloody Sunday" and by the arrest of the working men in the early days of March. The failure of the Government to grapple with the industrial discontent, together with the vanishing of these illusions, acted as a signal for the general uprising of the working class.'[11]

In the summer, when the war's end seemed in sight, a few new proprietors set up shop. One of these was Karl Alksne, who set up the 'Electrobioscope' in an empty store on Strastnoi Boulevard, seating fifty, where he served as cashier and ticket-taker, as well as announcing the programme and raising and lowering the curtain. General strikes in September and December indicated a people too sickened and angry with the mishandling of the war as well as with the severe suppression at home to give business 'confidence'. Neither the city's middle-class audience, nor the peasants and poor workers in the towns and countryside were willing to give time or attention to the 'illusions', so pressing were the realities around them. Too much was happening—physically and psychologically in this period of constant social storms.

Nineteen hundred and five had strengthened liberal and intellectual solidarity to the point where the Tsar and his government were willing to make any temporary concessions, just to remain secure. They consented to the formation of a representative governmental body—a Duma, which would form the Lower House of the Russian parliament, the Upper House of which would be the Imperial Council, partly elective also. As time passed, arrests and repressions returned in full force, until the Social-Democrats were forced to find secret ways of electioneering, as every speaker they put on the street was snapped up by the police. They discovered the advantages of the dark cinema-theatres, and Vsevolod Chaikovsky tells a typical incident of the 1906 elections:

'Before the elections for the First Duma, I remember how, during a film showing in one of the electric-theatres, a voice was heard from somewhere in the completely dark hall, appealing to the audience to vote for the Social-Democratic candidates. In consternation at this illegality, the theatre manager ordered lights up. In a few minutes a pale and shaking police inspector entered the theatre, followed by the manager, frigid with horror. The theatre was crowded and the audience, knowing the strength of its numbers, greeted his frightened search with derision. He finally beat a hasty retreat to an accompaniment of whistling and laughter, empty-handed.'[12]

---

* Georges Sadoul informs me that the English Gaumont catalogue of 1905 also lists such a restoration of the Potemkin mutiny, entitled *Mutiny on a Russian Battleship*, with an identical action.

In May, the First Duma opened, and by July, the Tsar felt powerful enough once again to dissolve it. Immediately there were expressions of distrust; Russian troops mutinied in Helsingfors and August brought within a few feet of Premier Stolypin a badly-aimed bomb. The Tsar see-sawed back and made gestures to distribute land to the peasantry, gestures he did not bother to recall at a later safer time. Through the whole of 1906 and 1907 there were conflicts between Duma and Tsar, culminating in the arrest of 169 members of the First Duma, charged with treason, and ending in the opening, in November 1907, of a purged and packed Third Russian Duma.

Under cover of the political disturbances of this period, the cinema-owners swarmed in from the fairs, where they had advertised 'The Latest Miracle of the Twentieth Century', to the city, where similar advertising methods seemed to attract the supposedly more sophisticated city crowds. Small business men in other businesses began to yearn for this easier money. A typical case of this sort was Hechtmann, an owner of a clock store, who, in the fall of 1906, opened two theatres, both called the 'Grand Parisian Electro Theatre', at Sretenka Gate and on the Arbat. Next to his Sretenka theatre was a furniture store, whose owner within a month turned it into a theatre called the Grand Electro, in order to attract some of the startling profits Hechtmann seemed to be making. Even the luxurious Hotel Metropole transformed one of its ballrooms into the 'Moderne' Cinema.

By 1908 the extension of this business reached a point where it had to be curbed by the authorities, and measures were taken to limit the growth of the film theatres. The new law read, in part: '. . . the electric theatres . . . in the light of their abnormal development must not be established closer than 1,050 feet from one another (this includes show-booths, theatres and other places of distraction) . . . the number of electric theatres in the city of Moscow is not to exceed a total of seventy-five.'

The theatre took fright at this new rival and used all its political influence to have laws passed limiting the hours when electric theatres might function. They brought to the assistance of their growing economic problem all the resources of journalistic and editorial comment. *Moskovski Listok* reminded its readers of the great threat the cinema represented to all the arts. 'Particularly,' it said, imagine what life will be when drama, performed by first-class actors, is replaced entirely by the screen, on which we see only colourless, expressionless simulation!' Although the electric theatres could begin work at any time after noon that they pleased (usually one or three) they were obliged to close at nine p.m. The position of the 'legitimate' theatres became so ridiculous in view of their pretended scorn of the upstart attraction that they compromised at ten-thirty, and capitulated at eleven. Their final humiliation came when a few Moscow theatres included a film programme as an added attraction.

The electric theatres changed their programmes once a week, until competition forced some to change two or three times a week, and one theatre tried to find a new programme every day. An average programme included two, sometimes three dramas, a 'scientific' film, one or two scenics, and three or four comics and 'féeries' all of which lasted about thirty minutes with intermissions to clear the house—a custom that persists till today in Russian film theatres. One technical distinction between the two chief items should be noted; a drama would be confined to four or eight shots, one for each change of scene, while a comedy required ten to fifteen shots, even though its total length was less. The films were yet neither tinted nor toned, which is curious, since all French producers used one or the other colouring processes in their Paris laboratories. Pathé and Gaumont probably were so sure of their Russian public that they felt no need to add additional attractions. Another explanation may be that none of the showmen or theatres was willing to pay the extra amount demanded for tinting or toning. Titles remained in French and adaptation or change was unthought of.

It may be interesting to mention two great sensations of this period. One was *La Vie et la Passion du Christ*, made for Pathé in 1902. This drew the attention and the wrath of the Holy Synod upon it, and over it was fought the first battle of the never-ending war between the Orthodox Church and its fresh rival. When it was first brought to Russia it was censored as a 'violation of the Gospels'. Re-released in 1907 it received wide circulation. Its greatest rival in popularity and sensation was *La Civilization à travers les Ages*, made in 1908 by Georges Méliès.* Beginning with the murder of Abel by Cain it traced murder and inhumanity down through the ages—a forerunner of Griffith's *Intolerance*. The hysteria and fainting fits this film produced made it the constant object of censure, but did not diminish its popularity.

In the general effort to quiet popular anti-government feeling after the disastrous end of the Russo-Japanese War and the uprisings, all press censorship was relaxed. In April 1906 five months after this gesture, all the instruments of government suppression returned in fuller force than ever, and films too were found to need more careful watching. The reaction intensified the pre-revolutionary conservatism which Mirsky has described as 'an intense fear of change, and the conviction that if a stone was touched the whole edifice would fall. It was thus one of the aspects of the degeneracy of the monarchic power, and a sign of growing impotence.'[13]

The forms of film censorship were extremely primitive. Ordinarily, at the first showing of a new programme, the theatre would be visited by the police-inspector to make sure that everything was all right, collecting an appropriate fee for his supervision on his way out. At one time, Gaumont's film adaptation of Turgenev's *Fathers and Sons* was confiscated, making a serious loss to Khanzhonkov, who had imported twenty prints. Later the importers introduced a system of showing to the police single copies of films that had been brought in 'on approval'. One subject was forbidden from the earliest days—that of the French Revolution, no matter how indirectly it figured in the action of the drama. Along with it was banned any film showing the guillotine or the violent death of royalty. Even a film including the execution of Mary Stuart was confiscated. Pornographic films (called 'the Paris genre') were officially declared

---

* Although I find no record of a Russian distributor for the films of Méliès, these were probably distributed (illegally) there, similarly to Lubin's use of them in America. Méliès' *Voyage dans la Lune* (1902) was popularly shown all over Russia, and there is, in the archives of NIS, the Scientific Research Institute, a splendid collection of Méliès films.

illegal in April 1908, and when the film theatre 'Mephistopheles' tested the law by showing a full programme of the forbidden films, the theatre was closed. However, there was one theatre which the police did not visit. This was the 'Patriotic Cinema Theatre', organized by a reactionary, anti-semitic group, who called themselves 'The Union of Russian People.' The policies of the theatre and its powerful backers, actually the notorious 'black hundreds', were supported by the police with veiled approval in exalted quarters. In spite of this aid, the theatre closed when it could not find a producer willing to film the bloody pogroms the 'Union of Russian People' was provoking in all parts of the Russian Empire.

The primitive projector illumination caused acid explosions that injured and often maimed the operators. When electricity was adopted, these explosions were succeeded by far more harmful fires, due to careless protection of the projection booth, and the inexperience of the many hastily hired operators. Loss of life was a frequent occurrence. In magazines and newspapers of the time one finds phrases such as 'victims of cinematography' and 'the dangers of living photography'. This was another weapon for the press and authorities to use against the cinematograph. The medical profession added itself to the cinema's enemies, when audiences were subjected to shaking and chopped prints, due to the anxiety of the exhibitors to squeeze dry of value every foot of film they owned. The films found another, natural enemy in the clergy, who, after a newspaper had run a symposium on the subject, 'May the clergy attend the cinema?' categorically forbade attendance of their order.

Although the business spread, the quality and dignity of films descended, assisted downward by the press, the clergy, the doctors, and the greediness of the exhibitors, to a place on show-booth and vaudeville programmes. A similar situation was occurring in American metropolitan theatres where, once the excitement in *The Great Train Robbery* had died down, and no new film excitement had yet appeared, the upper-class audience avoided it. In a Russian trade paper of 1908, advertisements such as the following appeared:

> Variety numbers available for cinema theatres.
> LIVING PHENOMENA
> 1 Tattooed Lady—An American
> 2 Seventeen-year-old Giant—Weight: 450 lbs
> 3 Amazing Lilliputian—Weight: 35 lbs
> 4 Living Untamed Boa-Constrictors

This degradation was sure to affect the business. The foreign producers and the Russian distributors desperately sought to bolster their once sound investment.

Foreign companies had sent occasional cameramen into Russia to make their own product more international but the first of these to be shown on Russian screens were those taken by Gaumont cameramen* in 1907, whose Russian screening had far-reaching consequences. These four films: 1 *The Third State Duma in Session;* 2 *Review of the Troops by the Royal Family at Tsarskoye Selo;*

---

* 1, 2, and 3 were filmed by Kurt von Hahn-Jagielski whose regular camera job was as official cameraman to the royal family, a job begun in 1900.

3 *Review of the Troops in the Square before the Winter Palace;* 4 *Solemn Procession of Pilgrims at Kiev,* were the first Russians to have wide distribution on Russian screens. The general opinion was that 'we don't look so bad on the screen after all', and the air was full of projects for the production of Russian films. The most ambitious of these was for a film adaptation of Pushkin's *Boris Godunov.* The adaptation was to consist in filming the play's production at the Eden summer theatre, scene for scene, twenty-two scenes in all, which would automatically have meant twenty-two shots in all. 285 metres were shot before the project dropped from view.

Pathé and Gaumont created a more favourable situation for Russian native production than they realized when they built, for their own use, Russian laboratories to expedite the development and printing of their Russian newsreels and scenics, as well as to prepare Russian titles for their importations. All that the Russian film industry needed now, to be born, was an energetic man to take advantage of an already favourable situation.

In the autumn of 1907, newspapers and magazines carried the following advertisement:

FIRST IN RUSSIA

CINEMATOGRAPHIC STUDIO
under the supervision of the well-known photographer for
the Duma, A. O. Drankov
Manufacturers of films for cinema theatres.
Current subjects! Russian events on the screen!
Views of cities and countryside!
New subjects every week!
By request, films can be taken in any community that so desires

With this advertisement, Russian film production announced its first cameraman, and its first producer, Alexander Drankov. Drankov's photographic past was no less splendid than his announcement implies. He had been a photocorrespondent for Russian and foreign illustrated papers, including the *London Illustrated News, L'Illustration* and others. He occupied the honoured position of official photographer for the Duma and its members. Several Russian amateurs, after 1896, purchased and made private use of film apparatus,* but Drankov was the first professional Russian photographer to compete with foreign film-makers.

With this announcement by Drankov, the foreign companies feared a dangerous and perhaps ruinous competition, because the Russian press was expressing a popular demand for native films. As time passed with nothing apparent developing from Drankov's announcement, Pathé rushed into production and distribution (in February 1908) of the first Russian film, *Cossacks of the Don,* 135 metres long, consisting entirely of trick-riding and scenes of camp-life. Its success was prodigious. Every audience demanded to see it over and over. Two hundred and nineteen copies were sold in less than two weeks at seventy-four roubles apiece.

* The earliest recorded Russian cameraman was A. P. Fedetsky who filmed Cossack trick riders on 29 (o.s.15) September 1896, in Kharkov.

In the wake of this victory, Pathé immediately began the release of a series of twenty-one scenic films of Russian life under the general title of *Picturesque Russia*★ greeted with less enthusiasm however, than *Cossacks of the Don* received.

The other major European companies were awakening to the possibilities of the Russian market; the French *Théophile Pathé* and the great Italian firm *Cines* both sent representatives to Moscow. Gaumont realized too late the opportunity it had missed to dominate Russian subject matter, and hurried into the arena with two stop-gap films—*Rostov-on-the-Don* and *The Funeral at Vladimir of the Georgian Archimandrite Nikon*—with little more luck than the hasty attempt of a native Russian, Khanzhonkov. After three trial films—*The Opening of the Monument on the Site of the Murder of the Grand Duke Sergei Alexandrovich* and *Views of the City of Yaroslavl* and a short comedy too poor to be released, Khanzhonkov felt that the making of films was more risk than their distribution, and temporarily retired from the field, leaving it clear for the entrance of Drankov. Khanzhonkov's day was yet to come.

From February 1908, Drankov issued a series of seventeen films, one after another, bringing him a decisive victory over all his competitors, including the all-powerful Pathé. A comparison of the titles of the Drankov series† with those of the Pathé series indicates Drankov's keener appreciation of the film public's desire, particularly the Russian public's, for colourful active incident and variety of setting, than had the Pathé cameraman. Drankov thus became the undisputed monarch of the Russian cinema, and he immediately assumed the position of an important personage, one, by the way, with an unusual talent for publicity. His first move was to employ the customarily quiet summer to consolidate his place in the notice of the public. On June 8th, he invited himself to the wing of the Yelagin Palace where the Premier Stolypin was living. Drankov showed his films to the assembled guests, lunched with them, filmed them afterwards, and even went so far as to announce the film in the press. The Stolypin film was confiscated at once by the police, but Drankov, no wise intimidated, showed his power by having himself brought to Gachina Palace on June 20th, showing his films to the Dowager Empress Marie Fyodorovna and the royal family. The Empress was so enchanted by this first sight of the cinematograph that she demanded a repetition—of those films in which she appeared. Drankov's glorious summer was capped by the International Exposition of the Cinema Industry at Hamburg, where he took his films and captured the now customary acclaim. One result of his Hamburg success was the establishment of Paris connections, offering his 'views' for sale there. Thus Drankov added to his honours that of being the first Russian to export native films.

At this point Khanzhonkov grew impatient, seeing Drankov assume all the honours and power, and began a commercial duel to the death—a duel that was being fought within the young industry in every producing country; Pathé and Gaumont in France, Vitagraph and Lubin in America, copied their rival's successes, fought just as bitter a battle as Drankov and Khanzhonkov did in Russia. The new entrant's first move was to bring to Russia a representative of

---

★ A complete list of these titles has been included in the appendix.
† See appendix.

Itala-Film, planning to beat Drankov with a greater variety of films than he could manage, alone, to make. Drankov's answer was to create another sensation—filming Tolstoy 'himself'.

Alexander Drankov's first victory over Tolstoy's hatred of all photographers was on the occasion of his eightieth birthday. Drankov's aide, here and hereafter, was none other than Tolstoy's wife, Sophia Andreyevna, who had her own reasons for her assistance. In *The Tragedy of Tolstoy*, their daughter Alexandra tells of the birthday ceremonies on August 28, 1908:

'The precursors of every memorable event—the photographers—began to make their appearance at our house. I remember father sitting, exhausted, on the porch with his ailing leg stretched out, and mother coming in to ask him to consent to being photographed for the moving pictures. He made a grimace of pain and started to refuse, but the camera men swore that they were not going to disturb him and would not ask him to pose. They tried to photograph him from the lawn and from the verandah, while father sat motionless, looking before him with a melancholy stare.'

The five metres that Drankov captured on film did excellent business. Since Tolstoy's excommunication from the orthodox church in 1901 for his subversive teaching, he had become a figure who symbolized certain principles to be argued by everyone, often irrespective of his value as an artist. The appearance of Tolstoy on the screen provoked a furore. This 'wild beast in a zoo' glaring from the screen could not possibly be Tolstoy, sympathetic papers protested—'We have been deceived by some made-up actor'. Anti-Tolstoy papers were equally violent—one almost suspects the hand of a modern publicity agent—but all were silenced when the waiting Drankov finally and proudly displayed his proof, a statement from Tolstoy's wife, Sophia Andreyevna, insisting that the film of him be shown 'only on such programmes as are exclusively concerned with scientific and educational material.' If she made this request sincerely, it was at best a gesture; the Tolstoy family had no means of checking Drankov's sales, and Drankov was in business.

Khanzhonkov's move to counter this was a failure. His two small films of *The Mountains of the Caucasus* were met by Drankov, a better showman, with three typical Drankov films of sentiment and action. But Khanzhonkov's next move was a master stroke, leading eventually to Drankov's temporary retirement from active production.

France, at the beginning of the year 1908, had seen the organization of a new film company that was to advance the cinema as an industry, but was to deter its entire development as an art. This, 'Le Film d'Art', was organized for the purpose of presenting famous stage actors in film representations of their famous theatre productions. By the fall of 1908, their films entered the world market, and Khanzhonkov contracted for their Russian distribution. The first film he imported from them was *L'Arlésienne*, 'adapted for the cinema' from the play of Alphonse Daudet by his son Léon Daudet, enacted by the stars of the Odéon and the Comédie Française, and directed by Albert Capellani. *L'Arlésienne* was received with rapture by the Russian public, swelling the film audience with new devotees from the respectable classes, who now conferred dignity and artificiality upon the cinema. Khanzhonkov followed up this success with 'Le Film d'Art's first film *L'Assassinat du Duc de Guise*, which enjoyed an even more dazzling and snobbish success. Everyone interested in the theatre attended, in order to compare Le Bargy's characterization of Henri III with Moskvin's performance in 'Tsar Fyodor Ivanovich', then in its tenth year in the Moscow Art Theatre's repertoire.

Drankov was desperate when he saw that films he had not made were being applauded by a public he had never hoped to reach. He issued *A Fire in St Petersburg*, which, in spite of an intense advertising campaign and the fact that he was employing toned film in variously appropriate colours (blue for night scenes, crimson for the fire, amber for morning, etc.) for the first time in Russia, could not withstand the competition of the great French actors. He even stooped so low as to reissue his earlier film *The Moscow Rogues' Market*, with only slight re-editing, as a new film—*Creatures That Once Were Men—Gorky Characters*—all to no avail.

Other firms were rushing in to profit in Russia. The international 'Eclipse-Radios-Urban' made money with two films: *Catastrophe At Messina* and *The Operations of Dr Doyen* ('five amputations, 420 metres at the unprecedented price of ONE rouble a metre') which regularly sent the eager audience into shrieks and fainting-fits. Gaumont brought in a hopeful innovation—the first animated cartoons to be seen in Russia—the work of Emile Cohl. The British 'Royal Vio' brought to Russia its films of the Russo-Japanese War filmed in both camps, and only now permitted by the authorities to be shown. The war films were shown in the Field of Mars, St Petersburg, with a loud-speaker accompaniment of rifle and cannon-sound, etc. Drankov's position seemed really hopeless when Khanzhonkov imported a third Film d'Art, *L'Empreinte*, with Severin, Max Dearly, and Mistinguett, who was to Europe what Mary Pickford became to America.

B. S. Likhachov sums up this period thus in his history[14]: 'From this it is clearly seen that the cinema in Russia had reached a transition to a new era. Russian film production had not gone further than a "pompous parade" period, and the spectators were demanding dramatic films, as witness their eagerness to see *L'Arlésienne* rather than the arrivals and departures of the Swedish king.' Yet they had demanded Russian films, and were ready to respond immediately to any Russian film with an appearance of being dramatic. Drankov realized this and delivered a blow to his rivals by announcing a film about Stenka Razin; 'arranged with the participation of at least 100 persons—artists from St Petersburg's dramatic theatres in historical costumes with appropriate historical accessories.' In a vivid circular announcement of the film Drankov excelled himself in description. If he produced half of what he promised, the excited public would have had their expectations exceeded. The Duc de Guise and Dr Doyen were forgotten in the excitement, Drankov received advance orders from all corners of the Empire, and a success was prophesied by the whole film business. This was at the end of September 1908. A new epoch was entered. Independent Russian production was about to become a fact.

CHAPTER II

The Costume Business

1908–1911

How charitable are clothes, how beneficient, how
puissant, how inestimably precious. Mine are able
to expand a human cipher into a globe-shadowing
portent; they can command the respect of the whole
world—including my own, which is fading. I will
put them on
          —from *The Czar's Soliloquy* by MARK TWAIN

Drankov, as ever, knew his public well. His choice of the subject and atmosphere
for the first Russian dramatic film was calculated to appeal directly to the romantic
needs of that class of people which composed the film audience. This film
audience had experienced a revolution and, though temporarily defeated, was now
conscious of a strength they had not dreamed of before. Drankov chose to attract
and conciliate them with the character of Stenka Razin, an almost legendary
figure of heroism, a symbol of the Russian people rising against their oppressors.
Conscious, as he was, of his audience's nature, he was even more conscious of
his own class affiliations—and proceeded to water down the hero of the Volga
to the dimensions of a gay, singing, drunken brigand who meets a sad end.
Drankov found opportunity within the ten minutes that the film lasted to
encourage the audience to sing a song that had long been connected with the
fumes of the saloon and with sprawling in gutters—'Down the Mother Volga',
familiarly called the drunkard's ballad. The film was a success in every way
known to our film industry today—it made money, and sent its spectators away
warm but empty.

Stenka Razin was released October 15, 1908,* and showed good results so
quickly that Drankov attempted two Russian film comedies, whose utter failure
engendered the long-standing superstition that Russian film comedies could not
possibly compete with foreign products in this genre. With his government
connections and his success with *Stenka Razin* as levers, he obtained the consent
of the Imperial Alexandrinsky Theatre to film episodes from *The Marriage of
Krechinsky* as played by the great actor Davydov. With this and former victories
to his credit, there were few to dispute the position he assumed as the highest

---

* Theatres were offered with it an overture 'especially' composed by Ippolitov-Ivanov,
that could be performed by chorus, gramophone, piano, or orchestra.

authority on questions of the cinematograph, and he went so far as to give a pompous lecture at the 1908 conference of the Imperial Technical Societies on the subject: 'The relation between the story and the making of a cinematographic film.' But Drankov still felt unsure and shaky in the new field of dramatic production and, deciding to rest on his laurels and consolidate his authority, suddenly announced his temporary retirement from the market while rebuilding and re-equipping his studio. Reluctant to take any retreat without a journalistic effect, he announced that he was too busy organizing the first cinema exposition in Russia (held in the spring of 1909) to produce and rent films.

Within the next two months his old rival Khanzhonkov began dramatic production, and a third new firm was started that was to become a dangerous competitor both to Drankov's future ventures and to Khanzhonkov. On January 1, 1909, Paul Thiemann left his position as director of the Russian office of Gaumont and opened an independent renting office as the Russian representative of Lux and Le Lion of Paris, Warwick of London, Messter of Berlin, Ambrosio of Turin, Vitagraph of New York, and Nordisk of Copenhagen. Thiemann was shortly after joined by another German, a successful tobacco manufacturer named F. Reinhardt, and their first releases, *The Merchant of Venice* and *Saul and David* were as successful as *The Assassination of the Duc de Guise* had been. Shylock and Saul were followed by the first grandiose Italian films to be seen in Russia. Cines showed its two Dumas films *The Three Musketeers* and *The Countess Monsoreau*, and Ambrosio sent in through Thiemann & Reinhardt its *Nero*, whose grand manner and extravagant sets left Russian audiences dazed—until the next and bigger Italian film arrived.

In this new wave of pretentiousness Khanzhonkov's attempt to make such a simple film of Russian life as *Drama in a Gypsy Camp near Moscow* passed unnoticed. Likewise his *Song of the Merchant Kalashnikov*, an experiment with a film drawing upon the Russian past, was a few months ahead of its time and, unfortunately, appeared simultaneously with Pathé's widely publicized introduction to Moscow of the tinted film, *The Manufacture of Bamboo Hats on Sunda Island*. A man with a wide education and considerable knowledge of the arts, Khanzhonkov lavished artistic attention upon his *Kalashnikov*, adapted from a poem by Lermontov. Besides employing as director the scenarist of *Stenka Razin*, Vasili Goncharov, he persuaded Ippolitov-Ivanov to write a special score to accompany the film—but the Russian audience was too preoccupied with the big Italian surprises and with Pathé's marvellously tinted bamboo hats to recognize the film style that was to dominate the next three years. Luck did not return to Khanzhonkov until summer, when he added to his repertoire of topical films a compilation of film records of the royal family taken formally and informally by the court photographer Kurt von Hahn-Jagielski, from whom Khanzhonkov was permitted to buy a selection. These he made into a sentimental little topical of the home-life and official duties of the royal family.

Before there was time for any real competition among the Russian manufacturers of dramatic films a new factor made its appearance. After 1906 Russia presented an even more attractively conservative vista to foreign capital than had the Russia of the late nineteenth century. German, French, English and Belgian capital in the search for extensions of their interests felt more confidence in a Russian government that promised more stable, forceful constitutional conditions. Their confidence led to the formation, between 1909 and 1913 of 1,379 new limited companies[1] based on foreign capital largely from those four countries. The French may have met with equal competition from the English and German manufacturers in their race for Russian markets and raw materials, but the French were without rivals in one very large and profitable business—the business that looked least like business: i.e. all matters of style, including style in the theatrical arts.

There had been constant Franco-Russian cultural exchange ever since the reign of Catherine the Great. Up to the war French stock companies occupied the Mikhailovsky Theatre in St Petersburg, and even though great theatrical figures from Italy and Germany brought their troupes on tour, the ovations, the fashionable audiences, the great triumphs were achieved by French troupes, by Bernhardt, Réjane, Mounet-Sully, Guitry. The success in Russia of the exploitation of these names and figures by the Film d'Art has already been remarked. Now the French film was ready for the next stage of theatrical warfare —occupation.

The Franco-Russian exchange had worked both ways. Turgenev had introduced modern Russian novelists to France: they had been enthusiastically accepted by the French reading public. It was only natural that the French film, with its dependence at this time on adaptations, would arrive at Russian literature. No one expressed any particular anxiety about the errors in the early adaptations, but when, after the merger of Film d'Art as a subsidiary of Pathé Frères, an ambitious production of Tolstoy's *Resurrection** was released in France and in Russia, the ridicule and irritation it caused provided the motivation for the inevitable next move. Pathé and the Film d'Art decided that it was unnecessary to risk further serious errors in judgment of Russian manners and habits when it would be so simple to produce Russian films in Russia itself. So, with the characteristic contradictions of film-producing minds, they dispatched an entire production crew to Russia including not only the necessary technical workers, but also French directors and adaptors. The directors, MM. Maurice Maître and Kai Hansen, were to employ Russian actors and artists, and eventually Russian directors—not to make the product more authentic—but to increase the studio's productivity. From the start M. Maître (who stayed in France through each Russian winter), played the role of a missionary carrying to the barbarians the lowest and most superficial French theatrical culture. Throughout his Russian career he refused to learn the Russian language (he was heard to use in the studio only two Russian words—those for 'pig' and 'hurry') and ignored the inspiration of the Russian theatre which he rarely attended. He could not bear any pause in the filming in order for a conscientious actor to attempt to learn more about his role or try to feel it. Pathé were more fortunate in their technicians, especially in the chief cameraman appointed to their Russian studio. Joseph Mundviller, an Alsatian who spoke German, a more familiar foreign

---

* *Resurrection* furnished film material to many foreign companies at this time, including American Biograph (5/20/1909) directed by D. W. Griffith, who was even less concerned with accuracy of detail.

language in Russia than French, had worked in the Pathé Paris studio for a year before going to Moscow in January 1908.* (For reasons of his own he took the name of Georges Meyer in Russia, only resuming the name of Mundviller when he returned to France in 1914.) On the whole the Russian venture of Pathé proved a financial success, and soon after they applied the same plan of establishing branch studios in Germany, America and Japan.

One of the more ingenious French exploitations in 1909 of the exotic setting afforded by Russia was managed by the nineteen-year-old René Plaissetty, who had recently organized the Filma Company, where he was owner, producer, director and writer of all product. His claim to fame at this time was a serial detective film issued in episodes of two reels a week, *Les Aventures de Harry Wilson*, with Edmund van Daele as Wilson, the detective to whom no crime was a mystery. Plaissetty was no less ingenious than his creation, for he saw in him a perfect outlet for his own wish to travel by staging Wilson's adventures against genuine foreign backgrounds. His first choice was Russia, deep in November snows, and for this excursion he devised an adventure for Harry Wilson—trailing a beautiful woman jewel thief through St Petersburg, Moscow and Warsaw and catching her only on the train back to Paris. Plaissetty arrived, armed only with a letter of introduction to a French resident of St Petersburg, and accompanied by his assistant and cameraman, Gravier—made arrangements in a completely French manner—sent for Van Daele, and took all the film he wanted.

The first Russian Pathé films were shown in September 1909. In their choice from all the Russian material at hand for that which would be most exotic and attractive to foreign audiences they instinctively chose the Russian past—glorious and colourful in retrospect. Their choice was really fortunate, not only to Pathé but as well to the Russian press, which at last found in these films the popularizing illustrations of its nationalist policies. The first films were: *An Episode in the Life of Dmitri Donskoi*, a hero of the fourteenth century, the conqueror of the Khan Mamai and his Golden Horde—*Mazeppa*, a hero of the seventeenth century celebrated in poetry by Byron and Pushkin—and the natural, *Peter the Great*. All of these Russian epics were directed by the Franco-Dane Hansen, who consented to Russian collaboration in *Peter* because of its unprecedented length for Russian production—two reels. This collaborator was Goncharov, who was beginning to get the idea of what was needed, and for Pathé made his own adaptation of a nostalgic fragment—the song, *Ukhar-kupets*.

Following the tremendous success of these films abroad and at home, an Italian firm, Gloria, established a Russian studio, producing *The Death of Ivan the Terrible* ('a tragedy in nine scenes') enacted by artists from the Imperial Theatres. The new company Thiemann & Reinhardt attended to its Russian distribution, which proved disastrous. After its Russian première on October 17 it was mercilessly and unanimously attacked by the press (this was not what it wanted) and the film was withdrawn on October 25th. *The Death of Ivan the Terrible* did

---

* Many of the first cameramen were imported. Also from France came Tapis and Louis Forestier (who had photographed *L'Arlésienne* and *Nero* for 'Le Film d'Art'). Gaumont brought in Alphonse Winkler. Serrano came from Spain and Giovanni Vitrotti came from the important film studios of Turin, when Arturo Ambrosio joined forces with Thiemann & Reinhardt.

a fine business abroad, capitalizing on its Russian censure. Seeing the success of productions made in Russia by foreign firms for foreign audiences, Khanzhonkov determined to reach the rich foreign market too. As in most of his experiments, he anticipated a later successful genre, but, as usual, was ahead of his time. For this attempt to widen the range of his profits to the international market, he chose a popular ghost story entitling it *Midnight in the Graveyard, or The Fatal Wager.* The film depicted a young man who bets his companions that he can go to the graveyard at midnight, and there demonstrate his bravery by plunging his dagger into one of the wooden grave crosses. Everything goes well until he turns to leave—his cloak catches on to the cross, and, imagining that someone is holding him there, he goes mad from fright. If Khanzhonkov had made this film four years later it would have been welcomed in the flood of madness, sudden death, crime and horror dominating the Russian film during the war, but in 1909 it received a lukewarm reception, and never reached its intended market. The titles of Khanzhonkov's next films indicate his realization that at this time the press and public would assist films only of the romantically dim past; *The Boyarina Orsha* (from a poem by Lermontov); *Yermak Timofeyevich, Conqueror of Siberia* and *Russalka* (a fairy-tale poem by Pushkin).

The triumphs in history of Pathé Frères and Khanzhonkov released onto the screen a flood of historical or legendary heroes, armoured processions, and stalking, gesturing, padded heroines. Many mushroom producers appeared with bad and worse imitations of this genre. Costume store-rooms were ransacked and every film producer maintained a stock of discarded theatrical costumes, regularly carting away the costumes, scenery, props—and sometimes actors—of bankrupt theatres.

Gaumont hastily opened its own Russian factory for the manufacture of the costumed product: *Napoleon in Russia, General Toptygin, Easter Scenes at the Time of Tsar Alexei, Life and Death of Pushkin,* and even a faltering 'rendition' of *Crime and Punishment.* Slightly more astute than Pathé, Gaumont hired at the start a Russian director, Goncharov again (Goncharov was now elevated to the position of 'specialist' for historical films). With a business-like regularity no less admirable than Pathé's, Gaumont turned its Russian films into the world market—one every two weeks. We have an indication of what was sacrificed in this efficient haste—in a feuilleton report of Goncharov's filming of the fatal duel scene in *Pushkin*:

'. . . The camera is set up in a broad glade. Everyone is unloaded. What fuss and confusion. . . . The director yells again: "Cameraman, come here! . . . Pushkin, go away! The seconds . . . where are the seconds ? . . . " Three crumpled figures step out from the crowd. They look like wolves, cornered by hounds. Someone ironically remarks: "All you have to do is wash your mug and right away you get cast as a second. . . ."

'The sleigh with "Pushkin" goes off a ways and turns around to come back. "D'Anthès" strikes a pose. "Pushkin" does, too. The pistols are raised. "Pushkin" looks doubtfully at the snow on the ground. "Well, *fall !*"—the director encourages him. "I'll fall later. Why should I roll about for nothing ? . . . " "No, fall *now*. . . . Don't worry about it. . . . Are you some sort of ballerina ? . . . Seconds, put out your cigarettes. Now let's do it cleanly. . . ."

'Again the sleigh goes off and turns back. "Don't hurry, fellows, don't hurry . . . For God's sake. . . . Where are you going!" he screams at one of the seconds, who doesn't know what to do. The second is thrown into complete confusion by the scream. "Pushkin" has grown blue with cold since flinging his coat aside. "Hurry up," he says hoarsely, "hurry. . . . " "Seconds, don't stand on that junk-pile. . . . D'Anthès, lift your arm! Pushkin! . . . Well ? . . . *Fire!* . . . Fall. . . . Go ahead, *fall!* . . ."

' "Pushkin" first turns around, and then plumps down on the ground foolishly. The seconds run towards him. One snorts at the other: "Can't you keep off my feet, you devil!" . . . "Shoot, shoot!" "Pushkin" presses the trigger too soon and shoots somewhere in the general direction of the sky. Then he sits down, stares at "D'Anthès" and begins to aim. "Take it in your hand. . . . Lively. . . . Aim it at the sleigh. . . . *Where are you turning your head*," roars the director. The seconds embrace Pushkin and carry him off. The camera stops clattering.'[2]

Maître continued to satisfy Pathé and continued to draw upon well-known historical episodes, poems, and novels for his Russian output; *Mayoress Marfa* (*The Fall of Great Novgorod*), *Princess Tarakhanova*, Gogol's *Taras Bulba* (disguised as *The Love of Andrei*), Pushkin's *Gypsies*, Turgenev's *Lieutenant Yegurnov*, and Kuprin's *Duel*. Khanzhonkov maintained a remarkably high standard for his literary selections, using Nekrasov, Lermontov, and Pushkin. His version of Pushkin's *Queen of Spades* (directed by Chardynin) won the first critical approval on what could be called artistic grounds. The critic 'sensed something new here', for its taste and care distinguished this film from the other Russian films. If Khanzhonkov had wanted to try again with contemporary authors and subjects, he would have been discouraged by a newly passed law guaranteeing authors' rights—and the idea of asking an author if a cinematograph company might use his work had not yet occurred to anyone.

Another obstacle to any Russian company's desire to make films with contemporary subject matter was the ever-present censor. While the press watched to catch any misdemeanours in the historical films, such as Gloria's *Ivan the Terrible*, the censor kept guard over all matters concerning the delicate present. Newsreels were minutely examined; even the powerful Pathé-Journal (shown in Russia as *Mirror of the World*) appeared on Russian screens minus any news of real importance. A newsreel of the funeral of a Duma deputy was forbidden on the grounds that its showing might be used as a pretext for a demonstration in a theatre; a newsreel of Maxim Gorky in his Capri exile was prohibited in several cities on the pretext that Gorky was not celebrated enough!* The police were taking no chances. Their timorous attitude to the film industry of this time

* This footage of Gorky had been made by Drankov at the suggestion of Tolstoy's daughter Tatyana (when Drankov came triumphantly to Rome with his Tolstoy footage), but not with Gorky's co-operation; Gorky did everything to discourage Drankov, including beating him up and offering him money to be left in peace—but Drankov got what he came to Capri for. Gorky's own film-going tastes are described in Weisfeld's interview with Zhelyabuzhsky (*Iskusstvo Kino*, March 1958); when Lenin visited Gorky on Capri in 1908 they both enjoyed an ironic little film with the French comedian, Prince.

resulted in one notorious, almost tragic farce. On August 11, 1909, a balloon carrying not only Dr Brinkmann, an experimental aeronaut, but also Oskar Messter, the German film inventor and producer, rose from Berlin on a flight to film the environs of Berlin from a balloon. The wind rose unexpectedly and carried professor and cameraman to Breslau and, in spite of their efforts, 200 metres across the Russian border. Russian border guards in a panic fired upon the balloon and the falling occupants barely escaped with their lives. The soldiers arrested the Germans, looking upon the camera as conclusive evidence of a heinous anti-Russian crime, searched the balloon for bombs, and turned the suspects over to the local police. When the St Petersburg police heard about the moving-picture camera, they were fully confirmed in their suspicions of poor Dr Brinkmann and Messter, and it required several days and special representations from the German Ambassador, carrying proofs of the suspects' innocent pasts, to release the prisoners. As the editor of the French *Ciné-Journal* remarked[3] 'N'y avait-il pas, d'ailleurs une grosse imprudence à voyager en Russie sur un ballon *libre?*'

Tolstoy was still a touchy subject for the film censors, but as his years seemed to be coming to an end, the press devoted considerable space to his activities and pronouncements, in preparation for his posthumous sanctification. Interviews and conversations with distinguished Russian and foreign visitors to his retreat in Yasnaya Polyana were featured in the newspapers. It was inevitable that Tolstoy would become a film figure, whether or not he relished the idea—as long as Sophia Andreyevna saw advantages in it. From the sensational newsreel of the Tolstoy celebrations up to his very death-bed, newsreel cameramen (with secret aid from Sophia Andreyevna) and film enthusiasts dogged Tolstoy's steps.

'On September 3, 1909, Father, Dushan Petrovich, Ilya Vasilyevich, and I went to visit the Chertkovs at the estate of their relatives, the Pashkov family, at Kriokshino. Father wanted to see Vladimir Grigoryevich and to rest awhile from the life at Yasnaya Polyana. But people dogged his every step. Several days before our departure, a moving picture company [Pathé] requested permission to photograph his departure from Yasnaya Polyana. Mother liked being photographed and made no objections, but for Father it was annoying.

' "What for?" he said. "It's so disagreeable, so embarrassing! Couldn't we arrange it so that they would not come?"

' "Let's send them a telegram, very simply," I said. "Why should we have any compunctions about them?"

' "That would not be right at all," Mother argued. "Why should we hurt people's feelings? They will come and photograph, and it won't be any trouble whatever."

'But Aunt Maria Nikolayevna, who was visiting us just then, supported Father so energetically that Mother had to give in. I sent a telegram in Father's name, asking them not to come. But to our amazement and indignation, on the eve of our departure, the cameramen nevertheless made their appearance.

' "You ask my consent to be photographed," Father said to them, making an effort to control his irritation. "I cannot give this consent. And if you do it without permission——"

' "Our firm would never permit itself to do that!" one of the men [Mundviller] replied.

'Next morning as we drove to the station, the photographers were waiting for us at the gates of the estate. We reached the station just ahead of them. The railroad gendarme forbade their photographing on the railway premises, but they telephoned to the authorities at Tula and received the necessary permit. Again their cameras buzzed.'[4]

Mundviller says that he later showed this film to the Tolstoys, 'apparently the Count's first contact with film'. News of Pathé's coup reached Drankov, who hastily followed the Tolstoy party to Kriokshino. He knew that anything he could catch would be given world distribution. Taking his Pathé camera and a suitcase of film, he quietly moved into a village near Kriokshino—and rented a room from the driver employed by Chertkov to take care of the Tolstoys! This private spy brought him information on Tolstoy's movements, and a few days later told Drankov, 'You can catch Lev Nikolayevich every morning at five o'clock. He goes walking, alone, before breakfast.'

Next morning Drankov arrived (at *four* o'clock) at the edge of the woods. No sign of Tolstoy at five, but at about five-thirty Drankov saw the great figure approaching, stick in hand, and head down. Drankov told me that he could have photographed Tolstoy without being noticed, but for a variety of reasons ('I felt guilty') he decided to ask permission, 'Allow me to film you for the cinematograph.' Tolstoy replied with the curious phrase, 'I am at liberty,' and Drankov ran to pick up the heavy apparatus. In his haste, the tripod was not securely set and the whole apparatus fell to the ground—scattering over the ground the ruined film from the opened film-magazine. Tolstoy came over to the stunned Drankov and asked, 'What has happened?' Drankov, almost in tears, began the whole tale of his woe, 'For five years I've been trying to film you. I've tried so often, and now——' Tolstoy was more practical, 'There's a blacksmith three or four versts from here, where you can get your camera repaired. We can arrange a filming at some other time.'

The blacksmith was a good one, the lens was not injured, and Drankov innocently presented himself at the Chertkov house the following day, now that he had Tolstoy's personal permission. But Chertkov paid no attention to this fact, and drove him from the estate 'as if I had been a scabby dog'. So Drankov retreated to his observation post, and waited for Sophia Andreyevna's leg injury to improve so that he could catch them at the railway station at Kriokshino. His spy eventually reported, 'Sophia Andreyevna is better—they're leaving today.'

Drankov was finally successful. He got good footage of each of the Tolstoys as they crossed the platform to the train—and when Lev Nikolayevich saw Drankov at work, he smiled broadly at the camera as he boarded the train. This smile gave Drankov renewed courage; when the whole party had entered their compartment, Drankov followed them—a little thing like a missing ticket could not be allowed to stand in the way of this great moment. The few words he exchanged with Tolstoy were more than worth all his trouble. Tolstoy greeted him, and asked, 'Well, are you happy now?'

'Oh, yes, Lev Nikolayevich, very happy—I know what these films will mean to the people who see them. If they turn out well, I'd like to bring them to you and show them to you.' It was agreed that this could be arranged. When the train arrived in Moscow, Drankov joyfully exploited his new film monopoly on Tolstoy's face by hiring a drozhsky, and jumping out every three streets to film the Tolstoys as they walked along the Moscow streets.

'In Moscow Father was cheerful and in good spirits. In spite of the multitude of people, he had rested up at Kriokshino. I believe it was Maklakov who suggested going to the theatre.

' "Why not ?" said Father. "I would like to go to the ballet."

'Everybody was surprised. "Why to the ballet ?"

' "I have two followers who dance in the ballet, I should like very much to look at them."

'But the Bolshoi Theatre was closed for the summer. We went to a movie on the Arbat. The audience recognized Father at once, whispered, and craned their necks. It was stuffy, and a stupid piece was on the screen.

' "What a pity," Father said, "the film might be one of the mightiest means of spreading knowledge and great ideas, and yet it only serves to litter people's brains. And geography! How fine it would be to use the movies for the study of peoples and countries!"

'We left the picture early and went home. . . .'[5]

On January 6, 1910, Drankov took to Yasnaya Polyana cameras and projection apparatus and all the films he had ever taken of Tolstoy to show to the old man and to a full audience of village peasants whom Tolstoy had invited to the show. Although Tolstoy had seen at least one film previously, he was amazed to see his own life-like image on the screen. Afterwards, during a conversation with Drankov (with the peasants still present), Tolstoy learned something from him about the film situation in Russia, and (according to Drankov's subsequent publicity) expressed this opinion:

' "It is necessary for the cinematograph to record Russian reality in all its many-sided development. Russian life must be shown as it is by the cinema; instead of continuing to chase after fabricated subjects."

'At this, Lev Nikolayevich's daughter, Tatyana Lvovna, remarked that ancient Russian costumes are preserved in Tula province and that these might be recorded in a film. She suggested to Drankov that he come to her estate, where she promised him to arrange a series of interesting scenes from peasant life.

' "Yes, yes," resumed Lev Nikolayevich, "Tanya speaks the truth, listen to her advice: this would be very interesting because our peasants' life itself is very interesting and instructive."

'While saying this, Lev Nikolayevich had opened his book, "The Russian Peasant", and pointing to its illustrations [by N. V. Orlov], said, "You see how much work there is here for the photographer ?" '[6]

The agreement between Sophia Andreyevna and Drankov was progressing smoothly.

Tolstoy's opposition to films was further softened by a visit, on April 21, 1910, from Leonid Andreyev:

'At tea he talked to Lev Nikolayevich about the critic K[ornei] Chukovsky, who had raised the question of a special dramatic literature for the cinematograph. Andreyev was very enthusiastic about this. Lev Nikolayevich listened at first sceptically, but later he apparently became interested. "I shall most certainly write for the cinematograph!" he announced at the end of the conversation.'*

His interest possibly revived by reports of the Tolstoy-Andreyev conversation, Drankov wrote to Tatyana Lvovna to remind her (and himself!) of a remark made six months before:

'During my stay in Yasnaya Polyana, when I projected as well as photographed several new cinema shots from the life of Count Lev Nikolayevich with his family, you deigned to mention an idea that it would be desirable to film your peasants, dressed in the national costumes that they have preserved. I dare to remind you of this and to request your permission to come to your estate with the afore-mentioned aim.'[7]

Another letter, two weeks later, on June 28th:

'Am in receipt of both your letters, just as I am leaving Moscow this morning. I am deeply grateful for them. I knew from the papers that Lev Nikolayevich was visiting you, but I dared not come for I must go to Riga. I shall send in my place my brother and Mr Kozlovsky . . . All that you show them as necessary to put on film, they will. . . .'

On July 1st, Tatyana wrote to her mother:

'Staying with us are Drankov's silly and vulgar brother and his nice assistant. They don't have a drop of artistic or moral feeling. Orlov came over from his place to help them, but nothing will come of it. Today they muttered something about showing what they're filming in about two weeks, and sending for more film in the meantime, thus threatening to stay here forever.'

When the crew finally broke away and returned to Moscow, Drankov wrote Tatyana again:

'Allow me to express my profound gratitude for your kind reception and participation in the filming by my brother and Mr Kozlovsky. This picture, as an ethno-graphic survey of Russia, will surely offer great interest and I await permission, whenever convenient for you, to show this and others to you. I am very sorry that it will not be possible to employ the services of Mr Orlov, but I hope in the near future to use his artistic taste and knowledge of native life for the creation of some subject.'

* From V. Bulgakov's journal, quoted by Alexander Kaun in *Leonid Andreyev*. A story of this meeting was published in the newspaper *Ranniye Utro*, and reprinted in *Cine-Fono* in May 1910, under the sensational headline of 'TOLSTOY DECIDES TO WRITE FOR THE CINEMA,' giving a fuller version of Tolstoy's remarks, 'You know, I've thought a great deal about the cinema. And when I wake up at night I think about it. I decided to write for the cinema. Of course there must be a reader, as in Amsterdam, who would deliver the text. For it would be impossible without a text. . . .'

But the footage was neither complete nor satisfactory, and Drankov was obliged to finish the job himself, and on September 8th, Sophia Andreyevna records:

'Drankov filmed us again, and afterwards filmed a village wedding that was performed expressly for that purpose.'[8]

Drankov provided some reliable details of this filming in an interview, published in the *Peterburgskaya Gazette*, September 14th:

'On the initiative of Lev Nikolayevich scenes were arranged of a Russian peasant wedding—the match-making, the contract, the marriage ceremony, the feast and dancing, etc. to be filmed by the cinema. Lev Nikolayevich was very interested, especially in the peasants' mastering of their roles.'

This makes it quite clear that Tolstoy's function during the filming was no more than a 'consultant', but he was neither its writer nor director.

Sophia's business-like record of this event must be compared with her daughter Alexandra's and her husband's hectic picture:

'To comfort Father, I volunteered to accompany Mother. We stayed a few days as Yasnaya Polyana. Without Father, Mother was much more calm. But as soon as we returned to Kochety her nervousness returned . . . [Drankov] came and pressed us for a chance to photograph Father. This was enough to upset Mother. At any cost, she wished to be photographed with him, and she put as much emotion into the situation as if it were a question of life and death. "They printed in some paper," she said, "that Tolstoy has divorced his wife! Let them all see now that it is not true!" During the photographing, she begged Father several times to look at her.'[9]

Nor did she approve of the idea of filming Tolstoy (alone) chopping up firewood.* On this date, September 8th, Tolstoy made this entry in his last journal:

'Sophia Andreyevna becomes progressively more and more irritable. It is depressing, but I restrain myself. . . . Sophia Andreyevna insistently demanded that Drankov should film her and me together . . . .'[10]

Sophia Andreyevna's film associations continued after Tolstoy's death, as well. Her diary says, on November 28th:

'Health better. Anna Ivanovna Maslova, the cinematographer Drankov, and the correspondent Spiro, have come. . . .'

Could it have been at this conference that Drankov asked for Sophia's approval of his 'biggest deal' relating to Tolstoy? For the Tolstoy corpse was not very cold before a film entitled *A Peasant Wedding* 'written and directed personally

---

* A. B. Goldenweiser's diary quotes Sophia Andreyevna's sarcastic reaction to this wholly unplanned performance. This is how it happened: Tolstoy, walking, met some peasants chopping firewood. One of them wished to borrow certain books which Tolstoy said were at Makovitsky's and that the peasant should go there to get them. When the peasant said that he was afraid to leave his work, Tolstoy offered to take his place until he got back. As soon as the news reached Kochety that Count Tolstoy was, at this very minute, chopping firewood, Drankov raced with his camera to the spot.

by Tolstoy' was released by Drankov in Russia, and purchased for world distribution by the Italian company Cines. That Count Tolstoy had 'personally directed' this film ('No theatrical properties! Only exteriors!') a bare two months before his death was a 'publicity angle' not neglected by the film distributors. The widowed countess filed no protest against this distortion of the facts.

After this apparent contribution of literary prestige to the Russian cinema, a year passed before a living Russian writer of importance contributed to the film. Of defenders (often axe grinders) it had plenty, among whom Leonid Andreyev was the most powerful. The scenario-writing job continued to be pushed on to any one in the studio who didn't mind wasting time on this thankless task—whether it was the director (Goncharov for example wrote his own scenarios —actually little more than shooting schedules) or even the set-designer, as in Sabinsky's case.

Sabinsky took more creative interest in his job and every other job than was normal in the Moscow film studios of 1910. When Gachet and Maître opened the Moscow Pathé studios, a mixed French and Russian style was introduced that took many years and two revolutions to weed out completely from the Russian film. Maître stubbornly resisted innovations, and Sabinsky's attempts to change the French style of flatly painted sets (with stock, catalogued ornament) met obstructions at every detail. His suggestions for varying wall proportions and the use of real objects for decoration were not fully employed until increasing competition forced Pathé to make some changes in its system. Sabinsky was later responsible for the introduction to Russian film-making of miniature sets, and eventually his enthusiastic interest led him to direction.

Strict laws about the position of the camera prevented any film-photographic progress. Photography could hardly be expected to participate artistically (even in the bad sense of the word) when the camera was allowed to be neither higher nor lower from the acting floor than five feet, nor further than eighteen feet from the actors. Camera positions that cut the actor's body above the knees were rare in European production in general, not alone in Russia. From a single point within this narrow area of camera activity, often as much of a fourth of an entire film would be photographed. We find an extreme case of this restriction as late as 1915 when, in a version of *Revizor*, the prompter's box is visible throughout, at the bottom of the screen.

With the exception of Davydov's trial in Drankov's *Krechinsky*, only actors from second and third-class theatres would accept or seek film employment. This does not imply that a higher level of film art awaited the entrance of first-rate actors. That event was to be only another signal of the growing prestige of the cinema, and the breaking down of the former social barriers which were still restricting film appreciation and attendance to the lower and lower-middle classes. In 1910, and in the majority of the films of subsequent years, the general understanding of a film actor's methods was similar to his performance at a children's pantomime, where he would over-clearly delineate each emotion and situation with his face, his gesture and his pose. If he spoke words in his scene, he would enunciate them distinctly enough for his lips to be read by his future audience. It seems strange to us now that it was so long before it was realized that a film audience, via the camera, is invariably closer and more observant than a pantomime audience could be, in spite of the worst imaginable projection.

New cinematograph theatres appeared along the main streets of every large city. In St Petersburg alone twenty-two theatres were opened in 1910, which, subtracting the ten theatres destroyed by fire during that year, brought St Petersburg's film theatre enterprises to a total of eighty-four. But it must be remembered that none of these was especially built for cinema purposes. The exhibiting industry was still able to set up shop in almost anything with a roof over it to keep the rain and snow off the customers. The additional equipment was little more expensive than in the days of the first theatres. It was sufficient to buy, besides the projection apparatus and a book of tickets, fifty second-hand chairs and a sign to hang outside—now lit with red and green and yellow electric bulbs. And, unless you were unusually unlucky, you had a good business in hand.

Altogether, by 1910, there were fifteen 'studios' for the production of Russian films. These included the branches of foreign companies, such as Pathé, Gaumont, and others, which actually occupied the major place. During this year Ambrosio, the largest of the Italian firms, entered an alliance with Thiemann & Reinhardt, which provided Italian technicians in exchange for Russian history and exotica. Ninety per cent of this 'Russian' film industry was located in Moscow, the business capital of the Russian Empire. Foreign films dominated theatre programmes all over the country. No matter how popularly *Stenka Razin* was received, Cines' *Sack of Rome* or Pathé's *Cleopatra* attracted larger Russian audiences. The keystone of foreign film production at this time was the Holy Bible, which provided the film business with an unending source of subjects and plots. These holy films were staunchly supported by the Russian audience— jamming the theatres that were showing *The Resurrection of Lazarus* (Pathé) or *Daniel in the Lion's Den* (Éclair). The Orthodox Church encouraged attendance at these 'tableaux' until Les Films Esthetiques went too far, producing *Our Genesis* and a *Life of Christ*, whereupon the Synod revived its strictures against the blasphemous cinematograph. But the foreign companies had plenty of novelties to withstand any assault on their profits—Pathé showed its first Japanese film, *The Punishment of the Samurai*; the English firm, Kinemacolor, opened a success- ful Moscow office*; and less blasphemous historical chapters and literary classics were heavily drawn upon by all—influencing an imitative flood of 'classical adaptations' in the Russian industry the following year. At the end of 1910, the Danish firm, Nordisk, sent into Russia a two-reel film called *The Abyss*, with a new young actress named Asta Nielsen.† Within two years this and subsequent

---

* One Russian testimonial of Kinemacolor was that of the Dowager Empress, writing to her son, Nikolai, from London (April 29, 1912): '. . . We are lunching today with Georgie and May at Buckingham Palace. They both send you greetings. Last night we saw their journey to India. Kinemacolor is wonderfully interesting and very beautiful and gives one the impression of having seen it all in reality. . . .'

† *Afgrunden* was universally admired, influencing the films of every country. Besides Russia—France, Italy, and Germany succumbed to the deep impression made by the actress, just graduated from the Royal Dramatic School, and the director-author, Urban Gad. Both shortly after made Berlin their production centre. American films of shabby, realistic dramas of sin and crime were rarely produced until the Nordisk films were shown and imitated in the United States.

Nielsen films were to furnish the technical and moral base for all modern subjects treated by the Russian cinema, and Asta Nielsen, without crossing the Russian border, was to become the most popular and most widely imitated actress in the Russian Empire.

The 1910-11 season in the Russian theatre witnessed experiments of great importance. This season was as well the most reactionary in the cultural life of Russia and new work and new talents had to fight bitterly for recognition. Meyerhold's experiment in Molière's *Don Juan* at the Alexandrinsky Theatre was soundly trounced by *Novoye Vremya* and its followers. When Meyerhold produced Musorgsky's *Boris Godunov* at the Marinsky Theatre, with Golovin's sets, with Coates as conductor and Shalyapin as *Boris*, the production was used by *Novoye Vremya* as an excuse for a provocative article against 'the handful of aliens who control the Imperial Theatres'.[11] Meyerhold was referred to as 'that Jew'. It was during this season that Nizhinsky was dismissed from the Imperial Ballet because the Dowager Empress was insulted by his new costume designed by Bakst for *Giselle*. Diagilev firmly decided to centre his activities away from this stultifying atmosphere, in Paris, where Fokin's ballets and the Russian operas staged by Sanin and sung by Shalyapin, were adopted by the fashionable Paris audience, and thriving.

In 1910, the conniving identity between the Government and the Union of Russian People ('the Black Hundred') produced a maniacal series of anti-semitic pogroms throughout Russia which stirred the whole world to protest. There was universal anger against the Tsarist Government's policy and universal sympathy for the plight of the Russian Jew. The Kishinev massacre of 1904 had become the regular order of Jewish persecution. Foreign film companies produced quantities of agitational films based on the pogroms, usually as plot motivation for Russian terrorist or nihilist movements. With most of the protests emanating from democratic America, coupled with the fact of the large Russian and Jewish immigrant population in this country, it seems natural that the majority of these films were made by American producers. A typical one was *Russia, the Land of Oppression*, produced by Defender, and released in June 1910, a month after the expulsion of the Jews from Kiev. *The Moving Picture World* reviewed it thus:

'A very graphic reproduction of the terrible scenes of persecution which have been enacted among the Hebrew race in Kief and Kishineff. It is scarcely necessary to describe it. The newspapers and magazines have done this many times over. Happily the heroine of this picture has the general's son for lover, and she is saved from the unmitigated tortures and dishonours of Siberia by his intervention. There is a feeling of exultation when they are shown landing at Ellis Island, the gateway to the land where cruel persecutions of that character do not exist.'

Another American company, Yankee, seems to have been devoted to Russian subjects at this period—both its *Queen of the Nihilists* and *In the Czar's Name* were concerned with escape from Tsarist persecution to the U.S.A.

To be on the spot where these dramas were being enacted in reality, without being able to make films on these subjects, was a source of great commercial anxiety for Pathé. The circumvention of the censor was finally accomplished by making innocent films of Jewish life, which could be exhibited abroad as sensationally as the distributors found possible. For these first Jewish films to be made in Russia Pathé employed its regular staff of non-Jewish actors, using a few Jewish 'types' in the background. As un-Jewish and as poor as the results were, the two films—*L'khaim* (*To Your Health*) and *The Violin*, were welcomed abroad as authentic revelations, and were popular in France and the United States. A firm in Warsaw attempted to duplicate this move, in *A Cruel Father*, but did not have the advantage of Pathé's huge international connections. They were rarely seen in Russia however, where the restrictions on Jewish expression were so rigid that Russian and Polish Jewish newspapers and magazines making any real literary or social contribution had to be printed outside the country.

There was another way to circumvent the Russian censor and reach the foreign market. In the Cinémathèque Française is preserved the negative of a film entitled *L'Aurore de la Révolution Russe*, made in Russia at some time before the war, apparently only for export to France; its subject matter would be unthinkable on Russian screens. A nihilist is assigned to the task of assassinating an official on the street; his attempt fails and he is sentenced to hard labour; he escapes and returns to his family only to be arrested again; he dies in prison. The story seems harmless enough unless one realizes the several taboos the film violates. The artificiality of the painful prison interiors (in a painted Zecca manner) is heightened by some surprising glimpses of actual prison life. The film's historical significance is increased by the early appearance in it of two actors who were to make important contributions to the Soviet cinema: Ivan Bersenev, here the tortured nihilist, was to play more than twenty years later, the conspiratorial Kartashov in *A Great Citizen*, and Vera Baranovskaya, who plays the nihilist's innocent wife, was to make her role in Pudovkin's *Mother* unforgettable.

During the year 1911, the anxiety to put a large quantity of films on the market was replaced by the more commendable anxiety to better the quality of those few produced. The race for quality and audiences was rather equally run—by Russian Pathé, Thiemann & Reinhardt (supported by their link to Ambrosio) and Khanzhonkov. The films released by Khanzhonkov at the beginning of 1911 had considerable literary and artistic pretensions: adaptations of Glinka's opera *A Life for the Tsar*, Pushkin's *Eugene Onegin*, and Ostrovsky's *Vasilisa Melentieva and Tsar Ivan the Terrible*. Thiemann & Reinhardt and Ambrosio took their costume trunks to the Caucasus Mountains producing Pushkin's *Prisoner of the Caucasus* and Lermontov's *Demon*. At Pathé, the resourceful Hansen brought out a new novelty every week—one week adapting *Anna Karenina* and another week, Chekhov's funny short story, *Romance with Double-bass*. With few exceptions the films were evocations of the past. *Anna Karenina* was filmed in the costumes of the preceding generation.

Competition became increasingly keen, particularly from the new firms trying to get a foothold in the theatres. Rival firms would make films for the same occasion, hoping to cut each other's throat. For the fiftieth anniversary jubilee of the emancipation of the serfs, St Petersburg planned a formal celebration.

In preparation for this event, Pathé rushed into production a film entitled *Shield Yourself with the Sign of the Cross, O People of the Orthodox Faith* (the opening sentence of the emancipation proclamation) while Khanzhonkov filmed a scenario almost identical with this, but with a simpler title, *On the Eve of Emancipation.*

If an adaptation of an author's work proved successful in one case, other producers would speed into production other works by the same author, hoping for the same success. After the death of Tolstoy, Pathé's film of *Anna Karenina* was the first major work by Tolstoy to be filmed. Its success led the new association of Sphinx & Globus to make *The Kreutzer Sonata*. Cines gathered together all the newsreels of Tolstoy, and released a full reel called *Lev Nikolayevich Tolstoy*. The small firm of Persky felt that it needed a Tolstoy film too.

In his memoirs[12], Nemirovich-Danchenko has described the proud acquisition by the Moscow Art Theatre of Tolstoy's posthumous play *A Living Corpse*, and the jealous guard that was kept against a previous production by all other theatres until after the Art Theatre's premiere. Even Meyerhold's request for a simultaneous première in Moscow and St Petersburg was refused. Without reckoning on the keen business spirit and dulled scruples of a film producer, the theatre innocently allowed the newspapers to publish a synopsis of the new play—knowing that a synopsis would be useless for theatre thieves. But a synopsis was all that a film producer of that time needed. Limited in length he had to pare down any literary work to a series of its more active climaxes, so that the printed synopsis of *The Living Corpse* was just what Persky required for his stunt. As the long-awaited Art Theatre première was scheduled for September 23rd, Persky planned his sensational première for a week ahead. His announcement of this victory was not received as he had expected it to be. The first move from the defence was a letter from Alexandra, Tolstoy's daughter, sent to all the newspapers:

'According to the newspapers, the cinematographic theatres propose to show, on September 17th, a film of my father's play *The Living Corpse*. I feel it my duty to point out that no one has the right to prepare such a production. Aside from this fact, I beg those gentlemen of the cinematographic theatres to withhold their exhibition until after the appearance of the play on the stage of the Moscow Art Theatre and after the publication of the play—that is, until September 23rd.

August 30, 1911.   Alexandra Tolstaya.'

The newspapers, even the film trade papers, adopted her cause, and rallied to attack the man who allowed 'such a production to mock the memory of our great national writer'.[13] The film created a sensation beyond Persky's dreams. It was opposed as no other film had ever been opposed, and as yet no one had seen the guilty film! As can easily be imagined, no one paid any attention to its quality when it was released on September 27th; everyone was too angry. Its only result was to bring on Persky a virtual boycott, not only of this film, but of his entire production, until the scandal blew over. The following year brought on another Tolstoy film scandal, this time with the widow, Countess Sophia, as the martyr. At a preview, for Tolstoy's relatives and closest friends, of the *Departure of a Grand Old Man* with Shaternikov playing the rôle of Tolstoy, the Countess rose and accused the actor and the film of 'caricature'. The newspapers came to her aid, demanding the confiscation and destruction of this 'libel', and the innocent film was never shown publicly in Russia. Thus one of the first (and one of the most daring) films directed by Yakov Protazanov was seen only abroad.

On all Russian dramatic repertoires the good old remedy for any indications of dropping-off of attendance was Averkiev's play of the rich Russian merchants of the seventeenth century—*Old Times in Kashira*—a compilation of all the basic theatrical appeals—romance, patriotism, slapstick. When Thiemann & Reinhardt chose this play for a film, it was in itself a sensible move, and they elevated this move to the degree of a master-stroke by persuading a number of stage luminaries to join the cast. Their names were announced and billed conspicuously, establishing a precedent that the other companies were quick to follow. A production made with more care and technical adroitness than usual, a cast including the rising brilliant young actress Roshchina-Insarova, and the matinée idols—Maximov and Bestuzhev—all went into the making of a film that brought Thiemann & Reinhardt to the top of the Russian film market. Immediately afterwards Prodafilm launched a production of *Prince Serebryany and the Captive Varvara*. As the Imperial theatres forbade their actors to touch the cinema, Prodafilm turned to the acting staff of the People's House—crowding their poster with well-known names from that theatrical company. Alexeyev, the chief director of the People's House, consented to direct the film and the result must be admitted to be the best of the historical films seen up to its time. Naturally, there was a flock of bad imitations.

An unusually acute observer, Stephen Graham, made a tour through Russia in the summer of 1911, and left a record[14] of the firm place that the cinema had made for itself—particularly on the humbler levels of Russian life. In Rostov:

'The electric theatres do a most extraordinary business, and the people of Rostof take more interest in the programmes than any one dreams of in England. The items at these shows are bloodthirsty, gruesome murder stories, stories of crime, of unfaithful husbands and wives, and of course the usual insane harlequinades. The young men and women discuss these imported horrors—they are nearly all of French origin—as if they represented real life, and are much more interested in *The Horrors of Life* and *The Husband's Revenge* than in the works of Tolstoy, Dostoievsky and Chekhof by which Russia is famous. . . . The streets at night are full of what would generally be called rabble, all talking nonsense and surging from one glaring electric theatre to another.'

In Gelendzhik, a summer resort, '. . . there is a lumber-shed where one can see "la vie sur l'écran"; an absolutely new programme. . . .' On a highway near the Black Sea, he encountered a runaway sailor who, in an outburst of pent-up emotion, shouted,

'What is a sailor's life ? Yes, I ask God that question. Last night I was at the dim pictures (the cinematograph) and I saw how all the generals, and officers, and soldiers stood with their hats off and their heads bowed, saluting the Tsar, and the Tsar alone had his hat on, and looked around like a cock on a perch. Good to be the Tsar! Not good to be a sailor!'

And in the Urals, he found the cinema helping to divert the miner from thought of his condition—a condition that was to lead to the strike of the Lena gold-fields' workers the following year.

'The cinematograph teaches him that women can be bought, that they can be quarrelled over, and that a cruel and ugly revenge is noble and striking . . . Miass is a gold mining village of 25,000 inhabitants . . . two churches, four electric theatres, fifteen vodka shops, a score of beerhouses, and many dens where cards are played and women bought and sold to the strains of the gramophone.'

The foreign films brought into Russia during 1911 were rich in variety and in financial returns. Foreign film comedians had no Russian rivals. Since the appearance in Russia of André Deed, whose film situations became colloquial expressions (his French name was forgotten, and he was known in Russia as *Glupishkin*— 'Dopey'), Max Linder had joined him and surpassed him in popularity. In a questionnaire, run by one of the Russian fan magazines in 1911, Max was voted the most popular, followed by Asta Nielsen and Valdemar Psilander, another Danish star, known in Russia as *Garrison*. In 1911, America was represented among the Russian favourites by John Bunny, known there as *Poxon*.*

Within a single year the name of Asta Nielsen was powerful enough to fill a theatre half an hour after her name was put out on the front. Other Danish films, particularly those with 'Garrison', attracted new audience elements, even of the intelligentsia. Herman Bang's story of circus drama, *Four Devils*, already well known by Russians in literature and the theatre, was seen in the first of many versions of this story. *Zigomar*, the first of the great serial film detectives, appeared in Russia this year, preparing audiences for his successors—*Nick Carter, Nat Pinkerton, Fantômas, Pauline, Elaine*.

The grandiose Italian and French films were not relaxing their hold on the world's imagination and wish for luxury, and this year *Notre-Dame de Paris, L'Aiglon, L'Affaire du Collier de la Reine, Madame Sans-Gêne* (with the magnificent Réjane) came from France, and Italy sent her usual quota of Falls of Troy and Figaros, leavened only by an experimental 'psychological guignol'—*Ward No. 13*, which was to become another pillar in the influences upon the immediately pre-war Russian cinema. Russian production followed in the steps of these foreign examples, without taking the opportunity to discover new paths. Only one foreign type remained uncopied as yet—the grand spectacle *a l'italienne*, and the one Russian producer, whose work stood out as the most original and truly native, succumbed to this model. This was Khanzhonkov, who had always wished to draw upon his military background, and determined to make a historical spectacle equal in scale to those of Ambrosio.

Khanzhonkov and Goncharov began an intense system of contacting important

---

* Both these changed names were invented by Yakov Protazanov when working in the distribution office of Thiemann & Reinhardt.

persons outside the film business—in high business and in the Government—selling their great idea to the higher circles with the result that the following official announcement appeared:

'With the sanction of the Sovereign, his Imperial Majesty, the Tsar Emperor—the manufacturer of Russian cinematographic films, officer of the reserves, Captain of the Cossacks Khanzhonkov, enters into the production of a grandiose battle film, *The Siege of Sevastopol*. His Imperial Highness, the Grand Duke Alexander Mikhailovich, organizer and builder of the Sevastopol Museum (together with those officers of the various departments of the Museum) assumes the work of preparation of this film under his exalted patronage.'

The announcement aroused immediate excitement. Publicity was sent to all the film papers abroad. *The Moving Picture World*[15] informed its readers that

'The plans for the production of a film of the Siege of Sebastopol have met with heartiest approval of the Czar, who has signified his intention of being present at the taking. . . . An immense number of harmless shells are being constructed for the purpose of making the performance realistic.'

The preparation indicated a scale of film-making unheard of in Russia until that time. The director Goncharov, and the French cameraman Forestier, spent whole days inspecting the ruined fortifications to choose locations. Khanzhonkov himself, as an accredited army officer, rehearsed the battle scenes with the assistance of Admiral Boester and the choir of the Sevastopol cathedral![16]

Without waiting for the completion of the film, Khanzhonkov planned an extremely clever distribution system for the film. Instead of using his own limited distribution channels, he relinquished the rights, and sold the film to *all* the other Russian renting agencies.

After a royal preview on November 15th at Livadia, the Tsar's summer palace near Yalta, on which occasion 'his Imperial Highness, to the great joy of Khanzhonkov, asked many gracious questions,' the film received its first public showing at the end of November, under the heroic title of *The Defence of Sevastopol*. This showing, at the Moscow Conservatory of Music, was most solemn and grand—with an accompaniment of two orchestras, a chorus, the sounds of battle, etc. It was generally agreed, by foreign critics as well as the naturally enthusiastic Russian critics, that its quality was comparable to the *Fall of Troy* and *The Siege of Calais*, a new French film opened at the same time. It was certainly a great step from *Stenka Razin* and the whole genre of ciné-illustration—and a milestone in Russian film-history. Unfortunately the surprises of the large battle exteriors did not carry over the weaknesses of the interior dramatic scenes. The public wanted more battling and less of Napoleon III's general staff and the Royal Court at Constantinople. Goncharov and his actors contributed little to the filming; the real victory was that of the former Captain of the Cossacks—Khanzhonkov.

During this four-year period—the first stage in the development of the Russian film—351 films were produced. Of these 139 were dramatic and 212 newsreels and topicals.

In the Duma Cinema: Leapfrog, or Teaching Efficiency of Work,
in *The Grey Wolf*, St Petersburg, February 3, 1908

CHAPTER III

Enter—Author and Stockholder

1912–1913

> ... these romances that distort the truth and realities;
> provoke, cultivate and embellish all the morbid
> emotions, confusions, ignorances, prejudices and
> horrors; and purposely and skilfully pervert the
> hearts and still more the minds ...
>
> VANZETTI

Looking back on the years of reaction—1907-10 Lenin[1] thus characterized the period: 'Tsarism is victorious. All the revolutionary and opposition parties have been defeated. Depression, demoralization, splits, discord, renegacy and pornography instead of politics. There is an increased drift towards philosophic idealism; mysticism serves as a cloak for counter-revolutionary moods. . . .' Continuing, Lenin shows that it was precisely this physical and moral defeat that taught the revolutionary class a useful lesson.

Literature was the first of the arts to be infected by this dank and rotted social atmosphere. Tolstoy's death in 1910 seemed a last warning to Russian literary traditions, already overwhelmed by fascination with methods and devices; the new authors called their mystic gestures 'themes' and laughed at the old obligations of Russian literature to be realistic, to communicate ideas and to instruct. Audiences were finding the 'madness and horror' of Andreyev's works diverting. Describing the period after 1906, Masaryk wrote:

'In literature and philosophy, after the revolution, those tendencies were strengthened which, as we have already seen, were characteristic of the pre-revolutionary epoch, namely mysticism and a return to religion. With this religious revival was associated a turning away from revolution. The loudest preachers of these movements were deserters from the Marxist camp; but among the narodniki and the social revolutionaries Dostoevski and Soloviov now enjoyed enhanced prestige. In literature, decadence become conspicuous in the form of irritable and stimulating sexuality; the boundary between art and pornography was often blurred. . . . The disciples of decadence delighted in religious mysticism.'[2]

In one of his first articles after his arrival in America, Ivan Narodny[3] told of the transformation in Russian literature from a pessimistic realism (such as the work of Alexander Kuprin) to a new vivid impressionist erotic fiction, reeking with sensualism and typified by Mikhail Artsibashev's *Sanin*. Artsibashev[4] himself protests: '*Sanin* made its appearance five years too late. This was very much against it; at the time of its appearance literature had been flooded by streams of pornography, and my novel was likely to be judged with these.' It must have taken extraordinary fortitude to be a Gorky in such times.

Feeling in poetry seldom ran deep those days—preferring to remain on an impressionist surface. The world of Russian music switched its attention from native sources to romance, sentiment and mystic sensuality, exchanging the exotic for the erotic. In 1909 Skryabin, self-proclaimed theosophist, brought out his 'Poeme de l'Extase'. He had sharpened his sensitivity to the unknown and dulled his relationship to life about him to the point where he could later declare (in a London interview): '. . . through music and colour, with the aid of perfume, the human mind or soul can be lifted outside or above merely physical sensations into the region of purely abstract ecstasy and purely intellectual speculation.' Polite society was conferring near-sainthood on the late Madame Blavatsky. Nineteen hundred and ten had witnessed the début of two new art movements— the first show of the futurists and the grander exhibition of Diagilev's *Mir Iskusstvo*—both signs of the social times. Art was attempting to sever its last bonds with its popular sources.

As the decay spread to larger groups, the theatre became its headquarters. When Pavel Orlenev came to America for the second time in 1912 he displayed his disgust with the condition of the Russian theatre in terms that were amazingly frank, considering he was planning to return to Russia.

'The pornographic and the sensational are holding sway. The censor follows in the path that has been blazed by the policeman. Study clubs conducive to advanced thinking are discouraged, but shows of low moral standard are not interfered with. The kind of spectacle which corresponds to suggestive musical comedy on your stage is never suppressed. You can imagine what fruits such a policy has been bearing. Besides these unspeakable "psychological" plays, the old-time burlesque, rough and vulgar, is also flourishing. The intellectual awakening of the revolutionary years seems to have been followed by a still heavier slumber.'[5]

This disintegration of society and art had not spread to the degree where the cinema—infallible mirror of tastes—was yet expected to assist. The cinema had to wait for the widespread moral decay that was to follow war before the screen could demonstrate how strong an ally of rot it could be. In 1912, it ventured only a light seasoning of pornography* and welcomed the approaches that decadent literature was making to it.

It was at the height of their retreat from the real problems of contemporary society that literature and the theatre discovered a new topic for fierce discussion —the cinema. Leonid Andreyev headed the crusade. Andreyev's American biographer, Alexander Kaun, has remarked how Andreyev's search for 'another

* As witness this discreet advertisement in *Vestnik Kinematografiya*: 'Seances for adults! Films of the "Saturn" studio. Grandiose piquant subjects! Sales and rentals.'

reality' led him to adopt one short-lived infatuation after another; in turn he was passionately intense about colour photography, sea voyages, alcohol, the cinema, etc. In 1911, following a slack period in his theatre success, Andreyev outlined a plan for theatrical reform and renaissance written in the form of a brilliant exhortation, entitled *Letters on the Theatre.* Advising the theatre to concentrate its efforts exclusively on the 'inner soul-drama' and 'extensions of the pan-psyche', he pleaded with the stubborn theatre to relinquish activity, crowd movements, in fact, all 'the reproduction of visible, physical life',[6] relegating these to the cinematograph, where they naturally belong. These 'letters', actually a manifesto, were not published until the end of 1913, but Andreyev's crusading spirit brought the subject of cinema into every literary tea or 'evening' he attended. Although his first film work, an adaptation of his play *Anfisa* for Thiemann & Reinhardt (starring Roshchina-Insarova and Maximov), was not produced until 1912, it was undoubtedly Andreyev's powerful influence that was behind the earlier attempts by other well-known authors to write for the new medium.

The film business welcomed the authors with open arms. Literary interest may even have been fostered by the producers, so opportune was the authors' entrance. In Europe the industry was breaking down the prejudices of artistic circles for many materialistic reasons: the film's increased financial backing required less of a risk for its investment and a well-known author's name was considered a solidifying factor in the nebulous matter of attendance. In Germany, the Goethe Society, organized to combat the evil influence of the cinema, was falling apart, due to the acceptance of the films in 1913 by established as well as experimental writers. Gerhart Hauptmann adapted his novel *Atlantis* for a super-production made with Danish and German money, and Hans Heinz Ewers actively assisted Paul Wegener in the production of a series of supernatural subjects, beginning with *The Student of Prague* (1913). Italian films had won such universal praise that d'Annunzio and Henryk Sienkiewicz felt no diminishing of their dignity by their association with *Cabiria* and *Quo Vadis?* MM. Pierre Decourcelle and Eugène Gugenheim had organized their friends into *La Société Cinématographique des Auteurs et Gens de Lettres*, whose productions were financed and distributed by the omnipotent Pathé Frères.

Throughout the film world the idea was gaining strength that the supreme element in the making of a film was its scenario. In America alone the reliance was still placed on camera ingenuity, vivid acting and striking effects of movement. Griffith and Ince as well as many lesser directors were free, as yet, of the cramping literary classic. But Europe was firm in its dependence on the scenario, and every company avidly read the *Rules for Scenario Composition* published by Gualtiero Fabbri, an Italian professor. The mechanics for the gleaning of scenarios was not yet organized, and the first solution offered to them was the contest. In fact the first move of one newly organized Russian film company was a scenario contest, with cash prizes of 500, 300, 200 and 100 roubles. Such contests did not achieve the desired result, because no one, including the judges, really knew how to write for the films, and cash prizes were offered in vain. So it was that the single solution appeared to be the literary name. Russian Pathé and Khanzhonkov competed in the number of great names they could attach to contracts. Pathé managed to

rally Anatoli Kamensky, Mikhail Artsibashev, Arkhipov, Solomensky, and Semyon Yushkevich to their banner. Khanzhonkov signed contracts with Arkadi
Averchenko, Osip Dymov, Fyodor Sologub (his theories about the annihilation
of everything were thought charming), Amfiteatrov, Chirikov, Alexander
Kuprin and Leonid Andreyev—but it soon appeared that the majority of
these were to contribute no more than their names, for, as Mr Dymov has
said, Madame Khanzhonkova did all the real scenario work. Later, these
fashionable names were lent to the letterheads of these companies' 'literary
departments'.

Not only did literature give a different character to the films from 1912 on,
but the theatre established a new relationship with its former rival. The more
evident the limitations of the cinema, the more willing were actors and directors
to make a little extra money out of it, since their theatrical positions were not
threatened financially. Important dramatic actors, who had so recently been so
haughty to the films, now flocked into the film studios. During the 1911 convention of film business men, it was stated that the annual turnover of the cinema
exceeded 120 million roubles. In view of this fact, the lure of the cinema for
poorly paid actors does not seem so inexplicable. Perhaps more important, as
'prestige', was the growing interest, though still on the planes of condescension
and argument, of the theatre directors. Previous to the expression of this interest,
a smart small theatre of literary burlesques, called *The Crooked Mirror*, frequented
by the jeunesse dorée of St Petersburg, produced a *Parody on the Kinematograph*
in February 1911, telling the tritest story with a hash of emotional clichés and
mannerisms typical of the worst films of the period. Later when Nikolai Yevreinov
took over artistic supervision of *The Crooked Mirror*, he threw this skit out of
the repertory, remarking 'What a cheap pose—to be indignant with the cinema!'
Fyodor Kommisarzhevsky took a friendly interest in the cinema, defending it
against the attacks of the commercial theatre. Kugel, editor of the respected
weekly, *Theatre and Art* ran a series of *Lessons in the Cinema*. An examination of
Theatre and Art of 1912-13 reveals an explosion of interest occurring at this
time—expressed in articles, cartoons, letters to the editor, etc. Unfortunately
this same periodical gradually lost its pure motive of reader interest, for, by 1915,
it sacrificed its integrity, trading a column of film news for the film industry's
regular advertising space. The theatre was learning to suffer its cousin industry
that had been thrust unwanted upon it.

In contrast to this more tolerant attitude was the short-sighted (and short-
lived, since he himself was soon to succumb to the attractions of the cinema)
intolerance of Vsevolod Meyerhold. In 1912, he published a collection of his
essays entitled *About the Theatre*. The key essay, wherein he outlined his whole
theory of the theatre, was *The Booth*—exactly contrary to Andreyev's manifesto,
on the need of the theatre to return to primitive audience-actor relationships, to
the methods of the *commedia dell'arte*, employing the actor's body as an asset
equal in expression to the spoken word. Both Meyerhold and Andreyev con-
curred in one opinion, however, and that was vigorously to deny the term art to
the cinema. Meyerhold's trip to Paris the following year, at which time he met
the cinema-enthusiasts Gabriel d'Annunzio, Guillaume Apollinaire, and Edouard

de Max, opened his eyes to some of cinema's exciting possibilities, but in 1912 he was very stern:

'The importance of the kinematograph, this idol of the modern town, is greatly exaggerated by its supporters. For science this importance is indisputable; the kinema greatly helps here in making demonstrations appeal more strongly to the mind. The kinema can also serve as an illustrated newspaper. For some people (horrors!) it serves to replace travelling itself. But in the field of art there is no room for the kinema even when it might take only a subordinate part. If it is for some unknown reason called a theatre, this can be explained only by the fact that during the period of the sway of naturalism (at present the enthusiasm of its followers has considerably cooled) the theatre called to its service everything that contained in itself elements of machinery.'[7]

At first sight it may seem remarkable that the cinema made no use of the technical experiment proceeding in all the arts of that time. Meyerhold's theories of actors' movement seem from today's perspective ready-made for an adolescent cinema, and were indeed, later adapted by Kuleshov to film use. Andreyev's subtle shadings of horror and even Skryabin's experiments can be found echoing through another country's films of later period that has much in common with pre-war Russia—post-war Germany. But these Russian films plodded drearily past the art movements of their day without absorbing more than their unhealthy attitudes and subjects. The film industry—primarily and solely an industry—was firmly chained to a low level of taste above which commercial success was not so surely calculable. Evidently the technical development of the film medium was waiting for its own artists—and for higher motives.

The outside influences brought to bear on the Russian cinema of 1912 changed its character completely. The modern dramas from Denmark had, with their host of successful imitations from other countries, become the only models that it was profitable for the unsure Russian producers to follow. The entire world industry's capitulation to the dinner-jacket, décolletage, and sin, was complete. Even in Italy, the gorgeous gowns and languid modern sighs of Francesca Bertini were replacing, with a few notable exceptions, the crowds and porticos of the Italian spectacle film. During 1912, all the French imports were dressed fashionably, including the films of the great stage performers—Sarah Bernhardt (*La Dame aux Camélias*) and de Max (in Abel Gance's *Masque d'Horreur*).

Russian historical films thus almost disappeared. After this turning point the film industry referred to a past century only for the purposes of celebrating a great date, such as 1812 or 1613, the year of the accession of the Romanov dynasty, or for the purpose of adding colour to a 'timeless' emotional pattern. The Russian cinema that had begun with processions of the real great, and had then hired actors and costumes to continue these processions, now tried to galvanize its wearying audience with modish evil and the *guignol*.

The film *guignol* was growing popular abroad. It was the single unreality that the Danish naturalistic cinema allowed itself. From there to Russia came *The Bride of Death*; Italy followed its tentative *Ward No. 13* with *Rehearsal for Death* and *Love of the Tomb*. The Russian companies leapt to the occasion. Thiemann

& Reinhardt made *Nailed* and inaugurated the popularity of Maximov as well as their famous Golden Series with *Corpse No. 1346*. Russian Pathé turned out similar titles: *The Terrifying Corpse* and *The Goblet of Life and Death*. Pathé also produced the first Russian effort to combine the evening-gown with the guignol, *The Secrets of House No. 5*, a 'salon' detective drama sprinkled with mysticism, vampies, ghosts, etc. A device for this period of the Russian cinema would be an open coffin rampant on a field of stage blood, the whole garlanded with intertwined lilies and bats.

Khanzhonkov, who had failed to popularize this genre three years before, was too busy with a huge new enterprise to follow the fashion. Enlisting the financial support and world distribution facilities of Pathé Frères, he had begun production, in the winter of 1911-12, of *1812*, a suitable successor to *The Defence of Sevastopol*—a film to celebrate the centenary of the French defeat in Napoleon's Russian campaign. In the production of *1812*, many novelties were introduced into Russian film-making—for the burning of Moscow, Sabinsky employed a miniature set; wolves tamed by the famous Durov chilled the audience by their ferocious attacks on French dummy soldiers stuffed with chunks of raw meat. Previous films—Russian and foreign—had copied well-known paintings, but the two directors of *1812*, Uralsky and Hansen, made a wholesale business of this method—copying (by composing living tableaux which were ruined as soon as movement started) all the French campaign paintings of the war-painter, Vereshchagin.* On August 25, 1912, the eve of the anniversary of the battle of Borodino, the film had a simultaneous première in all the cities of Russia. In spite of its inferiority to *Sevastopol*, it was a tremendous success and was reviewed in every newspaper of the Empire.[8]

The success of *1812* showed big business that the cinema offered a fair risk of a return on investments, with perhaps a little additional to make the game worth while. Khanzhonkov has told the details of the negotiations that led up to the formation, on September 8, 1912, of the joint stock-company, 'A. A. Khanzhonkov & Co.' with a capital of 500,000 roubles. Keeping in mind the comparatively limited business range of the Russian cinema during the entire existence of its management by private capital, this step can be compared, in what it meant to Russian film-finance, with the formation by Adolph Zukor in America that same year, of Famous-Players. It was the turning-point in Russian film history from hand-to-mouth film production to a larger, freer scale of investment and turnover. Stocks and the celebrated author had entered the cinema the same year, and it was not long before they found that there was room for only one of them. Khanzhonkov retained control of his company as president of its board of directors, and the literary supervision remained in his wife's capable hands. But producers and stockholders were soon to lose faith in the attraction of an author's

---

* The results were strikingly convincing for at least one witness. Early one morning the actor Kachalov, considerably under the weather, was returning home through Red Square. The all-night party and the jogging droshky had made him doze off, and when he awoke with a start, he saw advancing towards him Napoleon and all his marshals! Pinching himself, Kachalov went temporarily on the wagon. It was explained to him later that this was just a film-crew taking advantage of the early morning to use a real background for their scene of Napoleon's entrance into deserted Moscow.

name on the screen, and soon switched their attention to the 'star'. From the audience's viewpoint, it was only natural that the face of the star, created by repetition and sustained as long as the audience could identify its desires with that face, would supersede the invisible author. Within two years the celebrated author as a scenarist had disappeared from the posters, leaving only in slightly smaller type than the star's name, the title of his best-selling play or novel, adapted by a movie 'expert'.

Nineteen hundred and thirteen immediately showed the results of the joint entrance of literature and high finance into the film industry in 1912. The first signal was the appearance—on all sides and in all formats—of periodical film literature. Broader and more intense film distribution schemes needed more regular salesmanship methods—and the magazine or newspaper was the film-owner's contacts with the theatre-owner and the movie-fan.

The first Russian effort to publish a specialized journal devoted exclusively to the cinema was among the earliest of such efforts throughout the world. This was the bold effort of the nineteen-year-old enthusiast, Vsevolod Chaikovsky, to write and publish, in 1907, a film magazine.[9]The first issue was not succeeded by a second, because his enthusiasms had not taken circulation into consideration. The first well-organized Russian film trade paper was (as was to be expected), published by a Pathé salesman, Lourié, later in 1907. By the end of 1913, nine Russian magazines and newspapers devoted to cinema affairs were in weekly and monthly circulation.

The producer, Persky, published and edited a magazine also—the *Kine-Journal*. Like Khanzhonkov's paper, Persky had started his modestly in 1910 and by 1913 it increased its format along with the ambitions of the film industry. Although he had no interest whatsoever in the art movements of his time, he often invited figures from art circles to liven his pages with original impressions or opinions of the cinema, and the publicity being received by the Moscow futurists attracted his attention.

The futurists themselves were adopting the cinema without being asked. On borrowed money, a group of the futurist painters headed by Burliuk, Larionov, and Goncharova succeeded in producing the first 'futurist film', *Drama in the Futurists' Cabaret 13*, a parody on the prevalent genre of the film-guignol. The nineteen-year-old Vladimir Mayakovsky, who had joined the futurists in 1911, was fascinated by the cinema; at the height of his brilliantly public year of 1913, culminating in the performance of his futurist tragedy entitled *Vladimir Mayakovsky*, Persky asked him to contribute some argumentative pieces to his *Kine-Journal*.* The young poet assumed Persky's interest to be serious, and wrote a scenario—the first of many:

'My first scenario—*Pursuit of Glory*—was written in 1913 for Persky. One of the officials of the firm listened attentively to my reading of the scenario and then said, hopelessly, "Rubbish." I went home. Ashamed, I tore up the scenario.

---

* In Nos. 14, 16, 17, 1914. These were entitled 'Theatre, Cinema, Futurism,' 'The Destruction of the Theatre by the Cinema' and 'The Relation of Theatre and Cinema to Art.' The first of these appears as an appendix to this volume (p. 412).

Later on a tour of the Volga region, I saw a film made from this very scenario. Evidently it had been listened to with a closer attention than I had imagined.'[10]

Mayakovsky was not to try again as a film-writer until 1918, encouraged by the post-revolutionary freedoms of the cinema.*

During 1913 St Petersburg made a serious attempt to shift the concentration of film production from Moscow. During this year three new companies were formed in St Petersburg: Vita, Tanagra, and the Russian Cinematographic Association—all planning to divert into the film business some of the wealth of theatrical talent in the capital.

A retired cavalry officer, V. F. Gelhardt, remodelled his private apartment into a primitive studio and made use of his wide circle of artistic acquaintances for the initial productions of Vita. Gelhardt's literary friend, Alexander Kuprin, wrote a series of slapstick comedies for Giacomino, the variety star, in which Kuprin himself playfully assumed small rôles in the same spirit that he organized wild parties. Another writing friend, Nikolai Breshko-Breshkovsky, established the fortunes of Vita by writing *The Fighter Behind the Black Mask,* a detective story dressed in fantasy. It was inevitable that such a man-about-town should approach his friends among the dancers of the Imperial Ballet. Gelhardt persuaded Marie Petipa, daughter of the great choreographer, to perform one of her numbers for the cinematograph, *A Night in the Harem.*

When Bistritsky formed the Tanagra Company, his first move was to place under contract the popular comedian, Varlamov, and the pretty ballerina, Smirnova, as his surest attractions. Obtaining these, he was unwilling to waste such fine assets on the poor equipment and studios of Moscow, and postponing the construction of his St Petersburg studio, he transported his stars and his stories to Berlin. There he hired space and technicians in the Bioscop Studios, making Russian films with an entirely German staff, including the director, Georg Jacobi.

The third of the new St Petersburg companies did not begin so auspiciously. The first films of R. K. T. (Russian Cinematographic Association) were received coldly, barely getting distribution, and its third film was censored irrevocably. This was a large-scale film version of Kuprin's naturalistic novel, *Yama,* which was never seen publicly until after the revolution. As the R.K.T. had staked all its remaining funds on this ambitious project, it was obliged to retire from production when *Yama* was shelved.

The Moscow firms added ballet as a novelty to their programmes, and competed for the services of the stars of the Imperial Ballet at the Bolshoi Opera. Most in demand was Yekaterina Geltzer, whose miming talent equalled her fame as a ballet technician. She made a short film for Pathé of the Bacchanale from *Samson et Delilah,* and a longer film of the whole story of *Coppelia,* with Zhukov and Riabtsov. She danced a Chopin *Nocturne* and Schubert's *Moment Musical* (with Tikhomirov) for Thiemann & Reinhardt. Ballet never found a stable place on Russian film programmes, although one of the film stars, Vera Coralli, came

* Persky's search for scenarios led him in 1915 to ask Vladimir Korolenko for a film story, but Korolenko offered him a story, 'Without Language'—of two Russian peasants in America—that was not 'suitable'. (*Iskusstvo Kino,* March-April 1950).

from the ballet (after an injury to her foot had temporarily halted her theatre appearances) and ballet dancers as heroines provided romantic interest even through the first period of the post-revolutionary film.

Dissatisfied with the half-hearted response to the *guignol*, Thiemann & Reinhardt adopted for imitation another genre from France—the drama of pathos, where plot-intrigue was replaced by the sentimental sensations of unreal figures clothed in the most exquisite sartorial taste. The titles alone of Thiemann & Reinhardt's Golden Series for 1913 (chiefly directed by Protazanov) are revealing: *How Fine, How Fresh the Roses Were* (an episode in Turgenev's life); *What the Violin Sobbed; The Shattered Vase; For Each Who Plays, Another Pays; How the Soul of a Child Sobbed; The Passing Dream, Caught but Once.* This sentimental period was epitomized by one of the Golden Series, *Keys to Happiness*, the greatest box-office success known to the pre-revolutionary Russian cinema. Made from the best-selling novel of its time, it owes its success more to its source than to its qualities as a film. The author, Verbitskaya, who also made the film adaptation, has been described as the Kathleen Norris of Russia— enjoying the same huge reading public, the same scorn from intellectual circles, relying upon the same sentiment and sex clichés. The film public doubled and quadrupled itself. In one St Petersburg theatre, the Gigantic, the prices of the 900 seats were increased as much as 30 and 70 kopeks, and the theatre made 28,550 roubles in a two-week run. In every theatre where *Keys to Happiness* played tickets were sold for several days in advance, and Standing Room Only signs were displayed day and night. With the proceeds of this one film, Thiemann & Reinhardt were enabled to install complete modern equipment in their studio.

The success of *Keys to Happiness* threw the formulas of the other producers into confusion. Self-conscious of his new financial responsibilities, Khanzhonkov switched from one type of film to another, trying out historical, contemporary life, comedies, fantasies, Jewish films, society dramas in hasty succession; the transition from the historical film to the modern 'psychological' drama was undertaken by Khanzhonkov with great reluctance. Only one thing was clear to Khanzhonkov and his stockholders, and that was that the films in which Mozhukhin appeared, no matter what their type, showed no financial loss. Although Ivan Mozhukhin had attracted little notice in his first excursions from the theatre to the film studio, now his large 'magnetic' eyes, clear features, and noble carriage were drawing together a 'Mozhukhin public'. His only rival, in quality and popularity, was Maximov, whom Thiemann & Reinhardt were clinging to ever since *Keys to Happiness*. It is doubtful if Maximov would ever have been 'starred' or if his star would have ascended to any height if he had not been so true a copy (in faultless evening dress—at all times of day) of a foreign favourite—the Danish actor, Valdemar Psilander ('Garrison'). The faces of Psilander, Asta Nielsen, and other Danish stars were to be found on more Russian postcards than any of the Russian movie faces. Actresses who might deflect some of Asta Nielsen's receipts to Russian production were sought everywhere. The 'Creo' Company in Warsaw, found a greater rival to Asta Nielsen than they could possibly have guessed. This was Apolonia Chalupiec, a sixteen-year-old actress with ballet training, attracting attention in the National Theatre. Beginning her screen career with *Slave of Passion, Slave of Vice* (advertised as 'autobiographical'!), this promising actress adopted a name easier for the posters —Pola Negri.[11] After less than a year of Polish films, Pola Negri interested German producers and was invited to come there.

Another greater film talent escaped from the periphery of the Russian Empire when a Russian army musician named Stiller took his son Mauritz from Helsingfors to Sweden, to evade his son's compulsory military service in the Russian army. Both the later Russian and Finnish cinema learned much from the original work that Mauritz Stiller accomplished in Sweden. Fortunately for the Russian cinema there was another move, in the opposite direction: one of its great contributors, Edward Tisse, was soon to move from his Swedish home to his mother's country, Russia.

Nineteen hundred and thirteen was the Jubilee year, the tercentenary of the Romanov dynasty. All the Imperial theatres prepared for the occasion special plays and productions: *The Choice of Mikhail Romanov for Tsar* at the Alexandrinsky, *1613* at the Malii. Meyerhold, perhaps not too innocently, prepared a production of Strauss' *Elektra* for the Marinsky, and had the reactionary newspapers crashing down on him with editorials about his impudence in presenting, on the 300th anniversary of the Romanov dynasty, a spectacle in which royal personages are beheaded. A bit too over-sensitive, also, was the sentimental disgust occasioned in some quarters by the postage stamps commemorating the tercentenary. These caused pain to patriots, for stamps have to be licked and postmarked. The Jubilee was celebrated in all the arts and industries, and naturally in the films, too.

Into the new encouraging atmosphere of an industry beginning to take hold, Drankov had returned from his retirement. Persuading A. G. Taldykin, the owner of a costume firm, to provide the capital and divide the profits,* Drankov again had money for grand enterprises. When Khanzhonkov announced the production of a grandiose (four-reel) jubilee film, *The Accession of the House of Romanov*, Drankov, with a whole costume firm at his disposal, attempted to undermine this project by procuring the patronage of the Tsar himself,† and launched a more ambitious project—*Tercentenary of the Romanov Dynasty's Accession to the Throne*—in seven reels, promising to bring the history up to the coronation of Nikolai II. Drankov planned to make use of the actual films taken of this coronation, but no one could find them, and it had become questionable if there actually had been a cameraman in Russia that early. The days of Lumière, Doublier, Mesguich had already become pre-historical to the Russian film industry.

Some idea of the methods employed in making Drankov's Romanov film, and of Russian film-making methods generally in 1913, can be found in Mikhail Chekhov's memoirs:[12]

'Shortly after joining the Moscow Art Theatre, I was invited to play for the cinema. I was flattered and excited. As soon as I consented, the man [Drankov]

---

* Drankov promised Taldykin the fulfilment of his fondest dream—to meet the Tsar!
† Not only did the Grand Duke Mikhail secure his brother's blessing upon the project, but he also opened the wardrobes of the Historical Museum for Drankov's use.

who had made the suggestion began to talk about fees. Waving his arms in the air, he advanced upon me, driving me into a corner. There we both halted. "Just think of it! What does the screen give you? Glory! You will be famous! Everyone will know you! And what makes this miracle? The screen! Understand? And besides you get thirteen roubles! Agree and everything will be settled." As far as I was concerned it was "settled" when that man began to wave his arms. I agreed. The man disappeared instantly.

'The film for which I was hired was to celebrate the 300th Jubilee of the Romanov Dynasty. Part of the picture was to be filmed in one of the small towns of Russia [Nizhni-Novgorod?]. It meant two days on the train and a stay of two days in a terrible provincial hotel. It was winter and there was a severe frost. Arriving there, we were sent to a cold barn-like building where we made-up and dressed in the required costumes. The actors were flippant, drank a lot and tried to ingratiate themselves with the leading man [Nikolai Vasiliev], who had grey hair, a swollen face, and the characteristics of a genius; for instance, he was afraid of the stairs and had to be supported on them while he closed his eyes and emitted piteous cries.

'For the first day I was placed on a high hill. The camera was at the foot, near a gate. I was impersonating Tsar Mikhail Fyodorovich. As I approached the gate, I heard exasperated voices shouting to me, "Abdicate the throne! Hurry up! There are only two metres left! Hurry up! Abdicate!" I abdicated as quickly as I could. At my left I suddenly found the leading actor. He was dressed as a priest, leading me by the hand, uttering thereby various obscenities. The "shooting" lasted quite a time. . . .

'The night in the dirty hotel passed very uncomfortably, and the following morning found me very wretched. The day began with the police chasing away the local villagers who, seeing our colourful costumes, had come to us with petitions in which their grievances against the local government were set forth. The petitioners having been driven away, the "shooting" began. They set me astride a horse and I was told to ride to the nearest clump of trees. . . . The "shooting" was distressing me more and more and I was ready to run away from my benefactors, giving up the promised glory and the thirteen roubles.

'That evening the producers gave a dinner in honour of the Chief of Police and other town officials. The Chief was a man of handsome presence, with a gallantly twirled moustache and a great number of medals on his chest. The dinner began with solemn speech-making. Anyone listening could imagine that the person upon whom each and every cinema-theatre owner, as well as the artistic and material success of the entire Russian cinema industry, depended and would ever depend, was this Chief of Police. In answering . . . he was not able to express his ideas as succinctly as the producers. Suddenly and surprisingly, the solemnity was transformed into an atmosphere of love, with everyone embracing everyone else and exchanging and signing photographs. The Chief of Police signed a photograph portraying some kind of monument.

'On the following day I was on my way back to Moscow. The filming was not yet finished, but I flatly refused to take any further part in the proceedings.

Another actor was engaged in my place, but he was photographed only from the rear, so that his shots could be combined with mine.'

As Pathé had not made its own jubilee film, it approached the two rivals with a plan to distribute both films. Thus they appeared simultaneously, and Khanzhonkov's more modest film was acknowledged the better—dramatically and historically. Drankov resumed his old war with Khanzhonkov. When he heard that his rival was preparing an expedition to the Caucasus to film *The Conquest of the Caucasus* with the Armenian actor Shakhatuni in the rôle of Shamil, Drankov found a new director, Chorni, an assistant to Max Reinhardt, and followed Khanzhonkov to the Caucasus. Both groups brought back practically the same film. Goncharov's novel, *The Cliff*, was put into production by both companies— Drankov with a cast lured from the staff of the Imperial Alexandrinsky Theatre and Khanzhonkov with actors from several Moscow theatres plus his trump card—Mozhukhin. Khanzhonkov won, and Drankov, after a few more attempts at importance, such as Pavel Orlenev in *Crime and Punishment* and the celebrated Jewish actor, Rafael Adelheim, in *The Secret of Professor Insarov's Portrait*, retreated to the less risky sphere of simple melodramas and vaudeville skits with Uncle Pud (V. Avdeyev).

Warsaw was assuming an important status in the European market, with its promising young actress, Pola Negri. It was from Warsaw also that the first genuine Jewish films came in 1912, employing actors from Jewish theatres, notably the famous Fishson, in *The God of Vengeance* by Sholom Asch and Gordin's *Satan*. The first Jewish companies in Warsaw were Sila (Strength) and Variag, established by two women, Yelizariantz and Stern. During 1913, two more firms were formed, Mintus and Kosmofilm, making only adaptations from the Jewish stage, even more tearful, if possible, than their contemporary Russian product. Often entire productions were carted to the studio, set up there and filmed exactly as staged. During this period Pathé produced several more Jewish films on their old plan, engaging as few Jews as possible. The Jewish films of most general interest were directed by Arkatov.

The steady film-audience was beginning to select its films by the producer and the actors, and even by the director. The audience attention given the foreign film directors—Urban Gad of Denmark, Léonce Perret and Louis Feuillade of France, Max Mack of Germany and Mario Caserini of Italy—was being divided as well among newly-known Russian directors. The 'name' directors in the Thiemann & Reinhardt studio were Vladimir Gardin (sharing the success of *Keys to Happiness*), Yakov Protazanov, and Alexander Volkov, learning their trade in the school of sentiment. From the weakening Russian Pathé, Sabinsky also joined Thiemann. Khanzhonkov had an equally-known group of directors—Pyotr Chardynin, entrusted with the bigger films, and Wladyslaw Starewicz, whom Khanzhonkov had discovered in an amusing way.[13]

One of Khanzhonkov's assistants had been delegated to keep a clipping service, not only of references to film business, but anything that might remotely interest an intelligent film producer, looking for story material and new people. One such clipping told of a young bookkeeper in Vilna, Poland, who, for three Christmas masquerades in succession, had won first prize for the most original costume. Interested, Khanzhonkov asked Vilna acquaintances to find out more about this young fellow Starewicz, and they reported his low pay, his success in art school, and his huge collection of butterflies and insects. An inquiry was sent him and he arrived in Moscow at once, ready for any work in the studio. While carrying out various jobs of designing, he learned everybody else's job as well. Without any previous training, he picked up still photography and motion picture photography. His infinite patience found ideal employment in introducing into Russia stop-motion photography, animating modelled figures. His first film in this technique was *The Beautiful Leukanida* (1912), performed entirely by modelled, jointed reproductions of his beloved beetles. After several experiments in this animating method, he turned his inventive mind to the drawn animation and produced the first Russian animated cartoon, *The Gadfly and the Ant*, from the Krylov fable. But it was the skilful animations of modelled insect and animal figures that brought Starewicz renown and gained for Khanzhonkov his first foreign success. The technique of modelled or jointed figures, animated by stop-motion photography, was not original with Starewicz; Emile Cohl, and British and American film-makers had employed this method at an earlier date, but rarely with as much gentle wit and charm as the films of Starewicz display. He delighted in giving human characteristics to his insect figures, as in *The Cameraman's Revenge*, where the bad-tempered insect-husband and beetle-butler suggest the engravings of Grandville.

Another director employed by Khanzhonkov was to rival Protazanov as a dramatic artist in the years before the revolution. Yevgeni Bauer had begun work as director and designer with the Pathé and Drankov studios; among other work he directed *The Secret of Professor Insarov's Portrait* and designed Drankov's big Romanov film. It was not until his association with Khanzhonkov, who gave his singular talents an almost free rein, that Bauer showed his best, and made a lasting impression on Russian film history.

The film audiences in the Russian theatres had a different appearance from that of metropolitan audiences of any of the other world film-centres. The amusement that the Tsar and the royal household found in the cinema was emulated by the Russian upper classes. It was well known that the court photographer was constantly employed filming the private pleasures of the royal family—the princesses playing tag, the Tsar and his male entourage splashing about in the lake, etc.* If the Tsar could be so personally pleased by the cinema as to have a private cinema-theatre installed in the palace at Tsarkoye Selo, there must be some noble pleasure to be derived from it. If the Grand Duke Mikhail Mikhailovich, an amateur photographer, Diagilev's sponsor at court and Drankov's support on odd occasions, could, for a hobby, run a cinema theatre in Tashkent, there must be something intriguing in the pastime, increasing the generally strange atmosphere around this Grand Duke. So film-going became à la mode and each new theatre built made exaggeratedly separated accommodations for the elegant element, and sometimes for the aristocracy. The rich furs and fashionable hats

---

* Several thousand feet, at least, were used in these 'home movies', of which the most revealing were incorporated by Esther Shub into her *Fall of the Romanov Dynasty* (1927).

had a natural scorn for native films. preferring anything foreign to its Russian equivalent. The Theatre Soleil ran nothing but foreign films, and *Quo Vadis?* at this theatre had the most moneyed audience, judging from the number of push-carts, selling kvass, candy, and articles of less filling uses, remaining in front of the theatre for the run of this film. The *Fantômas* serial began to arrive from France this year, and everyone, including the royal audience, followed the exploits of Fantômas and Juve with childish excitement. Outside the great centres, where a different audience paid humbler prices, two other foreign films were great favourites: *Les Miserables* with Henri Krauss, and a version of Zola's *Germinal,* butchered by the Russian censor under the ruling forbidding the representation of any form of hard labour,* but still with enough social value to attract the scrupulously protected working-class audience.

In its issue of April 19, 1913, the American periodical, *Moving Picture World,* published in its Projection Department an informative letter from a Nicolas J. Bluman, in the Moscow branch office of the M. P. Sales Agency:

'There are about 800 to 1,000 theatres here, the very largest only seating about 200 to 300 and are nearly always on the second floor. . . . As yet, there are no theatres here that can boast of having two machines, the nearest approach to this being two separate halls on the same floor with a separate machine for each. Half the programme is shown in one hall and the audience then saunters into the other for the remainder! ! ! ! ! The projection is invariably *bad* and there is only one show that transforms its current from the city three-phase to direct current for the projection arc lamp. Can you expect good pictures under these conditions? All the same we see the newest and best American and European films here, and it is noteworthy that the audiences are of a class far above any in the greater part of the rest of Europe. I have often seen high officials in uniform sitting in the local theatres and I certainly cannot say that of Germany or France. The prices charged for admission are high and there are always little open "boxes" at the back of the stalls, each of which holds from four to six chairs and costs five roubles ($2.50) the lot. . . '.

The editor's comment on this letter was, 'seems to me there would be a splendid opening for some enterprising Americans in the larger cities of Russia. . . .'

In July 1913, some sixty enterprising members of the Russian Educational Business Men's Association attended the Chicago convention of the Motion Picture Exhibitors' League for the purpose of studying exposition methods. They were astounded by the scope of an industry that they were only beginning to notice in their own country, and wrote to their friend in the Duma, F. I. Rodichev, directing his attention to the possibilities of encouraging this industry's growth in Russia. We next hear of this letter in a report by the police department (!) submitted to the Tsar!! Entertained as he and his circle may have

---

* An official circular, dated August 1913, demanded 'the strictest attention to films dealing with the lives of workers, and under no conditions whatsoever can there be allowed the exhibition of films depicting difficult forms of labour, agitational activity, nor those containing scenes that may arouse workers against their employers, films of strikes, of the life of indentured peasants, etc.' (quoted by V. Vishnevsky, in *Kino*, March 11, 1936).

been by films, the idea of films reaching the lower levels of his subjects made him panicky enough to write this note in the margin of the police report:

'I consider cinematography an empty, useless and even pernicious diversion. Only an abnormal person could place this sideshow business on a level with art. It is all nonsense, and no importance should be lent to such trash.'

In spite of the Tsar's private announcement, 'abnormal' persons continued to look at the film industry with the eyes of art, chiefly of literary art. A. S. Suvorin, wealthy St Petersburg publisher, had developed a theatre that was regarded with as much respect as the imperial theatres. Suvorin kept his repertoire fresh and international by sending each summer to Europe his manager and leading actor, Boris Glagolin, to inspect and purchase the new plays of Shaw, Hauptmann and Rostand. In the summer of 1912 Glagolin also inspected the Paris studios of Pathé Frères, and brought back to St Petersburg a new enthusiasm and a new hobby for Suvorin's literary interests. By the following year, in the scenery store-house in the Fontanka, directly behind Suvorin's Literary-Dramatic Theatre, the engineer Gakkel built a film studio in twenty-four hours, using equipment imported from Frankfurt. Glagolin's new film company was named 'The Russian Ribbon' (a film was called a 'ribbon') and sixteen friends and actors invested in shares at 500 roubles apiece—forming a basic capital of 250,000 roubles; 6,000 of this was invested by Suvorin.

Literature had motivated this film company, and literary taste was its chief claim to our attention. All Suvorin's 'name-authors', living and dead, were drawn into Glagolin's amateur scale of production during the next three years: Kuprin wrote an original film story on Jewish life, *The Coward* (which was sold to the United States); Leonid Andreyev adapted one of his stories as *The Story of a Girl*; Glagolin adapted two stories by Chekhov, *Illegal* and *A Daughter of Albion*; Burenin's dramatization of Boccaccio's *Fiametta* and Oscar Wilde's *Lady Windermere's Fan* gave 'tone', and Devereux's *Henry of Navarre* (filmed in Reval) gave 'size' to Glagolin's enterprise. He maintained his amateur status by relinquishing the larger profits and headaches attached to distribution—renting his negatives to distributors and larger companies for release. The amateur's entrance into an art indicates the growth of the art to adolescence, at least.

At a considerable distance from both the Winter Palace and the Fontanka there was an interesting polemic under way—in the Bolshevik press[14] Signed 'Ivan Petrovich', an appeal for the organization of a workers' theatre was introduced with this logic:

'. . . Due to his position in production the worker is a person chiefly active, and therefore he loves action, he loves the dynamics of life and he loves the theatre as an art dynamic to the core.

'That is why he fills suburban theatres, gratefully applauds untalented actors and animatedly accepts the contents even of anti-artistic and tasteless plays, offered to him by suburban entrepreneurs.

'That is why he goes to the kinemo and there roars over the stupid pranks of the cheap Glupishkin and sincerely re-lives the 'tragic torments' of the 'brilliant' Asta Nielsen.

'One can't ignore the serious and extremely harmful influence of the cheap theatre and kinemo on the proletarian psyche. . . .

'It is absolutely necessary to satisfy this thirst for aesthetic sensations unknown to the suburban theatre and kinemo of the existing type; *it is absolutely necessary to set up one's own workers' theatre.*'[15]

Pursuing this question, 'A.T.' agreed with 'Ivan Petrovich's' premises, but went to considerable lengths to clear up certain of his misconceptions, among them his total rejection of the cinema:

'The cinematograph of itself is not evil. In proper circumstances it not only can make misty pictures but it can also perform a task that we know—the development of the masses, and can even reach the level of a guide to art. The matter is only that the cinematograph is in the hands of persons who pursue a single aim—profit, and so, from the cinematograph to art is "a distance of enormous length".

'However, the cultural-educational societies can do something in this field, also. It is absolutely necessary for them to enter into agreements with proprietors of cinematographs [theatres], guaranteeing them on certain performances a definite number of customers, and distributing the tickets for these performances among their members, etc. Of course, the condition must be made that the choice of the film must be in the hands of the society. . . .'[16]

The final word—for the time being—and possibly the official word, on this subject, was published by Vladimir Osipovich Zelensky, writing under the name of 'Leontii Kotomka'. His article, entitled 'The Cinematograph and the Workers', opens by demonstrating the extraordinary 'accessibility' of film-theatres to *all* classes, including the working class:

'Good in idea, this democratic theatre would appear by its content to be an embodiment of bourgeois vulgarity, of commercial calculations, a slave to the tastes of the spoiled upper classes of society, a servant of capitalists. Falsely sentimental kinemodramas, with cloying philistine morality. Comedies that are primitive and devoid of content. The cinematographic press sees all this and realizes the relation to militarism and the Parisian mode [pornography]. But it is only on extremely rare occasions that it looks beyond this.

'Educational, historical and scientific films appear on the screen in only small quantities and modest lengths. Instead, cinematographic celebrities, with unnatural and exaggerated crude mimicry, teach the audience unhealthy, antiartistic tastes.

'Comedians force laughter from the spectators by grimaces, smashed crockery, damaged clothing, head-spinning falls, and a carefully cultivated primitive and crude humour, far from the noble "laughter through tears". When the modern cinema attempts subjects touching class interests, its leit-motifs are invariably either bourgeois-reactionary or hypocritically liberal.

'But the cinema can occupy a prominent place in the life of the working class. It can tell about the life of the working class.

'It can tell of the life of the workers of all countries, opening the pages of international artistic and scientific book-treasuries, reflecting all the phenomena of social life in living illustrations, in order to demonstrate the advance of the working class in all countries. The task of democratizing the cinematograph under present conditions is impracticable. There are a few improvements of the kinema-theatres possible on the way towards the establishment of workers' cinematographs. There has been a proposal made to demand the screening of classical, ethnographic and historical subjects. And it is necessary, therefore, to take care that the demand is large and serious. Gradually developed, workers' cinematographs can bring to life a corresponding film company. But all this will be only a partial improvement of the cinema.'

It would be interesting to know who, among Russian film-workers, read this programme on the day it was published—March 30, 1914.

Boris Glagolin
from Remizov's album, *Theatre and the Rest*

CHAPTER IV

A Crumbling Empire

1914–1917

Our last weeks at Peterhof were very crowded:
meetings, official receptions, two weddings, and the
manoeuvres—all this went on just like a moving
picture

NIKOLAI II

Russia's character of a semi-colony of Western Europe, with France, England
and Germany competing on business and diplomatic fronts for the upper hand
in 1914 appears boldly clear, in perspective. In looking back on these months,
some call them the most prosperous in Russia's history, while others see in this
prosperity only the outward signs of a growing subjugation to increased foreign
investments. The bustle of business, the transactions on the stock market were
creating profits that never saw Russian pockets. Although forty-nine per cent
of Russian business was done with Germany, the Franco-Russian alliance was
bound more tightly by the milliards of francs that Paris banks lent the Tsar's
Government.

The cinema industry of Russia also fed on this fortune. Stronger financial
ties abroad and at home gave it short-lived ease and comfortable grosses. Its
prestige grew in all quarters; the Court Chancellery presented awards and orders
to the managers of the Khanzhonkov and Pathé studios for their jubilee zeal,
and the ministries began to employ films in their departments. The Minister
of Agriculture ordered films taken in the provinces for inspection in St Petersburg,
and the Minister of Naval Affairs ordered a record made of the entire Russian
fleet and all naval fortifications. In the circles of the arts, the cinema, now a common conversational topic, reached a new intellectual height by being the object
of an official debate in a forum held March 9th, where the relative values of theatre
and films were settled once, but as we well know, not 'for all'. The chairman on
this occasion was Baron Dreisen, and the distinguished debaters included Meyerhold, Ozarovsky, Soloviov and Prince Sergei Volkonsky.[1]

But the opponents of the cinema still occupied high places, too. Whenever
V. Purishkevich rose to speak in the State Duma, his colleagues grew to expect
fresh scandals from this spokesman of the notorious 'Black Hundreds'. But on
May 21st, he surpassed himself. With the words, 'I propose to draw your particular attention to the new plague, to the cinematograph,' he hurled streamers

of film at the startled tribune. These were fragments of a newsreel in which he figured, but with such an 'insulting' portrayal of his appearance and actions, that he had confiscated it from a film-theatre. 'Beware! It may be I today, but it will be another tomorrow, and the day after loftier persons—in the service of the state—who will be ridiculed by this frightful weapon of propaganda, employed towards the revolutionization of the popular masses?' Almost as an illustration of the measures he proposed, the newsreels ran into trouble with the rising Rasputin, whose written permission had to be obtained before a picture taken of him could be shown. Film censorship stiffened—the strictures against the depiction of any form of hard labour were severely enforced.

Above all this, diplomatic gestures increased in pressure. In June, Admiral Beatty brought an imposing part of the English fleet on a demonstrative visit to St Petersburg. President Poincaré paid France's respects (with gentle reminders of the Russian obligations) to the Tsar during the particularly strategic days of July after the assassination of the Archduke Ferdinand. He found St Petersburg trying to cover up signs of the bloody suppression of a general strike that had grown out of the workers' resistance to speeded-up war orders.

There seemed only one answer to the French banks and the Russian people, and when the Tsar declared war on July 20th, the hope of the Russian autocracy to restrain the growing forces of revolution played no small rôle in the decision. All the stops of patriotism, religious fervour, and hysteria were pulled out, and Russian men marched off in the glory of this music and flower-strewn streets to die for a foreign cause. The war's inner domestic motives were manifested in many ways. A visiting English vicar writes of 'a huge crowd of "demonstrators", all carrying thick sticks and singing the National hymn at the top of their voices whose huskiness is readily traceable to the last public house.... There is shouting here and singing there, and everywhere the frenzied waving of national flags and the display of cheaply-printed portraits of the beloved "Little Father".'[2] Employing the old method of furnishing outlets for this spirit, the press assisted the first of several German pogroms. Using as a pretext the 'indignities' suffered by the Dowager Empress on her return to Russia through Germany, the rioters sacked the German Embassy. Anti-German orators and gestures were plentiful, but the grandest gesture was the Tsar's order to change the name of St Petersburg to Petrograd—from a German to a Russian name. Every voice opposing the war was silenced—the five Bolshevik deputies in the Duma were soon arrested and later exiled to Siberia.

Everything was swept along on this patriotic tidal wave. The war rapidly subordinated all cultural problems to the single question of their relation to war. When Khanzhonkov returned to Moscow after signing a contract for the unfinished *Cabiria*, he was 'reminded of a military camp. . . . In the city they spoke of nothing but the war, and only of those businesses that had acquired military significance. The cinema was no exception.'[3] The film industry's first move was a noble one—the financing of a hospital, but the war's commercial advantage to the industry became apparent so clearly that their support of the war can not be considered as disinterested. Closed frontiers meant closed foreign distribution offices in Moscow.

During the first fervour, theatre attendance dropped off slightly. A panic-stricken proposal to close all theatres until the end of the war was countered by the argument that such a move would depress the spirit of the nation. Meyerhold took advantage of the panic to write for the *Bourse Chronicle* a feuilleton entitled *Theatre and War*, saying 'Why should the entrepreneurs be so alarmed? It seems to me that they are frightened by the realization that the kind of art which they have been showing to the public isn't needed by that public any more.' And he turned to the production of the first of the symbolic war plays—*Fire*. Life quickly resumed its normal course. In Petrograd, the show-window of the Government and court, 'trade was brisk, carriages rolled along the avenues, and the Morskaya Prospekt was brilliantly illuminated. The theatres were filled to capacity.'[4] In Moscow, the business centre, the theatre managers turned into the staunchest patriots—without waiting for the autumn season, August brought on war spectacles and pageants by the dozen in every community that boasted a stage. The first six months of the war produced 175 war plays. Wagner, Schiller, etc. naturally were hurried from the repertories.

The cinema industry showed similar zeal. A special war newsreel appeared, called *Mirror of the War*, whose first issue comprised the following items: *Our Trophies in Lvov* (Lemberg), *Naval Engagement in the North Sea*, *Barbarous Destruction of Louvain*, *Barbarous Bombardment of Rheims*. Other war newsreels were soon made available to the eager theatres—*The Holy War*, and Gaumont's *On the Western Front*. The Skobelev Committee that was to assume greater film responsibilities, opened its first film department—for the filming and distribution of newsreels.

The war was an undisguised blessing to the Russian film industry. Freed from foreign competition, the industry was spurred to more intense production and greater efficiency. New companies were formed, new studios were built, new fortunes attempted. The most spectacular of the new producers was Yermoliev. The legend is that as a camera-assistant for the Pathé newsreel he had taken cameras 'to clean' over week-ends; with these and with short-ends of negative he produced the first films that launched his success. He built his studio near the Briansky Station; Taldykin, near the Donskoi Monastery, Vengerov, on the roof of the highest building in Moscow—the eight-story Rubinstein House. A new large laboratory was rushed to completion, the 'Svetosil'.

Turning on the German and Austrian films which had contributed to Russian film technique, they applied what they had learned to fighting the Central European Powers with every metre of film. Battles, attacks, spies were the first film subjects to come into the theatres to supply the emptied agencies and the audience's emotional needs. Typical titles of this period are *Under the Bullets of the German Barbarians* (Thiemann and Reinhardt); *For the Honour, Glory and Happiness of the Slavic Race*; *In the Bloody Glow of War* (Taldykin); *Secrets of the German Embassy*; *Glory to Us, Death to Our Enemies* (Khanzhonkov). Approaching Andreyev, to whom 'the war augured a revival of heroic aspirations and noble sentiments, rendering tragedy timely and desired',[5] Khanzhonkov persuaded him to adapt his war play, *King, Law and Freedom*, for his studio. All energies were poured into stimulating mobilization and morale, and the authorities encountered no widespread difficulties at first.

'In the same measure as the war with Japan, in 1904-05, had been unpopular in Russia, the war against Germany was in the beginning—before the manifestation and corruption of the military and civil authorities—popular and stimulating. It appealed as a conflict of ideas, and of course there was no doubt in the minds of either side as to which ideas were right and just.'[5]

To make sure that this idealism was followed logically by orderly mobilization, the Tsar made the supreme sacrifice of his liquor monopoly by raising the price of vodka beyond the means of the to-be-recruited soldier. The reformers praised this move so warmly that he was persuaded to stop the sale of vodka altogether, even closing the beer shops. Naturally the best intoxicants could still be had openly at expensive restaurants (where one drank alcohol from a teapot instead of from a bottle, following Mrs Gamp's example), but the lower classes must be guarded against themselves for the duration of the war. And thus the war again rebounded profitably to the film, a substitute for drink. If you couldn't get drunk you could while away an inexpensive evening at the cinema. At least it was more satisfying than kvass.

The mobilization did continue in good order, even though the common soldiers were very hazy about the reasons for the conflict. In these early stages of the war, it was simpler to maintain the class distinctions between the officers and the ranks. In 1914 the officers were drawn from the well-to-do and professional elements exclusively. The theatre surrendered many of its best young talents, and the officer casualties included film names as well (no casualty list of private soldiers was published). The film actors, Shaternikov and Pomerantsev, were dead or missing, the first wounded included enlisted film theatre managers, the actor-director Alexander Volkov, and the Skobelev Committee's cameraman at the front, Ercole.

The films had their 'publicity' victims, too. Late in August, the Russian office of Pathé released to the press the sad details of Max Linder's death. It was tragic—Max, being an Alsatian, was called to fight in the German army against his own French brethren. But death saved him from this horrible predicament, when he fell beneath the wheels of a motor lorry before firing a single shot. All Russian newspapers and magazines (no other country was informed) printed this story and Max's popular films won new admirers. But in November, the Russian press received a singularly contradictory communication, ending:

'. . . In anticipation of a gratifying meeting in Berlin with my Russian brothers-in-arms, I beg you to receive assurances of my sincere sympathy. Vive la Russe! Vive la France!

Voluntaire de l'Armée Française, Max Linder.'

The first war winter found Russian cities in an atmosphere of victory and gaiety. On the Eastern Front, the Germans retreated from one Polish city after another. No matter whose victories there were, the cities east of the Polish province became choked with refugees and wounded. The care of these victims was the object of innumerable Red Cross teas, charity ballet performances, receptions, and 'charming evenings'. While the poor of Petrograd gave unstintingly of their money and clothes to assist the soldiers and refugees, ladies out of the *Almanach de Gotha* sporadically operated private nursing homes, which they closed when they grew bored.[6] With the assurance that the end of the war was at hand, the several charitable organizations became careless. The gap between the increasing needs for hospitalization and the decreasing support was filled by the Government with taxes on all goods—whose prices were rising steadily anyway, because of the improvement in the methods of the profiteers. The collections made for the hospital run by the cinema industry fell with startling rapidity.

The war's wounded could not disturb the film industry's delight in its growing prosperity. Italy's entrance into the war withdrew another nation from the competition in the Russian market. Many of the German films of earlier date were withdrawn from the theatres through a special decree of the Council of Ministers. Others went on, disguised as American, Dutch, French or Danish. One newspaper detected Berlin scenes labelled New York. But these were further contributing factors to the rise of the Russian film industry.

The films were sought after and capitalized upon by their most scornful opponents. Although the Imperial Theatres forbade the films to their actors, and private theatres like the Korsh wrote this prohibition into actors' contracts, players lured by a little extra money managed to evade these restrictions. Success in films often created crises that resulted in departure from the theatre. The Moscow Art Theatre characteristically appealed to the individual conscience by forbidding its actors 'to take part in any film that does not have serious motives'. There were such edicts, usually stricter, from the great theatres in every film-producing capital; in New York the Charles Frohman office announced, much earlier, that any actor who worked in moving pictures could not work for them.[7]

Stanislavsky's personal feeling about films began as contempt, warmed into antagonism, and never went beyond tolerance, in later, mellower years. His kindest words were in an interview of 1913: 'I've never been an admirer of the cinema—I have even been what you might call an "antagonist" . . . But recently I begin to sense a possible superiority of cinema to theatre.' Yet in 1915, when he heard that Yevgeni Vakhtangov and Olga Baklanova appeared in *The Great Magaraz*, he refused to speak to them for six months. Even with a discipline harsher than this he could not have stayed the flood. A constant underground movement of his theatre's youngest actors to the film studios (and some extra money) was too strong to be countered by any measure short of dismissal. Even a young director of the theatre, Boris Sushkevich, took advantage of the theatre's 'conscience clause' to direct entire groups of his young colleagues* in films that he would not be ashamed to show to Stanislavsky—*When the Strings of the Heart Sound* (in 1914, with Vakhtangov, Baklanova, and Mikhail Chekhov), *Cricket on the Hearth* (1915), *Hurricane* (1916), and a Chekhov story, *The Flowers are Late* (1917). Another actor, Boleslawski, directed and played in more commercial films. Individual actors took their chances, often in ways that sound extremely

---

* After seeing *Symphony of Love and Death*, an effective adaptation of Pushkin's one-act play, *Mozart and Salieri*, with Geirot and Baklanova.

interesting: Maria Germanova made a film solo, *The Corner*, in 1916. The grandest project, worked out by Gorky and his actress mistress, Maria Andreyeva, was for an entire film production unit attached to the Art Theatre.[8] The millionaire Lianozov pledged his support, Gorky was to choose the stories to be filmed, Krassin was to superintend the technical departments, and Andreyeva was to be in charge of casting—but Stanislavsky or Nemirovich-Danchenko must have put his foot down. The death of Leopold Sullerzhitsky cancelled the most hopeful plan to link Stanislavsky to cinema. Stanislavsky had actually given his most trusted disciple formal approval to make a film for 'Russ'.[9]

Fyodor Shalyapin, who made life unhappy for the current Intendant of the Imperial Theatres, defied the rules again when he felt tempted by the multiplied audiences of the motion picture. In the summer of 1915 his impresario, Reznikov, formed the Sharez Company for the purpose of filming the great actor-singer in his most popular rôle—Tsar Ivan the Terrible in Rimsky-Korsakov's opera, *Pskovityanka*. A few years later Shalyapin angrily told the whole silly story to Lev Nikulin:

'What a robber he was—even his name was robberish—Ivanov-Gai. He was quite a talker, bright and crooked. We were introduced in the baths. People are naked at the baths and you can't see their souls.

'There was something about him that I liked. I can't remember who brought him to me. "Fyodor Ivanovich, there are millions of people dreaming of seeing you in the films, and even though they wouldn't hear you, just seeing you would satisfy them. And especially as Ivan the Terrible."

'So he talked me into it, damn him. Nothing but shame came of it. I go to the filming. There are some extras about, feeble folk on police nags. Who are they? I was told—"the tsar's falconers." They hold stuffed birds on their arms, and they are themselves stuffed pea-green birds. I suppose this means a falconing hunt is to be filmed. . . .

'That robber Gai tells me: "Don't worry, Fyodor Ivanovich, for God's sake! Although they look so unpresentable, they're all college students, intelligent people. . . ." So what of it, should I hire them as tutors? And what are those costumes they're wearing? "Those are costumes of the period, hired from Zimin's."

'Oh, well—I dress and make up for an Ivan younger than in *Pskovityanka*. I think out everything. I come out, and see two men aiming cameras at me, and there are rods stuck here and there in the field. "What are those for?" "Look, be so kind as to walk from here to there, no nearer and no farther than six arshins." Has he gone out of his mind? "Oh, no, Fyodor Ivanovich, that's the technique, optics and such."

'I looked at Ivanov-Gai, he was trembling. "I swear to God, it's a technical law, you can ask anyone. Here's a Frenchman—the cameraman [Winkler]." Well, I say, the rods can go to the devil, I'll walk and act, and let these people with the cameras follow me and film. "Oh, that's impossible, cinematography can't do anything like that. . . ."

'What sort of acting could you do—two steps forward, two steps back. I dropped everything and decided to give everything alike the same face, the same eyes, without any more fuss. We started filming—the sun is shining, a little breeze is blowing, there's an old church on a hillock in the middle of the green meadow— all real, not as in the theatre. I even became inspired and imagined that the Terrible himself might have ridden here to hunt. . . .

'Suddenly that man screams: 'Hold it, Fyodor Ivanovich, hold it!'' What's wrong? The sun had gone behind a cloud, you couldn't photograph. My whole mood was ruined. No, this is not for me . . . Others, like Mozhukhin or Polonsky, can do it—I'm just not lucky at it. I'll never act in a film. . . .'[10]

Shalyapin was paid 25,000 roubles; the production was expensive, but slipshod in quality, depending exclusively on the star, and the finished film was not popular. It was calculated to appear for the jubilee of Shalyapin's twenty-fifth year on the stage, and the star cannot have been very proud of his careless venture. The press was severe. One of the bit players was Richard Boleslawski, a young actor from the Moscow Art Studio earning a few extra roubles in an idle summer.*

The hasty ripening of the film industry was seriously hampered by the lack of raw materials. The war had interrupted regular shipments of raw film, and each company began to ration its reserve stocks. Positive film was scarce enough, but the situation was worse in negative stock. The raw film crisis was beginning— already—producing its expected crop of speculators. The Paris factories of Pathé had been completely disorganized by the war and could not promise French pro- ducers, let alone Russian, any constant supply. Mr Dunn, the cautious repre- sentative in Russia of Eastman Kodak Company, accepted orders only when paid in advance and without giving any guaranteed delivery dates.

However impeded the industry was by these obstacles, it blossomed as it never had before—in scope and in attendance. The early spring of 1915 witnessed the appearance and development of the greatest of the pre-revolutionary film actresses. Vera Kholodnaya, the wife of a poorly paid officer, applied for work at the studios as an extra. She had one black evening gown, whose appearance she changed by a judiciously placed flower at her shoulder or waist. The black gown and her dyed black hair set off a face whose paleness was accentuated by dead white make-up, making her heavy bottle-green eyes conspicuous even in a crowd of extras. At the height of her later fame, she said, 'My eyes are my bread.' She was to become a brunette star in a blonde country that contrarily worshipped dark Francesca Bertini and darker Asta Nielsen. Khanzhonkov's brilliant director, Yevgeni Bauer, discovered Vera Kholodnaya among the studio extras, and gave her a leading rôle in Turgenev's *Song of Triumphant Love*, which established her among the Russian stars. Fellow actors ascribe her fame to her plasticity in an intelligent director's hands (usually Bauer's), and a face and graceful figure that photographed well from any angle. Russian films and Russian film actors—the ballerina Vera Coralli, Natalia Lissenko, Vladimir Maximov, Vitold Polonsky, Olga Gzovskaya, Vladimir Gaidarov—were becoming powerful favourites of the Russian audience, though never wholly displacing Nielsen and Linder.

* Another bit was played by Mikhail Zharov, who had the experience of seeing himself in the film thirty years later when Eisenstein and he were doing research for another film on Ivan the Terrible.

Another of the Russian stars began a new stage in his career when Ivan Mozhukhin left Khanzhonkov, in whose studio he had learnt film technique since 1911. His feelings were hurt when the director Chardynin invited another actor to play a desired rôle, and he went over to the fine new studio of Yermoliev. But it was Bauer's originality that had formed Mozhukhin as a new type of screen actor; Mozhukhin's memoirs record the change:

'. . . one day Bauer had the idea of entrusting to me an important and very dramatic rôle in a film whose title I have forgotten [probably *Life in Death*, 1914]. In the course of the plot a woman, whom I was supposed to have loved, died, and I had a long scene of despair beside her body. Up to then, when an actor was given a scene of this sort, he expressed his grief with much wringing of hands, attitudes of dejection, facial contortions practised at great length before a mirror, and glycerine tears. In a complete break with this tradition, already entrenched in our studios. I contented myself with playing the scene in an absolutely motionless position, gradually bringing myself to the point where tears—*real* ones—suddenly welled up in my eyes and trickled down my cheeks. . . . What made me more happy than the success of the film was that I felt I now understood cinema.'[11]

The film industry was not sufficiently co-ordinated to make for complete security. It remained a speculation to the end of its history of private ownership. Recognized actors demanded a deposit in the bank before going before the camera —new actors had to take a chance, as the producer was as likely as not to run out of money in the middle of a film. Kholodnaya was the only actress to command a salary even comparable to modern motion picture salaries. Paid by the film, she obtained as much as 25,000 roubles ($12,500) for one production—that lasted as much as three months. The situation was so shaky that the most secure of the producers was glad to find a rich man interested 50,000 roubles worth in the career of a girl.

Film production boomed in quantity but without having any effect on its quality and with a positive decline in the worthiness of its subject matter. The war films were crude and tasteless, finally serving more to inflame the resentment than the fighting spirits of the spectators. And they were well prepared in their resentment by the news from the front. Inefficient generals, lack of munitions, delayed supplies allowed the German and Austrian troops to begin their recovery in 1915 of all the territory they had lost in 1914. Defeat at the front was accompanied by disintegration in the rear. The Tsar's insistence that the industrialists regulate production and consumption—and their incomes, released an open break between the autocracy and the capitalists that the future was able to mend only temporarily. Rumours spread rapidly, most of them with a basis of unpublished fact. The war was becoming unpopular, and certainly unwise as subject matter, for literature,

'Undoubtedly the great emotional impulse of the opening of the war in Russia has passed. This is reflected very clearly in current literature. The flood of printed lectures, war-pamphlets, and poems has ceased. Volumes of war stories are no longer printed, and indeed the war as a literary topic has become of minor interest.'[12]

for theatre,

'The interest in war themes in the theatre soon diminished. It became apparent that the public avoided war on the stage and sought peace-time subjects for their entertainment.'[13]

and for films.

The reaction here turned from the blood of very real thousands to the blood of a single theatricalized corpse, from the horrible reality of war to the fantastic irrationality of the murder mystery. On its lowest level this tendency was expressed by the sensational serial, derived from the accidentally perfect timing of the release in Russia of the French *Fantômas* and the American *Perils of Pauline*.* An omnipotent heroine is common to the several successful serials that Russian producers put onto the market. Drankov made *Sonka, the Golden Hand* in six chapters, with a Miss Hoffman. Gardin and Protazanov directed for Yermoliev *Petersburg Slums* in four chapters, and Bauer directed a more sophisticated arrangement of the same crimes and gangs in *Irina Kirsanova* for Khanzhonkov. Very few of the film firms pursued anything resembling artistic tasks; most of them had an appetite for money-making that seemed slaked only by detective films, adventure stories and crude farces. These titles adorned the lurid posters: *The Wolf of Moscow, How Women Promote Their Husbands,* (Weckstein); *Krivula the Bandit, The Scalped Corpse* (Russ). Alexander Drankov, whose *Sonka* led the field, laid it on pretty thick: *The Bloody Fortnight, The Seventh Commandment, A Ruined Life, Thirsty for Love, In the Claws of the Yellow Devil,* etc.

On a higher level (the highest then) were the firms of Yermoliev, Khanzhonkov, and Thiemann & Reinhardt. They made intelligent appeals to theatre people for assistance, unlike Drankov, who in hiring Alexander Tairov, chose from the Kamerny Theatre's repertory a subject that fitted into the studio's policy—*Le Mort,* by the Belgian writer, Camille Lemonnier. Tairov's decision not to employ any subtitles was, like all of his work, interesting but neither original† nor profound, an idea dating backward to the first films and dating forward to *Shattered* and *The Last Laugh.* The theatre world was accustomed to large sums being offered to its dramatists and its actors, but the invitations to directors were rare, and Paul Thiemann's offer to Meyerhold, the most stimulating theatrical figure of his time, was news.

When Meyerhold came to Moscow in May 1915, before his first film subject had been chosen, he outlined his proposed film methods generally in a newspaper interview:

'My first task will be to undertake a thorough research work into the methods of the cinema, methods which are still deeply hidden and unused. The cinema

* Pearl White is the only American actress whom war-time Russian movie-goers can remember.

† Max Reinhardt's film of the Vollmoeller pantomime *Venezianische Nacht* (1913) had been acclaimed for its lack of subtitles.

as it exists today is entirely inadequate and my attitude toward it is negative. I feel very indignant about what I have seen up to the present time. I have my own specific theoretical approach to the cinema about which it would be premature to speak now.'

His biographer, Volkov, provides more detail:

'Meyerhold was not satisfied with the existing form of the scenario—he wanted dialogue furnished for the actors, and guiding directives to the directors, designers, electricians. He found it necessary to attract non-professional actors to the films, his opinion being that the majority of dramatic, operatic and ballet artists had already demonstrated their utter unfitness for the screen.'[14]

Thiemann's first suggestions to Meyerhold were Hugo's *L'Homme qui rit* and d'Annunzio's *La Gioconda*, but the final decision rested on Oscar Wilde's *The Picture of Dorian Gray*. Meyerhold himself undertook to find in Wilde's 'golden embroidery' a consecutive film story without falling into the ghoulish errors that the French and Danish producers of this story had made. Like the true experimenter that he was, he threw himself into this new work with his full enormous energy and imagination. He employed every means to set this symbolistic tale of downfall in an atmosphere of luxury, decadence, and subtle horror. Vladimir Yegorov was employed to design the few built sets, and Meyerhold borrowed from his Moscow friends quantities of rich and tasteful 'properties'. The cast was largely drawn from outside the studio personnel—Meyerhold himself playing Lord Henry Wotton, and finally placing an actress, Varvara Yanova, in the difficult rôle of Dorian.* Meyerhold brought from his theatre theories elements into the photography and lighting that were original to all cinematography of that time. The entire film was composed in bold black and white masses—with dramatically lit figures against dark backgrounds or striking silhouetted figures against bright backgrounds, as in Dorian's caped figure outlined against a huge high-keyed theatre poster lit by a single street light overhead. One of the most vividly original episodes was a scene from 'Romeo and Juliet' shown as reflected in the large mirror of the loge behind the watching Dorian. As punctuation throughout the film, Meyerhold used Wilde's epigrams. The scene of Basil Hallward's meeting with Dorian is concluded with 'Laughter is not at all a bad beginning for a friendship and it is far the best ending for one.' A large close-up of Dorian and Lord Henry Wotton was preceded by 'The only way to get rid of temptation is to yield to it. Resist it, and your soul grows sick with longing for the things it has forbidden to itself.' Other epigrams performed similar functions.

The film was planned to be three reels in length with eighty-two different scenes, an unusually large number. Preparations included an unaccustomed amount of time spent in rehearsing the actors. The resultant film was acclaimed by critics of vision, and pretty generally disliked by the public at large. It was original and daring as few films before it or since have dared to be. Russian artists who saw it and then *The Cabinet of Dr Caligari* a few years later in Europe, tell me that if it had been shown abroad it would have surpassed *Caligari*'s

* This was a source of great irritation to the inimical critics later, as had been Meyerhold's casting of an actress in the leading rôle of Calderon's *Steadfast Prince* at the Alexandrinsky.

reputation as a heightening of film art. It was undoubtedly the most important Russian film made previous to the February Revolution.

With the lowest level in 1915 reached by the blatant sensationalism of *Sonka, the Golden Hand*, and the highest by the luxurious mysticism of *The Picture of Dorian Gray*, we find a prodigious number of forgotten middle films of an absurdity of 'high-class' sentiment that we may find difficult to visualize today. A fragment of a 1915 scenario[15] demands quotation here:

 1 Count Ozersky arrives at the gate of the villa in a luxurious automobile.
 2 Chauffeur gets out and bows low to Count Ozersky.
 3 Count Ozersky nervously takes a bouquet of lilies from the chauffeur.
 4 TITLE: '*You may return home, Nikolai.*'
 5 Count Ozersky smells the lilies and with a musing air walks to the door.
 6 Count Ozersky presses the door-bell.
 7 The hall-porter opens the door and bows.
 8 Count Ozersky speaks.
 9 TITLE: '*Is the baroness at home?*'
 10 The servant bows low and replies:
 11 TITLE: '*The baroness is not receiving anyone.*'
 12 Amazement and rage fill the countenance of Count Ozersky. He steps back, glaring fiercely.
 13 TITLE: '*What does this mean? Is it possible that you do not know with whom you are speaking?*'

The indignant Count Ozersky was very far away from Russian realities at home and at the front. As these realities forced themselves more upon the consciousness of the Russian population, the films dropped all pretences of reflecting life and Count Ozersky became Sir Reginald Bradwin-Arbuthnot or the Duc d'Amoulé wooing similarly fictional ladies in indefinite Western European vacation spots. When you entered the movie theatre (the 'Piccadilly' or the 'Parisiana'—or, in Harbin, the 'Decadence'), you departed from this drab world.* All the admiration for the foreign turned to a frantic attachment to a distant rosy other-world of Paris negligées and Mediterranean landscapes (filmed in the Crimea). Russian authors assumed names like Alexander Smith, or Jones or Higgins. One of Alexander Vertinsky's popular songs was 'Where Are You, My Little Creole with Purple Eyes?' Even the flowers mentioned in literature or song could not be Russian—they had to be rhododendrons or cactus.

The censors encouraged this departure from reality. Newspapers and magazines appeared with white or blackened spaces where news of any revealing factual sort had been. The theatre censors were dubious about the advisability of rare references to war. In June of this year the innocent Kursk Society for the Promotion of Popular Education was suppressed altogether. This society, with its 30,000 roubles of capital, its seventy reading rooms and public libraries, was one of the necessarily privately subsidized institutions for adult education, and its

* From a contemporary poem by Moravskaya:
'For those whom life has cheated,
Open the electric paradise.'

suppression is indicative of official fright. The cinema was especially censor-ridden. Max Reinhardt's film of his *Miracle* was found in circulation and stopped. Every film that spoke of Jews was confiscated or cut—*God of Vengeance, Civic Duty of Jews, The Beilis Case.** From *The Life of Wagner*, the Jewish cantor scene was cut, and the rest was allowed as *The Life of a Composer*. This was carried to its logically ridiculous extreme: all Biblical films were forbidden—*David and Goliath*, etc. ('Very dangerous to see so many Jews on the screen'). The Siberian prison scenes were cut from *Resurrection* and the grave-diggers were removed from *The Living Corpse!*

Anti-German riots went to new lengths. For three days—May 27, 28, 29, 1915—houses belonging to Germans or even with German names were burnt. Four hundred and seventy-five shops and 217 residences were attacked and looted, of which it was later established only 113 could even have been suspected of being German.

'For the first twenty-four hours the police could or would do nothing. Fires broke out in many quarters of the city, and, if there had been a wind, the disaster of 1812 might have repeated itself. On the Kuznetsky Most I stood and watched, while hooligans sacked the leading piano store of Moscow. Bechsteins, Blüthners . . . were hurled one by one from the various stories to the ground, where a high bonfire completed the work of destruction.'[16]

Rumours of high treason in high places were circulating and the police had been advised from extra-Governmental quarters that 'the riots would have a salutary effect on a lukewarm Government'.[17] In Kiev there was a special drive against 'German influence' in any form in the theatres and cinemas. In the press of this day, 'German influence' can usually be translated 'liberal tendencies', which could be interpreted without limits. There was a German spy uproar in Moscow's 'Union' cinema theatre. Other results of the provoked anti-German feeling were the forced departure of Reinhardt from the firm of Thiemann & Reinhardt and the warnings given Paul Thiemann, whose long Russian residence was in his favour. It was revealed that Nordisk received German financial support, and Asta Nielsen and 'Garrison' disappeared for a time from Russian theatres.

The energy of Drankov was equal to these new times. He conscientiously drew upon Russian literary successes—filming Andreyev's *He Who Gets Slapped* with Pevtsov (directed by Ivanov-Gai), and attracted café society into the movies —the Princess Vyazemskaya came to act and the Princess Bebutova offered her unwanted novels to the 'new art'. The enemy nobility were 'exposed' in an early *Mayerling—Maria Vetsera, The Secret of the Habsburg Court*. But these were only conscience-soothers. His income depended not on these, but on his *Secret of Loge A, Contagion*, etc. etc.

The raw film crisis was still in effect, but the first panic was over. Crannies in the frontiers were found and Kodak received regular shipments through Vladivostok and Denmark. Finished films filtered through at several points,

---

* This detailed reconstruction of the notorious trial of Mendel Beilis was filmed by Josef Soifer in the actual Ukrainian locations. It was not publicly released until after the February Revolution.

mainly Greece and Rumania. But the film industry had new troubles. The bad
spring had produced a worse summer at the front. In August, the Tsar dismissed
the Grand Duke Nikolai and assumed command of the already tottering army.
Russia's control of its enormous front required a greater efficiency of its economic
resources than its technical backwardness permitted. The whole clumsy edifice
of Imperial Russia was collapsing. Emergency War Industry Committees were
set up to handle all supplies. In October 1915 the Special Fuel Council decided
to requisition fuel stocks, and the theatres and cinemas were the first to be placed
under restrictions. Restrictions on fuel stocks meant higher prices on fuel, so
movie theatres were forced to raise their prices. Seats that had cost fifty kopeks
were raised to a rouble and fifty kopeks, or seventy-five cents. In the lower
scales, the lift from fifteen kopeks to twenty-five resulted in a serious loss of the
poorer customers and many smaller theatres had to go out of business.

Bourgeois circles were alarmed when the Grand Duke Nikolai's dismissal was
rumoured. The Tsar's answer to them and their spokesmen—the President of
the Duma, the Moscow City Duma, and other backed bodies—was not only the
execution of the Grand Duke's dismissal but the prorogation of the Fourth
Duma on September 3rd as well. Thus ended the last nationally representative
body allowed by the Tsarist Government. The remaining bodies had the character
of clubs and abstained from any political function. Such a one was the All-
Russian Union of Zemstvos, or County Councils, headed by Prince Lvov, and
dedicated to the care of wounded, hospitals, manufactures of clothing, munitions,
etc. In September the second category of recruits was called up. The approaching
winter of 1915-16 seemed dark and confusing.

It was at Khanzhonkov's initiative that the film industry revived at least a
wish to participate in the aid to soldiers at the front. In the foyer of his theatre
he placed a moving picture camera in front of the contribution box, filming each
donor and showing them on the screen the following week. There was an increase
of both contributions and attendance. A more ambitious but less practical plan
was formed at a meeting called by Khanzhonkov of all the Moscow film directors.
Chardynin proposed a film to be made jointly by all the studios and by all the
directors! A production committee was formed of Chardynin, Bauer, Protazanov,
Gardin and Krivtsov, the subject chosen was Tolstoy's *Fruits of Enlightenment*,
and nothing came of this enthusiastically conceived idea, whose purpose had been
to raise money for gifts to soldiers.

Conditions at the front must have exceeded in horror those of any other
European front. Sir Alfred Knox noted in his diary:

'I hear whispers that the Russian infantry has lost heart and that anti-war
propaganda is rife in the ranks. It is little wonder that they are down-hearted
after being driven to slaughter over the same ground seven times in about a
month, and every time taking trenches where their guns could not keep them.'[18]

There were refusals to attack in the army and mutinies in the navy in the winter
of 1915.

'The frightful horrors of war drove the soldiers to desert. The deserters were
constantly hounded, they lived in fear of being betrayed to the police at any

minute. Yet they preferred the life of half-starved deserters hunted like wild beasts by the military police, to life at the front. In 1916 there were already over one and a half million deserters from the Russian army.'[19]

The allies in the West sought every means of 'putting spirit back in the Russian army'. Naturally they turned to films. Throughout 1916, increasing in quantity as the war spirit of the Russian army and public declined, there was a frantic flood of foreign film propaganda. These predecessors of George Creel's 'battle of the films' came mostly from France. At the beginning of the war France had sent crude atrocity films that were not appreciated by the rapidly cooling Russian audience. Later the atrocities, decorated more subtly, enacted by famous actresses (Sarah Bernhardt in *Mères Françaises* and Réjane in *Alsace*) were more easily stomached by the Russians. Both French and British put most of their film faith in some semblance of reality, sending regular newsreels and feature films made largely of war newsreel material. Even the Italian Government sent a film propaganda mission to Petrograd on the eve of the February Revolution. Business interests were also at work in these films so successfully that the American Ambassador[20] repeatedly reported to his superiors that 'American merchants should get a firm foothold in Russia' before the English and French take full advantage after the war of the decline of German commercial influence. Until the entrance of the American Government and George Creel into the World War, the only American weapon was the bank. Among other cementing-friendship loans, the National City Bank lent Russia fifty million dollars in July 1916.

Inspired by the new ideas of foreign propaganda films, the Moscow and Petrograd studios were again enlisted by the Russian Government. Films appeared for many purposes (including Russian Liberty Bonds) and the usual technique was to use a body of newsreel material with a minimum of linking dramatic action. Most of these appeared from the production department of the Skobelev Committee, set up for charitable purposes, and sufficiently independent of Government policy to turn out a great variety of films. But these were for the public. The few films shown at the front were more cautious. In January 1916 General-Adjutant Ewert asked the film industry to provide every camp with film apparatus —to show only newsreels of the war and the army. The unreality of dramatic films of the war—or of any subject at that time—might have made for inconvenient states of mind among the soldiers. Even the newsreels showed a life at the front without the ugly detail that the soldiers knew too well, and the authorities soon found it safer not to show films at all.*

* I have found no further evidence of any general use of films for Russian troops in this war. Showings appear to have been arranged exclusively for distinguished visitors or for officers, as was the incident described by Bernard Pares, following the departure of a commission of military inquiry from General Baluyev's sector: '. . . when they had gone his staff felt they ought to do something to cheer [Baluyev] up, so they proposed a cinema show in the little garden. There we sat in the dark among the fruit trees, and the show began. The corporal who was operating was nervous, and the picture came on with great jolts upside down. A nervous voice came through the darkness: "Your Excellency, I beg leave to stop this picture; it's coming on upside down", and from the front bench of the spectators came Baluyev's gruff reply: "I command you to continue upside down." He then suggested that the whole thing should be done backwards.' (*My Russian Memoirs*. Jonathan Cape, London 1931. p. 378).

In the summer of 1916 the economic life of Russia considerably worsened; food shipments became less regular, and the price of all commodities gained twenty-five per cent over pre-war prices; the value of money dropped steadily. The administration demonstrated its disintegration by a series of new Prime Ministers and cabinet members, usually on Rasputin's recommendation. The cabinet under the régime of Baron Sturmer and Rasputin's protégé Protopopov as Minister of the Interior, was rumoured to be selling Russia to the Germans, and Sturmer was publicly charged with treason in the Duma by Milyukov. Along with keener privations the desire for coarse amusements grew; the farce theatres, the operetta, the café-chantant and the once-worried cinema thrived.

There are evidences from all over Russia of this prosperity. Visitors invariably remarked the busy cinema box-offices. Vladikavkaz in the south: 'In the evening I witnessed at a cinema building, made lively by an energetic band of music, a humorous fantasy which appeared highly popular.'[21] Archangel in the north: 'I fell in with various queer people; a speculator buying up land, a one-eyed man with smoky glasses seeking a site on which to build a cinema. Eight thousand roubles would buy a cinema with all fixtures, including an electric piano. It was bound to be a success, he argued, for there would be no other place to go in the long black winter.'[22] Even in Minsk, within the Pale, 'the shopping streets seemed composed, in about equal parts, of moving-picture shows, photographers' windows full of officers' pictures, and the officers themselves'.[23] The film theatres in Riga were full despite the German bombings. Hugh Walpole lived in Petrograd as an agent of the British Foreign Office in the interests of allied propaganda, and his literature on Russia abounds with references to the cinema as a pleasant habit. One of the best of these passages appears in his novel, *The Secret City:*

'We had arrived. The cinema door blazed with light, and around it was gathered a group of soldiers and women and children, peering in at a soldiers' band, which, placed on benches in a corner of the room, played away for its very life. Outside, around the door were large bills announcing "The Woman Without a Soul, Drama in four parts", and there were fine pictures of women falling over precipices, men shot in bedrooms, and parties in which all the guests shrank back in extreme horror from the heroine. We went inside and were overwhelmed by the band, so that we could not hear one another speak. The floor was covered with sunflower seeds, and there was a strong smell of soldiers' boots and bad cigarettes and urine. We bought tickets from an old Jewess behind the pigeon-hole and then, pushing the curtain aside, stumbled in. Here the smell was different, being, quite simply that of human flesh not very carefully washed. . . .

'No one could have denied that it was a cheerful scene. Soldiers, sailors, peasants, women, and children crowded together upon the narrow benches. There was a great consumption of sunflower seeds, and the narrow passage down the middle of the room was littered with fragments. Two stout and elaborate policemen leaned against the wall surveying the public with a friendly if superior air. There was a tremendous amount of noise. Mingled with the strains of the band beyond the curtain were cries and calls and loud roars of laughter. The soldiers embraced the girls, and the children, their fingers in their mouths, wandered from bench to bench, and a mangy dog begged wherever he thought he saw a kindly face. All the faces were kindly—kindly, ignorant, and astoundingly young. . . .

'The lights were down and we were shown pictures of Paris. Because the cinema was a little one and the prices were small the films were faded and torn, so that the Opera and the Place de la Concorde and the Louvre and the Seine danced and wriggled and broke before our eyes. They looked strange enough to us and only accented our isolation and the odd semi-civilization in which we were living. There were comments all around the room in exactly the spirit of children before a conjuror at a party. . . .'

In another place[24] he describes another usual feature of the programme: '. . . in the intervals between the pictures he has music-hall turns—the two dwarfs, the gentleman who sings society songs, the fat lady and her thin husband—all this for a penny or twopence.' All theatres used music—a pianist, or an accompanied violinist, or, in the case of smarter theatres like the 'Palace' or the 'Crystal', a chamber orchestra.

The Russian film industry of 1916 was a more solid investment than Walpole might have assumed. There were 164 production and distribution firms; 30 of these were actively engaged in making new films. The capital investment of the entire industry amounted to 4,100,000 roubles.

Paul Thiemann (now calling his company 'Era') again invited Meyerhold to make a film for them and this time the search was among the works of Edgar Allen Poe and Villiers de l'Isle-Adam. The choice fell upon a Polish writer with Poe affinities—Stanislaw Przybyszewski, and the first novel of his trilogy—*The Strong Man*. Working simultaneously on it and on a staging of Tchaikovsky's *Queen of Spades* for Nikita Baliev at the Chauve-Souris Theatre, Meyerhold's ideas on films became more articulate. After finishing the film he told an interviewer from *Teatralnaya Gazeta*:

'In producing a film adaptation of Przybyszewski's novel I wanted to carry out the same ideas which I attempted to realize in *The Picture of Dorian Gray*. I wanted to bring to the screen those specific acting gestures that respond to the laws of rhythm and to utilize in the fullest way the light effects that are natural to the cinema. My work in the field of light effects, to which I ascribe great importance, was considerably hindered last year by a cameraman who couldn't be persuaded to leave his conservative notions. This time, the firm has given me a more experimental cameraman with more understanding.* The technical side of the cinema plays a great rôle, but is far from completely known. As to the settings of the film I found a real artist and an inventive collaborator in Vladimir Yegorov. We agreed to show in the film not whole scenes, but only sharp fragments of the whole. We've cast out a mass of unnecessary detail in order to focus the audience's attention on the highest moments of the rapidly developing film. . . . As to the acting itself I want to point out that my aim was to avoid any excessive accents, the moving-picture apparatus being over-sensitive in catching and reproducing even the most subtle gestures.'

* His cameraman for *Dorian Gray* had been Alexander Levitsky; Samuel Bendersky photographed *The Strong Man*.

During production he wrote enthusiastically about the work, the cast (with Khokhlov and Zhdanova of the Art Theatre; he again played a secondary rôle himself) and the staff.

The Strong Man was finished in August 1916, but its harsh reality and cynicism prevented its release until near the October Revolution. Its honesty must have been strikingly apparent in this season of tasteless trash and tasteful unreality. The memorable films of the fall and winter of 1916 were of this latter category. Protazanov made an extremely decorative film of Pushkin's *Queen of Spades*—a good story faithfully rendered. Its film adaptation was made by a college student, Fyodor Otsep, working after school hours as an assistant editor of Yermoliev's movie magazine.

Not normal men and women, but devils, ascetics, vampires peopled the films of the Russian winter of 1916. One of the best of these really merits a detailed synopsis here. *Satan Triumphant* was directed by Protazanov, and played by Mozhukhin and Natalia Lissenko. In possibly Scandinavian surroundings, there lived two brothers, a minister and a hunchback painter of the chapel with a very beautiful wife. One stormy night a stranger who has asked for shelter, tells the minister of all the beautiful things in this world which he has not yet tasted. From then on, the minister can neither preach nor sleep for thinking of his brother's wife. The Stranger disappears. In the town, the minister finds in the window of an antique shop an old print of Satan in a jubilant, haughty attitude. His meagre salary cannot afford this luxury, but he is tempted to break into the shop and steal it. The print takes the place of the Stranger in his life. The minister no longer resists any temptation and he and the beautiful wife are drawn together. One sultry night, both are unable to sleep and discover each other's presence near the altar. They embrace—lightning strikes the steeple— and the illicit pair are buried in the debris of the fallen scaffolding. The film ends with a close-up of the old print, broadly grinning.

Strikes and demonstrations in the cities during this autumn frightened the administration almost more than the difficulties at the front. The jingoistic newspaper, *Russkoye Slovo*, proposed an extensive use of films for the purpose of giving the public 'a more healthy political and social outlook'. During December the autocracy closed the Union of the Cities and the Union of Zemstvos, and prohibited the most innocent of meetings—such as a meeting of the Society of Journalists and a meeting of the Society of Children's Doctors. In January 1917 new elections were carefully *planned*, under the supervision of Khvostov, a former Minister of the Interior. Eight million roubles were placed at the disposal of this election expert for the purpose of bribing the press, issuing literature, hiring printshops and organizing street displays and cinema shows.[25]

It was bread that upset the neat campaign. It was hungry women who decided the course of the several palace conspiracies. The rumblings grew into a general strike in Petrograd on February 25th. That evening, Nikolai II answered the cracking noises of the falling empire with the following telegram to General Khabalov, Commander of the Petrograd Military District:

'I command you, not later than tomorrow, to put a stop to the disorders in the capital, which are intolerable in this grave time of war with Germany and Austria.'[26]

When questioned by the Investigation Committee after the February Revolution, Khabalov testified:

'This telegram—how shall I put it?—to tell the frank and honest truth, it was like a thunderbolt to me. . . . How was I to put a stop to the disorders not later than tomorrow? . . . When they said "Give us bread!" we gave them bread—and that was the end of it. But when the flags said, "Down with autocracy!"—how could you appease them with bread? But what was to be done? The tsar had given his orders. We had to shoot.'[27]

That was on February 26th, and by February 27th, the insurrection had grown to such proportions that events moved at catastrophic speed. The Tsarina sent a series of telegrams from Petrograd:

'The revolution yesterday assumed frightful proportions. I know that other army units have joined. The news is graver than ever before.

'Concessions are essential. The strikes continue. Many troops have joined the revolution.'

One would like to speculate on the appearance of Petrograd that night. We know that shots emptied the streets immediately. We know that the brilliant audience at the long-awaited première of Meyerhold's production of Lermontov's *Masquerade* heard the shots through the gilt and red velvet of the Alexandrinsky Theatre. And we know something about the film posters on the emptied streets— screaming lithographs that were visible even on corners where the street-lamps had been shot out—advertising *The Festival of Night*; *Then She Decided Upon Revenge*; *The Torturing Enigma*; *The Bloody Exhalations of a Perverted Love*; *Fate's Puppet*; *How Madly, How Passionately She Wanted Love* and *Playing With Her Heart as With a Doll, She Broke Her Heart as She Would a Doll*.

Returning from General Headquarters, the Tsar got no further than the station of Dno, where he turned and went to Pskov. There he was informed of the victory of the revolution, and he resolved to abdicate. On March 2nd, he abdicated in favour of the Grand Duke Mikhail, who quickly abdicated in his turn. On March 8th he was arrested, and confined with his family to the palace at Tsarskoye Selo. There is an apocryphal cablegram of this period:[28]

'Nikolai Romanov
Petrograd Russia

'When I was poor boy in Kiev some of your policemen were not kind to me and my people stop I came to America and prospered stop Now hear with regret you are out of a job over there stop Feel no ill-will what your policeman did so if you will come New York can give you fine position acting in pictures stop Salary no object stop Reply my expense stop Regards you and family

Selznick, New York'

An Interlude

in which some personages of Russian history touch the film, each in his own way.

I

The Stavka—General Headquarters of the Russian army—was far enough behind the lines to be comfortable, but far enough from Petrograd to require its own entertainment facilities. The Tsar was at once the social leader and the reason for society in this small community. He had installed his favourite diversion at the Stavka immediately upon his arrival. True, the movie theatre there was not as elegant as his private theatre at Tsarskoye Selo, but when the lights went out and the machine started he could relax and forget the absurdly long drawn-out war that was keeping him from his wife for so long. Once a week his daily letter[1] to her would describe a visit to the cinema—no matter through what crisis Russia or the Russian army was passing. One such letter, dated April 6, 1915, ends thus:

'Well, my love, my little bird, I must finish; it is time to dispatch the courier. We are all going to the cinematograph.

Ever, beloved mine,
Your hubby, Nicky.'

It was here that the foreign powers tried to exert cinematographic pressure on him, with a lukewarm reaction that can be judged by his reports to the Tsarina. 'We were shown part of a very interesting English military film . . . remarkably interesting and entertaining(!)' and for a film of Verdun, '. . . saw an interesting French picture at the cinematograph.'

In the letter (March 9, 1916) in which he tells her of the secret plans for the coming Russian drive—which undoubtedly she told 'Our Friend' Rasputin, at once—he writes:

'Yesterday I went to a cinematograph which was particularly interesting, because we saw many scenes of Erzerum immediately after its fall. The high mountains are amazingly beautiful; covered with deep snow, glistening in the sunlight. . . . After this we saw two amusing pictures with Max Linder—this would probably have appealed to the children.'

But this man whose habits of irrelevance and concern with trifles led him to devote whole letters to a leaky fountain pen saved his warmest enthusiasms for more important films. His favourite film was *The Exploits of Elaine*, whose chapters he saw regularly through the summer, fall and last fatal winter of 1916. The last chapter is reported in his letter of December 7, 1916:

'The cinematograph was extremely interesting last night. We know at last who is the "mysterious hand". Her cousin and fiancé, would you believe it? This caused tremendous excitement in the theatre.'

2

The Vitagraph studio in New York had hired Emil Vester to give authentic Russian atmosphere to a Russian spy melodrama—*My Official Wife*. The real reasons for this production were Clara Kimball Young and Earle Williams, but Blackton decided to make it a super with real costumes and real beards. Among other atmospheric properties Vester required some nihilists, and he did his casting in a Second Avenue café. He brought back to the studio some fine nihilist types who drew five dollars a day for glowering in an underground meeting-place. Vester says that one of these was Leon Trotsky, whose American name of Bronstein appeared on the studio register as Brown. The work would have been a not unpleasant way of adding to his small salary on the *Russkii Golos*, and it is said that he found time to play the same rôle again at Vitagraph before he returned to Russia.

3

When the extreme rightist conspiracy to depose Nikolai II, consign the Tsarina to a convent, crown the Tsarevich Alexei and appoint the Grand Duke Mikhail regent, was plotted, the first step in this palace revolution was to be the assassination of the key figure of Grigori Rasputin. As this part of the plot was outlined, it became clear that a decoy was necessary. The conspirators considered all their lady acquaintances, and the choice fell on a film actress. Out of that famous harem for Grand Dukes, the Imperial Ballet, the Grand Duke Dmitri Pavlovich had chosen Vera Coralli to grace his days. Able then to enter films without fear of losing her Imperial contract, she added to her ballet fame a film fame, and altogether she must have been a very tempting morsel whom Rasputin had long wished to meet. Well-armed with poison and revolvers, the Grand Duke felt safe in allowing her under the same roof with Rasputin.

So the Yusupov Palace on the Moika Canal was manned on the night of December 16th by Prince Felix Yusupov, the Grand Duke Dmitri Pavlovich and Purishkevich, supplied with biscuits sprinkled with arsenic and a well-mixed bottle of Rasputin's favourite wine, and baited with a film star.

4

One of the little film theatres of Zurich was sometimes attended by a man who didn't come for entertainment or forgetfulness or any of the well-known purposes of film attendance. He came to study Europe, to watch in the newsreels the appearance and spirits of the peoples of all the warring countries, the faces of the diplomats and generals—especially those generals who had decided that his death would make the world safer for war. This was Vladimir Ilyich Ulyanov, whom the Russian working-class and secret police knew as Lenin. After his day at the library, when it was not convenient to continue his work at home, Lenin came to films for information.

CHAPTER V

From February to October

1917

The time is at hand, an avalanche is moving down
upon us, a mighty clearing storm which is coming, is
already near and will soon blow the laziness, the
indifference, the distaste for work, the rotten boredom out of our society

Three Sisters, CHEKHOV

'The February Revolution was joyfully greeted by the film workers. Nevertheless, in the confusion everyone forgot to film anything on the first days—February 26th to 28th. Not until March 1st did the cinematographers collect their wits, and take their cameras out onto the streets.'[1]

When their cameras did come out in Petrograd there was little more to be photographed than the natural consequences of an outraged people taking immediate retribution—blown heaps of ashes where the official blackmailing records had been thrown, blackened walls of emptied, burnt prisons, crowds assisting in removing coats-of-arms from palace and barber-shop. Around the Hotel Astoria, which for the past six months had been the luxurious headquarters of the higher officers, 'the snow of Morskaya was cumbered with hundreds of broken bottles and soggy with spilt wine'[2]—not from an orgy of drink but of anger.

'The pavements were filled with excited and happy people. Everybody was wear-ing red badges and ribbons. Here and there automobiles and trucks filled with armed soldiers passed by. The people on the pavements welcomed them with cheers and the waving of hats. The soldiers answered them in the same way.'[3]

Detectives and policemen who had rushed into civilian disguise to escape this anger were caught and lined up in front of the cameras for future audiences to jeer and hoot. The film that was finally released to the joyful populace was a combination of all the material taken by the various companies' cameramen in both Petrograd and Moscow, and assembled in the Military-Cinematographic Depart-ment of the Skobelev Committee. This was entitled *Great Days of the Russian Revolution from February 28 to March 4, 1917.*

Another cameraman who came out after Petrograd's streets were safer was Donald C. Thompson, an American news-photographer, with a notable lack of scruples and disregard for facts. He has left some literary documents of his adventures, in one of which[4] his companion records the following fine remark, 'A photographic record of the French Revolution would be beyond price. This is my chance.' This was said 'while seeking shelter in a doorway from a burst of bullets that swept the Nevsky Prospekt' and thus began Thompson's biased 'document' of inter-revolutionary days that he brought back to America and showed in December 1917 as *Blood-Stained Russia.*

Moscow, too, was taken by this 'peaceful revolution'. An eye-witness of the Moscow events provides a revealing glimpse of the character of the February Revolution:

'All through, there had been no loud yelling—either cheering or quiet talking. No uproariousness, no hooliganism, and this you could understand when you looked at the crowd. They all seemed prosperous and well-to-do. All in furs. No roughs or toughs. All either good old mujiks or the intelligentsia. And all so very happy. Every one went home at night. When I went out this morning, the Revolution was over. Constitutional government was assured, and the whole people began to make holiday.'[5]

In Petrograd the revolution had left behind it not one government, one power, but two. The tsarist troops and police had been fought and overwhelmed by the women from the bread-lines, the men from the factories and the revolutionary soldiers and sailors. Although it was these who risked their lives to upset the autocracy, the upper classes behind the autocracy were too clever and well-organized to let working-men and peasants take away their power. Thus the Soviets, or Councils, of Workers' and Soldiers' Deputies that had been set up by the revolution allowed their power to be surrendered bit by bit to the Provisional Committee of the State Duma, which rapidly transformed itself into a Provisional Government, and in this form retained bourgeois power which had been so nearly lost. The capitalists and landowners breathed easily again.

The dual power was reflected in the film industry as in every Russian industry. The workers and professionals in this field, where before the February Revolution only one strong industrial organization existed—that of the theatre-owners, began to demand their own unions. The Revolution seemed to them a real one, and in the joy of the first days few saw that the fight for these rights still lay ahead.

'The March days of 1917 were days of sentimental hope and illusion for the cinema. Censorship was put aside temporarily. Now the cinema could speak in its true voice! Many hoped that the revolution would at last reconcile the owners with the studio workers and the creative workers, would wipe out rivalry, would eliminate friction between theatres and distributors; projectionists prepared to demand a vacation and an eight-hour working day; the directors and cameramen dreamt of enough raw film on which to film true, uncensored works of free cinematographic genius.'[6]

On March 3rd, the day of the declaration of the Provisional Government, the 'dual power' appeared in a Moscow film theatre where 350 delegates were attending a meeting of the 'All-Russian Society of Kino-Theatre Owners'. The speeches were cautiously fiery. The President of the Society, Mr Antik, sent a telegram of greetings to the Government from the meeting. To the Soviet of Workers' Deputies was delivered an offer of all the companies to work collectively on a film of the February and March days (finally assembled by the Skobelev Committee) for the sole benefit of political prisoners, freed by the revolution, and their families. A proposal with less disinterested motives was 'to organize, from the responsible workers of cinematography, for the aid of the Soviet of Workers' Deputies, a commission to dispose and circulate films in Russia and abroad'. This might give the means to break into that long-wished-for international market.

Not a word as yet on the union question. The next meeting was scheduled for March 6th, which would be open to all workers in the film industry for a discussion of 'problems common to all', but no particular effort was made to bring the workers to this meeting. It was assumed that the same theatre-owners would be the only ones to appear, which would make discussion much simpler and satisfactory. They must have been considerably put out when two thousand representatives of every department of the entire Moscow film industry turned March 6th into a mass meeting. Not only industrialists, distributors, laboratory owners, and studio managers appeared, but plenty of workers from the studios, agencies, theatres, laboratories, trade papers—directors, actors, designers, cameramen, to make the discussion really interesting.

Antik manoeuvred a Mr Igor Kistyakovsky (one of the Khanzhonkov Company's board of directors) into the chairman's seat in the hope that his profession of barrister and his political party, the Constitutional Democrat (Cadet), would make the right appeal to the liberals in the audience. The chairman's opening speech glittered with ambiguous classical quotations, and in coming to concrete suggestions, not very surprisingly dwelt on the need for the Government to resume its police functions and the film industry's need for smoother distribution facilities! He pleaded for the unity of all the forces of the film industry—the owners and the workers. The director, Bonch-Tomashevsky quickly took up this theme, passionately asking for labour and capital to unite in support of themselves and the Provisional Government:

'At such a time, when all Russia is pulling toward one aim, when Russia gathers together her last strength in order to overthrow the cursed, hateful structure and organize a democratic Russia, any move toward disunity is criminal!'

This was a thought, even in these exact words, that might have been heard in the Duma that day as a protest against any effort at basic reform by the Government temporarily in power.

All the artistic workers who spoke,★ with the exception of Bonch-Tomashevsky, voiced objections to such a single organization of owners and workers, and in so doing risked the hostility of their employers. When the owners continued to ignore this opposition, two workers angrily proposed that all workers leave the meeting. Representatives from the artists' group unsuccessfully begged them to

★ Viskovsky, Gardin, Perestiani, Azagarov and several less-known actors.

stay and support them for otherwise their voices would not carry any weight and in the confusion Kistyakovsky announced an intermission.

The final result at the meeting was a Temporary Committee (the words 'temporary' and 'provisional' became the key words of the February-October period) of twenty-four persons, including industrialists and theatre-owners (Kistyakovsky, Frenkel, Khanzhonkov, Aleinikov, Persky, and others), creative workers (Perestiani, Chardynin, Gardin, Bonch-Tomashevsky, Frantsisson, Azagarov, and others), and a couple of 'reliable' workmen.

Real results of a permanent character were obtained only away from the influence of the owners. Against a unionizing background of 130 new trade unions established in Russia during March and April, the workers in the film studios, agencies, and theatres formed nine professional organizations between March and July—not only in Moscow, but in Petrograd, Kazan, Minsk, and Odessa. The three important professional unions in Moscow to grow out of the dissatisfaction with the March 6th meeting were the Union of Workers in the Film Industry, the Union of Office Employees of the Film Industry, and a Union of Artistic Workers of the Cinema.

The most serious immediate problem facing this group of unions was the working conditions of the workers in the theatres. On April 25th, a leaflet, addressed to: 'Comrades mechanics, pianist-accompanists, and employees in the film-theatres' made workers and owners sit up with joyful and angry surprise, respectively. The leaflet read in part,

'. . . but we will be strong only when our membership includes all the workers in film-theatres, and for this reason, comrades, become members of the union. The larger we are, the stronger we'll be.'

The demands were for (1) the inviolability of active union leaders and seniority rights and (2) fifty per cent increase of pay. Everything proceeded according to the long-familiar pattern of strikes. The newly realized unity of the workers gave them a strength that rallied the staffs of twenty-five theatres to the strike. Theatre-owners promptly called in strike-breakers, and sometimes operated the projection-machines themselves rather than consent to talk over the demands of the workers. When the 'official' union (OKO) was approached to consider the strikers' demands, Antik refused to recognize the strike as anything more than an 'incident'. The union that led the strike gained enormous respect and authority with a successful settlement, membership boomed, and departments were set up for the workers in the rental agencies and in the laboratories. The owners had not accomplished their purpose, but they were soon to bring the fight into the open with the rest of their class.

The February Revolution brought about no change in the economic structure of the film industry. If anything, the tendency toward monopoly that the bigger firms had shown during the war was given fresh impetus by the 'new freedom'. Some of the old firms immediately reorganized themselves with new names and new policies phrased for favourable relations with the new Government. Antik was most ambitious of all. His 'Neptune Co.' with a new two million roubles of capital made wholesale offers to the best directors and actors throughout the industry in an effort to monopolize the field. Bauer and his entire production group were attracted away from Khanzhonkov by an increased salary offer, but found the new conditions offered by Antik so oppressive that they returned to the home fold in a few days. Vladimir Gardin, then one of the leading directors, gives us some idea of the conditions awaiting the creative workers in this new monopoly drive:

'I signed a contract with the "Victory" Studio for the production of three films "subject to our confirmation of the scenarios", and for this work, the three films, I received 3,600 roubles. Thus was defined the contractual relation between the director and the management. In five words 1917 made its methodological statement clearly and simply: *three films and money down*, but this "subject to our confirmation of the scenarios" was an innovation of the "liberal firms". Here was already a conquest of the February Revolution. I had written scenarios before but never did I have to write them under the management's supervision. Up till then, I had been given a title and I gave them back a film.'[7]

This censorship by the management of the director was an innovation. Investors of large sums in the capitalist film industry all over the world were already seeking to protect their investments by tightening controls over the talents that evoked the investments.

The foreign firms too acted as quickly as possible in taking advantage of this new situation. Broader distribution methods were devised, and the following comment from Chester Beecroft reveals the details of these methods:

'I went through Russia and Finland in 1917. The Scandinavian Film Agency, Ltd., of Copenhagen which I represent, was at that time the second largest rental concern in these territories. We had an enormous campaign laid out and believe that we would have been able to develop it from an eight to perhaps a twenty print territory. We had three offices operating in Petrograd, Moscow, and Odessa, and had worked out a scheme for connecting up several exhibition centres which have never had motion picture theatres for the reason that there have been no rail connections from town to town and that the roads were too rough to permit of automobile travel. There was no means of circulating the film for profitable distribution. One enterprising concern was at that time preparing to send out several operators with portable machines and a supply of film to pioneer vast territories and open the way for a regular circuit. The Bolshevik rule, however, nipped all these plans in the bud.'[8]

The spreading conception that the Russian film industry housed the great profits of the future can be detected everywhere, even in the *Matrimonial Gazette*, where the following advertisement appeared:

'FILM DIRECTOR-CAMERAMAN, 26 years of age, of medium height, energetic, enjoying social popularity, already securing for himself the production of the best plays for the cinema, a lover of art, nature, music, poetry and everything bright and beautiful, striving for friendship, aim—marriage, to a maid or widow, not older than thirty years, with the power to adorn and to provide the path to the accomplishment of his ideals, which will require a security of not less than 50,000 roubles, for his private production of films.'⁹

A force that had greater dreams and more solid ideals to realize was collecting its strength and organizing its activity on a new broader base. This was the Bolshevik Party, which was weakened organizationally at the time of the February Revolution, now tightening its old contacts with the masses, coming above ground, stepping up the pace and intensity of its work. Lenin and the exiles in Switzerland had not yet found the means of return to Russia, but Lenin's directives from exile were full of understanding of the changing situation and full of encouragement for the new stage of Bolshevik Party work. Stalin and Sverdlov, returned from Siberian exile with the other released political prisoners, sought out the Bureau of the Central Committee, which the Bolsheviks had managed to preserve throughout the war, with a leadership including Molotov. On March 5th, the newspapers, *Pravda* in Petrograd, and the *Social-Democrat* in Moscow, resumed publication, and the Provisional Government gained a new enemy in its campaign against the workers' and peasants' organizations, and above all, their Soviets.

In the demonstration on March 19th, organized by the League of Women's Rights, the newsreels taken show not only nattily dressed suffragettes marching, but hungry soldiers' wives. Alongside of pallid appeals for women's votes, one can see slogans 'against the imperialist war', 'return our soldier husbands to their home', 'votes and bread' that show that the Bolshevik Vera Figner was as active as the suffragette leader Shishkina, both of whom appear in the newsreel.

If ever a nation's women needed rights and the protection of those rights, it was the Russian women. They were shamefully handled by every bourgeois party and every official institution and got only promises from the Provisional Government. During this period, certain film companies treated the questions of family and marriage in a fashionably 'liberal' manner that smacked more of Henri Bataille than of needed realism. The alternatives open to women were usually posed as church wedding or unmarried love—both with equally tragic denouements. A typical film about women was *Woman of Tomorrow*, for which the advertising reads: 'The woman of tomorrow—Dr Betskaya, a strong soul, shunning the ordinary feminine private life, personifying in herself the features of the women of the coming generation.' Rosolovskaya points out that the medical work of this doctor is indicated only in her title and costume. More important was the rapidity with which she changed husbands. Even the Skobelev Committee, which was supposed to be devoting itself to progressive themes, tossed off this problem without so much as a single Ibsenish slammed door.

The Skobelev Committee had, perhaps, too many troubles of its own to bother with the troubles of a whole sex. In the midst of its attempts to obey its new double master—the Provisional Government and the Soviets—its important Moscow branch was involved in a scandal. Kara, the Moscow director, accused by everyone as a dark dealer, a bitter reactionary (not fashionable at the moment) and a profiteering speculator in both money and raw film, suddenly attempted to escape abroad with the funds of the Moscow branch. The result was a national overhauling of the cinema departments, with no real improvement in quality or function with one exception. Before the February Revolution, the Military-Cinematographic Department of the Skobelev Committee had no special newsreel section, but now a 'Department of Social Newsreels of the Skobelev Instructional Committee' was set up, with Grigori Boltyansky in charge of production. The amount of good that Boltyansky could do in this post was largely limited by the administrative heads over him. V. I. Dementiev, who had rushed leftwards away from his monarchism, was taken from the War Ministry, Ikov, a Menshevik, was appointed by the Provisional Government, and a Social-Revolutionary, Marianov, came from the Soviet. With this act and the addition of the word 'instructional', the Provisional Government considered the film problem finished.

These three saw to it that this liberally labelled department showed the official version of passing history. If a particularly courageous cameramen had brought back any troublesome pictures of protest meetings in the factories or army, strikes, workers' inspection of factory conditions, portraits of the Bolshevik leaders, the triumvirate of Dementiev, Ikov, and Marianov—plus the military censor—would never have allowed such material to get as far as the screen.

But Boltyansky preserved a record of the events covered by his department that show this work as being far from negligible in importance. The first of these events was the funeral of victims of the February-March days, held on March 23rd. Three thousand feet of film was used by two cameramen this day and the detailed record of the leaders of the first Provisional Cabinet gives it great historical value. It has another, emotional value that is probably as great today as when it was first shown—the total tragic effect of the Field of Mars, chosen as the burial ground, covered with a fine mist, which turns to a steady drizzle when the simple, unpainted coffins, draped in red bunting, are lowered in groups into the wet common grave.

Newsreels, and particularly the regularly issued 'Free Russia' newsreel from Boltyansky's department, became the steady diet of the Russian theatres. Where newsreels previously had spent most of their time on scenes of fantastically distant places, they now became living illustrations of the events as recorded in the newspapers, or as experienced by the audience last week. Across the screen streamed demonstrations, meetings, slogans waving over the heads of the demonstrators. The revolution had become the single theme of the newsreel, but this theme, like the rest, was temporary, and there was a noticeable decrease of such inflammatory material after the military censor had returned to work in April.

There was also for a while a steady diet of anti-Romanov films, made mostly of the sweepings of the multitudinous Rasputin scandals—*Dark Powers—Grigori Rasputin, People of Sin and Blood, The Holy Devil*, etc. Both pornographic and over-politicalized aspects of such films came under the ban proclaimed by the Government as 'a surveillance of public spectacles'. The censor was much more lenient to anti-Romanov films that went further back into the dynasty (Nikolai I, Peter III), showing despots crushing suffering masses who only dream about resistance. Such films were *Thus it Was and Thus It Will Not Be, Chained in the Claws of the Double-headed Eagle*, etc. A few films with an approximately revolutionary content did get made however, and were dangerously popular. One of these was *The Revolutionary*, produced by Khanzhonkov, written by Perestiani and directed by Bauer. Another was *Andrei Kozhukhov*, with Mozhukhin in the title rôle, directed by Protazanov. This was adapted from the autobiographical novel by the terrorist Stepniak, and in the making it was only natural that his revolutionary activity should be subordinated to the novel's thread of love story.

Rasputin could not be killed often enough to satisfy film audiences, and he re-appears constantly in the films of this period. It is not surprising that he is adopted by foreign film producers as an ideal, colourful villain in whom the entire Russian Revolution is easily explained, There are literally dozens of these, continuing to our own day, but the most lavishly produced contemporary version was *The Fall of the Romanoffs*, produced by Lewis Selznick in 1917 and directed by Herbert Brenon. This had a distinguished cast—Conway Tearle as Yusupov, Edward Connelly as Rasputin, etc., but certainly the most amazing actor in the cast was Iliodor 'the Mad Monk', who acted himself. He does not seem to have approached film-acting lightly, for he takes the trouble to dedicate his memoirs (ghost-written by Van Wyck Brooks), 'To My Good Friend the Admirable Herbert Brenon, Motion Picture Artist and Poet.'

As early as March 9th (o.s.), the Provisional Government had been recognized and greeted by the United States, followed two days later by France, Great Britain, and Italy. But Russia's allies were concerned over the effect of the revolution on the war schedule. If Russia should cease distracting the Central European powers from the East, the Allies in the West would face a doubly strong enemy. The 'dual power' in Petrograd again presented a dual picture. On March 14th, the Petrograd Soviet of Workers' and Soldiers' Deputies addressed an appeal 'To the Peoples of the World':

'Realizing its revolutionary strength, the Russian democracy declares that it will by every means in its power resist the annexationist policy of its ruling classes, and it appeals to the peoples of Europe to take joint action on behalf of peace.'

This appeal added to the natural fears of the Allies, and their Ambassadors in Russia demanded a clear statement from the Provisional Government. They quickly received this from Milyukov in a telegram sent to Russian representatives abroad, asserting that it was the aim of the Russian Revolution to fight the war to a victorious finish. Thus the Provisional Government disappointed the people in one of their chief aims in revolution—peace.

To bolster up the new slogan of 'war to a victorious finish' the Allied governments sent their socialist and labour leaders to convince the doubting Russian people of the wisdom of this course. These members of the Second International —Moutet, Cachin, and Lafond from France and the British Labour Party leaders James O'Grady and Will Thorne made the best of a difficult job—but returned home without any appreciable accomplishments. At the beginning of April the new French offensive on the Western Front began and ended ingloriously. America's entrance into the war was not yet showing results, except perhaps in the strikes in the munition factories of Berlin and Leipzig. Added ideological reinforcements were sent to Russia in the form of the French Minister of Labour, M. Albert Thomas.

Another arrival at this time counteracted all the possibly successful effects of the socialist speakers. Lenin and the Bolsheviks in Switzerland had been prevented from returning to Russia by England and France who controlled all the entrances, on the theory that was stated by the enemies of the Commune a half-century earlier: 'To surrender Blanqui to the Communards would be equivalent to presenting them with a whole army.' Milyukov had warned all Russian Embassies to check the 'military reliability' of all returning political exiles.

'Only one way remained open to Lenin, and that was to travel through Germany by getting the Russian Government to exchange Russian exiles for German prisoners of war . . . this method had already been tried. During the war an important bourgeois liberal, M. Kovalovsky, returned to Russia through Germany and in Petrograd was met at that station with great ceremony by Milyukov himself. . . . In his speech of welcome, Milyukov never even hinted that to travel through Germany was high treason. But this same Milyukov—now Minister in the Provisional Government—accorded Lenin an entirely different reception.'[10]

The plan, proposed by Martov, was accepted by Lenin only on the condition that every step in this return was supported by documentation, because he foresaw the uses that would be made of his return through Germany by the defencists and 'provisional' democrats. Through Fritz Platten, Secretary of the Swiss Socialist Party, an agreement was made with the representatives of the German Government which stipulated that places in this train were to be given to all exiles irrespective of their attitude towards war, that Austrian and German prisoners in exchange would be immediately demanded upon the return of the exiles and that the car in which the exiles travelled was not to be subject to search, examination or inspection, with any communications en route to be made through Fritz Platten. Thus arose the legend of the 'sealed car'.

Both the British and French Embassies submitted memoranda to the Ministry of Foreign Affairs warning them of the arrival of Lenin, and the Assistant Foreign Minister made a note for the press: '. . . the goodwill shown by the German Government towards Lenin and the others should be stressed.' Huge demonstrations gathered at the Finland Railway Station to await Lenin's arrival, utterly ignoring the mesh of slander woven by the press. The cameramen of Boltyansky's department were there too, but the train was late. Although it grew too dark to film, the camera crew and Boltyansky stayed on to join the greeting crowd.[11] The arrival, his speech from the armoured car in the square outside, had to wait ten years to be put on film—then a reconstruction by Eisenstein, in *October*.

Lenin's arrival immediately galvanized the forces that continued to fight for a people's revolution. The April Conference of the Russian Social-Democratic Labour Party (the Bolsheviks) made a sharp analysis of the world situation, the revolutionary situation, and what the Bolsheviks were to do about it, that panicked the Provisional Government. The offices of the Bolshevik fraction in the Tauride Palace held the strongest support that the Soviets had, and a stream of deputies and representatives visited Lenin there. Boltyansky tells that he made another attempt to film him,

'. . . I got as far as the door and heard him speaking to representatives from Kiev. He seemed too busy to bother and I was afraid to ask him. Besides I knew he would refuse, for he had to be so careful those days.'

The first May Day to be legally celebrated was an event. Besides the demonstration, the Skobelev newsreel men recorded a group of newsreel portraits, including the newly arrived Plekhanov, Kropotkin and his wife, Kamenev, and Trotsky. Surprisingly enough the faces of the Bolsheviks Kollontai and Lunacharsky were also allowed to be included. Although modern newsreel portraits are neither imaginative nor dynamic, the group and individual portraits of that period were many times stiffer. The subject would have to do something on his own initiative, such as smile, or lift his hat, or bow. Kropotkin cranked an imaginary camera in the air for his wife's amusement.

In Moscow the May Day film had a history of its own.[12] This first Moscow May Day film was made by the Moscow Soviet of Workers' Deputies without any assistance from the film industry. The holiday and demonstration were planned in advance, and a film had a rôle in these preparations. *Festival of Freedom* was a little document of the March 25th demonstration, and it was timed to be shown just before May Day. Although it had been made by the Mossoviet, they did not feel equal to the well-known complexities of distribution and placed it in experienced hands, those of the Platov brothers, theatre-owners. These experienced hands managed the job so badly, with more than a suspicion of sabotage, that the Mossoviet decided to handle its May Day film itself. The obstacles were not yet all overcome. When the Kodak store was approached with a request to release 1,500 metres of negative and 5,000 meters of positive stock, this was refused at the last minute. The film used was finally supplied by the Khanzhonkov Company. The greatest victory of this first film was not its quality (it was not shown theatrically, but to organizations, with lectures, etc., so there is no critical record of it) but in the response to the notice that appeared in the newspapers on April 17th: 'Comrade Cameramen who wish to assist the filming on May 1st are requested to obtain passes for permission to photograph freely on that day. Apply to the organizing commission, the soldier A. Prager.' Among those who participated in this filming were Alexander Levitsky, Grigori Lemberg, Pyotr Novitsky, and the tenacious Frenchman, Louis Forestier.

The rôle played by the Provisional Government was becoming too clear. It was tottering dangerously, when the liberals—Mensheviks, Social-Revolutionaries, Popular Socialists, etc.—decided to show their preference for any known type of government rather than the unknown of a workers' government by joining the cabinet of the Provisional Government. The new Coalition Government acted promptly before the surprise had worn off, negotiated a $100,000,000 loan from the U.S.A., and prepared the long delayed Russian military offensive on the Eastern Front.

The Russian offensive, scheduled for June 18th, had to be sold to the people with every cheap theatrical and propaganda method conceivable. Battalions of

Death were organized with the encouragement of the new coalition Minister of War and Marine, Alexander Kerensky, and the one Women's Battalion of Death among them was organized and trained by Maria Bochkarieva in the floodlights of international publicity. Emmeline Pankhurst came from England later this June to champion the Women's Battalion and to organize Russian womanhood against the Bolsheviks.

The English became the most energetic salesmen of war propaganda to the unwilling Russian people. Bruce Lockhart, in the Moscow Consulate, made himself sales manager:

'As part of our propaganda baggage-train we had a travelling film mission, of which the able chief was Colonel Bromhead, the subsequent chairman of British Gaumont. He, too, was enlisted to coax the Russians into fighting by showing them war films of the fighting on the Western Front. The effect of these war pictures on the mind of the now undisciplined Russian army can be imagined. Not unnaturally, they served merely to increase the number of deserters.

'It was not Bromhead's fault. He was a splendid fellow, who realized the futility of showing war pictures to men whose sole thought was peace. Still, he had his duty to do. Films were part of the Whitehall scheme for the regeneration of Russia, and shown they had to be.

'To Moscow, then, came Bromhead for a monster demonstration of the British effort. . . . We secured a theatre. We arranged a programme. And then the Soldiers' Soviet, infinitely more powerful than the Provisional Government, intervened. The show was for the Moscow troops. The soldiers might see the films. They were not to be exposed to the harangues of Imperialist jingoes. There must be no speeches.'[13]

Lockhart himself was finally allowed to make a short but well-calculated speech after the films. 'Our films were of two kinds; naval and military. Very wisely we showed the naval films last. They were impressive and free from all horrors.'

Temporarily impressed though the men in that auditorium had been, Mr Lockhart, Colonel Bromhead and their films had little influence over the broad masses of Russian people, and none at all over the organized workers. Their answer to the 'coaxing' was a wave of strikes, not only as a demonstration of strength, but because the owners were feeling safe again in bearing down on working conditions, cutting pay and adding hours. In the Moscow film industry, demands similar to those of the theatre-workers were made by the workers in the studios, were refused, and in quick succession the Khanzhonkov Studio, the Kharitonov Studio, and the Yermoliev Studio staffs as well as lesser studios struck. The Strike Committee placed the following statement in the newspaper *Social-Democrat*:

'In the struggle for the solidarity of those workers who have, till now, crawled at the feet of capital, no methods of struggle are ignored: with hitched-up aprons or dressed in smocks, thrusting their shears into their belts, they rose to the call of the workers in the carpentry shop and the scenery painting shop. The strike committee wishes to notify the comrades of the names of these gentlemen: regisseur Sabinsky, his assistant Bray, the cameraman Slovensky, [Slavinsky?], the actor Rimsky-Korsakov, the actor Tamanov, the employee Zakhar Ivanov, and the manager of the prop department Khusainov.'[14]

The anti-strike unions had established themselves in a club-café called 'The Tenth Muse', which became one of Moscow's gambling and speculating centres. What discussion took place there was centred around the duplication of scenarios by different companies (this practice had never ceased) and against pornographic and cheap films, although the leaders of these discussions continued to write such films under their own and other names. Above all, the regular topic was the soothing of studio-owners and theatre-owners. G. I. Leskes remembers an experience when a delegation of which he was a member came from the Projectionists' Union to 'The Tenth Muse' to discuss possible co-ordination of the work of the two unions for their mutual benefit.

'To demonstrate how wide the gulf between us was, the following fact is illuminating: When I and two members of our union board—the mechanic Gromov and the studio worker Seleznev—came to "The Tenth Muse" for the talk, the doorman, after carefully inspecting the clothes of my comrades, refused to let them in. I went in alone to find Nikandr Turkin to get him to permit my comrades to come in. Turkin, coming out to the doorman, spoke a historical phrase, "Let these people in, they are useful to us".'[15]

The Provisional Government had only one answer to the swelling resentment at continued war, and delayed improvements. When the dissatisfaction broke out into an enormous spontaneous demonstration on July 4th that took even the progressive parties by surprise, the Provisional Government answered with guns. They quickly followed this massacre with an attempt at physical annihilation of the Bolsheviks, their offices, their newspapers. Many leading Bolsheviks were imprisoned, Lenin escaped to Finland, and the party again went underground.

But this did not seem sufficient to those in power. They resorted to slander, not only of a political nature, but against the characters of known Bolsheviks and Bolsheviks in general. Lenin was called a doped idiot, Kollontai an erotomaniac, etc. etc. The notorious 'document' by Alexinsky, proving the planned treachery of Lenin, was vigorously supported by the Mensheviks and liberals in the Government. Throughout the press, it was made clear that more murderous provocations against the Bolsheviks would be a form of patriotism—lynching was repeatedly suggested. Captain Thompson has left us a record of his assistance to this campaign in *From Czar to Kaiser* in which he repeats as gospel the officially circulated legends that Germany had arranged and financed the overthrow of the Kerensky régime, paying ten roubles to each marcher in the anti-war demonstrations, and that Lenin, finding a shortage of red cloth in Petrograd, had ordered banners specially made in Germany. Nothing was too low: and still in control of the cinema, the governing class enlisted its services in the campaign.

First of all, a lengthy record was filmed of the funeral of those Cossacks who had been caught in their own cross-fire during the July 4th killing. These were now 'victims of the Bolshevik July mutiny'. Dramatic films were tried, too—

even though they had little more than gossip, anecdotes, and the legend of the 'sealed train' to build upon. The quality of the results can be judged by the fact that even the most reactionary theatre magazine could not stomach one of these films, called *Lenin & Co.*, whose author concealed himself under the signature 'The Man in the Street'. The reviewer found this 'a foolishly talentless concoction'. Drankov provided *Bolshevik*, Taldykin presented *A Stab in the Back*, and Savva—*Fatherland in Danger*, and that was the extent of these efforts, as their reception fell short of expectations.

On June 17th, the Government had placed the Skobelev Committee under the Minister of Charities, but by July 31st it, too, was enlisted in the reactionary ranks by placing the Committee in the care of the Ministry of War. Vishnevsky calls this 'the most eloquent decree on cinema of the Kerensky régime'. The cinema was to be asked to help the Government's agitation for a continuance of a war of conquest 'to the victorious end'. One story filmed was that of a revolutionary who has spent long years in prison exile, returns to new free Russia by order of 'Citizen Kerensky', and immediately enlists in the army of the 'democratic republic'. Boltyansky has preserved from the files of the Committee a plan outlined for the purposes of any party who wanted a film made. It begins with the motto of the party, 'dependent, of course, on the ordering party'. Then symbolic figures—'a figure or group, preceding the opening of the story, symbolizing the struggle of the party for its ideals. Example: the inspiring figure of a worker at a forge, as if he were beating out some new form of society, or a fiery spray, etc.' Further on 'a pretext is to be found to insert film showing the leaders of the party, its workers and its history'. The film was to end with a procession, showing the party flags and slogans, and the final caption was to be the chief slogan again. There is no record of this neat plan being employed, as the parties for whom it was intended were too busy squabbling to think of attempting to recover mass support.

By its unmistakable actions on July 4th, the Provisional Government had demonstrated its intentions to the watching world and those who became interested in the conflict—reformers, liberal journalists, etc., followed Mrs Pankhurst to Petrograd in droves. Rheta Childe Dorr, an American journalist, recorded as happy a picture as she could of the benefits of the Provisional Government's policy, but she couldn't help noticing that Petrograd was not a very happy place.

'Brilliant signboards . . . once added to the gay appearance of the streets, but just now it increases their anxious and ominous air. Hundreds of the shops are empty, the doors are locked and the brilliant signboards alone remain to indicate that business was ever conducted there.'[16]

The chief interest that Mrs Dorr holds for a historian of the Soviet cinema is to be found in her last chapter, containing recommendations for Russia.

'Russia needs wholesome popular amusements to entertain and instruct her adult population. If I were to write a detailed list of Russia's most pressing needs I should place near the head of the list plumbers and moving pictures. . . .'

After she sums up the sanitation problems, she continues:

'They have some moving picture theatres in Russia, but they are poor in performance and frightfully high-priced. You pay as much to go to the movies in Russia as you pay to hear a high-class symphony concert. I never saw a ten or fifteen cent motion picture house, nor could I learn that they existed anywhere in the empire. Mrs Pankhurst and I went to the movies one night, paying something like a dollar and a half for our seats. The play was a long dreary drama, ending in suicide and general misery. The acting was poor and the actors fat and elderly. For current events pictures they presented the Cossack funeral, reeled off at such a dizzy pace that it looked less like a funeral than an automobile race.*

'Moving pictures, carefully selected, offered for a small admission fee, would be a boon to Russia. They would teach the grown people a thousand and one things they never had the chance to learn, and they would get the Russian mind out of its ingrowing, self-torturing analysis that leads to nowhere. They would also give the Tavarishi something to do besides soap box spouting, and their listeners something more to think about than half-baked social theories. Because of the great illiteracy of the masses, Russia would have to introduce into her picture theatres an institution which Spain has already established. In Spain few people can read the titles and captions that run through the picture dramas, so each theatre has a public reader, a man with a strong voice and clear enunciation, who reads aloud to the audience, and also makes any explanations that are necessary.'

With very American enthusiasm for the detailed plan, she also suggests the People's House in Petrograd as a place for the films, 'without waiting for private enterprise to open theatres'.

In August all the political, economic and military issues became inescapably clear. The Provisional Government announced its absolutism, attempting to dissolve the Soviets and adopting Kornilov's programme for more restrictive measures in the army. The army under Kornilov suffered increasingly bitter defeats until finally Riga was surrendered to the German forces, and Kornilov turned to march on Petrograd for the purpose of setting up a military dictatorship—his solution for administrative confusion.

The second All-Russian conference of film workers was called on the eve of the Kornilov revolt and during a nation-wide transportation strike, but nevertheless representatives from all over Russia managed to attend. The conference was led by the theatre-owners and the union in their control, so the agenda included only safe questions, like juridical problems, material growth of the industry, and, grandly, the question of 'the cultural-educational significance of cinematography'. The chief accomplishment of the conference was to draw up the battle lines more clearly. Dementiev made a purely political and very frank presentation of the official policy—the cinema to aid in continuing the war to a victorious finish, to support the military dictatorship (although Kornilov was left unnamed), and the replacement of the death penalty and other repressive measures at the front. The conference closed with a resolution to hold a 'Liberty

---

* This sounds as though the projectionist had been a good union man and perhaps a Bolshevik sympathizer.

Loan week' and a 'Day of Russian Cinematography'. This matter was set for December 15th and, as Rosolovskaya concludes, 'the sun of that "Day" never rose on Russian cinematography'.

During this same month the Skobelev Committee was struck. The workers demanded, besides an increase in salary, the admission of workers' representatives into the administration of the Skobelev Committee, and the introduction of a workers' inspection of the financial operations and the hiring and firing of manpower. Two hundred and fifty persons participated in this most important of Russian film strikes.

The general organization of red guards grew up in the emergency situation caused by the refusal of the Provisional Government to defend Petrograd against Kornilov. After the failure of Kornilov,* Kerensky was appointed Supreme Commander—Generalissimo—and his first move was an attempt to dissolve and disarm the armed workers organized by the Central Committee of the Bolshevik Party. The move was unsuccessful, and, from September on, the Provisional Government faced an armed enemy that waited for its opportunity.

From the newsreels taken at the Government conference, held in the Alexandrinsky Theatre, one significantly characteristic shot has come down to us. This is of the Supreme Commander, Minister of War, Minister of the Navy, the Prime Minister—all embodied in the single person of Alexander Kerensky. He leaves his automobile and marches into the building, looking neither to the right nor to the left, and followed by two carbon-copy aides, fully equipped with the same sternness and the same portfolio.†

All the theatres suffered from the decrees rationing electric power and lumber for heating. Nothing but the temperature had changed much. The dramatic theatres made only superficial changes in their repertoires and drifted further away from topical subjects. The audiences who could afford it came for relaxation. They must have accepted the romantic appearances from a loge of Trotsky in the rôle of Prophet of Doom as part of the spectacle. Shalyapin tells of one such outburst:

'The blood of the people is running in the gutters, and you, you thickheads and vulgarians, you lower yourselves to listen to the stupidities and banalities that a pack of rotten actors spew at you. . . .'[17]

The films too had changed just as little as they felt they had to. After February there had been a fever of change—besides new 'revolutionary' films, old films were re-issued with fiery new subtitles‡—but this fever wore away as quickly as it did in the Provisional Government. The most irrelevant of war-time subjects must have seemed topical in comparison to the remote fantasies of this period.

---

* There is, in *Vechernaya Vremya* shortly after the Kornilov fiasco, an attack on Persky for announcing a Kornilov film subject, calling upon the Union of Film Workers to try him for this 'base crime'.

† The piece of film is very short, but its character is so clear that Eisenstein was able to base upon it the whole sequence in *October* of Kerensky 'mounting to glory'.

‡ The old favourite, *Keys to Happiness*, reappeared 'without tsarist cuts'. Khanzhonkov says of this, 'What could the tsarist censors have found to cut, other than protracted embraces and kisses?'

To the flourishing murder mysteries, detective dramas and tragedies of high society were added some new themes. One of these was the tragedy of 'bohemian life'. Set in a studio, backstage, the sordid cabaret or the garret, the story would expose the artist to the soiling influences of money, leaving him dying at the end, either having returned to his ideals, or repenting not having returned to them. This legendary, gay, sad life of the artist, among plaster casts, Turkish rugs, and draped living models, was repeatedly told under varying arrangements and titles: *Oh, If Only I Could Express in Sound*; *In the Name of Great Art, Curtain!* Other dramas drew upon the subjects and tastes of Henri Bataille, Georges Ohnet, William Locke, and the like. Bataille's play *La Vierge Folle* was filmed, with his permission, by 'Neptune' as *Keep Watch, If You Would Know the Day, the Hour.*

The decadent, the religious, the mystic writers and subjects were in their glory. Both literature and the 'symbolic' theatre were drawn upon by the cinema for this material. Satanism and demonism were favourite explanations of the world's confusion. The sources were as varied as Merezhkovsky's *Julian the Apostate* and Oscar Wilde's *Salome*, adapted by Nikandr Turkin, of 'Tenth Muse' fame, for 'Neptune'. Artsibashev was the spokesman for this group, when he placed the following philosophy in the mouth of a character in his *At the Last Frontier*:

'. . . neither revolution nor any government, neither capitalism nor socialism—nothing gives happiness to man, doomed to eternal suffering. Why should we concern ourselves with our social structure if death stands by every shoulder ?. . .'

We cannot, however, leave this period without calling attention to the exceptions to this general state of film affairs, to certain very definite accomplishments, artistically, and in technique and theory.

The artist working in film had, in spite of the shoddy material given him, become conscious of the potentialities of the instrument and bravely assumed greater artistic responsibilities. The success of one step ahead gave him the courage and the confidence of 'the front office' to make two more steps ahead. Thus, in the free-for-all chaos of this time's film production, we can find two talents ripening very quickly: Yevgeni Bauer and Yakov Protazanov. Bauer did not venture far in imagination, but he set an excellent example to his co-workers in his love for the medium and his wish to develop its technique more articulately and less haphazardly. In the three and a half years with Khanzhonkov, Bauer had directed sixty films, nearly all on contemporary subjects—he shunned history and the 'classics'. This modernity, despite Bauer's fixed ideas on white columns (even in a telephone booth, it was joked) and on the unvaryingly beautiful dress of his heroes and heroines no matter what their position, proved valuable to the many young film-makers who were soon to be handed a mass of contemporary subjects. When Bauer returned to the Khanzhonkov studio, Khanzhonkov took him down to Yalta to supervise the building of a permanent base for the annual filming expeditions to the Crimea. While there, Bauer fell and broke his thigh—complications set in, and before the summer was ended, Bauer was dead. It is a pity that the last film that he left behind was *The King of Paris*.

The anti-Romanov films served one useful artistic purpose. In the need to give the tsarist crimes of the past any conviction, the methods used in the other films' abstractions of setting and locale had to be sacrificed. One way of being historically rich and convincing was to photograph historical scenes in their actual settings. More documentation was done on the characters in history too than previous historical films had demanded. Altogether, these were forward steps and Yakov Protazanov immediately profited from these lessons in naturalism to give his films of historical settings more atmosphere and more life. It was at this time that Protazanov came to the production of the last and most important film made before the October Revolution—*Father Sergius*.

Tolstoy's story of *Father Sergius* goes into the mind of a handsome officer at the court of Nikolai I, a Prince Kasatsky who 'broke with his beautiful fiancée, a lady-in-waiting, and a favourite of the Empress, just a fortnight before the wedding-day, and giving up his small estate to his sister, retired to a monastery to become a monk'. Tolstoy examines the motives of pride and passion behind this move, and follows the prince, now Father Sergius, through the multitude of temptations he encounters as acolyte, priest, hermit, healer, and as a wandering holy man, begging for bread. The intimations the story contained about the private life of Nikolai I and its revelations of corruption and ordinary human weaknesses in the priesthood made it a literary scandal in its time. Protazanov and Volkov had considered filming it before 1917 but a film of this highly censorable material was an invitation to trouble. The February Revolution had loosened some of the earlier restrictions, particularly those on religion, as the bonds between the Greek Orthodox Church and the Government were not as tight as in tsarist days.

The finished film is still dramatic and compels more than an antiquarian's attention. Few concessions have to be made for its more than forty years of age. Only the actors' make-up obtrudes. Its episodic story is told and the stages in the life of Father Sergius are shown with a skill exceptional anywhere in 1917. It may not have the epic quality of Griffith's war-time work, but it is easily comparable to Sjostrom's famous *Berg-Ejvind*, produced that year, in intensity and character revelation. Mozhukhin never excelled this performance in its convincing complex ageing of a man eternally pursued by the desires of the flesh, and Lissenko portrays an astonishing sensual creature.

Father Sergius was finished before October, but for some reason it was not shown until 1918, months after its producer had fled south with his company. Perhaps the Provisional Government's censor hesitated to expose a nervous public to such a frank denunciation of the official church.

Bauer had had, in his group at the Khanzhonkov studio, a young designer named Lev Kuleshov, and 1917 gains another importance for the history of the Soviet film by being the year in which Kuleshov's first theoretical articles were published. One of these was on 'The Tasks of the Artist in the Cinema', printed in *Vestnik Kinematografiya*. It called attention to problems of the designer that were generally ignored and the main point he had to make was in great advance of his time. This was that the task of the artist in the film is not merely the painting of scenery, but of co-ordinating all the elements of composition and rhythm, in short suggesting an identity between the designer and director. 'The artist in the cinema paints with objects, walls and light. . . . It is almost unimportant what is in the shot, and it is really important to dispose these objects and combine them for the purpose of their final, single plane.' Kuleshov also wrote on the scenario.[18] He refuted the theory that the scenario is the sketch of the future film, contending that the artist ordinarily sketches in a medium very close to his finished medium. The only true sketch of a film would have to be on celluloid. This was a progressive attitude for a production period in which the whole dependence was placed on the written detail, the written action, and the written word. He went to the other extreme in concluding that only directors could really write scenarios. Another error of enthusiastic reform was contained in a suggestion for scenario notation by means of a certain shorthand and alphabet of symbols,* saying, 'Other regisseur-performers can carry out such notation, as a musician does the compositions of Beethoven and Mozart.' Dividing the functions of scenario-writing (composing) and direction (performance) was a mechanical separation that he did not cling to long.

The history of the Soviet cinema starts to grow before the date of the revolution just as the embryo of the government structure of the Soviet Union can be found in the local and factory councils of workers' deputies before October. In September a conference of workers' educational organizations was called by the Central Council of shop-factory committees to discuss the ideals of a proletarian, socialist culture, with regard to each of the arts. This meeting, attended by several leading Bolsheviks, including Lunacharsky, Kalinin, Samoilov among others, was the first meeting of the organization that was to become the Proletkult after the Revolution. The opinions of the meeting were summed up in a series of resolutions, and among them we find one on the cinema:

'Taking into consideration that the modern cinema, being a great technical conquest of human genius, is now in the hands of the bourgeoisie, displaying a school of corruption, crime and moral decay. Together with this it appears as the bearer of the ideas of the ruling class with the intention of the strengthening of bourgeois conceptions and morals among the proletariat. Under the conditions of genuine peoples' power the cinema can be formed into a real and potent weapon for the enlightenment of the working class and the broad masses of people, and one of the most important means in the sacred struggle of the proletariat for the release from the narrow path of bourgeois art. It will promote the development of class consciousness and the growth of international solidarity and it will invigorate the spirit and brighten the passionate ideals of the struggle of the proletariat for socialism.'

This first concrete statement on the differences between the aims of bourgeois and proletarian film production was made at the first conference to plan the rôle of the arts in the coming struggle. One can almost imagine that they sensed the rôle that cinema was to play in Soviet history.

---

* This is a problem that, with the added complexities of sound notation, still fascinates him.

October 10th: At a meeting of the Central Committee of the Bolshevik Party, attended by Lenin, armed insurrection is decided.

October 12th: The Executive Committee of the Petrograd Soviet resolves to form a Revolutionary Military Committee, while, in Moscow, Rodzyanko opens the Second Conference of Public Men.

October 15th: The Soviets of a number of cities declare in favour of the immediate transfer of power to the Soviets.

October 18th: Kamenev and Zinoviev, members of the Bolshevik Central Committee, warn the Provisional Government in a letter to the newspaper *Novaya Zhizn* that an armed insurrection is being planned.

October 22nd: The cruiser *Aurora* receives orders from the Soviet not to leave Petrograd.

October 23rd: The Revolutionary Committee appoints its commissars to the military units and to the key positions in Petrograd. The Provisional Government attempts to arrest the Bolsheviks for taking part in the July demonstration.

October 24th: The military schools are prepared by the Government. Bridges are raised and telephone communications with the Petrograd Soviet are cut by the Government. The *Aurora* is ordered by the Revolutionary Military Committee to lower the bridges across the Neva. The Revolutionary Military Committee assumes the offensive.

In the evening Lenin arrives at the Smolny Institute.

The next day one class had taken power away from another class, and Russia was in the hands of its people. It was an act that changed not a few lives, or most lives, but every life in Russia.

Insignia of Trofimov's film-company, 'Russ'

CHAPTER VI

Moscow—Odessa—Paris

1917–1920

Sporting, frisking, gadding fly
Warbled all the summer through,
Scarce had time to turn her eye:
There stands winter, full in view.
Now the fields lie bleak and dead,
All those days of sunshine fled,
When she found 'neath every blade
Bed and breakfast ready made

KRYLOV

Some fled before the revolution.

Along with the manufacturers and their Government fled the monarchists, who had not bothered to leave in February. Drankov and two of his actors hid for seven days in the basement of his Moscow apartment-house before finding the necessary costumes and courage to run away.

The arts that had become luxuries had severed many of their artists from the broad popular public. The ballet was shut off from the time's life and thinking by the still 'imperial' stage doors of the Marinsky and the Bolshoi Theatres, the stout latches of the Ballet School and the upheld inviolability of the box office. Most of the dancers who had the means to leave Petrograd and Moscow did so hurriedly. The exodus from the dramatic theatre was not so widespread. Misused as the Russian dramatic theatre may have been, it held on to a greater part of its creative workers than any other native art, by virtue of its relation to the progressive currents of its time. This was particularly true of the Moscow Art Theatre, which lost some of its actors but none of its leaders, so firmly grounded were its artistic policies in Russian life. The movie folks, elevated into an isolation equal to that of the ballerinas, allied themselves in flight with the ballet, both fearing that they were luxury items whose futures would be extinguished by this revolution. They were ideological descendants of the crew of gay actresses who delivered St Petersburg's mail in 1906 in smart sleighs and snug furs in order to break the postmen's strike.[1]

The stream of rich merchants, bankers, landlords, politicians, accompanied by their stars of the ballet and the cinema, and by confused crowds of smaller men who ran before the unknown caught up with them, started their race towards what they believed was safety. There were many ways 'out' (of Bolshevik-held territory) at first, but these rapidly narrowed down to three—Scandinavia, Siberia, and southwards. Most of the movie people who fled, fled south, because the southern sunny studios were there, and films still had to be made, no matter what happened to their audience. The Moscow studios were stripped of all portable apparatus, and the Russian film industry took its first fatal step away from Russia. Yermoliev prevailed upon his whole artistic staff to move with him and the apparatus. His actors, directors and cameramen joined him, many never to return. A few did contribute to the future Soviet film years later, and among these was Yakov Protazanov. But now, as the most distinguished director of the Yermoliev studio, he joined Yermoliev, Turzhansky, Strizhevsky, Mozhukhin, Lissenko, Kovanko, Volkov, Burgassov, Loshakov, and others on the crowded trains bound southwards. Vera Coralli left for Finland, followed later by Gzovskaya and Gaidarov.

The 'Committee to Save the Country and the Revolution' formed from a coalition of Petrograd's anti-Bolshevik groups of all shades, was defeated in the streets. Kerensky's forces were routed at Pulkovo and driven back to Gachina. A White military insurrection was put down in Moscow. A more crushing defeat: among the first acts of the Council of Peoples' Commissars were decrees for the eight-hour working day, the rights of all the peoples of Russia to self-determination, the abolition of class distinctions and civil rankings, the nationalization of private banks and the socialization of the land. Before the end of November 1917, the Bolsheviks had begun their most terrifying move—the publication of the secret diplomatic documents of both the Tsarist and the Provisional Russian governments.

The exposure of the true motives of Russian diplomacy and the unpleasantly revealing contrast between the oppressive social policies of the previous governments and the present sweeping change was a force that strengthened the people's cause and scared reaction further away. The more exposure and defeat, the further and more desperately did the old guard run. Out of the West to the East, the North and the South. Out of Russia into the Ukraine, where they gained the protection of the German occupation. When central Ukrainian affairs grew too turbulent for them, they moved further south. From Kiev to Odessa. The Russian film industry finally unpacked the equipment that it had removed from its Moscow studios and contemplated production schemes in Odessa. The Crimean resort of Yalta, where several of the southern film studios had already been built, became a temporary Hollywood.

Khanzhonkov gives us a telling incident of this confusing period. In the middle of January 1918, the Red Army approached Yalta and bombarded the White-held resort. After the Whites retreated, leaving the Reds in possession of the town, the Khanzhonkov group resumed the interrupted filming of *Lord Darnley*. The delayed ball-scene was first on the new schedule:

'To this ball, in addition to the participating actors, were also invited as many of the townspeople as possessed the proper costumes. The rehearsal began.

'Smart ladies' toilettes twirled with the evening clothes and military uniforms of their cavaliers. . . . Suddenly the street door burst open and three armed men walked into the studio: the first had only a whip, but his two escorts had grenades and ribbons of machine-gun bullets.

'The dancing stopped instantly. All waited for what was to come. I was sitting by the cameraman in my arm-chair and finally decided it was my duty to break the oppressive silence. I was listened to attentively. I explained to the new arrivals the reason for the "assemblage" and why there were persons here in "white-guard" uniforms.

'Apparently my explanation satisfied them fully, for the senior immediately released his convoy and, introducing himself as Neratov, commander of the Yalta district, requested permission to remain during the filming, as cinema matters interested him very much.'[2]

The German occupation of the Ukraine began on February 18th, answering the plea (dictated by the German High Command) of the counter-revolutionary Ukrainian Rada for help to withstand the advance of the Soviets. Following the departure on February 25th of the American and allied embassies from Petrograd, the Allied intervention, aimed at both Bolsheviks and Germans, began on March 5th, with a landing at Murmansk in the North. On April 5th, Japanese and English forces landed at Vladivostok. The Germans took Kiev (March 16th), Kharkov (April 5th), Odessa (April 13th), the Crimea (April 20th) joined by the Turkish occupation of Batum on April 15th. The circle was being completed, and the émigrés took refuge on the edges of the circle, shifting their national sympathies with the changing flags.

Odessa must have been an amazing place to live in for the next two years. Crammed with people from all over Russia who had run away from the same things for a variety of reasons, this pleasant looking Nice-like port actually seethed with emotion—bitterness at the past, frustrated anger at the present and fear of the future. No one knew what tomorrow was to bring, but as the city was repeatedly occupied (about fifteen times altogether) by German or French armies of occupation and White or Red Russian forces, the cooped-up population grew to care less and less about the future. The only precaution taken was to keep one set of papers in the right-hand pocket and another set of papers in the left-hand pocket. Along with the lowering morale came a slackening of interest not only in their personal fates but in the fate of Russia. Impermanence became a standing joke. One Russian, in recalling this period, was reminded of Murger's *Scènes de la vie de Bohême*, where one of the light-hearted Bohemians decides to keep an apartment on condition that the concierge will 'come up every morning to tell me the day of the week, the day of the month, the quarter of the moon, what kind of weather it is, and what form of government we are living under'.

The signing of the European armistice signalled new, more intense wars of intervention in Russia. Following the Germans and Petlyura, the French moved into Odessa from December 1918 to April 1919,[3] but by this time the temporary residents of Odessa could not distinguish between one temporary army and another. Each occupation brought a new liberator. But, until the final evacuation of the defeated anti-Bolshevik armies, little was changed each time except to throw a few criminals into jail, clean the sewers, establish new bank branches, and to change the names of the principal streets and squares. While the Ukrainian nationalists under Petlyura were masters, the Ukrainian language was irrationally forced on the heterogeneous Russian population. The first signs of every German period of power were German book-stores and a whole German officialdom. Throughout the variety of régimes, gambling and speculation never ceased. The men to whom money was their life could not resist trying to make more money, even though they were sitting on top of a volcano. Diamonds, gold watches, foreign currency and food became the only fixed values. The peasants in the district lost faith in all money and established a barter system—tomatoes for blankets, sugar for old shoes, etc. There was nothing precious enough to exchange for butter.

The film colony quickly acclimatized themselves to the unnatural moral and social atmosphere, more like the milieu of a film than of life. No one had any idea of how long they would have to stay, but at the same time Odessa seemed such a precarious station that any steady production schedule was unimaginable. Films were begun and left unfinished for lack of stamina and also for lack of financial security. The subjects drifted further away from the exciting drama of their real lives. Khanzhonkov completed *Lord Darnley*, Drankov made *Harrison's Career*.

The movie people became conspicuous in the cabarets and night resorts. The ranks were swelled by further retreats from the Bolshevik-held studios of Moscow. Vera Kholodnaya, who had remained in Moscow through February 1918,[4] finally arrived. The over-crowded city bred epidemic fiercely, and Kholodnaya succumbed not long after her arrival to a fatal attack of influenza, a war-born epidemic which killed many of the transients. As an illustration of the mental condition of the city, her death was promptly ascribed by rumour to a variety of more melodramatic causes—a rival's poison, etc. It was long before her Russian public heard of her death; the first genuine film actress of Russian film history lived on screens for years after her mortal end.*

During 1920 the southern White armies rapidly lost ground in spite of the support of Allied finance and French troops, and district after district was emptied of White guards and their civilian followers. We are provided with a cause of the rout by one of the defeated:

'While the evacuation of Odessa was taking place, the French Commander-in-Chief in Constantinople, General, now Marshal, Franchet d'Esperey, asked me to tell him what I knew about the situation in Southern Russia, where French troops were showing themselves incapable of holding their ground. I am afraid what I told the French General was not pleasant hearing for him, because the French soldiers and sailors in Southern Russia were themselves undermined by Bolshevik propaganda and did not live up to the hopes of the Russian civil population in them.'[5]

* In Boris Pilnyak's novel, *The Naked Year*, set in a central Russian small town in 1920, one finds this description of a film performance: 'Then the lights went out again, and once more and once more again Vera Kholodnaya loved and died in the most extraordinary way of ways.'

When the Allies abandoned Odessa, ships of all countries were sent to transport military and civilian refugees to the new haven of Constantinople. It was a British ship that carried Odessa's entire movie and theatrical colony to the relative security of the sympathetic Turkish capital, now in Allied control. On this boat were Protazanov, Yermoliev, Volkov, Rimsky, Loshakov, Lissenko and Mozhukhin and he has told, 'We had no baggage and the little gold that we had was stored in the heels of our shoes.'[6]

The influx of Russians into Constantinople was swelled in March by the army and followers of General Denikin from Novorossisk and the evacuation of General Wrangel's army from the Crimea. Wrangel arrived in Constantinople in November 1920, with about 50,000 troops and 60,000 refugees. It was the beginning of an undesirable Russian addition to the kaleidoscope of Stamboul, with results that are still floating about the Near East. A contemporary American report on the refugees describes the problem:

'. . . the great expense of travelling, as well as the drastic passport regulations of other countries, have made it very difficult to distribute them to areas where they can become self-supporting, and almost impossible to find employment for them in the city, as Constantinople has few and primitive industries, and the present crisis has curtailed production.'[7]

The results were inevitable. Housed in wooden barracks, in tents, in children's homes, in cheap lodging-houses, in temporary hospitals, in rest-houses, and in private houses and hotels, the situation of the refugees steadily worsened.

'The apathy and stagnation of unemployment are fruitful ground for the worst sort of reaction. The police records of the city show an increase in the population of the red light districts, coming from among Russian refugees.'[8]

A new cabaret, 'The Black Rose', opened by the ever-present Vertinsky, became the Russian market for girls, drink and dope. In spite of the film producers' efforts to scrape together a little production finance, rent studio space and restore the disintegrating morale of the actors, their Odessa pursuits became habitual in 'The Black Rose'. The futilely rented studio-sheds stayed empty.

When Yermoliev finally found the means and the boat to take his flock back to Europe, his baggage contained the beginnings and middles of a half-dozen films that the conditions of the Crimea and Constantinople had not permitted him to finish, in addition to prints of several of his most prized Moscow productions. Landing in Paris in August 1920, his first effort to gain security there for himself and his dependents was to prepare for distribution the finished or nearly completed Moscow and Yalta product. The first of his Paris releases was the 1916 success, *The Queen of Spades*, serving to introduce Mozhukhin to the French public, which was to adore him so intensely for a few years, and to introduce the original work of Protazanov to the French film-makers.*

The world-dominating French film industry of 1914 had been crippled, then shattered, by the following four years of war. With the rise of the film in peaceful

* A large group of these Yermoliev-Protazanov films was also offered in New York and London in 1920.

America and the appearance in France of the direct, intense Swedish film works, the slowly recovering post-war French film had become less a native medium and more one submissive to the influence of any unaccustomed film fare in the midst of their own discouraged cinema. In this process of influence and revival the French film-makers were spurred by a group of writers and *cinéphiles* who adopted the cause of the woe-begone French *cinéastes* as their own. The leading spirit of the newly-attracted intellectuals was the talented young writer, Louis Delluc, whose criticism, by virtue of its wit and good taste, did much to consolidate the discouraged directors, by making them feel that their best efforts were appreciated. Delluc placed emphasis on a study of the contributions of the foreign films, and the organizations and magazines in which he was active gave as much space to American and Swedish work as they did to French. Soon the German film was to come back into an enemy world, assisted by critical appreciation of its rapid succession of striking innovations. Beginning in 1920, Delluc played an influential rôle in encouraging a Russian film vogue, brought on by the arrival of the flood of film émigrés and their films into a novelty-seeking cinema industry.

Yermoliev's first move was to rent a studio to finish the Yalta projects and to begin work in the new environment. The hopeful new French firm, Ermolieff-Films, finally chose a studio in Montreuil-sous-Bois that had witnessed the many hopes and disappointments of its builder—Georges Méliès. Failure and bankruptcy were such common occurrences in the film industry that even the superstitious Russians did not worry about their predecessor's bad luck. The first film finished was one that had been begun in Yalta, and had been continued, a little at a time, at every stop in their wanderings (with easy revisions of the scenario) and finally appeared under the appropriate title of *Angoissante Aventure*. Its star, now known as Ivan Mosjoukine, rapidly ascended in Western Europe.[9]

It was inevitable that the Russian émigrés, a group of artists united at first by a common fear, would break apart into smaller groups, then into so many individuals separated by successes, failures, jealousies and the passing of time. There was no unity of purpose, artistic or otherwise, to cement them, once fear no longer bound them to each other. Anyone's promise of fame and an increase of salary was sufficient to draw one of the actors away from the colony.

More Russian producers found their way to Paris via Germany and the northern route. Paul Thiemann formed 'La Société Russe Paul Thiemann' and attracted several of the talented émigrés in Yermoliev's group to his new venture, notably Protazanov. French companies sought to capitalize on the Russian vogue and Pathé and Gaumont revived their old interest in Russian subject matter, assisted by the wanderers.

A natural interchange of material and techniques took place between the Russian and the French film-makers. The French avant-garde of the early 1920s found much to admire, imitate and borrow wholesale from the Russian work. Marcel L'Herbier, particularly, demonstrated this influence in his work of that time. When Delluc began direction on his own, his handling of Eve Francis produced results remarkably similar to Protazanov's direction of Lissenko. On the other hand, Protazanov, now Jacques Protozanoff, politely adapted French literature, Zola's *Pour une Nuit d'Amour* and Paul Bourget's *Le Sens de la Mort* for the Thiemann studio. Of the latter film Delluc pointedly said, '*Le Sens de la Mort* est un excellent film français. Il a été fait par des Russes.'[10] Quite aside from the quality of the film, it will probably be remembered solely for the appearance in a minor rôle of a young actor, René Clair, whose observation of Protazanov at work may well have been a spur to his own talents.

At Ermolieff-Films, the remaining directors, Tourjansky and Volkoff, were busily exploiting the Russian trump card, Mosjoukine, for all he was worth. When this company was re-organized by Alexandre Kamenka, the son of a Russian banker, as 'Albatros-Films', the productions grew more ambitious in scope and the best Russian talents were given a freer range. The first films to come from the Albatros studios were the last of the colony's contributions to merit critical attention.

The first of these large, successful films was made by Mosjoukine in collaboration with Volkoff, adapting the play by Alexandre Dumas, *Kean, ou Désordre et Génie* (1922), to the obviously appropriate gifts of Mosjoukine. His delight in the colourful story of the great English actor's life and death is clearly apparent in the finished film, largely composed of scenes from every actor's dream-rôles— Hamlet, Romeo, Tristan, Werther, Manfred, etc. No film actor could ever have such a holiday a second time, but Mosjoukine did manage to run an equally enviable dramatic gamut in a picture made the following year. This was his most famous tour-de-force, as writer, director, and actor of several rôles—*Le Brasier Ardent*. The film was experimental to an extreme degree, dressing a totally unimportant story in a pastiche of photographic and acting devices, all enlivened by striking imagination. In the subject-matter's macabre remoteness from all reality, it stems directly from the war-time Russian cinema. Its story

'. . . starts off with a nightmare in which out of a confused background a man materializes, calmly, now as a beggar, now as a bishop or a fashionable dancer. When the victim of this nightmare wakes she tells herself that it all came from the various disguises adopted by the detective X in the novel she had been reading before she fell asleep. But there is a burglary in her home, and her husband goes to consult the same detective X. The two characters now find themselves in situations which correspond to those of the nightmare, and Natalia Lissenko remembers, each time, the dream symbol (beggar, dancer or bishop) which corresponds to her present feelings.'[11]

By 1925, the Russian contribution to the French cinema was so completely assimilated as to be indistinguishable. Mosjoukine's best work this year was not in Tourjansky's *Michel Strogoff* but in L'Herbier's adaptation of a Pirandello novel, *The Late Matthew Pascal*. After this film, the star of Mosjoukine, who outlasted his compatriot actors, began to set. The first sign of decline was a retrospective of the star's remembered rôles, a 'Festival Mosjoukine', the next— an invitation from America, following the completion of Volkoff's extravaganza— *Casanova*.

The Berlin colony of Russian film émigrés went through a similar cycle of vogue, personal ambition, break-up and decline. Their greatest obstacle was the resentment of German actors, who were having a hard enough time making a living after the war. By 1922 the Association of German Artists made a formal protest to the Government about the influx of Polish and Russian actors depriving native actors of theatre and film work. The only working film group consisted of several actors who had not returned to Russia after the European tour of the Moscow Art Theatre. Under the direction of Conrad Wiene, this group made a ponderously theatrical film of Tolstoy's *Power of Darkness* and under Robert Wiene, an 'expressionist' treatment of Dostoyevsky's *Crime and Punishment** with Grigor Khmara as Raskolnikov, and Alla Tarasova as Sonya, before the group scattered.

Of the Berlin colony, only Khmara attained the temporary starring position of the Paris idol, Mosjoukine. He provided Berlin with the same romantic Russian flavour that Mosjoukine gave Paris. His popularity (heightened by marriage to Asta Nielsen) and his training in the Moscow Art Theatre gained him a wide variety of important rôles in German films, often opposite his wife—Christus in *I.N.R.I.*, the waiter in Pabst's *Freudlose Gasse*, etc., but Grigor Khmara was soon laid aside by the Berlin studios, as was also the Russian favourite, Osip Runich.

A less romantic, but more dependable Russian character actor was Vladimir Gaidarov, whose Moscow background included both theatre and cinema. In getting from Moscow to Berlin, Gaidarov had travelled via Constantinople where, a year after the previous film colony had passed through there, he stayed to direct two films, *The Life of a Refugee* and *Star of the Orient*, to raise money abroad for the refugees stranded in Constantinople. His work in Berlin was under the direction of F. W. Murnau (*Der brennende Acker*), Arthur Robison (*Manon Lescaut*), Joe May (*Tragödie der Liebe*) and others. He and his wife, Olga Gzovskaya, soon moved to the Paris colony, from whence they finally returned to the Soviet Union.

Aside from Gzovskaya, no other Russian film actress gained even a temporary success in Berlin. Olga Chekhova (Tschechowa), niece of Anton Chekhov, and by profession a sculptress, entered films for the first time while she was living in Berlin, making her début in Murnau's *Schloss Vogelod*. She gained a certain international reputation (playing in Clair's *Chapeau de Paille d'Italie* and Dupont's *Moulin Rouge*) among others and remained active in German films throughout the Hitler régime. The Russian film actress, Tamara, played bits in Berlin, and then disappeared from sight. Evidently, Russian film émigrés were no happier in Berlin than they were in Paris. Georgi Azagarov continued to get directing jobs and Vengerov continued to interest investors in new companies.

One Russian director with a reputation for being a lone wolf even in Russia, did make headway in Berlin. This was Dmitri Bukhovetzky, who sought employment as an individual with no obligations to his compatriots. Energetically making a fresh start abroad, he assisted Carl Froelich on *The Brothers Karamazov*† and got the direction job on *Danton*, *Othello*, and *Peter the Great*, all with Emil Jannings and big sets, and without a single Russian actor. His last German film

---

* *Die Macht der Finsternis* (1922) and *Raskolnikow* (1923) were both produced by Neumann, and later shown in England and America.

† With Fritz Kortner, Emil Jannings, Bernhard Goetzke, Werner Krauss, Hermann Thimig. This film was shown in Paris at the height of the Russian vogue, and to make the film more authentically exotic, Bukhovetzky was given sole credit for its direction.

was *The Passion Play*, acted by the Freiburg and Oberammergau Passion Players. His success with costume dramas brought him an invitation from Hollywood, which was gulping European directors and actors by the dozen.

As little success as the German and Swedish importations may have had in Hollywood, the Russians had even less. Arriving in Hollywood in 1924, Bukhovetzky lasted barely long enough to witness Mosjoukine's glorious arrival and hasty retreat. Bukhovetzky at least had some showmanship to give Universal in his work for them but had so little knowledge of the medium that when Metro engaged him for *Anna Karenina* he was dismissed half-way through it. Tourjansky and his wife, Kovanko, went to the States in 1926 but soon turned back, after he had made *The Cossacks* with John Gilbert, and her Rubensesque figure had found no welcome; Mosjoukine had nothing but a face in which the American public, unfortunately for dramatic or romantic expectations, found a resemblance to Larry Semon's. In films where Russia was concerned, Americans showed a preference for Lon Chaney's Russian whiskers and Cecil De Mille's Volga boatmen. Aside from Boleslawski the only Russian directors to maintain a hold in Hollywood were Gregory Ratoff, Anatole Litvak and Rouben Mamoulian, none of whom had touched films in Russia.

The end of the story of the Russian film émigrés is not a very happy one, no happier than the story of all the expatriated Russians. Paris, the headquarters of the 'White' Russians, has seen so many of the noble or wealthy Russians unwillingly descend to driving taxis, modelling clothes, becoming floorwalkers, cloakroom attendants, etc., that there was no pity to spare for the descending film great. Ivan Mosjoukine, retreating before the sound film and old age, hid in a Paris cabaret as a dancing partner, and after a prolonged illness, died January 18, 1939, surrounded by the relatives and few friends who could still afford bus fare out to the Courbevoie nursing home where he lay—Volkov, Strizhevsky, Loshakov. These had jobs. Wladyslaw Starewicz has a little studio in Fontenay-sous-Bois where dolls and animals are animated with the same ingenuity but less astonishment than the young Starewicz gave to the animations invented in the old Khanzhonkov studio. Kovanko and Coralli have disappeared from public life, and Lissenko has gone from the extra lists of the Paris studios to a rest-home. A Russian name no longer has the magic effect in French films.*

The emigrant film producers have fared no better. Yermoliev is the only one left to command respect in the studios of America and Europe. Kamenka made Albatros a thoroughly French studio, and a good one. Vengerov managed to maintain an office on the Champs Elysées, but Dmitri Kharitonov found more security in keeping a restaurant—Le Poisson d'Or—than in scraping up finances for film production. Drankov tried many things—went from high Hollywood hopes to a broadwalk café in Venice, California, and finally came full circle with a return to his first work, photography: when I last saw him he operated a small photo-finishing plant in San Francisco.

Several film émigrés are still alive and working, but few rewardingly. In all the studios of Europe and California, one is bound to meet Russian individuals or tiny groups, mostly employed as 'character extras'. Not all of them had film

* Two younger French film-makers are of Russian families: Jacques Tati and Vadim.

experience in Russia—some had been army officers, some engineers, some children when they left, but as a group they have exerted a temporary influence that must be reckoned in estimates of French and German film history. The experienced film émigrés transferred bodily to Paris a 'Russian morbidity' that one must seek today in French rather than in Russian films. In the years before the German occupation particularly there was a wave of Russian film subjects in France; the best known were *Les Bas-fonds* and *Crime et Châtiment*. But more significant was a 'Russian tendency' in French settings: in *Pension Mimosas, Quai des Brumes, Carnet du Bal, Lumière d'Été,* and in many others can be recognized attitudes born in Moscow film studios during the first World War. Russian attempts to continue their startling if mannered romanticism have never equalled their native efforts during those war years. It is not really profitable to try to imagine the consequences of this tendency if they—and the old government—had remained in control at home, but it seems possible that the course of Russian film history might have paralleled the events in Sweden: an emigration of artists towards Hollywood contracts, assimilation and destruction of unsure talents away from home—like the Swedish fate. In Sweden another generation had to enter film work before the tired patterns were refreshed.

In Russia that new generation could not wait for the proper time to pass—there was too much to be done, and too many glorious opportunities. Within a very few years after their arrival abroad the émigrés saw in the first film exports from Soviet Russia a promise of new vigours and new styles that later Soviet films more than confirmed. Even a film as unpretentious as *Polikushka* was concrete evidence that Russian films were being made outside of Paris and Berlin, and it was a revelation from which the Russian film exiles, who imagined they had brought the Russian cinema with them, never recovered.

Ivan Mosjoukine in *Casanova* (1927)

CHAPTER VII

Peace—Bread—Land

1917–1920

The convulsions in France are attended with some
disagreeable circumstances; but if by the struggle
she obtains and secures for her nation its future
liberty and a good constitution, a few years enjoyment
of these blessings will amply repair all the damages
their acquisition may have occasioned
BENJAMIN FRANKLIN

The day after power in the capital of Russia passed into the hands of the
Petrograd Soviet, the Second All-Russian Congress of Soviets adopted three
decrees introduced by Lenin. The decree on *peace* proposed an immediate
armistice for all belligerent countries. The decree on *land* proclaimed that
'landlord ownership of land is abolished forthwith without compensation'. The
decree on *state power* formed the first Soviet Government—the Council of
People's Commissars, with Lenin as Chairman of the Council. All three assured
bread for all, equally.

The next day—November 9th—though less world-shaking than the two
previous days, was one of immense activity, too. Out of the many movements of
the new state machinery came the first Soviet film organization: the establishment in the State Commission on Education, within the instruction section, of a
film sub-section—*kinopodotdel*—under the supervision of Nadezhda Krupskaya.

In his autobiography Vladimir Mayakovsky says, under the date of 1917—
October:

'To accept or not accept? For me (as for the other Moscow Futurists) this
question never arose. It is my revolution. Went to Smolny. Worked. Did everything that came my way. Meetings began to be held.'[1]

When the new government, within a month of the capture of the Winter Palace,
called its first meeting of Petrograd writers and artists Mayakovsky was one of
five who showed up. There were two other poets, Alexander Blok and Ivnev,
the painter Nathan Altman, and theatre was represented by Meyerhold alone.
The art that was to become the primary Soviet art in the eyes of the rest of the
world, as well as in Lenin's eyes, was not represented. The artists of the Soviet
film were still in the making. The 'princes' of the Russian film industry were in
retreat.

'The far-reaching thoroughness of the Bolshevik Revolution startled the intelligentzia. . . . A nightmare does not last long, was the consoling thought. "Two
weeks", became the whispered password; two weeks was the longest the bolshevik
bad dream was expected to last, what with the bristling hostility of the whole
civilized world, and the opposition of the "better" classes within the nation.
Lenin himself was not sure that the experiment would outlast the span of the
French Commune of 1871. This attitude accounts for the wide-spread boycott or
strike against the bolshevik "usurpers" on the part of the intelligentzia. . . .'[2]

Although it was in Petrograd that the first step was taken towards Government
participation or supervision, if not yet actual control of the Russian film industry,
Petrograd was not the industrial base. It had a single studio of any pretensions,
two laboratories, and a few distribution offices. It did have, however, 300 film
theatres in comparison with Moscow's 85, and *theatrical* control was quickly
put into effect in Petrograd. But the major producers and distributors in Moscow,
allied with a union of the cinema's intellectual aristocracy (the 'Tenth Muse'),
felt powerful enough to fight this threat to their peace of pocket.

Long before the first attempt was made at even partial nationalization of Russian
film enterprises, skirmishes took place that showed the antagonists clearly—
Government and private industry, employees and employers, the new and the
old. The younger antagonists were slow to organize and unite, and were thus,
for a while, at the mercy of the well-organized manufacturers' association, and
its tool, the Tenth Muse, more officially known as the Union of Workers in the
Cinematographic Art (which excluded all *workers* from its membership). In
response to the commandeering of a few scattered theatres by local or neighbourhood organizations, the Tenth Muse made its first open declaration of war against
possible Government acts, in Moscow's *Kino-gazeta* in January 1918:

'The council of cinematographic unions and congresses has discussed in one of
its most recent meetings the question of the commandeering of theatres by various
organizations, and it proposes the following measures for the defence of the
common interests of cinematographists:

'1 To require the film exchanges to cease providing films for the commandeered
theatres.

'2 In the event of an exchange breaking this rule, all theatres are to agree not
to rent any films from that exchange.

'3 In the event of film exchanges being commandeered, the theatres undertake
not to accept any film furnished by any of these exchanges.

'4 Individual producers and distributors of films agree not to furnish films to
commandeered film exchanges.

'5 To draw up an appeal in the name of all film organization-members of the
Federation, to boycott commandeered theatres.

'6 The execution of these measures is guaranteed by the organization committee, which will consider ways of aiding the victims of the nationalization.'[3]

In a later issue of the same trade-paper appeared evidence that these threatening
measures could be made concrete:

'Proprietor Solovyov of the "Furore" Theatre in Alexandrovsk (province of Vladimir) has notified us that the soviet of workers' and soldiers' deputies in Vladimir has commandeered his theatres with its projection machines and other equipment, and continues to operate the theatre for its (the Soviet's) profit, depriving the proprietor of his means of livelihood. Consequently, the distribution section asks the council of cinema firms to request all film exchanges to cease delivery of films to the "Furore" Theatre in Alexandrovsk.'

During the first months of 1918 the nearness of Petrograd to the front forced the new government to move itself, piece by piece, to the more protected capital of Moscow. In March Lenin and the Council of People's Commissars moved from Smolny to the Kremlin. Mayakovsky, ever eager to be near the source of energy, also came to the new capital. Moscow's film industry must have been encouraged by the Government's 'retreat' from Petrograd, but discouraged by the prospect of the Government's closer inspection of their anti-Government activities.

In the few months after the October Revolution before the Allied embassies and missions fixed their attitudes to Bolshevik power, Allied propaganda machinery continued, though with difficulties. The American films that were to accompany Edgar Sisson to Petrograd never got beyond Stockholm, but at the end of December 1917 he and Guy Croswell Smith managed to put together enough miscellaneous footage to make a programme entitled 'All for Peace' (to respond to the public's hopes), for which a theatre on the Nevsky Prospect was hired, with an orchestra to play 'The Star Spangled Banner' for the assembled guests.[3a] The theme of peace also limited British propaganda efforts; after a discussion with Lunacharsky, Bernard Pares tried to tour Russia with films of English life, but Colonel Bromhead could supply only one film about peace.[3b] The memoirs of the French Ambassador comment acidly on the 'films de propagande' sent to him in 1918 by the Quai d'Orsay to show the Russian people that France had perfected the machines and methods of work; the tractor given the place of honour in the films showed a conspicuous label: *Gemacht in Landau*.[4]

In view of the national crisis produced in February by the breakdown of negotiations with the Germans at Brest-Litovsk, and the resumed German offensive along the entire front, from the Baltic to the Black Sea, one might imagine Moscow's theatre-owners and film-distributors submerging their petty anxieties in the greater difficulty threatening all Russians. Nothing of the sort. At the beginning of March *Kino-gazeta* published an editorial:

'The newspapers announce the coming visit to Moscow of Lunacharsky, who intends to make a report to the Council of People's Commissars regarding the eventual nationalization of the cinema industry.

'At Petrograd this project is already in partial effect and the cinema studios and exchanges there are nationalized. Their personnel has been asked to remain in service and continue work. For the moment it is yet impossible to say to what extent Lunacharsky's reforms will have repercussions in other cities. If the reports from Petrograd are exact, it is strange that nationalization is taking place in isolated cities. All the cinema industry constitutes a homogeneous whole, and Petrograd especially is merely a geographic offshoot, a dependency of Moscow—the centre of the entire cinema industry. As for other cities, we have reports only on Yekaterinburg and Kharkov.

'At Yekaterinburg,* now the capital of the Ural Republic, all cinema companies have long been nationalized. The Ural Republic recognized the edicts of the People's Commissars insofar as they are advantageous to it, which is to say that nationalization has been put into effect at Yekaterinburg in an autonomous and disorganized manner. At present all cinema firms have been ruined, and struggle along with difficulty in view of the absence of films *which Moscow refuses to furnish*, as nationalization has purely and simply had the character of a monopoly in the Ural Republic.'[4a]

The 'proprietors' waged their private war against the inevitable. Quietly and systematically, theatre chains and film exchanges were being closed down, film studios and laboratories were being stripped of equipment and materials, and whole enterprises were being shifted to the 'safer' south—along the same route as those who had fled earlier. In the words of Henri Barbusse, *'Comme partout, les entrepreneurs de films ne cherchaient que le bénéfice immédiat du capital engagé et ne se souciaient nullement des intérêts moraux du troupeau qui regarde.'*[4b] The Presidium of the Moscow Soviet, with the possible encouragement of the newly arrived Lunacharsky, finally answered the industry's war declaration with the first Soviet legislative decree to affect the film industry—150 days after the Revolution:

'Decree on the introduction of workers' control over film enterprises in the city of Moscow.

'1 In view of the circulation of false rumours regarding the possible seizure of film enterprises, such as: studios, offices, laboratories, theatres, warehouses, etc., and in view of efforts on the part of individual proprietors to carry off, for the purpose of concealment, the implements and means of production, as well as raw materials, creating a situation that can wreck the base of the film industry, and that can increase the number of unemployed, the Presidium of the Soviet of Workers', Soldiers' and Peasants' Deputies of the city of Moscow and of the Moscow region hereby informs the public that no attempt at the seizure of cinema enterprises will be tolerated, no matter from where it may come. . . .

'2 The proprietors of all film enterprises are required to declare to the cinema commission before March 10th, between eleven and three o'clock, an inventory of negative and positive films, jupiter lamps, electric cables, film cameras and projectors, scenery, musical instruments, furniture and other accessories, chemical products and all implements and means of production, as well as raw materials possessed by their companies as of February 14/1.

'3 All transfers to new owners are forbidden as well as the reduction or interruption of production, the closing of film exchanges, theatres, laboratories, without special permission of the cinema commission. . . .

---

* Where Grigori Alexandrov (then Mormonenko) had begun his career, dividing his time between errands for the local opera house, and as doorman at one of the film theatres. Other careers were ending in Yekaterinburg—the Romanov family was interned near here.

'4 Citizens who disobey this compulsory order, whether in its entirety or in any part thereof, will be liable to penalties up to the extent of imprisonment and confiscation of all property.

Presidium of the Soviet of Workers', Soldiers' and Peasants' Deputies of the city of Moscow and of the Moscow Region.

Moscow, March 4, 1918.'[5]

Once the emergency situation was taken care of by this decree, other more basic decrees relating to the film industry were introduced. On March 19th the education commission of the People's Commissariat of Education decreed the nationalization of the Skobelev Committee and the transfer of the cinema section of the Moscow Soviet over to the Commissariat of Education. On March 20th *Izvestia* published an appeal by the cinema section to all professional unions, film-workers, and cultural organizations to exert their influence on behalf of a newly formed Cinema Committee, in its efforts to organize independent creative activity in the field of the cinema; on April 10th the Committee held its first meeting to plan its future activity. A similar Cinema Committee, headed by Dmitri Leshchenko, was set up in Petrograd on May 5th. And it was in April that the Government felt impelled to open at the Commissariat of Education a 'section of independent cultural-educational organizations—Proletkult'.

In all discussions of the direction films should take in the new society (barely six months' old), the word 'education' was heard more often than the word 'art'. It may have been thought that the quality of *art* had had its opportunity in Russian films, while the function of *education* not only in Russian but in all films had been neglected. On May 26th the functions of the film section in the Commissariat of Education were transferred to Moscow's new Cinema Committee, making it the sole responsible body in all matters of this vital but unfamiliar field: the film in education. There was no encouragement to relax this severe attitude on the part of the Cinema Committee; their sense of responsibility increased with the growing tension of the military crisis. In March the British landed troops in Murmansk, in April the Japanese established a new base in Vladivostok, and in May the Czech army corps, on their way back to the Western front, started hostilities at several points along the Trans-Siberian railroad. The Entente's ring was being forged.

As severe and purposeful as the Cinema Committee's educational attitude may have been, their movements must have looked more like groping than like organization. They needed time to formulate their ideas, they badly needed equipment to start *something* going, and there were human failings, as well, as Gardin's exasperated portrait of Chairman Preobrazhensky shows us:

'We listened to the chairman.

'He could speak by the hour and lull a raging tiger to sleep.

'All this was extremely boring, but at that time it was so necessary to be organizational that it was impossible to escape this ridiculous talking machine.

' "Why don't you draw people, informed people, from the unions?"

' "The unions are to be entirely reconstructed. Don't mix the work of professional unions with the Cinema Committee!"

' "Why have you put people over the sub-sections who can't tell a negative from a positive?"

' "This knowledge comes very soon. One learns from mistakes, comrade."

' "If you nationalize only the Skobelev Committee, you will give the signal for evacuation [of firms and equipment to the South]! "

' "Questions of nationalization will be determined by the Government."

' "You are losing the summer season! You won't have any pictures!"

' "We are opening our Literary-Artistic sub-section. Patience, comrades. Above all—order and organization. We are building a new life, etc. etc. . . ."

'Finally Anatoli Vasilyevich Lunacharsky arrived with the flaming Vlad. Mayakovsky. They had just become friends.

'A.V. was in love with the cinema and his words were exultant—amazing. . . . Fyodor Shalyapin is an extra player; there's not much to be said about Kachalov, Leonidov, Moskvin; they are bit players; estimates of the number of films soar into the millions, and the whole revolutionary people take part in mass scenes! Of course a raw film factory has been opened—why, it's imperative to have one's own raw materials for such grandiose dimensions; the technical sub-section offers plans for its own apparatus factories, and the gigantic growth of Soviet cinematography is secure. . . .

'A.V. swept aside both entrance and exit doors of the Cinema Committee. Mayakovsky roared a farewell. Preobrazhensky again sat down at his desk to draw deductions, and his eyes once again closed. . . .'[5a]

A new government, of necessity operating through inexperienced officials, with dozens of new functions and duties that no other government ever had had to face before was a tempting bait for smart business men, both Russian and foreign. A typical case, having a serious effect on the young Soviet film, was that of Jacques Roberto Cibrario[6]. Italian-born agent in Russia of several Italian firms. The details of this case may help us understand some attitudes of the years to come.

Cibrario's business, before foreign enterprises in Russia were upset by the October Revolution, was the renting of films and the sale of motion picture supplies. By the spring of 1918, Cibrario had recovered his equilibrium and business acumen and addressed the following letter to the Moscow Cinema Committee (of which Preobrazhensky was still Chairman):

'Cinematographic Committee,   May 10, 1918
Commissariat of Public Instruction, City.

Gentlemen:

I have been greatly interested in the development of the Cinematographic Committee ever since it started work.

As I know that the art of cinematography can be developed only when all the improved technical devices are applied, and taking into consideration that same are very scarce in Russia. I should be glad to enter into negotiations with you in the capacity of the representative of the cinematographic firm "Transatlantic," and I herewith have the honour of offering you the following articles. . . .'

Although the commercial motive behind the letter's charm must have been obvious, even to harried new committee-men, the Cinema Committee considered Cibrario a business man of no more than normal greediness and entered into an agreement with him in July, by which he was to go abroad and purchase for the Committee the following material*—a good indication to us of the Committee's interests and needs at the time:

20	Universal cameras
200	Fumagoli projection machines
1,500	Cormack school projectors
2	printing machines ⎱
3	cleaning machines ⎰ all Fumagoli, Pion & Co., Milan
2	titling machines
50	metrometers
20	American metrometers
50	Cormack portable projection booths
50	portable electric installations
300	educational film subjects of 200 metres each. (3 copies of each; titles attached)
1,000,000	metres of negative film (Kodak)
7,000,000	metres of positive film (Kodak and Brifco).

For this purpose the Cinema Committee deposited with the National City Bank at New York (for it was to America that Cibrario was to go), one million dollars. Cibrario received an advance of $10,000 on his future commissions, which were to be paid to him at Moscow, after receipt there of shipments of the material, which were to be approved by a Soviet inspection committee that was to follow Cibrario to the United States. Cibrario's commission would probably have totalled about $60,000. It was an excellent deal—for the agent.

When Cibrario arrived in the United States, in December, he lost no time in elaborating a scheme that would yield him more than his stipulated commissions. In collaboration with others, he proceeded to organize a number of different corporations from which he was to 'purchase' the film and equipment, and induce the National City Bank to honour his drafts on the credit deposited for him by the Cinema Committee. He proceeded to buy from the corporations controlled by him, large quantities of obsolete equipment and worthless film, paying, for instance, $70 for an ancient projection machine and billing it against the National City Bank credit at $227. The merchandise was not shipped, but accumulated in storage. He continued for months to buy and bill and store, profiting at every point, even on the insurance and storage charges.

* It is necessary to keep in mind that none of this equipment had ever been manufactured in Russia—there was no Russian camera, no Russian projector, no Russian raw film— neither negative nor positive. It was not until the summer of 1919 that Professor Sreznevsky and Engineer Gluskin were set to work on the development of Soviet-manufactured raw film stock.

Meanwhile, the credit was running low and the bank warned Cibrario that shipment must soon be made or there would be insufficient funds to meet storage and insurance charges, to say nothing of shipping expenses. Cibrario, now living in a luxurious Central Park West apartment, owning two Packard cars and flashing diamond rings, realized that he must take some action. If he shipped this rubbish abroad, there would be serious trouble when it reached Riga and his only excuse could be that he was unable to make previous shipment because of the blockade, which had also prevented the departure of the Soviet inspection committee. He hoped, no doubt, that everyone in Moscow with whom he had dealt had forgotten about the transaction or was dead. In the meantime, for safety's sake, Cibrario deposited his money abroad—in Italy, Holland, England—and tried to leave the country with the United States income tax investigators hot on his trail. He was compelled to come to an agreement with the tax authorities.

From his arrival in December 1918, through the years 1919, 1920 and part of 1921, Cibrario manipulated his purchases. It was not until July 1921 that the National City Bank ordered a shipment of some of the accumulated material to be sent to Reval. Neither that shipment, nor any other, was ever delivered at Moscow. Preobrazhensky, responsible for this fatal commission, was removed from the Cinema Committee.

In the meantime, the Soviet authorities had retained Charles Recht, a New York lawyer, instructing him to look into the Cibrario transactions and to take action to protect the one million dollar deposit in the National City Bank. In August 1921, a lawsuit was started on behalf of the R.S.F.S.R. against Cibrario and the bank, alleging improper payment against the deposit. On September 1st Cibrario was indicted by the New York County Grand Jury, and pleaded not guilty. On September 16th the New York court appointed a receiver for Cibrario's property; but by this time, nothing remained in the United States but his office furniture, and one of his automobiles. The indictment was shortly afterwards dismissed. Cibrario now lost no time in leaving the country. He was soon in Europe, purchasing castles in Italy. The 'profits' he had made were never touched by the processes of law. The Cinema Committee got a lesson in the technique and ethics of private business enterprise; but it got precious little material to carry on its projected cultural film programme.

In the making of films that could be called, to any degree, 'Soviet', the Government in 1918 was still largely dependent on the good intentions of those private producing firms that were waiting for the end of the 'two weeks'. It is more than likely that the need for total nationalization of the film industry was not yet apparent even to those most conscious of the Soviet film's possibilities. Workers' control, especially in film exhibition, and the formation of a separate Government film-producing organization (to compete with the private firms), were the maximum measures considered at this time.

One Moscow studio that had not yet vanished to the south was the firm of 'Neptune', and as Mayakovsky did everything 'that came my way' to help his revolution, he found time between March and May of 1918, to write and act in three films at this studio:

. . . 'Young Lady and Hooligan' and 'Creation Can't be Bought'—sentimental commissioned rubbish, adapted from *The Workers' Teacher* [*Cuore* by Edmond de Amicis] and *Martin Eden* [by Jack London].

Rubbish not because they were worse than others, but because they were not better. . . .

Director, designer, actors and everyone else did everything to strip these things of any interest.

The fourth scenario [counting from the unhappy *Pursuit of Glory*]—'Shackled by Film'. Having become acquainted with the technique of films, I did a scenario that could stand beside our work in literary innovation. The direction, also at 'Neptune', mutilated the scenario without the slightest shame.[7]

The first of this group, *Creation Can't be Bought*, was written in March and completed by the end of April. The director, Nikandr Turkin, despised the futurists and Mayakovsky in particular, which may explain the superficial execution of the two films he made with Mayakovsky. The poet himself played Eden (transformed into a more autobiographical rôle of Ivan Nov, poet), with David Burliuk, Vasili Kamensky, and Margarita Kibalchich in the other rôles. Burliuk gives us an account of the writing and filming of this lost work:

'I worked out the scenario, an adaptation of Jack London's novel, *Martin Eden*.

'The composition of a scenario for the "silent" screen was much easier than at present. Only the scheme of the story: only a description of the scenes. All the rebellious and revolutionary features of the American's epic work were brought out. The scenario was liked. Mayakovsky made several alterations, doing these very skilfully. . . .

'I was entrusted with the rôle of the rich debauchee, patron and discoverer of Mayakovsky [Ivan Nov] and admirer of his genius.

'I made my appearance under the blazing, burning eyes of the jupiter lamps . . . with my pockets full of bottles. Or I would take out an ancient volume of poems.

'Mayakovsky and I "drank" and I ecstatically listened to the declamation of this person I had just found on the street, on a bench in the boulevard—a homeless young genius—a poet.

'A poet of insurrection—of revolt. . . .

'And then "Ivan Nov" met a bourgeoise girl.

'He is captivated by her, he experiences the torments of love. Standing on the boulevard, in the ominous dark blue twilight, the young poet looks up at the house where she lives.

'Shots were taken on streets, in parks, still swathed in the snow-drifts of February. A tavern was built according to my design, which I did in a cubist, grotesque style.

'The film had to be . . . "futuristic".

'As director and designer they gave me a free hand in everything. I was stimulated. I made up my face in flat planes; I discarded the forms of "volume". I shortened or lengthened noses! . . .

'In the film Mayakovsky protests against the bourgeois, sugary art of his time. He leaves a classic ballet, stepping over the enthusiastic bourgeoisie. . . .'[8]

The memory of Victor Shklovsky, scenarist and critic, provides a few more details. Rejected by his beloved, the poet 'wants to end it all, plays with a revolver, balances on the edge of a balcony. Finally he leaves his top-hat on a skeleton that happens to be standing in his room—and goes out on the road, homeless and free, like Chaplin. . . .'[8a] At the first screening of *Creation Can't be Bought*, it was introduced by Lunacharsky.

Young Lady and Hooligan, the second of Mayakovsky's films for 'Neptune' in 1918, was written in April and filmed in less than two weeks. It was directed and photographed by Yevgeni Slavinsky, with A. V. Rebikova playing the heroine opposite Mayakovsky. Considered at the time 'a very revolutionary film', it was widely circulated in the period of War Communism. It was one of the films programmed for the mass open-air screenings on May Day, 1919, in Moscow—and it may be to this circumstance that we can be grateful for its preservation. Two French critics who have seen it recently—Georges Sadoul and Henri Langlois—report it rather as a curious relic than as a film of any importance.

The first scenario that Mayakovsky was really proud of was written early in May 1918, but Nikandr Turkin, in charge of its 'mutilation', shot it without one rehearsal. *Shackled by Film* had an original idea (not surprising coming from the poet who was to write *Mysteria Bouffe* three months later): the life of a film-character—the ballerina in an imagined film entitled *Heart of the Screen*—and her encounters in the real world. Lily Brik, who played this rôle, has said that Mayakovsky proposed a sequel, in which this ballerina was to live in a fantastic film-world 'behind the screen'. Indeed, the idea was so good that Mayakovsky tried it again in his next period of intense film enthusiasm, eight years later.

Another poet, Alexander Blok, willing to take an active interest in film-making, was more discouraged than Mayakovsky by the conditions of 1918. When Alexander Sanin, a director at the Moscow Art Theatre who had just completed his first film, *Maids of the Mountain*, wrote to Blok proposing their collaboration, Blok replied with thanks and good sense:

'I have nothing now ready for the screen, but I have more than once thought of writing for it; I always feel, however, that this will have to find a new technique for itself. In my opinion cinema has nothing in common with theatre, is not attached to it, does not compete with it, nor can they destroy each other; those once fashionable discussions "on cinema and theatre" seem quite unreal to me. I have long loved the cinema just as it was—then I lost interest when it fell into the hands of the Philistines and into the vulgarity of "high society" subjects.

'But it moves—it all moves, and the strip of film remains a strip of film. Nothing can stop it. An actor trained in Spazhinsky cannot play Shakespeare, but a mechanism can be trusted with anything, so long as you can use its services and not trouble the wheels and levers with things that they themselves would fling away squeamishly. . . .

'That's the sort of ideas that are fermenting, but I don't know how to put them to work. Time is needed, and concentration. Most immediately, though, will you tell me, (1) what would you expect from me? To adapt a known literary work, or provide something of my own—history, fantasy, psychology? Or something already in my mind?—(2) what material conditions? What sum of money could be counted on, and how would it be paid—at once, or in instalments?'[8b]

The first May Day celebration in Red Square was a memorable occasion. A young newsreel-cameraman was assigned to cover the event—a tall Swede named Edward Tisse, who has written his memory of that day:

'Workers came to Red Square from the factories. Over their shoulders were rifles and ammunition pouches, and they were girdled with ribbons of machine-gun bullets and cartridges. Red Square itself wore an unhappy appearance— shattered pavements, bombarded houses, glassless windows, pock-marked walls. Around the ends of the square stood trucks—the speaking-platforms. I came to the square early in the morning without knowing exactly what was to happen or which members of the Government were to participate in the demonstration. I had a large movie-camera and 120 metres of film, the maximum provided in those times. With these 120 metres I had to record that exciting day. I began by filming the workers—I had been told that they were leaving directly for the front after leaving the square. . . . Suddenly I sensed a new movement of the crowd. Without realizing yet what was happening, I rushed along with the rest towards one of the trucks. Around me I heard only one word—both children and adults, looking towards one point, repeated: "Lenin, Lenin, Lenin! Here he comes!" With a great effort I managed to squeeze my camera and myself to the side of the truck. And then I saw Lenin for the first time. . . . Vladimir Ilyich walked at an unhurrying, quiet gait. He had a thoughtful and concentrated air, but when he looked up at the people, his face lighted up with an affable smile.

'Ilyich was in his never-altered thin black top-coat and grey cap. Before reaching the truck he stopped, took out a little note-book, wrote something in it with the stub of a pencil, and put it back in his pocket. He came up to the truck and, seeing me with the camera, said quietly and seriously: "Film less of me, comrade, and more of those who are going to listen to me, the comrades on their way to the front". . . .'[9]

Spurred on by the tremendous need for appealing to the minds of the public through the film as well as through the press, the Cinema Committee began to solve its manifold problems in a more direct way. On June 27th the Moscow Cinema Committee began production on its first film—the first Soviet film: *Signal*, based on a story by Vsevolod Garshin (directed by Alexander Arkatov, photographed by Tisse and Novitsky). In October, Alexander Serafimovich, one of the two Russian novelists to risk offering his services to the Bolsheviks at this time,* submitted a script to the Committee. His finished film, *Underground* (directed by Vladimir Kasyanov and photographed by Alexander Levitsky),

---

* It was Serafimovich who, before the revolution, had dreamed of the day 'when men with hearts and consciences would come to cinematography'.

together with *Uprising* (a semi-documentary film directed by Alexander Razumni [one of the few members in the film industry of the newly named Communist Party] and Vladimir Karin), was ready for release by the first anniversary of the Revolution. Another timely subject, though of milder revolutionary content, was directed at the 'Russ' studio by Sushkevich and Boleslawski. This was *Bread*, with a distinguished cast: Leonidov, Baklanova, Zhilinsky; the company of the Habima Theatre were used in the mass scenes. The Petrograd Cinema Committee began its production activity in October with an 'agit-comedy' entitled *Congestion*, written by Lunacharsky. *Congestion* was filmed in eight days (not in a studio but on the street and in a real 'former private residence' into which the characters of the film are supposed to have moved) and was exhibited ten days later in most of Petrograd's theatres. Both Committees announced scenario contests: in Moscow for film adaptations of Turgenev works in connection with the hundredth anniversary of his birth, and in Petrograd for scenarios in honour of the first anniversary of Soviet Russia's birth.

More revolutionary and far-reaching in influence were two other moves made this summer.

One was a move away from the studio. The first 'agit-train' left for the Eastern Front, for Kazan, recently taken by the Czech army corps. The raw troops of the Red Army, sent to recapture Kazan, needed the most powerful moral support that their government could provide. For this purpose the 'agit-train' was evolved: it contained a printing-plant equipped for the publication of news-papers and leaflets, a theatre company prepared to write as well as to perform plays, and a film-crew, headed by the young veteran of both newsreel and studio work, Edward Tisse.* Later the film organizations of more elegant agit-trains were completely self-contained, carrying a film laboratory and cutting-room, but this first agit-train cameraman sent his footage back to the Moscow Cinema Committee, and they handed over the editing job to a fresh volunteer on their staff—a twenty-year-old experimental poet who had named himself Dziga Vertov.

The other move was the State Commission on Education's acceptance of Vladimir Gardin's proposal for a State School of Cinema Art.

On May 28th the Cinema Committee had called a conference of the stubborn 'great ones' of the Moscow film industry, who were still running things their own way outside Petrograd and Moscow. The aim was to establish some *modus vivendi* even temporary, for the two antagonists. The result of this conference was a series of decrees issued from the Moscow Soviet on July 17, 1918. The first ordered the compulsory registration of all film enterprises: (1) no transfers without permission, (2) limitation of electric current, (3) the care and pre-servation of apparatus, (4) *all* Moscow film theatres, including those run by Soviet organizations, were to be affected by this decree. The next series con-

---

* A witness has described Tisse's appearance on the Kazan front: 'Hard to get hold of. Possible only in the evening. In the railway-carriage of the Lenin train (on the Czecho-Slovak front). A lean blond fellow in a Red Army uniform is removing from his camera a film-container filled with explosions, attacks, smoke and flame. . . .' Leo Mur in *Sovietsky Ekran*, January 25, 1929.

cerned censorship: (1) all theatres were to submit two copies of the programmes, posters, librettos of their films the day before running them (penalties for disregard of rule: closing and a fine of 1,000 roubles), (2) distributors were to submit all material relative to each film they released, sale and exhibition permitted only after Committee's approval (fine up to 3,000 roubles). The third series concerned raw film stock: (1) all raw film stock in storage, whether for use or sale, was to be registered (the rule applied to private and Soviet supplies, and in case of infraction, both individual and owner of establishment were to be punished), (2) the sale of raw film was forbidden, and all unregistered film was to be confiscated (and a 3,000 rouble fine paid).

These decrees had an almost immediate result—the almost complete disappearance of raw film stock. Speculation had been prevented, but there was fraudulent manipulation of depleted existing stocks of raw film to the point of near-stoppage of all production. The political and military situation made further importation impossible. It is quite comprehensible that the tightening blockade and strengthening White and Entente offensive gave the Government little time even to consider a proposal made by a few of the most loyal members of the industry, to buy abroad fifteen million metres of positive and negative film stock.

The July 18th decrees scared the producers badly. While hoarding their most precious instrument, their raw film, they continued to assume polite attitudes before the Cinema Committee, offering to do any odd 'revolutionary jobs' that the Committee required. The Committee contracted a series of innocuous films from the firms of Yermoliev, Russ and Neptune—Andreyev's *Savva*, Pushkin's *Snowstorm*, two tales by Hans Christian Andersen, *The Little Match-Girl* and *The Emperor's New Clothes*, and Gorky's *The Three*.

It is interesting to note the number of attempts made by the Government film bodies to work with the existing private firms, before total discouragement in these efforts finally led to nationalization of the industry. Each Red Army victory would make the Cinema Committee feel more powerful and would make the firms sound more co-operative—and it was the Red Army that was winning in the summer, fall and winter of 1918. With the Fifth Ukrainian Army led by Voroshilov, and the defences of Tsaritsyn organized by Stalin, the Eastern Front had been cleared of White and Czech armies all along the Volga. More stringent property nationalization laws in December made the proprietors' outlook no brighter, either. But when the first well co-ordinated campaign by all Entente forces began early in 1919, the 'great ones' relaxed, and their faces assumed less co-operative expressions.

At a conference in December 1918, called in Petrograd by Education Commissar Lunacharsky on the question of organizing film production and film studios within the graphic arts division, the film of the future was represented by a strong voice—Mayakovsky's. He spoke with disgust of his experiences at 'Neptune'—'Even the fictional film stands on a level entirely too low to be permitted.' It is important to note that he did not favour nationalization: 'War cannot be waged on such a scale against the horrible vulgarity of the cinema.' He urged, however, the immediate organization of governmental film production, and proposed concrete measures for the participation in such work of the graphic arts division:

'Next there can be another programme: for the formation within the graphic arts division of a cinema section as a regularly functioning establishment with its own decorators, posters, productions. And there could be a third solution: the transfer of all such matters into the hands of artists. But there is no point in speaking of this now, because the cinema is faced not only with artistic problems, but colossal educational problems, on which we cannot linger. My concrete recommendation: demand that the film department (in Moscow) allow the graphic arts division to produce a certain number of films each year, the participation of representatives from the division in compulsory screenings, and the criticism of these films from an artistic standpoint.'*

Shouldering aside traditions, he called for new talents and new forms to express new ideas, and it is conceivable that the first distinctive form of the revolutionary film was stirred to life by Mayakovsky's booming voice—the *agitka*—the film leaflet.

Coming into wider and more familiar use was a word to which we are inclined to attach opprobrium—*agitation*. As a positive term of stimulation, inciting to thought as well as to action, we have already seen the word frankly applied to a number of forms and means—agit-comedy, agit-train, etc.† At the beginning of 1919 the word was used for a new film form—the *agitka* (literally 'a little agitational piece').

This term appears to have been used previously in another medium—applied to the sharp, folksy, agitational poems of Demyan Bedny, poet laureate of the Civil War period. It was one of Bedny's satirical *agitki* that the Cinema Committee filmed in the fall of 1918, and it may have been through this Bedny film that the term carried over to the film medium.

Bedny's narrative satire, entitled *The Tale of Priest Pankrati, Domna the Peasant Woman, and the Newly-Revealed Ikon at Kolomna*, became the base for the most outspokenly anti-religious film to be made up to that time. A decree of January 23, 1918, had officially broken the ancient and abused connection between the church and the state, but there had been little opportunity to reflect this new status of the church in films, aside from its exploitation as a 'daring' subject—as in *Father Sergius* (not theatrically released until May 14, 1918). Anti-church campaigns, directed particularly towards younger people, had not been pursued very energetically, so it is not surprising to learn that when the actor who was to play the priest in *The Tale of Priest Pankrati* realized the nature of the film being planned, he categorically refused to assume the rôle.

* These are not Mayakovsky's actual words, for the stenographer at this meeting recorded only summaries of what was said—and not very accurate summaries, at that. The entire project, for various reasons, came to nothing, and the last heard of it was its declaration (probably written by Mayakovsky) printed in *Art of the Commune*, in January 1919, beginning: 'The rôle of the artist in cinema affairs is tremendous. As designer and decorator he controls the artistry and appearance of a film. As regisseur he creates its dramatization that produces the effect on the spectator. . . .'

† Later it was applied to a theatre form that agitated with the more instructional aim of propaganda—the 'agit-prop' theatre.

If personal safety was his motive he was fully justified, because the crew and cast were actually threatened with stoning during the filming in Kostroma of their satirical version of a religious procession. Mayakovsky volunteered for the risky rôle of Priest Pankrati but it was finally played by Preobrazhensky himself. It must have been grimly humorous to see the Chairman of the Cinema Committee take off his military belt, from which an imposing Mauser dangled, in order to get into his priest's cassock and make-up.

The first intense use of the *agitka* came as the result of a general inventory of suitable film material for Red Army screenings—in training and at the Front. The Cinema Committee revealed a number of defects, after making this survey —available films were absolutely foreign to the needs of the new army; even those claiming worthwhile literary sources were too distant from the original intents of Zola or Tolstoy, etc.; many on the staff of the Committee itself were impeding the departure for the Front of each film and each projector for fear it would never come back!

In the interests of a partial remedy for this neglect of Red Army films, an announcement appeared in *Izvestia* on February 4th:

'The production section of the Cinema Committee in the People's Commissariat of Education, in preparation for the anniversary of the Red Army and the day of the red gift on February 23, 1919, is organizing the making of a series of films of an agitational-revolutionary character, the filming of which will take place both in the studio of the Committee as well as in the studios of private firms assigned by the Committee. At present the scenario sub-section invites private firms to take part in this work, which has a general governmental significance. . . .'

By February 23rd the Committee proudly released* thirteen single-reel *agitki* supervised by Gardin:

	Directed by
Daredevil	M. Narokov and Nikandr Turkin, written by Lunacharsky ('Neptune')
The Fugitive	Boris Chaikovsky, written by G. Nikolayev ('Khanzhonkov')
The Eyes Were Opened	Cheslav Sabinsky, written by F. Shipulinsky ('Yermoliev')
Comrade Abram	Alexander Razumni, written by F. Shipulinsky ('Yermoliev')
Father and Son	Ivan Perestiani, written by A. Rublev ('Khanzhonkov')
The Last Cartridge	Nikandr Turkin, written by A. Smoldovsky ('Neptune')
We Are Above Vengeance	Nikandr Turkin ('Neptune')
For the Red Banner	Vladimir Kasyanov, written by Smoldovsky ('Neptune')

* There was a special order to supply electric power to ten Moscow theatres that evening so that Red Army men could see the new films in their honour.

Glory to the Strong	P. Malikov, written by V. Dobrovolsky
What Were You?	Yuri Zheliabuzhsky, written by Dobrovolsky ('Russ')
The Dream of Taras	Yuri Zheliabuzhsky, written by M. Aleinikov ('Russ')
Red Star	Pyotr Chardynin, written by Pavlovich ('Neptune')
Deserters	Yevgeni Slavinsky ('Neptune')

Despite the banality of these titles, they do indicate a toughness and urgency that is welcome after the plush and sticky textures of pre-October titles.* However, these *agitki* bear a close resemblance to the agitational patriotic films produced in Russia (*and* elsewhere) during the period of 1914-17. These were posters in an urgent advertising campaign. Their subjects were drawn from one year of Civil War.

Daredevil: a circus clown joins the Red Army and 'one day' rescues some of his comrades from a White Guard prison by applying his acrobatic art.

Comrade Abram: a Jew who has survived the miseries of imperialist war and the horrors of the pogrom, takes his place beside the Bolsheviks and volunteers in a Red Army detachment that beats the Whites in a battle.

Father and Son: a Red Army man, Fyodor, is taken prisoner by the Whites, and who should be placed over him as guard but his father, who had joined the Whites; the son convinces the father of the latter's error and both escape to the Red lines.

We Are Above Vengeance: when the Red Army takes Kazan, soldiers discover a general's daughter, gun in hand, and she is condemned to be shot; before facing the firing squad she tells the story of her life, which so touches all Red Army hearts that she is released, whereupon she remains with the army as a Red Cross nurse.[10] The political and social revolution had not yet found a response in the art of film.

Furthermore, in turning to the names of their directors, we might well be looking at a list of pre-October directors. As widely various as the political sympathies of these men (from extreme right Turkin to extreme left Razumni who photographed and designed, as well as directed *Comrade Abram*), they are all men trained in the commercial film. It would be in the interest of their general security as craftsmen to preserve, as best as they could under the changed circumstances, the forms and techniques with which they were familiar. If we are seeking, among the men behind cameras during the Civil War, those who are to lead the film revolution, we shall have to look beyond Moscow and Petrograd studios.

This is not to say that there was a sharp division between the past and the future. The present was a mixture of both: older men with skills and imagination for which there would always be a demand, younger men and women who were

---

* Harry Alan Potamkin pointed out a more fundamental distinction in early Soviet films of this type: 'The themes in this preliminary period rejected the literary source. Although opposition to the adapted scenario is a sophistry, the direct transference of the social theme to the scenario attests, in this case, to a commendable desire for reality.' 'Pudovkin and the Revolutionary Film,' *Hound and Horn*, April 1933.

to take the long steps forward. Both groups were attracted by the area of greatest excitement and change—the Front. When such studio cameramen as Alexander Levitsky and Grigori Giber joined less studio-trained men such as Tisse at the Front, the older men lost contact with traditional methods, and were forced to think of new ways to photograph new events—even to indicate new meanings that were slow to find visualization. A student of these men, Vladimir Nilsen later demonstrated this process clearly:

'Certain cameramen were transferred from story-film cinematography to news-reel work, and became permanent travelling companions of Red Army detach-ments. In the foremost positions at the Polish front, in the Crimea, with Budyonny's cavalry, in the rear of the Czechoslovaks, everywhere the camera-man was to be seen, actively participating in military operations and battles. Already he was far from the neutral position of the bourgeois newsreel reporter who seeks sensational shots amid the circumstances of a fighting front. He became an active agitator and propagandist, frequently changing his camera for a rifle. In these harsh circumstances of the civil war he was subjected to an ideological transformation, for he recognized the importance of this rôle as a Soviet newsreel reporter, and distinctly understood his social obligations to millions of workers who thirsted to see on the screen genuine cinema documents of day-to-day events. In the process of this continuous active work a new type of cameraman was created, completely unlike the "artists of photography" of the days of Pathé and Khanzhonkov. . . .'[11]

Lunacharsky may not have been capable of realizing his film dream, but he never tired of outlining this future to visitors and other audiences. George Lansbury came through the blockade in February 1919, to provide us with a full reflection of Lunacharsky's prophesies:

'So far, cinemas are not much used owing to shortage of materials. There are great difficulties to be overcome before the "movies" are used as in other countries. When these difficulties are removed by the establishment of trade relationships with the outside world, the moving picture will be utilized to the very fullest extent for amusement and education. The story of humanity will be told in pictures, and heroic deeds recorded. There will, however, be no glorification of bloodshed and violence; no appeal to race or religious bigotry and hatred: the cinema will be used to teach citizenship and love of humanity.'[12]

This dream seems a wonderful example of what another visitor to Russia that winter, Arthur Ransome, calls the 'extraordinary vitality which persists in Moscow even in these dark days of discomfort, disillusion, pestilence, starvation and unwanted war'.[13]

Other foreigners who managed to see Russia in these first Soviet years note one thing in particular in their film observations. It is the unfamiliar concen-tration of Soviet films on education and enlightenment that captures their attention. It is what William Bullitt noticed in February 1919[14], Isaac McBride in September 1919,[15] and when Henry Noel Brailsford visited the tiny milltown of Sobinka, Vladimir Province, in the autumn of 1920, he recorded this inspiring picture:

'Without training or experience, amid war, civil war and blockade, sometimes half-starved . . . grappling with every imaginable difficulty, material and moral, this community had striven, as its own master, to lay the foundations of a human and autonomous life.
'Some achievements lay to its credit, and in these one may read its purpose. It had installed electric light in the barracks-dwellings, and the pipes lay ready for the introduction of drains. It had created crèches and kindergartens. . . . The inadequate old school was working "double shifts". By day it belonged to the children. In the evening it was crowded with classes for the youths and the illiterate adults including four hundred women. . . . A library had somehow been collected with nine hundred volumes. A small theatre had been erected . . . and here an amateur choir, a band, gave frequent performances.'[16]

The agit-train that had done duty on the Eastern Front at Kazan was now sent in the opposite direction—to the Western Front for a three-month tour. The chief film carried along was Dziga Vertov's first editing job, *The October Revolution*. Now not only an army was to be 'agitated', but the civilian population, as well. In its first month of work—from station to station—the train's staff gave seventeen screenings and twenty-eight special screenings for children. Resistance to the enemy was not the only subject taught in this travelling school—literacy, sanitation, anti-alcohol lectures were also demonstrated on the screen. *Pravda* described the train's method (in February 1919):

'During each period when the train was not in motion, the travelling cinema worked with hardly a break, with an ever-changing audience of hundreds of children, local workers, and peasants. In the evenings the films were shown on the streets, near the train. . . .'

Huntly Carter also records data on this first agit-train:

'On November 1, 1918, Lenin inaugurated the first "Red Train", which toured the towns and villages of Soviet Russia. From this "Red Train" of Propaganda over 20,000 pamphlets and books were sold for ready cash in the first seven days, and 60,000 educational books were distributed freely to various local Soviets. The weekly sale of *Izvestia*, also carried on this train, increased during the same period by 10,000 copies. Twelve mass meetings were held at various stopping places. Travelling with the train were cinematograph operators taking films, and painters making sketches of the life of each town visited. The films and sketches were exchanged in order to acquaint the people of the various districts with each other's mode of life, habits, and dress.'[17]

During the following spring, another agit-train (*October Revolution*), managed by Kalinin, was sent to help meet the fresh offensive from the East of Admiral Kolchak, 'supreme leader of the Russian State', and in the summer an 'agit-steamboat'—*Red Star*, was sent out along the Kama and Volga rivers. Managed by Molotov and Krupskaya, this towed a barge-cinema that seated 800 spectators, and carried a crew of cameramen, including Lemberg and Yermolov, who filmed a record of the entire three-month trip—edited afterwards by the Committee's now chief editor, Vertov.

The success of this one new educational device was at once extended. In preparation for the Seventh Congress of the Communist Party, the draft directives on questions of art and education were published in *Pravda*. In two divisions of these we find functions allotted to the new-found film. On popular education:

'Manifold government aid for self-training and self-development of workers and peasants (the formation of a network of non-school educational establishments: libraries, adult education classes, people's houses and universities, courses, lectures, cinemas, studios, etc.). . . . Similarly necessary to open to labourers and give them access to all treasures of art, built on a foundation of exploitation of their labour and till the present held exclusively at the disposition of the exploiters.'

And on cultural work in the country:

'Political propaganda in the country must be conducted both for the literates and the illiterates. . . . The cinema theatre, concerts, exhibitions, etc., as much as they will penetrate to the country, and towards this end all forces must be applied, must be used for communist propaganda directly, i.e. through their contents, by combining them with lectures and meetings. . . . There must be arranged for the illiterates regular readings in the schools, the offices of the Sovdeps, the reading-rooms, etc. . . . It would be desirable for such readings to be accompanied by graphic illustrations with the help of the cinematograph or stereopticon slides. . . . General education—in schools (artistic means are included herein: theatres, concerts, cinemas, exhibitions, pictures, and so forth), must be aimed not only at throwing the light of various fields of knowledge into the dark country, but must mainly promote the working out of a consciousness and a clear world-outlook—and must be closely linked with communist propaganda. There is no form of science or art which cannot be linked with the great ideas of communism and the infinitely diverse work of building a communist economy.'

With a timing that looked like direct support of the Party's cultural directives (on which, incidentally, Lenin may have consulted him), the greatest living Russian writer proposed an astonishing film project. Maxim Gorky had not immediately sided with the Bolshevik Revolution. It was only when he saw Soviet power used to broaden a systematic programme of unprecedented proportions in popular education that he joined forces with Soviet leaders, offering his energies in their support. By 1919 he headed a commission for improving the living conditions of Russian scientists, and undertook the supervision of two huge publishing projects: the *World Literature* series, and the many-volumed *Life of the World*. Accustomed to the almost limitless scope and thoroughness of these projects, Gorky saw nothing Utopian in proposing a film series that was no less ambitious.

On March 3rd, only a few days after the publication of the Party directives, Gorky delivered an address to the Theatre Division of the Petrograd Soviet on the necessity for a thorough overhauling of theatre and cinema repertories. A socialist audience needed a more responsible choice of subject matter. One of the means for unifying the most valuable materials in the existing miscellaneous repertories was the 'staging of the history of human culture in the form of theatrical presentations and pictures for the cinematograph'. At the first conception of this grandiose plan, Gorky had thought of a circus arena as the ideal stage for his endless series of cultural dramas which were to 'replace the dry, colourless telling of history', but by May he had fixed on the film as a medium more suitable for his pictures of 'the great sufferings, stubborn labour and fantastic accomplishments of the human brain, will and imagination', and had drafted the scenario for the first film in the series, on life in primitive society. His manuscript (and human culture) opens on this tableau of the Stone Age:

'A cluster of rocks, a cave, a few fern palms, beyond these a marshy expanse, on the horizon—forest. On a stone, at the entrance to the cave sits the head of the family, an old man, there are bones at his feet, the remains of a meal, there is also a bone in his hand; he examines it attentively, tests its toughness against the rock; a youth watches him closely. Half-drowsy children are rolling about on the earth. One of these turns from side to side; all have stuffed themselves to the point of drunkenness, they are hot. A grey old woman, dressed in the skin of a wild animal, is watching over a wounded man; he is also covered with an animal's skin, which has stuck to his wound; the old woman carefully tears it off; the wounded man softly growls; a young woman growls to him in the same tone—she is grinding some sort of plant on a smooth stone with a shinbone. A few more men and women of various ages lie about on the earth; one of these, with light pushes of his hands, rolls stones away from him and, noticing that the larger the stone, the further it rolls with a push of the same force, he picks up the larger stones and looks at them attentively. . . .'[18]

Vishnevsky found, among the papers of Alexander Blok, an unfinished sketch, 'The Boat', that he deduced may have been Blok's part in Gorky's ambitious project:

'A human family (man, woman, children) is wandering over a barren place. They have succumbed to exhaustion. Before them is revealed a great river and beyond the river—a blue land, where peaceful animals move, and fruit hangs from the trees.

'The river is a natural obstacle. The man attempts to swim it and is forced to turn back. The current is too swift.

'Assault by a beast of prey. Struggle with him.

'Another addition to the family.

'Together they look towards the far shore. New fruit ripens there.

'A fresh attempt to swim across. One of them drowns.

'One of the tribe leaves to seek a way across.

'They await him. He is lost.

'A new assault by a beast. Life in the trees. From there one can see even further into the fruitful land. There a herd of reindeer appears.

'Assault by a beast. Children are destroyed. A snake. Hunger. . . .'[19]

While there was still hope for realization of his plan, Gorky gave an interview to Isaac McBride, an American journalist:

'. . . Gorky has been devoting much time to the preparation of a series of motion-picture scenarios, composed with scientific historical exactness, showing the history of man from the Stone Age down through the Middle Ages to the time of Louis XVI of France, and finally to the present day. This work was begun in July 1919, and when I talked with Gorky in September of the same year, he told me that they had already finished twenty-five scenarios. He described the extraordinary difficulties under which the work was going forward; the actors and actresses who were often undernourished, persevered over all obstacles, inspired by an enthusiasm which Gorky thought would have been impossible in any other country. The Soviet Government was aiding the production in every way. The best actors and actresses in the country had been enlisted in this work along with historians and scientists. The films were being sent into the remote towns and villages, and thousands of small theatres already were being built.'[20]

In September Gorky made a last effort to promote his film idea, but when the 'reasonable men' demonstrated to Gorky that neither the Russian film industry, nor the new Soviet film organizations were equipped for such a project, he shelved it. If this dream had been discussed as little as one or two years later it might, at least, have been tried, but by that time Gorky, again ill, was sent abroad to a more healthful climate.

Half-hearted attempts continued to be made, both from Soviet and private sides, to prove that 'we can all work together', but there were too many indications that it wasn't possible. The big firms would make big announcements (*The Brothers Karamazov*! *Crime and Punishment*! *Torrents of Spring*! *Taras Bulba*!), would shoot a few sequences,* would ask for more film (although records showed they had plenty), and then would move off to the south under the pretext of 'location shots' or 'sunshine'. (Actually, most of their announced films were completed in Berlin.) For the May Day celebrations in 1919 the last results of this collaboration were shown. Comparing the productions of the Cinema Committee (*The Brain of Soviet Russia*, *Day of Universal Training*, *Children's Colonies in Russia*, etc.) with the 'collaborating productions' (Andreyev's anti-religious *Savva*, Tolstoy's *Power of Darkness*, Herzen's *Thieving*

---

* One such company arrived in Tula to film *The Time of Troubles*. The young poet, Boris Pasternak, whose only previous film experience had been to translate Kleist's *Broken Jug* for possible use as a scenario, was an interested, if horrified observer of the peculiar proceedings. In his *Letters from Tula* he reported the event as through the eyes of an old man standing by the river who can't understand what's going on across the river, 'looking at the boyars and voyevodes wavering on the farther bank, and the dark people who were leading men roped together, knocking their hats off their heads, into the nettles . . . at the Poles grappling up the slope behind clumps of broom, and their axes which were insensible to the sun and gave no sound. . . .' Pasternak dismissed the private behaviour of the company as 'the worst appearance of bohemianism'.

Magpie, etc.) it was obvious that the former were more worth the time and precious materials that went into them than the latter. Organizational hesitation came to an end. Nationalization of the Russian film industry was decreed:

DECREE

ON THE TRANSFER OF THE PHOTOGRAPHIC AND
CINEMATOGRAPHIC TRADE AND INDUSTRY TO
THE PEOPLE'S COMMISSARIAT OF EDUCATION.

1. The entire photographic and cinematographic trade and industry, their organization as well as the supply and distribution of technical means and materials appertaining to them, throughout the territory of the R.S.F.S.R., shall be placed within the province of the People's Commissariat of Education. 2. To this end the People's Commissariat of Education is herewith empowered: (a) to nationalize, by agreement with the Supreme Council of National Economy, particular photo and cinema enterprises, as well as the entire photo and cinema industry; (b) to requisition enterprises as well as photo and cinema goods, materials and equipment; (c) to fix stable and maximum prices for photo and cinema raw materials and manufactured products; (d) to exercise supervision and control over the photo and cinema trade and industry, and (e) to regulate the entire photo and cinema trade and industry by issuing decisions which shall be binding on enterprises and private persons, as well as on Soviet institutions, insofar as they relate to photo and cinema matters.

CHAIRMAN OF THE COUNCIL
OF PEOPLE'S COMMISSARS: V. Ulyanov (Lenin)

Moscow, Kremlin.   Executive Officer of the
August 27, 1919.   Council of People's Commissars: Vlad. Bonch-Bruyevich

The new-born Soviet film industry's first great success—artistically, at the box-office, and even politically—was not a Soviet film; it had not even been made in Russia. By one of the most extraordinary flukes in film history, at the beginning of 1919 a print of Griffith's *Intolerance* had found its way through the blockade to Moscow.

There are so many legends of the subsequent history of *Intolerance*'s significant Soviet career that it is very difficult to extract the true part from them at this late date; it may be wiser to list them all: (1) Lenin saw it, and personally arranged to have it shown throughout Russia; (2) the shortage of raw film stock caused by the evacuating firms held up this wide distribution of *Intolerance* until Guy Croswell Smith, representing an American condensed milk firm [!*] managed to import some positive stock; (3) Lenin at once cabled D. W. Griffith an invitation to take charge of the Soviet film industry†, but Griffith's new

* This story, by Gardin, is hardly credible, because Smith, representing George Creel's Committee on Public Information, left Russia with Edgar Sisson in March 1918, to set up shop in Scandinavia. Smith visited Russia ten years later, with Schenck.

† Arkatov informs me that this is half true, and that it was Cibrario (!) who was commissioned to see Griffith and to get him to Russia at any cost.

association with United Artists and the opening of his studio in Mamaroneck, N.Y., made his acceptance impossible; (4) dozens of Russians who had lived in the United States suddenly sought work at the Cinema Committee, each claiming to be Griffith's 'right hand'. (Gardin tells us that Preobrazhensky did, unfortunately, hire one of these 'right hands' [Zamkovoy] to head the Committee's production department.)

These are the legends, but the larger, though less specific facts that can be verified, are more important. We know for certain of the popular success of *Intolerance*, and we know as certainly of the tremendous aesthetic and technical impetus given to *all* young Soviet film-makers by this and subsequently-shown Griffith films.* No Soviet film of importance made within the following ten years† was to be completely outside *Intolerance*'s sphere of influence.† As to its political or social contribution to the Soviet film audience of 1919 there was no less relevance of theme and treatment in *Intolerance* than in *Comrade Abram* and its fellow-*agitki*.

The thematic flaws and illogicality of *Intolerance*'s four stories show up more clearly thirty years after the event, rather than when American audiences in 1916 and Soviet audiences in 1919 were dazzled and excited, either by the 'hail of images', or by Griffith's passionate portrayal of the four conflicts. Some may have been moved by the dimensions of the Babylonian story, but it must certainly have been the intense 'modern story' that moved the alert, embattled Soviet audience. Russian audiences had never seen such a believable tragedy of American working-class life—it must have given life to every slogan they had heard about the sympathies of foreign workers with the revolution in Russia. It was this core of sincerity in the film, rather than its philosophy (which would not have stood up under any objective Marxist inspection) that gave *Intolerance* its popular Soviet appeal.

The success of the *agitki* in meeting immediate tasks should not be underestimated. Formed under more strictly military auspices, the film section of the Ukrainian agitation-education committee in Kiev produced films in the spring of 1919 that were at once put to work in a Red Army recruiting campaign: *Listen, Brothers*! and *Peace to the Cottage, War to the Palace*! We are given a glimpse of the curiously autonomous procedure for producing Odessa's *agitki*—in some highly coloured memoirs of the period:

'On February 16th [1920], a special meeting of the *Politotdel* was called to devise means of combating the world-wide publicity given the Red terror. . . .

---

* There is also a curious pre-revolutionary Russian link to Griffith's influence: Protazanov's *Drama by Telephone* (1914) exactly follows *The Lonely Villa*, directed by Griffith in 1909 (with a script by Mack Sennett). It is also possible that Protazanov copied a Danish or German copy of Griffith's original.

† Iris Barry, in *D. W. Griffith, American Film Master*, says, 'It is true that Griffith is largely instinctive in his methods, where the Russian directors are deliberate and organized; but it was nevertheless in large measure from his example that they derived their characteristic staccato shots, their measured and accelerated rhythms and their skill in joining pictorial images together with a view to the emotional overtones of each, so that two images in conjunction convey more than the sum of their visible content.'

For nearly two hours, I had listened to a series of orations more or less to the point . . . when to my surprise, Commissar Kopolovich announced:
' "Now I would like to hear something practical, and so I shall call upon the *Amerikanetz*, Comrade Rubin. . . ."
' "The thing to do", I began, "is to fight the White guards with their own weapon. That is, show the world the White terror—the atrocities committed by the Denikin régime during its occupation of the Ukraine. The way to do this is by producing a moving picture, showing the pogroms upon the Jews, the raids upon stores and market-places, the cruelty, the injustice, the extortion, the graft, the many executions."
'My suggestion was received with great applause and unanimously adopted. Kopolovich appointed a committee of five, with myself as chairman, to write a scenario and submit it to the *Politotdel* at its meeting on February 23rd.
'At the next meeting the scenario was read. It was the story of my own experiences in Odessa—my arrival to negotiate with the Denikin Government, the jealousy of the English (Capitalistic) Consul, his scheme to arrest me, my prison life, my death sentence, my release and then the series of White atrocities I had witnessed or learned about before the capture of Odessa by the Bolsheviks. The picture was to be called *Between Two Flags*. . . .'[21]

500,000 roubles were appropriated for the production, Arkatov was appointed director, and Mr Rubin was given the rôle of Mr Rubin. Production began within a week and was completed in five weeks. The Moscow authorities were somewhat less enthusiastic about the film than was the Odessa Politotdel. Mr Rubin's book is illustrated with stills from this short-lived and local *agitka*.

When the Whites recaptured Odessa they made an open declaration of the effectiveness of the *agitki* being shown there: they staged a public burning of all the *agitki* they could find. They also arrested Mikhail Werner, who had directed a particularly pointed two-reeler, *Scared Bourgeoisie*, and they shot one of the actors, Insarov.

In the spring of 1919 the Petrograd Cinema Committee had begun work in their new studio (the former 'Aquarium') with a film for May Day—*The Victory of May* (directed by B. Svetlov and photographed by V. Lemke). By the following November this Committee was confronted by a much more serious task. The British-supported army of Yudenich, equipped for the first time with tanks, had already reached the suburbs of Petrograd. The 7th Red Army could not stop the advance without reinforcements. The Cinema Committee was called in to help with the city-wide recruiting drive, and the *agitka* produced for this purpose by Svetlov and Lemke—*All Under Arms!*—helped Petrograd's working men and women to turn the Yudenich advance into a rout. One of the few records of the Yudenich campaign was made by a Swedish Biograf cameraman just three hours after a battle on the Russo-Finnish border some twenty-five miles from Petrograd.[22]

The defeat of Yudenich allowed Red Army concentration on the Kolchak front, and Frunze's army (including the division led by Vasili Chapayev), along with its cameramen, stormed eastward. The battles with Kolchak's forces were not only filmed by Tisse, Lemberg and other Soviet cameramen. Along with Kolchak's other foreign equipment:

'Uniforms from England,
Epaulettes from France,
Japanese tobacco,
Kolchak leads the dance. . . .'*

there was a British cameraman, from Charles Urban's 'Kineto' Company. By the end of 1919 the Kolchak front was liquidated,† and the Admiral was captured and executed. The escape of Urban's cameraman must have taken time, for his films were not shown in London until the following summer.

These victories did not break the blockade, however. The new Soviet Republic and its infant film industry faced the worst winter of their lives. The hungry and cold year of 1919 was coming to its climax. At the beginning of December the New York *Times* quoted *Izvestia*'s announcement that the supply of wood in Petrograd would suffice for only twenty days, and that the Committee of National Economy had decided that 'in addition to the already closed factories it is proposed to close the greater part of the theatres and moving picture houses, to cut down the electric supply and water works and to stop the tramways'. Inflation gave each mouthful of food the value of a jewel: bread cost 300 roubles a pound, meat—600 roubles, butter—1,700 roubles.

'Such educated Russians as were too old or weak to be in the trenches had to grapple with a variety of problems in the rear, under conditions of hunger and cold. Visualize the great Pavlov carrying on laboratory experiments, dressed in his fur coat, his fingers numb and stiff; Meyerhold producing daring performances in unheated theatres; Glazunov raising his baton before a shivering orchestra and audience.'[23]

Moscow this December was no less hungry and cold and it seems nothing short of heroic that even one studio should have continued work under such circumstances. Although the nationalization of all private studios was decreed the preceding August, the actual transfer was not carried through until January. Any private film crew that continued work in this period was not only heroic, but must have been loyal or extra-enthusiastic, as well. 'Russ' had, apparently, such a crew, for they continued to use frozen cameras in a frozen studio—never sure of their next meal.

When Trofimov left Moscow in October 1917, he may have been able to take the funds of the 'Russ' Studio with him, but much of its equipment was left behind, as was its greatest asset: the talents of the people working in the studio.

* The final stanza of this Siberian song runs:
Uniform in tatters,
Epaulettes all gone,
So is the tobacco,
Kolchak's day is done.

† During the fighting at Irkutsk, a freight car containing Jesse J. Seadeck and the projection equipment of the 'Community Motion Picture Bureau' was under fire for thirteen days. Mr Seadeck had just completed a record run of Chaplin's *A Dog's Life*—67 nights in 67 different Siberian communities—the first Russians to see Charles Chaplin.

Aleinikov looked on the situation as an artistically golden opportunity. Now he could show the Russian film industry what it should have been doing all these years. He had talked about the idea of an artists' film co-operative before the October revolution. Immediately afterwards, in the early months of 1918, the talk was realized with the formation of 'The Artistic Collective of Russ'. Lunacharsky helped them hurdle the many formalities confronting this novel move in a suspect industry, and he agreed to support certain unwritten conditions: though there were no communist party members in the collective, no outside political control was to be exerted over the films produced, and all films were to have primarily artistic and not political aims.

The composition of the collective was as ideal as its aims. As chairman and production head, Aleinikov guided policies and administration; Otsep, Aleinikov's assistant on Yermoliev's old magazine, was brought in as artistic supervisor of production; Nikolai Efros, one-time head of the Art Theatre's literary department, was given the same responsibility here. The choice of a technical head was a little idealistic: Yuri Zhelyabuzhsky, son of the Art Theatre actress Andreyeva, was an energetic amateur photographer whose good sense and taste made the collective confident that he could photograph films in spite of his limited experience.* Agranovich, Aleinikov's brother-in-law, was designer and the three remaining members of the collective were all from the Art Theatre: actor Ivan Moskvin (a novice in films), actress Olga Gzovskaya (already holding the status of a film star), and an associate director, Alexander Sanin. Even without Stanislavsky's permission, this collective could be justly called the film branch of the Moscow Art Theatre.

The entire membership decided on the collective's first film. Tolstoy's story, *Polikushka*, was chosen because it was (1) a Russian classic, (2) against serfdom, and (3) offered an interesting rôle for Moskvin's film début. While Otsep and Efros worked on the film adaptation (Otsep, though far younger in years, was older in film experience), the administration organized a nation-wide search for that precious stuff—raw film. Operating on rumours that there were a hundred metres in a certain Kiev closet, or two hundred metres in an Odessa warehouse, etc., friends were sent to acquire, somehow, every decent metre of negative stock remaining on Russian soil. Later, in the filming, this made every re-take a calamity, but its makers are still proud that, despite the abnormal circumstances and Zhelyabuzhsky's inexperience, an 1,800 metre film was cut from a total of 2,000 exposed metres. Sanin directed, assisted by Otsep.

Fantastic is the only suitable word for the conditions in which *Polikushka* was produced during the winter of 1919-20. There was no transportation between the city and Petrovsky Park, where the studio was located. The collective managed to acquire the services of a single sleigh, horse, and coachman, but to conserve the energies of the hungry horse, only women were permitted its use. The men walked there and back each day. To live at the studio was unthinkable—its spaces

---

* However, between the formation of the collective and the start of their first film, Zhelyabuzhsky got some practice in the *agitki* (see page 136); he had also worked as an assistant cameraman before the revolution.

could not be heated, for there was no firewood available. Tiny protected bonfires were produced from the brushwood combings of the park, and were built inside the stages. The freezing actors would rush towards them at the end of a shot, to warm themselves, sometimes with a bowl of hot, but almost imaginary soup, while the next set-up was being arranged. The jubilant climax of this woodless winter was the discovery of an empty, unclaimed *wooden* house nearby. The collective 'liberated' it at once, and the entire membership raced over to help tear it down and chop it into firewood. Nothing could dampen the enthusiasm of these eager, youthful artists. The members received no pay during production, for they were willing to wait for equal shares in the eventual proceeds. Money itself did not seem worth much thought this winter—non-members who acted and worked in *Polikushka* were glad to be paid in potatoes.

The 'eventual proceeds' were a long time materializing, but they were worth waiting for. Cutting took longer than the filming, and then there was the matter of prints. For a long while after the completion of the cutting, the only print available for screenings was the work-print, for the members of the collective. It was shown to Lunacharsky who was not only personally moved, but was excited by this visible confirmation of his hopes for Russian films. He at once arranged for Aleinikov to go abroad, through the first crack in the blockade, to sell the foreign rights of *Polikushka*. With these funds, Aleinikov bought good negative and positive film, in Berlin, needed apparatus—and *stockings*, to send back to the collective. Simultaneously, two new films were put into production, and prints of *Polikushka* were made and released. Its theatrical success justified the wildest hopes of the collective and of Lunacharsky.

This simple, direct fable of an ignorant peasant, entrusted with a mission, failing, and hanging himself, must have had unusual poignancy for its audience. Probably the person most responsible for the deep impression the film made everywhere was Ivan Moskvin, who played the rôle of Polikei. Moskvin's later film work is more polished, surrounded as it was by more skilful film-makers and respectable equipment, but this comparatively crude film contains the clearest possible reflection of the qualities that made Moskvin one of the great artists of the Moscow Art Theatre. Every gesture, every glance of Polikei's is so *true* that one has to remind oneself to examine this as a performance by an actor. There are other talented players in the cast, including Vera Pashennaya (of the Malii Theatre) as Polikei's wife, and Rayevskaya of the Art Theatre, but they merely serve to help one date the film. Only Moskvin seems to have looked ahead to a period when the principles behind the best acting of the Russian theatre would be fully fused with Soviet film-making.

On January 15, 1920 the studios were officially taken over by the All-Russian Photo-Cinema Section, and what was left of Khanzhonkov, the Skobelev Committee, Yermoliev, 'Russ', 'Ekran', Taldykin, Kharitonov, and lesser firms, became instruments to be used by the Soviet Government.

Two days after a new agit-train left for Turkestan, on January 23rd, Lenin, still convalescing from Fanny Kaplan's nearly successful bullets, sent Comrade Burov a list of directives on improving the work of this instrument, examining the use of educational films with an attitude that is still advanced:

1 *Strengthen the economic and practical part of the trains' and steamboats' work* by including in their political sections agronomists, technicians, with a selection of technical literature, and *with corresponding subjects on motion picture films,* etc.

2 *Prepare,* through the Cinema Committee, *films* of manufacturing (showing various branches of production), agricultural, industrial, anti-religious and scientific subjects, ordering such subjects from abroad through Com. *Litvinov.* . . .

3 Draw attention to the necessity for a careful *selection* of motion picture films and a calculation of the action of each film on the audience during its projection. . . .

7 *Organize* abroad *representatives for the purchase* and shipping of films, raw film stock and all sorts of cinematographic material.

8 *Draw particular attention to the selection of the working personnel* on the trains and steamboats.

Among the many new forces put to work on increasing the effectiveness of the agit-trains was a young Red Army artist, Sergei Eisenstein, who had just been transferred from work on fortifications to the more congenial job of designer in a Red Army theatrical unit at the front. He had been in the army two years, after leaving the Institute of Civil Engineers in Petrograd to volunteer in those first doubtful months of 1918. After working on the defences around Petrograd, he had served similarly on the Northern Front (at Vologda) and the Western front (at Dvinsk). It was not long after he had been painting posters and caricatures for the agit-trains that he was released from the army to complete his schooling. By the autumn of this same year, 1920, he had dropped the career of engineer, gone to Moscow where his intention was to pursue his interests in Japanese arts, but instead he joined the staff of the exciting new workers' theatre—the Central Proletkult Arena—and his first step towards films had been taken.

'The flourishing phase of proletkult coincided with the lowest ebb of public well-being in Russia—years of civil war, intervention, blockade, famine, the period of "military communism". Proletkult reflected the romantically heroic notions, the half-baked extremism of the early stage of the revolution. The next stage meant sober reconstruction, under conditions of comparative peace.'[24]

Another aspect of the true significance of Proletkult's popularity—the determination to learn—was the new State Film School, that examined its first year's pupils and presented them in an agit-play on the night of May 1st. The school's director opened the examinations, and Lunacharsky spoke enthusiastically of the school's future. Kuleshov, the radical designer who had worked for Khanzhonkov, was also there, just returned from a period at the Eastern front as supervisor of a group of cameramen. Along with the newsreel footage, Kuleshov had also brought back some ideas, and the beginning of a group:

'. . . When the cameraman and I were returning from the front, through Sverdlovsk (then Yekaterinburg), we met a young Red Army man, Leonid Obolensky, with whom I had many talks about cinematography. I told him my attitudes on cinema, and a theory of mine, and we found we had a lot to talk about. Obolensky had just been discharged, and I gave him a letter to the State Film School that had recently opened in Moscow. . . . When I returned from the front, Obolensky was studying there. The teachers were experienced, but from my point of view, "conservative". They worked with a purely theatrical method (with the exception of Gardin, who was more "left"). They knew nothing about a specifically cinema technique, and considered it unnecessary. At the examinations, where I happened to be, one of a group of students who "failed" as being absolutely unsuitable was a girl named Chekulayeva. . . . I began work on an étude for the re-examination of Comrade Chekulayeva, being especially careful to work out each movement (I had as yet no theory for the actor's work), and the étude turned out very well. Incidentally, in working out this étude, I intuitively, without any theoretical base, applied a method of maximally accurate construction of movements—step by step, detail by detail. When the committee re-examined Chekulayeva, they were amazed. . . . I then went to work with all the students who had failed (they turned out to be the most talented students in the school) and these, too, received the highest marks in a re-examination.

'At that time I learned that two students had done a parody on the fragments I had prepared for the examination, and I asked to see this. It really was unbelievably funny and extremely well done. These two students were A. Reich and A. Khokhlova. . . .

'Soon I was invited to teach in the State Film School, and I was given a workshop—a separate class—to which, of course, all the students I had helped in the re-examination applied for admittance. . . .'[25]

The May Day ceremony at the State Film School is also memorable for another beginning: the first professional appearance of Vsevolod Pudovkin as an actor. As engineering lost Eisenstein to art in 1920, so did chemistry lose Pudovkin this year. At the comparatively late age of twenty-seven, Pudovkin abandoned the security of a laboratory job at the military plant 'Phosgene No. 1' for a completely unfamiliar field:

'As far as I can remember I doubt if I saw a single film before 1920. As a matter of fact I didn't even consider the cinema an art form. But the theatre was a different matter. I was much more interested in it than in chemistry or in my job. What attracted me most at that time, however, was painting. I spent all my leisure time painting. I was also very fond of music.'[26]

The preceding years had done much to re-arrange this chemist's outlook and sense of values. Just as he was graduating from the Moscow University (majoring in physics and chemistry) into the profession of chemist, the first World War broke out. Pudovkin enlisted in the artillery without passing his final exams. By February 1915 he was wounded and taken prisoner, and the next three years were spent in a Pomeranian prison camp, learning English, German and Polish in his spare time. He took part in one unsuccessful prison break, but a group of the Russian prisoners found a better opportunity during the German revolution, so that by the end of 1918 Pudovkin was back in Moscow, and soon afterwards was following the career he had dropped four years before. New artistic ambitions made him restless in the laboratory, however, and he even went so far as to apply for entrance into one of the Moscow theatres. He passed the examinations but held on to his chemist's job for a while longer. Within a few weeks he had made up his mind, but in a wholly unexpected direction:

'. . . I had seen D. W. Griffith's *Intolerance* which made a tremendous impression upon me. This picture became the symbol of the future art of the cinema for me. After seeing it I was convinced that cinematography was really an art and an art of great potentialities. It fascinated me and I was eager to go into this new field.'

Pudovkin applied to the State Film School and was at once accepted and put to work by Gardin in the May Day performance (where Pudovkin assisted as well as played bit rôles of a worker and a soldier).

'Then came the news that a new workshop, our own Soviet workshop, was to be opened. Kuleshov's workshop was located in a former private mansion on a small Moscow side-street. I went there one evening soon after I heard about it. There was a strange odour about the place, a mixture of lilac, celluloid and burned wires. Someone was improvising at the piano. . . .'

It was to be two years, however, before Pudovkin got around to joining Kuleshov's group. 'Comparative peace' was not yet in sight, for on April 25th the Polish army had opened a fresh attack on the Soviet republic and had seized Kiev. Among the many efforts made by the young Soviet film to help the resistance to this attack, both Kuleshov and Pudovkin took part, but in separate sectors.

The newsreel men went to work; the Cinema Committee announced a scenario contest on the Polish war; Mayakovsky wrote an *agitka* entitled *At the Front*, and both the Film School and the new workshop offered their services. The School was assigned to make a three-reel *agitka*, *Days of Struggle*, under the direction of Perestiani, in which the chief rôles were played by Andrei Gorchilin (the film's author) and Nina Shaternikova, with Pudovkin playing his first film rôle, a Red Army commander.

Kuleshov and his group had barely moved into their new quarters with the strange odour before they left on May 22nd for the Western front, with plans for a three-reel, half-newsreel, half-enacted *agitka* to be filmed as near the actual fighting as Comrade Smilga, of the Revolutionary-Military Council on the Western front, would allow. Smilga suggested that the crew set up headquarters in his train, and thus they would get as close to the front as he did. The entire crew, including Kuleshov, the cameraman Yermolov, and Khokhlova, Obolensky and Reich as actors, worked out a very simple script for *On the Red Front*, inspired both in structure and filming by American 'chase' films, particularly the finale of the 'modern story' of *Intolerance*:

'The spectator's attention was caught by the very opening of the film. In close-up, pliers are cutting a cable. A field-telephone, damaged by a Polish spy, stops operation. The commander of a military unit is obliged to send a secret dispatch to headquarters by a Red Army man. A horseman races along the road, while the spy, who has climbed a tree and is camouflaged, follows the rider in his gun-sight. There is a shot. The rider falls from his horse. The spy runs to the fallen Red Army man, takes the packet from him, races to the station and leaps onto the first train that passes. But the Red Army man has not been killed. Wounded, he trails the enemy as long as his strength lasts. Luckily, he meets a Soviet auto-mobile on the road. The Red Army man is taken into the car, and they chase the train, in order to cut off the spy's return to his base. The train is stopped. The Red Army man jumps onto the car's platform and runs through the cars, looking for the spy. Noticing his pursuer, the spy climbs up on the car's roof. The Red Army man goes after him. An unequal struggle ensues on the roof, finally resulting in the defeat of the spy, who falls from the roof. The intercepted packet is delivered at the appointed time.'[27]

There being no negative film available for this rush job, Yermolov bravely shot the entire film on *positive* stock. The printing of copies presented new problems, for foreign positive stock was getting too rare for ordinary use. Some ingenious mind had brought a method to the Cinema Committee for washing the emulsion from used film and recoating the celluloid by hand. It was on this home-made stock that *On the Red Front* and other *agitki* of its time were printed, which is, no doubt the reason why so few of these war-time films have been preserved.

For the several professional film-men (such as Perestiani) the *agitka* was a political kindergarten. For the others—those film-workers who were given their first creative responsibilities by the revolution—the *agitka* was a technological kindergarten. Kuleshov has remarked that in making *On the Red Front*, the actors regarded their work rather as students preparing an examination performance. Results were not uppermost in the crew's thoughts, but the finished film must have done its job, for Kuleshov was told that Lenin saw the film twice, and had praised it.

Earlier in May the cameraman Grigori Giber had been sent to the Western front, at the disposition of Tukhachevsky, the commander of the Soviet offensive. Travelling almost continuously by automobile, Giber filmed the battle at Molodechno, and the recapture of Borisov and Minsk. Even when his stock of raw film was exhausted, Giber went on reporting—now for the newspaper, *Red Front*.

On the opposite front in the Polish camp, was a man who, only two years before, had made the *agitka*, *Bread*. Richard Boleslawski had crossed the lines, volunteered his services to the romantic Pilsudski, and organized the filming of the Polish version of the war.* The resulting film (half-newsreel, half-enacted, as was Kuleshov's *On the Red Front*) was *The Miracle of the Vistula*, the miracle being the Soviet retreat, on August 21st, from their furthest point of advance on Warsaw.

---

* German cameramen were also at work on the Polish front, supplying footage for the newsreel, *Messter-Woche*. This circumstance gives a rather peculiar colour to a Chicago *Tribune* dispatch from Warsaw at the time of the Soviet retreat, reporting that a propaganda train had been captured by the Poles, and that the films carried on the train had *German* subtitles!

Behind the enemies' southern front, too, there was film activity, but less directly political in nature. The Menshevik government of Georgia was still in Tiflis. A French producer by the name of Piron came in and took over the film market. He hired the one cameraman available, Alexander Digmelov, and made a series of films, of which only the titles remain to indicate their viewpoints: *The Decapitated Corpse, Tell Me Why*, and the like.

The anti-bolshevik film front extended far beyond the military front, and its centre was the new film centre of the world—the United States. As late as January 1920, the U.S. State Department shipped films to Russia to counteract the effect of Soviet propaganda behind the interventionist lines. In the same month Secretary of the Interior Lane followed up the Palmer raids with an energetic 'Americanization' campaign, addressed to the film industry. Industry leaders were polite but cool to his requests for fifty-two Americanization pictures a year, in which there would 'run a golden thread of the American spirit through the web',[28] but their ears pricked up at his suggestion of anti-bolshevik propaganda films—now, there, at least, was a subject you could get your teeth into! The long familiar characterizations of black-bearded anarchists and bomb-throwers now had Government approval. Wharton at once produced seven reels called *The Red Peril*; Norma Talmadge played in *The New Moon* ('giving her an opportunity to play both Princess and Peasant'), and Lenin's life (?) was filmed as *The Land of Mystery*.

The centre of the centre was, of course, the Committee on Public Information's Division of Films. George Creel has told how 'the fall of Kerensky made Russian consignments a problem', and how an attempt to use the Y.M.C.A. as a channel to Petrograd and Moscow film audiences, broke down—allowing thousands of reels intended for Edgar Sisson's and Arthur Bullard's propaganda campaign to pile up uselessly in Sweden.[29] Thereafter, the Committee's film operations were located in the intervention bases of Archangel and Vladivostok. Although these operations, in their last Harbin stages, sound pretty pale,* we have Mr Creel's campaign to thank for a large part of our prolonged poor relations with Soviet Russia after the cessation of formal hostilities—even to the extent of cancelling out the friendship potential contained in American relief activities during the subsequent Russian famine.

This intense American film campaign did not, however, prevent older, more innocent American films from remaining in Russian circulation at the same time. The habitual film-going of the city public continued, unbroken by any discouraging war-time or revolutionary factors:

'Occasionally, instead of sitting at home in the evenings we used to go to the cinema. Once a few of us from the Schicksaal school decided to go to the "Cinema

---

* From the report of Malcolm Davis: 'The pictures which we had were mainly military and industrial, with a few travel pictures of America and some weekly news review films. We had an excellent film, "The Re-making of a Nation," and also much other film showing army-training in the United States. We divided the films off into programmes as well balanced as possible. . . .' (Creel, p. 389). Yet Herbert Griffin wrote enthusiastically from Vladivostock, 'Russia is virgin territory for the motion picture business, . . . big business will be done once order is restored.' (*Moving Picture World* March 15, 1919).

Soleil" in the Nevsky Prospekt Arcade. We had papers to prove that we were students, and with the help of these we were going to try to get in at reduced prices. When we asked the lady at the ticket-office, however, she said we should have to speak to the manager, and pointed out his office to us. When we opened the door, I saw to my surprise the priest who used to give us scripture lessons at school. He was dressed very elegantly for those times, in an almost new green suit, and when I greeted him, politely asking for the manager, he burst out laughing and said that he was the manager. And when, more astounded, I asked him how he had come to such a state, he chuckled and said that everybody has to find his way out of difficulties and to get on in life: he had abandoned one profession for another, similar. A cinema-manager, he said, was as much a curer of souls as a priest—he had merely exchanged a congregation for an audience. He seemed to find it very amusing, and finished by telling us that he felt much freer and happier in cinema than in church. In an access of jubilation and for the sake of old times, he pushed us genially into the hall where we thrilled and glowed, without paying a kopek, over an old, old film of Mary Pickford.'[30]

Despite the anti-bolshevik campaign in the United States, the Commissariat for External Affairs permitted the editor of the New York *World* to come in for the purpose of interviewing Lenin at the beginning of 1920. Along with the newspaperman came a newsreel cameraman who filmed the only intimate footage of Lenin—within his Kremlin office, cat in lap. On the other hand, the cameraman Flick, sent in by the Fox News through Reval, was imprisoned in Moscow before he could get his Pathé camera unpacked. The charge was suspected counter-revolutionary activity, and Flick was kept in prison till August 1921— a year later.

On October 7, 1920 a happier visitor, H. G. Wells, attended a meeting of the Petrograd Soviet, to which he made a brief statement clarifying his political position. The meeting ended with a debate on the production of vegetables in the Petrograd district.

'This business disposed of, a still more extraordinary thing happened. We who sat behind the rostrum poured down into the already crowded body of the hall and got such seats as we could find, and a white sheet was lowered behind the president's seat. At the same time a band appeared in the gallery to the left. A five-part cinematograph film was then run, showing the Baku Conference. . . . The pictures were viewed with interest but without any violent applause.'[31]

One result of this screening was that the Petrograd Soviet gave Mr Wells a print of this film to take back to London with him.

The last military anti-Soviet force, and its leader, Wrangel, left Russian soil on November 14, 1920. Their evacuation of the Crimea also removed the last remnants of Russian private film industry.

Within this Civil War period of the Soviet film only one film was made (*Polikushka*) whose title is remembered. There was in films nothing comparable yet to the sharpness of Lenin's oratory or to the fire of Mayakovsky's poems.

But in this period were born the basic principles and ideals that still sustain Soviet film art. The people who were to build this art were now coming home from the war, readied by the war for their new job. Fifteen years later one of them wrote:

'. . . we all came to the Soviet cinema as something not yet existent. We came upon no ready-built city; there were no squares, no streets laid out; not even little crooked lanes and blind alleys, such as we may find in the cinemetropolis of our day. We came like bedouins or gold-seekers to a place with unimaginably great possibilities, only a small section of which has even now been developed.

'We pitched our tents and dragged into camp our experiences in varied fields. Private activities, accidental past professions, unguessed crafts, unexpected eruditions—all were pooled and went into the building of something that had, as yet, no written traditions, no exact stylistic requirements, nor even formulated demands. . . .'[32]

We have seen the arrivals of the first 'bedouins or gold-seekers'—Vertov, Tisse, Kuleshov, Pudovkin. Eisenstein is designing scenery and costumes at the Prolet-kult Arena. Grigori Alexandrov's work in a front-line theatre on the Eastern front encourages him to seek fame and fortune in Moscow. Abram Room has moved from dentistry to journalism and is on his way to direction at the Theatre of the Revolution. Anatoli Golovnya's eyes are being trained, as a Cheka worker, in Dzerzhinsky's office. Victor Turin had been sent by his well-to-do family to America, where he moved from the Massachusetts Institute of Technology to the Vitagraph Studios, and is considering taking back what he has learned to a new film world. Two boys, Grigori Kozintsev and Leonid Trauberg, are excited by American serials and comedies, and organize their friends, including a painter, Sergei Yutkevich, into a boisterous ambulant studio-theatre. Esther Shub enters the cutting-room where she is to remain for more than five years. Alexander Dovzhenko, graduating from a teachers' college, is the political cartoonist on an Ukrainian newspaper, and is studying painting in his spare time. Mikhail Chiaureli is about to sacrifice his career as a Tiflis sculptor for that of a Tiflis actor. Mark Donskoy, a discharged soldier, contemplates the career of a professional boxer. Friedrich Ermler fought in the Red Army on the Northern front, and joined the Communist Party in 1919; while recovering from tortures inflicted when he was captured by White troops, Ermler recalls his boyhood fascination in films and enters the Leningrad Institute of Screen Arts. Another Red Army soldier from 1917 to the end of war, Sergei Vasiliev, also enters the Leningrad Institute. Mikhail Kalatozishvili enters a business school.

Insignia of VUFKU

CHAPTER VIII

Reconstruction

1921–1923

> Cultural problems cannot be solved as quickly as
> political and military problems. . . . It is possible
> to achieve a political victory in the epoch of acute
> crisis within a few weeks. It is possible to obtain
> victory in war within a few months. But it is impos-
> sible to achieve a cultural victory in such a short
> time . . .
>
> LENIN

An alert English visitor, Huntly Carter, who travelled in Russia in the summer
of 1921, brought back some newsworthy impressions of film and theatre activities
there. Despite his disgust with the films he saw then, against a background of
famine and confusion, he risked a prophecy:

'There is no doubt that the Russians would express themselves through the
film if they were given a proper opportunity to do so. I do not think the opportunity will be long coming.'[1]

In another article he made a bolder statement about Soviet films that might
stand as an epigraph on this chapter:

'Perhaps never in the history of civilization has a mechanical contrivance been
used more successfully under exceedingly difficult conditions to assist in the
construction of a new nation.'[1a]

Eight months after Wrangel's evacuation of the Crimea, the country was
plunged into what was

'. . . perhaps the most critical period in Soviet history, when exhaustion, caused
by civil war and foreign intervention and blockade, was about to culminate in
the great famine of 1921, and Lenin himself was compelled to make a profound,
if temporary, sacrifice of socialist theory and return to a system of private enterprise at first not superficially remote as Capitalism.

'This change, which was called the New Economic Policy (NEP), was officially
inaugurated by a decree published on August 9, 1921, but "free trade", as it
was called, that is private enterprise had already been in force for some months,
quite soon indeed after the revolts at Kronstadt and Tambov in the spring.

Lenin had a long struggle to convince his followers that the change was necessary. One of his arguments was that it would facilitate economic relations with the outer world, an inflow of foreign capital in the form of concession agreements.'[1b]

To this Dr Hammer adds a characteristic detail of the change wrought by NEP:

'Its immediate effect was to bring forth untold quantities of goods of every variety which suddenly appeared as if by magic. The shelves of stores formerly empty were overloaded with articles which had not been seen since the days of the Bolshevik revolution four years before.'[2]

After watching the behaviour of the film proprietors in the first months after the October revolution, we can expect to see all the equipment of film-making and film-distribution suddenly re-appear, as soon as its owners (what was left of them) were assured once more of profits. Not only did railway engines and looms move once again, but film exchanges sprang up in nearly the exact places where they had ceased functioning three years before. Lenin's reasoning had been sound:

'. . . The civil war slowed everything down and now we must start in afresh. The New Economic Policy demands a fresh development of our economic possibilities. We hope to accelerate the process by a system of industrial and commercial concessions to foreigners.'[3]

Translated into terms of the film industry, this meant that the first *producing* steps in the reconstruction period were to be subsidized by taxation of the NEP concessionaires while the *distribution* channels, choked by disuse, were to be flushed with the new films and the theatre renovation that would be the concessionaires' first investments. Both production and distribution were to be aimed at becoming self-supporting, once foreign capital had provided this necessary breathing interval. How seriously the film industry needed this temporary crutch is shown by this typical observation, made by a visitor earlier this year:

'The motion picture theatres in Moscow were as a rule gloomy and unattractive places, poorly heated, dirty, and, for the most part, displaying worn-out films from pre-war days. There were a few theatres where the Soviet news weeklies were shown together with a number of propaganda films, but the Government has been terribly hampered with regard to film production by the lack of technical material. The motion picture industry is controlled by the Kino Komitet, a branch of the Department of Education, and it has planned a wonderful programme on paper for popular amusement and education through the movies, but at present little can be done.'[4]

Kuleshov found the studios in an even worse state:

'They were ruined or half-ruined, the equipment having been taken abroad by the owners, or smashed and destroyed. I recall a visit that I made to one of these "film-factories" to ascertain whether it could be put to use or not: under the open sky, in a chaotic heap of wreckage protruding from the snow-drifts, I caught sight of a desk with a typewriter, rusted and covered by snow, and in the machine was an unfinished message on the letter-head of the former owners.'[5]

But the execution, now, of all 'wonderful programmes' was shoved back by a new national crisis, for in the wake of war, famine stalked the whole country—and set up its power in the most fertile region of Russia, the Volga basin. When in the first months of autumn 1921, the first terrible news came of mass deaths from starvation, carrying a threat of far wider catastrophe, three films were immediately put into production to gather sympathy and funds for the famine victims. Moscow sent out the first crew, headed by Gardin, with a scenario prepared by him and Pudovkin, *Hunger. . . . Hunger. . . . Hunger.* In Petrograd Panteleyev and the cameraman Kozlovsky went to work on a film called *Infinite Sorrow.* The world outside Russia was also to be appealed to, by Dr Fridtjof Nansen, who filmed the Volga famine in November and December of 1921 as part of his world-wide relief campaign. His film, *The Famine in Russia,* with no theatrical elements and photographed by an amateur, was perhaps the most devastatingly real and frightening of the three films. It was the one film made in Russia after the Bolshevik Revolution that was shown throughout the world without a word of political protest. Its Paris showing, at the Trocadéro, was supported by a statement from Anatole France.* In London it was shown at St George's Church in Bloomsbury. America was in a position to respond to Nansen's appeal, and did so, generously, forming its own relief organization and sending in its own cameramen to continue the campaign at home. Floyd Traynham, who spent seventeen months in Russia as official photographer of the American Relief Administration, left this note on his introduction to the famine area of Ufa in February 1922:

'Before leaving Moscow I had been told of the horrors to expect where the famine was bad, but having been a news-cameraman for some time I felt that I had seen enough horrors to be hardened for whatever was before me. This proved to be wrong. The first picture I made there, I remember, was of one of the kitchens. While making an exterior shot of the building I saw two men fall on the street within twenty-five yards of where I was standing. For a Southerner, it was terribly cold; about fifty degrees below zero Fahrenheit. These men were starved, and to fall exhausted in the snow meant death in a few moments. . . . A Ford truck had been placed at my disposal by the District Supervisor at Ufa, and into this we put the two exhausted men and had the chauffeur take them to a hospital. One died on the way and the other shortly after arriving at the hospital. After that, to see people fall on the streets became a rather common sight. . . .'[6]

Pudovkin's work with Gardin on *Hunger* was to be the last film on which they worked together. At their first meeting Gardin had sensed temperament and talent in the almost middle-aged entrant to the Film School. Immediately after Pudovkin's work in Perestiani's *Days of Struggle,* Gardin had sought his aid on the production of a more developed *agitka, Sickle and Hammer.* This scenario had been submitted by the author of the previous film, Andrei Gorchilin, but Gardin

---

* Gardin's *Hunger* was also shown in Paris in 1922, at the Ciné-Club organized by Louis Delluc.

considered an epilogue necessary, and Pudovkin's first job on the film was collaborating with the director on the composition of this epilogue. Before the film was finished Pudovkin not only played the leading rôle (a poor peasant whose character is strengthened by the revolution), but had also worked as an assistant (both to Gardin and to Tisse, their cameraman), as an administrator for the crew's affairs, and as a property-man. No negative stock could be unearthed for the film, so it was shot on various pieces of positive stock. When the crew returned from location in February 1921, the variety of Pudovkin's responsibilities increased: he helped repair the new building awarded to the School (Yermoliev's former studio); it was proposed that Gorchilin's scenario be published, and Pudovkin took care of this, too, writing a foreword in the name of the entire collective; he assisted Gardin in the adaptation of Jack London's *Iron Heel*, which was to be given a half-stage, half-film production at the Theatre of Revolutionary Satire, worked on its designs, and then played in it along with other students of the School, including Khokhlova and Obolensky. It is surprising that in the production of *Hunger*, Gardin gave only one scene to Pudovkin and Tisse to do without his supervision—a scene of the death of a peasant's baby.

Even before the inauguration of NEP, there was activity in the Commissariat of Nationalities that was to have an enormous and positive effect on Soviet films. The Commissar, Joseph Stalin, was one of the few persons in positions of authority who paid the cinema more than lip-service. Within a programme of increased cultural autonomy for the non-Russian states, Stalin, without fuss or pronouncement, gave the cinema equal standing with the other arts, and it was Georgia that was the first to take advantage of the blanket offer to assist in setting up national film-studios; in April 1921, a film section was established in the Georgian Commissariat of Education, and production was begun at once under the direction of Perestiani, who had originally come to Russian films from the Caucasus. The first new Georgian film appeared the following October: *Arsen Georgiashvili* (or *The Murder of General Griaznov*), directed by Perestiani, with Mikhail Chiaureli playing his first film rôle, Arsen.

By the beginning of 1922 the Ukrainian film industry reorganized itself as VUFKU—the All-Ukrainian Photo-Cinema Administration. Shifting from Kiev to Odessa to Yalta along with the advancing Red Army, the film section of the Ukrainian agitation-education committee had barely managed to stay in existence. Its chief director, Pyotr Chardynin, was not working for them out of any deep conviction in their cause, but mostly because he had stayed behind when the film industrialists fled from the Black Sea coast and the Crimea. After a year of *agitki* (seven of them, including *Hassan the Red*) Chardynin grew homesick for private industry, and not even the assignment of directing an adaptation of Andreyev's *The Seven Who Were Hanged**∗** made Soviet supervision less distasteful to him, and he emigrated to Riga, where he was instrumental in

∗ In an interview given by Chardynin in Riga, and published in *Cinéa*, May 26, 1922, he recalled a detail of the production: 'Extreme courtesies were extended to us—in fact they even offered us a real hanging. When I refused they said blandly: "It makes no difference whether condemned prisoners are shot or hanged and if you assent, you will have a very realistic scene".' Chardynin also mentioned another motive for his emigration: 'Ever since those days I have kept the memory of our poverty and our empty bellies.'

establishing the more agreeably commercial Latvias-Film. The most ambitious and controversial film produced in these post-Wrangel and pre-VUFKU months was made by Boris Glagolin, organizer of the earlier Russian Ribbon Company. The literary inclination of his old company was still dominant: the subject chosen was a novel on the Second Coming, by Saint-Georges de Bouhélier, and Glagolin's adaptation resulted in *Return to Earth*, a film emphasizing an identity between Christ's teachings and Communism.

One of the first moves of the new VUFKU was to invite experienced film-makers to work in the attractive but deserted studios of Odessa and Yalta. Such an offer was made to Gardin. He accepted and asked Pudovkin to work with him, first on the adaptation of Lunacharsky's play, *Chancellor and Locksmith* (revised to *Locksmith and Chancellor*), and later to assist in its production and to act in it. But by the completion of the scenario, Kuleshov's workshop was again in full blast, and Pudovkin made the second wise sacrifice of his career—he rejected Gardin's offer of quick success in order to become a student of an artist who was more stimulating for him.

After *On the Red Front* the Kuleshov group worked energetically for an entire year before Pudovkin joined them. They accepted the film crisis and found plenty of experiments that could be done 'without film'.

'Returning from the front, we continued work in the Government film school and it was here that a firm theoretic basis for the training of film-actors was begun; our first task was to develop a method for this training. . . . As part of this training we prepared several instructional *études* in the form of complete little plays, arranged with "montage" changes and without pauses. A demonstration evening was given at the school, and out of this developed a series of demonstration performances. . . . Why didn't we make films ? There was no raw film.'[7]

The four playlets given at the first performance of the Kuleshov class were unpretentious in subject, but extremely ambitious in presentation and style. 'At 147 St Joseph Street' concerned the kidnappers of a dancer (Khokhlova) who fight among themselves over the loot. Among the students in this were Pudovkin, Reich, and Chistyakov, a former bookkeeper who was forty years old when he entered the school. The second, 'The Venetian Stocking', was more complicated, with twenty-four 'cuts'. The scenario, by Valentin Turkin (first used in 1915 for a Chardynin film), told a story of jealousy; the chief characters were a doctor (Podobed), his jealous wife (Khokhlova), a gallant friend (Pudovkin), and a quantity of small rôles were played with professional polish by other students, later joined by Inkizhinov. The third *étude*, 'Apple', was much shorter, with Komarov, Khokhlova, and Kravchenko. The fourth was a grotesque, 'Circle', in which Fogel did his first acting. A later addition to the programme was probably the most important, as it foreshadowed the mood and material of *By the Law*. This was 'Gold', drawn from a Jack London story, 'A Piece of Meat'. Three criminals—Pudovkin, Komarov, Khokhlova—manage to kill each other over a stolen gold ingot. Throughout his subsequent directing career Pudovkin, who always enjoyed acting and actors' problems, boasted of the technically difficult fall he accomplished in this *étude*.

'We were not only cold, but hungry, as well. In 1920-21, learning "to film without film", and to pick up a little extra cash, we took out our classroom *études* to concerts. We'd go to these affairs with our own costumes and properties, made by the students and instructors out of any sort of rubbish that came to hand* or could be brought from our homes. We carried our equipment to and from the concerts on children's sleds—the trams weren't running, and we didn't have enough money to hire an *izvoshchik*.

'Thus we prepared cinematographers, thus we taught others, and taught ourselves.'[8]

On January 17, 1922 Lenin dictated a memo to himself:

'What functions in photo-cinema matters have been left at Narkompros [the Commissariat of Education]? Who in Narkompros is in charge of this?

'Ask him to come over and discuss it with me.

'In order to organize superintendence over all performances and to systematize this.

'All films shown in the RSFSR should be registered and numbered with Narkompros. For each film performance programme there must be established a definite *proportion*:

(a) entertainment pictures specially for advertising and revenue (of course with no indecency or counter-revolution) and

(b) pictures prepared under the title of 'From the life of peoples in all countries' —pictures with a specifically propagandist content, such as: the colonial policy of England in India, the work of the League of Nations, starving people in Berlin, etc. etc. More than cinema should be used for such displays—photographs with corresponding captions would also be interesting for propaganda. Make sure that film-theatres remaining in private hands turn over sufficient revenue to the state in the form of rent. The owner has the right to add to the programme or change it, but with certain censorship by Narkompros, and on the condition that the proportion is maintained between entertainment and pictures of a propagandist character under the title of 'From the life of peoples in all countries', in order to interest industrialists in the production of new pictures. Within these limits they should be given a broad initiative. Pictures of a propagandist nature must be checked by old Marxists and literary men so that we won't repeat the occurrence of those sad attempts in which propaganda achieves aims directly opposite to those intended. Particular attention must be given to the establishment of film-theatres in villages and in the East, where they are yet novelties and where our propaganda will thus be especially successful.'

These notes were drafted for a letter (now lost) to the vice-commissar of education, Litkens. Unsatisfied with the lack of immediate response and execution of his directive, Lenin summoned Litkens' superior, Lunacharsky, to his office:

'In the middle of February, or perhaps at the end of the month, Vladimir Ilyich suggested that I come and have a talk with him. As I remember, the conversation

* For 'The Venetian Stocking' Kuleshov made a hat for Khokhlova out of tin film-cans.

touched several current problems in the life of the Education Commissariat. He asked me what had been done to carry out the instructions sent to Litkens. In answer I gave a quite full account of everything that I knew in regard to the state of cinema in the Soviet republic and of the tremendous difficulties encountered in the progress of this matter. In particular I stressed the absence of means in the Education Commissariat for any broad set-up for film production, as well as the absence of managers for this business, or, to be more exact, manager-communists who could be depended upon. In reply to this Vladimir Ilyich told me that something would be tried for the expansion of the photo-cinema department's means, and *that he had an inner conviction in that great gains could be won in this matter, if properly handled.* Once more he emphasized the necessity of establishing a definite proportion between entertainment and scientific films. Unfortunately this is still weakly established. Vladimir Ilyich told me that the production of new films, permeated with communist ideas, reflecting Soviet actuality, must begin with newsreels, for, in his opinion, the time for the production of such films had not yet arrived. "If you have good newsreels, serious and instructive pictures, then it's unimportant that the public is being now entertained with useless films, more or less of the common type now available. Of course, censorship is necessary, all the same. Counter-revolutionary and immoral films should find no place here." To this Vladimir Ilyich added: "This all depends on how you put it on its feet, thanks to proper management, and perhaps, in the general improvement of the country's condition you will also receive a certain loan for this business, you must develop broader production, and especially promote healthy cinema for the masses in the city, and even more in the country." And then, smiling, Vladimir Ilyich added:

' "You are known among us as a protector of the arts, so you must well remember that, of all the arts, for us the cinema is the most important".'[9]

On May 21, 1922 the country saw a more than promising answer to the central demand of the 'Leninist film-proportion' when the first number of Vertov's *Kino-Pravda* was released. This famous series, actually a film-journal in a completely new and lively style that had evolved from Vertov's years at the cutting-table, in its turn was the training-ground for the bigger and more ambitious films that give Vertov a permanent place in all film history. Vertov always pointed to the twenty-three issues of *Kino-Pravda* as the first work in which his future development can be clearly foreseen.* He described the physical conditions under which these pioneering newsreels, which were to develop into an entirely original film genre, were made:

'We had a basement in the centre of the city. It was dark and damp, with an earthen floor and holes that you stumbled into at every turn. Large hungry rats scuttled over our feet. Somewhere above was a single window below the surface of the street; underfoot, a stream of water from dripping pipes. You had to take care that your film never touched anything but the table, or it would get wet.

* The *Kino-Pravda* circulated by the Museum of Modern Art Film Library is a synthesis made from several issues of 1922 found in a New York collection: 1 (June 5), 2 (June 12), 4 (July 1), 5 (July 7), 6 (July 14), 7 (July 25), plus some August items.

This dampness prevented our reels of lovingly-edited film from sticking together properly, rusted our scissors and our splicers. Don't lean back on that chair—film is hanging there, as it was all over the room. Before dawn—damp—cold—teeth chattering. I wrap Comrade Svilova in a *third* jacket. The last night of work so that the next two issues of Kino-Pravda will be ready on time.'[10]

During the actual filming of these series, Vertov himself was seldom on the scene. Instead he organized a group of cameramen-correspondents, stationed throughout the Union, whose movements from place to place he half directed and half left to each cameraman's imagination and quick thinking. And it was a method perhaps unthinkable before the invention of the compact, hand-held cameras, the Sept, Kinamo, etc. Thus, newsreel material on dozens of widely varied subjects continued to pour into his basement workshop, where he and his editor-assistant, Yelizaveta Svilova, shaped these film-scraps into atoms of Soviet life sharply observed from the many angles of the Kino-Eye.

Also in May, with less public attention, Lenin's other factor, industrial support from abroad, was hopefully furthered with the Moscow visit of Charles Recht, the American lawyer who had handled the Cibrario case. He, too, made a depressing visit to a fractionally functioning film-studio, and while he watched rain coming through the roof he listened to pleas for technical equipment of any sort, for any discarded or outworn American films. In exchange for help concessions were offered: if American film companies assisted the reconstruction of the Russian film industry, they were welcome to make pictures there with no further outlay of capital—and Lunacharsky agreed to this. On his way back, through Berlin, Recht told a correspondent of the New York *Times*: 'I am returning to the United States with my appointment as the attorney for the Russian Socialist Federated Soviet Republic, confirmed by the Commissariats of Foreign Affairs, Justice and Foreign Trade. Among the tasks with which I am charged is one by the Commissariat of Education to invite American moving picture men to assist in the building up of the film industry in Russia. . . .'[11] The first American moving picture man to consider the proposal was Joseph Schenck, at the Hotel Adlon with Norma Talmadge on their way to location filming in Egypt. His possible interest in Recht's plan was hindered from two sides: Miss Talmadge was against any trip to Russia because conditions were so disturbing; and Kaufman, Schenck's UFA representative, was discouraging for a more serious reason—UFA's interest in taking the concession themselves. Back in the United States Recht saw Will Hays, who agreed to call a conference of motion picture producers. This resulted in another visit of Recht to Moscow, in December, but no concrete exchange was ever agreed on, and Russian film history was to proceed along a tougher and more independent line of development.

Moscow's film-theatres had little to show of Russian production this year. Their programmes included a smaller proportion of Russian films than at any time since Russian film production began, and not one new Russian film. Though the first public showing of the finally completed *Polikushka* took place on October

23rd, Moscow's NEP-nourished theatres during the first half of November show no recognition of it:

1st GOSKINO (formerly the 'Artistic'), on Arbat Square: November 1-3, *La Dixième Symphonie* [directed by Abel Gance]; 5-7, *Greed* ('The Trust of the 15'), first chapter of a serial; 9-11, *The Reporters' Adventures*; 12-14, *Berlin, or The Millionaire's Joke*.

2nd GOSKINO, Theatre Square: 1-3, *The Woman in Grey*, second chapter of the serial; 5-7, *Scorning Death* [continuing with the same films shown by the 1st Goskino].

3rd GOSKINO, Tverskaya Street: 1-7, *The Kiss of Death*; 8-10, *Drama on the Equator*; 12-14, *Jola* [directed by Starewicz].

KHANZHONKOV Theatre: 1-3, *The Road to Death*; 5-7, *The City's Temptation* [directed by Bauer, with Vagram and Perestiani]; 8-17, *The Devil's Admirers* ('Secret of the Black Order').

KOLOSSUS (formerly the Conservatory Salle): *Nana*, by Zola [Cesar-film, with Francesca Bertini].

HALL OF MIRRORS (formerly the Zon): *Lady Hamilton* [directed by Richard Oswald, with Conrad Veidt as Nelson].

UNION, at Nikitsky Gate: *Judex* (*The Judge in Black*), in 6 series, 26 parts, 12 episodes [directed by Louis Feuillade]. This serial became an institution at this theatre.

PALACE, Strastnaya Square: *Mary Magdalene* [directed by Turzhansky, with Leonidova].

KINO, on Malaya Dmitrovka: 1-3, *A Night of Horror in the Menagerie* [directed by Arthur Robison?]; 5-12, *The House of Hate* [directed by George Seitz, with Pearl White, 1918] and 'The Lost City' (*Daughter of Tarzan*).

GREAT SILENT ONE, on Strastnaya Boulevard: 1-3, 'Aphrodite'; 5-7, *Panopta* (second chapter, 'The Terrible House at the Bottom of the Lake'); 8-10, third chapter; 12-14, *Evil Shadows* [Cines, with Lydia Borelli].

MAGIC DREAMS, at Pokrovsky Gate: 1-3, *The Adventuress*, fourth chapter; 5-7, *Secret of the Egyptian Night* [with Ellen Richter]; 8-10, *Carnival of Life and Death* [directed by L'Herbier?]; 12-14, *Merchants of Souls*.

The film-people of the past felt secure when the red necktie of 'Count Amori' again appeared in the waiting-rooms of the new firms. 'Count Amori' was the pseudonym of an energetic hack-writer, Rapgof, whose talent for writing 'anything' in the recognizable style of 'anybody' found steady employment in the film studios before 1918. Between then and NEP he either changed his habits or his costume, for his old associates missed him in those anxious years. Perhaps 'Count Amori' managed to get abroad? Now his black frock-coat and never-varying red necktie seemed an assurance that the past was here to stay.

This year NEP money and the revived interest in both local production and in new foreign films brought out a quantity of new film magazines. The most important and most belligerent of these was also the first to appear, in August 1922: this was *Kino-Phot*, the organ of the 'film constructivists', which seemed to include anyone who wished to experiment or to applaud experiment in films. Mayakovsky published his 'Kino and Kino'* in their October issue. In October the more luxurious magazine *Kino* appeared, open to both NEP distributors and the avant-garde (the February 1923 issue carried an article, 'Time in the Cinema', by Vsevolod Pudovkin). In November VUFKU's journal, *Photo-Kino*, and Sevzapkino's journal appeared, both sounding broader than mere house-organs. The first issue of the weekly newspaper, *Kino-Gazeta*, continuously functioning to this day, appeared in September 1923. Ideas were running on to paper faster than they could get on to film, but there was a dribble of fresh film-stock for the most persistent of the experimenters. Kuleshov describes three of his basic experiments[12] on the power of the editor:

'I made a more complicated experiment—and *on film* this time. Khokhlova and Obolensky worked in it, and this is how they were filmed: Khokhlova walks along the Petrovka near the Mostorg department store; Obolensky walks along the Moscow River embankment—three versts away. They each catch sight of the other, smile and hurry to meet each other. Their meeting is filmed on Prechistensky Boulevard—in an entirely different part of Moscow. They shake hands in front of Gogol's monument [in a fourth place] and look at something off-screen; here we cut in a shot from an American film—the White House in Washington. Next shot: they are on Prechistensky Boulevard; they decide to move on, leave the shot and climb the great staircase of the Cathedral of Christ the Saviour [a fifth place]. We film them, edit, and it appears that they are climbing the steps of the White House! We screened this edited sequence, and it was clear to all that Mostorg stands on the shore of the Moscow River, and between Mostorg and the river runs Prechistensky Boulevard, where Gogol's monument stands, and facing the monument is—the White House. In doing this we had employed no trick, no double exposure; this effect was achieved solely by organization of raw materials and cinematographic method. The scene demonstrated the incredible strength of montage that, apparently, was so powerful that it was able to alter the basic imagery of the material. We learned from this scene that the chief strength of cinema lies in montage, because with montage one can destroy, repair, or completely re-cast material.

'Another detail: when we filmed this scene we lacked the time to make one other shot—the handshake of Khokhlova and Obolensky. So we took the over-coats of Obolensky and Khokhlova, and against a background of Gogol's monument we filmed the handclasp of two other persons' hands. In editing we showed Khokhlova and Obolensky immediately before this shot, and the substitution passed unnoticed.

'This suggested another experiment. In the first experiment we had arbitrarily created our own geography, against which a single line of action was played. In

---

* For you Kino is—something to look at.
For me—it is almost a way to understand the world. . . .
But—Kino is sick. Capitalism has covered its eyes with gold. Smart producers lead it by the hand through the streets. They collect money by touching the heart with snivelling subjects.
This must come to an end.
Communism must confiscate Kino from the speculating leaders of the blind. . . .

the second experiment we maintained a single background as well as a single action, but now by re-combining the people themselves. I photographed a girl sitting before her mirror, making up her eyes and eye-lashes, rouging her lips, lacing her shoes. Solely by means of montage we showed a living girl, but one who actually did not exist, because we had filmed the lips of one woman, the legs of another, the back of a third, the eyes of a fourth. We cemented these shots, fixing a certain relationship among them, and we obtained an entirely new personage, using nothing but completely real material. This example also demonstrated that the whole power of cinematographic effect is in montage. Nowhere else can you achieve with nothing more than raw materials such absolutely unexpected, and seemingly incredible things. This is impossible in any form of spectacle other than cinema, in which the achievement comes not from tricks, but only through the organization of the materials. . . .

'When we sensed this fresh power, we undertook two more things. We had had a difference of opinion on the degree to which the psychological state of the actor is linked to montage. Some said that montage cannot alter that. To an important film-actor who held this view we said: imagine this scene—a man starving in prison is brought a bowl of soup; he is wonderfully happy and devours the soup greedily. Another scene: the prisoner is now fed, but now he longs for freedom, for birds, for the sun, for cottages, for clouds; the door is opened; released, he now sees all he dreamed of. We asked this actor: "The face reacting to the soup and the face reacting to the sun—will these, in cinema, be the same or not?" His answer was indignant: they will certainly be different, for no one would have identical reactions to soup and freedom.

'Then we filmed these two shots and—no matter how often I transposed them or how many people examined them—no one could detect any difference in the face of the actor, although his playing of the two reactions had been quite different. An actor's play reaches the spectator just as the editor requires it to, because the spectator himself completes the connected shots and sees in it what has been suggested to him by the montage.'

It is, of course, the first two laboratory experiments that have become standard practice for the experimental editor, just as synthesis of a compound is basic for the beginning chemist. The third Kuleshov experiment is too dependent on the actor's individual quality (despite Kuleshov's triumphant conclusion) to be often repeated under 'scientific' conditions. But this contest of actor's expression *versus* editorial manipulation, in other variations, is often cited in technical texts.* Kuleshov dates these montage experiments as January 1923, after he had set up an experimental laboratory in Ferdinandov's theatre—a step closer to actual film production.

Another theatre preparing a greater master for his film début was the Proletkult, where Eisenstein's production of Ostrovsky's *Enough Simplicity in Every Wise Man* required a short film interlude, 'Glumov's Film-Diary'. With Alexandrov, Strauch and Antonov playing rôles in it (as they were to play in

---

* Pudovkin's chapter on film-montage (in *Film Direction*, 1926) cites a similar experiment with three 'neutral' shots of Mozhukhin.

both *Strike* and *Potemkin*), this witty little film, made in March 1923, may be counted as Eisenstein's Opus 1 in a full but too brief career. Within five years he had completed the films that assured him international and permanent fame and it was then (without any suspicion that the tragic interval in his creative work had already begun) that he wrote amusingly about 'My First Film'.[13] The style of the interlude was to parody (and nothing in this production of Ostrovsky's play was gentle) *Kino-Pravda*, and when Goskino was asked to appoint someone to help the film-amateurs of Proletkult, the administration, in all innocence, gave this task to Vertov! 'But after watching us take our first two or three shots, Vertov gave us up as a hopeless case, and left us to our own fate.' The cameraman appointed also deserted the project: when Lemberg saw the scope of his responsibility, including Antonov's dive, in clown's costume, into a tank in the courtyard of the Military Academy, and Glumov's dangerous adventure (involving Inkizhinov) at the Zoological Gardens,* he resigned on the pretext that he was being asked to make dissolves without black backgrounds, and the more courageous (or foolhardy) Frantzisson took over the camera. The work had to be completed in one day's shooting—a Thursday—for the play's première on Saturday. The cutting was not complicated for, in order to have a film 120 meters in length, they shot exactly 120 metres. This year also opened Eisenstein's career as theoretician, also spurred by *The Wise Man* at Proletkult: his article on 'Montage of Attractions', based on a background of vaudeville and circus and a forecast of film, appeared in the extreme-left literary journal LEF in May.

At the beginning of June Proletkino showed its first films. The first and second issues of its newsreel were issued, and there was a gala performance of *At the Fighting Post*, *May Day in Moscow*, *The Work of MSPO*, *Needle-Workers*, and other short films. We have an eye-witness account of this occasion by an outsider, Huntly Carter:

'Last June the first Prolet-Kino film was exhibited. It was the signal for an outburst of great enthusiasm on the part of the young proletarians. When I arrived at the great hall where the film was shown the entrance was packed with a dense crowd of youths and maidens wearing the regulation get-up, blouses, caps, top-boots, head shawls, and red stars. The proceedings were opened by a fiery speaker, who told us what the new cinema would do in visualizing the 'Dreams of the Red Soldier'. I did not know exactly what this meant, but I gathered from the concluding picture that it was the liberation of workers throughout the world. The film was mainly topical—sports and fire-brigade drill displays, and great May Day and Curzon Note demonstrations, and a very skilful reconstruction of the murder of the Soviet delegate, Vorovsky, at Lausanne, in Switzerland, and his spectacular funeral in Moscow. . . . The Prolet-Kino films, then, will be sociological and life-centred, they will concentrate attention on the psychological, social, and industrial development of the workers. Special regard will be paid to current events, such as demonstrations,

---

* The surrealist silliness of 'Glumov's Film-Diary' may have encouraged the FEX eccentricities of *The Adventures of Oktyabrina* next year. The resemblance, however, to the Picabia-Clair *Entr'acte* (1924) must be wholly coincidental.

festivals, gymnastic displays, processions, protest meetings, political trials, and significant ceremonies of all kinds.'[14]

A successful purchasing expedition to Riga in June 1923, brought back to Russian film-theatres a collection of Baby Peggy comedies and, of more permanent value, Stroheim's *Foolish Wives*, which proved a memorable hit with Russian audiences, though I doubt whether Stroheim had ever expected his acid portraits of Russian émigrés to be seen in their home land.

On August 17th a step was taken that seemed backward to most of those working in the film industry, yet it seemed the only possible next step to those few who were to take part in the new Soviet period of that industry. All private film firms were liquidated and a state monopoly of film production and distribution (Goskino) was declared. The most positive of the private firms, the collective 'Russ', was merged with the film section of Mezh-rab-pom (Workers' International Relief) to become Mezhrabpom-Russ. The private firms at first took this sudden blow without believing that it could mean a permanent change to their increasingly promising situation. Their foreign offices, in 1924, to show their hopefulness, supported a new magazine in Berlin, *Ekran*, in four languages. The determined editorial in the opening issue (was there ever a second ?), after reminding the commercial reader that before the War foreign companies supplied to Russia as many as twenty to thirty copies of their most important films, declared that this must happen soon again, and continued, in the frank voice of the English translator:

'The everlasting struggle for new markets makes it only plausible that everybody in the cinema-world should look at that Country of Unlimited Possibilities as the Land of his Dreams'.

The 'News from Russia' mentions one of the last projects left undone by the NEP period of Russian production: *Crown of Blood*, set in the period of Boris Godunov and the False Dmitri. This was 'conceived on a colossal scale: for the scenes on Red Square before the Kremlin palace walls, the Government has promised to keep all traffic off the square for three days.'

The feature films produced and shown by Government firms during the last half of 1923 gave the 'Dreams of the Red Soldier' a distinctly adventurous colouring, however. Early in November Proletkino showed *Kombrig Ivanov*, made with the co-operation of a Red Army unit. Razumni had naïvely added direct propaganda lessons to an old-fashioned plot, achieving the curious contradictory effect of the first Communist films made in China twenty years later: new people and new ideas bound to antique and commonplace dramatic patterns. Those who later attempted to prepare *Kombrig Ivanov* for American audiences gave it the more exact title of *The Beauty and the Bolshevik*.

Another release, a few days later, was Sevzapkino's *Long Live the Power of the Soviets*, directed by Panteleyev, trained in the *agitka*. It was an adventure-film set in the period of Petrograd's defence against Yudenich's attacks in 1919. Goskino began its first productions, *Lifted on Wings*, the adventures of an aviator's life, and the more memorable first film of the Kuleshov Collective, which turned out to be an adventure-film with a difference. But the first Soviet film to compete successfully with all foreign product on the country's screens was directed by Perestiani for the Film-Section of the Georgian Commissariat of Education, with three young circus performers in the leading roles. This was also the first Soviet film to be reviewed in the New York *Times*—in a news dispatch from their Moscow correspondent, Walter Duranty:

' "Little Red Devils" [or *Red Imps*] is the appropriate title of the first real Bolshevik photoplay, which had its first presentation this week. Revolutionary films have been shown before . . . but nothing has been on such a scale as "Little Red Devils" . . . the play is a Russian revolutionary version of *Huckleberry Finn* or *Tom Sawyer* produced in a Tarzan manner and tempo. . . .

'The setting of the piece is magnificent—wild mountains, rivers, forests and cascades—wherein a supposed Red Army is waging guerilla warfare against the Whites and the bandit leader, Makhno. In point of fact, this struggle took place in the flat corn lands of the Southern Ukraine, but the Caucasus undeniably makes a better background.

'The "plot" is so light as hardly to count at all, but the idea is to portray the adventures of three children who, to avenge the murder of their parents by the Whites, act as voluntary scouts for Budyonny's Red cavalry (there is always a tremendous roar of cheering when the popular Cossack General is shown on the screen), and finally bring about the capture of Makhno himself. . . .

'The first section of the long play, which is in two parts divided into ten sections each, shows thirteen-year-old Ivan and his sister Kalya weeping over the ruins of their burned cottage and the bodies of their murdered parents. Amazingly enough, they are accompanied by a small coloured boy . . . from the fact that he is once shown dreaming of a white planter beating an adult Negro with a ten-foot pole one imagines he is a slave who fled to Soviet Russia straight out of the pages of *Uncle Tom's Cabin*. . . .

'There is no love in the play, but there are some excellent scenes of village life and faces with jugglers, acrobats, etc.; vivid pictures of the Red Army and a thrilling battle between the Cossacks and the armoured train. . . .

'Though the Reds naturally win at the end, there is no striving after "propaganda", and the final scene, when the three children are decorated with the Order of the Red Flag by Budyonny at the victory parade of the Red Army through the streets of a large city, compares favourably in restraint and effectiveness with similar French productions. . . .'*

In a more Georgian style the leading Tiflis newspaper hailed the film: 'Bravo—director, bravo—filmactors! Bravo—cameraman! Bravo—scenarist! Bravo—all

---

* On another page of this same issue of the *Times* (December 8, 1923), this 'society item' appears: 'A private view of the Russian moving picture "Psycha" was given yesterday at the Russian Eagle, 36 East Fifty-seventh Street. A musical entertainment provided by General Lodyjensky, Lieutenant Commander Makaroff and Wladimir A. Behr followed the picture. Among the guests were Prince and Princess Youssoupoff, Prince and Princess Christian of Hesse, Prince and Princess Francesco Rospigliosi, Count and Countess de Periguy . . . [etc.]' *Psycha* was made by Chardynin during his stay in Latvia, just before his decision to return to the VUFKU studio.

who worked on this wonderful film-poem of the recently past revolutionary storm!'

In the last year of the New Economic Policy the State regained its financial as well as political control over the cinema. NEP, as in the rest of the economic life of the Union, had exercised a restorative function in the film industry. The change to monetary economy, the advantages of new credits in foreign materials, and the recovery of a large part of the urban population's solvency had all contributed to a newly solid material base. Since this 'restoration' was aimed more at quantity than at originality it is triumphantly significant that the number of full-length films made annually in the USSR jumped from eleven in 1921 to 157 in 1924.

Goskino's advertisement for *Strike* (1925)

CHAPTER IX

The Youth of an Art

1924–1925

Everything in heaven and earth, in man and in story,
in books and in fancy, acts by Confederacy, by juxtaposition, by circumstance and place

CHARLES LAMB

At some time during the period from February 1924 to February 1925 all those
Russian* directors who were to assume places of prime importance in the
creative and theoretical history of the silent film had entered the Soviet cinema.
Pioneer innovators such as Lev Kuleshov and Dziga Vertov evolved, during this
period, films that were complete practical demonstrations of their previously
announced aims.

Lenin died in January 1924, but he had already indicated, by his close and
constant concern with the tasks of the young industry, the direction it must
take to become the communication medium fit for those tasks. Since Lenin's
nationalization of the film industry in 1919, it had remained under the direct
control, even during the period of NEP, of the People's Commissariat of Education, where Lunacharsky held the post of Commissar, giving particular
attention to the carrying on of Lenin's directives, developing them as time
presented new problems. Although the first All-Union Party Conference on
film questions was not held until 1928, every political leader took a definite stand
before 1925 on the needs and purposes of the moving picture in the Soviet
Union. People's Commissar of Nationalities Stalin, who had observed the
visible educational advance obtained by film-showings among the peoples
of the national minorities and the peasants, announced at the Thirteenth Congress
of the Communist Party: 'The cinema is the greatest means of mass agitation.
Our problem is to take this matter into our own hands'; and the Congress did
embody this resolution in a strongly worded decree to give material and financial
teeth to the monopoly (chiefly in principle) declared in the previous September.
On June 13, 1924, the Council of People's Commissars established a special
commission, headed by Leonid Krassin, to form the new company, Sovkino.
The new unity of organization and purpose behind the entire industry en-

* Similarly clear evidence of progress in the other republics, especially in the Ukraine
and Georgia, cannot be seen until somewhat later.

couraged the people working in the Soviet film to make both social and artistic progress that caused it to become, within the next three years, the most typical art medium of the Soviet Union, judging by its continuing popularity with audiences within the Union and by its fame abroad. What artistic forces appeared in 1924 that assured the international prestige of the Soviet film by 1926?

'Pioneer' is certainly an accurate word to describe Kuleshov, who co-ordinated the loose instincts of dramatic film-structure already existing throughout the film world, and Vertov, who literally revolutionized the newsreel. They were young pioneers: Kuleshov had directed his first film (*Engineer Prite's Project*, 1918) at the age of seventeen, and Vertov at the age of twenty had been put in charge of all newsreels filmed on the front during the Civil War. Although creative responsibilities were not entirely in the hands of such youngsters, it is true that the first great expressive advances in Soviet films came from film-workers in their twenties.

In preceding chapters there is some detail on Kuleshov's studio-work before the Revolution, his group of cameramen and actors at the front during the Civil War, and the formation of his 'workshop' where a group of enthusiasts* doggedly studied film principles without benefit of more than a reel of raw film. Their opportunity came in November 1923, when the First Studio of Goskino in Moscow, immediately after its organization, offered them a chance to show what they could do with the precious imported film-stock. Kuleshov decided that a comedy was the best form in which to make a public demonstration of what they had learned during their three years of preparation. This was *The Extraordinary Adventures of Mr West in the Land of the Bolsheviks*, made with a sense of humour in character and in action that is as fresh today as it was in 1924. It was not easy to make Soviet comedies, even with satirical content, then. Chaplin's work had been seen by almost none of the film-makers, but the pre-war comedies of Max Linder and André Deed were still in frantic circulation, and formed a concrete rival to any home competition. The collective was also testing their method against all other 'method':

'In 1923 . . . with trained actors, taught in a new method, we engaged in production for the first time. It was very terrifying—for suddenly nothing turned out the way we expected it to.

'The studio had just been organized, the heating system wasn't even working yet, there were no properties at hand, no technical personnel. We had to do nearly everything ourselves. Why was it necessary to make "West?" "West" had to be made to find out if we were right, and to confirm that theatre schools were unsatisfactory for the film, which required its *own*, *a specifically cinematographic school*. A decision on this question was extremely important. There were then very few adherents of a pure cinema method.

* In the order of their admission to the workshop: Leonid Obolensky, Alexandra Khokhlova, A. Reich, Porfiri Podobed, Sergei Komarov, Vsevolod Pudovkin, Galina Kravchenko, Vladimir Fogel, Pyotr Galadzhev, Boris Barnet, Valya Lopatina, Valeri Inkizhinov, Pyotr Repnin, Mikhail Doller, and others. Almost all members of the workshop took part in the production of *Mr West*.

'Everyone defended the theatricalization of the cinema, the Moscow Art Theatre was law, and only in it could be seen future production possibilities, and if not there, then in the continuance of the tradition of Maximov, Runich, Kholodnaya, Lisenko, Mozhukhin, and the like. It was a gloomy heritage. . . .

'Respect in our collective had fallen, but the most difficult task was to show that new actors, specifically trained for film-work, were far better than the psychological-theatrical film-stars. And it was necessary to show this practically, without films, without essential apparatus, without special staffs, and chiefly without production experience.

'Our first experience was recognized as successful. Of course there were many faults in the picture, but it could not have been otherwise in a first work.[1]

A proof of the success of *Mr West* with home audiences (the only ones to see it) is that thirty-two copies were put into distribution immediately on the film's initial showing—a number that was exceeded only by two dramas in Goskino's 1924 output. Alexander Wicksteed, an Englishman temporarily resident in Moscow, found the comedy 'perfectly delightful':

'In this an American tourist [played by Podobed] who is full of the horrors that the American press are so fond of describing in Russia falls into the hands of a gang, who proceed to "play up" to him and show him all the things for which he is looking. Finally as he is on the point of paying an enormous ransom, he is rescued by the G.P.U., who proceed to show him the real Moscow. One can but admire the skill and restraint of the producers in realizing that it was not necessary in any way to exaggerate the tales of the foreign press in order to reduce a Moscow audience to helpless laughter.'[2]

Before the bars of the international blockade against the young Soviet Russian Republic had come down, the country had been deluged with adventure and mystery serial films—such as were entertaining the Tsar at Headquarters in 1916, and Moscow audiences in 1922—the most lively ones coming from America. Kuleshov had tried to introduce not only American cutting methods into the Khanzhonkov Studio,* but had also tried to imitate the widely popular American adventure films. The first films to enter the U.S.S.R. after the lifting of the blockade, and with the help of the new NEP distribution channels, were also westerns and serials, because these were generally regarded as innocent of any harmful thematic content, depending as they did largely upon action, which the Russian public adored. Feuillade's *Judex* became a nationally recognized figure. The popularity of the new *Red Imps* was another persuasive argument for the Kuleshov collective in their choice of the subject for their second film. Based on an idea originating with Kuleshov, the scenario for the workshop's next film was written by Pudovkin—a framework that proposed to include in a Russian and European setting all the tricks and action of the best American and French serials, but to go one better than the lot by employing the workshop's efficient filmic methods.

* 'Fast cutting was then known as American montage—the slow montage was Russian.' —Kuleshov, *Art of the Cinema* (1929).

'The basic mistake of "West" was in several schematic performances by the actors, for what had seemed satisfactory in theory required greater polish in practice. It appeared that, with the less perfected actor, the construction of his action had to be more primitive, but as he matured technically, he could give a more "jewelled" treatment to each of his gestures. After "West" we got recognition and friends, as well as indifferent observers and, chiefly, enemies.

'In order to get more work we had to show that we could solve any technical problem; another pressure was that we must continue to demonstrate the work of the whole membership of the collective. With these aims in mind we sat down to work out a scenario [*The Death Ray*] ourselves:

1 To show that, technically, we could make a film no worse then the best American or European work (film technique was in the most deplorable state at that time).

2 To demonstrate *each* member of the collective, to display them as in a catalogue.

3 To try the "tricks" that the pre-revolutionary and early Soviet cinema could not achieve.

4 To prove that crowd-scenes could and should be filmed in an organized rather than in a hit-or-miss fashion.

5 To obtain the active participation of the working masses in revolutionary scenes (such scenes of workers were then very rare).

'To set such tasks for one scenario, inexperienced scenarists that we were, was really impossible. To get all this in packed the whole thing too full and drew it out too long. *But we did carry out the tasks we had set ourselves*, which was, most importantly, to push our contemporary film technique out of its rut. Even up to now [1929] the composition principles for mass-scenes, factory locales and scenes of uprisings are filmed in ways that derive from the methods of *The Death Ray*. Difficult montage, carefully clean cinematic acting by the players, a collection of tricks previously untouched by our cinema—all this was given by the so-called failure, *The Death Ray*.

'Comrades Komarov, Pudovkin, Fogel, Khokhlova, Podobed, Obolensky and others were subsequently given an opportunity to do independent, successful work, because they had been demonstrated as players and had been trained as film directors in *The Death Ray*.

'This was not generally comprehended. We were persecuted for our film. Especially for its lack of a firm ideology, and for its experimentalism. The comrades lost sight of the fact that in this film we were pioneering a *film-grammar*, that *The Death Ray* was primarily not a film, but a "primer".

'Though the press raged, *Ray* brought in good profits. There was no commercial fear of our experiments, nor of the unusual appearance of Khokhlova— the best of our actresses, to whom, unhappily, we have paid too little attention, on the mistaken belief that "good people always get along".

'So for a year and a half after *Ray* we did no work. . . .'³

The Death Ray was completed by the end of 1924, but not released until March 16, 1925. Kuleshov's judgment of the film's victories is just except that it leaves the faults of the film to be pointed out by others, and there was plenty of such pointing then, as there has been ever since. Its scenarist, Pudovkin, later writing of the importance of rhythm, an area in which all his own films were to show unusual sensitivity, said, 'Remember, for instance, how exhausting, and how extinguishing its effect, was the badly created, constantly confusing rhythm of that film, *The Death Ray*.'[4] In *Art of the Cinema* Kuleshov quotes a conversational critic: ' "For goodness sakes! you must be completely mad futurists—you show films made out of tiny pieces that to any normal spectator seem an incredible muddle— the pieces chase each other so fast that no one can possibly find out what's going on".' The film's technical deftness appears today, of course, more admirable artistically, yet the absence of emotion in this effort to condense all of Pearl White, Harry Piel, and Fantômas within one film also appears today as a danger signal in that youthful period of the Soviet film. Kuleshov himself was to follow *The Death Ray* with one of the most emotionally tense films ever made, but the *Ray* is the ancestor of a technically proficient and emotionally empty tendency that was to emerge too often in the history of Soviet films.

The Death Ray marks a turning-point in Pudovkin's development from the abstract enthusiasm with which he entered the Film Technicum and Kuleshov's workshop to his position as one of the leading creative artists in the film medium. This was his introduction neither to acting nor to direction—Gardin had previously given him a taste of both. *The Death Ray*, however, written by him, designed by him, and brilliantly acted by him, exhibited that full consciousness of the medium that four years with Kuleshov had given him. Now he left the group, to work for Mezhrabpom-Russ, but his last film for Kuleshov already marks Pudovkin's recognized entrance into history, during this 'rising' period. It is usually assumed that pupil and master parted because of basic differences, but Kuleshov himself helped Pudovkin to find and hold his new job, and later even helped with some difficult scenes in *Mother*.

After a few unhappy days as assistant to Eggert on *The Wedding of the Bear* (from an adaptation by Lunacharsky of a Merimée story), Pudovkin was assigned by Mezhrabpom-Russ, whose programme included purely educational films (they distributed Flaherty's *Nanook* in Russia) as well as dramatic films, to make a film popularization of Pavlov's studies in conditioned reflexes. Pudovkin's scientific background made him the perfect choice for the job and he approached the new work eagerly, less as an artist than as a scientist. Clearly as his 'psychological resemblance to Griffith' has been indicated by Harry Alan Potamkin, a parallel with Pabst's development is often inevitable—particularly in comparing *Mechanics of the Brain* (1925-26) with *Secrets of a Soul* (1925-26), both begun as instructional films and both furnishing the director with a foundation for a disciplined realistic aesthetic, Pudovkin on Pavlov, Pabst on Freud.*

During a pause in the filming of *Mechanics of the Brain*, Pudovkin was asked to make a topical comedy on the International Chess Tournament being held during November 1925, at Moscow's Hotel Metropol. The catch was that one could not

---

* Incidentally, Pavlov himself was as much against the making of *Mechanics of the Brain* as Freud was against the filming of *Secrets of a Soul*.

ask the contestants, least of all José Capablanca, to act in a comedy. Shots of Capalanca, taken by a cameraman pretending to be taking newsreel shots, were brought to the cutting-table with shots of other actors' hands and of objects, and a minor rôle was thus created by the Kuleshov method* that must have surprised Capablanca exceedingly if he ever saw it—which is unlikely as the film was never shown abroad until the Museum of Modern Art Film Library acquired it from Moscow in 1937. The film has a fund of simple satire and movie wit. The hero's extreme preoccupation with chess and the growing exasperation of the heroine (played by Pudovkin's wife, Anna Zemtsova) cannot be imagined apart from Kuleshov's ingenious cutting method. Although it was the first film by Pudovkin (co-directed with Nikolai Shpikovsky) to be released, there is nothing to distinguish *Chess Fever* from the Kuleshov *études* and films; this is Pudovkin's smiling farewell, a salute to his master.

The basic technical contribution of Kuleshov, the artistic legacy that he handed over to Pudovkin and Eisenstein for further investment, was the discovery that there were, inherent in a single piece of unedited film, two strengths: its own, and the strength of its relation to other pieces of film. In his text book[5] Pudovkin quotes Kuleshov as saying, 'In every art there must firstly be a material, and secondly a method of composing this material specially adapted to this art,' and Pudovkin goes on to explain:

'Kuleshov maintained that the material in film-work consists of pieces of film, and that the method of composing is their joining together in a particular creatively conceived order. He maintained that film-art does not begin when the artists act and the various scenes are shot—this is only the preparation of the material. Film art begins from the moment when the director begins to combine and join together the various pieces of film. By joining them in various combinations, in different orders, he obtains differing results.'

As proof Pudovkin cites the experiments described by Kuleshov. When Pudovkin said: 'The foundation of film art is editing', other Soviet film-makers could be relied upon to heed this maxim in proportion to the needs that had given birth to it. It was the foreign advance-guard, both in criticism and in amateur film-making that took this maxim out of its historic context, and made of it a law that cancelled all other natural laws of cinema. Much later Eisenstein made a more judicious definition:

'Photography is a system of reproduction to fix real events and elements of actuality. These reproductions, or photo-reflections, may be combined in various ways. Both as reflections and in the manner of their combination they permit any degree of distortion—either technically unavoidable or deliberately calculated. The results fluctuate from exact naturalistic combinations of visual, interrelated experiences to complete alterations, arrangements unforeseen by nature, and even to abstract formalism, with remnants of reality.'

* Film-professionals, unacquainted with Kuleshov's methods, could also be caught; when Mary Pickford and Douglas Fairbanks visited Moscow in July 1926 they innocently permitted another Kuleshov graduate, Komarov, to film them in enough random action to achieve a full-length comedy after their departure.

and added a brief, but unshakable analysis of the features resulting from an acceptance of his thesis, but concluded,

'Within normal limits these features enter, as elements, into any style of cinematography. But they are not opposed to nor can they replace other problems— for instance, the problem of subject.'[6]

The question of *subject* leads to the examination of other Soviet film pioneers, but the importance of Kuleshov's researches and contributions cannot be dismissed in any hasty way. First of all, he is still making films, each of which as it appears is an event even if not internationally, at least in the Soviet film world. The film recognized as his greatest work, *By the Law*, made in 1926, after the departure of Pudovkin from the group, will be discussed in the next chapter. His experiments in sound (*Horizon*) and in new narrative styles and structure (*The Great Consoler*) prove that the question of his place in 'historical perspective' cannot yet be regarded as closed. His formative influence upon and relationship to Soviet film-makers, among them both Pudovkin and Eisenstein, concerned more than merely handing on a formal technical discovery, or his minute investigation of the creative process of film-making. His high respect and sense of responsibility toward the medium which he helped to develop as an art is not the least of his lessons to other directors of greater accomplishment who went beyond their master. More concretely, he always made himself available for consultation on new problems that arose, ready with advice and with physical assistance (as when he helped Pudovkin with the crowd scenes in *Mother*). He keeps his friends; and his friends value him highly. In his first text-book, *Art of the Cinema* (1929), the introduction, signed by Pudovkin, Obolensky, Komarov and Fogel, concludes: 'We make films—Kuleshov makes cinematography.'

The new importance given to editing or 'montage' in the theoretical and technical history of the Soviet film is touched upon in a notable remark by Ivor Montagu, 'It is important to observe that its development is peculiarly associated with the Soviet cinema's need to reflect the external world with more reality than is usually attained by the Western cinema.'[7]

'Reflection of reality' is a phrase inseparably linked with the theories and work of Dziga Vertov. In 1929, a speech which he gave in Paris during his European tour began thus:

'The history of Kino-Eye has been a relentless struggle to modify the course of world cinema, to place in cinema production a new emphasis of the "unplayed" film over the play-film, to substitute the document for mise-en-scene, to break out of the proscenium of the theatre and to enter the arena of life itself.'

This struggle began back on the Civil War fronts, whence Dziga Vertov sent back to the cities and other fronts visual news of the progress of the war. This was then the most important task given to film-makers, and it was natural for Vertov to feel that every step made toward socialism, after the close of the Civil War, also needed to be made known immediately all over the Soviet Union, just as would newsreels of a victorious battle. The material for this new kind of news film was to be the life of the entire Union, and the instruments were to be: the brain of the *cameraman*, his eye—the camera, the hands of the *editor*, and the brain of the *author-supervisor*, or *composer*, as Vertov later signed his films. The other factors, linked to the invented stories of the normal film, were to be thrown overboard: Kino-Eye was to make a new beginning. Sergei Tretyakov wrote, 'The director ordinarily *invents* the plot for the scenario—Dziga Vertov *detects* it. He does not, with the aid of authors, actors, and scenery-carpenters, build an illusion of life; he thrusts the lens of his camera straight into the crowded centres of real life.'[8]

As early as 1919 Dziga Vertov wrote his first manifesto, extended and published in LEF, 1922, condemning the play-film as an entertainment form alien to the needs and wishes of the new Soviet audience. Until October 1924, the work done by him and his group of cameramen and editors was exclusively newsreel in purpose and content (though foreign newsreel companies would not have found many of the items 'news-worthy'), with a growing fund of theoretical and technical experience accumulating at the same time. At an open meeting which took place in Moscow in 1924, the Kino-Eye group brought to light Lenin's directive on the proportion of fact-films on every film programme. Hitherto unknown, this 'Leninist Film Proportion' (so designated by the Kino-Eye group) met with fierce opposition from the body of film workers, very nearly becoming the exclusive property of the Kino-Eye group and their several literary partisans (grouped around the journal LEF, edited by Mayakovsky), but it may have influenced the formation in October 1924 of a branch of Goskino, called Kultkino. The bulk of this new studio's production was supervised by Vertov and made by him and his group. Kultkino now took over those regular newsreel releases that the Kino-Eye group had formerly been issuing from Goskino's main studio: these were *Goskino-kalendar* and the series *Kino-Pravda*.

The degree of high enthusiasm as well as of bitter antagonism aroused by these manifestos and preliminary essays of the Kino-Eye group are in themselves sufficient testimony of the extraordinary amount of individuality which Vertov had bestowed upon the neglected newsreel. For all that the orthodox film industry cared, the newsreel could stay neglected. With the exception of those film-makers who were to go forward with the swiftly advancing Soviet film after 1924, the other authors, directors, actors and designers, whom Vertov's plan threatened, now took the offensive, attacking his proposals, manifestos, and films at every opportunity. There was genuine resentment at the trouble this 'futurist' was making for them: 'Isn't film-production tough enough at this time, without these Kino-microbes making it tougher for us?' was the general view.

But against this professional front there were two factors opposing it that counted for more than printed words. Audiences would write to the film trusts and to their local newspapers if *Kino-Pravda* did not arrive on schedule. It was often the single item on the film-programme that reminded the audience in what a new age and a new kind of society they were living. And, more valuably, it conveyed a wish to participate and assist in that life, which was the life of that same audience. Sensing this, the newspapers adopted the cause of *Kino-Eye*, and *Pravda*, central organ of the Russian Communist Party, printed on its front page an article by Mikhail Koltsov, pointing out the high political value of the *Kino-*

Pravda series. The upshot of this polemic was that Kultkino, before its absorption into the newly organized Sovkino (uniting the Moscow and Leningrad studios) gave Vertov the opportunity he was waiting for: the right to supervise every shot of a full-length film made in the Kino-Eye method. As succeeding events proved, this encouragement of Vertov's theories assisted the liquidation only of those same pre-revolutionary concepts of film-making that Kuleshov in his way was also attacking.

For this first full-scale demonstration of his theories, Vertov produced the first of a series that was itself called *Kino-Eye*. His plan for this first of a series* was to cover the following kinds of material: '(1) the new and the old, (2) children and adults, (3) the co-operative and the open market, (4) city and country, (5) the theme of bread, (6) the theme of meat, and (7) a large theme in which bootlegging, gambling, drinking, cheating, drugs, tuberculosis, madness, death, were shown as contrasted with health and courage.'[9] Working on a grand scale, sending organized expeditions to every part of Moscow and the vicinity, displaying the concentration of an inventor who has been given the chance to prove the value of his invention, Vertov with his brother and chief cameraman, Mikhail Kaufman, lived in a Pioneer camp, visited markets with concealed cameras, rode with ambulances to accidents, spied on criminals from behind windows, haunted the doors of beer-parlours, danced with rejoicing collective farmers—neglecting no technical device then known to camera work in order to transfer a sense of actual life onto a moving-picture screen. In speaking of their filming and editing devices, Osip Brik, holding up Kino-Eye as a model for all Soviet film production to follow, wrote: 'It is necessary to get out of the limited circle of ordinary human vision; reality must be recorded not by imitating it, but by broadening the range ordinarily encompassed by the human eye.'[10]

Marshalling his method against all other methods of film production in use at that time, Vertov pointed out that while the montage, or editing of 'artistic' films meant only the putting together of separate strips of film according to the scenario, his understanding of montage was 'the organization of the seen world', thus:

'1 Montage during the observation period (immediate orientation of the naked eye at all times and places).

2 Montage after observation (logical organization of vision into one or another definite direction).

3 Montage at the time of filming (orientation of the *armed* eye—the moving picture camera—during the search for the appropriate camera-position, and adjustment to the several changing conditions of filming).

4 Montage after filming (rough organization of the filmed material according to main indications, and ascertaining what necessary shots are missing).

5 Judgment of the montage pieces (immediate orientation to link certain juxtapositions, employing exceptional alertness and these military rules: judgment—speed—attack).

* There was no second, for in his following work, Vertov decided to apply the method to large single themes.

6 Final montage (exposition of larger themes through a series of smaller subtler themes; reorganization of all material while keeping the rounded sequence in mind; exposure of the very heart of all your film-objects).'[11]

Two shorter films, *Leninist Film-Truth* and *October Without Ilyich*, both of them finished and issued in January 1925, should be mentioned here, because they introduce a far from objective and apparently non-Kino-Eye pathos that was afterwards to be laid aside until 1932 when Vertov made his *Three Songs of Lenin*. This later film not only revives the forgotten pathos of the earlier films, but recovers the themes and methods used in 1924, expanding these to further breadth of material and depth of emotion. *Leninist Film-Truth* (issued as No. 21 of the series *Kino-Pravda*) uses a main structure of Lenin's funeral, developing from it parallel sequences of sorrowing peoples, and followed by a paean of pride in the accomplishment of Lenin's directives—in industry, in agriculture, in culture, in social life. *October Without Ilyich* has much the same Mayakovskian quality, using the annual celebration of the October Revolution as a base upon which to build both memories of Lenin's life and funeral, and to show his inspiration continuing after his death. As anyone will realize who has seen *Three Songs of Lenin*, this approach is almost identical, but none of his work between the two dates, as we shall see later, attempted this successful synthesis of fact and emotion.

Today it appears that Vertov's early bloodthirsty manifestos overstated the actual situation when they assumed that certain failures in the Soviet cinema of that time indicated a disease of the entire dramatic film. The fact was that the work he based upon the manifestos not only materially assisted the eradication of pre-revolutionary technique from the Soviet cinema, but also acted as a *conscience* throughout succeeding film history. While most films produced at that time approached revolutionary subject-matter of the past with attitudes strongly influenced by the cheapest theatrical and adventure-film traditions, both in selection and in method, Vertov's films dared to treat the present and, through the present, the future, with an approach as revolutionary as the material he treated. Willingly or not, Vertov gave new strength to his fictitious 'enemy'— the acted film.

Both in Moscow and in Leningrad, this period marks the entrance of complete newcomers into the Soviet cinema, who by their first works in it were to affect it radically. In December 1921, the city of Petrograd had been no wise rocked to its foundations by the manifestos and public declarations of a group of young stage actors and directors who claimed that they had discovered a means to reform the entire socialist theatre—to be founded on principles derived from the circus and vaudeville.* In the face of an utter lack of interest on the part of critics and theatre-people, the young group announced the formation of the Factory of the Eccentric Actor—or FEX, and until 1924 defied critics and tradition alike by their unconventional productions. One critic foamed when they 'soiled' Gogol's *Marriage* with a production that employed some film sequences. But the directors

* Their first manifesto quoted Mark Twain, 'It is better to be a young June-bug than an old bird of paradise.'

of the 'Factory', Grigori Kozintsev and Leonid Trauberg, attracted sufficient attention with their last staged production, *Foreign Trade on the Eiffel Tower*, in June 1923, to justify the Sevzapkino studio's invitation to the FEX group to make a short comedy on a similar fantastic plane.

'Their first film, which probably few remember, but which the FEX's love like a first-born child, was *The Adventures of Oktyabrina*.* This small film, which was made under heaven knows what conditions, does not belong among the important films of any genre. The *Adventures* made liberal use of all the tricks that the FEX-people had been panting to utilize once they had entered that paradise—the cinema. The least pretentious episode I remember from it is a crowd bicycling across roofs! Nevertheless the FEX's are right to love their *Oktyabrina*. It taught them not about "monumental epics" or "fundamental comics", where there were already footprints to guide them, but it helped them to discover, even to invent, elements of cinema, and without excess timidity they snatched at that thing around which the more respectful and less quick-witted had erected taboos: the cinema as an art.'[12]

Few took much notice of this modest, unsuccessful film-fantasy, and Sevzapkino (later Leningradkino) next entrusted the FEX group with nothing more important than a light, less fantastic, children's comedy, *Mishka versus Yudenich* (the tale of a boy, a bear, and two spies); even shorter than their first effort. It was not until 1926 that the style that we now identify as peculiar to the collaborations of Kozintsev and Trauberg began to develop, and to that end these eccentrics had to be tempered by a great many German films.

Out of the film experiments of Kuleshov and Vertov, as well as out of his own experimental innovations as designer and director for the Proletkult Theatre, there now emerged Sergei Eisenstein, whose first film, *Strike*, triumphantly closes this introductory period—which I have arbitrarily bounded between February 1924, and February 1925—and inaugurates the period of accomplishment and success.

In Eisenstein's theatrical work,[13] elements of reality had gradually assumed a more central and commanding position until finally, in the season of 1923-4, when planning the production of Tretyakov's play *Gas Masks*, about a gas factory, he decided to produce it in a real gas factory. The American poet, Babette Deutsch, on a tour of Moscow's theatres, reported the production in a way that almost prophesies Eisenstein's next move:

'The play was extremely crude, and the acting untutored and rhetorical. But when the men, facing certain agony and possibly death, went down the shaft to save the factory, "their" factory now, the minutes were tense with an actuality that no stage performance, with trained actors and modern lighting, could touch the fringe of.'[14]

The only step beyond this was towards the cinema—and so the young Soviet theatre was robbed of Eisenstein.

* The only surviving copy of this film is in the possession of Mr Trauberg. The plot concerned a fantastic, but symbolic, attempt by Curzon, Poincaré and Coolidge to rob the State Bank, and the robbers' frustration by a pre-school age Young Pioneer.

The most advanced group of writers and performers, working at the Central Moscow Theatre of the Proletkult, now deliberated the question of film work for the entire collective, and decided on the following plan: to make a series of films to be called 'Towards the Dictatorship [of the Proletariat]', to record all the lessons learned by Russian workers in their pre-revolutionary struggles—in strikes, underground activities, illegal publications, political organization, etc. The collective, supervised by Valeri Pletnyov and Eisenstein, began work on a scenario for the fifth in the series, *Strike*, the only film of the projected series* to be made.

'Our first film, *Strike* . . . floundered about in the flotsam of a rank theatricality that had become alien to it. At the same time the break in principle was so sharp that in my "revolt against the theatre", I did away with a very vital element of theatre—the subject-story. At that time this seemed natural. We brought collective and mass action onto the screen, in contrast to individualism and the "triangle" drama of the bourgeois cinema. Discarding the individualist conception of the bourgeois hero, our films of this period made an abrupt deviation—insisting on an understanding of the masses as hero. No screen had ever before reflected an image of collective action. Now the concept of "collectivity" was to be pictured. But our enthusiasm produced a one-sided representation of the masses and the collective; one-sided because collectivism means the maximum development of the individual within the collective, a conception irreconcilably opposed to bourgeois individualism. Our first mass films missed this deeper meaning. Still, I am sure that for its period this deviation was not only natural but necessary. It was important that the screen be first penetrated by the general image, the collective united and propelled by one wish. "Individuality within the collective", the deeper meaning, demanded of cinema today, would have found entrance almost impossible if the way had not been cleared by the general concept.'[15]

Another positive aspect of this transition is that the purely instructional bonds of the film's original aim were (involuntarily?) broken and the 'simple record' exploded into an original dynamic shape of ideas and emotions—a shape that was to be given a firmer graphic development throughout Eisenstein's career, and a shape that was to influence the next decade of Soviet film-making. Audiences who looked at the film were supposed to study it coldly as a document about the evolution of a strike in pre-revolutionary Russia—first the oppression that produced the need for it, then on through the process of organizing the workers into united collective action, to a new stage of oppression that butchered the strikers. But the film failed in this desired effect. It achieved something much greater and more valuable—it *moved* its audience. In *Pravda*, Mikhail Koltsov, who had supported Vertov and his work, wrote, 'In *Strike* we see the first revolutionary creation of our cinema.'

At this moment of triumph in an unsuspected corner of the film world, another great period was just ending in Sweden—with Sjostrom already departed for

* 1. *Geneva-Russia;* 2. *Underground;* 3. *May Day;* 4. *1905;* 5. *Strike;* 6. *Prison Riots and Escapes;* 7. *October.*

America, and Stiller providing a sort of swan-song with *The Story of Gösta Berling*. Germany had started to export most of its talent to America, too, leaving Murnau, whose *The Last Laugh* appeared that December, to wait for a later boat. Soon only G. W. Pabst and Fritz Lang remained to carry on the development of the German film, so important to the whole world during the earlier post-war period. France produced, this year, its best avant-garde cinema: *Ballet Mécanique*, *Entr'acte*, and *À quoi rêvent les jeunes films*, while in America, Griffith was making his last great spectacle, *America*, Stroheim his greatest film, *Greed*, and Flaherty his most wonderful, *Moana*. The film world outside the Soviet Union seemed at a peak. The Soviet film was just beginning its climb.

Beginning too was not only Eisenstein's film career, but the inseparable and harmonious collaboration between the artist-logician Eisenstein and the artist-craftsman Edward Tisse. Tisse, born in Stockholm in 1897, of a Swedish father and Russian mother, was educated, first, among the Swedish film-makers, masters of photographic dramatization, then, later, as a newsreel cameraman on World War and Russian Civil War fronts, where a quick eye and a brain for all emergencies not only saved his life but produced newsreel material that was the envy of more cautious cameramen—when they had time for envy. Between the newsreels and *Strike*, Tisse photographed other films,* but not until he met a director as swift and fearless as himself did his talent display itself fully.

Eisenstein based his film method on his theatrical principle of 'montage of attractions', meaning that every moment the spectator spends in the theatre should be filled with the maximum shock and intensity, within and between each episode. *Strike* is full of cinematic metaphors and images of sight, sound, touch, smell and taste; it is a deluge of real things and surroundings—the spying in the latrine, the union meeting in the row-boat, the hosing of the demonstrating strikers, the final débâcle. One of the secondary benefits of the preservation of *Strike* is that, aside from a few photographic records, it shows a manifestation of an artistic movement that ended only thirty years ago: 'constructivism'—less in surface design (*Aelita* supplies that aspect) than in the more important matter of *method*—building inventions with the essentials of reality. And in this view of the constructivist attitude of *Strike* we can find a vital source for the method of *Potemkin* that is otherwise difficult to trace either from painting, sculpture, or theatre. *Potemkin* seems so wholly 'filmic' in its materials that we are prone to look in it for the influences of science (particularly physics and psychology) rather than the influences of graphic or theatrical principles. *Strike* warns us to listen more attentively to Eisenstein's declarations of cinema as a synthesis of arts and sciences. *Strike* is no single experiment in approaching this synthesis—it is a whole experimental laboratory. To watch the experimental ideas and tricks that no longer 'come off' (if they ever did) is just as rewarding and fascinating as to see the bubbling retorts all through *Strike* that were to produce the full aesthetic success of *Potemkin*. This makes us more tolerant of experiments that often look

---

* For Gardin, *Hunger, Hunger, Hunger* and *Sickle and Hammer*; for Chaikovsky, *It Needn't Be Thus*; for Sabinsky, *Elder Vasili Gryaznov*. Between *Strike* and *Potemkin* Tisse photographed *The Gold Reserve* for Gardin and *Jewish Luck* for Granovsky; after *Potemkin* he filmed the prologue for Eggert's *Wedding of the Bear*.

like youthful horseplay. The precision of photographic expression so notable in
the later collaboration of Tisse and Eisenstein is only hinted here in their first
work together, but in its place is a wide range of less subtle trickery that often,
surprisingly, produces a piercing effect—changing frame dimensions, an iris used
with a maximum of 'eccentricity', dissolves used for almost every reason except
the ordinary reason of indicating the passage of time, double-exposures used with
stimulating effect, as in the accordion scene (to be later cited with approval by
Eisenstein [16]). Even though Eisenstein was always to use some actors in each of
his films, the manner of acting in *Strike* is so 'off-beat' as to awake our curiosity
about the 'circus style' in his theatre work that preceded *Strike*. This grotesquerie
of acting is accompanied by a grotesquerie of casting (such as the macabre
tangoing midgets in the bribery scene) that points ahead to Eisenstein's typage
theory. Ivor Montagu comments on the two poles of attraction for the makers of
Strike, the discovery of reality and the appeal of the circus:

'. . . these two aspects of his career are apparent in every foot of *Strike*. On the
one hand, here and there, actual material is arranged with economy and laconism
into a realism poignant in its universality; on the other, the fantastic clowning of
the circus shows itself in detail everywhere, and in the exaggerated, even hyper-
trophied, treatment of particular episodes and the plot in general. The twisting of
actual material, with an ironic air of naturalism, to express such fanciful, exaggerated, "propaganda-poster" ideas, works often with a confusing, indeed shattering,
effect on the spectator that must have delighted the young Eisenstein and flung him
passionately into love with the film medium and its potentialities.'[17]

Another English critic, David Sylvester, has characterized *Strike*:

'Its method is closely analogous to that of a poem with which it is almost exactly
contemporary—*The Waste Land*. It is alike in that it operates through the
rhythmic relationship of scattered images, each of them precisely concrete yet
also symbolic, the juxtaposition of which startles and surprises. . . .'[17a]

Once the shocks of experiencing *Strike* have been absorbed, one perceives values
not easily associated with a work so explosive—a broad, deliberate, three-part
form, almost symphonic in its division of the powerful first and violent third
parts by an idyllic interlude that grows more restless as if modulating into a
minor key, in preparation for the harshness and brutality of the final movement.
With shots of smokestacks, a bloated factory-owner, his hectic office staff, the
enormous shed of a real machine-shop, the first seconds of *Strike* juxtapose the
real and the grotesque whose combination dominates most of the film. In the
factory a strike is under discussion, and the discussions are under observation by
the factory-owner's lieutenants, and by detectives who spy on the workers outside
the factory. The suicide of a worker touches off the strike. After shutting up the
factory the workers experience the unusual sensation of leisure—strolling, singing, gambling—but as time goes on and their demands are ignored by the management, hardship and hunger increase. The strikers' last possessions are pawned
for food. The police attempt to isolate and divide the strike leaders with bribes
and brutality. Provocations are staged, with the employment of the city's under-

world. Unsuccessful in provocation, the police drop intrigue, invade the workers' quarters and organize a final massacre of the unarmed workers.

The original instructional intention can be seen at several points: for example, the touch-and-go organization of meetings at and away from work, and the use by a detective of a tiny camera disguised as a watch is shown with all the apparatus of the operation, through photographic darkroom to the arrest of the photographed suspect. There are also fully dramatized incidents, such as the family dramas (a wife holds on to a prized trinket that the husband needs for pawning; another wife curses the strike and her husband's laziness as she storms out of the room with her empty basket), that may have begun as information for audiences of 1925 about conditions not experienced since 1917.

The development of the two last violent sequences shows how far the young artists could go from the 'informational', though information must have sparked both sequences into being. In one, the police, though helped by hoodlums, have failed to lure a workers' demonstration to loot a burning tavern; a girl breaks through to the guarded fire-alarm; when the engines arrive, the police-agent has the fire-hoses directed against the workers. Their first reaction is to regard the streams of water as a joke, and then we see them learning that it is a new weapon that has been turned on them. The sequence builds on the evidence of the water's increasing force and the victims' increasing helplessness, until one of the strike-leaders is captured in the cross-fire of the hoses. At this point the action is brought back to 'normal'—but only in order to increase tension again ('more and more and more') up to and far beyond the degree reached in the hosing scene. The concluding sequences, beginning with a street scuffle and mounting through the Cossack riders' invasion of workers' tenements, end on the image that has become the only familiar—in print—portion of *Strike*: the equation of the police massacre with the butchery of an ox in an abattoir. The force and necessity of this image can only be estimated by seeing it in context, for brutality and violence have reached a tragic point where you *have* to ascend to imagery; the 'facts' have grown so harsh that they leave you no place to go but *up*, through actuality to a kind of poetry.

It is no surprise to see all of Eisenstein's future films 'introduced' in *Strike*; more surprising are the introductions in *Strike* of other Soviet films; *The End of St Petersburg* was to be especially full of echoes or tributes to *Strike*: the elegant automobiles and luxurious waste, the monarch capitalist lonely in the spaces of his office or home, the hysterical typist, the prisoner who enjoys another prisoner's beating. The admirations of *Strike* expressed in the words of Dovzhenko and Ermler have been expressed in their work, too. *Strike* also looks backward. The spontaneous street struggle of workers and their wives with the mounted police recalls the opening of *Intolerance*'s modern story, and the use of babies and other soft young animals has a Griffith touch, too. The conference of capitalists has a fantastic air that resembles passages in Lang's *Dr Mabuse*, on whose Russian editing Eisenstein assisted—as his first contact with film.

The first revolutionary-mass film entered the Soviet cinema at a point when the Soviet audience and the distribution apparatus were ready for it, though the release of *Strike* was delayed for lack of positive stock for prints. The 2,579 film theatres (2,115 urban, 464 rural, not counting about 5,000 travelling projection machines) operating in 1925 seem numerous neither in comparison to the 26,160 theatres operating in 1934, nor when compared to the highest point of pre-revolutionary film-going, in 1914-17, during which a little more than 2,000 film theatres were in existence throughout the Russian Empire. The real victories of 1925 in this respect were that all the old theatres, plus several new ones, were now back in operation, partly thanks to the NEP interval.

And it was the tickets sold by theatres that made production possible. Two American journalists, in the summer of 1925, were clearly offended by the ascendancy and appeal of American films:

'Russian reels were hard to find in Moscow last summer . . . four times out of five, I would be seeing another Hollywood product. I have seen scantily filled theatres snuffling and sobbing over Baby Peggy and the Japanese valet who loved her while her parents quarrelled and committed adultery. And I have gone away in high dudgeon that even a social revolution could not ban such films or change the sentimental audiences.'[18]

'For American films dominate, inundate, glut, overwhelm the Russian motion picture houses today. Clara Kimball Young has a theatre devoted solely to her in Moscow. In the Arbat, centre of the workers' quarters of the Russian capital, a new building celebrates the glory of Douglas Fairbanks in electric letters three feet high. In the leading workers' club and a dozen other places Mary Pickford holds forth. . . . It is a bit depressing. . . .'[19]

Miss Evans and Mr Hibben would have been less depressed if they had realized that Soviet film production depended entirely on film theatre admissions* paid into box offices all over the Union. Baby Peggy and Douglas Fairbanks were helping to make *Potemkin* and *Mother* possible.

A foreign sociologist-observer records some data at this time on the increasingly valuable rural cinemas:

'In order to meet the problem of extending the cinematograph to the villages, a special Cinema Section of the Political Education Section was instituted in 1924. One of the first tasks of this new department was to establish a standard type of apparatus which could be used in the villages where electric power is seldom available. It was also necessary to organize the service to a whole group of villages by a single apparatus. A study was made of the requirements and tastes of the village audience. Finally, an organized propaganda to spread the idea of acquiring an apparatus was started in the country districts. Films based on village life were prepared in the belief that these would appeal particularly to the peasant audience.'[20]

However, in choosing between unrealistic 'films based on village life' and un-realistic films imported by the NEP distributors, the peasant audience too often

---

* Money earned from the sparse sales of Soviet films abroad went into the purchase of equipment and raw film stock—and more foreign films to keep Soviet theatres in business.

showed a distinct preference for the latter. It was some time before the city people who made Soviet films learned how to show village life on the screen.

Another result of the solvency which NEP brought to the Soviet film industry was the transformation of some of the technical intelligentsia, even some who had run away after the October Revolution, into supporters of Soviet policy and, in turn, into beneficiaries of the new cultural policies; this may have been one way to bridge the often-noted 'difference between the ideological tasks of the foreign and the Soviet cinema'. Just before their merger with Mezhrabpom the Russ collective invited several film technicians to return from their voluntary exile. The most important of these was Yakov Protazanov, who had been working in Berlin and Paris since 1917.* One of the first films released by the new Mezhrabpom-Russ was Protazanov's *Aelita*, which though least important technically and socially of all Protazanov's Russian films, received more publicity abroad than any other Soviet film until the international success of *Potemkin*. Its method was fundamentally antique with a new use of stylization that he had brought back from the Berlin and Paris art and theatre world, though he borrowed too from the limited experiments being made at the Moscow Kamerny Theatre at that time. The film as seen today achieves its most memorable moments not from the over-vaunted theatrical settings and costumes of Alexandra Exter and Isaac Rabinovich (more expressive in stills than on the screen), but from the robust comedy performances (upon which Protazanov was so wisely to depend later) of Ilinsky and Batalov, who made his first film appearance in *Aelita*. Protazanov's reappearance in Russian, now Soviet, film history had a deeper effect than shows on the surface. True, he did not help the theorists or the experimentalists, but he did preserve a kind of healthy simple folk-humour in Soviet films for which they are very grateful in this age of sound.

Protazanov's second film of his Soviet period, filmed this winter and released in 1925, was more openly 'agitational'—*His Call*, written by Vera Eri on the theme of the Communist Party's appeal, after Lenin's death, to enlarge its membership. The surprise and contribution of this film was that both the 'good guys' and the 'bad guys' seemed credible human beings, reminding the spectators of people they themselves had met in life. *Strike* pointed a way towards a new film form, but while that future was still on its way, *His Call* served the more immediately useful function of showing how the traditional dramatic film could absorb realistic dramas of propaganda intent. Pudovkin learned something from it for his *Mother* and praised it generously.[21] Less expected praise came from an American visitor already quoted:

'Last summer in the projection-room of the Mezhrabpom-Russ, a Moscow concern operating with mixed capital, half private money and half a state grant invested in the name of the International Labour Defence Society, I saw one of the most impressive pictures of my life.

* In Berlin he made for UFA, *Der Liebe Pielgerfahrt*, and others. In Paris he worked for Yermoliev's new company (*L'Amour et la Loi*, etc.); for Gaumont and Le Film d'Art (Zola's *Pour une nuit d'amour*, *Justice d'abord* [a re-make of his 1917 *Public Prosecutor*] etc.) and for Diane Karenne *Les ombres qui passent*. The Russ Collective invited Protazanov back to produce *Taraz Bulba*—an unrealized project.

'The film, which was not quite finished, was shown for us by the director. . . . The story, simple and stirring, began in the Petrograd of the October Revolution, with fighting between cadets and workmen. When the heroine's father was killed, the little girl was taken back to the village by her old baboushka. The Baron of the village had fled to Paris, hiding his treasure first. The little girl grew up and went to work in the factory; a young Bolshevik fell in love with her. The Baron's son, after many scenes of *émigré* life in Paris, comes back to Russia, disguised, to get the treasure. The village girl is infatuated with him. . . . The troubled young Bolshevik did the best he could. Life and the revolution went on. The story became, somehow, not the tale of persons but the story of the village, of a school, a Soviet meeting, to which came news of Lenin's death. The waiting at the station in the bitter winter night for confirmation of the news. The grief of the people.'[22]

Another from the past, directing films for Mezhrabpom-Russ was Vladimir Gardin, who had remained in film production continuously, through the most hectic days, making during this period *Four and Five*, a melodrama of 'bourgeois elements' in Soviet life, and *The Golubin Mansion*, a film about tuberculosis. The latter introduced to film work a young writer who was to make a major contribution to the Soviet cinema—Nathan Zarkhi. Another at this studio from the Russ days was Yuri Zhelyabuzhsky, who graduated from cameraman's job to that of director without relinquishing his beloved camera, and now made a folk-fairy-tale, *Morozko*, and a modern comedy, *The Cigarette-Girl of Mosselprom*.

Zhelyabuzhsky's best-known film is his next, made in the winter of 1924-5. *The Station Master*, Pushkin's simple story of a loving father, a pretty daughter, and an unscrupulous hussar officer, was chosen by Zhelyabuzhsky and Moskvin as the film to follow Moskvin's international recognition in *Polikushka*. In making *The Station Master** the co-directors also made a valuable record of the method then used at the Moscow Art Theatre. They hired Simov, the most typical designer there, to do their sets, and cast the film with people either attached to or sympathetic with the methods of Stanislavsky. Moskvin himself, a leading actor at the theatre, spent himself for the film in a way that shows his great hopes for it. Much of the filming was late at night because he often had both a day-time rehearsal and an evening performance; he never showed the exhaustion plainly seen on the faces of the younger actors. His behaviour throughout was a demonstration to all of the dedication and concentration associated with his theatre:

'During the filming of *The Station Master* Moskvin would begin to live the life of Semyon Vyrin even in the automobile taking him to the studio. I noticed, as he stepped from the car, that his very movement had changed. Here, already, not yet in make-up or costumed, was the slightly stooped, domesticated, fussy gait of a "station-master, dictator of the post-station". He had entered the automobile as Moskvin, a man of 1924—he left it in the acted image of a petty official of Nikolai the First's Russia, for whom each detail of his humiliated life

* Filmed so recently before, by Ivanovsky for the Yermoliev Company in 1919, that Mezhrabpom felt obliged to alter their title when the new film was released (Sept. 22, 1925).

was cosy and sacred, ready to be irritated with the maid if she did not put his "favourite" cup on the table for him.'[23]

'The detail is ample compensation for the silence of the film', was one of Moskvin's most valuable remarks on his film experience. With more sympathy at both ends his remark might have suggested a bridge to the remote reaches being explored by Kuleshov and Eisenstein, who thought the methods of the Art Theatre then spelt anathema. For the final scene, the death of Vyrin in the snowy courtyard, Moskvin declined to have the scene transferred from the freezing exterior set to a partially warmed studio. Not only did he not want to hold up the schedule, but he felt that the studio's warmth would distract him from the feeling of the scene, though when the shot was finished (no second take was possible), the crew heard the pathetic corpse complain, 'May I get up now? Or am I to freeze to death——'

The Goskino directors of that time who parried the bold strokes of Kuleshov, Vertov and Eisenstein with tried and true pre-revolutionary film methods, were old directors like Alexander Ivanov-Gai, Cheslav Sabinsky, and Alexander Razumni (whose political advance left his technique far behind), and younger men who found security in less adventurous techniques: Leo Mur [Murashko] of the romantic background[*] and Yuri Tarich. Other new companies also used old directors—Dmitri Bassaligo worked at Proletkino, and Alexander Anoshchenko at Kultkino. In Sevzapkino, at Leningrad, the technical domination came from directors already established before the revolution: Boris Chaikovsky (1888-1924),[†] Vyacheslav Viskovsky, Alexander Ivanovsky, and Pavel Petrov-Bytov. Besides the FEX group, the only youngster here who felt the need at that time for a technical revolution in the cinema was Semyon Timoshenko, who was to become the Leningrad champion of the Moscow-born theory of montage. It was Ivanovsky who made the most significant, if old-fashioned, Leningrad film of this period; Alexander Wicksteed again provides a valuable outsider's view of *Palace and Fortress*:

'Unfortunately the photography in this film leaves much to be desired . . . but the excellence of the production makes it to my mind quite the finest I have ever seen. The hero is an aristocratic young officer who joins the revolutionaries [of the time of Alexander II], is arrested and confined in the Peter and Paul fortress of Petersburg; here you watch him slowly progressing through loss of mind to death. By some technique that I was not at all able to analyse an impression of an immense lapse of time is produced so that you really feel as if you had passed interminable years with him in this horrible place. Mixed in with the prison scenes are others from the court of the Tsar. . . . Then at the very end, when you are feeling almost overpowered with the weight of hopeless misery in an evil world, they show you a post-revolution view of a group of kiddies playing on one of the bastions of the prison that has stood for so much that it is intolerable to

---

[*] Mur was born in 1889, joined the Social-Revolutionaries in 1904, was arrested in 1907, sent to Siberia, whence he escaped to the East. By 1914 he was in Honolulu where Universal films were on location, and he returned with them to Hollywood. Worked in films there and with Griffith, as assistant and odd-job man, and in New York, whence he returned in 1923 to work for Goskino.

[†] His last film, *Behind the White Lines*, was released posthumously.

contemplate; and you feel that at any rate it is over and done with for ever. It is quite the most effective piece of propaganda I have ever seen.'[24]

At Proletkino Bassaligo made a similarly 'big' film, but far less successful, of the contrasts of the past, *From Sparks—Flames,* based on the history of the Russian textile workers' revolutionary activity. In addition to the large scale of its historical theme, its bigness was physically unusual, too—released in six full-length parts, to outdo *Intolerance* and Stroheim's dreams—it gives us a sense that the original multiple-film project for Eisenstein's *Towards Dictatorship* was by no means visionary. Bassaligo himself must have been at this time one of the brightest hopes of the new film industry. His political background was unique among directors then, for he had joined the revolutionary party in 1904, before the first revolution. In the Khanzhonkov Company he had worked as an actor and as Bauer's assistant, and had directed his own first film before the October Revolution. This, *From the Darkness of Tsarism to the Radiance of Freedom,* described by Vishnevsky as 'a naïve revolutionary drama', gave Bassaligo a prestige after October that made his *Fight for the 'Ultimatum' Factory* (1923) and his huge *From Sparks—Flames* possible, but the enlarged scale of these did not materially alter the dramatic level for his first work.

In Leningrad, other more important personalities entered the film-world in less responsible capacities, training themselves for their later, fuller responsibilities. One of these was Friedrich Ermler who entered the Leningrad Photo-Cinema Technicum in order to take small acting tasks. Sergei Vasiliev became a film editor, specializing in the re-editing of foreign films for Sevzapkino.* One who was to make a magnificent contribution to the cinema as well as to his already chosen art was Dmitry Shostakovich, who obtained a bread-and-butter job this year:

' "Our greatest misery," writes Marusia [Shostakovich] to her aunt Nadejda in October [1924], "is that Mitya is going to play in a movie house. This is a real tragedy for us, considering the hard work and his health. But he says that he cannot stand our life any longer and will feel much better if he could bring home some money every month. . . ."

'The little theatre was old, draughty, and smelly. . . . Three times a day a new crowd packed the small house; they carried the snow in with them on their shoes and overcoats. . . . The heat of the packed bodies in their damp clothes, added to the warmth of two small stoves, made the bad air stifling hot by the end of a performance. Then the doors were flung open to let the crowd out and to air the hall before the next show, and cold damp draughts swept through the house.

'Down in front below the screen sat Mitya, his back soaked with perspiration, his near-sighted eyes in their horn-rimmed glasses peering upwards to follow the story, his fingers pounding away on the raucous upright piano. Late at night he trudged home in a thin coat and summer cap, with no warm gloves or galoshes, and arrived exhausted around one o'clock in the morning . . . It was in the midst of this that Mitya began composing his First Symphony.'[25]

---

* At this time Esther Shub was editing foreign films at Goskino. This training as editors stood both in good stead in their future work.

And that may have been the reason Shostakovich left this job in January 1925, and resumed it in the fall, presumably for more bread and butter, only to quit it for good soon after. The composer's wife later described the circumstances of one of these exits:

'Dmitri's direct spontaneous nature caused his downfall. An American comedy was being shown with huge success three times daily. Every time certain scenes flashed on the screen, the piano was silent and the audience heard the piano player burst into laughter, enjoying the antics of the comedian. For this unseemly behaviour, the administration decided to part company with the youthful pianist.'[26]

The national cinema industries were not to blossom for a couple more years. In the Ukraine, old Pyotr Chardynin was in artistic control; in Georgia and Armenia, Ivan Perestiani (*Red Imps* and its sequels) and Amo Bek-Nazarov (*The Lost Treasure* and its sequels). Alexander Dovzhenko had not yet quit his painting, Ivan Kavaleridze his sculpture, Georgi Stabovoi his writing, or Mikhail Chiaureli his acting (in the theatre and films). These were the young directors that the national film cultures were waiting for. Meanwhile, even in the work of the established directors the historical and local colours of the national surroundings were finding an expression that hinted at greater futures. There were some timid and imitative experiments at VUFKU (*A Spectre Haunts Europe* (1922) and *Order Number—*(1925)) that may have laid a foundation for the later acceptance of Dovzhenko's greater, original poetics. The experience of Amo Bek-Nazarov helped him to find the national subject and new actors for the Georgian *In the Pillory* (1924), and encouraged him to develop the Armenian film industry into an increasingly important contributor to Soviet arts. His *Namus* (*Honour*), made jointly in 1926 by the Tiflis and new Erevan studios, was the first Soviet Armenian film.

Throughout the Union, film production was almost catching up with its audience, both in quantity and in its gauge of the audience-temper. The quantity was to remain less than adequate up to the present day. But, by the end of 1924 (climaxed in *Strike*), the administrative gauge of temper and needs began to provide a constantly revised and flexible measure for film planning and film-making that has continued up through the present. The Soviet film had become a conscious mirror of Soviet life, and its successes and failures from this point onward have been dependent upon the accuracy of its reflection of Soviet thought. Only a year had passed since the production, if not acceptance, of such *technically* progressive films as *The Death Ray* and *Adventures of Oktyabrina*, and an original technical basis was already available to the bravest and most alert film-makers. With this instrument the new Soviet film could set about its main task, posing and answering the questions of the main body of Soviet citizens, often illuminating these against the revolutionary-historical background of the new society.

Examined at another, deeper level, however, we can see that the Soviet film had now entered the period of its greatest conflicts. Artists who had learned to use the film as a creative instrument, offered themselves and their newly sensitized instruments to a fresh society whose aims they recognized as identical with their individual decisions. And so long as they had maximum encouragement from their employer-society, they made their greatest efforts, stimulated their audiences at home and abroad to disturbingly new sensations and new ideas, created works of enduring value, and served the world well. But the more intense the social engagement of the film-artist, and the greater the service he wished his films to render to society, the more inevitable his approaching conflict with the administration of the industry within which he worked. This conflict would be expressed variously, in terms of money, or form, or social function, but beneath the argument would be heard a fundamental clash between the natural need of any industrial administration for efficient continuing uniformity, and the natural need of the responsible artist for patience and trust—time to try the untried—for how else was he to reach the social goal that was the understood base of every contract to work for a Soviet studio or to produce a Soviet film? The second-rater, the hack-artist, he with the least (ironically) to contribute, would encounter the least friction.

This was not an exclusively Soviet problem; the medium itself contains mutually hostile elements—art, persuasion, profit, education, hypnosis, stimulation, and so on. It was not enough for successive administrations of the Soviet film industry to announce periodically that such contradictions had been successfully resolved and subordinated to the larger needs of the Soviet audience; recognized as such, or not, this was and is a permanent struggle that requires constant adjustment to changing powers and conditions. The only temporary resolutions of the medium's elements occur in time of war or similar urgency. Such armistice in this inner war comes to an abrupt end when the crisis ends; see how these contradictions jumped shockingly into view at the end of the second World War—especially in Hollywood were the employee-artists caught off guard.

When the removal of crisis pressures brings this deeper war to the surface, champions always appear to fight for each element's domination of all other film elements. Each except art can assemble a large, well-armed party, but the artist alone knows his own potency—a potency that seems so impotent when it is challenged. There is not one important Soviet artist who did not, at some time, enter this conflict, occasionally with tragic results for the world that needed his work. Blame can sometimes be put on him, sometimes on his administrative opponents—but to recognize the nature of the conflict is more essential than any condemnation.

It was just now, as the critical conditions of the Civil War were receding into history, that the individuals who were to establish the Soviet film as a powerful new art medium, brought closer, with every step of their applauded progress, the confusion and humiliation of a conflict with 'authority'. Their very recognition of new responsibilities, new freedoms, new horizons, new powers was to bring troubles that would repeatedly obscure and delay these victories—as often as they were to produce them.

Skating Rink, an animated cartoon by Vano and Cherkes (1927)

CHAPTER X

Theory into Practice

1925–1926

Would I had phrases that are not known, utterances
that are strange, in new language that hath not been
used, free from repetition, not an utterance which
hath grown stale, which men of old have spoken

KHAKHEPERRESENB (2000 B.C.)

Strike made a great impression not only on Soviet film-makers, but on its own maker. It convinced Eisenstein that his chief interest was cinema. So long as he remained at Proletkult he would have to divide his attention between theatrical and film work. On completion of his first film (but before its general release) Eisenstein resigned from the direction of Proletkult's Central Theatre, and went to work at the Moscow studio of Sevzapkino, where he began the preparation of a film on the First Cavalry Army's rôle in the Civil War, a project that must have been dear to Tisse, who had filmed and fought with Budyonny's cavalry during the war.

Nineteen hundred and twenty-five was an anniversary year. It was one of the duties of the appointed jubilee committee to assign and supervise the production of films to celebrate the 1905 Revolution. The two most important scripts, *Ninth of January* and *Year 1905*, had been approved as early as June 1924, but the committee found themselves well into 1925 without having decided on a director for the latter, larger, scenario. Nina Agadzhanova-Shutko had sketched a panorama of the events of 1905 that seemed too huge for any of the established directors to tackle. After pre-release screenings of *Strike* in March the jubilee committee and the Commissariat of Education felt that, at last, the director for *Year 1905* had been found. Eisenstein was withdrawn from the Cavalry Army film before shooting was started, and assigned to the *1905* panorama.

We often have occasion to note the extraordinary speed of the Soviet film's development as communication, as art, growing in the power of its propaganda and its aesthetics. This growth seems even more remarkable when we watch it through the leading individuals of this period. As sophisticated as Eisenstein's approach was to the Proletkult staging of Ostrovsky's *Wise Man*, the twenty-five-year-old artist who did that seems many years younger than the twenty-six-year-old artist who directed *Strike*. And the making of *Strike* had speeded up the process of his artistic maturity to an astonishing degree that can be measured only by looking at *Strike* and *Potemkin* on the same day. There have been other instances of such swift growth in young artists, but the leap between those two works is as great as the leap from theory to full realization. The plunge into the new medium brought new light to his whole theoretical approach to the problems of art. The psychological basis of artistic creation, always important to Eisenstein after the profound impression made upon him by Freud's essay on Leonardo da Vinci, now had a new world to be applied to. He later said that Marx and Lenin furnished the philosophical basis for his psychological researches, which were drawn from Pavlov (reflexology) and Freud (psychoanalysis)—and *Strike* had, apparently, come, at just the right time in his theoretical development, as the incentive he needed to transform his next material into a masterpiece. Kuleshov, as he would, explained Eisenstein's swift development in a much simpler way—'will, persistence, and sharp eyes'.[1]

As handed to Eisenstein by Goskino, the scenario of *1905* covered the Revolution from the Russo-Japanese War to the armed uprising in Moscow.* Filming began March 31, 1925. The first episodes to be filmed were of a demonstration in St Petersburg and incidents of the general strike—and then film history was changed by the continued concealment of the sun, both in Leningrad and in Moscow. Towards the end of his life Eisenstein wrote a memoir[2] on the making of *Potemkin* that tells of the group's decision to work on episodes that could be filmed in the south, and of their chase after the last rays of summer sun there. Odessa was to be the setting for a strike of dock-workers and the demonstration after the mutiny of the battleship Potemkin. In the script forty-two shots were to cover the Potemkin mutiny and consequent events. But when Eisenstein saw the great flight of marble steps leading down to Odessa's harbour, he knew that this was the stage for the Cossack massacre of the Odessa crowd:

'I believe that nature, circumstances, the setting at the moment of shooting, and the filmed material itself at the moment of montage, can sometimes be wiser than author and director. . . .

'The fragments [to precede the battleship's cannonade] had at first been planned to develop the harshness of the Cossack reprisals through various ascending stages (on the street, in a printshop courtyard, on the outskirts of the city, in front of a bakery) into one monumental flight of stairs, the steps of which were to serve as rhythmic and dramatic links for the victims of the tragedy, scattered about the steps.

'No scene of shooting on the Odessa steps appeared in any of the preliminary versions or in any of the montage lists that were prepared. It was born in the instant of immediate contact.

'The anecdote about the idea for this scene being born as I watched the bouncing from step to step of the cherry pits I spat out while standing at the top, beneath the Duc de Richelieu's monument, is, of course, a myth—very

* 1. Russo-Japanese War; 2. January 9th and the following wave of strikes; 3. Peasant risings; 4. General strike and its liquidation; 5. Reaction attacks—Jewish pogroms, Armenian massacres; 6. Krasnaya Presnaya.

colourful, but a downright myth. It was the very *movement* of the steps that gave birth to the idea of the scene, and with its "flight" roused the fantasy of the director to a new "spiralling". And it would seem that the panicky *rush* of the crowd, "flying" down the steps, is no more than a materialization of those first feelings on seeing this staircase.

'And, too, it is possible that this was helped by some looming from the womb of memory, some illustration in a magazine of 1905—a horseman on a staircase veiled in smoke, slashing someone with a sabre. . . .'

Out of this decisive idea grew another, as the actual filming began: to make the Potemkin mutiny the central episode of '1905'; in the cutting-room, or even later, it became apparent that this single episode contained all that was typical of the whole revolution. In the final cutting, all material but *Potemkin* was dropped, and thus evolved what has been called the most perfect and concise example of film structure.

Eisenstein's memoir tells of the discovery of a surviving sister-ship of the *Potemkin*, the *Twelve Apostles*, by 1925 anchored in a Sevastopol cove as store-ship for mines, and of its transformation into the battleship *Potemkin*, for the great scene on the quarter-deck. Another ship, the cruiser *Komintern*, was used for the episode of the maggotty meat, and most of the other action requiring a busily functioning ship. As for the scenes near the end of the film, showing the whole naval squadron, that later caused such an anxious debate in the German Reichstag on the size of the Soviet Navy, Eisenstein revealed the surprising source of these shots: 'old newsreels of naval manoeuvres—not even of the Russian Fleet, but of a certain foreign power' (probably the British Navy).

Many of the accomplishments in *Potemkin* can be ascribed to the understanding with which Eisenstein and Tisse worked together. Aside from the almost in-credible efficiency with which *Potemkin* was filmed (all shots of the funeral procession completed in one morning, the whole drama on the quarter-deck filmed on their last day),* Tisse's ingenuity was ideal for Eisenstein's invention. The slaughter on the steps needed filming techniques as original as the new montage principles. A camera-trolley was built the length of the steps—dolly-shots were then almost unknown in Russian films. Several cameras were de-ployed simultaneously. A hand-camera was strapped to the waist of a running, jumping, falling (and circus-trained) assistant. Many realities put on film for the first time, such as the scene in an actual ship's engine-room, have long since been absorbed by documentary techniques; John Grierson's work on the American version of *Potemkin* lends veracity to the story that the British documentary film movement was born from the last reel of *Potemkin*.

Although this is the classic example of a non-documentary film without 'rôles', *Potemkin* was introduced to the United States as 'played by Moscow Art Theatre actors'! There are a few actors in the film, chiefly all of Eisenstein's assistant

---

* The tumult around the steps during the filming led a French traveller, André Beucler, to suppose that Civil War had again broken out. (*Les Nouvelles Littéraires*, 15 October 1927).

directors from Proletkult*, and Vladimir Barsky, a film director who played the part of Captain Golikov, but the Moscow Art Theatre can hardly claim the Sevastopol gardener who played the rôle of the priest or the furnace-man who was cast as the ship's doctor[3], not to mention the dozens of vivid 'bit' rôles, played as much by Eisenstein's compositions and Tisse's camera as by the sailors and citizens whose faces we see.

The importance of cutting and editing as a creative process was perhaps the most widely recognized revelation of *Potemkin*. The sensations of fear on the quarter-deck, panic and machine-like murder on the steps, tension on the waiting ship could only have been communicated by this revolutionary cutting method. What must be remembered is that the total construction and the frame-compositions of *Potemkin*, notwithstanding all spiteful legends about 'happy accidents'† to the contrary, were gauged and carried out with most of the eventual juxtapositions in mind. The shots taken on the steps were filmed looking forward to the cutting-table as much as were the famous shots at the end of the fourth reel—three different marble lions which become one single rearing lion in the editor's hands and the audience's eyes. Heretofore, the movement of a film had depended largely on the 'logical' progression of action within the sequence of shots. Eisenstein now created a new film-rhythm by adding to this content the sharply varying lengths and free associations of the shots, a technique growing directly from his interest in psychological research. Besides the behaviouristic stimulation made possible by this method, a new range of rhythmic patterns and visual dynamics was opened by *Potemkin*.

The story of *Potemkin*'s public release is one that has never been told fully, possibly because it would reflect small credit on the administration of the film industry at that time. On December 21, 1925, *Potemkin* was shown for the first time, at the 1905 jubilee evening held at the Bolshoi Opera Theatre.

'When the day of the solemn jubilee meeting came, we were still editing the film [after eighteen days in the cutting-room].

'When the hour for the screening struck, the last reels were not yet ready.

'Cameraman Tisse left for the Bolshoi Theatre with the completed first reels, so that the screening could be started. Eisenstein followed him as soon as the next to the last reel was ready. I stayed behind to splice the last reel. As soon as I finished I started off with it, but my motor-cycle refused to go beyond the Iberian Gate, and I had to run from there to the Bolshoi.

'As I raced up the stairs to the projection booth, I was overjoyed to hear the

---

* Levshin plays the first ship's officer whom we see; in a manner almost identical with his characterization in *Strike*, Alexandrov plays Chief Officer Gilyarovsky; Antonov plays Vakulinchuk; Gomorov plays the sailor whom we see oftenest. Matyushenko is played by a former naval officer who was also the technical advisor on the film's period details.

† Agadzhanova-Shutko apparently never forgave the cavalier treatment of her ambitious script, and some stories can be traced to her friends.

noise of applause coming from the theatre. This was the first happy sign of our film's success.'[4]

It is a pity that there is little contemporary evidence on the opinion of that first of many audiences to see it, for this invited audience must have contained all the leading members of the Government and representatives of all the arts. Between this occasion and the date of the film's public release, January 18, 1926, would seem a normal interval to prepare the release prints and distribution apparatus, though it does appear that Goskino might, with a little haste, have released the film within the anniversary year. On December 25th, Goskino released, instead, the other anniversary film, *Ninth of January*, directed by Viskovsky. This delay gives some substance to a story (told after Eisenstein's death) by Waclaw Solski,[5] then assisting Goskino in foreign sales. His errors may be due to a faulty memory, natural after twenty-five years, or to a less excusable tendency toward 'angling' his story. The most credible portion of his story concerns a private screening that may have taken place between the two public showings:

'Vladimir Mayakovsky, the famous Soviet poet, saw *Potemkin* with me. His friend, the poet Aseyev, had written the titles for it, and he was always loyal to his friends. Immediately after the showing, Mayakovsky and I went to see Sovkino's president, Konstantin Shvedchikov, a party man who once had hidden Lenin in his home before the Revolution.

'Mayakovsky took the floor first. He talked, as usual, in a thunderous voice, pounding the table with his fists and rapping on the floor with the heavy cane he always carried at that time. He demanded that Shvedchikov immediately export *Potemkin* and told him he would go down in history as a villain if he did not. Several times Shvedchikov tried to get a word in, but in vain. Nobody ever could say anything when Mayakovsky spoke. The climax of his speech was rather dramatic. Having finished, he turned to go.
' "Are you through?" Shvedchikov asked. "If you are, I would like to say a few words myself."
'Mayakovsky paused in the doorway and replied with great dignity: "I'm not through yet and I won't be for at least five hundred years. Shvedchikovs come and go, but art remains. Remember that!"
'With that he left. I stayed behind and tried to argue with my boss in more reasonable terms, but in vain. It was only later, under the pressure of an ever-growing group of writers and journalists as well as some influential party men who liked the film, that Sovkino finally did agree to send *Potemkin* to Berlin.'

Whatever the story behind it, the fact of *Potemkin*'s triumph in Berlin is indisputable.[6] This was the beginning of a series of shocks and triumphs in every country where the film was shown—a series that shows no sign of yet ending. What is more doubtful is that *Potemkin*'s Berlin success made Soviet critics pay more attention to the film; this seems to strain probability, and is based on the fact that all Soviet critical reactions were published after the later public release rather than after the Bolshoi showing. In a later detailed complaint at Sovkino executives Mayakovsky said, 'On its first showing *Potemkin* was relegated to second-rate theatres only, and it was only after the enthusiastic reaction of the foreign press that it was put into the best theatres.'[7] And Lunacharsky also gave evidence on this point:

' . . . we have many examples of Soviet films that do not pay for themselves, and have no success. It is true that some of these deserve such a reception, but there are also facts of an opposite significance. It is commonly hushed up that *Potemkin* had no success with us. I remember the strange impression I had when I entered the First Sovkino Theatre on Arbat Square, decorated with a display representing a ship, and with ushers costumed as sailors. I found the theatre half-empty. And this was the first run of *Potemkin*. Only after the German public enthusiastically greeted *Potemkin* was it properly shown here. Its greatest publicity came from the wish to see a film that had brought us our first victory in the foreign film-market.'[8]

Before *Potemkin*'s foreign acclaim there was a never-disputed concept in the Soviet film industry: that no Soviet film with 'agitational value' could be shown abroad with success. Obviously the revolutionary material saturating *Potemkin* had not interfered with its success abroad; even in those countries, such as France and England, where it was forbidden publicly, the private screenings were to attract enormous interest. This was an unpleasant shock to those directors who had defended their 'minimal-agitational' films by this myth of foreign coolness to Bolshevik art.

Potemkin has been the subject of more *post facto* examination than any other film. Eisenstein himself has provided the best of these analyses in his later theoretical writing; in one article he concentrates on the over-all structure and content of his masterpiece:

'*Potemkin* looks like a chronicle (or newsreel) of an event, but it functions as a drama.

'The secret of this lies in the fact that the chronicle pace of the event is fitted to a severely tragic composition. And furthermore, to tragic composition in its most canonic form—the five-act tragedy. . . . This was further emphasized by the individual titling of each "act".* Here, in condensation, are the contents of the five acts:

'Reel 1—"*Men and Maggots*". Exposition of the action. Milieu of the battleship. Maggotty meat. Discontent ferments among the sailors.

---

* From the first years of the Soviet film, with its emphasis on travelling and rural film exhibitions, rarely equipped with more than one projector, the film-makers planned each reel as an independent unit that could be followed by a (hopefully) brief pause. Scenarists and directors exploited the dramatic possibilities of this physical part-structure. In both *Strike* and *Potemkin* Eisenstein went a little further by giving each reel a title.

'*Reel 2—"Drama on the Quarterdeck"*. "All hands on deck!" Refusal to eat the wormy soup. Scene with tarpaulin. "Brothers!" Refusal to fire. Mutiny. Revenge on the officers.

'*Reel 3—"Appeal from the Dead"*. Mist. The body of Vakulinchuk is brought into Odessa port. Mourning over the body. Indignation. Demonstration. Raising the red flag.

'*Reel 4—"The Odessa Steps"*. Fraternization of shore and battleship. Yawls with provisions. Shooting on the Odessa steps. The battleship fires on the "generals' staff".

'*Reel 5—"Meeting the Squadron"*. Night of suspense. Meeting the squadron. Engines. "Brothers!" The squadron refuses to fire. The battleship passes victoriously through the squadron. . . .

'From a tiny cellular organism in the battleship to the organism of the battleship itself; from a tiny cellular organism of the fleet to the organism of the whole fleet—thus flies through the theme the revolutionary feeling of brotherhood. And this is repeated in the structure of the work containing this theme—brotherhood and revolution.

'Over the heads of the battleship's commanders, over the heads of the admirals of the Tsar's fleet, and finally over the heads of the foreign censors, rushes the whole film with its fraternal "Hurrah!" just as within the film the feeling of brotherhood flies from the rebellious battleship over the sea to the shore.'[9]

One of the curious effects of the film has been to replace the facts of the Potemkin mutiny with the film's artistic 'revision' of those events, in all subsequent reference, even by historians, to this episode.* It is partly the history of the film's evolution that explains such a 'revision', for as the whole material of the '1905' film was gradually replaced by the single episode of the mutiny, that episode had to work as a synthesis of the whole 1905 Revolution. One result has been to transform an episode of the revolution into the symbolic episode of the whole revolution. In the process *Potemkin* often sacrificed the lesser historical facts for the dramatic essence of history. In actual fact, for example, other ships did join the *Potemkin* in mutiny, and the Cossack slaughter occurred quite differently. Eisenstein once received a letter from one of the mutineers, thanking him for the film, and identifying himself as 'one of those under the tarpaulin'. Eisenstein did not have the heart to tell him that the tarpaulin had been a dramatic invention—but he was interested in how even an eye-witness, a participant, after exposure to the power of empathy, could revise his memory of the fact.

Another, greater anniversary was to be celebrated soon—of the October Revolution—and to this end it was announced at the end of 1925 that Vsevolod Meyerhold was to film for Proletkino John Reed's historical account, *Ten Days That Shook the World*. But this came to no more than had another Meyerhold film project boosted to an American journalist earlier that year:

'Meyerhold whose "Path of Steel" is to cover the development of the steel industry and exhibit the titanic conflict of man with metal, is captain of a group

* When a *Potemkin* opera was later composed, it was the film, not the fact, that the librettist followed.

of four directors chosen from among his own followers who are making this picture in the very mines and blast furnaces and rolling mills. . . .'[10]

The inventor of this team idea issued another manifesto this year:

'Kinodrama—is an opium for the people. Kinodrama and religion—are deadly weapons in the hands of the capitalists. The scenario—is a tale thought up for us by literary people. . . . Down with the bourgeois tale-scenario! Hurrah for life as it is!'[11]

Only age and obscurity made Dziga Vertov less shrill. Even success did not make him relinquish the employment of Mayakovsky's loud voice, but without the literary ingredient that Vertov so scorned. And *Kino-Eye* had been a distinct success, so that Vertov's next two films were both commissioned by Soviet organizations outside the film industry. *Stride, Soviet* was ordered by the Moscow Soviet as an informational film to be shown before the election of 1926. *A Sixth of the Earth* was commissioned by Gostorg (the Government trade agency) as an internationally circulated advertisement of Soviet resources and possibilities. Both jobs were, fortunately, freely interpreted by Vertov, as opportunities to make film-poems of pride. *Stride, Soviet* employed a simple structure of parallelism: this is the way things are now, that is how they were then; or, this is the way things are with us, and that is how they are in capitalist countries. *A Sixth* was the first Vertov film to be generally well received by the Russian press. Its publicity purpose was lost sight of in the grandest and most complicated system of travelling cameramen that Vertov had yet had at his disposal. If the viewer of Vertov's feature-length films should have the same trouble that I sometimes experience—of not being able to identify an extract or a still from 'a Vertov film,' any more than one could give the correct number to an issue of *Kino-Pravda* —he can always distinguish *A Sixth* for its preponderance of exotic material, for Kaufman and Vertov's other cameramen reached further points of the Soviet Union, and more of them, than they ever had before. Gostorg must have had a hard time 'using' Vertov's film for sales purposes (the film calls its audience to look at 'our victories'), but the film found a pleased public wherever it was shown; its first showing was to the delegates at the fifteenth party congress in November 1926.

In 1925 and 1926 the film-theatre, as supporter of the film-studio, ranked equally with it in authority. For example, a theatre could advertise a film in any way it thought it could attract an audience, and no one but film-makers and film magazines would protest, but powerlessly. While *The Wedding of the Bear* was banned in Berlin, a Moscow theatre advertised it as 'playing with huge success in forty Berlin theatres'. Another Moscow theatre announced: 'Charlie Chaplin plays leading rôle in *Woman of Paris*', while a Perm theatre must have irritated Vertov by advertising his *Stride, Soviet* as, 'Played by the best actors in Russian films.'

Fortunately for Russian film-makers, the end of NEP in the film industries did not mean the end of foreign films on Russian screens. The film-making country whose post-NEP connections stayed firmest was Germany, while French films dropped to a lesser place, as they did generally in the post-war film world. In Russia Gance was the most admired French director, Griffith and Cruze represented the serious American film, while the whole range of German work was familiar, to a remarkably full extent—Lang's *Dr Mabuse* and both parts of his *Nibelungen*, Pabst's *Freudlose Gasse*, Murnau's *Letze Mann* had all been seen in Russia by the end of 1925; Lubitsch was known both for his comedies and his historical spectacles, and Oswald for his social films and handsome costume tragedies. It is to this tremendously influential array of German styles and methods that the changed appearance of the FEX films in 1926 can be linked. On March 3, 1926, after the interval of a year, appeared their first popular film, *The Devil's Wheel* (originally titled *Sailor from the Aurora*), a drama of the gangster bands that preyed upon Petrograd during the Civil War. The clash between the realistic material and the eccentric treatment by the FEX seems to have increased the force of the film. All disparate elements were pulled together by the dramatic, expressive, Germanic photography of their new cameraman, Andrei Moskvin, who was to identify himself with the whole film career of Kozintsev and Trauberg. Typical of the successful mixture of real and eccentric was the scene in a Leningrad amusement park:

'Amidst roller-coasters, giant swings, devil's wheels, and a thousand crowding pleasure-seekers, under the din and the laughter, the ringing of hammers and gongs, squeaking hurdy-gurdies, glaring fireworks, moved the lyrical theme of love and chance encounter.'[12]

Another step in the progress of the FEX was due to their exposure to the Kuleshov films, to *Strike* and to *Potemkin* (though the films of Ince could have taught them this much), to judge from this fragment of a shot-list, a sequence showing Vanya Shorin, the sailor, barring a gang from a workers' club:

1   Door of workers' club.
2   On the steps, leading to the door: Vanya Shorin and group of gangsters.
3   One of the gang makes a slow move towards Shorin.
4   Puts his hand in his pocket.
5   Face of Shorin.
6   Crowd of gangsters.
7   A few of the gang, closer.
8   One inhales cigarette-smoke, and blows it out.
9   Behind Shorin the figure of a hooligan slowly approaches him.
10 One of the gang inhales his cigarette. . . .[13]

and so on. This reads so normally today that we find it difficult to realize what a commitment to the Moscow school this Leningrad film then indicated. After seeing *Strike*, Kozintsev addressed the FEX group, 'All that we're doing is childish nonsense, we must all see *Strike* again and again, until we can understand it and adopt its power for our own.'[14]

In *The Devil's Wheel* the eccentric tendency had found its happiest outlet in the peculiar lesser figures of the story. It was natural for the FEX to search for material that would give even greater opportunity in the direction of eccentric

portraiture and behaviour, even of the central rôles—and they next found what
they needed in the most natural place, the stories of Gogol. Gogol's technique,
too, which furnished so much inspiration to modern Russian novelists and
dramatists, became a source for the Soviet cinema. His grotesque characters
and high-lighted detail were ready-made for a group of young actors and directors
seeking literary material for formalized film action. The interest of the FEX
in Gogol was clearly formal as well as literary. Their subtitle to *The Cloak* explains that it is 'a comedy in the Gogol manner'. In addition to that famous
story the scenarist, Yuri Tinyanov, drew upon another Gogol story, 'Nevsky
Prospect', to make a three-reel prologue, showing a frustrating youthful adventure
of the pitiful clerk of *The Cloak*.

It is in the direction and acting that the style of the film, a romantic brand
of expressionism, is most clearly established. Andrei Kostrichkin as Bashmachkin
is stylistically the piteous sleepwalker from *Caligari*, experiencing rather than
producing terror. The tailor and his wife give performances that might have been
obtained from two well-directed acrobats. Andrei Moskvin's photography, as
romantic or grotesque as the scenes call upon it to be, maintains the cloak's
character as a fetish, observing the clerk with heroic and powerful camera-
angles so long as he is wrapped in it, and photographing him mercilessly from
above after it is taken from him. Moskvin's treatment of the robbery in the snow
is especially expressive. Enei, the designer, assisted both the spirit and the
functioning of the film by sharply characterized interiors and street scenes.
The co-ordinated effort of all participants achieves a unity that reminds one of
the more perfect result of the collaboration of Mayer, Murnau, Freund, Herlth-
Röhrig, and Jannings in *Der letzte Mann*, perhaps a model that the FEX followed
here.

Many years later Kozintsev described the effect of making their first 'costume'
film in a studio distinguished for its stilted costume films:

'When we came to work in the Soviet cinema, we found the Leningrad cinema
factory full of historical pictures taken on a naïvely naturalistic principle.

'All the generals, tsars, soldiers, etc., were shot primarily in order to emphasize the products of the costume department of which the factory was so
proud. They shot the costumes, with the actors inside them. That was the basic
attitude of the time.

'Now we wanted primarily to replace this parade of historical costumes
across the surface of the film by a feeling of the epoch, in other words purposively
to replace it with a general style, and not the naturalism of details. From the
cameraman's viewpoint we were interested in obtaining an extremely pictorial
photography. We wanted to get away as far as possible from the external form
of the costume, we wanted to convey to the audience the atmosphere of the
epoch.'[15]

For Kozintsev and Trauberg *The Cloak* was a satisfying excursion into the exotic,
faintly ridiculous past, an excursion that was to find many successful sequels in
their future. Before spending several years in that past they made another attempt
at a contemporary subject, in *Bratishka*, 'a comedy about a truck', with all the

elements that one would expect the FEX to employ in this subject: startling shots of modern city vehicles, an unsmooth love affair between a chauffeur and a girl street-car-conductor, and lyrical scenes played in an auto-dump.

The campaign against religion was one that, logically, could have employed the dramatic and satiric means of the cinema successfully. Yet the only attacks on the Orthodox Church that had force are passages in films of broader scope, such as Eisenstein's *Old and New* or Dovzhenko's *Earth*. The purely anti-religious films have been uninteresting as films, evidence perhaps that it takes more than a negative slogan to inspire a good film-maker. Soviet policy on this matter has altered so often that the scenarist or director prefers to avoid it as a central theme rather than see his script or film, produced within one policy, be shelved in a reverse of policy.* One of the earliest of the 'godless' films, *The Miracle-Worker* (directed by Panteleyev, released November 22, 1922) long remained in circulation on the strength of Lenin's approval: his widow reported that he had seen and praised it. Others were *Father Serafim* (also directed by Panteleyev in 1922) and *The Elder Vasili Griaznov*, made by Goskino in 1924 (directed by Sabinski and photographed by Tisse), showing the manufacture of 'holy relics'. The most ambitious released film on this subject was Gardin's *Cross and Mauser* (released November 8, 1925), on the espionage of Catholic priests for a 'foreign power', and their provocation of pogroms.

Policy on the Jewish religion was less ambivalent, for here there was the matter of a minority culture to be encouraged and protected. A religious character in Soviet films of Jewish life was just as likely to be the comedian of the piece as its villain. Even Zionism was not too touchy a subject for film treatment; and once the Jewish Autonomous Region of Birobidjan existed (1934), it was given considerable film attention. Later, after the state of Israel was established, with its lean towards the United States, the problems of Soviet Jewish films grew more complicated. But in the more innocent 1920s Alexander Granovsky could make a good-humoured adaptation of a Sholom Aleichem story, in *Jewish Luck*, without causing undue anxiety in any quarter. This was also the film début of the distinguished Yiddish actor, Solomon Mikhoels.

Gradually, as production facilities widened, the Soviet film was catching up with the foreign film on Soviet screens. Samuel N. Harper noted some progress in the showing of native films, as well as the consequent greater care taken with their scenarios:

'In 1924 only 28·5 per cent of the pictures shown in the Soviet Union were the so-called Soviet films, the balance being foreign. In 1925 the percentage had increased to 30. . . . For Soviet films a special Art Council for the Kino attached to the Political Education Section gave the ideological direction with respect to content. During 1925 some three hundred scenarios were submitted to the Art Council, and of these less than half were passed. The majority of the scenarios

---

* This was a factor in the fate of *Bezhin Meadow* (1935-37). There was a similar risk taken with the subject of international relations. I have known of film-attacks on Poland and Turkey that were quietly laid aside before production or release when relations with those countries improved. And, of course, the 1940 pact with Germany resulted in the temporary shelving of all anti-Nazi films and even of *Alexander Nevsky*.

submitted were either "politically illiterate" or they had no relation to social themes or they were purely agitational in character, besides being utterly devoid of artistic value, it was reported by this committee. Of the scenarios passed, six related to the history of the struggle of the working class, eleven were based on episodes of the civil war, nine described in general contemporary social conditions, and fourteen were descriptive of village life. There were six films based on the culture and customs of national minorities. Educational films numbered forty-six. Only two films were classified as based on exploits or adventures, and eight were indicated as comedies. The balance, about forty, evidently did not lend themselves to classification. . . .'[16]

Mezhrabpom-Russ, where the scenario department was more forceful than in other studios, had nothing prepared for the anniversary year. They made grand announcements of the literature made ready, this year, for the indefatigable Protazanov: a scenario by Maxim Gorky on the Stenka Razin rebellion (the manuscript was found among Gorky's papers after his death), a film of Dosteyevsky's *Eternal Husband*, and, grandest of all, a collaboration by Protazanov with Nemirovich-Danchenko on Tolstoy's *War and Peace*.* None of these projects was ever seriously begun. Instead, Protazanov made films that were far less grand and possibly more interesting, the first two in a form that became associated with his name—the satirical comedy: *The Tailor from Torzhok* (commissioned as publicity for the State Lottery Loan) and *The Three Million Case* (or *Three Thieves*, from the Italian novel by Umberto Notari†)—both with much the same cast, Ilinsky, Ktorov, Zhizneva, who were also to play in his later comedies. Though *Three Thieves* was frowned upon as 'an ordinary drawing-room comedy', the two comedies were agreeably successful at the box-office, but his next film went beyond his studio's expectations. This was *The Forty-First*, based on a story by Lavrenov of the Civil War in Turkestan.

In the desert war a Red Army detachment encounters a caravan escorting a White Guard officer. The best sharpshooter of the Red soldiers is a girl. She fires at her 'forty-first' victim, the White lieutenant, but she misses. Capturing the caravan, the Reds take the lieutenant, a courier, with them. Circumstances and adventures eventually separate the girl and her captive from the others. A desert island romance is ended by their rescue, but before an enemy ship can reach the lovers' shore, she carries out her oath and shoots her 'forty-first'—the only man she has ever loved.

The unusual demands on a cast of two, for most of the film, made the rôles of the girl and the officer vital, and two seasoned actors were given the rôles, Vera Maretskaya and Ivan Koval-Samborsky, whereupon Protazanov went to the Caspian Sea to select locations for the exterior scenes. Preparations were in fine shape, when Maretskaya took ill. Protazanov's assistant, Yuli Raizman, had the difficult task of replacing her, and quickly. He sent film-tests of candidates to Protazanov, waiting in Baku, and the actress chosen for the rôle was Ada Voitsik,

* This project was briefly revived in 1928, with a scenario by Lunacharsky and Protazanov.
† Filmed twice before: in 1916, as *Thief*, with Maximov and Baranovskaya; in 1923, as *Candidate for President*, directed by Chardynin.

just graduated from the film-actors' course at GTK. Raizman had seen her playing in a student film, directed by her brother. She has described her girlish fears at the test and at her first meeting with Protazanov in his Baku hotel, and it is to him that she gives full credit for her extraordinary, almost savage performance as Maryutka.

'Yakov Alexandrovich would always explain every thing to us in advance, and in the fullest detail: not only what shot was to be filmed and how many metres it was to be, but also what in the finished film would precede and follow it, and even why we were filming that particular shot at this time. Protazanov explained to us the technical as well as the creative process of the film medium, even to letting us in to photographic mysteries—why we were waiting for this shadow, or why Yermolov was using that lens.'[17]

Despite all the unusual filming aspects of *The Forty-First*, it was filmed in record time, two months, including the distant location shooting. Its character, as an original Russian love story in the style of an Ince 'western', helped to make it an international success—so complete, indeed, that thirty years later it was remade, possibly for the same market.

Within this period there were two important non-commercial contacts with the foreign film world. The 1925 international exhibition in Paris of decorative arts gave recognition, but in a peculiar way, to four Soviet films. Protazanov was awarded an honorary diploma (2nd class) for *Aelita*; Eisenstein, a gold medal (3rd class) for *Strike*; Bassaligo, a gold medal (3rd class) for *From Sparks—Flames*; and Vertov, a silver medal (4th class) for *Kino-Pravda*. But these awards were not made to the films, for no films were sent to Paris, but to the photographs and posters for these films—so it is difficult to give either the films or their directors much credit for these honours.

More direct and tangible honours were given by Mary Pickford and Douglas Fairbanks on their visit to Moscow in July 1926. It appears that they made the trip more through curiosity than for business reasons (and crowds of their Moscow fans showed equal curiosity), but one important piece of business was done: Fairbanks took *Potemkin* to the United States, and his praise of it swelled its audience everywhere. He also asked Eisenstein to follow it to Hollywood, the first of several such invitations. No other film shown to the visitors made such an impression on them, and they were shown everything new of any interest. Much was made of their reactions, and it was never forgotten of *Three Thieves* that Pickford and Fairbanks had nothing to say about it as they left the projection-room. Leningrad made a reciprocal gesture to the international film in an exhibition in January 1926, commemorating the thirtieth anniversary of the Lumière invention. A related project (but not realized) was proposed by Yutkevich and Levshin: F.O.F., *Film About Film*, on the history of cinema, and describing how films are made.

The director who was to make one of the grand images of the 1905 Revolution was busy with his own education during most of the anniversary year, for once Pudovkin actually began work on *Mechanics of the Brain*, in May 1925, it proceeded at a leisurely and often interrupted pace for the next year. The wide range of experiments to be filmed, the shuttling between the studio in Moscow and the Pavlov laboratory in Leningrad, consumed more than normal production time, particularly as there was never a formal scenario to work from. To cause further delays, the delicately 'conditioned' animal actors were easily put off their carefully nurtured habits by the unusual apparatus and noise of the filming.[18] Eventually the crew learned to hide themselves and the cameras from the animals as they did from the children who were shown in the film. Pudovkin's enthusiasm for the scientific subject, and the care and attention given by him to each detail of the scientific observations demonstrated, all indicate *Mechanics of the Brain* as the appropriate post-graduate work for this Kuleshov student. Professor Burankov, at the Pavlov Institute, was so impressed by Pudovkin's concentration and method that he offered him a post as his assistant. Another who showed himself as temperamentally right for the work was the cameraman of the crew, Anatoli Golovnya, and his work with Pudovkin on this film determined his almost exclusive career on the films of Pudovkin. Their first work together, when Golovnya was Levitsky's assistant on *The Death Ray*, was continued on the comedy of *Chess Fever*. *Mechanics* showed them that they were exactly right for each other, just as Tisse and Eisenstein made an ideal partnership. Twenty years later, Pudovkin told an interviewer:

'The only significance this first film of mine has is that it made me realize that I could work on my own. Up to then such an idea seemed absolutely impossible to me, although Kuleshov assured me that I was fully able to. . . .'[19]

While Pudovkin continued his exposition of Pavlov, his best scenarist prepared their first collaboration, long before Pudovkin knew that he was to direct *Mother*. Nathan Zarkhi's first try at adapting Gorky's novel did not satisfy him—it seemed too sentimental. Furthermore, the director first assigned to the film, Zhelyabuzhsky, was unable to find the right actress for the title rôle. He even asked Zarkhi to rewrite the scenario, transferring the character of the *mother* to a *father*, to be played by Moskvin.[20] Zhelyabuzhsky and Moskvin put the idea aside, and then Aleinikov, of the Mezhrabpom administration, proposed the film to Pudovkin. In another of the pauses during the filming of *Mechanics*, one of which had already resulted in *Chess Fever*, Pudovkin accepted enthusiastically and began work with Zarkhi before the completion of his scientific film.[21] They returned to the original scenario, hoping for better luck with the chief casting problem, and developed its simple theme of a down-trodden working-class mother rising to political consciousness through her son's revolutionary activity. Zarkhi was also encouraged to treat the Gorky novel even more freely than he had, making his scenario a transformation of the original rather than an 'adaptation'.* Drawing on memoirs of the revolutionary movement of 1905 and 1906, particularly in the city of Tver, Zarkhi created a script that purified and simplified

---

* Gorky was not happy with the news of his novel's transformation into a film that was only generally related to his work. He asked to see the finished film. Although Soviet films were forbidden in Italy a copy of *Mother* was admitted to Capri for a private showing to Gorky. I have never seen a record of his reaction, but the story is that he gave his approval reluctantly. Another hint of his feeling can be found in a later speech: 'Men of letters should take a more active part in the work of the cinema. We literary men should make the scenarios ourselves; that is our business.'

Gorky's looser novel to an almost classic structure. The character of the father, for example, who illuminated the film both dramatically and socially (and figures importantly in the first three reels) is not in the novel. The dramatization of the trial scene was modelled on the trial in Tolstoy's *Resurrection*. Zarkhi provided Pudovkin with the perfect material and form not only for a demonstration of all that he had learned under Kuleshov, but for an unforgettable demonstration of Pudovkin the film-artist—the man whose three penetrating film experiences had been *Intolerance*, *A Woman of Paris*, and *Potemkin*.

In the scenario, Zarkhi and Pudovkin consciously established a sonata outline: first and second reels—*allegro* (saloon, home, factory, strike, chase); third reel—a funereal *adagio* (dead father, scene between mother and son); fourth and fifth reels—*allegro* (police, search, betrayal, arrest, trial, prison); sixth and seventh—a mounting, furious *presto* (spring thaw, demonstration, prison revolt, ice-break, massacre, death of son and mother). This early consideration for tempo is a contributing factor to the notable rhythmic harmony of *Mother*.

Most of the difficult casting problems were solved by Mikhail Doller, Pudovkin's excellent assistant, whose theatre work for the past thirteen years had acquainted him with the acting personnel available. Not only was he responsible for the casting of most of the vivid 'bit-rôles' in the film, but it was he who brought both Baranovskaya and Batalov from the Moscow Art Theatre.

The administration of Mezhrabpom-Russ had proposed for the rôle of the mother (Pelageya Vlasova) one of Moscow's most popular 'character-actresses', Maria Blumenthal-Tamarina. She did not fit Pudovkin's image of the mother, but he was inexperienced in authority, and, besides, he himself had no one to suggest. It was only Doller's support and encouragement that resolved this dilemma. He chose Vera Baranovskaya for the rôle—but she did not consider it right for her, and neither did Pudovkin! Yet stubborn Doller dressed her for the rôle as he imagined it, and asked her to sit on some studio steps in any way suggested by the clothes she was wearing. When he brought in Pudovkin to see her, it only needed a glance at that immobile figure to convince Pudovkin that this was the only actress for the rôle. Furthermore, she made the whole character come alive to him as it had not before. Nikolai Batalov, too, resisted the rôle of the son, Pavel, but was argued in to it by all, including the studio, for whom he had worked in *Aelita* and, briefly, as the hero of *His Call*.* It was also Doller's suggestion to cast Chistyakov, the Kuleshov student who had been a heavyweight athlete, for the father. The smaller rôles were filled with just as much care, usually by Doller. For the colonel in the scene of Pavel's arrest, he found a former officer of the tsarist army—who played himself. The subordinate officer in this scene was played by Pudovkin, who thereafter always played a small part in his pictures (also a superstitious habit of Alfred Hitchcock) and enjoyed working in the films of other directors, as well.

'I regard as comparatively successful the little piece I played in *Mother*, where I represented an officer, a police rat, who came to search Pavel's home. I remember

---

* Batalov's illness (tuberculosis) required his replacement in this film by Koval-Samborsky (who plays Pavel's friend in *Mother*).

that for this rôle, by habit of my old training [with Kuleshov], I based myself principally on the external traits of its image. I began by cutting my hair *en brosse*, grew a moustache, and put on a pair of spectacles, which, it seemed to me, by their contrast with the military uniform, which always lends a certain air of bravado and masculinity to the wearer, would especially emphasize the weak and degraded character of a typical police-officer rat.

'I remember that the only inner mood on which I tried to base my acting was one of sour dreariness and boredom, such as seemed to me should cause the spectator to feel vividly the dourness of police mechanism. . . .

'I remember that all the work on this tiny part was most closely bound up with its editing development. The somnolent, bored, and dreary figure of the police officer, mainly shown in long shot and medium shot, was purposely changed to close-up and big head when, in the course of the rôle, I began to show glimpses of interest in the chase as I scented the spoor.'[22]

After casting was largely settled, another obstacle appeared; details of this problem have been helpfully recorded by M. N. Aleinikov, the executive who greatly admired the finished script of *Mother*.[23] The budget for the production of *Mother* was estimated at 85,000 roubles and the Prom-Bank balked at this amount, as it was higher than the studio's average budget (*The Station Master* cost 50,000), and as a seemingly inexperienced director was to handle this risk. News of their objection nearly ruined Pudovkin's morale, and only Aleinikov's suggestion that he get started anyway, and let him go on arguing with the bank, restored his capacity for work.

Partly because of his fear that certain actors, needed for the climax of the film, would obtain other work before those scenes were taken, Pudovkin began the shooting with the last reels. The first shots filmed were of Pavel being brought to the court-house for trial, and of his departure, when his mother begs his forgiveness. These exteriors were shot in Moscow, using the façade and steps of the First City Hospital. The first 400 feet accomplished two large purposes: they established the style for the film—one of these first shots, the powerful composition of the standing policeman, has been called 'an example of fore-shortening which has become "classic" in cinematic practice'[24]—and they convinced the book-keeping department; the Prom-Bank granted the 85,000 roubles with no further hesitation.

In Yaroslavl where the crew went to film the breaking ice on the Volga, Doller showed himself the ideal assistant director. For the scene of Pavel escaping across the broken ice Batalov refused to endanger his life, and a local sportsman was found to double for him:

'Boots with crampons were ordered for him; he was instructed and rehearsed in how to run. Two weeks they waited for the ice to break. One morning the Volga began to move. The sportsman quickly put on the costume of Pavel and the whole group ran excitedly to the river and prepared to take this vital moment for the film. The sportsman walked down to the shore, looked at the ice, tested it with his foot, and announced, "The ice is too spongy—impossible to run on it." No pleas would sway him. Pudovkin was desperate—he least of all was prepared for such a decision. And the ice flowed on, crackling and breaking. Then Doller, without a word, dressed in Pavel's costume and stepped onto the ice. He ran along the river, jumping across a gap in the ice, and stepping from floe to floe. And Golovnya filmed it all. . . .'[25]

For the scene of the May Day demonstration being run down by the mounted police, the studio permitted only two hundred paid extras, but Doller felt that such a thin crowd would hurt the significance of the scene; he went from factory to factory in Tver, where they were shooting, and explained the film's story, its revolutionary theme, and asked for volunteer extras. When the scene was made, seven hundred Tver workers appeared. When they were shy about running along the street, both Doller and Pudovkin led the crowd, racing ahead of the horses. When Pudovkin was not satisfied with the effect of panic produced by his volunteers, he created a real one by an unannounced change of direction taken by the horses—with both him and his ideal assistant running in the midst of the crowd.

Towards the end of his life, in the interview with Jeanne Gauzner, Pudovkin gave an amazingly negative motive for the making of *Mother*:

'In that picture I first of all tried to keep as far away as I could from Eisenstein and from much that Kuleshov had taught me. I did not see how it was possible for me to limit myself, with my organic need for inner emotions, to the dry form which Kuleshov preached. . . . I had a strong instinctive inclination for living people whom I wanted to photograph and whose soul I wanted to fathom, just as Eisenstein had fathomed the soul of his *Battleship Potemkin*.'

It was no doubt a dejected mood that Pudovkin was in at the time of this interview that accounts for its negative tone, and for its rejection of influences that helped make *Mother* the strongly individual work that it is. In another, earlier, interview, given before the release of *Mother*, Pudovkin (or possibly the interviewer) was more helpfully naïve in describing the compositional approach of the film—one not dissimilar to Andrei Moskvin's camera work in *The Cloak:*

'The cameraman and I have tried to use camera angles to strengthen the impression conveyed by the actor. A man with an arrogant lift to his head would be filmed from below—a head drooping with exhaustion would be filmed from above, and so on.

'In composing the shots we aimed to fill them efficiently with the required action. Whenever we noticed some dead place at the edge of a shot, we would eliminate it, to have nothing useless or superfluous in the composition.'[26]

In the following year, during work on *The End of St Petersburg*, Anatoli Golovnya wrote to the same purpose:

'In showing a developing situation in a film one usually alters the psychological image of the protagonist. For example, the downtrodden woman (in *Mother*) was transformed into a heroine, willing to sacrifice herself. On the path that the actor must take to accomplish this he must be accompanied by the cameraman. We would film her initial image of an oppressed, humiliated woman from slightly above, with a harsh, flat lighting and miserly, dry compositions. . . . Her final image, of a heroine filled with titanic strength, would be filmed from below, no longer concentrating on the texture of her face, but giving the whole head and face its maximum power.'[27]

It was while working on *Mother* that Pudovkin formulated his compositional aim in one of his most elevated and helpful statements:

' . . . the greatest artists, those technicians who feel the film most acutely, deepen their work with details. To do this they discard the general aspect of the image, and the points of interval that are the inevitable concomitant of every natural event. . . .

'In the disappearance of the general, obvious outline and the appearance on the screen of some deeply hidden detail, filmic representation attains the highest point of its power of external expression.'[28]

Among his examples of selected significant detail are scenes from both *Intolerance* and *Potemkin*. Pudovkin's other favourite, *A Woman of Paris*, could easily have been quoted in respect to this same power.

'Pudovkin heard and saw each shot of his films before it was filmed. . . . In filming the scene of the mother sitting by her husband's bier Pudovkin and [Baranovskaya] sought for the pose that would convey the feeling that the mother had already sat there a long time, erect and immobile. Pudovkin wanted to convey graphically the sense of empty and silent surroundings. Kozlovsky and I removed everything superfluous from the set. Left in the composition were only the black figure of the mother, the white sheet over the corpse, the open coffin, the grey walls. [See still of this scene (Plate 19).]

'In filming it we spoke in whispers, walked on tip-toe. The wash-stand was filmed separately. Pudovkin gave [me] only one direction: "Film it so that the dripping water can be heard".'[29]

Throughout *Mother*, unusually unified in graphic style as it is, the image often seems to have been scientifically stripped of every distraction, forcing the small, apparently involuntary gesture or flicker of an eye upon you, and in this Pudovkin had the collaboration of Golovnya and of the equally sensitive designer, Kozlovsky. It was, of course, Kuleshov who first taught Pudovkin the dramatic value of such cinematic *pointing*, yet Pudovkin's practice on *Mechanics of the Brain* must have reinforced the lesson. By comparison with these stripped images, their many sources appear almost cluttered or ornamental—Velasquez' 'Bollo' that brought the famous camera angle of the monumental policeman into being; Van Gogh's 'Prison Courtyard' (after Doré), inspiration for the scene of the prison exercise hour; the carefully composed realism of Degas, the haggard blue-period paintings of Picasso and the prints of Käthe Kollwitz, that all contributed to the graphic representation of the mother; Rouault's three 'Judges' that helped to characterize Pudovkin's three judges.

More important than any individual compositions in *Mother* is its continuation of the Griffith-Eisenstein tradition of camera as active *observer* rather than mere spectator. Lunacharsky remarked that the film carried a conviction as though an extraordinary cameraman had been present at actual events. The photography of the actors is especially emotional in effect. Pudovkin has told how he establishes personal relationships with each actor in his films,* a method that, particularly in *Mother*, renders them intimate to the spectator, helping to make this the most lyrical and immediate film of this first rich period of Soviet films. It was probably *Mother* that inspired Moussinac's famous comparison: 'Un film d'Eisenstein ressemble à un cri, un film de Poudovkine évoque un chant.'

During the production of *Mother*, Pudovkin completed two booklets for a series of practical manuals on film-making published by Kinopechat: *The Film Scenario* (64 pages) and *Film Director and Film Material* (92 pages). The Russian circulation of these was enormous: the second was published in April 1926, in a first edition of 7,000 copies at 50 kopeks. It is truly difficult, now, to believe that the articulate, assured voice in these booklets was that of a man who had produced almost no independent artistic work. The two manuals were published together abroad[30] and have become standard international reading in film-theory as well as film-practice, accepted and gospelized far beyond their author's expectations. In fact, after *Mother*, Pudovkin moved so far beyond his views of this period, that correction of these manuals was a wish he cherished but never realized.

The most startling (at the time) statement to foreign readers opens the introduction to the German edition: 'The foundation of film art is *editing*' and, 'The film is not *shot*, but *built*, built up from the separate strips of celluloid that are its raw material.' The editing process is not the only one that made *Mother* great, but one can learn more of the value that Pudovkin placed on it from this film than from the masses of *The End of St Petersburg* (1927) or the technical tour-de-force of *Storm Over Asia* (1928). The expert cutting on human movement of *Mother* has been more widely absorbed into general film technique than its more abstract cutting propositions. The clearest example in all of Pudovkin's work of the 'associative' editing of logically unrelated scenes to form a 'plastic synthesis', is still the episode of Pavel's joy at the news he receives in prison:

'The photographing of a face lighting up with joy would have been flat and void of effect. I show, therefore, the nervous play of his hands and a big close-up of the lower half of his face, the corners of the smile. These shots I cut in with other and varied material—shots of a brook, swollen with the rapid flow of spring, of the play of sunlight broken on the water, birds splashing in the village pond, and finally a laughing child.'[31]

The whole film demonstrates that senses of smell (saloon, early morning), feeling (mud, blow of a fist), and sound (water drip, swollen stream) could not have been so strongly communicated with any other method. *Mother*'s editing is the logical outcome of the disjunctive cutting introduced by Edwin S. Porter, enlarged by D. W. Griffith and others, and analysed by Kuleshov. Although in direct theoretic

---

* So much so that when he played his small rôle in *Mother*, Baranovskaya had great difficulty in working in that scene with him; she was used only to Pudovkin the friendly director, and missed him.

opposition to Eisenstein's *shock* montage, Pudovkin used a *linkage* method beyond Kuleshov's 'brick by brick' construction.

Aleinikov mentions a personal trait that tends to substantiate the critical importance for Pudovkin of the editing stage:

'It is interesting to note that the calm and confidence that never deserted Pudovkin so long as he was actually shooting his film, changed suddenly at the cutting-table. In the heat of filming, while in close contact with the dramatist, the actors and the cameraman, Pudovkin could easily endure opinions coming from the camp of his former partisans. But while editing Pudovkin was so nervous that he would react to every remark relayed to him about being the captive of such an "old-fashioned" dramatist as Zarkhi, or of such "old-fashioned" artistic methods carried into his film by the Art Theatre.'*

When audiences abroad saw *Mother* a year after *Potemkin*, they were amazed that two such powerful works, so different in style, could come from a country that had not shown the world any particular national character in its films. These now were both Russian films, indubitably, but the only dominant characteristic they shared was that they were both Soviet films.

Kuleshov's other students were also making more headway this year than was Kuleshov. Komarov was offered a job by Mezhrabpom. Boris Barnet collaborated with Otsep on the scenario of a serial adventure comedy written by Marietta Shaginyan (her pseudonym, 'Jim Dollar'!), *Miss Mend*, and he adapted the Kuleshov method so well to the familiar material that he was off to a good start in Soviet films. Leonid Obolensky also accepted two comedies (both with the titles of popular songs—*Kirpichiki* and *Ekh, Yablochko*)—with which his more pedantic personality did its merely satisfactory best. All these scattered jobs were signs of the Collective's demise, and Goskino considered dropping Kuleshov and the remnant of his group still attached to him. Criticism of *The Death Ray* still rankled, and in an economy drive then in progress Goskino, after keeping them waiting for a year and a half and rejecting their scenario, *Pavel I*, told Kuleshov that they were giving the group a third and last chance.

Kuleshov and his literary adviser, Victor Shklovsky, sought a subject that would offer an opportunity for a serious experiment but would require a minimum of expense. It had to be done cheaply and quickly—with few actors, few sets, and no sumptuous costumes. A cast of three characters offered the cheapest dramatic possibilities, but there had to be some natural reason for isolating the three: they had to be in a desert,† or snow-bound, or flood-bound, making the unsalaried elements play rôles. They chose Jack London's grim Alaskan story, 'The Unexpected', in which three people, joined by murder, are isolated from civilization by winter storms and spring floods. The Alaskan atmosphere was understandably of less importance to Kuleshov than the essential drama of Jack London's story. Although the finished film shows faithful respect for the idea of

* Aleinikov, op. cit.; typical of the comment that upset Pudovkin is Shklovsky's devastating 'centaur' remark, published in *Poetics of Cinema* (1927): '*Mother* is a peculiar sort of centaur, altogether a centaur—the queer animal starts out as prose with expository subtitles that get in the way of the images, and ends up as absolutely formal poetry.'

† In a similar fix this year, this was Protazanov's choice—for *The Forty-First*.

London, its visualization seems to us peculiarly Russian. Incidentally, Shklovsky has told how he drew one of the added episodes—the birthday party—from a scene in Dostoyevsky. The writing team finished the adaptation and shooting-script in one night and submitted it to the studio, which rejected its subject and its proposed heroine, Alexandra Khokhlova, as 'not attractive enough'. These obstacles were overcome by placing the production in the category of an 'experiment', on a restricted budget. *By the Law* was filmed precisely according to the scenario with only one omission: at the start an Indian was to have been shown executed for some infringement of the law, to show rigid adherence to the law.

Only one interior set was built, in the courtyard of the studio. Three actors, Khokhlova, Komarov, and Fogel, were put on salary; the other two smaller rôles were filled by Galadzhev and Podobed, former members of the Workshop, who helped out by taking time off from their regular jobs. As the studio had assigned Alexander Levitsky to photograph another film, he supervised a younger camera-man, Konstantin Kuznetsov. Evenings were used for rehearsals of the action and camera set-ups for the next morning's shooting, a great economy of time and raw film. *By the Law* is still the least expensive feature film ever produced in Russia.

When released (December 2, 1926) and exported, the studio was amazed at its reception by critical opinion abroad.* The absence of all orthodox film devices (no hero, no villain, no variety of locale, no parallel action, etc.) surprised and attracted advance-guard film-goers, much as the early Thomas Ince-William Hart films had excited perceptive Parisians. Above all, its physiological tension was unique on European screens. A record of its unusual effect is provided by H.D.'s review in *Close Up* (May 1928), communicating the sensations of catalepsy and hysteria she experienced on seeing it in a little Lausanne cinema. It is interesting that no effort was made to analyse the experience or understand the technique that produced it, although its influence on foreign film-making can, perhaps, be detected in Carl Dreyer's *Passion de Jeanne d'Arc* (1928).

Tretyakov comes close to the means by which the film's intensity was achieved: '*By the Law* was worked out in the spirit of an algebraic formula, seeking to obtain the maximum of effect with the minimum of effort.' The mathematical precision of every gesture and movement contributes to the total effect of each character and episode. Kuleshov taught his workshop that the hands, arms and legs are the most expressive parts of the film actor's body and we can observe that their movements create as much of the film's tension as does the facial expression. The same intensity of 'performance' by Khokhlova and Fogel that amazed critics only proved how correct was Kuleshov's avoidance of 'performance'. Even Shklovsky, who had worked in all stages of the film's preparation, confessed, 'Kuleshov made more out of the film than I expected.' To paraphrase Edmund Wilson's estimate of Turgenev, Kuleshov in one film had perfected 'the modern art of implying social criticism through a narrative that is presented objectively, organized economically, and beautifully polished in style'.[31a]

The unexpected quality of the film did not resolve Kuleshov's lifelong battle

* Well known in English film-criticism under many titles—*Expiation, Sühne, Dura Lex—By the Law* was not shown in any English-speaking country until 1939.

with hampering 'tradition', but the appearance of *By the Law* seems to coincide with a sort of truce between innovators and traditionalists. From now on they had too much respect for each other's problems and accomplishments to continue their rather fruitless bickering or to encourage Vertov—whose personal campaign showed no sign of truce.

One of the 'masters of repertory' (the polite term for traditionalists) was Yuri Tarich who, after his move from scenarist* to director in 1925, directed ten silent films, nearly all of them vigorous period pieces that took little notice of any basic change going on in the art of Russian films, for there was always a steady market in and out of the Soviet Union for efficiently told tales of the Russian past. The best of these was the first film that Tarich directed independently, released November 16, 1926, *Wings of a Serf* (shown abroad as *Ivan the Terrible*), a drama of the time of Ivan IV: the unhappy fate of a serf who is so unwisely clever as to invent an apparatus for flying through the air. Yet when this story leaves the memory, what stays is the extraordinary portrait of Ivan, as played by Leonid Leonidov. Of his place in the film, shrewd Shklovsky, who worked on this script, had this comment:

'In the case of *Wings of a Serf*, a film made conscientiously and, I suppose, with archaeological exactitude, talented Tarich did not realize what richer material he had at hand in the face of Leonidov; the director's hands were busy with all sorts of things, while Leonidov was left at the side.'[32]

Another factor in the lasting quality of the film may lie in the composition of the crew. One of Tarich's assistants was Ivan Pyriev, who was not to ripen as director until the sound period; and the film was cut by Esther Shub, who was to show a new form of film—*her* quiet invention—in the following year.

One new director startled the Soviet film world with three original and conspicuously successful films, all made between the summer of 1925 and the winter of 1926. Abram Room's film career had begun in 1924, but his modest films of that year had prepared no one (but himself) for the excitement and melodrama of *Death Bay* and *Traitor*, or even less, for the completely fresh 'chamber-work', *Third Meshchanskaya*, more familiar to the world as *Bed and Sofa*.† Within this same period Room taught at GTK, where he had his own workshop. This turned out to be the most productive period of his entire career. Room had worked in amateur theatres since 1914, including his three years (1915-17) at the Leningrad Institute of Psycho-Neurology, where he had directed the student theatre. After the October Revolution he had worked in Saratov with Bauer's communist assistant, Bassaligo. His last provincial work, in a children's theatre, was ended in the summer of 1923 by an invitation from Meyerhold to work in the Theatre of the Revolution, on the staging of Faiko's *Lake Lul*. From Meyerhold to cinema was but a step, quickly taken by Room.

In *Film Problems of Soviet Russia* Bryher gives a detailed summary of the action

---

* The scripts of Tarich were directed by three of the anti-innovators: Razumni, Sabinsky, Mur.

† It was the Berlin distributors of Soviet silent films that were responsible for this and other altered titles that became familiar abroad: *Ten Days that Shook the World*, *Storm Over Asia*, *Village of Sin*, *The Yellow Pass*, etc.

of *Death Bay* that is almost as direct and sharp as the film itself. It is a melodrama, but one played by credible people (except for some villain-grotesques), with psychologically justified behaviour and motives. But, she concludes, it is 'perhaps a succession of flashes, of great but loosely-knit moments rather than one coherent film; the drive of the idea loses impetus between moments. . . '. The story, by Lev Nikulin and Victor Shklovsky, of Room's next film, *Traitor*, follows the tracing and exposure of a tsarist police provocateur who had been responsible for wiping out a pre-revolutionary circle of Bolshevik sailors.

Room's next film, the film by which he will always be remembered, was a masterpiece of intimate relations, minutely observed. Many good people collaborated on *Third Meshchanskaya* (*Bed and Sofa*)—the scenarist Shklovsky, Room's assistant and designer, Yutkevich, the cameraman Giber, the excellent cast of three: Semyonova, Batalov, Fogel—but history must give the chief credit for the result to Abram Room, despite the absence of comparable films by him before or after *Bed and Sofa*. Bryher's synopsis of the 'plot' of *Bed and Sofa* is unusually helpful in pointing to its crowded implications in every glance and gesture. The film begins:

'It opens in a room: a quite familiar room, not completely of the slums, but too crowded with things to be comfortable. Moscow, we are reminded, suffers from a housing shortage. A husband and wife are in bed together. It is morning. A cat stirs them. The husband (Nikolai Batalov) snatches it up, he is young but settled, seeing his wife now as something stable like the chair, not as something alive and full of movement like the animal. And the wife (played by Ludmila Semyonova) is aware of this. She is brooding and resentful. Bored with the constant nagging succession of household duties, cooking in the tiny room, keeping it clean when so encumbered and having nowhere to put her clothes. Hundreds of daily trifles that prickle like pins. The husband rushes out to his work on a building high above Moscow. There are trams in the distance and a sense of work and space.

'A printer (Vladimir Fogel) sits on a train coming towards Moscow. His bundle of belongings is beside him. Work is easily got, they say, but they cannot give him a room . . . until he gets tired and his bundle heavy, he wanders about, asking for a room without result, but examining everything with interest. Suddenly he and the husband meet; they used to know each other. "No room, but we have a sofa", the husband says. So there are to be three now in the tiny room that has scarcely been wide enough for himself, his wife and the cat.'[33]

The wife is naturally resentful of this intrusion, another symptom of her husband's lack of regard for her and for their relationship. The printer, more sensitive, tries to make up for his invasion with assistance and gifts. The husband is called away from Moscow, the printer wishes to leave, but the husband won't hear of it. As Bryher says, 'the inevitable happens', and when the husband returns the wife is so changed that it is clear to him what has happened. He leaves, looking for another room, unsuccessfully; when it rains, he goes back to their room for his coat, and his wife, pityingly, suggests that he stay—on the sofa. Room gets the most out of the subsequent involvements until the wife realizes she is pregnant, without being sure which is the father. Though she goes for an abortion, she changes her mind and, instead, leaves both men without a woman to 'wash and cook for them'.

Even without an opportunity to see this film, the reader may judge what a delicately balanced combination of comedy and drama it is built upon. And how rarely such a combination works! Such material, and in such realistic surroundings, has no comparable sequel in Soviet films, or elsewhere, for that matter. Soviet critics and historians have taken little pride in this offshoot of Soviet film tradition, and its contemporary reception was one of resentment rather than of satisfaction. In writing of Room's 'enemies', Tretyakov gave this reason for their bitter antagonism:

'Room works with many realistic objects, and his realism is all to the good, because with its anti-aesthetic effect, he routs the canonized formulas of movie romance out of their fortified positions. . . .

'In his film [*Bed and Sofa*] not one of the men or women is handsome or beautiful. Woman is not even romantically displayed, and Love no longer has the look of a courtesan with polished, powdered skin, but more like a tired washerwoman with a grey, sad face—which is what love is in most cases.'[34]

After one more realistic film Room seems to have experienced some revulsion against that style, for thereafter he indulged in extremely handsome, almost stylized film-manners. Sad to say, his positive contribution to the Soviet film ended a little more than two years after it began. His fate almost makes one take seriously the doctrine of 'formalism as artistic poison'—but I have always wondered how much help was offered him in his dilemma. Room's last realistic film, *Ruts* (released January 10, 1928), attacked a psychological problem as serious as that in *Bed and Sofa*—how a marriage can be broken by the difficulties that a new child brings into a home.

Slower to start and longer and more valuable to stay was the steadily growing contribution of Friedrich Ermler. The little boy who ran errands for a pharmacist and organized the other children of the neighbourhood to act out his filmscripts in the back-yard, was at last prepared to put his dreams and hopes on celluloid. His days as bit player (in Viskovsky's *Red Partisans*) and student of the Leningrad Film Technicum ended with a clear position of his future 'fundamentalist' approach to realism. Being the only communist among the students led him to take a position for 'revolutionary content' as against 'revolutionary form', then being noisily declared by the FEX group. To oppose this emphasis on outer effects Ermler organized KEM (Experimental Film Workshop) among the students; the group planned and staged films without film-stock. On graduating from Technicum he and another beginner-director, Edward Johanson, proceeded to put their principles on film. Their first jointly directed film was *Children of Storm* (released August 17, 1926), on the rôle played by young communists in the defence of Petrograd during the Civil War; the adventures of one Komsomol group captured by the White Guards, and of another group endeavouring to rescue them, kept the film moving, but with no especial revelation of character. The two young men were still learning their craft. Their next effort was more memorable, more quiet in tone, and closer in spirit to Ermler's mature work, still to come. *Katka's Reinette Apples* concerned a girl, Katka, who comes to Petrograd in the first days of NEP to find work, is reduced to selling apples on the street, where she encounters the underworld of the city. She is seduced, cheated, deserted, before she meets a gentle protector, Fyodor. In this rôle Fyodor Nikitin played the first of his touching series of atypical characters in Ermler films.

On November 7, 1926, there was an instructive summing-up in Leningrad. For this ninth anniversary day more than seventy Soviet films were exhibited in the city's cinemas and clubs.

This was the first period when the export of Soviet films became a secure factor in their continuance, as well as in their growing world prestige. The days when *Polikushka* or *Kombrig Ivanov* would be sold to any passing purchaser were over. After March 1925, when Sovkino took over the business systematically, a world market was aimed at, and by now the whole world, including those countries where the censorship was frightened and unchecked, wanted to see these new films. The list on page 218 is intended to show films exported during 1925 and 1926[35] would not, of course, show private or purely political screenings. This may explain why Vertov's films are missing altogether. There may also be inaccuracies in this list.

National studios were still contributing little, either to Soviet theatres, or to Soviet exports. Many new nationalities were coming to film life at this time, or at least showing signs of life. Though first films are pleasant to note, they are usually better left undusted. Yet *The Starving Steppe Revives* deserves mention, not only as the first Uzbek film (released in March 1925), but as one of the rare Soviet films made by an amateur, in this case, one N. Shcherbakov. In January the Azerbaidjan studio began work, and in September, the first Chuvash film was started, *Volga Rebels*. One of the most productive of the national studios, in Byelorussia, was not initiated until 1927, when their first film, *Prostitute*, was released. The two oldest nationality studios, in Georgia and the Ukraine, were soon to show mature and characteristic work.

In the Ukraine film-literature advanced more boldly than film-production. In December 1925, the Kharkov studio of VUFKU began a monthly magazine, *Kino*, that in any country at that time would certainly have been labelled *avant-garde*, aesthetically and politically. Not only were foreign films reported, but film-experiments, too, in Germany and France; and the experimenters themselves were sometimes its foreign correspondents; Eugene Deslaw reported regularly from Paris. The autobiography of George Grosz ran serially, and German-trained portraits by a young Ukrainian, Dovzhenko, were reproduced in colour. When Léon Moussinac visited Kharkov, he had difficulty asking questions, for most of the time was taken by the questions asked him, chiefly about the films of Clair, Cavalcanti, Epstein, Dulac, Man Ray, and Léger. Though the artistic tendency at VUFKU remained stodgy (in the spring of 1926, the twentieth anniversary of Chardynin's film activity was celebrated with the release of his biggest and most easily forgotten VUFKU film, *Ukrazia*), it is comforting to look ahead to see VUFKU taking greater chances on unknown artists and peculiar projects than any other Soviet studio was then willing to underwrite.

FILMS EXPORTED (TO FEBRUARY 15, 1927) IN THE ORDER
OF THEIR DOMESTIC RELEASE.

	Germany	Poland	Latvia	Lithuania	Estonia	Finland	France	Belgium	Switzerland	Austria	Hungary	Czechoslovakia	Sweden	Norway	Denmark	Holland	Rumania	Britain	Greece	Bulgaria	Yugoslavia	Japan	China	bloc of Latin American [countries]
Red Imps																							×	
Morozko	×	×	×	×	×	×				×	×				×			×						
Aelita	×	×	×	×	×	×				×	×	×			×									×
Cigarette-Girl of Mosselprom	×	×	×	×	×																			
Palace and Fortress		×										×												
Strike	×										×													
Station Master	×	×	×	×	×	×	×	×	×	×	×	×					×	×	×	×	×	×		×
Cross and Mauser																	×							
Jewish Luck			×	×	×						×												×	
Ninth of January	×	×	×	×	×					×		×												×
Battleship Potemkin	×	×	×	×	×	×	×	×	×	×	×	×	×	×	×	×	×		×	×	×			
Wedding of the Bear	×	×	×	×	×	×				×	×		×	×	×			×	×	×	×			×
Death Bay	×								×	×														×
Abrek-Zaur	×	×	×	×	×					×	×	×												×
The Cloak												×												
Mother	×	×	×	×	×	×					×													
Wings of a Serf	×		×	×	×	×	×		×	×	×				×									×
By the Law												×												

One of the young directors given his first opportunity by VUFKU was Nikolai Okhlopkov, whose entrance to films had been as an actor in Room's *Death Bay* and *Traitor*.* His basic training had been in Meyerhold's classes in bio-mechanics, and in his first film interview Okhlopkov took occasion to bewail the absence in film the solid training that Meyerhold, Stanislavsky and Vakhtangov had provided his generation of theatre personnel. Erdmann, the playwright whose *Mandate* Meyerhold had staged recently with great success, wrote Okhlopkov's first

* He was also to have had Fogel's rôle in Room's *Bed and Sofa*.

scenario, a comedy, *Mitya*, and stayed with the filming in Odessa—not a customary procedure. Obviously the two young artists worked well together on *Mitya*:

'Actors always blame the director. This is easy and fair. In this I am both acting and directing—not so easy and not so fair. Erdmann wrote a tragedy about people whose pictures happen to be side by side in the show-window of a provincial photographer. There's nothing funny about Mitya [a telephone mechanic], except that the GPU mistakes him for Glupishkin [André Deed]. I'm still learning about films. I fully understand Erdmann's wishes and aims—but it's one thing to understand and quite another, to do. I can't say more about this until the work is finished. Work is based on: actor plus object plus costume plus elements of the milieu, meaning the director. The quarrel among actor, director, dramatist, is insoluble. The acting method used is —'slight'. I do not declaim this as the only true principle—it's simply my method of work. No engineers here. No defined terminology, not even an undefined one.'[36]

Another of the modestly entering directors in 1926 changed the nature and scope of the medium he walked into. And Alexander Dovzhenko did just that, walk into films, after a decision as sudden and intense as a typical moment in his films:

'Before I began to work in films in 1926, I had been a painter. I was not yet a master of my craft, but felt fairly confident that in another ten or twelve years I might be. At that time, however, the leftist papers and periodicals carried articles on the uselessness of painting and its expected demise as an art, and these led me to reflect on my chosen profession.

'In June of 1926, after a sleepless night of examining my accomplishments up till that time, I left my Kharkov apartment and my painting materials behind, took my stick and suitcase [containing a copy of Rolland's *Colas Breugnon*], and started for Odessa, where I joined a cinema studio. I stood on the shore of the Black Sea like a naked man, thirty-two years old, starting life from the beginning again. The cinema, I thought, was the one art which was fresh and new, with enormous creative potentialities and opportunities. I knew little about it—indeed, I very rarely saw films. I may have been mistaken about painting, but I was quite right about the part that film would play in our Soviet life.'[37]

If anyone at the Odessa studio of VUFKU guessed that a genius had walked in, it must have been entirely on the strength of Dovzhenko's commanding personality; surely his first two efforts in films gave little hint of the power to come. His first job must have been accepted and filmed immediately, for the film made from his script of *Vasya the Reformer* was released July 17, 1926, only a few weeks after his arrival. It is also possible that he was given the job of doctoring an earlier script for this mild social comedy (about an adventurous boy), whose production might even have begun before the new writer was hired. The only facts about the film that now seem significant are that Dovzhenko had a taste of film—and stayed—and that the cameraman for his script, Demutsky, was to be associated with his greatest work. Dovzhenko's next script was a short slapstick comedy, *Love's Berries*, written in three days and directed by himself. A year and a half later, after Dovzhenko had made a film at last manifesting characteristics of himself, he wrote an autobiographical sketch that should be quoted in full:

'I was born in 1894, for which I still grieve. I should have been born in 1904—I would be ten years younger!

'In Sosnitsa, in the province of Chernigov.

'My parents were unlettered, farm folk, middle-class.

'My education: public school, secondary, teachers' institute, four years' training in physics, natural science, athletics. And then the university, one and a half years of biology, three years at the Commercial Institute where, between terms, I switched from economics to technology, and then back again, till I came to my senses and had done with the whole of it.

'Chased the Poles out of Kiev. Took part in the organization of the Kiev section of the People's Commissariat of Education, and for a long time was secretary to the Collegium and directed the city branch. At the same time I worked as a member of the Kiev Administration of People's Education.

'In 1921 I was transferred to the People's Commissariat for the renovation of Kharkov. From here I went abroad, working in Soviet embassies.

'Worked for the Ambassador in Poland and as Secretary at the Berlin Consulate. I left to study painting with Professor [Erich] Heckel.

'Came back to Kharkov at the end of 1923. Worked on newspapers and other periodicals as an artist.

'Well, and then—VUFKU.'[38]

As the world's praise of *Potemkin* swelled, it became difficult for Goskino to agree on a subject worthy of the twenty-eight-year-old director who was now acclaimed as the most important of the Soviet film's assets. One project was pursued for a half-year by Tretyakov, who returned to Russia from revolutionary China in the autumn of 1925, and was now determined to return there with a film-crew headed by Eisenstein:

'It is possible that to send such a film-expedition would have meant taking several risks, for there was the possibility that the Chinese revolutionary movement could take a sudden turn, even reversing itself. But I considered that such a risk should be taken. I was so determined to have modern China (not its past) filmed, and absolutely as it is, that we came very close to a realization of this project. This was my chief reason for sharing, with S. M. Eisenstein and with the administration of the First Goskino Studio (where I worked with L. M. Karakhan), the wish to go to China. Unfortunately, neither in 1925, nor in the first half of 1926, could these intentions be carried out.'[39]

A year later Eisenstein explained the situation to Joseph Freeman:

' "When I finished *Potemkin*, the Russian cinema faced two burning questions: events in China and the development of the Soviet village. The Chinese workers and peasants are going through a life-and-death struggle for freedom. There is a profound need for the fighting film. Concrete agitational material is needed in China itself. Perhaps for the first time in history, the film has become as terrible a weapon as the hand grenade. . . ."

'Eisenstein went on to explain how he planned a gigantic Chinese film in three parts, but had to give it up for technical reasons. There remained the theme of the Soviet village. . . .'[40]

By the summer of 1926, the Eisenstein group and the studio (now Sovkino) had agreed on the subject of their next film—nothing less than the Communist Party's policy on the collectivization of Soviet agriculture. The film was to be called *The General Line*. But it was in production only a few months before the group was hurriedly transferred to a more urgent subject, a film to celebrate the tenth anniversary of the October Revolution, to be ready for screening on November 7, 1927.

'Project of a monument to Dziga Vertov'
a cartoon by Lavinsky, in *Sovietsky Ekran*, January 1927

CHAPTER XI

Anniversary Year

1927

> . . . a work of historical fiction is much more a docu-
> ment on its own time than on the time portrayed
>
> T. S. ELIOT

Vsevolod Pudovkin began work on his film for the October Jubilee while *Mother* was still in production. The idea for the film came from a suggestion by Golovnya, who had just read Pushkin's *Bronze Horseman*, and had seen the quantity of sketches and drawings of old St Petersburg made by Alexander Benois in pre- paring an illustrated edition of the poem. Golovnya proposed a film that would cover two centuries of St Petersburg's history, through the years of Petrograd up to Leningrad; Pudovkin was immediately enthusiastic, seized upon the idea as a jubilee film that offered the scope and epic quality of *Potemkin*, and started Zarkhi to work on a script that would embody Golovnya's vision. During the last weeks of work on *Mother*, Zarkhi sought a dramatic form to show the birth and history of the great city; Pudovkin saw in the grandiose scale of this idea an oppor- tunity to escape from the dependence on skilled, theatrically trained actors, for which his *Mother* was being criticized even before it was seen. Even while Zarkhi sought a shape for his scenario, Pudovkin delighted in planning the quantity of vivid small rôles—especially of figures of nineteenth-century revolu- tionary activity, bomb-throwing terrorists, self-sacrificing teachers of workers' circles—that would relieve his need for such dramatic, continuing images as Pavel and his mother in *Mother*.

But Zarkhi was defeated by the breadth of two centuries,* was forced to reduce the time covered to 'our times', and gave Pudovkin a script entitled *Petersburg, Petrograd, Leningrad* that demanded sustained drama—and actors. This first script, with which they began to work as soon as *Mother* was cut and released, approximately corresponds with the material in the first four reels of the finished film, ending with the peasant boy's attack on the steel magnate, Lebedev. But Pudovkin's original wishes and needs also found an outlet in the dramatic structure of the revised idea; *The End of St Petersburg* became the most deliberately symbolistic of Pudovkin's films, and the influence of Alexander

---

* At Eisenstein's request Zarkhi returned to this problem in 1933, when they planned a similar film on the history of Moscow.

Blok's poetry and of Andrei Byely's novel, *Petersburg*, can still be detected in this rich film.

Before the film was shown to the jubilee audience in November, its scenario was to undergo many and hasty alterations. Shooting even began without a final script, and while Pudovkin and Zarkhi struggled to get their ideas on to paper, Doller was sent off to the country to film the first sequence of the peasant family who are forced, by hunger, death, and the arrival of a new mouth to feed, to send a young widowed son to find work in St Petersburg. Doller had also found the actor for the film's central figure of the peasant lad—Ivan Chuvelov, then acting in the theatre, though his stolid peasant portrait gives the impression of a non-professional playing himself, a triumph for his director as much as for him. Chistyakov and Baranovskaya played the other chief rôles of a worker and his wife, in politically conscious characterizations diametrically opposite to their portrayals in *Mother*. After completing the country exteriors all other location work was done in Leningrad, where the actual place of the two revolutions of 1917 was to affect the structure of *The End of St Petersburg* almost as much as the Odessa steps affected *Potemkin*.

By early spring of the anniversary year all the other films planned for the celebration were under way. Mezhrabpom's other large project, *Moscow in October*, was assigned to Boris Barnet, then completing his first lively and success-ful comedy, seasoned with satirical situations and 'bourgeois left-overs', *The Girl with the Hat-Box*. It was probably with relief that Barnet returned to comedies after his jubilee task was done. Even the newly-born Belgoskino had an anniversary film under way, an undistinguished long cartoon, written by G. M. Boltyansky, *October and the Bourgeois World*. Sovkino's biggest display was to be *October*, for which they ordered the Eisenstein group away from *The General Line*.

'Eisenstein and Tisse are to begin work January 1st on filming a grandiose jubilee film. The film will be in production nine months and will include: pre-parations for October, October at the centre [Petrograd] and other places, and episodes of the civil war.'

This announcement, in the newspaper, *Kino*, on November 6, 1926,* hints at so broad a scope for the project that it is not surprising that work on the scenario consumed the first three months of the tight schedule. The absence of Alex-androv's name from the announcement may be explained by the short-lived hope that Alexandrov could continue work on *The General Line*. He was soon rushed into the *October* project as co-author and co-director. The first scenes of *October* were filmed on April 13, 1927—for the sequence of fraternization between Russian and German soldiers, with Tisse playing his only film rôle, a benevolent German officer.

A modest but extremely important October anniversary project could not begin until Esther Shub had completed her film for the anniversary of the February Revolution—*Fall of the Romanov Dynasty*—but as both her anniversary

---

* The same newspaper, five weeks later, announced another project for Eisenstein! This was Tretyakov's scenario, *Five Minutes*, about a strike on a foreign ship at the time of Lenin's death. 'Filming will take place at Moscow, Leningrad, on board ship, and at sea.'

films required the examination of old newsreel footage, it is possible that *The Great Road* (working title: *10 Years*) was simultaneously prepared. Both films were made by Sovkino in co-operation with the Museum of the Revolution, where the responsibility had been given of preserving film materials of documentary importance. Newsreels that had been filmed with as little thought of permanent value as is put into a daily newspaper were to be given by Shub the dramatic shape of historical chronicles.

'But to get a chance to put this idea into practical actuality was not so easy. It was long before the Sovkino administration would consent to approve my application to make such a film on the tenth anniversary of the February Revolution, and it was not until August 1926 that I began work on my first independent large work—*Fall of the Romanov Dynasty*. . . .

'This and my following two films filled three years with the joy of searching, finding, "opening" historical film-documents—but not in film-libraries or archives, for there were no such things then. In the damp cellars of Goskino, in "Kino Moskva", in the Museum of the Revolution lay boxes of negatives and random prints, and no one knew how they had got there.'[1]

More sensitively than Vertov and more carefully than any newsreel editor in the world, Esther Shub examined the whole archive of preserved newsreels, frame by frame, finding the implications and connectives in each shot that only a skilful editor is trained to do. Trained primarily in the editing of 200 foreign fictional films and ten Russian films,[2] Shub gave the newsreel a new dimension when, in *Fall of the Romanov Dynasty*, she brought back to life, or brought newly to an artistic, dramatic life, footage that had hitherto been regarded as having, at the most, only the nature of historical fragments. By the juxtaposition of these 'bits of reality', she was able to achieve effects of irony, absurdity, pathos, and grandeur that few of the bits had intrinsically. The *Romanov* film drew upon the quantity of private as well as public film chronicles[3] of the imperial family and their activities, to add to Shub's reconstruction of the events leading to the overthrow of the dynasty in February 1917.

For *The Great Road*, her October anniversary film, Shub combed all the newsreels made in the past ten years, beginning with the footage made of the Revolution itself by the former cameramen of the Skobelev Committee. The Museum of the Revolution did not solve all her needs, for that institution's collection tapered off at the end of the Civil War. And then Shub encountered a problem that has made trouble for all historians—the neglect of documents related to the recent past. She found that newsreels of recent years had not been systematically filed; they were scattered, left to disintegrate, and it was rarely possible to determine when or where a particular shot had been made. After looking over 250,000 metres of old newsreel footage, Shub concluded:

'After 1921-22 the trouble worsened. From that date newsreels were shot without much plan, and quickly put aside with little comprehension of their historic value, which of course increased with each passing year. Even worse is their change of tone after the Civil War; suddenly the concentration was chiefly on parades, meetings, arrivals, departures, delegates, and such—and almost no record was kept of how we transformed the country to a new political economy—or of the resulting construction.'[4]

Her surest help came from the cameramen who had filmed the newsreels, and she often applied to Novitsky, to Tisse, to Giber, for needed information on date and place. She was able to bring together shots, from several sources, that had been filmed on a significant occasion, such as the funeral of the twenty-six Baku commissars. She found some lists but these were often discouraging, as they sometimes indicated only what *had* been, before the damp and other enemies had eaten into it. One list showed that a large quantity of early Soviet newsreel material had been sent to the United States, in gratitude for the work of the American Relief Association. She followed this, conscientious researcher as she was, found that it had been given away or sold to commercial companies—and she followed *those*, too, with deserved rewards:

'I'll always remember one day. On my recommendation some negatives had been purchased from America, through Amtorg, for $6,000. In this lot I found material of the imperialist war, of the funeral of victims of the February Revolution, and—six completely unfamiliar shots of Lenin. Soviet audiences saw these intimate scenes* of Lenin for the first time in *The Great Road*.'[5]

An important conflict in Russian history to receive almost as much attention this year as the October Revolution was the Decembrist revolt of 1825 in St Petersburg. Two large-scale films on this event appeared this year—*The Decembrists*, directed by Ivanovsky; and *S.V.D. (The Club of the Big Deed)*, written by Tinyanov and Oxman for Kozintsev and Trauberg. Both films subordinated the drama of underground conspiracy to the handsomeness of the period's architecture and costume. Even in this common weakness they make an interesting comparison: the Ivanovsky film's use of all the traditional methods of performance and photography and design—opposed to the FEX group's assimilation of their increasingly relaxed stylization with the lessons avidly learned from the sombre, shadowed contemporary German film. The photography of Ivan Frolov in *The Decembrists* seemed pale and timid beside the bold shadows and high-lights of Andrei Moskvin's photography of *S. V. D. (The Club of the Big Deed)*. Perhaps the FEX group aimed to beat the traditionalists at their own game; for work by admirers of Eisenstein, it is impossible to realize, on seeing *S. V. D.*, that its makers had ever seen *Potemkin*. St Petersburg-Leningrad, as the identical setting for so many of this year's films, now provides an interesting basis for comparing the artistic viewpoints of several Soviet film-makers. How widely different the same city looks, as shown us by the FEX group in *The Cloak* and *S. V. D.*, and as shown in *The End of St Petersburg* and, even further away stylistically, in *October*.

Nineteen hundred and twenty-seven was a good year for Soviet film-literature, by now appearing on many levels, from the popular to the theoretical. In Paris the first detailed, documented history of the Soviet period appeared in a series, *L'Art dans la Russie Nouvelle: Le Cinéma*, by René Marchand and Pyotr Weinstein,

---

* Filmed in 1920, at the time of an interview given to a correspondent of the New York *World*.

with a preface by Henri Barbusse, who was growing more interested in the medium's possibilities. The only misleading 'tendency' in this short history comes from the fact that one of the authors, having worked close to the Leningrad studios, felt obliged to picture the Leningrad film-makers as heroic victims of a bullying Moscow power in the first Soviet years (though a rivalry between the two cities' film industries has always existed). A first Soviet history came out in September—B. S. Likhachov's *Film in Russia* (1896-1926), but unfortunately the reliable first volume, concluding in 1913, was never followed by the other announced volumes, a strange disease that was also to cut later Soviet film histories short. Likhachov's publisher, Academia, had previously issued a translation of Léon Moussinac's handy international history, *Naissance du Cinéma*. In theory and criticism much of importance appeared, supported by the excellent periodical, *Sovietskoye Kino*, begun in 1926. Some of the most stimulating writing, often in the form of journalism, came from Victor Shklovsky, a writer intimate with film-work and film-people. His two brief books, *Rewind* ('a booklet *not* for cinematographers') and *Their Realities*, on the work of Kuleshov, Eisenstein and Vertov, are both models of intelligent writing about films; neither, unhappily, ever appeared outside Russia. An important anthology, edited by Boris Eichenbaum, was *Poetics of the Cinema*.

At the base of all this film-literature was, of course, the strikingly articulate writing by the film-makers themselves, a contrast to the general silence of the other large body of film-makers, in Hollywood, where the taboo on open discussion of film problems is rarely broken. The Pudovkin manuals were followed by a quantity of articles and interviews;[6] Eisenstein's ideas were already to be found in print as well as on the screen, but his basic theoretical writing was to come later, in his teaching period. There is, in fact, no Soviet director of importance, who has not spoken and written frankly about his work—a fact that I have often blessed in preparing this history of a developing art. Frankness in print sometimes was turned against the authors by the seekers of dangerous unorthodoxies, but that does not appear to have stemmed this tide, at any time, of revealing words.

Symptomatic of the Soviet film administrators' increasing distrust of the unorthodox is the frustrating history of Vladimir Mayakovsky's efforts to turn his enormous enthusiasm for the film medium into actual films. Of all the film projects proposed in the last four years of his life, only two children's films were made, and these in a manner remote from the spirit of his scenarios.

The most persistent attempts to employ Mayakovsky in films came, not from Sovkino, but from VUFKU. On his tour of the south, lecturing about his trip to America, he visited the Jewish agricultural project being conducted in the Evpatoria District. At this time Abram Room was making a short film of the project, *The Jew on the Land*, and Mayakovsky offered to collaborate with Shklovsky on writing the subtitles for the film. (Some of the ideas in these titles can be found in his poem written at the same time, 'The Jew'.) And then, while in Yalta, in August 1926, Mayakovsky contracted with the local studio of VUFKU to write two films based on his observations of modern life in the Crimea: *Children*, about life in a Pioneer Camp (but with some ideas borrowed from an

O. Henry story, possibly 'The Ransom of Red Chief'), and a satirical comedy, *Elephant and Match*. After several revisions the children's film was finally made as *Three*—the satire was shelved. But before these unpleasantnesses, and while Mayakovsky and the VUFKU executives were on good terms, he signed a contract for two more scenarios: *Electrification*, and *The Heart of the Screen* (a revision of his 1918 scenario, *Shackled by Film*). Still extant is a script, with several alternative titles (*Two Epochs*, etc.), which may have been the first of these; neither was produced. In September 1926, Mayakovsky proposed a film (to be written with Osip Brik) for the tenth anniversary of the October Revolution, using the metaphor: Child = USSR:

' . . . a little story of two brothers (perhaps, sisters), chased from home by red bullets—one finds himself abroad, the other, who leaves his trousers hanging on a wall that he tries to climb over, stays willy-nilly in the USSR. In the subsequent history of the two brothers, for the first half of the film things get better for the foreign one, and worse for the one who stayed. The last half of the film reverses this. The story develops out of the foreign brother's efforts to get permission to rejoin his Soviet brother.

'Against this outline can be shown, vividly and realistically, our victories and struggles, leading to an apotheosis of the tenth anniversary.'[7]

This film was made, under the title of *Decembrists and Octobrists*, but there is little resemblance between the scenario and the childish, rather than children's, finished film, which added little lustre to the 1927 anniversary.

Mayakovsky's next scripts for VUFKU were left unproduced: *Story of a Revolver*, about decadent tendencies among the Komsomol membership; and *Down with Fat!* on 'psychological preparation for the defence of the USSR'. From the second script Mayakovsky salvaged only a character, whom he made the central figure in his play *The Bath*. His last script for VUFKU concerned English operations in Iranian oil-fields: he collaborated with V. Gorozhanin (who knew Iran) on *Engineer D'Arcy*.[7a] On December 17, 1926, Mayakovsky signed a contract with the film publishing house to print three of his scenarios, but he must have been too discouraged by his film failures to go through with it. His worst disappointment was caused by the script in which he placed his largest hopes, *How Do You Do?* written at the end of 1926.

Subtitled 'A Day in Five Film Details', the script of *How Do You Do?* was first submitted to the Moscow studio of Sovkino—with results that made Mayakovsky write his most trenchant film essay, 'Help!'[8]

'I wrote a scenario, "How Do You Do?"'

'This scenario was based on principles. Before writing it I asked myself a series of questions.

'*First question:* Why do foreign films beat ours, both generally and in artistic quality?

'*Answer:* Because the foreign film finds and uses special means that derive from film technique, and cannot be found in any other medium of expression. (The train in *Our Hospitality*, the transformation of Chaplin into a chicken in *The Gold Rush*, the lights of the moving train in *A Woman of Paris*.)

'*Second question:* Why must one defend the newsreel against the acted film ?

'*Answer:* Because the newsreel shows real things and facts.

'*Third question:* Why is it impossible to endure an hour of newsreel ?

'*Answer:* Because our newsreels are haphazard arrangements of shots and events. The newsreel must be organized and must organize itself. That sort of newsreel you could endure. Newpapers offer that sort of organization of events, and without newspapers you can't live. To reject such organization is no wiser than to propose the shut-down of *Izvestia* or *Pravda*.

'*Fourth question:* Why is *A Woman of Paris* so dazzling ?

'*Answer:* Because, in its organization of simple little facts, it achieves the greatest emotional saturation.

'The scenario of "How Do You Do ?" was planned as an answer to these questions about film language. . . .'

This introduction to Mayakovsky's article raises, today, many other questions, for one would never guess from it that *Potemkin* and *Mother* had already been made, or that Vertov had proposed and demonstrated any new organization of the 'newsreel'. Mayakovsky goes on to report that before submitting his script to Sovkino he consulted Kuleshov about whether it could be produced. Kuleshov replied, 'It can, it should, and it won't cost much.'

'As I hated to be parted from the new-born scenario I myself read it to the chief and literary department at Sovkino—Comrades Blyakhin, Shklovsky, and the departmental secretary. The reading went on over continuous amusement and laughter.

'After the reading.

'*Blyakhin:* Wonderful! It must be produced—no question of it! Of course there are unsuitable spots, but you could re-do those, of course.

'*Shklovsky:* I've read a thousand scenarios, but I've never seen one like this. It has the breath of fresh air. It opens windows.

'*Secretary:* Ditto.

'This brilliant response is matched by brilliant speed. Two days later I read the scenario to the Sovkino executives, including Shvedchikov, Trainin, Yefremov, and the secretary; from the first audience Comrades Blyakhin and Kuleshov.

'The assembly listened gloomily. Com. Yefremov rushed away (ill ?) at the beginning of the second part.

'Afterwards, discussion. I can only report the essence of this from my own notes; unfortunately no stenographic record was made of this proud occasion, inspiring the entertainment industry to new heights.

'*Com. Trainin:* I know of two types of scenario; one deals with the cosmos in general, the other—with man in the cosmos. The scenario we've heard conforms to neither type. To speak of it at once is difficult, but it seems clear that it passes the ideological test.

'*Com. Shvedchikov:* Art is a reflection of reality. This scenario does not reflect reality. We don't need it. Orientate yourself to *The Tailor from Torzhok*. This is an experiment, and we have to be self-supporting.

'*Com. Yefremov* (who came back as Trainin began his speech): Never in all my life have I heard such nonsense!
'*Com.* Secretary looked around the circle of executives and then took the floor:
'—The scenario will not be understood by the masses!
'*Com. Kuleshov* (while the discussion goes on): How can you talk with such people ? See what I mean ? After their speeches my head will ache for two weeks!
'The scenario is not accepted by Sovkino.'

Mayakovsky concludes this embarrassing record with several embarrassing queries: How can the choice of scenarios be the responsibility of people who know nothing about them ? How can artistic matters be decided by administrators ? How can the book-keeping department handle artists if artists are not allowed any voice in the book-keeping department ? If film-experiments cannot be made by the Sovkino monopoly, where can film-experimenters go ?

And Mayakovsky brought his queries out of the pages of *Novy Lef* into the open forum. When, in mid-October 1927, there was a discussion, organized by the Communist Party and the newspaper *Komsomolskaya Pravda*, on the failings of Sovkino, Mayakovsky was one of the last and most pointed speakers:

'Comrades, I did not, I'm sorry to say, hear the introductory report of Com. Blyakhin—(*Voice: Nothing to be sorry for.*) Sovkino is now being attacked from several directions. It's necessary to take up these directions separately, for they are now too interwoven with such questions as to whether the director of such-and-such a newspaper called on Shvedchikov, and whether Shvedchikov received him or threw him out—We shouldn't forget that we are discussing matters of cinematography. But we go on talking about Trainin, Blyakhin, Shvedchikov—Yet we should be sorry for such people. Why place them in positions for which they've had no training ? (*Applause*). . . . Each of us can only do all that he knows how, or understands. (*Applause*). . . . I don't reject the idea that at some time in the future Com. Trainin might issue good films, but that is now in the realm of experiment. . . . Here is organization without correct basis. We see financial organization, administrative apparatus, and everything else, starting to trade with nothing to trade. We do not have the merchandise and we won't have it, until the question of cinematic culture is settled. Take this very moment, for example, when in the Ukraine they don't show pictures made by Sovkino—but they have just now signed an agreement to show them. We should be sorry for the Ukraine. (*Applause*) "Mr Lloyd's Trip" will now travel even further. Of course, the Ukraine evens accounts—VUFKU sends us "Taras Trasilo". This is not Sovkino's exclusive problem, for there's little to distinguish it from our other cinema systems. I did several scenarios—just to begin at the ugliest end—and they were turned into films that I couldn't bear to see. . . . You submit a scenario, it's passed through Glavrepertkom, the scenario arrives at the factory, it's worked over and turned into a practical scenario, various hands get a try at it—and something emerges that you can't recognize . . . Sovkino films receive both praise and anger. Take "Poet and Tsar" for example. The picture is liked—but when you stop to think about it, what bosh, what a monstrosity. . . . Sovkino is a monopoly and it's bound to become even more of a monopoly—

so that if Sovkino won't encourage experiment, everything we've gained will fade away. They point to Eisenstein and to Shub to show you how mistaken your fears are. These directors are our cinematic pride, but they became that in spite of Sovkino. . . . They speak of Shub's triumph. Her art was in finding a completely unnoticed principle at the base of the film materials she uses: allowing her to edit real shots with no re-shooting. And what does Sovkino do? It refuses to give Shub author's rights. "You just select shots—anyone can do that."

'*Trainin*: It wasn't that way. . . .'

As for *How Do You Do*? Mayakovsky submitted the scenario to Mezhrabpom-Russ. There things seemed to be going well, with Kuleshov as director, and both Mayakovsky and Khokhlova assigned rôles, but the project was cancelled. Mayakovsky next tried the Leningrad studio of Sovkino, with a new comedy called *Forget the Hearthside*, a title borrowed from an old success with Vera Kholodnaya and Maximov. Kozintsev and Trauberg accepted it at once, announced that they would make it simultaneously with *New Babylon*; it was given to another director, and then shelved. Here, too, Mayakovsky salvaged something to use in a more familiar, less hedged medium—the scenario became the basis for his successful play, *The Bug*.

One of the greatest prose writers to emerge from the years of revolution made an equally persistent and equally blunted effort to work in films. Isaac Babel would have made the ideal scenarist for a film of the First Cavalry Army, except that Budyonny, heading that army, had made it clear that he despised Babel's stories of the Red Cavalry. Babel's first scenario, and his best known one, was an adaptation of motifs in another collection, his Odessa stories; *Benia Krik* was so fine a script that Eisenstein recommended it to Ivor Montagu for English translation,[8a] but so poor a film, directed by Vilner for VUFKU, that I have never found anyone who could tell me about it. Two more scripts for VUFKU were *Wandering Stars*, from a Sholom Aleichem story, and *Jimmy Higgins*, based on Upton Sinclair's novel of the American intervention. Babel wrote an original scenario, *Chinese Windmill*, for Sovkino, and his public film career was ended; two later scripts were for unreleased films, the last version of Eisenstein's *Bezhin Meadow*, and a documentary film of Odessa made by Jean Lods.

Whatever difficulties the Soviet cinema had in pacifying administrators versus artists, its social inventiveness and initiative were indubitable. The educational and 'cultural' film had never had such encouragement to show its usefulness. In February 1927, the first Moscow theatre to show culture-films exclusively was opened, and Leningrad opened a similar theatre in November. Wicksteed had nothing but praise for Moscow's

'. . . picture-house where they show nothing but definitely educational films. In this place the prices range from about fivepence to one and sixpence, and I think I am right in saying that members of Trade Unions are admitted at half-price. This is a most excellent institution, where you can see all the best educational films of the world; I myself saw the Everest film there. There is a regular afternoon performance for the benefit of children, who are admitted for a very small sum.'[9]

Similar concentrated work was done in the field of children's films. Tretyakov had published a frightening article,[10] prophesying what the children of 1926 would be like by 1940 if they continued to see the harmfully violent adult film fare on view in all theatres. He proposed special theatres to show a careful winnowing of all films available at all distributors, to choose those with appeal directly to children, from the works of Jules Verne and Mark Twain, or on subjects like *Robinson Crusoe*. Films intended only for child audiences were already produced in Soviet studios, but this section of cinema did not have a regular outlet or audience, like the popular children's stages in Moscow and Leningrad. But on October 10, 1927, the first children's film theatre was opened in Moscow, and the Soviet cinema had taken another social step in the right direction.

The film surprise of the anniversary year came from an artist self-trained in the specialized area of children's films. Olga Preobrazhenskaya had been a successful actress in the pre-revolutionary film—a 'star' in fact, featured in some of Protazanov's best early films, *Keys to Happiness* and *War and Peace*, among many other Russian films, and she had ventured to direct, as early as 1915. Believing that she, too, had learned something then about film-making, she asked for a trial in making modestly budgeted films for children. Her first three films were considered so good (notably *Kashtanka*, from Chekhov's story), that she was given a more ambitious film in 1927 that she turned into an international success.*

Bryher calls *Women of Ryazan* 'the most moral film I have ever seen'.[11] The tragic implications of this country tale of a father's desire for his son's bride would satisfy Eugene O'Neill, and the hopefulness of the social change suggested by the end was realistic enough to satisfy any viewing committee, yet 'utterly free from propaganda', as Bryher points out. The sophistication of its subject is not matched (perhaps fortunately) by any equivalent sophistication of film treatment. It is one of the best products of neat story-telling traditions from the pre-revolutionary film, depending entirely for its strength on a simple but careful plot (the scenario is by Vishnevskaya and Boris Altschuler) and credible performances. Whoever made the decision to soak the whole film in the folk traditions of the Ryazan district contributed a great deal to this best example of Russian rural exotica. The homely beauty and sense of open air, largely contributed by the clean photography of Konstantin Kuznetsov, is one element that was rare in the pre-revolutionary ancestors of this film.

The research for *October* was broader and more varied than that for *The General Line*, but less leisurely. The materials used, however, may have been more exciting. Esther Shub showed the group all her collected footage taken in Petrograd during the war and revolutions (a period, incidentally, of Eisenstein's own knowledge, as architecture student, of the city), and there were, of course, hundreds of news photographs to consult. One of these, taken by a news photographer from a roof-top looking down on the July demonstrators fired upon by

---

* Its profitable success at home was important; *Women of Ryazan* cost 46,000 roubles, and in 15 months returned 210,000 roubles. Compare with *Decembrists* that cost 340,000 roubles and in two years returned only 300,000 roubles. (Mikhailov, in *Sovietsky Ekran*, September 3, 1929).

Kerensky's soldiers, was so exactly duplicated in action and quality that Sigayev's still of this episode in *October* is as often reproduced as the news photo—*both* as the same historic document!*

Tisse's preparation for the work involved fresh problems. Thorold Dickinson gives some details:

'In *October* Tisse never hesitated to use light artificially to create dramatic effects without attempting to account for a realistic origin for the source of light. . . . Tisse strung up his lights all over the square for the attack on the Winter Palace, and he did so in a manner that would make a military tactician shudder. Thus works the artist who has graduated from the school of actuality. The camera artist brought up in the theatrical tradition of the film studio would probably have chosen to shoot these night scenes in daylight, using filters in front of his lenses. But he would have produced a much less harsh negative and a gentler effect. . . .'[12]

Some of Tisse's inventiveness would not have suited his announced photographic policy of 'utter simplicity' for *The General Line*,[13] and it is to the greater freedom of *October* that we can be grateful for such dramatic distortions as Nilsen (one of his assistants) analyses in his *Cinema as a Graphic Art:*

* Even before completion of *October* the Los Angeles *Times* reproduced another still from it, of the looting episode in the Winter Palace cellars, as evidence of 'continuing Bolshevik crimes'.

For this shot a sloping platform was constructed, up which the people pulled the cannon. Tisse modified the frame by tilting the camera sideways, so as to bring the sides of the frame into alignment with the angle of the slope—producing a graphic strain to match the physical strain shown.[14]

Golovnya, also, had opportunities for technical expansion on Pudovkin's jubilee film, but as most cameramen seem less articulate than most directors, his statement of this period has to be searched patiently for indications of this growth, which is, of course, far clearer on the screen. He begins with an argument that is as useless as determining who is responsible for a good portrait—the sitter or the painter:

'There are two attitudes to the function of the actor in films. The first is that he is the chief element, as in the star-system of American films, or the Russian-German psychological principle that builds a film around the photographic rendering of the actor's performance. The second attitude is that the actor is one of the elements that make up the composition of a film, and along with the other elements—objects, architecture, landscape, etc.—he must be photographed not merely while he performs, but only at those moments in his acting that are necessary and most expressive.'[15]

Golovnya goes on to apply this to the easier problem of the 'non-actor', and he does not attempt a choice or resolution of the two attitudes that he describes. He then returns to ideas that both he and Pudovkin made clear at the time of filming *Mother*:

'If we need to film, for instance, the statue of Alexander III, as an embodiment of autocracy, we would film it from below, choosing a camera angle to make the monument look monolithic and raised high in the composition. If an armoured car is to be filmed, it's absolutely necessary to do this with several shots from various angles, to convey an image, made of a series of film-moments, of terrible and swiftly advancing attack.'

He concludes by citing the changing photographic attitude to Baranovskaya in *Mother*, to indicate her changing character, cited above, pages 209-210, and we can see a similar treatment of Chuvelov's rôle in the new film.

This was the first year of graduation from all three major film-training institutions. In May the State Film Technicum (GTK) in Moscow graduated sixteen directors, thirty actors, nineteen cameramen and eight laboratory-workers.* In November the Leningrad photofilm technicum graduated a class of twenty-five cameramen, light technicians and laboratory men. And VUFKU's film technicum placed almost its entire first graduation class in positions in their expanding studios. The Leningrad studios were also able to absorb most of their newly trained technicians, but the Moscow graduates were scattered throughout the Union, chiefly in the new national studios. Many of the graduate directors went into educational film-work, and even into administrative posts, where some knowledge of the actual medium was badly needed. Some of the young

* From this first class came the directors Feinzimmer, Gendelstein, Nemolayev, and Tatyana Lukashevich, and the cameramen Kosmatov and Kabalov.

actors who could meet the higher standards of the theatre moved there. The totally new character of the Soviet film industry after the entrance of all this young blood, did not materialize—certainly not visibly, nor immediately.

An educational programme on a smaller and more effective scale was the workshop opened by Kuleshov and Khokhlova in the Georgian studio. Their new film, *Your Acquaintance*, was released in October and in the same month they left for Tiflis. The Georgian film industry also gave a warmer welcome to Sergei Tretyakov and his script-ideas than they had ever received in the Moscow studios.

Circumstance and temperament had combined to turn the Soviet cinema's two leading directors into rivals. Eisenstein and Pudovkin were friendly rivals on the personal plane, but bitterly combative on questions of film theory:

'In front of me lies a crumpled yellowed sheet of paper. On it is a mysterious note:

"Linkage—P" and "Collision—E".

This is a substantial trace of a heated bout on the subject of montage between P (Pudovkin) and E (myself).

'This has become a habit. At regular intervals he visits me late at night and behind closed doors we wrangle over matters of principle. A graduate of the Kuleshov school, he loudly defends an understanding of montage as a *linkage* of pieces. Into a chain. Again, "Bricks". Bricks, arranged in series to *expound* an idea.

'I confronted him with my viewpoint on montage as a *collision*. A view that from the collision of two given factors *arises* a concept.' [16]

Naturally this quarrel was so entertaining to the spectators that it was fanned and nourished in the film press and at public discussions, where disciples represented their absent, more sensitive leaders. Provocative questionnaires would be addressed to both, in the hope of obtaining opposing responses, but both Eisenstein and Pudovkin were careful to discourage aimless wranglings in the Kuleshov-Vertov manner.

Despite all caution, the rivalry came excitingly into the open in the anniversary year. The two men were engaged in making the two most important films for the October Jubilee—at the same time, and in the same place. For both shooting schedules brought the crews of the two films to the streets and palaces and squares and monuments where their chief subject—the October Revolution—had taken place ten years before. Both men were conscious that the identity of their films' subjects would heighten all their differences of approach and treatment, and the public saw this as an approaching test of the validity of each method. Furthermore, their respective studios and managers kept them at fever pitch to meet the deadline—the jubilee screenings of November 7th.

With the late start and the delay of hammering out an acceptable, workable scenario from the huge mass of material handed to them, the Eisenstein-Alexandrov-Tisse group tried to work miracles of organization, filming different episodes simultaneously; for example, while Eisenstein made the scenes at Smolny Institute, Alexandrov worked on the studio-filming of the Bolshevik messengers to General Kornilov's 'Wild Division', ending in the famous dance sequence, which was later edited by Eisenstein. Because of Tisse's group of quick-witted assistants, including Vladimir Nilsen, he could actually divide himself between such parallel filming. Ivor Montagu says that the work was so intense that their working day was dangerously lengthened, with 'the three doping themselves to stay awake'. It is possible that the unusually unified photographic quality of *October*, despite the separate unit work, was born of this haste. There was plenty of physical co-operation, as reported by Eisenstein to the *Nation's* correspondent:

'Night after night from four to five thousand Leningrad workers volunteered to participate in the storming of the Winter Palace. . . . The Government supplied the arms and uniforms, as well as the army. . . . The state lent us the *Aurora*. . . . We likewise had the use of tanks and artillery.'[17]

Though Pudovkin's earlier start could have made the schedule less of a burden to him, his nervousness took up this slack, and made him worry about the scope and effectiveness of his entire film. Faced with the actual stones that witnessed the October Revolution, Pudovkin persuaded Zarkhi to reorganize completely the structure of the scenario. Some central episodes already filmed were discarded in the process, and the whole final section, from the anchorage of the *Aurora* to the taking of the Winter Palace, was added, almost extemporized, on the spot. The two crews found themselves on each other's heels:

' "I bombarded the Winter Palace from the *Aurora*", says Pudovkin, "while Eisenstein bombarded it from the Fortress of St Peter and Paul. One night I knocked away part of the balustrading of the roof, and was scared I might get into trouble, but, luckily enough, that same night Sergei Mikhailich broke 200 windows in private bedrooms".'[18]

Mezhrabpom and Pudovkin won the race to November 7th. Though parts of *October* were shown to individuals before that date, the jubilee audience at the Bolshoi Theatre saw only *The End of St Petersburg* and *Moscow in October*. Shub's *Great Road* had been publicly released the day before. One critic who had seen the three films at earlier screenings made the inevitable comparison:

'All have the same theme, the same material, but used in three different ways: we have the *film of documents and facts*, edited from old newsreels that fix events of ten years ago (*The Great Road*); the *film of pseudo-facts*, artificially recreating the events as accurately as possible (*Moscow in October*); and the *film of images*, constructed on principles of the fictional film (*End of St Petersburg*).'[19]

All agreed in finding that Barnet's film was the least successful of the three, and this critic gave as his explanation that Moscow had so changed in ten years that in order to reconstruct events, the changed locations had to be photographically evaded with the use of 'un-newsreel angles'.*

---

* Ivor Montagu, who attended this Bolshoi screening, offers another explanation for Barnet's failure: in his haste to finish the film for this occasion, Barnet had not had time to photograph the several explosions needed; instead, his cutter inserted the same newsreel explosion shot at every spot, producing uproarious results.

In this same issue of *Novy Zritel* the editor commented on the advance screening given by Mezhrabpom-Russ of their two films at the Bolshoi Theatre a few nights before, on October 31st:

'The organizers of this screening managed to fill the parterre, the loges, the baignoires, and the bel-étage with "ladies" in evening-gowns and diamonds, but did not find time to invite any genuinely proletarian society, workers' organizations, or students, to the screening.'

This complaint was a significant one to make at a screening of *The End of St Petersburg*, for this film was soon to be the centre of a serious corruption scandal. Apparently so much money flowed through the departments of Mezhrabpom and the Leningrad offices of Sovkino during the making of the 'rich' scenes in the film that quite a lot of it clung to some fingers,* and Darevsky, production manager of Mezhrabpom, had to take most of the blame, for not watching the behaviour of his subordinates.

The scenes that had most tempted the jobbers in the filming of *The End of St Petersburg*—the flower-bedecked trooping off to war, and the elegant assumption of power by Kerensky—were perhaps worth a little graft, for they are among the most striking moments in the finished film. The artificially induced hysteria that follows the declaration of war in 1914 is one of the most graphic anti-war statements in film history. Indeed, the film's comments on 'war' seem far more meaningful than its comments on 'revolution'. The man who made the agonizing battlefield scenes of *The End of St Petersburg* had seen both real battlefields and the battlefields shown in *The Birth of a Nation*, but the man who related those scenes to the frantically grabbing scenes at the stock-exchange, in a brilliant image of 'encouragement', had stepped intellectually beyond his master Griffith.

Yet Pudovkin could still match richness of imagery with economy of dramatic means, as Tretyakov noted:

'Chekhov once said that anything not used should be omitted from the staging of a play. If, for example, a gun is shown in the first act, by the time we get to the last act that gun should be going off.

'Everything that Pudovkin puts on the screen is like Chekhov's gun, except that Pudovkin can get more than a shot from a gun. For instance: the glass of hot tea on the table in the worker's home, in *The End of St Petersburg*. It is never tasted, and no one drinks it—so as to its primary purpose, it isn't functioning.

'But this same glass serves to measure time, by showing the steam coming from it as thinner and thinner.

'And this glass all by itself on the empty table indicates lack of food, poverty.

'And this glass is finally thrown through a window as a signal of danger—and saves a man's life!'[20]

---

* Accusations moved from Pudovkin's film to the other expensive film then in production at Leningrad's Sovkino, *New Babylon*.

Another who saw the jubilee films in advance of the jubilee was Mayakovsky. He was asked to write a greeting to the film industry on the jubilee, and he used the opportunity to distribute some praise but more passionate blame:

'The best wishes for the Soviet cinema on the tenth anniversary of the October Revolution would be to disown such stuff as *Poet and Tsar* and, since there's little point to complaining about such films, to provide broader means of making newsreels of our revolutionary labour. This would secure the making of films in the future like *Fall of the Romanov Dynasty*, *The Great Road*, etc.

'I take this opportunity, in speaking about films, to protest once more, and in every way, against the portrayal of Lenin by such simulations as Nikandrov's. When a man who resembles Lenin reinforces the resemblance with poses and gestures, one senses in all these superficialities a complete emptiness, a total absence of thought, and it's disgusting to watch it. I heard one comrade put it correctly—that Nikandrov resembled not Lenin but a statue of him.'[21]

Nikandrov, a worker from the Urals, impersonated Lenin in two of the jubilee films, *October* and *Moscow in October*, and it could be his performance in the latter film that so irritated Mayakovsky.

Both these films, incidentally, showed the real people who participated in the Petrograd and Moscow uprisings. Except for the impersonated Lenin, Barnet was able to secure the co-operation of the surviving leaders of Moscow's October; an advertisement for his film promised: 'To be seen in the film: Stalin, Rykov, Bukharin, Yaroslavsky, Ulanov, Skvortzev-Stepanov [and others]'. Eisenstein proceeded differently, by finding doubles for *all* the well-known participants, even the members of Kerensky's cabinet;* he must have known that a paid actor, or non-actor, would be more flexible, even, dramatically, more credible, than a leading figure playing himself. This eagerness to manipulate all the materials of reality, including familiar faces, was understandable in Eisenstein, but the timing was accidentally unfortunate. A crisis in the Communist Party and among Government leaders coincided with the completion of a film in which both the now-divided factions were unmistakably represented on the screen.

In January 1925, a year after Lenin's death, Leon Trotsky had been relieved of his duties as People's Commissar of War and given industrial administrative posts. The damage to the ego of this individualist must have been great. Differences between him and other Soviet leaders grew wider until two factions appeared within the Party—the 'Government' group, and the 'Opposition', led by Trotsky and his friends. On every event, in and out of the Soviet Union, the two groups took opposing views, and the discussion remained open and frank, whether on the General Strike in England, or the domestic policy of collectivization, or Chiang Kai-shek's bloody coup d'état in China. But in the anniversary year, with the approach of the Fifteenth Congress of the Communist Party, set for the end of the year, the Opposition, partly in fear and partly in desperation, adopted underground, conspiratorial tactics to gain control of the Party

* Because of his resemblance to one of the cabinet ministers there is even one actor from the Moscow Art Theatre (at last!) in the film; Boris Livanov accepted the rôle because of his friendship for Eisenstein.

apparatus. Trotsky's ego made him lose sight of the greater political aims of the Party, and the fat was in the fire. He made trials of his strength, at a Leningrad demonstration in October 1927, and in Moscow on the day of the jubilee, November 7th, and defied the Government group to do their worst.

It was in this disturbing conflict that Eisenstein's film was inadvertently caught, for he had made no distinction, in reconstructing the events of ten years before, between the revolutionary parts played by members of the present Government group and members of the present Opposition. When *October* was not shown at the jubilee, and when Trotsky's open anti-Government campaign began, the wildest rumours flew around Eisenstein and his film, believed even by people who saw Eisenstein arriving at the studio cutting-room every day: that Eisenstein and Alexandrov had joined Trotsky's faction, that the film had been destroyed, that parts of it had to be remade, that Eisenstein was forbidden to touch his film, etc. etc. By the end of November the rumours were wild enough for the newspaper *Kino* to ask Eisenstein to explain the delay of his film's release. We can imagine him writing his reply in the corner of the cutting-room, in some pause while waiting for a sequence to be spliced together for screening:

'Why Is *October* Late?'

'This question, that has begun to sound like a rebuke of our group, is being asked everywhere films are talked about. Around this question circulate the most various, most contradictory and—let's be frank—the most absurd rumours.

'We consider it our social duty to give a little more information on this subject, to illuminate the circumstances and to relieve the idle film-gossips from the burden of inventing more of their not-quite-amusing notions about the film, *October*.

'It should be noted, first, that when we interrupted our work on *The General Line* and accepted the Government's assignment to make the film *October*, we were immediately conscious of the heavy responsibility that our group had assumed. Even the preliminary sketches for the scenario required far more time than had been allocated to this stage of the work.

'Our choice: to make a hurried job, or put ourselves on an incredibly hazardous schedule.

'We chose the latter. The group decided to show within a five-month period that there is nothing impossible to film-workers.

'But purely technical obstacles could not be overcome by naked passion: our technical poverty, our lack of sufficient lighting equipment, the accumulation of tasks never before faced by Soviet film-production—these could not vanish before our determination. . . .

'Some reels of the future film were shown at the time of the anniversary, both to our own people and to foreign guests—so we have often been reminded that the film *October* was on its way to completion!

'To the stories already in circulation we can add:

1 We are making two films: *Before October* and *October*. 13,000 feet in all. This should also tell something of our situation.

2 The purely editorial work to be done on *October* is extremely difficult, demanding a great deal of time—for we are confronted with a whole series of quite complicated and unprecedented approaches to the various sequences and themes (and we plan to write about these for *Kino* in the near future).

'In the general delay of our work's emergence into public view (and we are far from being to blame for this) we see no factor that should disturb the completion and polishing of our film. In the opinion of the jubilee commission our film was not intended for the shelves of the film-distribution offices after a few showings in the October celebration days* . . . No, we made the film with everyday spectators in mind. . . . The film was not orientated to the tenth anniversary alone; in this sense it was not "a jubilee film".

'It was calculated to show us, every and any day, the living and permanent jubilee of the October victory!'[22]

The statement did not stop the excited rumours, which continued in the foreign press. Opposition figures may have been cut from prominent emphasis in the film, but it is not true that Trotsky was completely eliminated—he can still be seen clearly in two episodes. The difficult 'purely editorial work' was completed by February 1928; while the negative was being cut, Eisenstein, Alexandrov and Tisse were sent to Germany to examine sound-filming systems before resuming work on *The General Line*. It was many months later, however, that Eisenstein kept his promise to discuss these cutting problems. The quoted reference to a film in two parts, 13,000 feet altogether—compare with the released 9,100 feet—was the only published reference to such a plan,† but it indicates how much material for *October* we have never seen.

Before the public release, in March 1928, of *October*, the last of the specifically anniversary films, there were two film achievements of considerable dramatic and propaganda value, not directly connected with the jubilee of the October Revolution: *Two Days* from vufku, and *The Parisian Cobbler*, from the Leningrad Sovkino.

Two Days is the only film directed by Georgi Stabovoi seen outside the Soviet Union, and its simple effectiveness makes one wish to have seen more of his work, even should it not match the quality of his best-known film. *Two Days* is also the only film by him mentioned in Soviet histories of the cinema, though the records show several other Ukrainian productions directed by him, following *Two Days*. Before entering vufku Stabovoi was a journalist and his first film work was as a scenarist; he could not have been very proud of his contribution to Chardynin's *Ukrazia*. *Two Days* was the first film he was given to direct, yet the scenario was not by him, but by Lazurin. Its well-shaped story of how forty-eight hours of the changing fortunes of Civil War also change the life and ideals of a faithful caretaker (resembling Firs of *The Cherry Orchard*) reminds

* A reference to the fact that *Moscow in October* already seemed destined for the archives.
† Until October 1957, when Eisenstein's notes for such an arrangement were published in connection with the scenario for an additional reel of *October* never filmed (*Iskusstvo Kino*).

one of the similar transformation of the heroine of *Mother*; for both heroes, the fate of their revolutionary sons determines the course of their own selfless lives. Bryher, in summarizing the action of *Two Days*, in her *Film Problems of Soviet Russia* (1929), calls it 'the most uncompromising of the Russian films I have seen', and it is true that beneath the richness of the film's execution and performance, the naked little story never swerves from its cruel revelation of character.

If Friedrich Ermler had not been noticed before, *The Parisian Cobbler* brought him attention. Here was a fearless treatment of a delicate theme. There is an antagonistic but reasonable account (by a former Soviet film writer) of the film and the motives of its authors:

'The major theme was the struggle of a Komsomol cell to improve the morals of its members and to make them more considerate in their relations with other human beings. Before production began the scenario [by Nikolai Nikitin and Boris Leonidov] was discussed at Party and Komsomol conferences and passed up through the various levels in the hierarchy until its "sensitive" theme was finally approved by the Komsomol Committee of the Leningrad Oblast. The heroine of the film, pregnant and abandoned by the young man involved, also a Komsomol member, cannot obtain help either from the Komsomol cell or from representatives of the Party, all of whom are indifferent and callous to her. Turned away everywhere, she finds friendly aid and shelter with the non-Party Kirik, a deaf mute who keeps a small shop of his own called "The Paris Shoe-maker". . . . The contrast drawn between Party and non-Party characters to the honour of the outsider explains in large part the heightened interest of the public in this film. . . .'[23]

Director Ermler and actor Nikitin, beginning their harmonious work together in *Katka*, were to continue together through three more notable films.

Mezhrabpom's non-anniversary films were modest personal stories into which, with some effort, could be read larger social meanings. Protazanov made *The Man from the Restaurant*, largely distinguished by Mikhail Chekhov's reluctant performance of the title-rôle* of a waiter whose pretty daughter (Malinovskaya) is persecuted by the restaurant's wealthy clientele, and *Don Diego and Pelageya*, a comedy about a small-town bureaucrat who loses his sense of proportion and arrests an old woman for an infinitesimal breach of the law. Fyodor Otsep made what was to be his last Soviet film, *Earth in Chains* (known abroad as *The Yellow Pass*), where the involuntary absorption of the heroine (played by Anna Sten) into commercial prostitution is shown with more drama than logic.

Of Eisenstein's four completed silent films *October* was the chief target of his Soviet critics. Its reception abroad in 1928 was gratifyingly warm, but at home it was used in the attacks on Eisenstein and his methods that were to continue, with only brief respites, for the rest of his life. Typical is the conclusion reached by the historian Lebedev: 'Both *October* and *Old and New* emerged as con-spicuous failures of the experimental cinema.' As proof of *October*'s weakness,

---

* Originally intended for Moskvin, who declined it; Shmelyov's novel had been filmed four times before the Revolution.

Lebedev writes: 'Eisenstein considered that the basic facts of the October days were generally known, so that he presented not these, but, by his own admission, "my own associations, my visual puns", that those facts called to mind.'[24] And yet one of the lasting values of *October* is its remarkably personal attitude to a great historic change, and from this attitude derive the vital emotional moments of the film, sometimes ambiguous, but always penetrating one's consciousness at some level. The brilliant photography and 'newsreel reconstructions' give *October* an air of objectivity, but it is Eisenstein's personal attitude that gives the film its focus.

There is one visual association in the film that has always struck me as stemming directly from Eisenstein's first architectural memory of St Petersburg. To cut off the escaping demonstrators who are being fired upon, the bridges are raised to separate the centre of the city from the workers' quarters. The Provisional Government's bullets find some victims and these bodies slide to the bottom as the divided bridge lifts. The last to fall are the corpses of a girl and of a horse; as the bridge lifts to its maximum height, the dangling horse plunges into the water, the carriage slides down and the body, seen from a great distance, falls with a sickening thud. At that moment the strange planes of the lifted bridge combined with the brutality of the act to suggest *Egypt* to the former architecture student and he cut to the stone eyes of one of the sphinxes that decorate the river-front. The specific Egyptian transition may not come through to the spectator—perhaps no more than an abstract stony chill—but the purely personal association paid a rich filmic dividend. *October* is full of such multiple-level moments. The divided bridge itself is an ample symbol. It is even possible that the whole extraordinary sequence of the suspended bridge is a successful visualization of the physical and dramatic connotations of the term 'suspense'.

Soon after the release of *October*, and while the new approach to *The General Line* was in work, Joseph Wood Krutch interviewed Eisenstein in Moscow, and recorded something of his ideas at that moment:

'. . . every work must be judged according to its usefulness at a given time in a given place. He himself is no longer interested in "Potemkin" which is more or less passé and not as purely cinematographical in its methods as he would like it to be. One can get an idea of what he wants to do from certain scenes in "October" where dynamic ideas are translated into pictures. The scene, for instance, in which the overweening Kerensky is shown, all alone, mounting up and up the successive flights of stairs in the imperial palace . . . or that in which the [idea] of religion is suggested by a series of flashes beginning with a picture of the fully developed God on an icon and descending through a whole series of representations to the grotesque idol of a savage.'[25]

Progress was announced more simply in the interview with Louis Fischer:

'Potemkin' was a poster. 'Generalnaya Linya' and 'October' are subtler. They are nearer life. We are learning. . . .'

Alexander Dovzhenko completed the direction of his first feature film in 1927, but it bears little relation to his basic film-ideas, and in later years he omitted it from the list of his work. VUFKU gave him a spy-film script by Zats and Sharansky, *The Diplomatic Pouch*, close in subject to the superficial *Mr Lloyd's Trip* that Mayakovsky so scathingly found typical of Sovkino's product. The VUFKU administration must have thought Dovzhenko's service in Soviet embassies had given him the right background for this material. The first part of the script was based on an actual crime: a Soviet diplomatic courier is followed and murdered by the police agents of a foreign power (the action indicates England). His pouch with 'vital papers' is stolen, but is recaptured by the sailors on a passenger ship to Leningrad, and returned to Soviet authorities. The story has nothing of Dovzhenko, but its treatment occasionally hints at his approaching invididual style. The actors play with an intensity at odds with their silly tasks; the small rôles are cast with the sharpness of caricature, reminiscent of FEX. Dovzhenko himself plays the small rôle of a stoker on the ship—and this performance marks the end of his brief acting career. Dovzhenko learned something from all the preludes to his mature work, and he always remembered the advice of his cameraman, Nikolai Kozlovsky, on *The Diplomatic Pouch:* ' "Never accept compromises", he said to me—to which I still try to adhere.' This film also taught him that his initial excitement in the film medium could not be maintained by commonplace material; he could be satisfied only with complete responsibility for the films he made:

'*Zvenigora*, my next film, for all its stylistic disharmony, did give me some estimate of my capacities for film making. It was then that I began to dream of doing independent film work, of being responsible for an entire film from script to screen.'[26]

His next film may, in the eyes of posterity, fall short of being a masterpiece, but *Zvenigora* was completely his own, despite the fact that its scenario is credited to the two writers, Mikhail Johansen and Yuri Yurtik; Dovzhenko would always claim it as the first of his films.

The film is a legend, or rather, a whole anthology of legends, linked by the symbol of hidden treasure. Because it ranges so widely through history, from the period of Viking invasion up through post-revolutionary Ukraine, it gives the impression of a larger scale than it actually has—at the time, it was referred to as 'an Ukrainian *Intolerance*'. This is not an apt parallel, for the structure of *Zvenigora* (for which the poet Johansen was probably responsible) is much looser: Grandad feeds Pavlo, a grandson, on such extravagant stories of Zvenigora, the treasure-hill, that the boy, blind to the revolution and dreaming only of sudden wealth, grows up to become a bandit and an émigré-adventurer. The wandering story's climax mounts in a Paris theatre, where Pavlo has attracted a paying audience to witness his public suicide. Instead, he escapes with the box-office receipts, to be used for counter-revolutionary sabotage in the Ukraine. When Grandad (symbol of the past) fails to derail the train (symbol of progress), Pavlo's postponed suicide finally comes off, and Grandad joins his good grandson, Timosh, whom we have watched through the film fighting in the war and staying with the revolution. There is an apotheosis of socialist industry, a neutral conclusion to which Dovzhenko manages to give some personality. But such an account of the film's 'story' conveys nothing of the film's character, full of fantastic surprises, lyrical passages, and a wealth of technical experiments that remind one of the similar wealth in *Strike*. Both films, too, each in its own way, are full of humour. Grandad, for example, in his story-telling, usually assumes the hero's rôle: he can outwit generals and decimate Viking forces with equal ease.

Dovzhenko had an answer ready for all complaints about his complicated story:

'Do I hear the objection that some people in the audience may not understand my film? Well, I cannot help it. I cannot very well appear before them at each performance and say "Look here, fellows, if there is anything you do not understand it does not mean that my film is bad or unintelligible. The reason why you don't understand it is within yourself. Maybe you simply are unable to think, whereas my purpose is to prompt your thinking while you see my film." If your girl friend whispers to you that she finds it boring, do not hesitate, get up and take her to another movie—because my film is a Bolshevik production.'[27]

If Dovzhenko had been a respecter of omens, he might have given up his film career with *Zvenigora*, for everything went wrong during the 100 days of its filming in the Odessa studio. The administrator suffered a nearly fatal stroke, Professor Krichevsky, the artistic supervisor, had a nervous breakdown, and in shooting the last sequence the cameraman Zavelyov and his assistant dropped two stories in a faulty elevator and broke their legs. But Dovzhenko has never been an easily discouraged man, not even when the VUFKU representatives in Moscow were stunned and helpless at the sight of *Zvenigora*. This impasse led to an historic occasion, the first meeting of the three masters of the Soviet cinema. It is Eisenstein who recorded the memorable encounter:

' "I beg you, please come", the VUFKU representative in Moscow repeated over and over on the telephone, "I beg you—come and see this film they've sent us. No one here can understand it, it's called *Zvenigora*. . . ."

'We enter the Hall of Mirrors in the Hermitage Gardens, where the Moscow Art Theatre began their work on *The Sea-Gull*, and where this incomprehensible film is to be projected for us. Here a young Ukrainian director is to receive his baptism of fire. "Is it or isn't it good? Help us decide", the VUFKU man implores. . . .

'I sit down beside Pudovkin. We both had just come into fashion—and weren't yet venerable. . . . In the crush we meet the director—his name is Alexander Dovzhenko.

'On to the three screens of the Hall of Mirrors—the true one and the two side ones that reflect it—*Zvenigora* leaps!

'Mama! What goes on here!

'Out of some peculiar double exposures swim figures in ancient armour.

'A white paint brush changes the colour of a black stallion.

'Brandishing a lantern a terrifying monk comes out of the ground. . . .

'The curiosity of the audience is intense. There is whispering.

'Already I reflect sadly that the film must eventually end and that I'll have to find something intelligent to say. For us "experts" this is also an exam—But with the tripled image emphasizing the fantasy, the film races on. . . .

'I may be (no, I really am) uncertain about the content of the scenes (I hope Sashko will pardon me), but I can't forget the impression they made upon me.

'As the film goes on it pleases me more and more. I'm delighted by the personal manner of its thought, by its astonishing mixture of reality with a profoundly national poetic imagination. Quite modern and mythological at the same time. Humorous and heroic. Something Gogol about it. . . .

'The screening is finished. People get up. Silence. It is clear to all: there's a new film person among us. . . .

'Pudovkin and I had a wonderful task: to answer the questioning eyes of the auditorium with a joyful welcome of our new colleague. And to be the first to greet him.

'And then this man, especially well-shaped and well-thatched, with the erect carriage of one no longer young in years, broke into a half-guilty smile—and Pudovkin and I clasped his hand heartily. . . .'[28]

Dovzhenko himself, as usual, made the most penetrating observation on *Zvenigora* in his short autobiography (dated December 1939): '*Zvenigora* was a catalogue of all my creative possibilities.'[29]

Insignia of VUFKU

CHAPTER XII

The Cost of Virtuosity

1928–1930

> . . . this new machine mass art cannot develop for
> its own sake: . . . it cannot rise to its obviously
> potential heights without lifting and being lifted by
> the human race
>
> LINCOLN STEFFENS

The Communist Party's attitude to the most clearly important of the Soviet arts called for more definition than could be entrusted to those party members who happened to fall into film-administrative posts. The semi-official conference on Sovkino's failings in October 1927 had been welcomed by film-workers as an airing of troubles long bubbling beneath the public surface. At the Fifteenth Party Congress at the end of the year everyone seemed to have something to say on this popular topic, adding up, usually, to the hope that the Party would watch over film production more attentively than in the past. The cinema's rôle in the first Five Year Plan, whose announcement was the chief contribution of this Congress, was less firmly defined and advocated. The concrete effect of the Five Year Plan on the cinema was to come later. In March 1928, the first All-Union Party Conference on Film Questions attempted to formulate the several directions taken by the discussion at the Fifteenth Congress, and party members in the film industry joined the larger number of lay critics and provincial delegates to talk about 'what's wrong with our films'. After the introductory speeches the first delegate to speak, a comrade from Siberia, got down to specific cases. He hoped that film distribution in his Irkutsk area was not typical, for they were sent nothing more appropriate on the anniversary of Lenin's death than *Lucrezia Borgia* and Buster Keaton's *Three Ages*. As for Soviet productions, they don't seem to think ahead how these will be received by non-city audiences:

'You show a film like *Bed and Sofa* in the country, and the peasants come out, spitting—"Ah, so that's how they behave in the city." And that's how Sovkino promotes the bond between city and country.'[1]

Inevitably the conference turned its energies to continuing the attack on Sovkino begun the previous year, for complaints always sound more useful than praise and, also inevitably, the complaints were aimed more at the foreign films chosen by Sovkino for distribution than at Sovkino's own productions, though plenty

was said about these, too. Cde Meshcheryakov, from the political education
section, quoted his own opinions of the scenarios of the criticized films to prove
that he had early recognized their faults, but that his advice had not been taken
by the producers. Of sixty-five films made by Sovkino, he thought only nine any
good. Nadyezhda Krupskaya, Lenin's widow, tried to bring the discussion back
to something helpful; she considered that insufficient attention was given to
educational and informational films. One of the rare cheerful notes was struck
by Cde Krinitsky in his summary of the first day's session:

'It's true that Eisenstein is non-party, Alexandrov is non-party, Pudovkin is non-
party. They made *October, Mother, Potemkin, The End of St Petersburg*. Who will
deny that these men understood the line of the Communist Party and expressed
it excellently in their work?'

Cde Ermler, the only film-maker to address the conference, refused to divide
directors into 'party' and 'non-party'—to him they were 'old' or 'young'.* He
saw a more serious obstacle in the fact that too many young people in studio
jobs have neither training nor any particular qualifications for them. 'In the Leningrad studio I know of four instances where work was given to people solely
because they are Komsomols.' *October* came in for its large share of political
criticism, so that one Ukrainian comrade came to its defence, saying that if Soviet
audiences did not find films like *October* or *Zvenigora* popular, that should not
cause their withdrawal from distribution, for it is these films that spur cinema
forward, and would always be counted among our achievements; it would be
a serious error to reject such films. But the Sovkino administration, represented
by Cde Greenfield, continued to express scepticism of Eisenstein, referring
sarcastically to his announced wish to make a film of *Capital*:

'We have no ideological supervision, nor can we say that ideological supervision
is in the hands of Cde Eisenstein, who hopes to find the correct ideology hidden
in Marx's *Capital*. Who is going to criticize his *Capital*? But how can each of
our directors make films about Karl Marx or V. I. Lenin?'

Some delegates showed the direction of future conferences by throwing blame on
non-party film workers who had been deluded by 'decadent' approaches to their
work. This particular 'formalist' handle of blame was not yet sternly wielded.
The 1928 conference was content to conclude that 'fictional films must be made
in a way that can be appreciated by millions'.

'Millions' was no exaggeration, for there were, by 1928, 9,000 film theatres in
the Soviet Union (to be doubled within two years), not counting travelling
cinemas, and annual attendance at the permanent theatres alone was approaching
the thousand million figure. Little was altered in the administrative offices of
Soviet film studios;† the viewing and reviewing apparatus for all scripts and

---

* Ermler's *House in the Snow-Drifts* was released during this conference. Of the three
stories told of the three floors of a Petrograd house, the emphasis is placed on a musician's
realization that the new society needs the art of the past.
† The Mezhrabpom scandal was resolved by fines and demotions, without radical
change except in name: Mezhrabpom-Russ became Mezhrabpomfilm.

finished films was broadened in an attempt to give the 'millions' more of a voice in film-production, but the wise Bryher was correct in warning that this was no guarantee of progress:

'All films when finished are submitted to about twenty people to ensure that they are sound from a Communist viewpoint. This does not mean that the films must be political in character, but they must not contain diametrically opposed ideas. The film is then submitted to an audience of workers, and if they do not care for it, it is then sent back for alterations. . . . I question myself, however, whether the multitude of criticism will be good for cinematography; not now, but in five years' time, as insensibly a tradition will develop which will mean that films may be rejected because they present a new point of view. But perhaps the situation will be adjusted.'[2]

A concentration of lay supervision over *subject* or *content* made for increased suspicion of other less tangible factors of film-making. Style, method, technique, the whole artistic embodiment of the subject, in fact, sounded to the lay critic as so much mystification or chicanery, an excuse for wasting the people's money, and his worries worked back to the film-makers. Yet there was one formal element that provoked pride rather than suspicion. Film-makers began to cultivate a showy photographic manner, the sort of conspicuously handsome photography that has always won prizes. Weaker film-makers found it easier to let their camera-men make a film look pretty than to learn how to give original dramatic substance to difficult and delicate problems of modern life. Current and future attacks on 'formalism' were not aimed at this evasive handsomeness (generally approved as another technical victory), but hit at elements of fantasy, unorthodoxies of structure and treatment, or almost any departure from the approved naturalistic norm. The materials of this victory were still foreign, for all cameras and most other apparatus continued to be imported, along with all negative used for dramatic films—chiefly from Germany (Agfa) and Belgium (Gevaert). Raw film was now manufactured at home, a large factory at Shostka was completed in September 1929, but this domestic product was used only for newsreels, teaching films, and some domestic prints. The dependence on foreign materials did not sour the effect of a socialist victory—'we'll use their techniques better than they can!' Contrary to expectation, the new beautiful photography gave the films an impersonal, machine-made quality that characterizes most of the well-known films made in this last period of the Soviet silent film. The approaching upheaval of the sound-film, as threatening as it seemed at the time, was actually a drastic medicine, except that it tempered the photographic obsession without altering the narrowing dominance of naturalism. The films of this period that survive longest— *Arsenal, Old and New, Earth*—derive their permanence from beauties more fundamental than photographic and from ideas more dynamic than naturalism.

What was it in Pudovkin that made him such an easy victim to the charm of surfaces?

'After finishing work on *The End of St Petersburg*, I was simply worn out. I dreamed of a long rest, of a trip to the sea-shore. I wanted to get away from the studio. But the director [Aleinikov] called me in and said, "Pudovkin, I'm giving you a vacation—for a month. Be ready to start on a new film just as soon as the month is over." I protested that I was tired and that I was sick of everything, but that man knew how to get around me. He told me that I was to go to Mongolia to make a picture there. I must tell you that besides my tremendous fondness for cinema as such, I also have a passion for going on location. So of course I agreed to his proposition.'[3]

The Novokshonov story that Aleinikov offered to Pudovkin told a Civil War incident of 1920, when the English army of occupation in Mongolia took a partisan fighter prisoner, and found on him ancient credentials that gave him the status of a descendant of Jenghis Khan. The English command decided to exploit these credentials to assist their rule: they seated their captured partisan on the throne of Mongolia. But the partisan, unattracted by the glory of his mighty ancestor, escaped from his regal captivity and rejoined the partisans to fight against the occupation army.

Aside from the exotic temptations in this material, the element that attracted Pudovkin was not the historic incident, but the story's quality of fable. Without much deliberation on its problems, he accepted the idea, counting on Zarkhi's help in deepening the anecdote. But Zarkhi was not interested in Novokshonov's theme, and declined to work on the project. Doller, too, preferred to work on a film of his own—so that Pudovkin lost two valuable members of the group responsible for his two first triumphs. Golovnya, however, was as attracted by the fresh material as was Pudovkin, and stayed with him. Osip Brik was invited to work on the new scenario; he accepted on the condition that he could accompany the expedition and compensate for his ignorance of Mongol customs, etc. Brik's job ended only with the release of the film, for Pudovkin and he revised the film throughout the location shooting in Siberia and Buriat-Mongolia, and even in the last stages of production, back home in the Moscow Mezhrabpom studio.

One possible reason for Pudovkin's quick acceptance of Novokshonov's story is that he was sure of casting its central rôle, Bair, the Mongol; his old Kuleshov group had included an actor perfect for the rôle, Valeri Inkizhinov, Buriat-Mongol by birth, though Russian by education. (The Mongol who plays Bair's father was, indeed, Inkizhinov's father, filmed in the place where he had always lived.) Without Inkizhinov the film might not have been made, but there was no question of his interest, even though the rôle required him to begin a completely new training: he had to transform himself into a 'restored' Mongol. His first task was to learn to ride freely in the Mongol manner, and he studied with a specialist for a month at a cavalry school before leaving for location. In their first conversations Pudovkin laid down these acting principles to neutralize Inkizhinov's westernized behaviour:

'*Reserve*—a deliberately narrowed range of movement to indicate emotion; *explosions* of accumulated energy in sudden fury; *many shy smiles* (or rather, as defined by Pudovkin, "reasons for smiling"); and *no needless naturalistic details*, no matter how justified by actual Mongol habits (Bair doesn't scratch himself, or blow his nose in his fist, or punctuate his talk with the long hissing classic sigh).'[4]

Once the expedition reached Verkhne-Udinsk, the capital of the Buriat-Mongolian Republic, Pudovkin grew so absorbed in the new work that he quite forgot his exhaustion. It was here that he met the local political worker, Ashirov, who provided Pudovkin and Brik with stories and details that put cinematic flesh on the bones of Novokshonov's narrative. 'After hearing his stories', Pudovkin said later, 'I could see my film exactly'.[5] The first sequence of the film—the arrival of guests at a yurta—was written and filmed exactly as Ashirov told it to them. The most delicate problem, filming at the lamasery of Tomchinsk, almost produced an impasse: before the group came, the lamas had divided into two camps, one absolutely opposed to the filming, and the other willing to wait and see, but with no enthusiasm for relaxing the institution's rules. The group asked the intercession of the Grand Lama of Buriat-Mongolia, and his word to the Tomchinsk lamas settled everything: even to the unimaginable extent of performing their annual ceremony before July 26th, its traditional date, to accommodate the travelling schedule of the crew; they also obligingly repeated any parts or details of the dance needed for the filming! Before returning to Moscow, the crew filmed the scenes of Bair's first flight and of partisan warfare near Lake Baikal and on the Bargoisk steppe.

The acting problems of the film were interestingly new for Pudovkin, but the Kuleshov approach was just as easily adapted to the acid impersonations of English 'types' as it was to the manipulation of Mongolian 'non-actors'.* Measured by the means and successes of Kuleshov, Pudovkin's third dramatic film can look like a luxurious expansion of them, especially luxurious in Golovnya's display of photographic riches. The finished film is a glittering flow of polished, glossy images that could leave breathless a spectator accustomed to the 'normal' film. The lyrical element in *Mother* that had grown to such power in *The End of St Petersburg* now flowered with dangerous brilliance in the exotic problems of *The Heir to Jenghis-Khan*.

As finally assembled, the film tells a half-heroic, half-ironic story of Bair, a hunter who brings a rare silver-fox skin to market, where he is cheated out of it by an English fur-trader protected by the British Occupation Forces. When Bair protests, he escapes capture by the army and joins a partisan detachment fighting the interventionists. When Bair's partisans defend the population against a military requisition of cattle (while the command, at a religious ceremony, declare their friendship for the Mongolian people), Bair is captured and executed. In going over his effects, a silken document (that he had been given by chance) is interpreted to identify its wearer as a descendant of Jenghis-Khan. The not quite dead body of Bair is hurriedly recovered and patched up for use as an impressive native front for the intervention. Climaxing an accumulation of revealing

---

* 'I wanted to have a crowd of Mongols looking with rapture on a precious fox-fur. I engaged a Chinese conjuror and photographed the faces of the Mongols watching him. When I joined this piece to a piece of the shot of fur held in the hands of the buyer I got the result I required.' ('Types instead of Actors,' a speech to the London Film Society, February 3, 1929, published in *Film Technique*).

incidents, Bair's rage breaks out against his British 'protectors' and the film ends in a great Mongolian army and symbolic storm sweeping away the interventionists.

It was the finale that provoked the hottest discussion. After a Samson-like image of Bair pulling down the British headquarters on their alien heads, he leaps from his captivity on to a Mongolian pony, summoning the waiting hosts of Asia to follow him against the invaders. The swiftness of the appearing riders is at once translated into the image of a storm blowing against the English, rolling them helplessly away with all the dust and debris that Pudovkin could imagine. Almost unanimously the Soviet critics condemned this conclusion as silly and schematic. Foreign critics were more enchanted with these technical fireworks. To all who were interested in the content-excuse for the film, this end was an evasion. But how else was Pudovkin to end a film subject whose attraction for him had been its fable and exotic imagery, except by hyperbole? A realistic revolutionary end would have been inconsistent with the tale-spinning character of the film, and would have been as jolting a sensation as Pudovkin's own well-known example of a made-up face against a real landscape—though here it would have seemed a real face against a painted landscape. Golovnya's field-day may have been Pudovkin's compensation for deficiencies in ideology and structure. Critics who worried about the finale as a symptom of trouble found ample (and, no doubt, gratifying) justification for their anxiety in Pudovkin's next film.

As *Storm Over Asia* the film was unusually successful abroad—after one large political alteration: when British protests were heard, not only in England, but in the foreign ministries of countries that permitted the film's exhibition, all foreign sub-titles indicating a British army were altered to mask it as 'the White Russian army', yet it is hard to believe that anyone was fooled, so biting are Pudovkin's English caricatures. There were, as usual, other 'improvements': the German editors cut the hundred shots in the storm finale down to twenty-seven.

Pudovkin's progress from utter simplicity to pictorial luxury, before any new discipline had been exercised, seems a natural development, but to see a similar process in Vertov is more shocking. In him it may have been encouraged by his fanatic dependence on artificially limited factors of film-making—the camera and splicer—and eventually this artifice assumed control. Within this same period Vertov, too, grew precariously virtuoso. His first film for VUFKU, *Eleventh*, was his last silent film to associate his Kino-Eye methods with the concrete victories of socialist industry and society. After *Eleventh*, in Eisenstein's words: 'formalist jackstraws and unmotivated camera mischief'; even in *Eleventh* the increasingly oblique approach catches the attention. A fragment of his diary shows him as an artist who thought 'in shots'—and even in sound track. This fragment records the filming of one of *Eleventh*'s most effective moments:

'Trumpet blast. Pause. Workers scatter. Horsemen patrol the area of explosion. A bell is struck. Pause. Slow ringing of other bells. Some toy-like figures are prepared to light the fuses. Swift ringing of bells. People light the fuses and run to shelters. Explosion. And another. A series of explosions, one on top of the other. Stones and dust gush up. Fragments fly far, landing on rails, on cars, on cranes.

Fragments drum on the roof of the car where we are hiding. They reach as far as an opened tomb, where a Scythian has lain for 2,000 years. Alongside the skeleton are spears, bronze-tipped arrows, with slots for poison. A broken pottery cup. At the head are the bones of a sheep (eaten) and the skeleton of a war-horse. The Scythian looks with hollow eyes, black openings in his skull. As if waiting for the explosion. Sky over him. And clouds. Rails go right through the tomb. Waiting on the rails are 40-ton cranes and loaded freight-cars. . . .

'*Scythian in tomb and the crash of advancing new life.*

'Scythian in tomb and a cameraman, focussing on a 2,000-year silence!'[6]

Such intuitive simple sensuality did not control the completion of the film. In Eisenstein's comment, the metric beat of its montage was 'mathematically so complex that it is only "with a ruler" that one can discover the proportional law that governs it'.[7] A European critic has characterized this period of Vertov's work:

'Theorists mostly love their theories more than fathers love an only child. . . . Vertov, also, has waged fierce, vehement and desperate battles with his material and his instruments (i.e. reality and the film camera) to give practical proofs of his ideas. In this he has failed. He had failed already in the era of the silent film—by showing hundreds of examples of most cunning artistry in turning: acrobatic masterpieces of optic jigsaw, brilliant conjuring of filmic association—but never a rounded work, never a clear, proceeding line. His great efforts of strength in relation to detail did not leave him breath for the whole. His arabesques totally covered the ground plan, his fugues destroyed every melody.'[8]

These harsh words are most applicable to Vertov's most brilliant film, his next.

My memory of *The Man with the Movie Camera* is not reliable; I have not seen it since it happened to be, in New York in 1930, the first Soviet film I saw. It was such a dazzling experience that it took two or three other Soviet films with normal 'stories' to convince me that all Soviet films were not compounded of such intricate camera pyrotechnics. But I hope to be forgiven for not bringing away any very clear critical idea as I reeled out of the Eighth Street Playhouse—I was even too stunned to sit through it again. The apparent purpose of the film was to show the breadth and precision of the camera's recording ability. But Vertov and his cameraman-brother, Mikhail Kaufman, were not content to show any simple vocabulary of film-practice; the cameraman is made an heroic participant in the currents of Soviet life. He and his methods are treated by Vertov in his most fluid montage style, establishing large patterns of sequences: the structure resembles that of *Kino-Eye*, with a succession of 'themes'—the audience, the working day, marriage-birth-death, recreation—each with a whirling, galloping climax, but the execution of the two films, separated by less than five years, are worlds apart. The camera observation in *Kino-Eye* was alert, surprising, but never eccentric. Things and actions were 'caught', but less for the catching's sake than for the close observation of the things themselves. In *The Man with the Movie Camera* all the stunts that can be performed by a cameraman armed with Debrie or hand-camera, and by a film-cutter armed with the boldness of Vertov and

Svilova—all can be found in this full-to-bursting film, recognized abroad for what it really is, an avant-garde film, though produced by VUFKU, a state trust.* VUFKU also produced Mikhail Kaufman's independent and more modest documentary, *Spring*.

The first masterpiece of the Ukrainian cinema broke entirely with traditional film subjects and structures. Dovzhenko's *Arsenal* grew out of *Zvenigora*'s material, compressed and deepened, but with an enormous leap into a new freely poetic and intensely personal quality. *Zvenigora*, for all its ranging through strange layers of the past and references to the (then) present, still clung to a 'logical' progression; movements from level to level were still justified by its story, or by the device of story-telling Grandad, or even by dream. But *Arsenal*, as Eisenstein pointed out, is *the* example of a 'liberation of the whole action from the definition of time and space', of 'a dramaturgy of the visual film-form'.[9] Dovzhenko was not the inventor of a new film-language of 'illogical' connections, for Kuleshov's 'creative geography' had been used even by Vertov,† and Pudovkin's emotional symbols and the 'intellectual' vaults of *October* had all suggested a new form; Dovzhenko was the first to lift all the suggestions to the level of mature poetry. By 1928 the international film had several such suggestions to offer him, but Dovzhenko saw fewer foreign films than most other Soviet filmmakers. I cannot determine if he was present at the exhibition of avant-garde extracts that Ilya Ehrenburg brought back from Paris in 1927, though it is tempting to relate some of *Arsenal*'s surprises to the seemingly remote surprises of *Ballet Mécanique*. In this connection one recalls the continued interest shown in the foreign avant-garde by VUFKU's journal. Yet the search for explicit influences is pointless; film-poetry, like the revolution sniffed by *Arsenal*'s horses, was 'in the air'. By the time Dovzhenko was ready to require this language, it was ready for his voice.

'I wrote the scenario in a fortnight, filmed and edited it in six months. . . . *Arsenal* is completely a political film. In making it, I set myself two tasks: to unmask reactionary Ukrainian nationalism and chauvinism, and to be the bard of the Ukrainian working class that had accomplished the social revolution. At that time, however, I lacked the necessary theoretical knowledge for an integrated handling of such a grand theme. As far as I was concerned, there were no questions of style or form involved. I worked like a soldier who fights the enemy, without thought of rules or theory. I dare say if I had been asked

---

* Through the courtesy of the Cinémathèque Française I have recently re-seen this inexhaustible ancestor of the modern documentary film, and found it just as dazzling and ingenious as twenty-eight years before, with a strain of wit and irony that I had forgotten. Its cutting seemed unusually bravura on this seeing, and on several occasions one sees the practical application of Vertov's discovery that two frames of a shot are visible in projection. But above all it is the cameraman who is the protagonist and it is his camera that is thrust into the emphatic foreground. There are two passages of possibly symbolic significance, both for Vertov's method and for the camera heroics of this period: at the end there is a trick sequence of a camera walking about on its tripod without human aid, and near the beginning one senses the stillness of all existence, waiting to be brought to life by the camera.

† In *The Man with the Movie Camera* Vertov opens a montage-phrase with a shot made in Moscow, followed by one in Kiev, ending with an Odessa shot.

then what I was thinking about, I should have answered, like Courbet to a lady's question, "Madame, I am not thinking—I am excited".'[10]

The one Ukrainian piece of reporting I have seen on the filming of *Arsenal*[11] gives little idea of what Dovzhenko was doing in the three summer weeks he spent working near and in Kiev: of the three filming days observed by the reporter we learn only that Dovzhenko joshed the soldier extras before working with them, that he grew angry when rain interrupted work in Sofia Square, and that he was unafraid among the explosive charges representing the artillery barrage and gas attack of the opening sequences. The best evidence, the film itself, exists exactly as Dovzhenko made it. Some years after his completion of the film he was asked to transcribe it in words; this is a sequence close to the beginning of the film:

'Tsar seated at his desk. His brow shows that he is deep in thought.

'A mother sows. The bag of seed pulls her toward the earth. She has no more strength. She falls.

'The Tsar thinks.

'A worker at his machine. He closes his eyes. Painful thought.

'The Tsar writes:
> *"I shot a crow. The weather is fine."*

'The Tsar signs his signature:
> *"Nikky."*

'The mother lies on the dry earth.

'The Tsar thinks, puts a full-stop, strokes his moustache.

'Face of the mother, covered with sweat.

'A field of grain. Amidst the grain stands a policeman, his silhouette blocking out the sky.

'A war factory.

'A field. Weak-looking grain. A shabby, gaunt, one-armed ex-soldier with inflamed eyes, leading a gaunt horse. They stop.

'They stop and look at each other.

'Sparse, dry wheat-ears.

'In a hut. A mother, standing. At her feet, children with swollen bellies.

'The children cry, weep, demand. The mother stands motionless.

'The field. The man—the ex-soldier—stands there.

'The mother stands. The children weep.

'The ex-soldier stoops and plucks a small, pitiful wheat-ear.

'Looks at it.

'A child weeps.

'The ex-soldier suddenly turns. Taking the lead-rope in his teeth, with his one arm he desperately begins to beat the horse with a stick.

'The mother beats the child in the same way.

'The ex-soldier brutally beats the horse.

'The mother beats the two children.

'The one-armed man beats the horse.

'The horse pulls away. The one-armed man falls to the ground.

'By a stove the child stands, crying.

'The horse stands still. The ex-soldier lies there, worn by his effort.
'The ex-soldier gets up heavily. The horse says to him:
  "It's not me that you should beat, Ivan".'[12]

The powerful determination of Dovzhenko's art bowled over the quibblers and bureaucrats who worried about *Arsenal*'s risks. (Something of his compelling force is seen in his persuasion of Ambrose Buchma, the most revered of Ukrainian actors, to play the bit of a gassed German soldier.) With the simplicity of great poetry *Arsenal* narrates the tragedy of a defeat. This film-poem of the Ukraine takes us from the unreality of trench warfare and the smaller agonies at home, through the shifting allegiances produced by news of the February and October Revolutions in Russia, to the bloody suppression of a revolt of workers barricaded in a Kiev munitions factory, in January 1918. The film is concerned entirely with conflicting forces rather than with individuals in conflict.

As Coleridge's genius fused the most miscellaneous of reading into great poetry, so the widest variety of elements became grist to the mill of Dovzhenko's excited experiment. Folk-songs and tales, political caricature (has anyone ever collected Dovzhenko's newspaper cartoons?),* the majesty of monuments, the immediacy of political tracts, memories of home, even Nikolai II's correspondence—all were subjected to the heat of a powerful artistic personality and made into a single experience. The elements and subjects of *Arsenal* fit into no ordinary film form— Dovzhenko has said that 'it contains material enough for five or six films'[13]; it pretends to no unity of form, but employs a miscellany of methods including some never before seen in films, and yet it is unified in purpose, and accomplishes a totality of effect beyond that of more formal directors. Its cameraman, Danylo Demutsky, illuminated the multitude of concepts and symbols with a photography so real and brilliant that the most universal statements in the film have the grip and conviction of tangibility, but Demutsky's brilliance, here and later, was always controlled by Dovzhenko's needs.

James Shelley Hamilton, who made the sensitive American adaptation, wrote, 'It is a picture that, like sublime music or poetry, gives up its meanings slowly, more and more eloquently and movingly the more often it is seen.'[14] And Henri Barbusse devoted an enthusiastic chapter in his Russian travel narrative to *Arsenal*, in which he comments on its structure:

'. . . even when the connecting thread seemed to disappear, the sense of drama was never absent; it grew in cumulative effect, and it carried with it the unity and the coherence necessary for the understanding of the drama. . . .'[15]

In a few instances the 'connecting thread' hangs on an immediate recognition of an image with local meaning, such as the ikon-portrait of Taras Shevchenko carried in the nationalist parade. The nationalists had adopted the nineteenth-century Ukrainian poet-patriot as the hero of their cause, and our bard's comment on this is to have Shevchenko's haloed portrait blow out his own ikon-lamp in

---

* In Dovzhenko's autobiography of 1939: 'Comedy scenarios that I never realized were *Native Land*, about Jews in Palestine, *Lost Chaplin*, about Chaplin's life on a desert island, and *Tsar*, a satire about Nikolai II. But circumstances somehow so worked out that I was never able to make a comedy.'

disgust at the misuse of his memory. But the majority of images need no foot-notes—the penetrating war-time scenes of nightmare horror at the front and mutilation at home; the train carrying the desperate, careless returning soldiers (suggesting the leaderless People's Republic); Timosh (brought from *Zvenigora* and passionately played by Svashenko), representing the Ukrainian worker who fought somebody else's battle and learned to fight his own; the speaking horses and the frantic dash to the waiting grave; questions addressed directly to the audience; and the arsenal—both historic fact and embracing symbol of the encircled fighters for socialism. *Arsenal*'s images and gestures sweep all dis-tractions aside, holding the intensity at a constant high pitch, ranging in move-ment all the way from reflective shots as still as death, to episodes as breathless in speed as a heart-beat in panic. When the gun-carriage delivers the dead fighter to the waiting woman and the new black earth dug in the snowy field, the words of his comrades might stand as epigraph over Dovzhenko's film: 'Here he is, Mother. No time for explanations! Such is our revolutionary life and death.'

Arsenal was released on March 26, 1929 to a public that accepted it more readily than most of the critics—and accepted it on its own terms, according to criticisms offered by a group of Moscow workers:

'The director should take into account that a symbolic style is more difficult to assimilate than an ordinary story-telling style, and he should provide more explanatory sub-titles, especially in the second half of the film where they are most needed. Another slight fault is that almost nothing is said in the film about what bearing the sequence of "self-demobilization" has on the arsenal; this is left open for speculation . . .'

and

'*Arsenal* is not a story, but a poem. Even the first words in the film actually sing— "Ah, the mother had three sons", when we see the infinitely sad face of the mother of three soldier-sons. A knot rises to the throat, as if we were hearing the sad song of a mother's grief. . . .'[16]

Abroad, at the time of its release, *Arsenal* had an extremely limited circulation. It was known and admired less in Europe than in the United States, where it acquired the same steadily widening audience, with similar reasons, that Picasso's mural of 'Guernica' gained when exhibited in America. The two works have much in common—a belief in human progress despite the barbarism of war, expressed in metaphors of pain and anguish that repel and attract at a first seeing.

Even while making *The Diplomatic Pouch*, Dovzhenko told an interviewer that he sought simplicity, and his artistic course since has been a process of increased directness, condensing his statements and stripping them of technical ornament— from the fantasy of *Zvenigora* to the epic-poem of *Arsenal* to the philosophic hymn of *Earth*. That a Dovzhenko could grow so consistently and accomplish so much, even alongside superficial works—that a non-naturalist artist continued to work freely amidst the mounting acceptance of naturalism—this is the proudest episode in the history of Soviet films.

It is difficult to detect the influence of *Arsenal* on the films of its time. A lovely surface continued to be the goal of the lesser films, and while loveliness grew standardized, so did 'realism' in less responsible hands. A realistic film with originality became as rare as a beautiful film with substance. Following a caricature in *Sovietsky Ekran* on 'Standard Types in Foreign Films',* came a more biting and pointed caricature, 'Standard Types in Soviet Realistic Films':

'*Alcoholic*. Beast, tormentor, bad union member. Usually ends badly: in delirium tremens.

'*Bureaucrat*. Clumsy, pot-bellied, bad union member. Tears young inventors to pieces. Chews apprentices for dessert. Ends badly, thanks to Worker and Peasant Inspection.

'*Hooligan*. Half-corrupt element. Terror of neighbourhood. Ends badly: gives up drinking, becomes a vegetarian and active member of the Auto-Club.

'*She*. Bacillus of corruption. Powder-puff and lip-stick. Scourge of all active union members. Ends somehow: marries a Nepman.

'*Kulak*. Monster. An oppressor, and generally a blood-sucker. Does not belong to a union. Ends badly: dies in horrible agony.'[17]

Neither of the masters of Soviet film realism can be associated with such stereotypes, common enough in films of the late 1920s. Abram Room's last film in his realist manner, *Ruts*, was released in January 1928. Though a compromise in its resolution of domestic crisis, its treatment remained uncompromisingly real and well-observed. It was this year that Room gave an interview that summed up all his best work: 'I believe that the principal value of the film is conferred on it by the diversity and complexity of personality and of human emotions.'[18] Room's former assistant, Sergei Yutkevich (whose first direction was of the street and factory scenes in *Bed and Sofa*), issued his first independent film, *Laces*, in June 1928—a lively film, with a tendency that was to characterize Yutkevich's subsequent films: a pleasure in plastic effects that sometimes diluted the dramatic aims of his films. His second film, *The Black Sail*, in 1929, was also good-looking and reinforced his standing among the young directors who were soon to be handed the new medium of sound-film.

In some unaccountable way the next film of the master, Room, carried further, not his own original realism, but the exceedingly handsome manner of his former assistant. The literary base was a story by Henri Barbusse, *The Ghost That Will Not Return*, about a political prisoner somewhere in a Latin American oil country. The grotesque prison authorities grant José Real the day of freedom with his family that is legally due him; no paroled prisoner has ever returned alive to the prison, for a police agent is ordered to follow and shoot at the end of twenty-four hours. The authorities trick Real into accepting their offer, and the agent that follows him lets him squander precious hours needlessly. Real finally reaches his family, but instead of returning to prison, or being shot, he leads an armed revolt, presumably against the oil companies, with consequences so ambiguous as to leave his future unclear—at least in my mind. Room made a wonderfully clever film out of this story, reflecting its refined cruelties with some of his own. It may

* This was in an issue headed 'Down with Foreign Trash!' One of the first visible results of the Party Conference in March was a wholesale and temporarily indiscriminate denunciation of the imported films.

have been the geographical or atmospheric remoteness of the material that led Room and his associates into the unnecessary exaggeration of all elements and the incredible lapses .of logic, for surely the blame cannot be put wholly on the textural proficiency of the cameraman Feldman, or the designer Aden (whose foreign prison was more elegant than forbidding). The good group of actors, too— all theatre people—behave in an unreal stylization that is only occasionally punctuated by an unexpectedly right gesture from Room's past, untainted by cliché. One of the few sequences to communicate any emotion is that of Real's last night in prison, when his cell is occupied, one after another, by visiting visions of his wife, his father and the men he worked with.

Friedrich Ermler's last and best silent film also shows elements of stylization, but, because they are controlled within the clear propaganda aim of the film, they never obtrude or take over the style of the film. In the tradition of the propagandist film, *Fragment of an Empire* deals with urgent social problems, but differs from the majority of the type in the quantity of problems touched and in the depth and acuteness of its criticism. Ermler and Katerina Vinogradskaya wrote into their scenario the most serious problems of the period—the human aspects of socialist construction, questions of new working relationships, of mass culture (and its misuses), and of marriage and modern family life, since private discord reacts upon social well-being. These several themes, affecting everyone in the Soviet Union, were focussed by the film through the experiences of a man who had lost his memory in the war, regaining it ten years after the revolution. We see him first in a prologue, as a simple helper at a provincial railway station during the Civil War. The Red Army is retreating before a White advance, leaving the dead behind. As he pulls off the boots of the corpses, one body shows life and he takes it inside, saving this boy from summary execution.

The film proper begins on the platform of the same station in 1928, with the helper still unaware of any social change in the country. In the film's most intense episode, his memory of his wife, the war, and his name—Filimonov— returns, and he loses no time in getting back to St Petersburg—but it seems strangely altered in every way: its buildings, its money, its habits are not those he remembers. His former employer (played by Viskovsky, Ermler's former director!) no longer owns the textile factory where Filimonov worked before the war. Now the factory is in the hands of a whole group of people, not at all like the masters he was used to. They smile mysteriously at his multitude of troubles. When he demands to know what has happened, who is master, they tell him that he, as everyone, is 'master' now. He gives his most prized possession, his war medal, to the property room for factory club theatricals. When he has grown accustomed to the new ways, the chairman of the factory committee (the young soldier of the prologue) helps him to find his wife, who has married a hypocritical cultural worker, and to face the most difficult problem of all—to watch his wife struggle unsuccessfully with an ancient set of conventions. When Filimonov leaves, his wife sobs 'The end', but Filimonov turns to the audience saying: 'No, it is not the end, there's a great deal yet to be done, comrades,' and the film closes.

The treatment of this material is a model of realism, presented without any sophistication—almost as if Filimonov were telling a parable in the terms of Rip

Van Winkle or Enoch Arden—although its technique recalls both Eisenstein and Dovzhenko, and even Pabst. This seems a more logical development from *Bed and Sofa* than *The Ghost That Will Not Return*. An indication of Ermler's aim for *belief* was in his insistence that Fyodor Nikitin appear in his Filimonov rôle in several public places until his costume and make-up attracted no notice. For his characterization Nikitin was disguised as a doctor's assistant in the Forel Psychiatric Clinic, where he studied the patients suffering from amnesia. And it was Ermler's sharp observation of both mental disease and of war that makes the fantastic sequence of the return of memory so compelling. An accidental juxtaposition of objects and movements brings back scraps of images, dimly remembered sounds, swinging a kaleidoscopic cluster of images into a recognizable pattern of the past—and Filimonov is himself again. Eisenstein's advice on the cutting of this sequence has been distorted into a story of Ermler's 'bungling' of his film,[19] a story to which his previous and subsequent films give the lie.

The last half of the film is really a comedy, beginning with the tram ride during which Filimonov is bombarded by new sensations—till the final episode in the apartment of the cultural worker, who is given a cruelly acid treatment. Without his spectacles he becomes a coward, identified with the other cowards and enemies of the film; his portrait of Lunacharsky is hidden by tasteless statuettes, and his complete set of Lenin's works is clearly unused. In this half of *Fragment of an Empire*, Ermler devised a modern approach to the folk-comedy, intended more for local than international audiences.

If handsomeness clashed with the painful material of *The Ghost That Will Not Return*, the equally handsome surfaces of *The New Babylon* seem more in harmony with its story of the Paris Commune of 1871, for the story's central setting is the luxurious Parisian department store, the 'New Babylon', where the heroine Louise Poirier, played by Elena Kuzmina, is a sales-girl. It is through her eyes that we see the contrasting sectors of French society, much as we see contrasting levels of past and present through the eyes of Ermler's Filimonov. Louise is the link between the poor people she lives among and the rich whom she works for and serves. The film's climax is made from their contrasting attitudes to the German advance on Paris, with the rich bargaining and capitulating, and the patriotic poor willing to sacrifice themselves for their capital. When these defenders of the city find authority in their hands, they establish their own city government, and the heroic tragedy of the Paris Commune brings the film to a more rhetorical conclusion than the similar fight against odds that concludes *Arsenal*. It takes this tragedy to convince Louise's lover, Jean, of the Versailles army, that her ideals were stronger than his peasant belief in authority. Kuzmina wrote of her Louise:

'I loved and cherished Louise as one can only love and cherish one's own child. I played the rôle on "naked nerves"—each new filming day bringing the joy of work as well as such a horror from the consciousness of her reality that I can't face it now. . . .

'Louise is not to be found in the literature of the time. We sought her in the whole epoch. This was a synthetic image of a communist girl at the time of the

Paris Commune, and to create it we had to know all we could about the history and events of the Commune, to transport us there and communicate its sights and aroma. While working on *The New Babylon* it was Zola who gave us the most. All of us read all his works.'[20]

The execution of *The New Babylon* is a consistently magnificent climax to the silent films of Kozintsev and Trauberg. The performances have just the right mixture of warmth and caricature, and the chiefly studio photography of Moskvin (assisted by Mikhailov) is as irreproachable in its way as Golovnya's exteriors in *Storm Over Asia*. It is a glittering film in which the glitter plays a calculated dramatic rôle. It is one of the most sardonic of Soviet films, and succeeds where most Soviet films about the past or the capitalist world do not; the trip to Paris made by Kozintsev and Trauberg just before filming their scenario must have been an extremely rewarding excursion. For the completed film young Dmitri Shostakovich wrote the first of his many film accompaniments, here scored both for large and small groups of musicians, but rarely used in the film's circulation, and quite unknown abroad.*

During the filming of *The New Babylon* Pera Attasheva watched the work with a distinguished bit-actor:

'In one interval between shots Enei, the ubiquitous and tireless designer, completes his set for an oriental department in the "New Babylon" store. Exotic objects have been borrowed from the ethnographic museum—fierce masks, gay lanterns, brocades, fans and parasols, brightly alluring kimonos.

'They are now ready to film the director Pudovkin in a tiny episode.

'Pudovkin is agitated. It appears that his most cherished dream is to act, not to direct.

'Monocle, striped waistcoat, curly wig, moustaches, artificially blackened teeth—director Pudovkin has disappeared; here is a salesman, in love with his job. With fan in one hand and a paper dragon in the other, unable to keep up with the race of his own temperament, he gasps for breath, he screams, possessed by the spirit of the sale:

' "Dear ladies, genuine Japanese fans, buy them! Buy! Buy! Look—what colours, what delicate tints! And here is a dragon, a genuine Japanese monster—just look at his eyes and tail. . . ."

'But the brittle, aged dragon, not subscribing to Pudovkin's enthusiasm, falls to the floor in pieces. Pudovkin is embarrassed and turns to another object. . . . To the great relief of the visiting director from the oriental division of the ethnographic museum, the film-makers announce that they have all the footage they need for this modest shot.'[21]

Pudovkin played enough film rôles to suggest study of his own acting style. After the Mongolian expedition he added to his earlier rôles in Kuleshov films not

---

* In his article on this score (*Sovietsky Ekran*, March 12, 1929) Shostakovich describes his principle of *not* illustrating each scene: 'For example, at the end of Reel 2, the important moment is the German cavalry's advance on Paris, but the reel ends in a deserted restaurant. Silence. But the music, in spite of the fact that the German cavalry is no longer seen on the screen, continues to remind the audience of the approach of that fierce power.'

only this *New Babylon* bit, but a 'magician bit' in Kuleshov's *Gay Canary*. He was offered and he accepted the leading rôle of Fedya Protasov in a joint Soviet-German production of Tolstoy's play, *A Living Corpse*—made twice before in Russia (in 1911, by Persky, and in 1918, by Sabinsky, with the galaxy of Maximov, Kholodnaya and Runich). Now Prometheus and Mezhrabpom jointly assigned Fyodor Otsep to direct the new version. The filming was begun in Moscow (chiefly of the gypsy scenes and exterior locations) and the crew took the film and cast to Berlin for completion with the non-Russian members of the cast, Maria Jacobini and Gustav Diessl. Golovnya, as cameraman, was assisted there by Piel Jutzi (who had improved *Potemkin* for its German distribution) and Pudovkin's designer, Kozlovsky, acquired a German collaborator. Though Pudovkin appears to have left full directorial control in Otsep's hands, his skill as an editor seems to have been employed in the film's completion. Pudovkin's work in Berlin coincided with the success there of *Storm Over Asia*, and before returning to Moscow he accepted a lecture invitation in England, where the Film Society was showing *St. Petersburg*. Ivor Montagu says that he took the opportunity there to point to the evidence around him that his English characters in *Storm Over Asia* were not exaggerations of reality.

One artist, in one film, moved against the tide of shimmering photographic perfection. Victor Turin knew how to make good-looking studio films, but in *Turksib* he seemed to turn his back on 'all that' in order to reclaim a direct style that was even disappearing from the 'documentary' film. I have never learned, not even in talking with him, how Turin happened to make this change. The push into the open air might explain this fortunate back-sliding, except that other open-air films of this period are just as elegant as its studio films. Was it because Vostok-kino was too young and poor to afford photographic riches?* Or was the schedule too tight to allow Slavinsky and Frantzisson time to make the desert look pretty? In any case, *Turksib* emerged as a documentary film that by its firm aim, firmly expressed, will always remain a landmark in that form. On its release, in October 1929, *Turksib* looked amazingly fresh; with its good humour, bounce, vitality, purpose, *Turksib* was a popular and immediate success abroad—and a surprise at home, both to the makers of culture-films and of studio-films, especially when this modest film was received with enthusiasm wherever it was shown. Critics explained some of this success in their admiration of the project's organization. With the remarkable comment that 'one of the most instructive things about *Turksib* is that it was realized exactly as its author visualized it', one critic printed some revealing extracts from Turin's original plan, submitted to Vostok-kino on April 9, 1928:

'The greatest defect in most of the culture-films produced up to now seems to be the absence of a precisely articulated theme. . . . The usual result is a tiresome hodge-podge of shots spliced together with merely mechanical links. . . . This makes even the sharpest facts grow dull on the screen, and leaves the spectator unmoved. . . . From the very outset it is necessary to approach the work of filming

---

* Vostok-kino was organized March 26, 1928 to produce films for those eastern republics that did not yet have film studios of their own.

Turksib not as one would approach a culture-film, even in the broadest interpretation that can be given this term, but as a film without actors, demanding no less attention than the making of any story film. If we do it this way we may be sure that our film on the building of the Turkestan-Siberia railway will be not only useful and cultural, but entertaining and emotional as well.'[22]

Turin's application ended with a thematic outline and a rough libretto for treatment, and these were, apparently, sufficient guides for the entire production. Even the working title was retained, though the studio wished a 'bigger' title— *The Steel Road.* In seeking a source for the clean simplicity of *Turksib*'s structure, it may be necessary to go back to Turin's education, perhaps to some inspiringly logical professor at the Massachusetts Institute of Technology. Turin's reward for *Turksib* was a studio production post, organizing other people's films.

Esther Shub made the last piece in her great trilogy on Russian history. With *The Great Road* covering the years 1917-27, and *The Fall of the Romanov Dynasty* the preceding period of 1912-17, there remained the more fragmentary and therefore more tempting newsreel material from 1897 to 1912 yet to use. 1928 was the centenary of Tolstoy's birth, and Shub's first thought was to bring together the filmed footage taken on the several occasions when Tolstoy co-operated with cameramen—chiefly Drankov. But in her basic source, the film library at the Leningrad Sovkino, she found very little negative and additional print of this material. Much that was known to have been filmed could not be located. In totalling her footage, she realized it was too meagre to depend on:

'only 160-200 feet of Tolstoy alive (period of 1906-10)
'325 feet of Yasnaya Polyana and its people in Tolstoy's time
'325 feet of Astapov
'about 1,000 feet of Tolstoy's funeral'

Shub decided to work on the *epoch*, using Tolstoy as a central figure, a spokesman for his time. One of the minor achievements of her film, *The Russia of Nikolai II and Lev Tolstoy*, is that the Tolstoy footage does not look as sparse as it actually is, so skilfully is it embedded in the more general footage. Handling the oldest films was a problem in which she was assisted by Kuligin, a laboratory specialist at Moscow's Sovkino, who supervised the transfer of old negatives and prints to modern stock with the delicacy of a craftsman. After her trilogy Shub's work has been in extremely well-organized and well-edited documentary films, with only occasional uses of her own speciality. An anniversary film for the Komintern was announced for her,[23] but this opportunity to use a wider range of existing newsreels was not realized. Instead, there is some striking employment of foreign newsreels in her *Today* (a 'film-feuilleton', 1930), shown abroad as *Cannons or Tractors*.

Exploit on the Ice, more familiar as *Ice-Breaker Krassin*, was a documentary film of this pre-sound period that also depended on editing skill. The cameramen who accompanied the ice-breaker *Krassin* on its mission to rescue the crashed crew of Nobile's arctic dirigible, did not work with any particular plan—they shot everything they could, brought it back to Leningrad, and Sovkino put the miscellany in the hands of Sergei and Georgi Vasiliev, two cutters with the same name but unrelated, who had assumed the 'pseudonym' of 'the Brothers Vasiliev'. Their film was released in October 1928, and its success helped them to realize their ambition to direct. Another personal triumph in documentary films was Yakov Blyokh's *Shanghai Document*. Blyokh's promising career had begun as *Potemkin*'s production manager, and after the release in 1928 of his bright reportage on Shanghai, great things were expected of him, but it was years before he was given commensurate responsibilities.

Before the last silent film by the Eisenstein group was released on October 7, 1929, under the title of *Old and New*, that great experimental film had undergone many vicissitudes, the most serious being the year's interval spent away from it on the production of *October*. Though I have often been told that *The General Line*, on being resumed after *October*, had a completely different plan, I find it hard to conclude that there was any total alteration in its general character or treatment or emphasis. There were stills reproduced in 1926 attached to the personal story that is the backbone of the final film, and most of the basic casting was done also at that first stage of production. Putting together the available evidence, I should say that when the crew returned to *The General Line* in spring 1928, there was no more than further shooting on the long-before determined story. At this point, and in the cutting-room, there was, of course, the always painful whittling process that reduced twice too much material to a normal running length of film. Here, as in both *Potemkin* and *October*, Eisenstein had to throw away almost as many ideas as the best ones that the finished films retained. If the treatment, published in Germany (as *Der Kampf um die Erde*)[24] at the time of the world release of *Old and New*, was written by Eisenstein and Alexandrov before the shooting script was done in 1926, the differences between this original plan and the post-*October* realization are so minute as to seem revisions of the least radical sort. (There was, however, a considerable change made *after* the montage of *The General Line* was complete.)

There are two articles by Tisse, written more than two years apart, describing approaches to the photographic style of *The General Line* that are fundamentally the same. The first, written before the crew moved to *October*, declares an aim of strict simplicity:

'In this film we resolved to get away from all trick camera-work, and to use simple methods of direct filming, with the most severe attention to the composition of each shot. Only exception to this rule: when we sometimes employed artificial lighting in exterior scenes—and this was to gain more control over final compositional unity. This gave us the means to determine all degrees of light, from day to night, without resorting to a chemical process at the laboratory, to achieve such gradations. . . . Our aim in this film: to gain artistic and technical effects by entirely new methods of filming reality with simplicity.'[25]

Tisse also mentions that for economy of time and maximum use of each filming day, some scenes were filmed with five cameras: 'With such filming for editing, there must be maximum accuracy in each camera's composition, so that each will supplement all other cameras that are recording the same scene.' He also voices a feeling that many cameramen have suppressed when he says that 'animals are more difficult to work with, but they are more patient than human beings'.

By the time Tisse wrote his second article, during the montage of *The General Line*, at least one important animal actor had joined the impatient human actors. The great bull, Fomka, developed a dislike for the camera, or for Tisse, and on one occasion broke away from the six men holding him, to charge at the camera. Tisse and his precious Debrie were saved by the men manipulating the reflectors, who used them as glittering distractions, as if they were cloaks in the bull-ring, to change Fomka's mind. This anecdote appears in an article on the difficulty of maintaining photographic unity in the film:

'Moscow—Rostov-on-Don—Baku—the Mugan Steppe—the Persian border—Leningrad—Ryazan province—Penza. . . . That is the road travelled by this camera.

'From bulls and hogs like armoured tanks to tiny new-born chicks, from black patent-leather shoes and silk stockings to black-earth country and bast-shoes, from 16-seater stylish aeroplanes, from tractors to carts and primitive wooden ploughs, from poor huts without chimneys to perfected glass houses and state farms, from tropical blossoms to harsh northern shores, from the freezing Kivach waterfall to the eternal fires of the oil-fields.

'All this varied material was filmed at different times of the year on the broadest of scales, compelling particular attention to the maintenance of a unified artistic style.

'Till now, both here and in the West, the opinion has been cultivated that rural material is not "photogenic". As *The General Line* is constructed exclusively from the materials of the countryside, it will be at some disadvantage if this should happen to be true, but I believe that it will demonstrate the contrary: that rural material gives very rich "photogenic" possibilities.

'On completing our location shooting, last autumn, we began our studio work. It was at this time that experiments began in the West with a new type of lighting apparatus, using lamps of half the power used formerly. We learned from these experiments and continued them in some of our studio work for *The General Line*.'[26]

The faces in *Old and New* had always given me the impression of having been found 'on the spot'—in the places being photographed—so I was quite unprepared to learn that they were the result of an immense casting operation that swept through cities and countryside to bring possible faces to Eisenstein for final choice. Most of the people in the famous religious procession ('prayer for rain') were found in and brought to the country from Leningrad's flop-houses* It was only when I became a part of this great casting apparatus on a later film, and saw the unstinting expenditure of time and effort, that I realized how this search for the precisely 'right' face was as important to an Eisenstein plan as a

---

* 'What a night! We have examined five night-lodgings from midnight to 6 a.m.—the time when they are fullest—and we found the participants for the procession. We looked at more than a thousand people.'—Maxim Strauch, 'In Search of Actors for "General",' *Sovietsky Ekran*, February 12, 1929. The procession was filmed outside Leningrad.

montage-list or a shot-composition. The discovery of the most important face
for *The General Line*, that of the film's heroine, was so long in being made that
everyone became worried:

'The filming went on, but the heroine had not been found. For two months
the directors of *The General Line* combed railway stations, night-lodgings,
factories. They rode through the country. They summoned women for inspection
by ringing church-bells. They looked at thousands of faces and tested some of
them.

'No heroine.

'In this extremity Eisenstein even decided on a step directly contrary to all
his principles originally formulated on beginning this film—he decided to test
actresses for the rôle. Interviews of actresses began. Nothing came of this.
Actresses looked insulted when they were asked whether they could milk a
cow, or plough, or drive a tractor. They would proudly answer, "No!"—and
that would end the interview. The directors resumed their search wherever
they went. At last, perhaps in exhaustion, they began filming anyway. Yet
nothing seemed quite right. They noticed that they tended to film people from
behind.

'And then, one fine day, they found her. . . .'[27]

Marfa Lapkina came to the filming that day only because everyone did. She had
been a farm-labourer since the age of nine; after the revolution she worked on
the state farm of Konstantinovka. She was illiterate, but once her remarkable
face was discovered by Eisenstein, he and the crew found in her an intelligence
and alertness that more than made up for her inability to read. At first she refused
to leave her work to travel with strangers, but finally agreed on the condition
that she could take along her year-old baby boy. The baby was always kept near
her, and between takes Marfa would sometimes run to change his nappy. When
the crew left to work on *October*, Marfa returned to her husband at Konstantinovka, and was again pregnant when *The General Line* was resumed, so that
most of her last scenes were shot to conceal her state; the new baby was born
just as the film was finished. Four years before the film was begun Marfa had
tended a healthy calf at the Konstantinovka farm, and when the crew arrived at
the Ryazan farm for the scenes with Fomka the bull, Marfa discovered that he
was the calf she had taken care of.

The kulak's rôle was played by Chukhmarev, a Moslem and former meat
contractor for the army. Father Matvei was found in Leningrad; before the war
he had played the cello at the Marinsky Theatre, was drafted into the army and
later joined the Red Army and suffered a concussion in the fighting at Kronstadt. The lovely sad wife in the scene of the divided hut* was found in Nevezh-

* This scene was suggested, indirectly, by Shub, via Shklovsky: 'I told Alexandrov
that E. Shub wanted to film Byelorussian life without staging anything, and in order to
show a genuine *izba*, she did not want to build one in the studio, but to take a real one and
simply saw it in half. Alexandrov replied, "It would be good if the sawing itself were to
be shown".' (*Their Realities*, 1927) Apparently this exchange lingered in Alexandrov's
memory, for that is how the wasteful divisions between the sons of a peasant family are
shown in *Old and New*: the family house is literally sawn in half.
It is curious that this scene, the product of many minds, should have been used so often

kovo, a village of Old Believers. One big beard that was found for the procession also worked in the *October* scene of Kornilov's 'Wild Division'.

It is perhaps for the last stage of *The General Line*'s creation that it will hold its place in all histories of film art. Several film-making generations from now the montage of Eisenstein's fourth film will be just as unique in its range of 'sensual montage' as *October* is unique for its vocabulary of 'intellectual montage'. Eisenstein himself realized the nature of *The General Line*'s montage only at a late stage of the film's completion, apparently at the time of its last revision:

'It was on the cutting table that I detected the sharply defined scope of the particular montage of *Old and New*. This was when the film had to be condensed and shortened. The "creative ecstasy" attending the assembly and montage—the "creative ecstasy" of "hearing and feeling" the shots—all this was already in the past. . . .

'And there, examining the sequence of the religious procession on the table, I could not fit the combination of its pieces into any one of the orthodox categories, within which one can apply one's pure experience. On the table, deprived of motion, the reasons for their choice seem completely incomprehensible. The criteria for their assembly appear to be outside formally normal cinematographic criteria.'

Defining 'orthodox montage' as editing for the *dominant* or surface elements of the filmed material, Eisenstein discovered that many sequences of the film had been edited for less visible associations, for their 'collateral vibrations', for their *overtones*.

'The montage of *Old and New* is constructed with this method. This montage is built, not on *particular* dominants, but takes as its guide the total stimulation through all stimuli, that is, the original montage complex within the shot, arising from the collision and combination of the individual stimuli inherent in it. . . . The whole intricate, rhythmic, and *sensual* nuance scheme of the combined pieces [of certain sequences] is conducted almost exclusively according to a line of work on the "psycho-physiological" vibrations of each piece.'[28]

In an essay written shortly afterwards Eisenstein simplified this definition to the term, 'tonal montage'.

'In tonal montage, movement is perceived in a wider sense. The concept of movement embraces *all affects* of the montage piece. Here montage is based on the characteristic *emotional sound* of the piece—of its dominant. The general tone of the piece.'[29]

as evidence against Eisenstein. Even twenty years later Ivan Pyriev wrote: 'Eisenstein approached the solution of this theme [Soviet agriculture] not with a national form, corresponding to the socialist content, but with the old formalist method of "montage of attractions", which he failed to overcome and shake off till the end. Naturally he suffered failure, misrepresented reality and characters of Russian people. It is enough to recall the scene of the two bearded peasants sawing their hut into half with a saw, or the character of the main and central figure of the film—the peasant woman Marfa Lapkina. What a mutilated, unreal and offensive character!' (In *Thirty Years of Soviet Cinematography* [Moscow 1950], translated in *Soviet Films* [Bombay 1951]).

Eisenstein's basic approach to the editing process—as conflict—had deepened in this stage of his work; he describes the delayed harvest in *Old and New* as an example of tonal montage:

'Emotive structures applied to non-emotional material. The stimulus is transferred from its usual use as situation (for example, as eroticism is usually used in films) to structures paradoxical in tone. . . .

'Therefore, the thematic *minor* of the harvesting is resolved by the thematic *major* of the tempest, of the rain. Yes, and even the stacked harvest, itself—traditional major theme of fecundity basking in the sun—is a resolution of the minor theme, wetted as it is by the rain. . . .

'The gathering of the skies into a black, threatening mass is contrasted with the intensifying dynamic force of the wind, and the solidification implied in the transition from currents of air to torrents of water is intensified by the dynamically blown petticoats and the scattering sheaves of the harvest.

'Here a collision of tendencies—an intensification of the static and an intensification of the dynamic—gives us a clear example of dissonance in tonal montage construction. . . .

'In some sequences *Old and New* succeeds in effecting junctions of tonal and overtonal lines.'[30]

The example of this, the religious procession, he gives again ten years later as an example of another term, 'polyphonic montage'; using the analogy of orchestration, he identifies the several instruments, or lines:

'1 The line of heat, increasing from shot to shot.
'2 The line of changing close-ups, mounting in plastic intensity.
'3 The line of mounting ecstasy, shown through the dramatic content of the close-ups.
'4 The line of women's "voices" (faces of the singers).
'5 The line of men's "voices" (faces of the singers).
'6 The line of those who kneel under the passing ikons (increasing in tempo). This counter-current gave movement to a larger counter-stream which was threaded through the primary theme—of the bearers of ikons, crosses and banners.
'7 The line of groveling, uniting both streams in the general movement of the sequence, "from heaven to the dust. . . ."

'The general course of the montage was an uninterrupted interweaving of these diverse themes into one unified movement. Each montage-piece had a double responsibility—to build the *total line* as well as to continue the movement within *each of the contributory themes*.'[31]

It was during the cutting of *The General Line* that Eisenstein made a serious beginning on a second career that in time would rank beside his film-making career—his work as teacher and theoretician. Even before his first film he had balanced—and in public print—the compelling intuitions of an artist with the inquiring mind of a logician; his teaching, too, had begun in the Proletkult days, when he had given a class in theatre direction (chiefly to show a method distinct from that of Meyerhold). And now his work on the montage of *The General Line*, with all the technical maturity that it represented, required words and print to explain his new steps to others—and to himself. I believe that the propaganda purpose for the unusual quantity of writing that began in 1928 and 1929 was less important than the personal reason: to find and define the reasons behind the thoughts and acts of excited creativity, to prepare himself for *next* steps. There are magazine and newspaper articles, prefaces, and notebooks dating from this time, dealing with everything from theory to polemic, various enough for several active minds. Engaged in production twelve hours a day, with some of the remaining time spent in detailed preparation for the next day's shooting, he yet found time to write, for example, an analysis of the relation between the arts of Japan and his theory of montage, followed by a vigorous (and effectual) attack on the methods of certain complacent scenarists.

There were many outer stimulants, too, at this time—some of them can be identified in his essays. One of the most impressive of these was the visit to Moscow from Tokyo of the Kabuki Theatre in August 1928, just as *The General Line* crew returned to Moscow for studio work. Eisenstein, who had studied Japanese culture at a distance, was already sharpened for every stimulating subtlety in this fresh theatre experience, and found in it, as he was to find in so many cultures and arts, justifications and precedents for the new forms he wished films to take. Soviet theatre activity, with Meyerhold in the vanguard, was competing with the cinema as the most vehement Soviet art. The new poetry of Mayakovsky and Pasternak was at its peak of popularity, and there was a new wave of study of the literary techniques of past generations. In painting and sculpture there was still room for more than the naturalistic norm that had always dominated these arts in Russia. And all the arts were clamouring for more responsible rôles in the propaganda and instructional jobs needed by the new industrial intensity of the Five Year Plan. This is a constant theme in Eisenstein's writing, especially in the quantity of forceful journalism that appeared alongside his theoretical essays.

The *General Line* crew returned to Moscow just as a school year was starting at the State Film Technicum, and Eisenstein, full of energy, offered to direct a workshop course there, simultaneously with his completion of the film. Eisenstein threw himself totally into this job, as if it were an extension of his creative work. One of the last leading directors to teach at the Technicum (Pudovkin had begun the first of his many classes there at the time of *Mother*'s release, and Abram Room had opened a workshop there the same year), Eisenstein eventually became the creative head of the school. This, though, was several years and many frustrations later; now he poured more and more of his time and ideas into eager young ears, and even went to battle the administration of the film industry for more authority and facilities to be given the school programme:

'Bismarck said, "To wage war successfully, three things are needed: Money. Money. And more money."'

'The Iron Chancellor of the Soviet cinema [Shvedchikov] has also taken this for his formula; he says the Soviet cinema needs only three things—money, money, and only money. And all would be well.

'Not true. It's true that money is needed, but there are three things far more needed:

'School. School. And again, school.

'The school of ideological supervision. The school of high sta.idards of production. The school of Marxist principles and theory of cinema. (Without the last, the two first are soap bubbles.)'[32]

His passionate interest in the education of future Soviet film-makers changed the emphasis of the curriculum of the directors' course. Heretofore a manipulation of the instruments of film-making had been the aim; Eisenstein changed this, now and in the future, to a preparation in the principles of all creative work, based chiefly on theatre experience. He even invited one of the Kabuki actors, Chojuro Kawarazaki, to give a supplementary course in movement. Among the members of this first of Eisenstein's important seminars were the two editors, the Vasilievs, eager to try direction. In addition to the instruction from Eisenstein, they obtained from Alexandrov a scenario for their first film, *The Sleeping Beauty*. Alexandrov also provided the scenario for another graduate, Yevgeni Chervyakov.

In the spring of 1929, the montage of *The General Line* was finished, the various inspection screenings had begun, and the Eisenstein group were planning a trip abroad to learn about sound-film, when a conversation took place that occasioned further alteration and delay in the film's release. Ten years later Alexandrov published his account of this event:

'One day when Eisenstein and I were lecturing to the students of GTK, the guard ran into the lecture-hall and told us that Cde Stalin was on the telephone, asking for us. We reached the phone in an instant.

' "Forgive me for interrupting your work", said Josef Vissarionovich, "I have wanted to talk with you, comrades. When would you have some free time? Would two o'clock tomorrow be convenient?"

'The idea that we, young Soviet film-makers, were to see the great leader of the people, to talk with him personally, filled us with excitement and joy.

'Next day promptly at two p.m. we were admitted to Cde Stalin's office, where we also found Comrades Molotov and Voroshilov. We were greeted warmly and kindly. An unconstrained discussion started.

'With great sensitivity Josef Vissarionovich gave us his critical comments on *The General Line*.* Then he went on to the general question of film art.

' "The significance of Soviet film art is very great—and not only for us. Abroad there are very few books with communist content. And our books are seldom known there, for they don't read Russian. But they all look at Soviet films with attention and they all understand them. You film-makers can't imagine what responsible work is in your hands. Take serious note of every act, every word of your heroes. Remember that your work will be judged by millions

* Alexandrov gives no information on this criticism.

of people. You should not invent images and events while sitting in your office. You must take them from life—learn from life. Let life teach you!"

'After a brief pause Josef Vissarionovich continued:

' "In order to estimate this properly, you see, Marxism must be known. It seems to me that our artists still show insufficient understanding of the great strength of Marxism." Cde Stalin spoke heatedly about the slight acquaintance that masters of Soviet film art* had with the works of Marx. . . .

'Cde Stalin showed interest in questions of film technique. Knowing about our planned trip to America, Josef Vissarionovich told us: "Study the sound film in detail. This is very important for us. When our heroes discover speech, the influential power of films will increase enormously."

'Towards the end Josef Vissarionovich again spoke about *The General Line*, advising us to change the finale.

' "Life must prompt you to find the correct end for the film. Before going to America, you should travel through the Soviet Union, observe everything, comprehend it and draw your own conclusions about everything you see."

'And he gave orders to the cinema administration, to organize a trip for us through the new construction projects. . . . We were sincerely sorry that the talk with Cde Stalin had not taken place before we made our film. It would have been a very different film. . . .'[33]

Amidst these platitudes and worshipping attitudes some things of interest reveal themselves—most importantly, that Stalin respected the medium of cinema more than he did the artists who worked in it. The effect of Stalin's 'orders to the cinema administration' was to delay the completion and release of *The General Line*. The crew travelled, filming, through the Soviet Union for two more months, achieving only an ordinary peasant-and-worker-bond epilogue that could have been attached to any other film. The original conclusion, in homage to *A Woman of Paris*, still showed the chance meeting of Marfa (now a tractor-driver) and the tractor-driver (now a farmer.)† Even as altered, the authorities were cool to *The General Line*, and to prevent its identification with any Party policy, scaled down its release title to the less specific *Old and New*.

In August 1929, three months before the release of *Old and New*, the Eisenstein group left the Soviet Union for a stay abroad of undetermined length. By now there was an accumulation of reasons for the trip: a study of sound-film techniques in European studios was possibly the primary reason, and the one usually advanced, but there was also the hope of working in the world's best-equipped film industry, Hollywood; Eisenstein had received many invitations to go there, the latest being from Joseph Schenck who visited Moscow in the summer of 1928; a trip to America was looked upon as a deserved vacation for a group that had worked so continuously without leave. A more pressing reason was connected with Eisenstein's project to film *Capital*: he felt that he could not honestly undertake such a task without seeing the capitalist world at its zenith

* Not identified.

† A copy with this conclusion, and other episodes removed to make room for the new epilogue, is preserved in the collection of the former Film Technicum. There was also an earlier conclusion which may not have been preserved.

(this was just three months before the crash of the American stock market!) and it was to that world that the group headed, each of the three carrying $25.

There must have been several private sighs of relief at the departure of the *enfant terrible* of the Soviet film: the administration of the industry lost its most irritating critic, and the makers of convenient, 'useful' films could work more comfortably without the constant challenge of Eisenstein's original ideas. To make the occasion even happier for the conservatives, the group left under a cloud of controversy caused by advance screenings of their new film: a controversial film has never been recognized by Soviet authorities and critics as a symptom of artistic health.

Throughout this last silent period there were plenty of good-looking non-controversial films that gave offence to no one. Tarich and Roshal pursued their sober ways. Nothing with which Preobrazhenskaya followed *Women of Ryazan* caused as much interest, not even an adaptation of Sholokhov's popular *Quiet Don*. Kuleshov's brightness, too, had settled into a fixed look. (Barbusse described *Gay Canary* as 'an amusing picture of the fever of revels and intrigues which took possession of Odessa during the foreign occupation ten years ago'.)[34] And Timoshenko made films on Eisenstein's principles, but without spirit.

It was however the oldest practising director who was not seduced by the tried-and-true. Each of Protazanov's last silent films was, in its quiet, solid way, an experiment. All three scenarios were written in collaboration with Oleg Leonidov. *The White Eagle*, based on Andreyev's story, 'The Governor', was the first Soviet film to show an official of the Tsar's government in a moral dilemma, a conflict between his private conscience and his official duty—and the film was, therefore, accused of misplacing its sympathies. Today its subject seems less extraordinary than its cast: in it Kachalov and Meyerhold give their only surviving film performances.[35] Protazanov's next film added performances by Moskvin and Tarkhanov to this display of Moscow Art Theatre history, yet the invention of *Ranks and People* was a formal one: its gathering of three short stories by Chekhov* into one film was an idea ahead of its time—a decade was to pass before other film-makers in other countries were to try such collections of 'miniatures'. This first Soviet film to draw from Chekhov was to be followed by many, but his serious plays continue to resist adaptation.

Holiday of St Jorgen showed the first successful approach to an anti-religious subject—laughter. As in *Three Thieves* where the methods of petty crime and big business are compared satirically, so in *St Jorgen* the business methods of thieves are paralleled with the financial and political pressures of the church—all in a richly vaudeville manner calculated, not so much to convince the spectator as to amuse him while making him a little more sceptical than before. Two thieves arrive in town at the time of the annual holiday of the local saint, an event efficiently exploited by town and church—only this time the two thieves exploit it for their own benefit. The film opens on exactly the right note (an episode not in the novel by Bergstedt), with the production of a propaganda film to attract worshippers to the shrine of St Jorgen. As if to underline the success of *St Jorgen* a serious anti-church film, *Judas*, appeared at the same time.

* 'Anna on the Neck,' 'Death of a Petty Official,' 'Chameleon'.

Another satisfying comedy was made by a newcomer to films, Alexei Popov, whose career since 1930 has been exclusively in the theatre. *Three Friends and an Invention* shows the adventures of a pair of young workers whose invention (a box-making machine) does not interest their factory, so they take to the road, accompanied by a jolly girl, to find someone who will give their invention a trial. Popov's second and last film, *Extremely Unpleasant Incident*, was a mildly anti-religious comedy.

A more sharply satirical comedy was made by Boris Barnet, *The House on Trubnaya Square*,* about the tangled relations of the occupants of this house. Central in the tangle is the servant-girl Parasha, the first large rôle played by Vera Maretskaya. What is extraordinary about this simple satire on contemporary Moscow life is the huge staff of skilled scenarists needed to complete it: Zorich, Marienhof, Shershenevich, Shklovsky, Erdmann. And this was the last film acted by the versatile actor, Vladimir Fogel, whose death on June 8, 1929, was the first loss from among those associated with the Soviet cinema's years of growth.

In the late 1920s there were an unusual number of departures, especially among actors, and these led in most cases to the elimination of their names (though not their faces) from Soviet publications. Of the several important émigrés from the Soviet cinema, those who did not make anti-Soviet films or anti-Soviet statements were not so completely erased. One actor who appeared in so many Soviet films that the elimination of his name (until recently restored) was physically awkward was Ivan Koval-Samborsky. He went to Berlin to appear in a Prometheus production of a Bela Balazs scenario, $1 + 1 = 3$, but arrived four days too late, so waited for another rôle, in *Schinderhannes*; he later returned to Moscow, but disappeared again for a while. Both director and cameraman of *Kira Kiralina* left VUFKU for abroad: Boris Glagolin ended in Hollywood, piteously unwanted, and Farkash remained employed in Paris studios. Alexander Granovsky, leaving behind the Jewish Kamerny Theatre and his one film, *Jewish Luck*, found both theatre and film work in Berlin and Paris. After *The White Eagle*, Anna Sten left to continue her starring career in Germany and at the Goldwyn studio in Hollywood. The last published Soviet word on her was in 1932, in *Proletarskoye Kino*: an irresistible but ungallant comparison of her Soviet autobiography with the version of her life (and adjusted birth-date) that she gave to German journalists. Vera Baranovskaya's departure was a sadder event, but there has never been any question of her elimination from *Mother* and *The End of St Petersburg*. Her last Soviet rôle was a comparatively minor one in Room's *Ruts*, and her departure to play for Terra in Berlin was partly justified by the Soviet press protests, at the time, that other major work could not be found for her. She did not give the Soviet film another chance. After playing in a Kuleshov film and an attempt at direction (*The Brand of the Cross*), another Pudovkin actor, Inkizhinov, vanished to Paris where he remained employable up to the present on the strength of *Tempête sur l'Asie*. Most of the Russian members of the cast and crew of *A Living Corpse* returned to Moscow, but Otsep stayed abroad to work in sound-films; his *Murder of*

---

* I have not seen Barnet's last silent film, *Thaw* (released June 20, 1931).

Karamazov had a greater effect on international films than any Soviet film he directed.

There has always been a steady supply of new acting talent, some even from the film schools, coming into Soviet studios. And young directors, eager and able to take the places of Glagolin, Granovsky and Otsep, were asking for chances to prove themselves. A young man who worked as an assistant on *October* made one of the most promising films of 1929. Ilya Trauberg, younger brother of Kozintsev's partner, and soaked in film talk from his boyhood, made his first effort in 1927, a documentary, *Leningrad Today*. After his job on *October* he was given a chance to show what he had learned from working with the Eisenstein group, made the most of his opportunities, and directed a really effective melodrama about the colonial powers in China—*The Blue Express*, more familiar abroad as *China Express*. A microcosm of the political world hurtling through the night on rails towards a certain geographical point and an uncertain destiny is such a dramatic idea that it is no wonder that it has been often repeated in film history, almost as effectively in Sternberg's *Shanghai Express*. In Trauberg's film the class divisions of the train fix the political divisions of the film, with the Chinese heroes travelling third-class and his alien villains in the luxurious first-class compartment. A mercenary's attack on a Chinese girl precipitates a clash that spreads through the train, and brings train and revolt roaring to its destination. (Workers in the audience wondered how, after the fireman left the engine to lead the revolt, the train got along without him.)

Another effective début was made by Raizman with *Katorga*. In 1927 Yuli Raizman left Protazanov and Mezhrabpom to work in a studio with no outstanding directors and no artistic reputation, Gos-voyen-kino (State Army Films), where he first made an unremarked comedy, *Circle* (announced as *He, She, and a Dog*). Then he quietly prepared a big film that was remarked by the whole industry when it was released November 27, 1928. *Katorga* (*Penal Servitude*) was written by Yermolinsky and photographed by Kosmatov, two talented people who were to remain with Raizman through his next several films. *Katorga* is set in a Siberian prison-camp early in the century; its climax is an unsuccessful revolt of the prisoners against the sadistic warden that was severely criticized for its 'pessimism' of content and its 'expressionism' of treatment. But the film found needed support in the Moscow section of the Society of Political Exiles who endorsed the film's reality and story.

In 1928 at another young studio, Byelgoskino (whose first film had been released in 1927—*Prostitute*, by Oleg Froelich), the young writing-directing team of Mikhail Auerbach and Mark Donskoy made *In the Big City*, about a peasant poet (modelled on Sergei Yessenin) who lands in city life with less tragic results than Yessenin's. This was followed with *Value of a Man*, but Donskoy's first independent films were a three-reel comedy, *Fop* (1930) and the full-length *Fire* (1931). Also at Byelgoskino Alexander Feinzimmer began his directing career with *Hotel Savoy*. At the Leningrad Sovkino the team of Alexander Zarkhi and Josef Heifitz, recent graduates of the Leningrad Technicum of Screen Arts, worked as scenarists before getting a direction job. Their last script was *Transport of Fire*, directed by Alexander Ivanov, and in the same year, 1929, they made their first film, *Facing the Wind*. In Moscow a graduate of the 1928 class of GTK was given his first film to direct by Mezhrabpom: Nikolai Ekk made such a good thing of *How and How Not to Do It*, an enacted culture-film on skins and leather, that more important films were predicted for him. Ivan Pyriev's first film, after leaving Tarich's crew, was *Strange Woman*, in 1929. But all these young directors would show their most interesting work in sound-film.

The Georgian studio showed a number of new talents in this period. After collaborating on two films to learn the medium, Nikolai Shengelaya left his literary career completely to work in films; his first independent film, *Eliso*, was a triumph. It was suggested by an anecdote recorded by the Georgian writer Kazbegi about a Tsarist scheme in 1864 to evict a village that occupied a desirable piece of land. The film makes the whole village its hero rather than any individual, and a richness of exotic folk-material* in it reminds one of *Women of Ryazan*. Two young directors with separate distinguished futures worked together on a Russian story of the Civil War, *First Cornet Streshnev* (1928), and each of the partners took Georgian stories for their next films: Mikhail Chiaureli, who came from acting and painting efforts, made *Saba*, a modern story attacking alcoholism, and Yefim Dzigan made *God of War* (or *The White Rider*) and *Woman*. Mikhail Gelovani, a director whose success was to come as an actor of one repeated rôle, made *Youth Wins*. A more important Georgian director, Kalatozov, came to films at this time as a cameraman. There were some ambitious films of this period that are now remembered only for their literary sources: *Woman at the Fair* (1928) was an embarrassing adaptation of Eugene O'Neill's *Desire Under the Elms*, in which the setting was unhappily retained as a peculiar version of rural United States; and *Law and Duty* (1927), an adaptation of Stefan Zweig's 'Amok'.

One young artist was lost to the Soviet cinema, but neither by death nor by emigration. After the domestic satire of *Mitya*, Nikolai Okhlopkov tried his sharp wits on a foreign subject, a story-fable by the French Marxist, Paul Lafargue— *Un appétit vendu*. A young worker who cannot support the excellent appetites of his family on his income sells his appetite to a rich man who cannot enjoy the wondrous foods his wealth can buy. The contrasts and ironies of this tale were developed by the scenarists, Marienhof and Erdmann, into a broad burlesque on capitalist contradictions, and filmed by Okhlopkov in a strikingly uninhibited style. The reactions to *The Sold Appetite* in the one country, France, that might be expected to enjoy its novelty and fantastic realism, were cool. One Parisian critic, Claude Jeantet, was quite discouraging:

'The heaviness of its manner, added to the basic *bizarrerie* of its subject, makes this film one that would, we believe, be impossible to show in ordinary theatres. It's regrettable that its surprising virtuosity and the forceful originality of some shots are almost unusable.'

The Sold Appetite, produced by VUKFU, was the last Okhlopkov film released.

* Eisenstein told Ivor Montagu that there were only two good filmings of the exciting Caucasian dance, the *lezginka*, and that Shengelaya's in *Eliso* was better than the *October* one.

Okhlopkov wrote his third scenario with G. Pavlyuchenko, *Way of the En-thusiasts*: through an episode of the Civil War it showed how crisis overcame the mutual suspicions of peasants and city workers. The film was produced by Moscow Sovkino, but was never released. The one foreigner who had a chance to see *Way of the Enthusiasts* was H. P. J. Marshall, then studying at GTK; he described the film as 'decidedly intellectual'.[36] Otherwise all that remains of this film are a published fragment of its scenario,[37] rumours of its fresh wit and originality, intriguing accusations of its attempt to apply Eisenstein's 'intel-lectual' methods to comedy problems, and Okhlopkov's refusal to direct another film. Thereafter he was willing to work in films as an actor, but his inventive talents he took to the theatre, making good the theatre's loss of Eisenstein in 1924. Okhlopkov's work at the Realistic, or Krasnaya Presnaya Theatre, with its new ideas of stage space, showed everyone what the cinema had lost. One of the greatest richnesses of the Soviet film was its extraordinary variety of approaches; Okhlopkov's withdrawal was a dangerous symptom of a narrowing range.

The Russian stop-motion film, begun so brilliantly before the revolution by Starewicz, was slow to grow afterwards; neither industry nor press paid much attention to these puppets and flat drawings. Late in 1923 Bushkin and Ivanov produced the first Soviet animated cartoon, *Soviet Toys*, made for Vertov's series at Kultkino. In 1924, a producing workshop for animated films, using both cartoons and dolls, was organized at the State Film Technicum, and their first film was *Interplanetary Revolution*, a parody on *Aelita*. Regular production dates from the workshop's second film, *China Aflame* (1925). Until then the animated film had been regarded by Soviet studios very much as it was regarded abroad, merely as a programme-filling novelty. The writers and artists of this film, however, aimed to make an effective political film. This first 'social ani-mation' was made with jointed dolls, filmed with the stop-motion camera, but the workshop soon adopted the cartoon as a more flexible medium, and exercised the animated dolls only occasionally, as in *Moidodyr* (1927), adapted from Chukovsky's poem about clean children. Once the technicum workshop had collected and trained a group of artists—such as Vano, the Khodatayevs (brother and sister), the Brumberg sisters, Suteyev and others, the workshop was absorbed by Mezhrabpom as a production department. Of these artists, Vano was the quickest to grasp the needs of the cartoon medium. In collaboration with Cherkes, he made a delightful white-line animation, *Skating Rink* (1927), recalling one of the earliest cartoonists, Emile Cohl, and *The Adventures of Baron Munchhausen* (1929), that achieved tones and depth that would have surprised foreign audiences. Political cartoons were further developed, during the silent period, by Antonovsky in Leningrad, who left newspaper work for films in 1929. He began with a harsh anti-religious satire, *Crusade*, followed by *Look at the Root*, *They and We*, and *The Good Soldier Schweik*. Some measure of importance seemed granted to the cartoon by the appearance of both Lunacharsky and Kalinin in Ivanov's series of 'Tip-Top's' excursions through Soviet life, in 1928. To see a photographed Lunacharsky greeting a cartooned 'Tip-Top' would, if translated into the officials and cartoon characters of any other country, have meant success, but the animated cartoon here, as everywhere, awaited the sound-track for its full arrival.

The story of Dovzhenko's *Earth* is so slight as to be almost plotless: the young peasants of a Ukrainian village want to buy a tractor to bring the future a little faster to their village; the kulaks of the community fear this strengthened unity and one of them kills the young village chairman. Yet this story scarcely hints of all the qualities and passages that have made *Earth* one of the few acknowledged classics of the Soviet and world cinema. The lyricism of the whole, sustained by Dovzhenko's philosophical sense of 'the earth', of life and death, is what remains in the memory of everyone who has seen this beautiful film. Before we remember what the film was about, we think of the prologue where the peacefully dying old man bites joyfully into an apple; or the funeral procession with the branches of the apple-tree sweeping over the dead face; or Vasili's dance of happiness through the summer's dust of the moonlit village, a dance that ends with a bullet; or the murderer's mad dance among the unhearing graves. A part of our reluctance to face the whole meaning of *Earth* is suggested by Ivor Montagu:

'For the key to all the poignancy in Dovzhenko's films is death. Just that, the simplest thing of all. Death apprehended never as an end, a finish, dust to dust. But death as a sacrifice, the essential one, a part of the unending process of reviving life. . . .

'Pantheism? No. Nature worship? Not at all. Sound Marxist dialectics: the union of opposites.

'Dovzhenko's films are crammed with deaths. No artist in any medium has torn more rawly at the heart-strings. But no death in Dovzhenko was ever futile.'[38]

How strange that on opposite sides of the planet the two greatest Soviet film artists should be filming the same theme: death as part of life—Dovzhenko in the utter simplicity of *Earth* and Eisenstein in the complex structure and grand range of *Que Viva Mexico!* Both artists had resolved the conflicts between beauty and content, each with a noticeable reduction of action, yet in neither case did his resolution effect the course of the Soviet film—for his American backers never permitted Eisenstein to finish his film, and Dovzhenko's film caused such a public furore as to frighten away any eager followers in his own generation, though there was appreciation of its unique beauty.

Demyan Byedny, the Bolshevik 'folk-poet', was so outraged by *Earth* that he devoted a three-column article in *Izvestia* to denouncing it as 'defeatist'. This and other attacks resulted in some cuts in the film,* and a shortening of its distribution life. Another poet left no record of the impression *Earth* made on him: within a week after Mayakovsky saw it at the Writers' Club he was dead by his own hand. Montagu summed up the offensive:

'Hot discussion': yes, within his own country and outside it. Within, the pundits could perceive and approve his love of country as a son of the Ukraine; the

* A copy in its original version is preserved at Gosfilmofond, and was shown abroad for the first time in Brussels, October 1958; the negative was destroyed in the German invasion.

poetic message they could only sense. Feeling its power, outside their narrow range, mistaking for pantheism its truly dialectic perception of the oneness and continuity of the universe, the puritans and careerists, alarmed, were nervous. Without, that same passionate love of man and all nature was misunderstood, and applauded, as a sign of indifference towards the contemporary struggle or the standards of the artist's socialist homeland, a sign that he was not *engagé*.

'Nothing could have been more false. This artist was the most *engagé* of all the talents in all Soviet art.'[39]

Eisenstein, whose *engagement* was also underrated at the time, had left Hollywood with Alexandrov and Tisse after their contract with Paramount had lapsed in repeated rejections of their proposals, and arranged to make a film in Mexico, financed by Mr and Mrs Upton Sinclair. Before the unfinished *Que Viva Mexico* was taken from him Eisenstein had poured all his ideas and hopes into a six-part epic of Mexican thought and history. It is now easier to guess his intentions from discarded unedited sections than from the several films cut by other hands: those hands inevitably imposed their own wishes on the material. What appears is more easily related to Eisenstein's subsequent work than to his silent films. The artist, trained as architect and engineer, who had derided his colleague's approach to film-making as mere 'building', found himself in the surprising position of a builder, too. The building of his Mexican epic, though, was of far more intricate a character than any work by Pudovkin: *Que Viva Mexico* employed both the great solid blocks of contrasting sections and the intricate lacy geometry of a growth that could be found in plant-life as well as in mathematics. The separate stones or cells of this elaborate structure were sometimes as minimum in movement or drama as shots in *Arsenal* or *Earth*, Eisenstein's movement being planned as successive impacts of these lightly breathing compositions. This was the logical development from his analysis of certain montage schemes in *Old and New*: 'The concept of movement embraces *all affects* of the montage piece.'

And *Que Viva Mexico* was to be as crammed with metaphors as *Earth* was crammed with deaths. Eisenstein later examined Dovzhenko's masterpiece on this plane of metaphor. One of the censored scenes in *Earth*, the naked agony of Vasili's fiancée, was criticized by Eisenstein as an aesthetic error, reasoning that Dovzhenko's wish to give an 'image of a life-affirming beginning' could not be realized naturalistically:

'. . . the spectator could not possibly separate out of this concrete, lifelike woman [a] generalized sensation of blazing fertility, of sensual life-affirmation [during the funeral] . . . This was prevented by the ovens, pots, towels, benches, table-cloths—all those details of everyday life, from which the woman's body could easily have been freed by the *framing of the shot*—so that representational naturalism would not interfere with the embodiment of the task of *communicating the metaphor*.'[40]

It is in this light that the tragically unrealized fragment compositions of *Que Viva Mexico*, magnificently organized as they are, must be examined—not for their seeming completeness, but imagining the structures they were to rear.

The first film photographed in Russia, May 14, 1896, by Charles Moisson for the
Lumière catalogue: 'Les souverains et les invités se rendant au Sacre (escalier rouge).'
frame enlargement: Cinémathèque Française

Lev Tolstoy, photographed at Yasnaya Polyana by Alexander
Drankov, 1909. *photo: Cinémathèque de Belgique*

The Cameraman's Revenge, 1912, an animated model film designed and directed by Wladyslaw Starewicz.

Moment Musical, 1913, danced by Yekaterina Geltzer and Vasili Tikhomirov, directed by Yakov Protazanov.   *frame enlargements: Museum of Modern Art*

L'khaim: Scenes of Jewish Life, 1910, produced by the Moscow studio of Pathé Frères.

frame enlargements from original negatives: Cinémathèque Française

L'Aurore de la Revolution Russe, ca. 1913, produced only for foreign distribution, with Ivan Bersenev and Vera Baranovskaya.

Singed Wings, 1915, directed by Yevgeni Bauer, with Vera Coralli and Vitold Polonsky. *photo: Photoplay Magazine*

Romance with Double-Bass, 1911, adapted from Chekhov's story and directed by Kai Hansen. *photo: Mr Mundviller*

The Queen of Spades, 1916, adapted from Pushkin's story and directed by Yakov Protazanov, with Mozhukhin and Shebuyeva. *photo: Photoplay Magazine*

A camera team of the Skobelev Committee, filming the May Day demonstration in Petrograd, 1917.
photo:
  Brown Brothers

Father Sergius, 1917-18, adapted from Tolstoy's novel and directed by Yakov Protazanov, with Ivan Mozhukhin.   *frame enlargement: Museum of Modern Art*

The Bloody Jest, from a series of Jewish films produced by Alexander Arkatov in Odessa in the summer of 1917, using actors with non-actors.   *photo: Mr Arkatov*

The Young Lady and the Hooligan,
1918, adapted by Vladimir Mayakovsky
from *Cuore* by Edmondo de Amicis,
with Rebikova and Mayakovsky.
photo:
  Lily Brik and Cinémathèque Française

Bread, 1918, an *agitka* directed by Sushkevich and Boleslawski for the Moscow Kino-
Committee, with Boleslawski, Leonidov, and Baklanova.   *photo: Mme Soloviova*

Return to Earth, 1921, directed and
played by Boris Glagolin.
            photo: Mr Glagolin

Adventures of Oktyabrina 1924,
directed by Kozintsev and Trauberg,
with Sergei Martinson as Poincaré.
*photo: L'art dans le Russie nouvelle:
Le Cinéma, by Marchand and Weinstein*

An echo of German Expressionismus.
Order Number —, 1926, from a studio in Rostov-na-Don.

Ivan Moskvin in *Polikushka*, 1920.

photo: Picture Collection, New York Public Library

Aelita, 1924, directed by Protazanov for the Russ Collective; *right*, Konstantin Eggert and Yulia Solntseva as Martian royalty; *below*, Nikolai Batalov, Igor Ilinsky, and Nikolai Tseretelli as Earthmen.   *photos: Ernestine Evans*

The fighting children in *Red Imps*, 1923, directed by Perestiani for the Georgian Film-Section.

photo: Cinémathèque Française

Left: Sergei Eisenstein in 1924.
photo: Eisenstein Collection, Museum of Modern Art

Strike, 1924-25, directed by Eisenstein with the Proletkult
Collective for Goskino.
frame enlargements: British Film Institute

The Cigarette-Girl from Mosselprom, 1924, directed by Yuri Zhelyabuzhsky, with Anna Dmokhovskaya and Igor Ilinsky.

Chess Fever, 1925, directed by Vsevolod Pudovkin and Nikolai Shpikovsky, with Ivan Koval-Samborsky, Vladimir Fogel, Anna Zemtsova and Natalia Glan.

The Girl with the Hat-box, 1926-27, directed by Boris Barnet, with Pavel Pol and Anna Sten.

Three Thieves, 1926, directed by Yakov Protazanov, with Olga Zhizneva.

The Cloak, 1926, adapted from Gogol's story and directed by Kozintsev and Trauberg for Leningradkino. *frame enlargement: Museum of Modern Art*

The Ninth of January, 1925, directed by Vyacheslav Viskovsky for Sevzapkino. *frame enlargement: Cinémathèque Française*

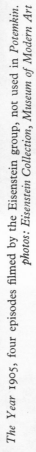

The Year 1905, four episodes filmed by the Eisenstein group, not used in *Potemkin*.
photos: Eisenstein Collection, Museum of Modern Art

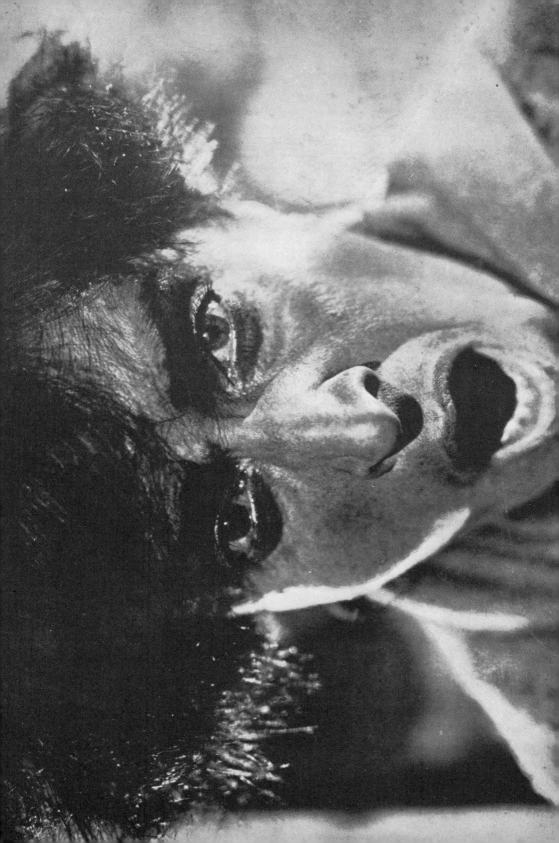

Women of Ryazan, 1927, directed by Olga Preobrazhenskaya and Ivan Pravov.

Jewish Luck, 1925, adapted from a Sholom Aleichem story and directed by Alexander Granovsky.

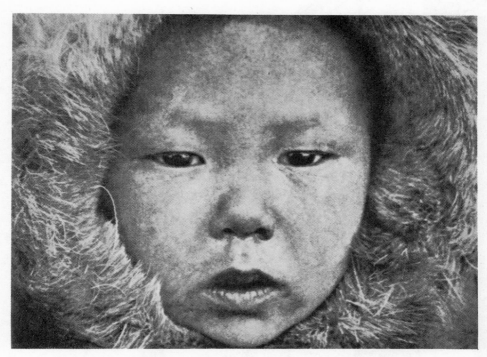

A Sixth of the Earth, 1926, directed by Dziga Vertov for Gostorg and Kultkino.

Mechanics of the Brain, 1925-26, directed by Vsevolod Pudovkin for Mezhrabpom-Russ.

By the Law, 1926, directed by Lev Kuleshov, with Alexandra Khokhlova, Vladimir Fogel, Sergei Komarov.

Mother, 1926, directed by Pudovkin; *right*, from the first sequence to be photographed by Anatoli Golovnya; *below*, the bier of the husband and father.
Photos by Alexandra Orlova

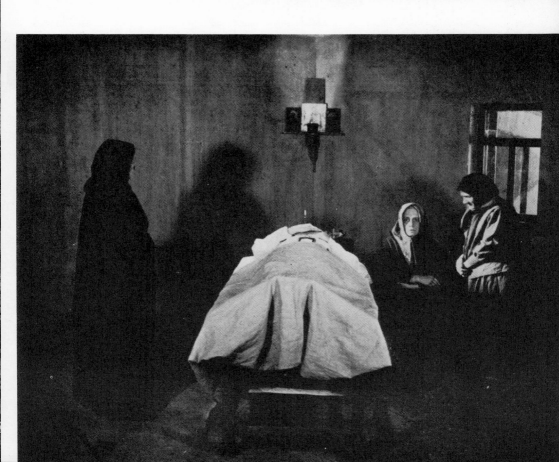

Wings of a Serf (Ivan the Terrible), 1926, directed by Yuri Tarich and Leonid Leonidov.

Elisso, 1928, directed by Nikolai Shengelaya for Goskinprom-Georgia.

photo: Cinémathèque de Belgique

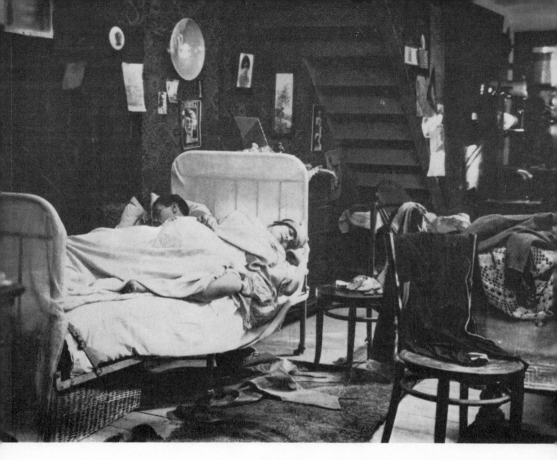

Third Meshchanskaya (*Bed and Sofa*), 1926, directed by Abram Room; *above*, the opening shot, with Nikolai Batalov and Ludmila Semyonova; *below*, the set designed by Sergei Yutkevich.

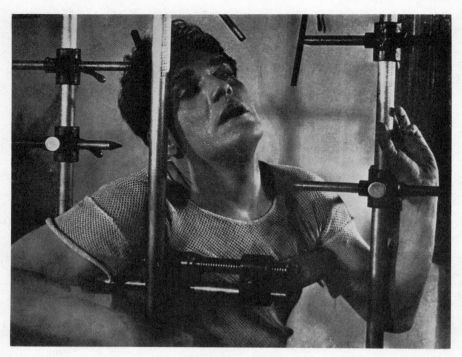

The Sold Appetite, 1928, directed by Nikolai Okhlopkov, with Ambrose Buchma.

Two Days, 1927, directed by Georgi Stabovoi, with Ivan Zamychkovsky.

The Diplomatic Pouch, 1926.
Alexander Dovzhenko playing a
rôle in his first full-length film.

Zvenigora, 1927, directed by Dovzhenko. Nikolai Nademsky as Grandad.
frame enlargement: Cinémathèque Française

ROLES PLAYED BY VSEVOLOD PUDOVKIN

As a German soldier, in an omitted episode of *The End of St. Petersburg*, 1927.
photo by Wenz

As a salesman, in *The New Babylon*, 1929, directed by Kozintsev and Trauberg.
photo by Yezersky

As the Abbé Revo, in *The Death Ray*, 1925, directed by Kuleshov.

As Fedya Protasov (with Nata Vachnadze as Masha), in *A Living Corpse*, 1928, directed by Fyodor Otsep.
photo by Orlova

The Heir to Jenghis-Khan (Storm Over Asia), 1928.

The End of St Petersburg, 1927.   *photos by Wenz*

The Man with the Movie-Camera, 1928-29, made by Dziga Vertov and Mikhail Kaufman.

Eisenstein, Alexandrov and Tisse filming a proposed prologue for the first
version of *The General Line*, 1926.

photo: Eisenstein Collection, Museum of Modern Art

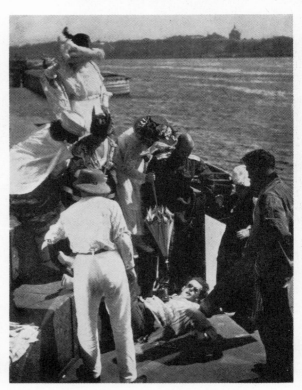

Eisenstein rehearsing a scene for
October, 1927; his inscription (to
Léon Moussinac): 'Le métier de
metteur en scène n'est pas toujours
trop agréable!' *photo by Sigayev*

Arsenal, 1928-29, written and directed by Alexander Dovzhenko; an effort to get food to the besieged arsenal has failed.

28

Fragment of an Empire, 1929, directed by Friedrich
Ermler.   *photo by Bushtuyev*

Salt for Svanetia, 1930, directed and photographed by Mikhail Kalatozov.

photo: Close Up

Pudovkin directing Yevgeniya Rogulina in
A Simple Case, 1930-31.

Katorga (Penal Servitude), 1928, directed by Yuli Raizman.   *photo by Khalip*

Earth, 1929-30, written and directed by Dovzhenko.

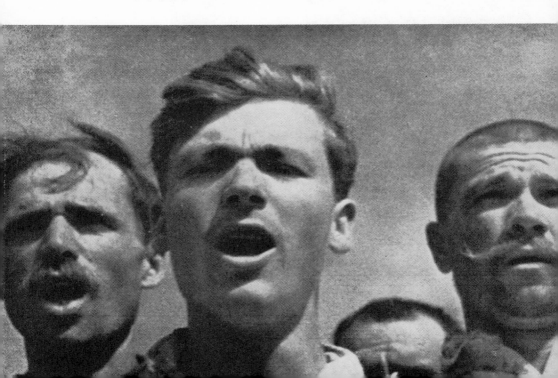

Eisenstein lecturing to his class at
GIK, 1934.   *photo by Debabov*

Pudovkin editing *Victory*, 1938.
photo: Sovfoto

Dovzhenko speaking to villagers in Western
Ukraine, during the making of *Liberation*,
1940.   *photo: Sovfoto*

Industrial Revolution

1930–1933

And, mind you, emotions are among the toughest
things in the world to manufacture out of whole cloth;
it is easier to manufacture seven facts than one
emotion

MARK TWAIN

The next great change in Soviet film history and, indeed, in world film history,
was caused by the financial anxieties of a small American film producer in 1925.
The school of 'inevitable' historians will say that the sound-film was bound to
come some day, but the fact is that it came when it did because the firm of Warner
Brothers needed a novelty to keep the company in business alongside its major
American competitors.

There had been inventions, ideas, schemes, dreams to synchronize pictures
and speech from the time of the invention of film itself. And just as several
inventors had arrived at the motion picture camera and projector almost
simultaneously, so several widely separated inventors were tantalizingly near
the realization of sound-film in the early 1920s. But the earliest practical
achievement in synchronized picture-sound recording and theatrical reproduction to attract investment was produced in the laboratories of the Bell
Telephone Company. When their device, Vitaphone, was offered to the major
American film companies, it was rejected for various reasons, chiefly economic;
it was such a reason that made the smaller firm of Warner Brothers decide
to invest in it all the capital they had and could borrow. The device was
given its first public test on August 6, 1926 when a musical synchronization of
the film *Don Juan* was introduced by various short films of singers and instru-
mentalists. The Warners' gamble did not really pay off until October 1927 when
they showed *The Jazz Singer* in New York, The three songs sung by Al Jolson
with a brief attached piece of dialogue changed the history of films. By the
beginning of 1928 another American producer, Fox, had bought and used
another process, Movietone, and before that summer ended the revolution in
Hollywood was victorious, with every studio installing sound equipment.
Audiences had shown their preference for the sound-film, and the silent film,
at least in America, was declared a thing of the past.

Less swiftly, this technical revolution spread to European studios and theatres, and many discouraged sound-film inventors there were welcomed in offices formerly barred to them. The two most persistent Russian inventors, P. G. Tager in Moscow and A. F. Shorin in Leningrad, were given fresh facilities and funds. Tager's systematic work on his invention dates from November 1926, a month before a kindred German process, Tri-Ergon, was demonstrated in Moscow and Leningrad. Throughout 1927 and 1928 Tager's progress was shown in a series of lectures and semi-public demonstrations. Whatever the influence of foreign progress on Tager and Shorin (who began his demonstrations in 1929), the delay in their work had certain advantages, chiefly in avoiding mistakes already corrected abroad. For example, Soviet engineers never had to suffer with the sound-on-disc method, the original Vitaphone process that was eventually discarded; both Tager and Shorin worked with the sound-on-film method that became universal by 1930.*

The late arrival of this technical revolution coincided with such great industrial changes in the Soviet film industry that it is natural to consider the sound-film as a 'reason' for the obvious change that took place in the artistic character of the Soviet cinema. But the full reason must be sought in all the changes that took place at this time. The emphasis of the first Five Year Plan on the development of heavy industry gave a new propaganda job to the comparatively light film industry, and geared film-making to the basic industrial programme. A symptom of this was the large new plants built at the major film production centres (except Leningrad); the new studios in Moscow, Kiev and Tiflis were begun in 1927, months before the programme of the Five Year Plan was announced, but the probably accidental timing of the construction, now ready for new responsibilities and new equipment, was perfect. The changed film industry centralized its financial structure and acquired a new industrial administrator, Boris Shumyatsky, whose primary task was to develop the Soviet film industry as an industry. Shumyatsky's ignorance of the nature of art and the psychology of artists may have recommended him for the new job. The two most vocal defenders of the artist's place and function within a socialist film industry were somewhere else: Mayakovsky was dead and Eisenstein was in Mexico.

At the height of the confusion in the international film world Eisenstein had proposed a programme for integrating the technological advance into the logical aesthetic development of the Soviet cinema. His bold warning against the temptations of the 'all-talking' film was subsequently ridiculed, but in August 1928 it was endorsed by Pudovkin and Alexandrov and appeared over their three signatures:

'We who work in the USSR are aware that with our technical potential we shall not move ahead to a practical realization of the sound-film in the near future. At the same time we consider it opportune to state a number of principle premises of a theoretical nature, for in the accounts of the invention it appears that this advance in films is being employed in an incorrect direction. Meanwhile, a misconception of the potentialities within this new technical discovery

* Tager's system used a variable density track, and Shorin used variable area.

may not only hinder the development and perfection of the cinema as an art, but also threatens to destroy all its present formal achievements. . . .

'Sound-recording is a two-edged invention, and it is most probable that its use will proceed along the line of least resistance, i.e. along the line of *satisfying simple curiosity*.

'In the first place there will be commercial exploitation of the most saleable merchandise, TALKING FILMS. Those in which sound-recording will proceed on a naturalistic level, exactly corresponding with the movement on the screen, and providing a certain "illusion" of talking people, of audible objects, etc.

'A first period of sensations does not injure the development of a new art, but it is the second period that is fearful in this case, a second period that will take the place of the fading purity of a first perception of new technical possibilities, and will assert an epoch of its automatic utilization for "highly cultured dramas" and other photographed performances of a theatrical sort.'[1]

Fortunately for the Soviet cinema, the chief mistakes of this 'second period' had been generally recognized by the time the sound-film reached Soviet studios. But other future troubles were more subtle, and this collective 'Statement's' suggestion that 'The first experimental work with sound must be directed along the line of its distinct non-synchronization with the visual images' is of historic interest but not of great help in the crises to come.

In the summer of 1929 both Tager and Shorin began practical film-studio use of their respective systems—Tager with Mezhrabpomfilm and Shorin with the Leningrad studio of Sovkino. In August Mezhrabpomfilm appointed Leonid Obolensky to work with Tager on the first attempt at open-air recording, when they tried his apparatus on a Moscow street. And in August the first sound-stage was completed at Leningrad Sovkino. At each of these studios the first directors to ask for the new device were responsible artists—Pudovkin at Mezhrabpomfilm, and Room and Vertov (for Ukrainfilm) at Sovkino.

Even before Pudovkin went to Berlin with the *Living Corpse* crew, he had decided that his next film was to be based on a scenario by Alexander Rzheshevsky, *Life's Very Good*. When he returned to Moscow in the spring of 1929, after a European tour that included lectures in England and Holland, he read the revised scenario against a background of all his new ideas about sound-films, ideas reinforced by disappointment in the sound-films he had seen abroad, and felt more deeply convinced of the artistic challenge in this scenario. However, after reading it, Golovnya was unconvinced, and he declined to work with such a 'loose' script. Yet it was the deliberate looseness and suggestiveness of Rzheshevsky's script that endeared it to precise Pudovkin.[2] Even more than with his Mongolian fable, the outer attractions of the scenario were stronger than its subject—the marital relations of a couple linked by common revolutionary experiences. Though Rzheshevsky based his idea on a newspaper feuilleton by Mikhail Koltsov, the general structure reminded Pudovkin's biographer, Yezuitov, of Cecil De Mille's *Why Change Your Wife*? In both films a husband leaves his wife for another woman and then, after the failure of the new relationship, returns to his first wife. Working with Kabalov as cameraman, and with the support of Doller, returned to the group after filming began in September 1929, Pudovkin dressed his variant on this subject in all the sensual poetry at his command, and tried all the experiments to which his months away from direction gave an extra relish, including the free use of slow-motion photography he wrote about in 'Close-Ups in Time'.[3] And as he began the new film just as his studio's hope in the Tager experiments was at its highest, work on *Life's Very Good* was inevitably scheduled as Mezhrabpom's first sound-film, and Pudovkin heard in his imagination a whole new scale of subtlety and sensual communication to add to his film. On a visit to Moscow, Margaret Bourke-White, the American photographer, found him 'working night and day on a new film'; he told her:

'. . . the sound film is a new medium which can be used in entirely new ways. Sounds and human speech should be used by the director not as a literal accompaniment, but to amplify and enrich the visual image on the screen. Under such conditions could the sound film become a new form of art whose future development has no predictable limits.'[4]

But the work with Tager showed, first of all, that his contribution was still a primitive and mechanical device, far from the subtle instrument that Pudovkin's imagination required,* and the crew revised the film's plan again on the basis of silence, rather than wait for the perfecting of sound-film manipulation.

Fortunately, Abram Room's first use of sound required no particular subtlety. His *Plan for Great Works* was a series of documentary episodes about the Five Year Plan, using almost entirely footage from previous films (such as Vertov's *Eleventh*, Shub's *Great Road*, and various issues of the Soyuzkino-newsreel), tied together with decorative animations by Tsekhanovsky. The sound-track was stripped down to music and agit-prop declamation, with some studio-manufactured sound effects.[5] The first Soviet sound-film was hurried efficiently through production, from its initiation in July 1929 to its release in March 1930. I have never seen the film, but it sounds quite unrelated to the rest of Room's work.

When *A Plan for Great Works* was released, there were only two theatres in the Soviet Union equipped to show it, the 'Giant' in Leningrad (1,000 seats) and the 'Artistic' in Moscow. An earlier experimental theatre in Leningrad had been used on October 5, 1929 to show a programme of Shorin's experiments,† but this seated only fifty persons, and helped little in this crisis of waiting for more sound theatre equipment to come from the factories. By the autumn of 1930 the distribution of *Plan* (and its accompanying animation, *Tip-Top, Sound Inventor*) had reached all major cities of the Union, and a new programme of sound shorts, made in all the native systems, was ready to follow it: a documentary, *The Fortieth May-Day*, an agit-prop, *Section of the Front*, the instruc-

---

* One sound episode described by Yezuitov: a farewell at a train window is made more broken and awkward by *expected but unreal* sounds of the starting railway engine, an idea that would demand a very delicate cutting and balance of sound and speech.

† These are concert and vaudeville numbers, and a synchronized fragment of *Women of Ryazan*.

tional film, *A Sound-Film Alphabet*, and various musical shorts—all of which disappeared as swiftly as the first Warners' programme when better stuff was available to the now waiting sound-theatres. The American films brought in for demonstration in September and November 1929, (including the musically synchronized *King of Kings* and the Technicolor *King of Jazz*), were not either available or suitable for public use. The next long film, the documentary *Olympiad of Arts*, tried an economy of money and time that was mistaken: to record this theatre festival that took place in Moscow in the summer of 1930, director Yerofeyev and cameraman Byelyakov made both picture and sound recording on a single film, preventing *all* the flexibility of cutting the picture and track separately. This was programmed with the earliest Soviet sound-film to be enjoyed by an international audience, *Post*, an animated cartoon by Tsekhanovsky (based on a children's book by Marshak and the artist Lebedev), made as a silent film but so rhythmically that Deshevov had little trouble composing a score for it. *Post* remained in circulation at home and abroad long after its Soviet contemporaries had vanished from the screen. Tsekhanovsky's next film started with its sound-track, a recording of Honegger's descriptive 'Pacific 231', and illustrated the music with a pleasant semi-abstraction of a speeding train. An interesting development (though without a long life) in connection with animated sound cartoons was the experimental work on artificial, or drawn, sound-tracks. In September 1931, the composer Arseni Avraamov was rewarded for his advances in this field, and by January 1933, there was a screening of *Symphony of the World*, an experiment in real and artificial sound, animation and colour. This gave encouragement to the 'Ivvoston' group of artists (Ivanov, Voinov, Sazonov) working on drawn sound-tracks, but after a few startling small achievements they found themselves in a dead end.

Each of the three documentary features released during the first half of 1931 had a different approach to the use of sound. Poselsky's *Thirteen Days* was a direct day-by-day record of the trial of Ramzin and the other engineer-leaders of the 'Industrial Party', accused of forming a counter-revolutionary organization and employing industrial sabotage as a political weapon. Nothing more than a simple recording of the trial proceedings (conducted by Krylenko as public prosecutor) was needed by this material to make audiences want to see it. Kopalin had a more artistic problem with his *One of Many* (or *The Country*). He wanted to record all the normal activity of a collective farm, choosing a farm near Moscow, 'Liberated Labour', as typical. Lebedev comments on the film's naïveté in con centrating exclusively on actions that made a recordable sound, but praises this recording for showing that natural sounds recorded on location were far richer and more interesting than the studio-manufactured sounds that were then considered obligatory.

It was Vertov, however, who showed 'natural sounds' in the fullest way, in *Enthusiasm*, or *Symphony of the Don Basin*. Theoretically, this film was to show how the miners of the Don coal basin were aiming and able to fulfil in four years their part in the Five Year Plan, but, practically, the film for Vertov was a demonstration of his lyrical method enhanced by sound and music. It was at the beginning of 1930, at the time Room began work on his *Plan*, that two of Shorin's assistants had been assigned to Ukrainfilm and Vertov's crew, and the sound-tracks they brought back from mines and factories astonished all with their vividness and novelty*. Vertov cut these sound-images as freely as he cut his visuals, with a great deal of superimposition, both of picture (the cameraman was Zeitlin) and track. The result must have had a sensual excitement novel to all viewers, but Soviet audiences were not conditioned to spend money on such a decorative film that was neither dramatic nor informative, and *Enthusiasm* had a longer public life on a few foreign screens. Vertov's intoxication with his new instrument often got the better of him and obstructed a normal perception of his new film by even its most sympathetic audiences. As evidence of his statement that 'Vertov was probably the most obstinate film personality of all time', Thorold Dickinson instances his behaviour at the London showing of *Symphony*:

'When Vertov attended the presentation of his first sound film, *Enthusiasm*, to the Film Society of London on November 15, 1931, he insisted on controlling the sound projection. During the rehearsal he kept it at a normal level, but at the performance flanked on either side by the sound manager of the Tivoli Theatre and an officer of the Society, he raised the volume at the climaxes to an ear-splitting level. Begged to desist, he refused and finished the performance fighting for possession of the instrument of control, while the building seemed to tremble with the flood of noise coming from behind the screen.'[6]

To counter the severe criticisms of his film at home, Vertov marshalled all the compliments that he and *Enthusiasm* received on their European tour in a defensive article entitled 'Charlie Chaplin, the Hamburg Workers, and the Injunctions of Dr Wirth',[7] but this did not protect him from the attacks that had grown harsher ever since *Man with a Movie Camera*. It was three years before Vertov showed his second sound-film.

To speed the introduction of sound-film while waiting for adequate supplies of theatre equipment, expeditions went out to far corners of the Union with a comparatively portable sound-projection machine and a programme of sound-films thus far released, showing *Plan*, the concert programme, *Thirteen Days*, and *Enthusiasm* to remote and smaller communities. The first such expedition started out in April 1930, and a month later the factory making Tager's portable equipment began production and subsequent expeditions were rendered less cumbersome. The Association of Workers in Revolutionary Cinema organized a conference on the artistic problems of the sound-film, to bring film-workers up to date on industrial progress; the speakers were distinguished, including Zarkhi, Obolensky, Vertov, Pudovkin, Turin, Ermler, but little was said to alter the industrial and technical emphasis. To prevent future crises of this sort, investigation groups were set up in March 1931, to consider problems of colour-film, stereo-film, and television. Artistic solutions for sound were to remain in the trial and error stage.

The first dramatic sound-film shown was Raizman's *The Earth Thirsts*, originally

* Portable sound-recording apparatus had not yet been devised, so that these tracks were recorded by microphones hooked up to Radio Centre. Vertov later assisted Shorin in perfecting a portable recording apparatus.

released by Vostok-kino in a silent version in the autumn of 1930, and equipped with a synchronized sound-track of music, song, and noise for release in May 1931. The film had an extremely simple story: a group of young communist irrigation engineers (a Russian, a Turkoman, a Jew, a Ukrainian, a Georgian) arrive in a Turkmenian village from their training centre, Ashkhabad, to construct their first canal; the bey of the district does everything to obstruct their work by trying to turn the villagers against them, but the group stick together, eventually win the villagers to their side, and complete the irrigation system triumphantly. This story is told with a minimum of ornament by Yermolinsky and photographed with a maximum of effect by Kosmatov; it is one of the last examples of the pretty photographic period of Soviet films, made by the same trust, Vostok-kino, for whom Turin had made the anti-pretty *Turksib*.

The first sound-film by Kozintsev and Trauberg (released October 10, 1931) was planned and photographed as a silent film, completed in that state in May 1930. The added sound-track of *Alone* played a more important rôle in its final structure than in Raizman's film; certain musical themes recurred for dramatic reasons, with a song representing the ideals of the heroine. There were also fragments of dialogue set into the otherwise non-speaking photography. *Alone* and *The Earth Thirsts* had remarkably similar subjects; in each the central action concerns eager but inexperienced Soviet youth encountering class warfare in remote regions. In *Alone* a young graduate from a Leningrad teachers' training school is assigned to the wilds of the Altai with nearly fatal results for her. Her yearning for the civilization of Leningrad and her repulsion from the strange conflicts and behaviour around her made for an effective dramatic contrast that Kozintsev and Trauberg carried too far, possibly because they themselves felt the sharp change from the comfortable Leningrad flat where they had composed the scenario (inspired by a newspaper item about the air rescue of a sick woman) to the four months of winter work in the Altai. (The only member of the crew to enjoy himself was Moskvin, who was experimenting with a deliberately narrowed range of photography, concentrating on the high and white tones.) The heroine, played by Elena Kuzmina, became almost as isolated a victim as she had been in *New Babylon*. However, the slow, tense, subtle and almost insinuating presentation of the film story seems more important now than its faults. Technically the film was satisfactory and the Shorin system did enough justice to the exciting score by Shostakovich for the film to gain an international audience largely on the strength of its music. A young man trained in music and wild to work in films was put in charge of the recording—Lev Arnstam's first film job.

Because of the slow groping towards a fully flexible new medium, Soviet film-makers could avoid the artistic absurdities of early sound-films elsewhere, just as the Soviet engineers had been able to skirt their early troubles. They never had to suffer through the period of the 'all-talking' craze that had struck the rest of the world in 1929,* and even the craze for musical shows was over by the autumn of 1930, before a single Soviet dramatic sound-film had been made. There is merely an historical remnant of that period in the number of projects for films

---

* The only Soviet relic of the 'all-talking' phase was a comedy, *The Mechanical Traitor* released October 6, 1931), with a phonograph in the leading rôle.

built around a musician hero—adaptations of Korolenko's *Blind Musician* and Turgenev's *Singer* were never realized, thanks to inadequate recording. Even Ermler prepared a scenario, *Song*, that was left unfinished.* The adolescence of the new art had been weathered before there was any Soviet contribution to it; with *Hallelujah* and *Blackmail* in 1929, *All Quiet on the Western Front* and *Sous les Toits de Paris* in 1930, it could be said that the chief dangers were passed, though the phantom of the 'highly cultured drama' predicted by Eisenstein still lurked as a Russian possibility.

Between the releases of *The Earth Thirsts* and *Alone* appeared the film sometimes regarded as the first Soviet sound-film, *Road to Life*, released June 1, 1931. True, it was the first Soviet sound-film to have been conceived and written in that form, despite its superfluity of sub-titles. Though there were quibbles at the time about its 'sentimentalism', *Road to Life* keeps a high place in Soviet film history, for its fusion of technical, dramatic and political achievements. Central in the film is the group of 'wild children' who had lost their families in the years of civil war and famine. In actuality, as shown in the film, these 'sparrows' collected themselves into roving bands that stayed alive by virtue of ingenious, bold thievery, and constituted a major social problem even up to the time of the film's production. The film is kept from over-simplification by showing the *bezprizorni* (neglected) band as a tangle of good and evil with, on one side, a hardened criminal trying to hold them within his control and, on the other, a teacher who encourages every 'good' instinct among them. This simple humanist position of the film has kept it valid far beyond the immediacy of its problem. And unlike its several American derivatives, *Wild Boys of the Road*, *The Wild Ones*, *Blackboard Jungle*, the sensational elements in *Road to Life* never stray from artistic control.

The subject of the 'wild children' and their social taming had been attempted in two minor previous films, but the authors of *Road to Life*—Ekk, Yanushkevich, Stolper—studied their material more thoroughly and trained themselves (chiefly at the GPU labour commune of Lyuberets) in the teaching methods used by their good angel, the experimental teacher Sergeyev, played by Nikolai Batalov. Between the professional actors Batalov and Zharov, who played the evil angel, the rôles of the *bezprizorni* were chiefly cast from non-acting boys who had graduated from the labour communes. None of these temporary actors, not even the remarkable Chuvash boy, I. Kyrla, who gave such colour to the rôle of Mustafa, ever again appeared in films. Nikolai Ekk himself is identified only with this film; all his later work and projects depend on some innovation as striking as this first manipulation of sound—the first Soviet colour film, the first Soviet Shakespeare film, etc. There are passages in *Road to Life* so filmically satisfying that Ekk's later retreat into novelties seems a great pity; Catherine de la Roche cites:

* In a recent essay Yutkevich mentions a new and more serious aspect of this failure: 'Why did Ermler, after the indubitable success of *Fragment of an Empire*, suddenly lose faith in his creative powers, and leave films without completing work on the scenario of *Song*, to return only after the urgent appeals of his friends (including Arnstam and the author of these lines) who always believed in the great power of his talent?' (In *Questions of Film Art* [Moscow 1958]) Ermler's return, with *Counterplan*, was in collaboration with Yutkevich.

'. . . the night scene on the railway where Mustafa was murdered: the metallic noise of wheels and Mustafa's carefree song, as he rides alone in a rail handcart; further along the line, the stillness of the night, broken only by croaking frogs and the light clinking of tools while the murderer loosens a rail; then Mustafa's distant song becoming louder and louder as he approaches danger.'[8]

The sound operator, Nesterov, deserves a share of the universal praise that came to *Road to Life*, for his deft use of the obviously primitive means at hand.

The next two dramatic sound-films (released in November) took other directions. Protazanov's first attempt, *Tommy*, was a comparatively safe adaptation of Ivanov's successful Civil War play, *Armoured Train 14-69*. Protazanov eliminated some elements to give more emphasis to the episode of the captured British soldier, through whose eyes (and ears) we observe the courage and character of the partisan fighters. This always intelligent director avoided the pitfalls of the 'adapted play' by filming *Tommy* in the winter exteriors that could only be suggested on the stage. Yutkevich's first sound-film, *Golden Mountains*, was more ambitious in theme and treatment; its interesting idea (transformation of a peasant's attitude on being exposed to city and revolution between 1912 and 1917) was sometimes obscured by the more immediately interesting execution of each scene, cleverly staged with a touch of stylization (it is one of the few films influenced by Dovzhenko), and photographed by a group of young cameramen whom Yutkevich encouraged to do their best. The sound-track of *Golden Mountains* was also 'advanced', with a serious attempt at the audio-visual counterpoint proposed by the Eisenstein-Pudovkin-Alexandrov 'Statement'. The film was cast with the customary sensitivity of Yutkevich: Pyotr, the peasant who came to the city to make his golden dream come true, was played by Boris Poslavsky; Boris Tenin played the hearty accordionist that one associates with Shostakovich's music for the film.

Though the sound-film was now accepted as the usual way to make and see films, the Soviet transition period from silence extended over more years than in other countries. One sign of acceptance was the number of silently produced films that were given sound-tracks and even additional dialogue sequences—*China Express* (whose track was added in Berlin, with a score by Edmund Meisel), *The Ghost That Will Not Return*, *The Quiet Don*, *St Jorgen*—and later, the Georgian *Eliso* and the Ukrainian *Karmeluk* and *Night Coachman*. On the other hand an occasional sound-film was issued in a silent version, to reach audiences that had not yet wired their theatres for sound. And as late as 1935 certain important films were produced and distributed without sound, and without being regarded as freaks.

The newsreel took on new life with sound, and sound 'firsts' were a matter for pride: the November 7th celebration of 1931 was filmed with sound and shown the same night to audiences in ten Moscow theatres; on January 26, 1932 the first newsreel interview—with Maxim Litvinov on his way to Geneva; Gorky recorded a speech on the tasks of Soviet cinema* to be included in a documentary

---

* 'It seems to me that film-makers must apply all their powers to make the cinema into a vigorous weapon of culture, a weapon that would help give our masses the qualifications to sense what is necessary and unnecessary for our country, what must be affirmed and what must be discarded.'

about him; a supplementary newsreel series was begun in 1933, called *Soviet Art*, benefiting from the possibility of communicating music and speech—new poems and musical compositions, fragments of recent theatrical productions, interviews with artists and critics; the outdoor screenings of the 1920s were now revived in the squares of Moscow with new documentary films—and loud-speakers. Sound and the Five Year Plan together spurred the documentary film to a group of accomplishments at this time. Two Arctic expeditions, on the *Sibiryakov* and the *Chelyuskin*, resulted in the first good Soviet films about the polar region. Edward Tisse (returning to the 'chronicle' for the first time since the Civil War) joined Roman Karmen on the Kara-Kum expedition to film an effective record of the drive from Moscow to the desert and back. The young Dutch film-maker, Joris Ivens, was invited to make a film about the new industrial centre at Magnitogorsk, staffed chiefly by Komsomols. His film, *Song of Heroes*, with a score by Hanns Eisler, showed the Soviet makers of industrial films a sharper, more personal style than they were used to with such subjects, and demonstrated the advantages of a track-picture relation that was as free as anything used in the fictional film up to that time.

Yet the most important step taken by the 'non-studio' film in this period was taken without benefit of sound-track. Its initiation may not sound exciting:

'*Order of the People's Commissariat of Transportation, December 29, 1931.*

'In order to implement the decisions at the October meeting of the Central Committee of the All-Union Communist Party on the improvement of rail transport and the development of technical propaganda through visual acquain-tance with the basic activities of rail transport, it is necessary to employ new methods and forms of mass work in technical propaganda, using the cinema to mobilize the working masses around the tasks of socialist construction and the renovation of rail transport.

'The all-union trust, "Soyuzkino-newsreel", has introduced for use the first Soviet film-train, which is a film-studio on wheels, completely equipped for the production of films under conditions of rail transport. Working on the assign-ment of the Central Committee, the film-train of "Soyuzkino-newsreel" gives, in its production plan, primary attention to rail transport, and the first three-month route for its operation specifically attends to the question of improving rail transport. . . .'

The order concludes with instructions to all railway points and station masters to give priority of attention to the needs of the film-train.

The film-train was made up of three railway cars, the first carrying living and dining quarters for a crew of thirty-two persons, the second a projection-room, storage for apparatus, and a complete installation for producing animated car-toons; the third car was filled with a laboratory and film-printing machinery. Pulled and tended by the railway system, this was a self-contained film studio that could maintain itself on location for months at a time without requiring supplies or even communications from a central base. It was the logical develop-ment from the agit-train of civil war days, and the films it produced were related, but on a higher stage, to the *agitki* of that earlier period.

Alexander Medvedkin was put in charge of the film-train; without him the innovation might not have had such memorable results. He had trained as Okhlopkov's assistant on the ill-fated *Way of the Enthusiasts,* and all his subsequent work can be regarded as a continuation in that genre of satire and fantastic comedy. During the first half of 1931 he produced a remarkable series for the Moscow studio of Soyuzkino—original short film-farces on social and industrial questions. These, with such titles as *Stop Thief!, What a Fool You Are!, Fruits and Vegetables,* were hailed by Lunacharsky[9] as a form of genuine importance, and led directly to Medvedkin's next assignment, the film-train. Okhlopkov and Mack Sennett had found a worthy heir.

Wherever the film-train was sent Medvedkin and his crew had a several-sided task. In addition to making instructional films to help local problems, for example, overcoming winter conditions to speed up freight shipments, the film crew was also to produce critical films on local conditions (bureaucracy, inefficiency, nepotism, etc.) that they or the local political workers judged to require their ungentle attentions. The prime audience for these, as for the instructional films, was the local one, who would greet these barbed film vaudevilles with welcome laughs and blushes. Out of all these hasty productions some were to be chosen for national distribution.

The first five months of 1932 were spent by the film-train on trips to railway centres (and problems) at Dniepropetrovsk and Krivoirog and from these two trips they brought back more than twenty new films. The third journey (August 6th-19th) was to Ukrainian collective farms, where Medvedkin made one of the best of his satires, *Tit,* or *Tale of a Big Spoon*—a two-reeler about a lazy dreamer, and his social reward. The fourth journey of the film-train was to the X military district where the crew not only made information films on new fighting formations, but also an improvised comedy, *The Snare,* or *Extraordinary Adventures of an Artillery Observer.* Anyone who makes films will envy the variety and quantity of work achieved by Medvedkin and the film-train in such a short time. After six journeys in 1932, the train was taken out of service for re-conditioning, and resumed its travels in July 1933 at transport centres, the North Caucasus, the farms in the Kuban area, and the railways of the Don Basin. Through its two years of work, though hoping to add sound to its programme, the train got along very well without it—perhaps fortunately. For the entertainment and instruction of future generations, I hope a group of the film-train's satires has survived the destructions of war and house-cleaning.*

There was a useful aspect of the opening period of the sound-film's evolution that the Eisenstein-Pudovkin-Alexandrov 'Statement' did not take into account: before selection and manipulation of sound there had to be perfection of its recording facility, especially in human speech, just as the photographed image could not be handled until there was an image that communicated, visually, everything that was before the camera. A group of films made in the second stage of sound served this purpose: *Men and Jobs* (October 1932), *Counterplan* (November 1932), *The Return of Nathan Becker* (December 1932) and *Okraina*

---

* I had not seen anything similar to Medvedkin's satires until recently, in the student work of the Polish Film School.

(March 1933). All but the last were subjects from modern Soviet life, with stories and characters that employed a minimum of rhetoric. Their aims were to sound as natural as possible, and their success with Soviet audiences depended on the shock of recognition—much as a community looking at the film-train's reflection of their problems or foibles.

The Return of Nathan Becker was made in both Yiddish and Russian versions by Byelgoskino, and the Yiddish version extended that pleasurable shock to many parts of the world, especially as Nathan Becker's Americanized speech was contrasted with the speech of his native village, personified in the rich complex character of Nathan's father, played by Mikhoels. The realistic story of the mixed blessings of such a return was written by Perets Markish and was directed by Shpis and Milman; the film grew less real when it moved to Magnitogorsk from the ancient Jewish community. A similar situation, of a Jew (played by Batalov) returning from America to his homeland, was made into a far less realistic film in *Horizon*, directed by Kuleshov, but his film, surprisingly, turned melodramatic at each opportunity. Kuleshov was to be more proud of his second sound-film.

In *Men and Jobs* the shock of recognition was a little too shocking for some ears. It was accused of being too rude and crude in its behaviour and speech, especially in the speech of its protagonist, the worker Zakharov, played brilliantly by Okhlopkov. Though some acute critics, Yezuitov for example, saw in *Men and Jobs* the distinct indications of the next period of Soviet film style, others criticized the first naturalistic Soviet sound-film as over-naturalistic (one critic found the influence of John Dos Passos!), and a certain playfulness of juxtapositions was blamed on the old theoretical whipping-boy, the 'intellectual cinema', and on Okhlopkov's counsel. But audiences in and out of the Soviet Union enjoyed its original, robust manner of telling a story that could so easily have taken itself too seriously: at Dnieprostroi a Russian worker (Okhlopkov) and an American engineer (Stanitsin), champions of two methods of doing things, clash personally and ideologically and understandably. If the film started from the popular slogan, 'Overtake and surpass America', the humanity of its author removed it entirely from the realm of slogan. The whole material of the film derived not from pre-determined dramatic patterns, but from modern people and their problems, and was almost as directly derived from its material as a Flaherty film. For a film set in a great industrial project it is amazing how little dependence is placed on handsome machine compositions. Alexander Macheret, whose first film this was,* was wary of this:

'One of the basic tasks facing me, as scenarist and director, appeared to be a struggle against the fetishism of giving the surface milieu some independent existence beyond its relation to the inner world of people. Cinema has evolved a certain language of conventions, a substitute for analysing linked expository situations, a language that resolves formal-aesthetic values instead of social values. Spectators are so used to this that when they see some object on the screen,

* Macheret's whole film career had been in sound-film, beginning as sound-director for *The Earth Thirsts*.

they can immediately determine that it is good or bad, depending solely on the way it is presented. A blast-furnace, interlaced pipes, a soaring bulwark of machinery—all this, rearing upwards, or at a camera-angle, lives its own feverish life, born from a barber-virtuoso rhythm of scissors, and produces through repetition a conditioned reflex of sympathy to the building of socialism.

'One blast-furnace may be differentiated from another blast-furnace by indicating that one is in capitalists' hands and the other in workers' hands, that one smokes and another doesn't smoke, that one smokes intermittently and another heralds with flames the victory of the shock-brigade—though in general a blast-furnace can show nothing more than that it is a blast-furnace—but all these glimpses are fixed into a conventional array of *film-symbols*, and over the years they slide into *film-clichés*.'[10]

Macheret continued to work both as scenarist and as director, but he never again made so personal a film. In spite of the unwieldy new apparatus, the introductory period of sound may have offered some extra freedoms to an assured artist. Macheret's assistant on *Men and Jobs*, Mikhail Romm, had moved from work as scenarist on his way to a long and substantial career in direction.

Counterplan set itself more difficult psychological tasks, an over-abundance, in fact, of them: the nature of collective work, the mutual responsibility of workers and party organizers, the relations between young workers who had grown up with the Revolution and older workers trained under capitalism, the ambivalence of professionals (or intelligentsia) torn between selfish aims and social demands, the restless idealism of the young. 'We must learn to show the party not as a *deus ex machina*, appearing at any right moment, in any crisis, but as a fundamental real moving force in struggle. . . .' Perhaps because of this multiplicity of tasks, the film had two directors—Ermler and Yutkevich who, from the beginning of their work on the scenario (written with the collaboration of Arnstam and Dell, and based on the rivalry in a Leningrad factory building a giant turbine in 1931), divided the characters and problems between them, Yutkevich in charge of the young people and Ermler taking on the tougher problems of the older generations: Babchenko, the old foreman, and his cronies of the machine-shop, and the traitorous engineer, Skvortsov, played by Poslavsky. The actors themselves may have had something to do with maintaining this division, for Gardin, whose performance of Babchenko is always placed among the great Soviet film rôles, reports that he could get nothing sympathetic from Yutkevich, and that his only scenes to stay in the finished film were those directed by Ermler. Babchenko and all other rôles were constructed from minute observation of their real-life models. Writer-directors and actors drew so much detail from reality that a repeated criticism heard at the time was of the excessive 'ornamentation' of the film. The subdued naturalism of its speech and appearance have since raised *Counterplan* to the status of a precursor of 'social realism', and its success fixed its style as the proper one for the 'improving' function of the Soviet cinema. The music by Shostakovich helped to bind the many separate scene-pieces effectively and his theme-song went far beyond the film's life when it was adopted twelve years later as the United Nations' hymn. This was the only film made specifically

to celebrate the fifteenth anniversary of the October Revolution; its original title
was *Greeting the Future*. From the start Sergei Kirov, party head of the Leningrad
district, concerned himself personally in the project with advice and physical
assistance. It was Ermler's acquaintance with Kirov in these years before his
murder on which the director based his last peace-time film, *The Great Citizen*.

After the packed tasks of *Counterplan* it is rather a relief to turn to the tragi-
comedy of divided national loyalties in *Okraina* (*Outskirts* or *Borderland*),
directed by Barnet. The setting is a small Russian community during the years of
war, and the story, written by K. Finn, does that extraordinary thing so rare and
valuable in films—it seems to tell itself without anyone pushing it. You can't be
sure whether the next scene will be funny or pathetic, gentle or violent.

'In the pictorial structure of *Okraina* there is something of Chekhov's plays,
with an action of interior development as well as an outer action. In it an important rôle is played by everything that goes on *beneath* the words—the concealed
and repressed emotions of its characters, the pauses and hints, the circumstances
and atmosphere of events, the combination of comic and dramatic elements, all
building a profound inner rhythm.'[11]

The performances are given the same spontaneity by Barnet and an excellent cast,
all from different professional backgrounds: Kuzmina, whose whole training had
been in pathos with Kozintsev and Trauberg, blossomed out as an unexpected
comedienne; there were Kuleshov's Komarov and Pudovkin's Chistyakov, who
played the cobbler; one of his sons was Bogolyubov from the Meyerhold Theatre,
the other son was Kryuchkov, a novice in films; in smaller rôles there were
Zharov from the Maly Theatre and Yanshin from the Moscow Art Theatre.
The ensemble playing of this varied cast remains a great credit to Barnet. His
admirers from the days of his farces and satires, weathering the crisis of his *Moscow
in October*, had at last a film to justify their patience.

Those were the naturalist triumphs of the first years of sound. Ranged opposite
them was an equally strong group of artists with aims beyond naturalism:
Dovzhenko, Shengelaya, Kalatozov, Pudovkin. The chances they took brought
them less triumph but more lasting credit in an art that cannot afford not to take
chances, if it wants to stay alive—no matter how much power pulls in the safer
direction.

The encounter between poet-director Dovzhenko and the great hydro-electric
project on the Dnieper River resulted in a film that fits no easy category—'a
Dovzhenko film' is the only adequate description of *Ivan*. Just after the release of
Earth Dovzhenko visited Berlin and Paris, a rounding of his first period of
artistic maturity: Berlin, scene of his embassy post and his painting lessons—
Paris, the setting of *Zvenigora*'s climax.

'I went abroad where I stayed about four and a half months. On my return I
proposed to the administration of Ukrainfilm a scenario, in brief form, on our
heroes in the Arctic, on the material of Nobile's tragedy and the loss
of R. Amundsen. The administration rejected this; they asked me to write
"something similar" on contemporary life in the Ukraine, rather than in the

Arctic. I hastily dislodged Amundsen from my consciousness and in twelve days wrote the scenario of *Ivan*, and began its filming. Work on *Ivan* was difficult for me. The film was shortened, and I was numbered in the camp of the biologists, the pantheists, the diversionists, the Spinozaists.'[12]

In Paris he had given a summary of his principles to *La Revue du Cinéma*:

'It is not the story alone that interests me. I take this to be a maximum means of communicating important social forms.

'That is why I work on typical documents and apply the synthetic method. My heroes are representatives of their class, as is their behaviour.

'At times the documentation of my films is concentrated to an extreme degree; at the same time I project it through a prism of emotion, which gives it life and sometimes eloquence.

'I cannot remain indifferent to documents. One must love much and strongly, and hate—otherwise one's works would remain dogmatic and dry.'[13]

These are principles most strikingly in evidence in *Ivan*, his first sound-film, full 'much and strongly' with love and hate—love for his 'unheroic hero' Ivan, hate and laughter for his powerful anarchist 'idler'. Despite the change in his medium *Ivan* is consistent with the growth of Dovzhenko's method. This is clear, not only in its beauties—in the introductory poem to the Dnieper, in the magnificent sense of space at the construction site, day and night, in the sculptural figures of workers there,* and in the images of pain: the plume of slow black smoke to tell us of a death, and the mother's abandoned agony of protest. There is also, aside from these visual beauties, Dovzhenko's ceaseless search for simplicity of statement, leading him to such a direct connection between one sequence and the next, in his demonstration of 'the reconstructed psychology of the new Soviet man', that the spectator, unwarned that this is 'simplicity', finds it the most puzzling sort of complexity. This unorthodox and non-naturalist approach made Soviet critics suspicious and limited the world audience for his film; even the simplicity of the words used in the film, thus juxtaposed in Dovzhenko's completely personal way, added an obstacle to the communication it sought. In America mistaken efforts were made to pare away the least understood words and moments, but this only mutilated the film, and made it no easier to comprehend. Nevertheless, the few American audiences that had a chance to see *Ivan* had no trouble with its beauties and with its laughter, especially the fantastic derision of the 'idler', made by Dovzhenko and Shkurat into a great figure of film comedy. Yet there is certainly more than comedy in this fascinating figure. He may even represent Dovzhenko's attitude to the current Ukrainian party purge of Ukrainian 'nationalists' from influential posts, a purge that affected many film-makers, including Stabovoi, Lopatinsky and several other colleages of Dovzhenko. There is more than 'idling' in the 'idler'; he should be examined together with Shkurat's rôle—a less passive criminal—in Dovzhenko's next film, *Aerograd*.

* At Dnieprostroy the work of the cameramen, Demutski and Yekelchik, was supplemented by Mikhail Glider's hand-camera.

In a public discussion of *Ivan* and *Counterplan* Dovzhenko made a prophecy that sums up all his film work:

'It is possible that we are still in a pre-historic stage of cinema, for the great history of cinema will begin when it leaves the frame of ordinary artistic representation and grows into a tremendous and extraordinarily encompassing perceptive category.'[14]

In Shengelaya's *26 Commissars* there is just as much love and hate, fiercely expressed in a more immediately comprehensible way, with an equal attention to graphic and sculptural beauties—but with little of the belief and perception that is in each Dovzhenko film. Yet in its monumental narrative of the actual tragedy of Baku in 1918, seized alternately by English and German-Turkish forces that tried to hold the coastal oil-fields, and of their Bolshevik victims, there is an original extravagance of style, pictorially and dramatically, without which the Soviet cinema would have been poorer. Shengelaya was not encouraged to persist in his extravagance, and the only noticeable pursuit of this manner is in the later Russian work of two Georgian compatriots, Chiaureli and Kalatozov.

The tragedy of the murdered twenty-six commissars is a subject that had been considered for years as film material. For a year Meyerhold kept Mezhrabpom expectant that he would undertake it. Then Room was prepared to film Blyakhin's scenario for it, following *The Ghost*. But it was not until the tempestuous Shengelaya, hot after his success with *Eliso*, took Rzheshevsky's scenario to the new Azerbaidjan studio, that work began. There was a hope that the film would have sound, but Azerfilm was not sufficiently equipped for that, so the film was finished and released, silent, in 1933.

Following Pudovkin's published appreciation of Rzheshevsky's idea of the 'emotional scenario', and his acceptance of the script for *Life's Very Good*, but before the débâcle of the finished film, the work of Alexander Rzheshevsky was in great demand among the youthful elements of Soviet studios. Shengelaya's excitement with Rzheshevsky's oblique look at the Baku tragedy was supported by all his young colleagues—by Yutkevich, for whom Shengelaya had played a small Baku rôle in *Golden Mountains*, and by Igor Savchenko, the young Ukrainian director who played the villainous rôle of a social-revolutionary for Shengelaya's film. With two scripts in production, Rzheshevsky embarked on the direction of a third, *Ocean* ('first part of a trilogy', at Ukrainfilm)—but this project had only a short life before the Rzheshevsky 'tendency' was frowned on by the film administration. He was to come back into prominence four years later, with more unhappy results, with a script for Eisenstein.

In the Tiflis studio at this time was a new Georgian talent with a great future. Mikhail Kalatozishvili, who simplified his film name to Kalatozov, was educated as an economist; his first film training was as a cameraman, and one can always sense his controlling hand on the camera, from his earliest to his current films. The two first films he directed in 1930 are both connected with Tretyakov's excursion to Georgia. The first, *Blind*, is a studio-made film that I have not seen. It is one of the scenarios that Tretyakov brought to Tiflis and adapted there. Tretyakov's next libretto for Kalatozov derives from a Caucasian tour,[14a] and was made even more purely local by Kalatozov's departures, on location, from the paper-plan. Its subject is Svanetia, once almost totally isolated from the rest of the Caucasus except for a brief snowless period on their one mountain-pass. Their ancient defence against the raids of feudal princes from the river valley is still witnessed by Italianate stone towers that also hint a link with the crusaders. The first film (*Svanetia*) to record this strange remnant of a medieval culture was made by Zhelyabuzhsky and Yalovoi in 1927, but the film that will always be identified with that people, as *los Hurdes* of Spain are identified with Bunuel's *Land Without Bread*, is Kalatozov's *Salt for Svanetia*. The two films are always linked in my mind—they are both sur-realist in the literal sense of the term, both with a harsh pity for the tragedies of their subjects that is far more moving than any appeal for sympathy. I wish that Kalatozov's early masterpiece were better known, but it is one of the several victims of the international transition from silence to sound*. The film appears in the export catalogue, but I have never heard any foreign comment on it. Even this catalogue description suggests a surprising film:

'Life is patriarchal, primitive; the struggle for existence among the snow-capped mountains entails such constant want and hunger, and particularly, the torment-ing hunger for salt, that each new birth is regarded as a terrible curse, while death becomes a solemn feast. Bloody offerings were made at the graves of the dead; horses and beeves were slaughtered in honour of their pagan gods, Salema and Dala.'[15]

One perceptive foreign critic, Harry Alan Potamkin, saw the film at several stages of its making, but his propaganda efforts on its behalf did not widen the film's audience; it was he who suggested that the film's misleading title, *Jim Shuante*, be changed to the more explicit *Salt for Svanetia*, but the film remained buried in lists of ethnographic films, and even now is rarely mentioned in Soviet film-histories. Potamkin's article on his Russian trip[16] contains the clearest indication in print of the film's worth:

'Kalatozov has established his point-of-view at once in the bold image and stern grand angles. . . . It is unrelenting in its exposure of the dread life of the Swans, exploited and hopeless, incarcerated by the mountains. The funeral of the tuberculosis victim is excruciating in its dire grief. The widow, dripping her milk into the grave, condemns the collusion of paganism and Christianity conspiring against human happiness. "We will not give our milk to the grave", the women cry in revolt. The film calls and we respond: "These people must be saved—roads and salt!" The last part shouting this slogan directly is a weak addendum—the entire film cries that convincingly enough.'

There were, of course, objections. Twenty-five leading citizens of Svanetia denied that the peculiar customs shown in the film had ever existed, and claimed that it was more important for a film to show the modernization of Svanetia than old customs; their objections were understandable, but not completely plausible—

---

* The film may have been the victim of a greater crisis: in the German invasion of the Caucasus the negative appears to have been destroyed. Prints survive in Gosfilmofond.

this reaction was later used against Kalatozov in the more serious crisis of his next film.

My information on *Nail in the Boot* comes entirely from the critical attacks and Kalatozov's defence in *Proletarskoye Kino*[17]. The stills reproduced in these articles have the Georgian intensity and compositional originality of Kalatozov's known films; this, together with the simple but ambitious theme, makes one regret that it can never be seen. The setting for the film is the realistic climax of Red Army manoeuvres in which an armoured train is 'captured' and 'destroyed'. The film's illustration of the old story that ends, 'For want of a nail the battle was lost', gains extra point here in that the soldier who wears the boot with the bad nail, and whose consequent injury leads to the 'capture' of the armoured-train, is in civilian life a shoe-factory worker who may have been responsible for the faulty boot. This possibility is revealed in the scene of his court-martial for the 'lost' armoured-train that concludes the film. When pressure from the Army resulted in the ban of this 'negative' film, Kalatozov protested that *Nail in the Boot* was not a film about the Army, but about industry, and the dependence on industry and its workers of every phase of Soviet life. But the ban held, and Kalatozov withdrew from film direction for the next seven years. His training as an economist and his talent as an organizer fitted him for the less painful job of administrator in the Tiflis studio.

After a year's work on *Life's Very Good* Pudovkin showed it to workers' groups who were bewildered by the film. The problem of ethics that Pudovkin declared to be his foremost aim was actually submerged in a splendour of sensual experiments that always moved their maker more than they did any audience. The lay audiences to whom the film was submitted challenged its ethics, its reality, its logic, its usefulness, everything about it; they asked, 'For whom is life "very good"—for the philandering husband? for the deserted wife? for the author?' If a film was to be judged only by its content, Pudovkin had made an extremely vulnerable film. Beside himself there were a few admirers, notably Shklovsky, who saw the value of its experiments, but the film was doomed to a series of revisions, delays, frustrations and denunciations.* Rzheshevsky's experiment in masking emotions with casual words and behaviour was damagingly compared to the methods of America's 'literary decadents', especially Hemingway, in such a story as 'Hills like White Elephants'. By the time the film was released, in December 1932, the drastically revised version had a more modest title, *A Simple Case*, and even Pudovkin was suspicious of its worth. There are stories of Pudovkin's hasty withdrawal of the film from the Moscow and Leningrad theatres where it was first shown, but this may have been only for more cutting, as the film was certainly in circulation later, and was exported, unsuccessfully—abroad, a silent fiction film, even by Chaplin, was already a mere curiosity. Significantly,

---

* Dario Vidi, in *Paris-Midi* (February 19, 1931), told a story of Pudovkin's troubles that is journalistically suspect, but may have some truth in it: that Gosrepertkom had turned over the original scenario to Lelevich, an official of RAPP, to give it a more Marxist base, that Pudovkin spent ten months on this revision which, when filmed, was shown to party chiefs (including Stalin and Voroshilov) who greeted it with some applause but more irritation, and thereafter Pudovkin was in trouble. The dates in his story can be reconciled with the known chronology of the film's production only with difficulty.

everyone who remembers *A Simple Case* recalls not its subject but some extraordinary moment in it. From the London Film Society showing of May 1933, Thorold Dickinson recalls

'. . . small details of masterly visual and editorial virtuosity: for example, the tiny detail of the putting on of an overcoat from which the audience received the impression of overwhelming, enveloping warmth. And there was a moving impression of a delirium, built out of a cascade of factual images of natural objects and processes, first of drought, decay, death and then of the living power of water welling up, breaking the dead earth crust forcing new growth.'[18]

Kabalov's camera contribution to this was considerable. He gave body to all the pictorial talents, even the pictorial vagaries, that Pudovkin yearned to put on the screen. The 'cascade of factual images' described above was actually made as an experiment unrelated to *A Simple Case*, but it turned out so well that Pudovkin re-arranged the script to make a place for it in his catch-all film.

In March 1931, between the two versions of *A Simple Case*, Pudovkin visited Hamburg with the idea for a new film. Two young journalists, Lazebnikov and Krasnostavsky, had shown Mezhrabpom and Pudovkin a carefully documented script on the life and struggles of Hamburg's dock-workers—*S. S. Pyatiletka*, to be made both in Russian and German versions. When Pudovkin returned from Hamburg, and went to work on his new subject, he asked Nina Agadzhanova-Shutko to strengthen the script. Hitler's coup in January 1933 not only caused the cancellation of the planned German version, but it also made the script, soon renamed *Deserter*, into a more militant film. The Communist hero, Karl Renn, given the choice of living a safe, protected life in the Soviet Union, sees himself as a deserter of his comrades and prefers to return to the fight in Germany. Golovnya approved this script from its earliest stages and accompanied Pudovkin on his trips to Germany; after January 1933, all further exterior shooting had to be done in Odessa and Leningrad. There were interruptions from the troublesome *Simple Case*, but the actual filming of *Deserter* was done speedily and efficiently.

The finished film, more than any other, embodies Pudovkin's wishes for contrapuntal sound-film structures. Some of the experiments with speech are too delicate to make a dramatic impression:

'In the first reel of *Deserter* I have a meeting addressed by three persons one after the other, each producing a complexity of reactions in their audience. Each one is against the other two; sometimes a member of the crowd interrupts a speaker, sometimes two or three of the crowd have a moment's discussion among themselves. . . .

'I sought to compose these elements by the system of montage. I took sound strips and cut, for example, for a word of a speaker broken in half by an interruption, for the interrupter in turn overswept by the tide of noise coming from the crowd, for the speaker audible again, and so on. Every sound was individually cut and the images associated are sometimes much shorter than the associated sound piece. . . . Sometimes I have cut the general crowd noise into the phrases with scissors, and I have found that with an arrangement of the various sounds by cutting in this way it is possible to create a clear and definite, almost musical, rhythm. . . .'[19]

Another example comes from a later, simpler scene, when Karl Renn (played by Boris Livanov) addresses a Soviet audience on the struggle in Germany, on the 'forces that brought him to the Soviet Union':

'During the whole of the film his worse nature has been trying to stifle his desire to escape these forces; therefore this moment, when he at last succeeds in escaping them and himself desires to recount his cowardice to his fellow-workers, is the high-spot of his emotional life. Being unable to speak Russian, his speech has to be translated.

'At the beginning of this scene we see and hear shots longish in duration, first of the speaking hero, then of his translator. In the process of development of the episode the images of the translator become shorter and the majority of his words accompany the images of the hero, according as the interest of the audience automatically fixes on the latter's psychological position.'[20]

Yet when there is a larger, overall image or movement to be conveyed by Pudovkin's principle of asynchronism, his experiment was eminently successful:

'The quiet streets of Hamburg; street traffic; the traffic policeman in control. Suddenly symptoms of disquiet. The policeman's eye catches sight of a distant banner. Panic on the streets. They empty. The demonstration approaches. Its step is sure and confident. The mass of workers grows. . . . Mounted and foot police hurl themselves at the workers, a battle begins, centring around the red banner carried at the head of the demonstration. The banner falls, but is raised again and again. . . . The banner crashes to the ground with the hero clinging to it and a policeman clinging to the hero. Those arrested are beaten up and led away. Then suddenly . . . the banner, torn from the hands of the enemy, soars once again above the crowd. . . .'

He goes on to describe what the music for this sequence might have been if it had *accompanied* the images—a waltz, a march tune, a danger theme 'strengthened each time the banner falls and rousing fanfares each time it rises', then music of despair followed by the music of victory.

'The composer—Yuri Shaporin—and I decided to follow another road. The score was written, played, and recorded for the whole of the sequence as a single-purpose unity, a workers' march tune with a note of stern and confident victory, firmly and uninterruptedly rising in strength from beginning to end. . . .

'Marxists know that in every defeat of the workers lies hidden a further step towards victory. The historical inevitability of constantly recurring class battles is bound up with the historic equal inevitability of the growth of the strength of the proletariat and the decline of the bourgeoisie. It was this thought that led us to the line of firm growth towards inevitable victory which we follow in the music through all the complications and contradictions of the events shown in the image.'[21]

Deserter is a film very rich in visual substance; it contains a quantity of shots, about 3,000, where the usual sound-film has 800 to 1,000. This great attention to the image, plus the experimental precision of the sound-track,* left it, too, open to attack that was not long in coming. A group of Leningrad film workers published a collective view of *Deserter*, attacking its intellectualism. Pudovkin was greatly disturbed by this; he agreed that the film contained mistakes, but he could not believe that this was their cause.† His normal sensitivity to criticism was heightened just now by an important personal matter. While *Life's Very Good* was being filmed Pudovkin had applied for admittance to the Communist Party, and in 1932 he was accepted as a candidate.

In a lecture at the Film Institute on November 3, 1930 Pudovkin had developed a corrective attitude to his earlier remarks on acting in *Film-Director and Film-Material*. In the autumn of 1933 after the release of *Deserter*, the cinema section of the State Academy of Art Research proposed that Pudovkin expand this lecture into a book, and during four days in December Pudovkin read his manuscript to the Academy. *The Actor in the Film* (English edition: *Film Acting*) appeared in September 1934, in a first edition of 10,000 copies.

After the fiasco of *Horizon*, Kuleshov, recalling the economic motives and artistic success of *By the Law*, made a sound-film experiment that was, primarily, an economic victory with full artistic compensation. Working with the scenarist Kurs, whose idea it may have been, he planned the only impressive Soviet film that has ever been made about the United States‡—a film about O. Henry who, before entering his career as a writer under that pseudonym, spent three years in the Ohio State Penitentiary for embezzlement. In those years William Sidney Porter met many of the characters and heard stories that he later used. In a book by Al Jennings, *Through the Shadows with O. Henry* (New York, 1921), Kurs and Kuleshov found the actual Jimmy Connors on whose life Porter based his story 'A Retrieved Reformation' (that became famous as the play, *Alias Jimmy Valentine*), and their film became a comparison of the raw truth with the rosier, albeit sardonic treatment given it by O. Henry, drawing inescapable conclusions about artistic process—making it a film unique in this respect, too. However, the aspect of the film, entitled *The Great Consoler*, that most astonished the industry was *how* it was produced:

* 'For the symphony of siren calls with which *Deserter* opens I had six steamers playing in a space of a mile and a half in the Port of Leningrad. They sounded their calls to a prescribed plan and we worked at night in order that we should have quiet.'—'Rhythmic Problems in My First Sound Film,' in *Film Technique*.

† Yezuitov, *Pudovkin*. As another example of Pudovkin's extreme sensitivity to opinion, H. P. J. Marshall told me that it was as the result of a suggestion from him at a screening of *Deserter* that Pudovkin changed the position of the demonstration scene described above, from the middle of the film to its conclusion.

‡ The most ambitious of several projects for American film subjects had just collapsed: a film about American Negroes, for which several Negro actors had come to the Soviet Union. One of these was Wayland Rudd, who stayed on for an active career on the Soviet stage and in films, beginning with a rôle in *The Great Consoler*.

'*The Great Consoler* was filmed in forty days. Its montage and sound-track were completed in sixteen days. It was photographed [by Kuznetsov] entirely on Soviet manufactured negative. It did not exceed either the film-stock or the money originally allotted to it. In its production Kuleshov and the production collective used a new and original rehearsal method, demonstrating its usefulness to all producers.'[22]

Pudovkin described its famous rehearsal method:

'All the shots in [Kuleshov's shooting] script, numbered and in their numerical order,* were transferred to a miniature studio floor. In fact, prior to the shooting of the film, he staged a performance consisting of very short scenes each in length identical with the piece later to be edited. As far as possible Kuleshov played each scene through on the studio floor in such a way that subsequently, after most careful rehearsal, it could be transferred back to and shot without alteration on the actual floor used in shooting.

'His rehearsal system attained three results. First, it achieved the preliminary work with the actor to the deepest possible degree. Second, it gave the executives the opportunity to "see" the film, as it were, before it was shot, and make any correction or alteration that might be required. And third, it reduced to a minimum the waste of time usually spent in setting up each shot. . . .'[23]

And Pudovkin gave a serious warning to those who advocated the adoption of this method throughout the industry:

'First and foremost, in striving at all costs to make the rehearsal performance an exact pattern of the future screen performance, Kuleshov undoubtedly not only rehearsed his actors, but also to some extent adapted his film to a form more convenient and simple for the carrying out of the rehearsal.

'It is not a coincidence that Kuleshov's film contains few dramatis personae. It is not a coincidence that Kuleshov has no crowd scenes. It is not a coincidence that the extremely sparse and limited exteriors take the shape either of empty country roads or of city streets on which one never meets a soul save those few dramatis personae.

'Kuleshov, of course, wrote his script in this way, set the action in these scenes, chose this subject and this number of characters precisely to give himself the chance to fit the film rapidly and easily into the framework of a stage performance, one, moreover, of necessity played on a stage rather especially primitively fitted out.

'I do not think this work of Kuleshov should be treated as wrong in principle. The effort was undoubtedly a most interesting experiment . . . but any mechanical deduction that might be made from it along the line of converting the method into a dogmatic recipe to be used in the shooting of any and every film would most undoubtedly be wrong.'[23]

---

* As distinguished from the usual production method of re-arranging the shots for convenience of the shooting schedule. Kuleshov here was using experience from the first years of his workshop, when film projects were *staged*. For *The Great Consoler* Kuleshov also prepared a drawing of each camera set-up (see page 300).

The 'mechanical deduction' was, fortunately, not made into an industrial law. Only Kuleshov and his disciples continued this method, and in a modified form.

The Eisenstein group was back in the Soviet Union by April 1932; Eisenstein's last act in America was to look (though he did not know it was for the last time) at the Mexican footage in a New York projection room. Then and for months later he believed Upton Sinclair's promise that all the Mexican negative and work-print would follow him to Moscow, so that, unaware of his own developing Mexican tragedy, Eisenstein spoke hopefully of *Que Viva Mexico* and of other projects to interviewers on his way home through Berlin. In Moscow, while waiting to begin work on the Mexican film, he started the scenario for a comedy, *MMM (Maxim Maximovich Maximov)*, Tisse went off on the Kara-Kum expedition, and Alexandrov, who had left his experimental sound short *Romance Sentimentale* in Europe*, made another short film, *Internationale*, chiefly as a vehicle for Vladimir Nilsen's experiments with rear-projection filming.

Boris Shumyatsky, heading the Soviet film industry with increasing personal privilege, showed Eisenstein in a series of actions that he was to be disciplined and 'brought into line', that he was no longer the respected leading artist of the Soviet cinema. He indicated no interest in *Que Viva Mexico*, and, indeed, it later appeared that he had encouraged Sinclair in *his* disciplinary action against Eisenstein. Though he allowed him to continue work on *MMM*, even to testing actors for it, he announced another film for Eisenstein in the export catalogue of Intorgkino. This was a film on the Haitian Revolution that had long interested Eisenstein; he had certainly mentioned it in conversation with Shumyatsky, and the idea of Paul Robeson's appearance in it became an essential part of the project. *MMM* was shelved and so, later, was *The Black Consul*, even after Robeson came twice to Moscow to discuss it. Shumyatsky's 'discipline' extended to the film press, too; Eisenstein's own published articles of this time are far more modest and far less 'theoretical' than before; only the most grudging references to his first films appeared, and every defect in them was emphasized as a warning to the young; as in other cases there was a tendency to credit an acknowledged victory (such as *Potemkin*) to society, while placing all blame (as for *October*) on an individual; the influence of the 'intellectual cinema' had become a cliché of accusation. Behind the deep personal antagonism between Eisenstein and Shumyatsky there was also the powerful political pressure exerted by RAPP's influence in the arts. Begun in the years of Proletkult as an almost instructional agency for proletarian writers, it had inflated its position to an artistic dictatorship, smelling out every 'anti-proletarian' heresy, and throwing its weight around dangerously. In April 1932, came the welcome liquidation of all self-styled proletarian art organizations, but it took longer for individuals who had suffered their attacks to resume full public artistic activity.

When the news came that Sinclair had turned over the Mexican footage to a Hollywood company to cut and distribute ('to recover our investment'), Eisenstein came as close to despair as he had ever been; the fact that *Thunder Over Mexico* was shown as 'Eisenstein's film' meant less to him than that the negative was being

---

* Tisse, too, had directed a film in Europe—a fiction feature, on abortion, in Switzerland.

irreparably harmed. There was one positive move, to balance all these pains—an invitation to Eisenstein to conduct the directors' course at GIK, beginning in September 1932. His first programme for this important work, 'The Granite of Film Science', was published in *Sovietskoye Kino*, 5-6, 7, 9, 1933. He continued to plan films, and it was understood that his teaching schedule would always be adjusted whenever he and the administration of the industry could agree on a film subject.

The Great Consoler (1933)
A composition-sketch by Kuleshov

CHAPTER XIV

Witnessed Years

1934–1937

> Realism does not take everything from life, but only
> what it needs for the reproduction of a given scene;
> that is, it brings to the stage only what has histrionic
> value; it takes living truth and gives back genuine
> feelings
>
> YEVGENI VAKHTANGOV

On September 14, 1933 I landed at Leningrad on my way to the Moscow State Film Institute. I was equipped with the Institute's letter of invitation, some photographs I had taken in America, and camera and typewriter for the demands I hoped would be made on me in the next months. A short film I had made was sent on ahead; that and the persistence of a friend had procured me the invitation. I was twenty-three years old, and I remained in the Soviet Union (which the United States had not yet recognized) for three years. There are diaries and correspondence of these years that I'll quote without reference, and without apologies for their naïveté or personal intrusions.*

After a rainy glimpse of Leningrad, the Hermitage and its 'Eisenstein arches', I reached Moscow which was for me then the home of the only film school in the world. Out of curiosity, more than for any research reason, I began to see old Soviet films as well as new, even before introducing myself at GIK. On my first day in Moscow I noticed a poster for *S.V.D.*, and dodged in to see it (diary records disappointment).

'*September* 19*th* . . . on to a tram in which one could almost stand comfortably. On the way out (and GIK is *way out*, in a building once the Yar restaurant, huge place, probably the closest thing to a Tsarist roadhouse) S. told me that Lusha [the cook] had come to them in the farm famine six months ago, when the small farmers and kulaks refused to reap their crops. S. described Lusha's swollen belly and sunken face then in a way that brought famine into the tram. At GIK we waited. The day before we had met a cameraman, Shelenkov, in Revolution Square, who told us that we should ask about the H. A. Potamkin scholarship, but the commissioner we talked to now had heard nothing about it. Finally

---

* Or for the space devoted at the end of this chapter to a film that does not appear in Soviet film histories.

established that I was to enter the first regisseurs' course in December. This means intense language study until then and after . . . found Museum of Modern Western Art—dazzled by quality and quantity of Matisses, Picassos, Cézannes. . . . To the ten o'clock performance of *Deserter*. Before the show the waiting audience circled and circled scrapingly. Never saw this ritual before. Intensely interested by *Deserter* but discouraged by audience's obvious impatience with it.'

Celebrated my first week in Moscow by landing in a hospital for a few days, before returning to room-hunting and Russian lessons, while staying with my friends in the suburb of Pushkino. Finally met the senior foreign student at GIK, the Englishman, H. P. J. Marshall.

'*Early October*. Marshall took me to the big new Soyuzkino studio. Back to the Udarnik Theatre, where we found Vertov filming scenes for his Lenin picture. Conversation (brief) between V. and me in extremely bad French. . . . Next night to Eisenstein's. Books and a pyjama top. Marshall idolizes E. E. is infallible. E. is mighty. E. asked me what I thought of his drawings at John Becker's. I told him. (A BIG mistake.) Kara-Kum motorists came back today, bringing Tisse, who came in later to report to E. More diplomatic errors by me and we went home.'

I had seen Eisenstein only once before, lecturing at Columbia University in 1931. The most productive result of the first touchy meetings with Eisenstein was that I acted on his suggestion to see as much as I could of the large number of Moscow's repertory theatres, and I did, without realizing that this was the beginning of my course with him. Mrs Edith Isaacs of *Theatre Arts Monthly* had given me a roving commission, and I began years of intense theatre-going at the right place:

'. . . to the First Moscow Art, and *The Cherry Orchard*. Missed the first act, but got standing-room for the other three acts and I had one of the most wonderful times I've ever had in a theatre. John and Auriol would gasp at such production. . . . A day of Eisenstein's lectures at GIK. Beautiful, charming, logical. No wonder his pupils idolize him, but I couldn't. And I have gotten off on a completely wrong foot with him. He thinks I'm making fun of him—perhaps he's as shy of me as I am of him.'

The Mexican film was rarely mentioned in our first talks, and I was too young and brash to guess the seriousness of that wound. Once he asked me about *Thunder Over Mexico*, and then, perhaps regretting his momentary trust of me, changed the subject as I began to answer. Weeks later, when our relation was improving, and when I began to hear of his several film ideas that had come to nothing since his return from Mexico, I had the brass to ask for an explanation. He gave me the most genuinely anguished look I ever saw on his face and shouted at me: 'What do you expect me to do! How can there be a new film when I haven't given birth to the last one!' And he clutched his belly with an equally painful gesture. Some of this pain was surely to avoid blaming anything on Shumyatsky, but there was a basic pain, too, that I heard about only when it was safely past. It was also later that I heard of Shumyatsky's rejection of another Eisenstein project of this winter, *Moscow*. Nathan Zarkhi was working on this script simultaneously with a play of similar subject, *Moscow the Second*—seeing the history of Moscow through several generations of a family. Eisenstein was to direct both film and play, but Shumyatsky's veto squelched both projects.

Though my personal feelings about Shumyatsky tempt me to put the whole onus on him for keeping one great artist idle and imposing mechanical standards on less powerful artists, I know that actually Shumyatsky was on a lower echelon of authoritative control, the 'total' supervision coming from persons of far greater political responsibility, ruthless in their application, to all arts and artists, of a single doctrine of socialist realism, which in practice usually amounted to an idealization of each character and every element. The fact that every finished film, no matter how slight, was seen and weighed at the Kremlin, is of considerable interest to future historians of the 'Stalin epoch'.

'*October 9th*. Letter from Jack tells me that Lincoln was thrown out of a *Thunder Over Mexico* showing. Must tell E., since I'm running out of books to lend him. E. seems to feel better about this impertinent Leyda and is going to look at the film tomorrow at 3.30. So 3.30 tomorrow will mark a beginning or an end.

'*October 10th*. Two lectures at GIK *and* showed the Bronx film to E. who liked it more than I hoped he would. He had probably heard how lousy it was, so he didn't expect anything of it. He has changed his whole attitude towards me and things are looking up generally.'

One important effect of the change: after getting me permission to attend the lectures without waiting for December, he now gave me summaries of them in English after each session. The murder in *Crime and Punishment* was being staged for a single camera position.

'*October 13th*. Lectures by tireless E. His pupils adore him. He keeps them excited with new ideas expressed by his short, sturdy body, his rasping voice, and his amazing indicative face and head. Am to work with his assistants on a sequence of *The Black Consul*, regardless of whether it is to be produced. . . . A production of *Razbeg* at the Krasnaya Presnaya Theatre [directed by Okhlopkov]. Extraordinary richness and variety. By means of new demands and shocks, by levels, by light, by sound (speech, music, noise), by the balanced use of every space and object, by terrific control of actors, by playing at all levels of intensity, by being surrounded (literally) by the play—an exciting evening.

'*October 17th*. Finished E's copy of *Black Majesty* and my scenario assignment. . . . At the Paustovskys, met the beautiful Jennie (Eugenia) Rogulina [the deserted wife of *A Simple Case*]. She's now working in the film that Balazs is directing.

'*October 19th*. Lectures. E. genial. Weeded out the foreign books in the library, found a good magazine collection, and behold! a letter postmarked July 25th from Amkino telling the director of GIK about Harry Potamkin's library. The letter had been thrown among all the other old and non-understood papers. M. and E. seized it as the straw to break bureaucracy's back. . . . After Russian lesson with [blind] Mme Mitrova, met H.W. at the Krasnaya Presnaya and saw the first lovely act of *Mother* before rushing off unwillingly to an evening of cartoons at Mezhrabpom.

'*October 21st.* School and an amusing movie in the evening—an early Yutkevich, *Laces.* A light touch. Unexpected place for a kino—a wing of the Museum of Revolution. Met Mme Stanislavsky at the First Art who will kindly help the article, if any. To Meyerhold, where I arranged seats for the whole current repertory.'

I sent important news to a friend:

'GIK is going under the general supervision of Eisenstein this year—with his plans (at least for the regisseurs' courses) and unifying method. Part of his plan is the formation within GIK of a foreign section with lectures and lessons in foreign languages. The first part to set up will be one in the English language. (Getting excited?) It should begin functioning about the first of December under his supervision and the direct leadership of Marshall. The patron of the foreign section is Mezhrabpom, who will take care of entries into the country, tuition at the school, and small monthly stipends for each pupil.'

Though a few more foreign students arrived, nothing further came of this plan. Perhaps the 'test case' was a disappointment or warning. Mezhrabpom had far greater problems at this time, attempting to shelter and employ the film refugees from Germany.

In late October I attended my first two 'horrible' parties, where I had my first sight of a distinguished drunk foreign correspondent; saw the German version of *Road to Life*, a dramatic reminder of the sudden removal of the largest foreign audience for Soviet films; and I finally saw all of Okhlopkov's perfect production of *Mother*:

'Must write about the Krasnaya Presnaya. Okhlopkov seems the most important unknown element in the Soviet theatre. I must see the films he made. I managed to see Pudovkin alone on the 26th. We got along very well together. An interpreter is always like eating through a sieve.'

As I did not then know of Pudovkin's plan to follow *Deserter* with a two-part film called *Intervention*, I didn't ask him about it, and he volunteered nothing on the subject. By then it may have been replaced by the idea of a Kirshon script about aviation. When the contrapuntal principles of the 'Statement' and the contrapuntal trials of *Deserter* were mentioned, he assumed an air of tolerant dismissal, as to acts of one's youth.

'*November 7th.* Today had time of my life marching for hours in Walker's boots in the celebration—the GIK contingent.

'*November 13th.* In the morning to *Conveyor of Death* [by Pyriev], an impossible solution for an international film style. Attasheva (for E.) arranged my afternoon's job—to take Ivor Montagu and his wife to the Museum of Modern Western Art. . . . SME's party—Pera, the Moussinacs, the Montagus, Tisse, Shub, Louis Fischer, Alexandrov, newly returned with oranges. . . .'

I have forgotten where Alexandrov was returning from, probably a vacation in the south; his visits to Eisenstein now became more rare. Shumyatsky had proposed to him the same musical comedy idea that Eisenstein had rejected, and Alexandrov accepted it—without consulting Eisenstein. This was one more stab, but received with the calm comprehension of a Freud learning of another defection.

'*Late November. Fear* [by Afinogenov] is not a good play, which made my conversation with Mme T. and the author somewhat strained. Coming back to First Art tonight for *Figaro*. . . . Had a marvellous time at the Meyerhold the other night, seeing *The Last Decisive*. Read that Meyerhold was criticized for not building enough socialist construction in his theatre. Sweet (too) dramatization and production of *Dead Souls* at the First Art. *Revizor* at Meyerhold is truer Gogol. Kachalov remains ill, so *Resurrection* has to be postponed again. *Turandot* at the Vakhtangov turned out to be museum piece, but valuable. *Intervention* much more stimulating.

'*November 30th*. Had to stop my lessons with Mme Mitrova when I ran out of roubles. Must find an income. VOKS is moving ahead with the exhibition [of my photos]. Hear that Meyerhold is starting production of *La Dame aux Camélias*! On Sverdlov Square a street fight incident, as completely and meaningfully detailed as a good movie episode. . . .

'*Mid-December*. Gorky's *Yegor Bulichov and Others* at Second Art (bad theatre and good play) and *Dostigayev and Others* at Vakhtangov—both have fascinating tangled construction which finds its progress in cleaning itself up. Great deal of Jewish Theatre lately, so far only the old Granovsky productions: *Benjamin III* (1927), *200,000* (1923), *The Witch* (1922). Of these the last was best and purest. In rehearsal: *Lear* and the Labiche play that Moussinac is directing. Seeing more rehearsals, gratefully—*Camille* at the Meyerhold, *Romeo and Juliet* at the Theatre of Revolution. Funny party at Mezhrabpom. Everybody. Strange to see unheroic Svashenko foxtrotting, Eisenstein playing the fool, good food.'

To see the whole Soviet film product, instead of the few best that were exported, was a new experience to which I adjusted slowly; I had not seen any country's *whole* product except America's. A letter of January 31, 1934:

'I'd want to be the Russian film correspondent for *New Theatre* except for the embarrassing circumstance that I have not liked any of the new Soviet films. I have even declined to write an article for Mrs Isaacs on the Hope of the Soviet Cinema. . . .

'It's not that I'm judging them on standards set by the Soviet masterpieces, or even by the effectiveness of other contemporary production. They leave their audiences COLD, and that's condemnation enough. The last fine one shown in America was *Patriots* [*Okraina*], and the only one of any interest since then was Pudovkin's *Deserter*. The only recent film of any lengthy popularity is a children's film, *Torn Shoes*, which is worth some attention abroad. But Protazanov's *Marionettes* is not funny—*Great Tokio* uses interesting material uninterestingly— the new film acted by Gardin, *Judas Goloviov*, excuses its sloppy sentiment with the novel it's based on, but why pick that novel, Russian classic or not? *Conveyor of Death* never gets anywhere in the effort to get everywhere, and some of the new ones can't even be remembered—that's the sort of films *they* were. The best film that I've seen here (and for the first time) is the old *Bed and Sofa*, which should be fought about in the States, instead of letting the censors say No and end the matter. . . .

'Excuse me, but I'd be glad to write as much as you want on the Moscow and Leningrad theatres, which I enjoy enormously, but I don't want to write a bunch of half-truths about the Soviet kino.*'

For me that was as shocking a surprise as my first view of the total film product; to find that the theatre, that I had thought an outmoded medium, interested me more than the new films, where all my hopes were, was confusing. To compound my irritation there was a thick smear of antique theatre in the 'important' films of this winter—Eisenstein's prophecy of 'refined talkies' finally come true. In an article written this year Eisenstein made a distinction between the Soviet films before 1930—a 'predominance of poetry'—and after 1930—a 'decisive turn to prose'.[1]

This group of heavily theatrical and heavily sentimental films—*Judas Goloviov*, adapted by Ivanovsky from Saltykov-Shchedrin's *Messrs Goloviov* (prejudicing me for years against this good satirist); *Petersburg Night*, expanded by Stroyeva and Roshal from ideas in Dostoyevsky's stories, 'White Nights' and 'Netochka Nezvanova'; *Thunderstorm*, adapted by the director Petrov from Ostrovsky's most 'classical' play—were all released in the first three months of 1934. All the studios share this guilty period, for Mezhrabpom gave the first taste of this trend two years earlier with Fyodorov's film about Dostoyevsky, *House of the Dead*, and Eggert's Balzac film, *Gobseck*, was one of the embarrassments of 1935; and even in Armenia Bek-Nazarov filmed one of its classical plays, *Pepo*, with improper reverence. But the chief offender would seem to be the Leningrad studio of Soyuzfilm, for two years later Ivanovsky filmed Pushkin's story, *Dubrovsky*, and Gorky's play, *Enemies*, with the same heavy hand, and Petrov built his more grandiose *Peter the First* on the same principles that made Pudovkin refer to *Thunderstorm* as 'definitely reactionary' in its anti-film method. Pudovkin also noted 'that the theatricalized style of *Thunderstorm* transforms the few exterior shots in it to the appearance of mere painted backcloths'.[1a] All these films employed the best actors of the Soviet theatre but contributed little more to Soviet cinema than lessons in what not to do. Such a wise veteran as Protazanov avoided this pitfall of theatricality; his Ostrovsky adaptation, *Without Dowry* (1936), has a film life outside its dependence on a well-known play.

In the fields of comedy and musical films the same tug-of-war continued between the theatre of the past and the cinema of the future, and here the film's defeats and victories were more equal. To balance the failure of *Marionettes* (one of the few occasions when Protazanov faltered), the success of *Lieutenant Kizhe*,

* I resolved this fear of over-optimism nine months later by proposing a regular page of reviews of new Soviet films, both good and poor, which we tried for a while with no visible effect on anybody. I tried to communicate some discoveries: 'The first empty period I get, I want to write for this page a group of landmarks in Soviet films—ones that never got to America—*Strike, By the Law, Salt for Svanetia, Bed and Sofa.*'

using similar elements of irony and exaggeration, was encouraging. What *Kizhe* would have been without Prokofiev's biting score* is difficult to imagine. Tinyanov's story of a fictitious scapegoat and Alexander Feinzimmer's direction treated Tsar Paul and his period with a satirical attitude that made no pretence to historical profundity or to any analysis of economic and social conditions. Even Lubitsch's film about Paul, *The Patriot*, had been more serious than this. *Kizhe* was unlike any Soviet film I had seen, though the treatment of its actors reminded me of the FEX tradition.

The next film to use music prominently lacked the advantage of Prokofiev's great art, but it had the asset of youth in its makers and in its ideas. Coming from the Baku Theatre of Young Workers (TRAM), Igor Savchenko was twenty-three when he made this first film, *Accordion*, after a short propaganda film, *People Without Hands*. The professional reception accorded to *Accordion* (Savchenko dared to call it 'a musical comedy') was reserved and rather sour, but the public greeted it as a blessing and justification for sound-films; singing and dancing were tied closely to its story. The film was produced at Mezhrabpom by an entirely Komsomol brigade whose work from idea to released film took eight months, at a time when the average schedule was stretching into years. The young poet Zharov worked with Savchenko on the rhymed dialogue and on the script, which has a story as simple as in Clair's best films. On one collective farm the best worker and the best accordion player are united in one person, Timoshka. For his good work he is made the secretary of the village Komsomol unit, and is elected to the village soviet. But he makes the serious mistake of burying his frivolous accordion in the hay of the barn. Village life turns dull, and into the breach step a band of young kulaks, with a leader (played by Savchenko) who has proper respect for the power of an accordion. The young kulaks and their songs disorganize village and farm to a point where Timoshka considers bullets. Then he digs out a better weapon, his accordion, and drowns out the kulak songs with his own songs of belief and hope, routs the enemy, and wins back his girl. There is no effort to inflate this modest material beyond its natural proportions. Compared with the huge musical comedy machines to come, *Accordion* is a real credit to the Soviet film, despite its neglect then and since. Savchenko's career did not progress until, years later, he returned to his native Ukraine.

Alexandrov's first musical comedy established him as a power in the Soviet film industry, but it is difficult to be really happy about it as a film, enriched though it was by the clever camera-work of Vladimir Nilsen who introduced some Western camera-tricks—models, glass-shots, combination photography, etc. An important sound-device used in American and European productions was also introduced here: to film the action of whole sequences to pre-recorded musical accompaniment. Yet despite the clever application by both cameraman and director of lessons learned, the film scarcely touches its spectator with its breathless flood of effective moments, gay music and spectacle, and its absence of comedy timing. It is a film of borrowings, including some from the surrealist

* This score recently had the curious experience of being re-used in a film it never dreamt of, *The Horse's Mouth*.

films of Bunuel and Dali. Made as *The Shepherd of Abrau*, it appeared as *Jolly Fellows*, with various other jolly titles abroad—*Jazz Comedy*, *Moscow Laughs*, etc. The hero, a shepherd-boy who reaches lofty heights as a jazz-orchestra conductor, was played by Leonid Utyosov, the jazz-conductor—and his brief film career was ended. But his heroine (originally written for a dancer) was played by Lyubov Orlova, a singer who had made her film début in *Petersburg Night*; she actually reached the 'lofty heights' of the film's fiction, establishing herself as the first recognized 'star' of Soviet cinema, playing in the whole succession of Alexandrov's musicals, and becoming Mrs Alexandrov. The score by Isaac Dunayevsky increased the popularity of the film even after it was revealed that his best tune was a Mexican song brought back for *Que Viva Mexico*. For the next year and a half Alexandrov worked on his second musical comedy, *Circus*, which had a more 'serious' plot, fully equipped with villain, persecuted heroine, and darling baby.

'My next picture will be an eccentric comedy based on a scenario by Ilf and Petrov. I expect it to be a real side-splitter. . . . We have worked out everything in advance and know where and under what conditions we shall film each episode and shot. . . . We have even decided on the kind of lens for each shot. In this way we can dispense with "creative hold-ups".'[2]

The result was unfortunately disappointing. Apparently the only valid way to import a foreign form, such as the musical comedy film, into the Soviet cinema, was to re-invent it in Soviet terms, as in *Accordion*, rather than to translate it into Russian with a Soviet setting, as in *Jolly Fellows*. Fortunately Alexandrov was not too blinded by his successes to realize this, and his work after *Circus* grew more conscientious.

Another foreign form that withstood imitation but begged for transformation was the animated cartoon, given more attention now that it had a sound-track. Sound added nothing to the work of Khodatayev, whose ambitious *Organchik* looked like a silent cartoon to which sound had been forcibly applied, but Vano's work matured with the simple rhythms demanded by the music and speech of *Black and White* (from a Mayakovsky poem about Cuba) and *The Tale of Tsar Duranda*, on which the Brumberg sisters collaborated. It was Tsekhanovsky in Leningrad who showed the greatest promise of originality and put up the greatest resistance to the industrial methods introduced from abroad. After *Post* and *Pacific 231* he began work, in partnership with Dmitry Shostakovich, on a full-length animated cartoon comic opera, based on a satirical poem by Pushkin, *The Tale of the Priest and His Servant, Blockhead*. The work might have gone faster if Tsekhanovsky had been willing to adopt the American methods that one of the assistants of Max Fleischer put into general and uncritical usage in Moscow and Leningrad cartoon studios. Their best effect was to show how cartoons could be made efficiently, and their worst effect was to turn out poor imitations of Disney and Fleischer characters, with superimposed Russian details. Tsekhanovsky felt, and rightly, that such a wholesale adoption would mean a sacrifice of many of his own standards and techniques. For three years he and Lenfilm were content to increase and reorganize his group of animators along American lines, but he stubbornly resisted the gelatin method in preference to paper, with which he accomplished such individual results. If his *Tale* had been finished, the Soviet animated cartoon of today might look very different, but the *Tale* had an unhappy end. Tsekhanovsky's opposition to the generally accepted industrialization, plus the increasing suspicion of 'formalism' that was directed at his graphic style and at Shostakovich's music prevented their completion of *The Tale*.* It is a capitulated and less interesting Tsekhanovsky that has worked since then.

Thanks to Starewicz the idea of three-dimensional figure animation can be considered a native Russian form. Sound gave this, too, an impetus, and Alexander Ptushko took advantage of it. He had worked in this difficult medium since 1929 and his first short sound-film, *Master of Existence* (1932), was acceptable. Even those familiar with his past work were unprepared for the magnitude and ingenuity of his first full-length film, *A New Gulliver*, the result of three years of gruelling work with moulded wax dolls. Swift's story is framed by a reading in a Crimean camp of Young Pioneers; their dreams bring it up to date with amusing details (a newsreel cameraman photographs the hauling of sleeping Gulliver into the capital, modern engineering solves the problem of feeding Gulliver, etc.) and a class-war in Lilliput, with Gulliver aiding the oppressed.

Foreign prestige and domestic film-making morale were bolstered by the appearance of a Soviet delegation, headed by Shumyatsky, at the second international film exhibition of Venice in the summer of 1934—a competition not attempted since the Paris exhibition of 1925. Of the films entered, Alexandrov's *Jolly Fellows* and a portion of the unfinished *New Gulliver* attracted the most attention, chiefly for their inventiveness. The *Chelyuskin* voyage, filmed in the Arctic by Shafran and Troyanovsky, seemed an exotic document. The gloomy, polished style of *Thunderstorm* and *Petersburg Night* fitted the audience's notion of what Russian films should be, and even Mikhail Romm's first film, *Boule de Suif*, silent though it was, was praised politely, though it is little more than an acceptable, stiff student adaptation of Maupassant's story. At home the cameraman, Boris Volchok, had been congratulated for his use of new Soviet manufactured negative exclusively, and this technical achievement was boasted at Venice, too, where half of *Boule de Suif* was shown with half of Dovzhenko's *Ivan*.

It was at this time that I first met Dovzhenko in Moscow. He had weathered the complaints made about *Ivan* and was planning a new film that would, the first time for him, be made outside the Ukraine. The film was to be produced jointly by Ukrainfilm and Mosfilm, where the studio work was to be filmed after the location expedition to Siberia. I knew little about the project until he read me the script of *Aerograd*. His voice, as powerful and convincing as I imagined Mayakovsky's must have been, filled his hotel room to the bursting point. His dynamic person exactly fitted my imagined maker of *Arsenal* and *Earth*. When I later watched him work at Mosfilm I saw that his relation to actors was to infect them with his immense enthusiasm in the same way that he swept me off my feet

---

* Another animated cartoon on *The Tale of a Priest and His Worker Balda* was made in 1940 by Sazonov.

with his reading. It was an exhilarating experience and I was ready to accompany the expedition to Siberia as assistant to this emotional hero. I was looking for a summer job, a practical experience ['praktika'] after the winter's immersion in lectures and theory.

But my obligations were to Mezhrabpom, that had sponsored my admittance to GIK and authorized my student's stipend there. It was at that studio, too, that foreigners were accepted more readily than elsewhere into film-crews. There were, just then, as many foreign directors, mostly German refugees, working there as there were Russian directors. Piscator was just completing his first film, the heavily experimental and effective *Revolt of the Fishermen*, from Anna Seghers' novel. Bala Belazs, too, was trying out a lifetime of film-theory with a first film, *Tissa Burns*, that was on its way to the shelf where *Metal* already lay, along with the American Negro script that Piel Jutzi had prepared. Gustav von Wangenheim was beginning a film about German resistance to Hitler, called *Fighters*, and Joris Ivens had a plan to make a Soviet film around his *Borinage*, a sharp and sensitive reportage on Belgian coal-miners, by shooting sound-sequences in Soviet mines and in the Moscow subway construction. As all my previous work had been in documentary films, I had more admiration for and familiarity with Ivens' work than with any of the other non-Russian directors at Mezhrabpom. Thus, I bragged in early May 1934, to a friend:

'I have a chance to work with either Ivens or Dovzhenko, but I've about made up my mind to work first with Ivens, who is closer to what I'm able to do and understand, instead of taking the risk right away of being overwhelmed by D., who is really overwhelming personally. Neither film expedition will start until July. . . .'

After the school term ended I visited Tiflis for the tenth birthday celebration of the Rustaveli Theatre, this in connection with my duties for *Theatre Arts Monthly*. The excursion turned out to be one of the highest joys of my whole Soviet stay, partly because I met Kalatozov at the Tiflis studio where he showed me *Salt for Svanetia* and told me how it came to be made, details that I passed on at once to a friend in America:

'Instead of going to Paris I went down to Tiflis to see a swell theatre that lived up to the extravagant praise I had heard, and saw one swell movie (and a half dozen bad ones). This is the film that Harry [Potamkin] always talked about—*Salt for Svanetia*—with such enthusiasm. It is absolutely the most powerful documentary film I've ever seen, and that includes *Turksib*, which is only more direct and more energetic. The film itself has a curious history. Its maker (regisseur, scenarist, cameraman), Kalatozov brought a film, his first [*Blind*], to Moscow the year that Harry was here, and showed it to Attasheva and a few friends who saw nothing amazing in it. He mentioned at the time that he had brought a lot of material with him from a couple of months he had spent in Svanetia, going there with a camera on the advice of Tretyakov. Attasheva asked to see it and asked if Harry and another American (Lozowick perhaps?) could come too. So about ten reels of unedited material were screened, with the result that

Pera A. and Harry jumped on to Kalatozov and insisted that he make the great film of this material that they saw in it. . . . It would stun any private film society that had the opportunity to see it, but some day it will have to be seen abroad.'

That 'some day' has not yet arrived. My scorn of the newer Georgian films shown me then, alongside the unfair competition of Kalatozov's film, might have been considerably tempered if I had seen a film then in production, released the following autumn: *Last Masquerade*, directed by Mikhail Chiaureli. This and Chiaureli's next film, *Arsen*, assure him a place in Soviet film history no matter how low, in our judgments, his later 'big' films about Stalin may sink. Both of Chiaureli's best films are set in the vivid past of the Caucasus. *The Last Masquerade* is laid in the recent past of the birth of the Georgian Republic, seen through the conflicting and often crossing biographies of Mito, a young worker, and Prince Rostom. The swirling action culminates in one of the most dramatic dance sequences in films. *Arsen* goes further into the past, into the story of the legendary bandit-rebel, Arsen, a figure that recurs in Georgian art, for it synthesizes the most basic elements of Caucasian character and independence. Indeed, Chiaureli himself had played this rôle in 1921, the first year of Soviet Georgian cinema. Kalatozov's own attempt to return to active film-making two years later, with a scenario on another Caucasian hero, Shamil, was quashed with denunciations of the scenario's 'distortion of history'.[3] Kalatozov's purgatory in administration was to be prolonged so long as the current central film administration lasted.

July brought the news that GIK was next year to become VGIK (Higher State Institute of Cinema) with new entrance requirements that I could not meet, for I had neither the minimum years of college or film practice. So the summer employment would have to cover the winter, too, if I was to remain in Moscow, attending Eisenstein's classes as an auditor. The plan for a foreign section in GIK had been abandoned and we few foreigners gathered there by chance, including an Italian, an Indian, and a Swede, were on our own. The older foreign students, Marshall in the director's course and Yolanda Chen in the camera course, were able to finish their training. My rationalization may have had the taste of sour grapes, but I told myself that I would be happier at work than at school. And Dovzhenko had expressed doubts about the usefulness of a long film education, on which he disagreed with Eisenstein, and put it this way in a speech two years later:

'. . . it does not take a long period of study to make a cinema regisseur. Five years would be harmful. One year of study and then to work. Otherwise, the student dries up, becomes 'wise'. He knows everything, the peculiar mistakes of every regisseur, and becomes a mediocre average of them all.'[4]

The Ivens film was not ready yet, so Vertov, then cutting *Three Songs of Lenin* at Mezhrabpom, took me into his group that was making, with no more than a sense of duty, a series of short films for Intourist, starting with one on Leningrad, where I was sent in August. Every Leningrad evening was spent catching up with any films I had never heard of, and seeing the few theatres that were sweating out the summer there. On grey and rainy days I wormed into rehearsals and ballet classes, and visited the proudly unmodern studio of Lenfilm in a building that still showed its original function—an amusement palace, with sound-stages now filling the skating-rink. Luckily for them, the directors I most wanted to see at work were on location outside Leningrad, Ermler on *Peasants*, and Kozintsev and Trauberg on *The Youth of Maxim*. I didn't know enough then (who did ?) to ask for the makers of *Chapayev*, then in the cutting-room. Through friends at the Children's Publishing House I met Tsekhanovsky, already deep in his comic opera cartoon. The most important film information I picked up concerned the film-training programme begun by Yutkevich. I saw a screening of Vostok-kino's *Song about Happiness*, the first film Yutkevich supervised, about the Mari people on the Volga. The heroine was played by Yanina Zheimo, a skilful young actress of children's rôles, and the young hero was a boy, Viktorov, whose only previous experience was a bit in *Road to Life*. The two directors were almost as young—Mark Donskoy and Vladimir Legoshin. The film's subject was education in general and music education in particular (Gardin played a Germanic music professor) and the whole had such a pleasant, unforced good humour that Yutkevich's art as teacher-producer was obvious. Both directors told me how much credit should go to him for the success of their film—Donskoy had been about to leave cinema entirely when the job was offered to him. Their subsequent work must have made Yutkevich proud: Legoshin's next film was *Lone White Sail* and Donskoy, after directing the Russian dubbing of the American *Invisible Man*, began work on his great trilogy of Gorky's youth, one of the noblest achievements in the pre-war period of the Soviet cinema. On a later trip to Leningrad I met the people working on the next film that Yutkevich supervised—*Girl-Friends*, the first film made by the musician-scenarist, Arnstam, in collaboration with the film's designer, Levin. I was back in America before I saw the third film from 'the Yutkevich workshop'—an adaptation of Gogol's comedy, *Marriage*, directed by the Meyerhold actor Garin, with his wife Lokshina (an assistant on *The Youth of Maxim*). These three films alone are a credit to any teacher or producer.

The first exciting film experience after getting back to Moscow in September was the new film of my temporary boss, Vertov. After three years of anxiety and hesitation and false starts, he had produced his greatest film, *Three Songs of Lenin*—and for once no one was left unmoved. His original idea of a film about Lenin had grown into a film about the effect of Lenin's life and teaching, and this led him to show this effect on some who had changed most—the women of central Asia. From the mass of folklore born from the revolution, Vertov found his vehicle in three anonymous songs of Uzbekistan, 'folk-songs' about Lenin. For those women, as expressed in their songs, Lenin meant freedom, his death a dreadful blow, and his teachings the basis of their future life. These three subjects shape the structure of the film.

The film opens with the first song, 'My face was in a prison black . . .' a song about women, imprisoned in the terrifying black horse-hair 'veils' of the past. This part of the film is heavy with the weight of oppression, the chains of tradition that burdened the women of the Asian colonies of Tsarist Russia; the section ends in brightness and hope. The second song, about the death of Lenin, achieves an emotional impact seldom realized in the film medium. 'We loved him. . . .' Afterwards one wonders how the suffering was conveyed. '. . . we never looked upon his face, we never heard his voice, but he loved us like a father—no, more than that, for no father ever did for his children what Ilyich did for us.' The third song opens with the triumphant chords of 'In a great stone city,' expanding into a glowing lyricism that Vertov's work, alongside its proclaimed factuality, had always hinted. The dependence on songs (later done into English by W. H. Auden) also determined the emotional tone of the film, a new tone not so much for Vertov, but for the international documentary film form.

Even before 1918, when Vertov entered the cinema in a professional capacity, he had dreamed of making an art of the sights and sounds of the world around him, arranging harmonies and dissonances out of these realities. It is interesting that, working as a poet when a boy, he became interested in films for their *partial* realization of his dream. His first use of the sound-film, almost a miraculous answer to that dream, was still linked to 'pure' documentation, in *Enthusiasm*. It was in his second sound-film that the boy-poet, Vertov, was recalled. Vertov's former 'absolute' dependence upon montage of otherwise untouched material had developed into a wish for more concrete images than the pure document can ever accomplish, but without discarding his long experience with archive material and with the untouched document. *Three Songs of Lenin* contains a quantity of archive material, moulded so deftly into the whole that it ascends beyond its specific historic source. It is really remarkable how the same footage brings such different results in the hands of Shub and Vertov. An example of the latter's lyrical method occurs in the second song where newsreel material of Lenin's funeral is juxtaposed to a series of faces, of many times and places, flooded with sorrow, creating a passage of genuine tragic beauty. There is a use of the untouched document in the third song when three spontaneous speeches are recorded. The strength of these uses of archive and untouched materials lies in Vertov's experience. He knew how far the pure document can be useful, because he had advanced beyond it.

The documentary films to follow *Three Songs of Lenin* showed little of its influence; apparently it was too personal a style for others' use. Esther Shub made two films in this period, *K. S. E.* (*Komsomol—Patron of Electrification*), and *Country of the Soviets*, both good jobs but without the surprise of her archive films. Yutkevich and Arnstam collaborated on a travel documentary about Turkey—*Ankara*. The *Chelyuskin* film and Mikhail Kaufman's films, *Air-March* and *Great Victory* (on the new ball-bearing plant), were conscientious, well-organized reporting. Even Joris Ivens' new version of *Borinage* was less powerful than the original silent version. Yet for me I should confess that *Three Songs of Lenin* made all other documentary films of the period a little ordinary by comparison. In this field it was outstanding for now and a long time after. Vertov's next film was released three years later, in November 1937, after I had left the Soviet Union, and I have always regretted not seeing that next step in his development, even if it did not move ahead from the Lenin film. It was entitled *Lullaby*, and I have read no account of its content beyond that it was concerned with the women of the Soviet Union and of Spain.

For the anniversary on November 7, 1934, the Soviet audience was given a long-remembered gift, the film *Chapayev*, the first sound-film written and directed by Sergei and Georgi Vasiliev.* Its reception was unanimously joyful; public, industry and film-makers joined in its praise, and it was known that the heads of Government and Army had endorsed it at earlier screenings in the Kremlin. It was an easy film to love; the deliberation that had gone into its two years of production was concealed behind a smooth surface of spontaneity and casualness, yet there was almost no gesture or glance that had not been calculated to give every figure a larger meaning than his function in the film's story. It was only later that the hard labour that went into *Chapayev*'s making became generally known. Fragments of its scenario's several stages have been published. The source was one of the most modest and lasting literary works to come from the Civil War, Dmitri Furmanov's *Chapayev*, an account of this individualist Red Army commander by the man sent to him as political commissar. In 1924 Furmanov had prepared a film treatment and submitted it, shortly before his death, to the Leningrad studio, where it was lost and forgotten.† Early in 1932 Furmanov's widow submitted her own treatment to the same studio, where it was turned over to the Vasilievs. They found it good material in an unfilmic form and asked her permission to return to her husband's book as a base. Anna Furmanova agreed and turned over to them all her notes on the Chapayev days. From this new beginning the Vasilievs' painstaking work on the script, and their willingness to discard good ideas for better ones, may be the key to the film's total effect. Their first idea for opening the film was in an outline:

Prologue.

Animated map—the republic encircled [by attack]
Railway station—seeing-off [of Furmanov].

I.

Furmanov's dream.
Acquaintance with Chapayev. . . .

The next step was the 'literary scenario', equivalent to our 'treatment':

Reel One.

A lyrical Russian landscape.
Its calm and clarity are suddenly shattered by an explosion.
A great burst of shell.
In the clouds of smoke and flame, clumps of earth fly up and slowly, slowly (slow-motion camera) fall to the earth.

* Their last silent film, *A Personal Matter* (1932), is compared by N. Lebedev in material and theme to *Counterplan*. Another pre-*Chapayev* work, *Unlikely but True*, directed by Georgi Vasiliev alone, is not characterized by Lebedev.
† After the canonization of the Vasilievs' *Chapayev* there was a search for this lost script, remembered by Furmanov's widow. In 1939 the script was found with other rejected scenarios by Furmanov. Their high quality embarrassed people who had worked in that earlier administration.

The explosion is accompanied not by a horrible roar, but by a sort of trombone drone. . . .

On a small hill, in clouds of smoke issuing from some unseen source, are two armed horsemen.

The group has the effect of a monument.

The horses stand as if rooted to the spot.

With binoculars the horsemen survey the field of action.

They are—Chapayev and commissar Furmanov.

Chapayev, a man of great height, mounted on a colossal steed (filmed from below), produces a grandiose effect. . . .

Thus begins what turns out to be 'Furmanov's dream' (see outline), from which he is waked by the real Chapayev. But this whole amusing idea of an heroic parody, that perhaps consumed more time and attention than it was worth, was dropped in preparing the first 'regisseur's scenario', or shooting-script:

Reel One.

Introductory titles. One and a half minutes of music (theme: Chapayev's song, 'Black Raven').

STUDIO. IZBA No. I. CHAPAYEV'S HEADQUARTERS.

With a restless shake of his head Furmanov wakes, and at once springs up.

In the middle of the room stands a man of medium height with the splendid moustaches of a sergeant-major.

He looks attentively at the man who has just waked and says, simply: *Hello. I'm Chapayav.*

Furmanov, not quite awake, one hand pulling on his trousers, holds out his other hand to Chapayev: *Hello, I'm Furmanov—appointed to you as division commissar.*

Chapayev's lips form a slightly ironic smile: *I know. . . .*

The final shooting-script, prepared for the second summer's location work, changes the setting for this meeting:

Reel One.

Down a hill, straight at the camera, races a *troika.*

It drives at an approaching crowd of running men, some without rifles, a few are barefoot.

The *troika* dashes into the crowd. A man in it stands up: *Stop! Where are you going?*

The crowd surrounds the carriage of their beloved commander. This is Chapayev. One of the breathless partisans 'reports': *Czechs drove us from the farm!*

Chapayev swings toward him: *Czechs?—And where's your rifle?*

The partisan waves his hand, embarrassed, back in the direction from where he had run with the others: *The rifle's there!*

And he starts to run back to the farm—to the Czechs.

Chapayev gestures and shouts to the driver: *Come on! let's go!*

The crowd follows—one feeble runner grabs and hangs on to a fender.

Along the road comes a crowd of retreating partisans.

Ahead of them appears a cloud of dust—coming closer. The partisans halt, and one of them recognizes the *troika*.

Chapayev!

And the crowd turns to run with the carriage.

The *troika* and the racing crowd, growing like a snowball, overwhelms the Czech picket and bursts into the farm. The driver pulls up—it is Petka, faithful orderly of Chapayev—and mounts the machine-gun. Fade-out.

It is at the recaptured farm, on a little bridge beneath which the embarrassed partisans are fishing out their rifles and machine-guns, that Chapayev and Furmanov first meet. An element common to all versions of the opening is a light humour, an important ingredient of the completed film.

The first version of the scenario was read at the apartment of Illarion Pevtzov, to whom the Vasilievs had proposed the rôle of Colonel Borozdin, commander of the Kolchak armies opposing Chapayev. Among those present at this first reading was an acting pupil of Pevtsov's, Boris Babochkin, who had been considered, privately, for the rôle of Chapayev, but who was offered ('as a test', Sergei Vasiliev later said) the rôle of the orderly, Petka. Babochkin, an actor at the Leningrad Dramatic Theatre, had played several small film-rôles. He was thrilled by the scenario:

'The two Vasilievs read it in turns. Georgi Vasiliev sang the songs. In its first version the scenario was so long that we sat from ten p.m. to three a.m. The material was so fascinating, intimate and exciting, that it already contained the seed of the film's future success. This very night, walking home, I showed how Chapayev would wear his cap, and I suggested the 'Black Raven' song to the Vasilievs. Frankly, the image of Chapayev was clear to me, but Petka, whom I was to play, was not so easily imagined. Nevertheless, I agreed to play Petka, for the interests of the film were now mine. It did not occur to me that I might be asked to play Chapayev. I only urged the Vasilievs to make no mistake in casting this rôle. I was eager for them to persuade Khmelov to play it. In describing the inadequacies of several candidates, and with no ulterior motive, I showed them how this or that actor would handle the rôle. They asked me to try the make-up, so I put on the cap and moustaches of the commander. A few days later I signed the contract to play the rôle of Chapayev.'[5]

Babochkin's memoir contains the only published account of the filming of *Chapayev*, in which he is frank on his 'endless arguments' with the Vasilievs, on the interpretation of his rôle, on the value of rehearsals, etc., 'and I am very sorry now that I was not always able to win them over to my way of thinking'. The first summer on location at the Volga camp of the 48th Division was almost a total loss—much rain and little sun. Only one scene from this summer's work was retained in the finished film: the parting of Furmanov from Chapayev, where the overcast sky gave the scene an extra colouring of sadness. One of the best ideas in the film, the 'potato scene', was accidentally found this wet summer:

'In the summer of 1933 we were sitting in a farmer's hut in the village of Marino Gorodishche, waiting for the sun—our usual occupation that summer. The peaceful hut had been transformed into one of our sets, the headquarters of the red partisans. On the table were grenades, bullet-belts. . . . While we waited the farmer's wife brought us a hospitable dish, baked potatoes. As she spilled them out on the table, one ugly one, all bumps and rough skin, rolled ahead of the others. Someone said, "There goes the detachment in marching order—and prancing ahead on his fiery steed is the commander." The wife placed some cucumbers on the table. "Ah, there comes the enemy", someone else added.'[6]

The film is founded on such sparse, but vivid, homely, and usually humorous details. Even the rôle of Anna, Petka's machine-gunner sweetheart, is presented without one maudlin touch. The photography by Sigayev (an assistant and still photographer on *October*) is similarly simple, natural and efficient. The central relationship, between Chapayev and Furmanov, is one of almost constant friction, illuminating both characters as well as the basic subject of the film— the rôle of the Communist Party in the Civil War. Nothing seems schematic. There is a repeated accent on human fallibility that somehow heightens the courage in and of the film, without diminishing the legendary Russian hero features in Chapayev's rôle. The enemy, too, represented by Colonel Borozdin, is shown with a subtlety that magnifies his ruthless effect: for example, in the 'Moonlight Sonata' scene in which, while he plays the piano, his servant, polishing the floor to the rhythm of the music, discovers the signed condemnation of his brother. It was a similar contradiction between beauty and cruelty that was the basic idea of the Vasilievs' first film, *The Sleeping Beauty*.

Between the lost summer and the extremely productive second summer on location, the final version of the shooting-script was fixed and all studio work was completed. The montage, calculated from the start by these directors trained in the cutting-room, was swiftly done. As evidence of their concentration on final form to the exclusion of individually effective shots, there is Babochkin's reaction to the famous scene of the 'psychological attack', which 'made the most depressing effect on me when the uncut footage was first screened'. The finally edited scene has been compared to the troops descending the Odessa steps in *Potemkin*.

Eisenstein, whom no one thanked for his early guidance of the Vasilievs, was unstinting in his praise of *Chapayev*, pointing to it as the first example, the model, of a 'third period' in Soviet film history, synthesizing the mass film of the first period with the individual, naturalist stories of the second (or sound) period. All the Vasilievs' training had prepared them for this deliberate victory, but some element of genius was lacking that would have made their subsequent work as memorable or as original. After *Chapayev*'s success their temptation, in which they were encouraged by everyone above, was to repeat its success, rather than to discover new *Chapayevs*—a mistake never made by the creator of *Potemkin*.

Chapayev's most immediate benefit was to give reason and focus to the coming fifteenth anniversary of Soviet cinema, dating from Lenin's decree of August 1919, transferring all film industries to the Commissariat of Education. To the organizers of this celebration *Chapayev*'s timely arrival must have seemed a nearly divine dispensation. It provided a proud peak for the January celebration as well as for the International Film Festival held in Moscow a month later. In preparation for the celebration the Dom Kino (Cinema House, for film-workers) presented a review of Soviet film history in a series of screenings through December, in which I saw some complete films and fragments of other films of the past that I missed in my school screenings, or at the Museum of the Revolution or in random cinemas. It was at these Dom Kino screenings that I saw Protazanov's *Father Sergius*; it, together with his *Queen of Spades* at GIK, gave me a clearer idea of his importance than had his recent films. At the close of the creative conference these retrospective screenings continued throughout January, in the special areas of children's films, animated cartoons, military, instructional and expedition films.

The celebration began with a most ambitious conference on creative problems, opening on January 8th. Though unpleasant for Eisenstein, who appeared the chief target of its criticism, there was a frank airing of fundamental problems. When Eisenstein prepared his first speech at the conference for publication he emphasized one little-publicized anxiety that the discussion brought into the light:

'To many it seems that the progressive development of the Soviet cinema has stopped. They speak of retrogression. This is, of course, wrong. And one important circumstance is underestimated by the fervent partisans of the old silent Soviet cinema, who now gaze bewilderedly as there appears Soviet film after film which in so many respects is formally similar to the foreign cinema. If in many cases there must indeed be observed the dulling of that formal brilliance to which the foreign friends of our films had become accustomed, this is the consequence of the fact that our cinematography, in its present stage, is entirely absorbed in another sphere of investigation and deepening . . . into the direction of deepening and broadening the thematic and ideological formulation of questions and problems within the content of the film. . . .

'The Soviet cinema is now passing through a new phase of yet more distinct Bolshevization, a phase of yet more pointed ideological and essential militant sharpness.'[7]

The substance of his report was a review of the parallels for certain fundamental methods found in other arts and sciences. Through many of the speeches and discussion, often quite personal and emotional, one could sometimes guess that a bitter remark about Eisenstein stemmed from the speaker's awareness of Shumyatsky's attitude toward this 'difficult' artist. Yet to this next stage of the administration's discipline of Eisenstein some sincere expressions of pity and fear were contributed, such as in Dovzhenko's heart-felt speech:

'When I heard Eisenstein's report I was afraid that he knows so much, and his head is so "clear" that it looks as if he'll never make another film. If I knew as much as he does I would literally die. [Laughter and applause.] I'm sorry you're laughing. . . . I'm also afraid that his laboratory may explode from an overwhelming confusion of complicated, mysterious, and enigmatic material.

'I'm convinced that in more ways than one his erudition is killing him, no! excuse me, I did not mean that word; I wanted to say is disorganizing him. . . .

'Sergei Mikhailovich [D. turns to him]: If you do not produce a film at least within a year, then please do not produce one at all. We won't need it, and neither will you. . . .'[8]

The Soviet cinema never had so much public attention as on January 11, 1935, with complimentary greetings from Stalin, Kalinin, and top party organizations featured in all Soviet newspapers, and a ceremony at the Bolshoi Theatre that evening, resembling an Academy Award evening in Hollywood, without jokes. I don't remember how I gained admission to these solemnities, but I was there. The positive aspects of the occasion were somewhat lost on me, because the next phase in the disciplining of Eisenstein darkened the celebration—just nine years after the first showing of *Potemkin* in this theatre. When the honours were announced, his name was not among those given the Order of Lenin: the Leningrad studio of Lenfilm 'for the production of films of ideological, artistic and technical distinction' was the first to be awarded, followed by Shumyatsky, Gruz (manager of the Photo-Chemical Trust), Tager, Pudovkin, Ermler, G. Vasiliev, S. Vasiliev, Dovzhenko, Chiaureli, Kozintsev, Trauberg. The Order of the Red Banner of Labour went to several administrators, including Valeri Pletnyov, once Eisenstein's associate at Proletkult, and now Shumyatsky's assistant, Yukov, another assistant in charge of fiction films, Dznuni, manager of Armenkino, and (No. 14) K. M. Shvedchikov, 'former organizer and chairman of the Sovkino board'. Nor was Eisenstein's name among those awarded the Order of the Red Star: Vertov, Kavaleridze, Bek-Nazarov, Bliokh, Alexandrov. I felt that everyone watched the man on the stage not yet named. He rubbed his nose in a signal recognized only by Attasheva in the audience: it was his code for '*je m'en fou*'. The title of People's Artist was bestowed on Gardin and Babochkin. The title of Honoured Art Worker was bestowed on Zarkhi, Eisenstein, Tisse, Kuleshov, Preobrazhenskaya, Protazanov, Roshal, Tarich, Shengelaya, Yutkevich, Golovnya, Andrei Moskvin, Piotrovsky (a 'producer' at Lenfilm), Enei (designer), Poselsky and Kaufman—an honourable company, surely, but no one missed the public slap at Eisenstein. The title of Honoured Artist of the Republic was given to twenty-six artists, chiefly actors and actresses, but including V. Petrov, Ptushko, Shub, Barnet (identified as 'actor'), and Yulia Solntseva, formerly an actress (in *Aelita*, *Cigarette-Girl*, etc.) and now the beautiful wife and assistant of Dovzhenko. The last category in the list of awards was of superannuation pensions—to Perestiani, Sabinsky, and Khanzhonkov, among others—men who were mature film-makers before Lenin's decree. The rest of the evening's programme—greetings from the Red Army, from artists of all media, and the theatres of Moscow, concluding with the third act of *Swan*

Lake!—was an anticlimax to the personal drama of the evening,[9] that I reported a few days later:

'He hasn't taken the rebuke easily about his not getting the Order of Lenin. And the rebuke has not done him nor his work any good. What has been said about it in America? As far as I'm concerned, the incident had a dampening effect on the fifteen years of Soviet Kino jubilee. Everything in connection with the jubilee has been treated with a generous but tasteless hand.'

At the closing session of the creative conference Eisenstein showed something like his old fight and polemic strength:

'No one here has had to listen to so many compliments about high brow wisdom as I. Almost all spoke of it quite sweetly: "Dear Sergei Mikhailovich ... what you are doing in the academy and in your study is nonsense. You've got to produce pictures. All your other work—all that is nothing."

'I feel it important to produce films, and I will produce films; but I feel that the work of making films must go parallel with intensive theoretical work and research. . . .

'I want to touch upon something that nobody speaks about openly and which disturbs you all. . . . I want to speak of that point in the Government announcement that relates to the honours awarded, and which pertains to me. . . . I interpret it this way: The hub is—and this you know—that I have not been engaged in film production for several years, and I consider the decision as a signal from the Party and the Government that I must enter production. . . .

'Comrades, today you have given me much credit for my brains. I beg you from this day to give me credit for a heart. [Great applause.] Whether Comrade Yutkevich meant his remarks about me or not, such films as *Potemkin* are made with the heart's blood, and what I now say to you is aimed at putting an end to all the gossip and comment about the one who was passed by and underestimated. . . .

'You know that we have quarrelled and argued with Comrade Shumyatsky in our speeches and in the press; but yesterday, at the meeting for those who were honoured by the Government, we all embraced Comrade Shumyatsky, and Ermler said that this opens a new stage in all our work. . . .'[10]

He was determined on another effort to break through the antagonisms, in order to create again; by spring he had an announcement to make.

Before the international film festival at the end of February, *The Youth of Maxim* happily appeared, to aid *Chapayev* in holding up the reputation of the new Soviet cinema and of Lenfilm. Though *Maxim* and the next two films by Kozintsev and Trauberg were finished over a period of four years, they demand consideration together: the *Maxim* trilogy was conceived as a unit. The plan to make three films about a synthetic party worker evolved from their dissatisfaction with *Alone*—if we are to work with personal material, let it be central and important.

'We began work by carefully reading memoirs by old Bolsheviks. . . . We quickly realized that all previous experience in the so-called "revolutionary adventure" film—such as *Red Imps*, *Traitor*, *Gay Canary*, and the like—was no help to us, neither in dramaturgy, nor in direction, nor in acting.

'All those enigmatic provocateurs, those effective escapes from prison, underground secrets and the rest of the romantic paraphernalia, not only did not come from the documents of revolutionary activity, but were actually distortions of that material, adapting images of Bolsheviks into heroes of adventure fiction.'[11]

Out of their search for a more truthful dramatic representation of revolutionary and underground activity came, also, a fresh dramatic form. Their 'story' is a free-flowing series of episodes that often seem accidentally or arbitrarily chosen, leaving possibly more central episodes of Maxim's life unshown. But this obviously selective process increases the pleasure of the film, which is built on artistic selection—of words, gestures, faces, moments. Begun as a synthetic biography (the script was first entitled *Bolshevik*), the film grew in this selective process with an individualizing of Maxim's character. This jolly, hardy, resilient, stubborn, hopeful being is no longer 'typical'—he is Maxim. In search of a song for him, they spent a month listening to the repertoires of accordion-players in the area. Boris Chirkov, as Maxim, would try each possible song; when they heard 'Whirling and twirling the sky-blue globe', they agreed this was *his* song, and the choice, in turn, made Maxim's character clearer to all.[12]

The careful process of selection continued to the very release of the film. Trauberg has told how, in the montage, whole sections were sacrificed, and how he never stopped worrying about some sections left in:

'The film now begins with smart sleighs racing along on New Year's Eve [1910]. This is an effective opening, yet we were always very dubious about these sleighs. They come across excellently, even to an audience of old Bolsheviks, but whenever I see these racing sleighs, I experience a slight chill, seeing them as a detail that I always wanted to omit but never could. Not only the sleighs but other things, as well, especially in the Prologue.* Many things, after being filmed, were not retained, but some are still there to witness my struggle with myself.'[13]

Kozintsev told Pudovkin that they rehearsed for the film in a way that also demonstrates the selective process. Instead of risking the mechanical effect of Kuleshov's rehearsal method, they chose to rehearse the actors in episodes that were *not* to be filmed—episodes possibly as vital as those shown. This concentration on parts of each rôle *outside* the film's action was suggested by Stanislavsky's preliminaries in shaping a rôle. The music, too, has been deliberately narrowed in range. It is only the Prologue that uses Shostakovich; the body of the film depends on songs and accordions, possibly the limits of music in the actuality of the film's setting, the slums of St Petersburg. Even Moskvin's photography shows a new 'emphasis by focus'—the selective process on another plane. Another clever decision was made for Moskvin's photography of buildings

---

* The troublesome Prologue, in which Maxim does not appear, shows the social-democratic underground organization in the period of reaction, and introduces the two experienced political workers, Polivanov (played by Tarkhanov) and the adaptable Natasha (played by Valentina Kibardina). An early script for the Prologue, published in *Sovietskoye Kino*, No. 9, 1933, was completely reorganized; it does not mention the 'smart sleighs'.

and streets: to see them through Maxim's eager humorous eyes—the police attack on the demonstration takes place beneath a gigantic wall advertisement for 'ARA PILLS'. Yet there was constant care to avoid photographic 'effectiveness'. There is not one virtuoso shot that can be applauded for its own sake.

The finished film has, essentially, as instructive a purpose as the similar material of Eisenstein's *Strike*—showing the growth of organization and heroism among spied-upon workers. The gaiety and keenness of the earlier film's method has been largely transferred by Kozintsev and Trauberg to their characters, yet the style shows the same spirit and wit that invented Maxim and Natasha. Their reconstruction of the recent past is made lightly, but acidly, with little of the 'expected'. In the fun it has with serious matters (such as Maxim's police registration, or the scene of Natasha's 'study-group'), *The Youth of Maxim* pressed home *Chapayev*'s lessons in humour.

In *The Return of Maxim* he is a fully formed Bolshevik revolutionary working in the months before the war. To avoid the dramatic pitfalls of merely illustrating the history of the party during years when socialist deputies were elected to the Duma and then sent off to Siberia, Kozintsev and Trauberg asked the dramatist Slavin to help with this second part of the trilogy. Yet their own imaginative method of research continued to be an important factor. The new figure of the clerk, Dimba, St Petersburg's billiard king (played by Zharov), came entirely from newspaper files of 1914. The drama of logic versus hysteria in the Duma scenes came from the Duma records. And their original rehearsal method continued:

'A student-Menshevik, played by Merkuryev, figured in our scene of the underground meeting. As he read his lines nothing particularly characteristic emerged. So we imagined his surroundings—the way he lived. A dirty garret, unaired for years, filled with old cigarette-smoke. Strewn with butts. Underfoot shreds of old newspapers, forgotten bits of bologna-sausage, empty tin-cans. On an incredible couch lies an unshaven and unwashed person, wrapped in a faded overcoat. He is reading Kautsky. None of this was in the scenario. But from it grew the image of a theology student who can quote Marx by heart without understanding him. Out of chain-smoking, nervous scratching, a bad taste in the mouth—came a general sense of a turbid brain. A certain slyness and malice, unclear words and confused diction. And thus a scene we never wrote helped the actor to a more explicit comprehension of his whole image.'[14]

The time of the last* film in the *Maxim* trilogy—*The Vyborg Side* (the workers' quarter of Petrograd)—extends from the moment when the Winter Palace is captured, to the dispersal of the Constituent Assembly. The theme for this part is Lenin's question, 'Can the Bolsheviks hold governmental power?' Two portraits were sketched in this film that were to become solid fixtures for years in Soviet films—Maxim Strauch's portrait of Lenin (shared simultaneously

* At the end of the trilogy Chirkov was not through with Maxim—he had become so identified with the rôle in the public eye (not entirely to his joy) that he entered Ermler's *Great Citizen* as an older Maxim (now on the Central Control Committee), and war-time brought him and his song again to the screen.

with Shchukin's portrayal of Lenin in Romm's films), and Mikhail Gelovani's more wooden portrait of Stalin. In *The Vyborg Side* the realistic prose of the trilogy continues to the end, flavoured still by the sharp choice by Kozintsev and Trauberg of words and images for their peculiar brand of 'prose'. Maxim is put in charge of the State Bank (as political commissar); Natasha's new duties as a judge require all her old wisdom in emergencies; even the gay billiard king leads a more serious life as an anarchist 'activist'. All the enlarged issues of this film have also dulled its style. In *The Return of Maxim* the special film humour with its old touch of FEX grotesquerie of the wonderful first part was already dimming in the film's (and Maxim's) increased responsibilities. And there are few scenes in *The Vyborg Side* that stay in the memory as long as the whole substance, three years earlier, of Maxim's *Youth*.

At the Moscow International Film Festival at the end of February 1935, *The Youth of Maxim* shared the attention of the foreign visitors with *Chapayev*. Politeness and diplomacy gave way before the pride of the Russian jury, which gave the First Prize to Lenfilm, to add to its Order of Lenin. Of the foreign films competing (released since the Venice Exhibition of 1934) Clair's *Dernier Milliardaire* took the Second Prize, and Walt Disney the Third. Since the Pickford-Fairbanks trip, film visitors to Moscow had been chiefly American—Cecil De Mille looking for a new subject,* or Lewis Milestone to clear his rights to an Ehrenburg novel (film unrealized)—but the Festival attracted European film people and helped Soviet film business on European screens. If this, as part of the fifteenth anniversary celebrations, was Shumyatsky's idea, it was the outstanding personal accomplishment of his administration. Inevitably, its success lured him to more inflated projects and to his downfall.

There was an especially poignant moment for Eisenstein at the Festival. Part of MGM's *Viva Villa* had been photographed at the hacienda he had used for the 'Maguey' story in *Que Viva Mexico*—a bitter reminder of the film held out of his reach. And *Viva Villa*'s sequence of revolutionary battles showed details that he had planned for the unrealized last story, 'Soldadera'—freight cars that carried soldiers, their families, their whole lives and hopes. What Jack Conway did with this material was far from Eisenstein's great concept, but Eisenstein always expressed his affection for this lesser film and even assigned an episode from it (the judgment of the dead) to his student-directors. There were rumours that Sinclair had sold background footage to MGM, but if so they didn't use it—there is not a foot of Tisse's photography in the film, though its reflection is often there in James Wong Howe's admiration for Tisse.†

Shumyatsky's efforts to compete commercially with foreign films led to the visit of a delegation, headed by himself, to Europe and America in the summer of 1935. Some delegates (the Vasilievs, Raizman and Shorin) returned home without seeing New York and Hollywood, where Shumyatsky, Ermler and

---

* 'Feet—marching feet—millions of them marching endlessly,' he tried to explain his feeling to me. 'If ever I do a picture about the new Russia, that would be its *motif*—feet in leather and feet in rags and bare feet, but all marching, moving, flowing—Feet!'—Eugene Lyons, *Assignment in Utopia* (1937).

† Similar rumours about the sale of footage to *The Kid from Spain* are based on that crew's study-screening of Tisse's bull-fight material.

Nilsen found a more organized antagonism prepared for them than, after being told of the increased popularity and circulation of Soviet films in the United States, they had expected. It was precisely this fact of increased popularity that should have warned them of probable hostility. After reading New York reviews of *Three Songs of Lenin* the leading trade weekly *Motion Picture Herald* published three frightened pages, beginning:

'The American screen, already burdened quite with its own sins and faced with endless problems of political regulation, taxation and general bedevilment of all sorts, now unwittingly adds entanglement in the web of propaganda woven in Moscow in the cause of chaos and the Third Internationale.'[15]

The Hearst Press developed this campaign; after *Motion Picture Herald*'s survey, published February 23, 1935, 'Soviet Pictures Showing in 152 Theatres in US.', a commendably factual account (in four pages), the Hearst *American* (March 6, 1935) described the 'multi-armed Octopus in Moscow' to its readers:

'The avowed purpose is the complete annihilation of the United States of America and its democratic institutions and the substitution of the dictatorship of the proletariat, the complete destruction of personal liberty, and, finally, as a matter of course, THE TRANSFERENCE OF THE NATIONAL LAW-MAKING BODY FROM WASHING-TON TO MOSCOW.[!]

'The latest propagandist move in this attempt of Russia to conquer America is in the field of the motion picture.'

The Soviet delegation ate pleasant lunches and dignified banquets on both sides of the continent, but little concrete negotiation was accomplished beyond talk of newsreel exchange and conversations with Hecht and MacArthur (possibly pulling Shumyatsky's leg) on 'a series of features' to be produced by them in Russia. The most visible effect that the expedition had on Soviet film history was damaging: it showed Shumyatsky an industrial ideal, a factory method that he envied and proceeded to adopt as quickly as possible, a little more quickly than possible, as it turned out.

A more productive excursion abroad was that by the cameramen Yeshurin and Zeitlin, to France to film the Lumière jubilee ceremonies in October 1935; before they turned homewards, the Italian invasion of Abyssinia had begun and they took their cameras there—the first Soviet newsreel cameramen to report a war outside their borders.* It was a bloody prelude to the deeper tragedy next year in Spain, whither the cameramen Roman Karmen and Boris Makaseyev flew, to record the defence of Spanish democracy.

Studio films were also ranging more broadly, to untouched corners of Soviet territory, and beyond. Vladimir Schneiderov, trained in the documentary expedition film (*Pamir, El-Yemen, Great Tokio*), applied his experience to a more demanding genre:

'In 1934 I decided to make my first film with actors. I chose adventure, for adventure films had not been previously made in the USSR. After eight months of

---

* At a screening of the London Film Society these Soviet reels on the war in Abyssinia were alternated with Italian reels, with startling effect.

work I finished an adventure talkie called *Golden Lake*. . . . The writer, A. Pere-gudov, lived and worked together with my expedition in the distant taiga of the Altai. He wrote the scenario right on the spot. . . .'[16]

A practice that led the story to more adventures and effects than to good sense or shape. But it was successful, and Schneiderov's second, *Julbars*, was more controlled. Its adventures were with guards on the border between Tadjikistan and Afghanistan; the hero was a police dog, Schneiderov hoping to repeat the the Russian success of Rin-tin-tin. A more domestic film, set in the Siberian Jewish region of Birobidjan, was *Seekers of Happiness*, directed by Korsh. The novelty of its setting contributed as much to its American success as its warm story and performances. The most exotic film of this period was commissioned by the Republic of Buriat-Mongolia. Made bilingually (in both Russian and Mongolian) by Ilya Trauberg and a borrowed crew from Leningrad, *Son of Mongolia* cannot be called the first Mongol film, but it was certainly the most entertaining one I have seen. Trauberg and the authors found a film method to reflect folklore forms. The entire film is related as a ballad sung and acted by a hero—of the strange places he has been, the things he saw and encountered, and his struggle with evil forces in their various shapes. Siven, a Mongolian shepherd, loses his way in a hurricane, and finds himself in Japanese-controlled Manchuria, where he dodges and harries the Japanese and the puppet Government. A simple, almost naïve tale, it is full of ideas and action—a valuable experiment. In this period there was even an excursion, by no means the last, into outer space and science-fiction, with *Cosmic Journey*.

In a period immediately following the 'local excesses' against large sections of the peasant population in Russia and the Ukraine, it took courage and wisdom to make films about 'the peasant problem'. Two remarkable ones appeared, almost together, early in 1935, and two less similar films would be difficult to find. At one end of the stylistic scale—*Peasants*, by Ermler; at the other, *Snatchers*, by Medvedkin.

Peasants was Ermler's most realistic film to date. The term 'naturalism', though applied to comparable work by Zola, seems too mild for this passionate, earthy film about hate and love and desperation. In *Counterplan*, possibly hindered by collaborating with another's values or by the novelty of sound, Ermler had made a less bold film than his silent work had led one to expect, but in *Peasants* he was as raw and fearless as his conscience and subject demanded. He lived on collective-farms for a year with the co-authors of his scenario, Bolshintzov and Portnov, and his film touched the most basic aspects of the peasant difficulties. Some may call his film 'repellent', but no one can dismiss it as evasive. It presents the whole Communist rationale behind the drive towards collectivization and the 'liquidation of the kulaks as a class'. The film is set in a hog-raising collective. A fodder crisis leads to a distribution of the hogs to the members. This is an idea that the audience, followed by the political department representative, traces to Gerasim, a stock-breeder who has concealed that he grew up in a now dispossessed kulak family. His brother-in-law, Yegor, a formerly poor peasant, is his unwitting instrument. There is a murder and another attempt at murder before Gerasim is arrested, and his dupes finally see his true motives. Ermler makes no effort to show this prettily or neatly. There is a brutality of style that harmonizes with this violent story and its milieu. The 'meat dumpling' scene requires strong stomachs, not only in the actors who gorge themselves perspiringly through this eating contest, but in us spectators, too, when Ermler ruthlessly tops the scene with the entrance of Gerasim, carrying the newly butchered head of their prize hog. This is a slowly, surely prepared shock that is quite sickening—intentionally. There is a more traditional scene of violence that is just as well executed: Gerasim, returned from a wild wagon-ride to get his mother out of sight after her unexpected appearance at his home, listens with disgust to his wife talk of their coming child's Communist future, and kills her with a realistic force that reflects Ermler's hate of Gerasim's class. The film had exactly the effect wanted by its makers:

'We showed the picture in some collective farms of the Azov-Black Sea province and in Kiev and Moscow provinces. . . . The regional Party organizations placed critical discussion of *Peasants* on the agenda of their meetings. After seeing the picture peasants told me, "Such a picture about our lives, about our struggle for collectives, we never saw before. Your picture is absolutely true to life. When we saw it, we were reminded of our own collective farm, our own mistakes. We saw ourselves on the screen." Such comments were the highest possible reward for the collective that made the film.'[17]

The only realistic element in *Snatchers* was its ideas. Otherwise and visually (it is a silent film) it was a fantasy that stopped at nothing in the communication of those ideas. Medvedkin employed exaggeration, farce, vaudeville, burlesque, surrealism (making Alexandrov's dabbling in that mode look juvenile), even expressionism and bawdy jokes. It is one of the most original films in Soviet film history, particularly remarkable in appearing in its most orthodox period. Its story—'tale' would be more proper—is here quoted from a piece of advertising:[18]

'Once upon a time there was a poor man, Khmir. For many years he patiently waited for a good life. And when it all got too much at Khmir's hut, his stern wife Anna sent him out to seek happiness.

'And Khmir found a purse with money.

' "Here's happiness!" he shouted, wild with joy. And Anna and he went to buy everything that seemed essential to make a happy life. They bought a horse to help the farming; they bought a dog to guard their future wealth; they bought a safe so that robbers couldn't steal from them; they bought ikons, flowers, geese—in a word, everything that they had seen through a hole in the fence of their rich neighbour, Foka.

'But somehow, no matter how hard Khmir tried, a happy life didn't arrive. The horse turned out to be a shameless over-eater and lazy, too. He ate up the straw roof on Khmir's hut, and refused to plough. Khmir tried harnessing Anna alongside the horse, but that didn't help.

'On top of everything Foka, his well-fed neighbour, thrived on Khmir. He fed him, lent money, gave seed, and wrote up the debts. And when Khmir finally brought in a harvest, it was all snatched, before you could wink, down to the last grain, for taxes, interest, and debts.

'Khmir grieved. In addition, his horse was stolen—and he decided to die. He began to hew his coffin. But the Tsarist chiefs were frightened. They forbade Khmir to die, and the governor decreed: "Let him be flogged until he's unconscious. But make sure he stays alive".'

He is kept alive to make war and do other dirty work that the 'chiefs' prefer not to do themselves. Even after revolution, numbed 'Khmir obstinately refused to believe that there could be happiness for him on this earth. That's why Khmir was the worst collective farmer.' Things work out for Khmir but the lesson remains with us, much as, in *Peasants*, the hardships of Yegor (a character resembling Khmir) evoke a pity that extends into other scenes. It was strange and exhilarating to watch *Snatchers* with pity and amusement at once, to laugh *and* understand. Medvedkin's education on the film-train must have been thorough. A slightly theatrical air about sets and costumes is offset by an effect of witty improvisation throughout—the cheering masks of the recruiting soldiers and the transparent gowns of the pretty nuns who collect Khmir's last coin seem spur-of-the-moment notions in a literate cabaret.

Eisenstein, too, announced a peasant and collective farm film, and began work on his long-awaited 'next' film in the spring of 1935. The scenario was by Alexander Rzheshevsky; his idea and title—*Bezhin Meadow*—from one of Turgenev's stories in *Leaves from a Huntsman's Notebook*. I was one of four students attached to the film as apprentice directors. Our main job was to be available for all emergencies, errands, consultations. My particular duties were to help with actor-selection, take the stills on location-trips, and to keep a production diary. The following extracts were written in 1935 during the production of *Bezhin Meadow*:

'Turgenev's story told how he lost his way home from a hunting hike, and stayed the night at a bonfire kept by boys watching the horse herds. The ghost-stories they told to keep themselves awake, revealing so much about the Russian peasant child of 1850, were recalled by Rzheshevsky when he was commissioned by the Communist Youth League to write a scenario on the theme of the farm work done by Young Pioneers [younger than twelve, minimum age for Komsomols]. He went to live in Bezhin Meadow for two years to observe and record the contrast between the Russian peasant child as Turgenev knew him, and as he is today.'

The central figure in Rzheshevsky's scenario was modelled on Pavlik Morozov (known in the film as Stepok), who organized the children so well to guard the harvest that the sabotage planned by his family was threatened and they killed their boy, become an enemy of their class.

'E. describes it as a film about children and adults for adults and children. To widen the child audience, he is making a second version for children, not differing in story, but playing up all sequences of action, and playing down all complex dialogue. . . .

'E.'s work on the shooting script is done alone, with occasional consultations with scenarist and cameraman [Tisse], discussions on technical questions of music (with *Chapayev*'s composer, Gavril Popov), of sound, re-recording (Bogdankevich and Obolensky are in charge of the sound), of rear-projection and other trick camera-work that Nilsen* is superintending.'

The stream of drawings, that was a normal part of all his thinking and private conversation, had turned into a flood in this period of preparation. There were sketches for all purposes—

'. . . for movements of separate bodies and massed bodies, for ideas that are drawn before they go into the scenario, for series of compositions to maintain a part of the narrative in one key, for series that are building a climax, for faces that he is looking for and faces that he has found and is fitting into the scheme, for backgrounds to be sought, settings to be built, costumes, objects, details, everything. As practical as these drawings are, as exercise or as plan, E.'s reliance on them is not a hampering thing [as I later saw "production designs" being used as blue-prints, both in Moscow and Hollywood]. The drawings are as loose and elastic as the scenario will remain to the last shot. I have seen more than one filming day pass without E. referring once to the script—so reliant is he upon the firm mental images he keeps with him. He says that all plans are to prepare you for the new ideas that the day's work brings.'

The process of actor-selection began on an enormous scale that seemed to surprise no one but me. Apparently Eisenstein's precision in this work exceeded that of any other Soviet director.

'Two days a week, for four steady hours, those chosen during the week by the assistants and agencies are shot into his view, five at a time; the second (his first) selection is indicated, these are photographed and registered. Those for mass scenes are chosen with almost as much care as for the speaking rôles. Out of more than 2,000 children, the assistants choose 600, which E. narrows down to 200, and still the boy to play the hero hasn't been found. No one made a deep enough impression on E. to be given a screen test. Attasheva, working as an assistant, was sent to Leningrad to look for possibles, but Stepok wasn't there, either. Crisis. The expedition was to start any day, and Stepok was a vital part of the episode to be filmed on location. Of the four leading characters, only one had been decided upon—the boy's father. At the first reading of the scenario, Boris Zakhava, director of the Vakhtangov Theatre and without previous cinema experience, was given this rôle.

'And then, in the next to last prepared viewing of children, E. saw Vitka—"He IS Stepok." He is a quiet eleven-year-old, interested in mathematics, but not movies—the son of an army chauffeur, Kartashov. He seemed to have everything (and everyone, including Rzheshevsky) against him: his hair grew in the wrong way, insufficient pigmentation of the skin gave him great white blotches on his

---

* Vladimir Nilsen was just then completing his comprehensive and reasoned examination of the cameraman's art, *The Cinema as a Graphic Art* (English translation by Stephen Garry). Throughout his book Nilsen placed an emphasis on artistic distortion as an expressive necessity in cinema.

face and neck, and at the test his voice grew stiff and dull—until he was told to ask us riddles, when he produced a clear, fine, almost compelling voice. Only E. was able at once to see the positives, later clear to all. A make-up man was some help; more importantly, Vitka expressed the rôle as E. imagined it, not as an actor, but as a child, as a Young Pioneer, with a quick and broad intelligence, an expressive face, and a surprising emotional range.'

While we waited for the location scouts (assistant Gomarov and administrator Gutin) to return from the south, we took advantage of the season to film the short poetic prologue: an evocation of Turgenev, blossoming fruit trees and church spires. On May 5, 1935 the first shots for *Bezhin Meadow* were taken in the often filmed old apple orchards of Kolomenskoye, associated with the memory of Ivan the Terrible.

'These first shots were taken with an understanding of Turgenev's place in and contribution to the history of literature and art. In the wake of romanticism, Turgenev was attracted by the impressionists, who were in turn attracted by the Japanese print-makers; Turgenev's introduction of impressionism into literature was the key the episode needed. As Turgenev extracted the essence of an already extracted Japanese accent on detail, on isolation, on the perfected ensemble of seemingly chance selection, so out of Turgenev's style and background a cinema approach was extracted. The problem for these first few compositions became one of showing the audience *how* Turgenev saw the things around him. The impression of this brief prologue must not be that of turning over a collection of Japanese prints and Chinese drawings, but of examining, lovingly, the corners and details of a landscape lit by the soft last light of romanticism, selected by an artist fascinated by the eye of the Orient.'

After a look at the present village of Bezhin Meadow, the producers had decided to compose a 'synthetic' village, using Kuleshov's 'creative geography' to pull together locations found anywhere in the Union. On the return of the location scouts, this plan was announced: Armavir and the Stalin State Farm for two weeks, where the biggest mass scenes for the 'Highway' episode were to be made, and then to Kharkov for about a month, to film the acted scenes for this episode, with the help of the Kharkov Tractor Plant. One of Eisenstein's aims, in the whole production scheme, was to prove that a good film could be made efficiently and quickly with no loss (perhaps a gain) in artistic value. Since *Chapayev*'s triumph, schedules had been lengthening ridiculously and wastefully.

At six a.m. on June 15th seven of us, including Eisenstein and Tisse, took off from Moscow airport in a chartered plane carrying all our cameras and apparatus, flew south over our studio and by four o'clock found ourselves near the Azov Sea, on the second largest state farm in the Union. The next day and the following seven days we photographed the thousand workers of the state farm riding to the harvest on tractors, combines, fire-wagons, motor-cycles, bicycles, autos and trucks.

'Our working day began at six a.m.; though Tisse would let no filming be done before the sunlight was soft enough (at about ten), it took that time to get to the filming spot, prepare for the day, and watch Tisse climb into his hole dug under the road to film different combinations of the traffic arranged the night before. The day ended at seven p.m., at the little hotel on the sovkhoz, washing up for dinner hilariously. After dinner each day there was a conference on the day's accomplishments and the next day's plans, in E.'s room, with a basket of straw-berries at one end of the table and a pail of cherries (with the compliments of the sovkhoz workers) at the other. "Well, have we come up to the record set during *Potemkin* when seventy-five different shots were made in one day's filming on the steps?" "No, but forty-five on three cameras and a hand-camera is also pretty good." "Not good enough, not good enough. Don't let the old battleship shame us".'

I have rarely experienced such a joy as at Armavir, as we lay on our stomachs among the dusty cabbages with several hundred horse-power pounding a few inches away.

'Although three and sometimes four cameras were filming constantly, very few of these shots will appear on the screen as they are being taken. E. explained the mystery: "On the editing table this episode will be handled in the same way a composer works on a fugue in four voices. The material we're filming here is only one of the voices. Most of it will be used for rear-projection and trans-parencies when the second voice will be worked out—with figures and close-ups in the foreground. That is why the Armavir compositions are incomplete; spaces are being left for the use of the second motif of the image. The third and fourth voices (or motifs) are in sound—sound and speech" . . . mounting up to the climax of the encounter on the highway, where the visual clattering and the sound clattering will pause so suddenly that the audience will be jarred, as in an unexpectedly halting train.'

Because the 'Highway' episode was the most difficult part of the film, Eisenstein had chosen it for the first to be filmed, so that the rest of the film could then be built around this accomplished climax. It occurs midway in the film, which covers a twenty-four hour action, from the morning of one day to the morning of the next, harvest day. The highway itself is one of the repeated uses of a 'road' symbol; at first, the wagon path along which Stepok and a tall peasant called 'Big-black-beard' bring the body of Stepok's mother (dead soon after giving birth to Stepok's sister) early in the morning.

When the story opens, four fugitive incendiaries (a fanatic, an anarchist, a kulak leader, and a poor peasant), having barricaded themselves in the village church, fire on the villagers who come to arrest them, are dislodged and, guarded by two militiamen, are being taken to the city to jail. They attempt to cross the highway amid the procession to the harvesting camp. When the farm workers realize that if these four had had their way the ripe fields around would now be a smoking waste, they toss the militiamen aside and prepare to take the law into their own hands. The leader is Big-black-beard, armed with an axe. The more self-controlled Komsomols, farmers and tractor-drivers reason in vain with the crowd until the child Stepok walks up between Big-black-beard and the four men and, with a joking remark, makes the harvesters laugh. With the tension broken the militiamen are allowed to proceed.

But Stepok's rôle in the drama is essentially tragic. At night while the village boys keep watch over the horses of the collective, Stepok goes to stand guard over the harvest. He has heard his father plotting with the four incendiaries to burn the crop, and has asked for guards to watch his hut until the harvest is complete. His father escapes and shoots his son, who falls from his watch-tower.

'Taking advantage of the generosity of the State Farm and the fine weather, and because we were way ahead of schedule, we used the marvellously filmic acres of ripe grain to film some shots for the finale of the film, when the body of murdered Stepok is brought back to the village: Young Pioneers from their watch-towers salute as the body is carried past, in a series of unusually beautiful and bare compositions, a pair of guards high in their towers and another pair, in close-up, below. Almost invariably these shots were taken with the 28. lens. When I asked E. to explain the choice of the 28. lens for these compositions, he said that lenses can be used as instruments in orchestration. Different lenses produce different tensions. There are "flat" lenses, such as the 150., which produce little depth, little tension and little emotion. Then there are the less corrected lenses, such as the 28. and the 25., which give a wide and sharply rounded image, producing a positive sense of strain in the spectator. These shots, coming near the end of the film, should bring a calculated, gradual expansion of the heart, and here the greatest tension of both lens and of composition (far and near) may be advisable. This exquisite precision in the choice of lenses is one of Tisse's contributions to the Eisenstein-Tisse partnership.'

One of the realizations of the non-theatricality of the subject we were filming remains as my last memory of Armavir. Around these watch-towers we would have to do some trampling down of the grain to get our work done, cameras set up, mirrors and shades adjusted, etc. As our truck would pull out to go to the next shot, we would look back, and see the real child-guards of the harvest emerge, and carefully prop up each bent stalk.

On our departure from Armavir, Eisenstein and Tisse flew to Moscow, promising to join us speedily in Kharkov. In Moscow, however, Eisenstein had an attack of ptomaine poisoning, making the first of an eventually fatal number of delays. From Moscow others of the group joined us, including the sound, make-up and costume chiefs, and the actors needed for the Highway episode, including Vitka.

'We were now a group of twenty-one, and made quite an impression on the village of Russkaya Lozovaya, out on the billowing Kharkov road, where we established our colony in the village school, left empty for the summer. We made our food arrangements with the collective farm, put up our volley-ball net, and settled in for a month.'

For two weeks after Eisenstein's delayed arrival, half-well, the weather turned bad and nothing could be done but evening and night shots of the tractor procession along the Kharkov 'Highway,' material that was to last only twenty seconds on the screen.

'Confinement made us irritable, and we displayed all too plainly our "basic characteristics". . . . Very special care was taken of Vitka, in regard to diet, sleep and amusements, to keep him healthy and normal. On the whole he was a good boy, especially if Maslov (one of the practicants, who plays the anarchist incendiary) would tell him the plot of one American movie comedy each night, but once in a while even he put on airs.'

On hopeless days I drove in to the city to catch old films and search book-stalls for Ukrainian film-books, and to see Eisenstein, still taking care of himself at a hotel. Then continuously clear weather and hard work made it possible to complete the whole enacted Highway sequence in scheduled time.

'After one full day of filming we rushed the four incendiaries to the Kharkov airport. I was mystified for I thought our only use of airplanes [flying over the tractor procession] was finished. E. showed me a new notation in his script. When the procession recognizes the four, their indignation is first expressed by hooting, shouting, whistling. The script had indicated a less and less realistic sound-track, climaxed in a volume of boat-whistles and factory sirens. The sound track goes so far into imagery that the image now has to keep up with it: the new notation reads 'the four under a high wind' and then, 'the four as in a hurricane'.

Back in Moscow we heard news of the other great director whose resumption of work had been delayed. Pudovkin was happily working again with Nathan Zarkhi, on a scenario about aviators and the nature of socialist heroism, *Birth of a Hero*. They were completing the script in a cottage several miles outside Moscow. On July 18, 1935 Pudovkin, who had become an enthusiastic motorist, drove Zarkhi to Moscow. There was a bad accident, and both men were taken to hospital. Zarkhi died, saying to his nurse, 'Such plans I have, devil take it, such plans . . . excuse me for the "devil", nurse. . . .' Pudovkin lived, but it was months before he could resume work. He knew he was at least partly responsible for Zarkhi's death.

'In the spring a field in a hollow near the Mosfilm studio had been ploughed and sown (by E. with proper ceremonies) for use this fall for filming, and in this field with its surrounding forest of silver birches overlooking the Moscow River below, we spent full cold nights (it was already late August) from sunset to sunrise every night for three weeks. The only change in this life of hissing, blazing Jupiter carbons came when the few houses for the set of the village street were built in the other end of the field, and then we filmed there from noon until time to start the night filming.'

The sequences for these weeks were 'Night-Fires' (Turgenev's boys guarding the horses of the Turgenev Collective Farm), and the events following the discovery of the fatally wounded Stepok—the chase after the escaped incendiaries, their capture, and Stepok's death at dawn.

'Each night's shooting began with the mass scenes of the boys leaving the fires and tearing along through the birch forest to head off the fugitives . . . furious to have been so near without preventing the murder of Stepok, whipping their horses and almost crying with desperation. . . .

'Behind the camera was as curious a picture as in front. Ranged along around the back were the crew—and the guests: friends, relations, managers from all the studios, other regisseurs (friends or disciples of E.—Kuleshov, Ermler, Savchenko, Barnet, Macheret, Trauberg, Shub, the Vasilievs), French writers, English aesthetes, German émigrés, American tourists. Whenever Tisse would pick up his camera and E. his candy-pink wand, and move to a new spot in the fantastically lit forest, the whole assemblage would move their auditorium (two wicker chairs and twenty old boxes) right along, adjust themselves to the new pits and puddles, and stare at E. making next year's magic.

'Each morning, to catch the first light of dawn, Stepok lay stretched out dead for the few minutes allowed us for the exactly right light. It was no joke to die in the clammy morning mist, but Vitka, as Stepok, made us forget the beds we were to rush off to in a few minutes, with the intensity and amazing realism he put into this scene each morning. . . . And through the sputtering of the carbons, and the scarcely heard directions of E. (his voice during filming is always the quietest of the group), the crew and guests began to forget that Stepok was Vitka and that he was not really dead. Then the chief [of the political department] picks up the body and starts towards the village, carrying it across his arms. This is the funeral of light, killed by the darkness, and forever renewed by the morning.'

The first of the sound sequences in the studio was of Zakhava, as the maddened father, interrogating his son (whom he has just shot) on God's methods, especially on His punishment of sons who betray their fathers.

'The make-up of Zakhava emphasizes features for which he was cast in this rôle. Nothing but his enormous beak-like nose and glassy eyes can be seen over a short curly beard. Before each shot of the figure of Stepok, each finger, each fold of his white blouse, each hair is carefully arranged. The compositions as seen in the rushes—triangular platform of watch-tower, ghostly heads of wheat, body of Stepok, and the father's eyes—maintain the increasingly nightmare atmosphere of the sequence. The struggle for the rifle will surely be an unforgettable moment of the film. . . .

'An Eisenstein sound film will be visual-sound counterpoint, in his own words —the highest plan for the realization of conflict between optical and acoustical impulses. He has also said that the ideal form for the sound film is the monologue. In the "Family" sequence both of these ideals find expression. The father is taunted by the presence of the boy who has "betrayed" him. His only outlet, being weak, and not quite drunk enough to beat the boy, is to goad him with scorn and anathema into making some move that can be answered with a blow. The dialogue for the scene is literally a monologue by the father, and the sequence will be edited as a conflict between the rising hysteria of the father and the increasing calm of Stepok, culminating in shrieking drunken fury and Stepok's decision to leave home forever. In an interior set, built in exaggerated perspective, you sometimes *see* the back of Stepok's upright head, and *hear* the new pitch of anger it provokes in the father. Sometimes the conflict appears in the same shot: Stepok's face and the father's face dancing behind it in frustrated brutality. Sometimes two visuals convey the same side of the conflict, but expressed in opposites—as in the shot where the father's hysteria is shown alongside the silent, still and concentrated hate held by the grandmother for the boy. . . .

'The woman-president of the collective farm has been finally cast: the rôle is played by Yelena Teleshova, a regisseur working in the First Art Theatre* and at the Red Army Theatre. She is the fourth theatre regisseur that E. has cast in the film: Zakhava, Teleshova, Garin of the Meyerhold plays the president's husband, and Okhlopkov plays a comic bit. This may be chance, and then again, it may be because E. knows that other regisseurs are likely to comprehend his wishes faster. . . .

'E.'s directions are the most sensible I have seen in practice. With both skilled and unskilled actors, he first solves their physical problems: What are my torso and limbs and head doing at this point? How will my movement over to there be managed? Does this movement convey the desired meaning? With skilled actors, and this now includes Vitka, he talks over the scene, uncovers the scene's emotions (but never once showing how a face must *act*), and goes through it once or twice without the camera, enlarging on details and making changes, seldom drastic ones. Then the camera is brought into action, the shot set up, and while Tisse arranges the lights and Bogdankevich the microphone, the scene is played through several times. When it is taken, if E. or Tisse or the actor is not satisfied, it is re-taken. In customary manner, a long dialogue sequence is filmed first straight through for sound-strip and *mise en scène*, before being broken into the more telling middle and close shots.'

Filming came to an abrupt halt when Eisenstein came down with smallpox. In his personal selection of every object that was to decorate the next interior set, the church, some germ waiting on an ikon or holy banner chose the atheist Eisenstein for the only case of smallpox known in Moscow for about two years. The last entry in my production diary is dated October 20, 1935:

'After a quarantine of three weeks (with daily radio bulletins), he'll convalesce for a month. . . . Mid-December will see work resumed on *Bezhin Meadow*, with scheduled completion in May 1936. In the hospital he celebrated his thirty-eighth saint's day.'

The most important film released this fall—to the usually varied reactions—was Dovzhenko's *Aerograd*. Between the expedition and studio work, Tisse had left *Aerograd* (when he was replaced by Gindin) to work on *Bezhin Meadow*; as both films were produced at Mosfilm we saw much of each other's work; nevertheless, I was surprised to see, in the finished *Aerograd*, so many parallels with *Bezhin Meadow*—in large elements, such as the identification of religion with an anti-Soviet action, and in smaller ways, as in the rhetorical conclusion to

---

* She was co-director, with Sakhnovsky, of the 'sweet' dramatization of *Dead Souls* I saw in November 1933; Alexandrov told Marie Seton that Teleshova, a friend of his wife's, had first met Eisenstein at their home

both films: an older man ceremoniously carries the body of a young victim. Another reason I felt disappointment on first seeing *Aerograd* was that it seemed a paler reflection of the passion that I had heard in Dovzhenko's reading of the scenario, and in his ringing direction of the studio scenes. But time and repeated viewings have made all my first objections petty, for it now seems to me one of the great original films. The studio work itself, which at first seemed an impediment, has turned into a demonstration of Dovzhenko's achievement in absorbing even the artifice of the studio into his main emotional line.

Discussion of *Aerograd* was as oblique as itself. At a three-day critical conference on it at the Dom Kino, Pudovkin declared that it stirred him too deeply to make a cool professional judgment. Dovzhenko was happy with the divided reactions, hoped that his next film, *Shchors*, would arouse even greater discussion, and contributed very little to information on his purposes:

'After studying the region [of the Soviet Union's Far East], I became convinced that the existing administrative and economic centres in the Far East are inadequate—that a road should be laid from the Sakhalin Ridge to the sea, and a socialist, Bolshevik city built on the shores of the Pacific Ocean. That city should be called "Aerograd" and I regard the title of my film as a forecast of the future. I soon decided that this film should be a defence film and that's the way it turned out.'[19]

Even this defence aspect is expressed obliquely, in the constant imagery of beasts in the dialogue, or in the lovely scene of the aviator's new child. Despite the difficult situations and concepts in *Aerograd*, it is more directly related to its audience than *Ivan*. Dovzhenko used music (by Kabalevsky) more freely—as another colour. Speech itself is more bold and stripped—sometimes addressed straight at the audience without pretext or inhibition. One of its extraordinary moments is only a gesture: Stepan Shkurat, as Khudyakov, discovered collaborating with a Japanese interventionist plot, is taken into the forest for execution by his best friend; as he passes the camera, he hides his face from us! Throughout the film Dovzhenko shows his delight in the strong beauty of the Siberian landscape, and his device of linking its variety by a singing traveller is almost a key to his idea of form.

With Dovzhenko absent from Kiev, the Ukrainian film showed little progress at this period. Ivan Kavaleridze, a mature sculptor turned film-director, and with enough standing to have been awarded the Red Star at the fifteenth anniversary, is a man whose early work I know only by repute. Stills of his films give me the impression of monumental, isolated figures, literally translated from his earlier medium, and his non-realistic style eventually brought trouble. When *Pravda* attacked his new film, *Prometheus*, on February 13, 1936, a change was predicted for him or for his style. He stayed in film production by making almost characterless Ukrainian operettas—the only work by him that I've seen.

At the opposite pole, of youth and realism, stood a Komsomol production collective, headed by Leonid Lukov, at Ukrainfilm. I must have missed the earlier films of the Lukov group, for I was completely and pleasantly surprised by their third film, *I Love*, an adaptation of the first part of Avdeyenko's novel about Donbas miners. This realism had a poetry and passion that made the best possible case for realism as a film style. I had seen no naturalism as stimulating as this since Barnet's *Okraina*; Barnet's new film, *By the Blue Sea*, seemed an affectation by comparison. And *I Love* made Yutkevich's more ambitious film of similar material, *Miners*, look strained in its over-hearty realism; the realistic comedies by Abram Room (*A Stern Young Man*) and Macheret (*The Private Life of Peter Vinogradov*) were embarrassments alongside the natural humour of *I Love*. There was sympathy when Room's film was taken from Soviet screens, with reprimands to him and the author, but for once the punishment fitted the crime. The most popular of the new naturalist films was *Party Card* by Pyriev, but it was difficult to take this agit-melodrama seriously; Pyriev's best films were to be his least serious and least real. Medvedkin's *Miracle-Girl* may have resolved the rift between reality and artistic validity, but it appeared after my departure and never reached America. It was in the theatre, as I had learned to expect, that realist subjects were customarily handled with more artistic control and dramatic belief than in the cinema at this period. It was cruel to the younger medium to place Chervyakov's film of Pogodin's play, *Aristocrats*, about the prisoners who built the White Sea-Baltic Canal, beside Okhlopkov's production at the Realistic Theatre; even the film's change of title to the flatter *Prisoners* was an indication of a lesser accomplishment. There was something wrong if normally effective films of modern Soviet life were so rare. One of the rare consolations in this period was the youthful originality of *The Bold Seven*, directed by Gerasimov, until recently an actor with the FEX group.

When realism went further into the past, especially the past of revolution and civil war, results were happier. The two films that led to make the style (that might be called 'historic realism') an accepted, even a standard style, were *We from Kronstadt*, directed by Yefim Dzigan, at Mosfilm, and *Baltic Deputy*, at Lenfilm.

The most progressive aspect of *We from Kronstadt* was its conscientious effort to find a more vital film style than the increasingly standard naturalism. *An Optimistic Tragedy*, Vsevolod Vishnevsky's poetic play of a Bolshevik defeat in the Civil War, had prompted Dzigan to approach the author for permission to adapt it. Vishnevsky responded with a combative eagerness to tackle a new medium, with a proposal to work on a scenario of related subject, and with three years of the most enthusiastic co-operation any film director ever had from a playwright-scenarist.[20] In this collaboration I am inclined to find Vishnevsky's share the more original; it was certainly his prestige and political authority that permitted that much deviation from the naturalist rut. His letters to Dzigan are stimulating work-documents, viewing each new problem from all sides, probing the most delicate issues of his subject, battering the conventions to find strong, new treatment. In one letter chiefly devoted to finding true, unhackneyed images for the Red Army, *beyond* the immediacy of Kronstadt in 1919, he sums up Soviet film victories:

'Here are the truest treatments:

'In *Potemkin*—explosion of the mass.

'In *Arsenal*—fearlessness, denial of death.

'In *End of St Petersburg*—evolution of individual, and of mass.
'In *Earth*—pantheism, eternity.
'In *Ivan*—tragedy of peasantry plus a gleam of the new.
'In *Chapayev*—personal tragedy plus warfare.
'In others—*Deserter* and such—insignificant. . . .'[21]

Vishnevsky's honesty and responsibility were not matched by his associates—director, cameraman, actors. Their search for a non-naturalist form led towards the very rhetoric that Vishnevsky guarded himself against—a rhetoric of pictorialism and movement, an employment of *all* the means at cinema's disposal, almost indiscriminately. The Tisse skill in gauging the correct lens for each degree of dramatic tension was a discipline not exercised by Dzigan and Naumov-Strazh. Everything is at maximum pitch, with an exhausting effect. Yet the material of the film overcame its distorted execution to make it popular on Soviet and foreign screens.

Josef Heifitz and Alexander Zarkhi, the Komsomol team at Lenfilm, made an important contribution to 'historic realism' with *Baltic Deputy*, a film that became a model for the style. This youthful film about an old man derived its style from both *Chapayev* and *Maxim:* the full-bodied personal drama of the one, and the wise, selected reconstruction of the other. The style, so simple as to appear easily imitated, conceals itself behind the figure of Professor Polezhayev, acted by Nikolai Cherkasov, to whom this film brought world fame. He had played a clowning rôle in the previous film by Heifitz and Zarkhi, *Hectic Days*, and their assistant, Shapiro, showed Cherkasov the new script, by Rakhmanov and Dell, more out of politeness than with any hope that he could manage the central rôle. He was at the time fully employed as the Tsarevich Alexei in Petrov's lavish production of *Peter the First*, so he too was 'not over-enthusiastic' about the suggestion—until he read the script:

'Sooner or later every actor comes across a rôle that opens up new vistas before him, that perfectly suits his abilities. I was sure that Polezhayev was just that kind of rôle. It was the chance I had been longing for.

'The studio tested several well-known actors for the rôle. I decided to do my best to get the part. I do not recall any other instance when I tried so hard or worried so much. . . . I virtually forced myself on the directors, giving them scores of reasons why I was sure I would succeed. I was told, and quite rightly too, that Professor Polezhayev was seventy-five while I was only thirty-two, but I countered this by saying that he was so young in spirit that only a young actor could play him. . . .

'My first test was not successful. But the second proved much better. The directors favoured me and I got the rôle, despite the fact that the top officials of Lenfilm and certain other film workers had no confidence in me. . . .

'The underlying idea was clearly expressed in the script. It dealt with the fate of the progressive, democratic intelligentsia in the early stages of the October Revolution.'[22]

At Lenfilm Lev Arnstam, working closely with his designer, Moisei Levin and under the supervision of Yutkevich, tried like Dzigan, a less naturalistic film of these Civil War years, *Girl-Friends*, and I have always preferred it to *Kronstadt*. At Mosfilm there were several worthy followers of the *Chapayev-Baltic Deputy* tendency, but Roshal's film of the Paris Commune, *Dawn in Paris*, showed that it was safer to keep 'historic realism' on home ground. (Even in such a grandiloquent film as *Peter the First* there were touching elements of humanity in characterization and situation, for which thanks are due more to Alexei Tolstoy than to Vladimir Petrov.) Roshal's wife, Vera Stroyeva, made one of the best examples of the style with dignity and a sense of the period in *Generation of Conquerors*. A poor example in this style, vying with *Dawn in Paris*, was Ekk's *Nightingale, Little Nightingale*, whose title was changed, just before release on June 11, 1936, to *Grunya Kornakova*—supposedly to reduce the film's pretensions. This was the first Soviet dramatic colour-film, for which Ekk prepared with a 'variety' film called *Colour Carnival*. *Nightingale* showed that the two-colour process was adequate, but that Ekk was not. The subject and its incidents (a revolt of women workers in a china factory) had been too tailored to a colour display. After dropping the rest of a planned trilogy around Grunya, Ekk announced *Hamlet* as his next colour-film, but fortunately he did not make it. Three days before *Nightingale* was released Mezhrabpom was liquidated, to be replaced by Soyuzdetfilm, a studio to specialize in films for children.

Since the assassination of Kirov, in Leningrad, in December 1934, the organizational links to his murderer, Nikolayev, were under investigation and, following some disturbingly unpublicized arrests, there were even more disturbingly publicized trials of a large group of well-known political figures, in which Bukharin and Radek, among many others, were accused of plotting an overthrow of Stalin and Bolshevik leaders. Because the plot was linked not only with Trotsky and other anti-Bolshevik groups, but also with foreign governments, a certain xenophobia became evident. Foreign residents, students and workers were asked to choose between Soviet citizenship and departure. The most significant effect this had on films was the elimination of Mezhrabpom, a base for foreign film workers. When I was faced with the choice of leaving now or staying forever, I could not face an émigré's life; when Eisenstein's film ran into another snag, he advised me to accept a job offered me in New York. He sent some documents with me, including his unrealized scripts of *An American Tragedy* and *Sutter's Gold*, to be deposited at the Museum of Modern Art, and arranged for the Film Library there to have one of the original copies of *Potemkin*; the negative had been literally 'printed away'.

The pauses forced on Eisenstein by sickness had created new problems. If his original schedule had been met the film might have been finished without major crisis, and judged as a whole. As it was, during his long confinement with smallpox and a consequent influenza, there were inevitable changes, both in his own ideas about *Bezhin Meadow*, and in official policy, especially in blunting the anti-religious campaign in rural areas. When he was ready to work again, both factors demanded a large revision of the script, though sixty per cent of the original script had been filmed. One of my last duties on the film was to work as messenger between Eisenstein and Isaac Babel, who was helping him in the revision. Filming continued with the new script, but more pauses for illness and further revision accumulated tragically, and his colleagues were not very surprised when on March 17, 1937, Shumyatsky halted the production of *Bezhin Meadow*. Shumyatsky then attacked both film and director in print and at a three-day discussion of the unfinished film, where the fault-finding was sadly uniform. Eisenstein's last public statement on *Bezhin Meadow* was a piece of published self-humiliation, 'The Mistakes of Bezhin Meadow'.[23] Though he said in this confession, 'The work had to be discontinued; additional shots and retakes could not save it,' I suspect that the total halt was not necessary, that the work could have been saved by a less drastic edict, and that in making the decision to *stop*, Shumyatsky had some other motive than the discipline of a recalcitrant artist. The theatre had just gone through an anti-formalism campaign, with Meyerhold playing the devil so vividly that political accusations were added to his artistic crimes; Shumyatsky's scheme for a grand step-up of the Soviet film industry was in more urgent need of a scapegoat:

'While establishing the style of Soviet film art, our directors and scenarists are at the same time waging a struggle against all manifestations of trends alien to Soviet art, especially against so-called formalism, which these trends use as a cloak for playing for play's sake, for bare "technicism", for external prettiness.'[24]

The logic of this, not immediately apparent, is that Shumyatsky had projected a 'Soviet Hollywood' to be built on the shores of the Black Sea; in this place, as isolated as Hollywood from the main stream of national arts, Shumyatsky would purchase his right to reign supreme by turning out, for a beginning, about three hundred films a year. Anything that would interfere with this smooth flow of product must be silenced or eliminated now; 'anti-formalism' made a perfect cloak for Shumyatsky's industrial programme, and Eisenstein was the suitable sacrificial victim. Of course this road to the Black Sea was paved with the best Bolshevik intentions, and Shumyatsky was certain that he had the best interests of the Soviet cinema at heart.

Yet it was an industrial mistake that proved Shumyatsky's undoing. The twentieth anniversary of the October Revolution was at hand, without a film to mark the date. Raizman's excellent *Last Night*, about the crucial hours of revolution in Moscow, and the popular *Baltic Deputy*, both released early in 1937, could have been regarded as anniversary films, but Stalin wanted a film that showed the act of October and the men responsible for it. As soon as Alexei Kapler's scenario was approved by 'the highest authorities,' *Lenin in October* was put into production on August 10th, already late in the year. The only director available for the rush job was Mikhail Romm, whose career had moved promisingly, after *Boule de Suif*, with *Thirteen*, a well-made 'desert adventure'. Dmitri Vasiliev, a dependable assistant, related to neither of the 'Vasiliev brothers', was assigned to Romm as associate (and second-unit) director. With constant prodding from above *Lenin in October* was ready for release on November 7th—three months after shooting commenced! *Bezhin Meadow*'s efficiency campaign had been realized by *Lenin in October*—and Shumyatsky's administration suffered a severe blow. Why had there not been other films made this quickly, this economically, and this well? There were grand plans, but look at your record, Comrade Shumyatsky—of the 120 films announced for 1935 forty-three were released, of the 165 scheduled for 1936 only forty-six appeared, and even 1937's more modest goal of sixty-two could result in only twenty-five releases. The film administration was dismissed almost *in toto*, Shumyatsky was denounced in *Pravda* (January 9, 1938) as 'politically blind' and a tool of enemy wreckers around him. He was put in charge of a small provincial factory and nothing further was heard of his assistants—or of his 'Soviet Hollywood'. I heard from friends that all of Moscow's film-makers gave parties on the night of January 9th.

We from Kronstadt (1936)
A design by Vladimir Yegorov

CHAPTER XV

Full Capacity

1938–1939

> . . . a great public is entitled to our respect, and
> should not be treated like children from whom one
> wishes merely to extract money. By accustoming
> them to what is good, we may lead them gradually
> to feel and appreciate the excellent, and they will
> pay their money with double satisfaction when their
> reason and understanding approve the outlay
>
> GOETHE

The structure of the cinema industry was completely overhauled, for the ninth
time since the October Revolution. After the Shumyatsky years all agreed that
this was a change for the better:

'With the aim of improving and unifying the management of cinema affairs and
of regulating the film industry, its production and distribution, a Committee on
Cinema Affairs is decreed to be formed directly subject to the Council of People's
Commissars of the USSR.'[1]

Stalin's happy experience in personally supervising the success of *Lenin in
October* was behind this reorganization, making the new Cinema Committee
(headed by Semyon Dukelsky) directly responsible to the top.

'The Council of People's Commissars has come to the conclusion that in the
production of fictional films there are serious deficiencies, which result in repeated failures in carrying out plans for the release of pictures, in mismanage-
ment and waste of funds, in the production of a large number of worthless
films, and in the increase of expense and delay in making pictures. One of the
most objectionable practices is poor planning, and making "standard units"—
without title or scenario. . . .

'There is no carefully worked out production procedure, and the period
between preparatory work and actual "shooting" is too long. Films are often
started without accepted scenarios, plans for sets, or estimates of costs. . . .

'To improve the organization of motion-picture making, the Council has
banned the practice of making films without prior confirmation by the Cinema
Committee of scenarios and cost estimates. A special scenario division within
the Committee will provide scenarios for all films planned, and will always have

some in reserve, for regular release to groups of actors and technicians. . . . Studios are forbidden to make any changes in the accepted scenarios, without prior permission of the Chairman of the Committee. . . .

'The present system of financing pictures out of receipts for exhibition of those previously made shall cease. . . .

'A special fund shall be created to pay premiums to creative workers, engineers, technicians, and outstanding studio workers, the fund to be made up from economies realized by reduction of costs of production.'[2]

On the same day a group of new orders were announced for the makers and leading actors of *Lenin in October* (Shchukin, Romm, Okhlopkov, Volchok), *Peter the First* (Tolstoy, Petrov, Simonov, Zharov, Cherkasov, Tarasova), and of *The Rich Bride*. This last was Ivan Pyriev's pleasing continuation of the original 'musical comedy' genre begun by *Accordion*, a genre that Pyriev was to prolong successfully through four films. *The Rich Bride*, made in Shumyatsky's régime, appeared a month after his exit, too late for his name ever to be mentioned in connection with its popularity.

The Ukrainian scenarist and recent VGIK graduate, Yevgeni Pomeshchikov, and the Russian composer Dunayevsky provided the good-humoured materials for *The Rich Bride*, and Pyriev made the most of these assets. The 'rich bride' of the title is Marina Lukash, outstanding worker on her Ukrainian collective farm. The farm's book-keeper sees her as the best catch to secure his future comfort, and when a handsome tractor-driver threatens to upset his plans by attracting Marina to himself, the book-keeper juggles the driver's production figures so that the marriage of such a 'shameful' worker to the prize-winning Marina will be obviously a poor match. But love and the inspection system triumph, all accompanied by songs and dancing that smell of the fields rather than of the stage. A year and a half after *The Rich Bride* (a short schedule these years), the Pyriev-Pomeshchikov-Dunayevsky combination produced another winner, *Tractor-Drivers*, made jointly by Mosfilm and the Kiev Studio. With a different intrigue the heroine (again played and sung by Marina Ladynina) ends the film in marriage to the farm's best tractor-driver.

Another unpronounced credit to Shumyatsky's administration, and another musical comedy that improved on all its maker's previous work (as *The Rich Bride* on *Party Card*), was Alexandrov's *Volga-Volga*. Writing his own scenario this time, Alexandrov based it on the recently increased efforts to reveal the rich theatrical talents among non-theatrical workers—amateur singers and dancers who earned their living as farmers, miners, book-keepers. This was a more original and profitable field for humour and entertainment, than the foreign jazz of *Jolly Fellows* and the worn excitements of *Circus*. Supported by new situations, the fantastic style of an experienced Meyerhold comedian, Igor Ilinsky (as a bureaucrat), and the music of Dunayevsky, both Alexandrov and Orlova were at their best in *Volga-Volga*. Their work before and since never showed them as so worth the support of the film industry and the film audience. Alexandrov celebrated his merited triumph by supervising the colour-filming of the May Day parade this year.

This was a year for youth. *Komsomolsk* is the name of a new industrial community built in 1932 on the Amur River by a crew of Young Communists, and the film made to show the drama and satisfaction of the undertaking was directed by Sergei Gerasimov, whose favourite leading figures were always to be young people,* and whose chief interest was in their training as film-actors. His methods may have been less radical than Kuleshov's, and less exaggerated than Kozintsev and Trauberg's, in whose group he had gained his first training, but the resulting films are of a controlled naturalism, always subordinated to dramatic needs, that gives us as tangible an idea as anything else in films of what was meant by 'socialist realism'. Gerasimov's *The Bold Seven* had been a model of selectivity and restraint. It too had shown a group of youths conquering the wilds, in that instance Arctic wilds, and the temptations of melodrama were skilfully avoided, more skilfully perhaps than in the larger scale of *Komsomolsk*. Kozintsev praised *The Bold Seven* as 'the only manly and calm style in which to speak of heroes'.[3] With these two films Gerasimov moved into the category of 'important directors'.

The noticeable passing-over in the March awards of the Vasilievs' new film, *Volochayevsk Days*, and of the first part of Ermler's *Great Citizen*, was repaired a week later when their actors were also awarded orders, their makers having had the highest orders pinned on in 1935. Yet the Vasilievs' first post-*Chapayev* film was the disappointment it was doomed to be, so long as its manner and subject echoed that of its inimitable predecessor. *Volochayevsk Days* described an episode of the Civil War in Siberia, with the partisans fighting the Japanese intervention. Emphasis was not so much on character as on the purely physical sensations of the battle for Emelkin's Hill, as if *Chapayev* had been built around its 'psychological attack' sequence. Aside from this over-effective icy battle, the most memorable contribution to the film was by Lev Sverdlin (another Meyerhold actor), who gave bite as well as subtlety to his rôle of the Japanese commanding officer, Colonel Usijima. Sverdlin has given an account[4] of his training for the rôle, including his memory of the visiting Kabuki Theatre (from which he took the idea of the Colonel's nostalgic performance of a geisha song), and a dinner at the Astoria Restaurant in Leningrad that he ate twice so that he could observe the behaviour of a Japanese diner at the next table.

Ermler, however, could not make the Vasilievs' mistake of self-imitation, for his profoundly political subjects always forced him into fresh materials, and sometimes into fresh methods. *A Great Citizen*'s style had none of the shock of *Peasants*, but the originality of its subject made up for it. Inspired by the murder of Kirov, both parts of *A Great Citizen* took us into the remote world of intra-party conflicts, showing Shakhov (Kirov) versus the concealed enemies who required his destruction. The scenario, on which Bleiman and Bolshintsov collaborated with Ermler, presented the official version of the assassin's motives, a version with which there was, by no means, unanimous agreement, either at Lenfilm or in the Leningrad party organization. After the release of Part One, the scenarists described their obstacles:

* The subject of his first attempt at direction, *Do I Love You* (1934), was the morals of Soviet youth.

'In January 1937 our scenario was accepted. It seemed at last as though we could begin filming. But not yet. For six more months we continued our fight to make *A Great Citizen*—and in so doing gained a graphic lesson in class struggle. The recently exposed saboteurs of the Lenfilm administration adopted the most varied means of interference with this film. They couldn't give the scenario to the production department without further revisions; they couldn't give the scenario for production because there were sudden doubts as to its political accuracy; and so on. And then, finally, the rumour that it was counter-revolutionary. . . . But we never gave up because we knew they would not dare to forbid the production outright.

'Once the film was on the studio's schedule, every sort of production delay was invented. Money was not granted to the film, nor actors; the crew could not be formed, sketches never arrived. Almost half of the scheduled shooting period had passed before anything was filmed.'*

A Great Citizen was so intimately attached to the substance of the Moscow trials that actors were understandably reluctant to play the enemies' rôles. Even Ivan Bersenev, of the Second Art Theatre, who finally accepted the rôle of Kartashov, 'one of the most loathsome representatives of the Trotskyite-Zinoviev gang', accepted it as his social duty. He played it well and was honoured for his work. I wonder how often his memory linked this rôle to his 1911 bomb-thrower of *L'Aurore de la Révolution Russe*.

There had not been such an unrelenting flood of words on the screen since the first American 'all-talkies', but Ermler used the flood for argument, instruction, exposure. The words are harsh. Dramatically they almost make one forget the seeming neglect of the pictorial element. Part One, released in February 1938, concentrated on the events of 1925, when the Bolshevik Party prepared for its Fourteenth Congress, the 'congress of industrialization'. The opponents of the programme, exposed by the end of Part One, establish contact with foreign agents. Part Two, released November 1939, is concerned with the events of 1934, and the Seventeenth Congress. It shows the enemies' techniques in a union. This mounts to Shakhov's assassination—with a full resumption of movie means in showing its preparation. With *A Great Citizen* advertised over the world as 'the film to explain the Moscow trials', the two parts became the most depended upon and most explicitly propaganda films of the pre-war period.

The trials themselves had repercussions among film-making personnel. There were disappearances that have never been publicly explained. I do not know what Vladimir Nilsen, the most articulate of Soviet cameramen, was accused of or arrested for. I only know that he disappeared abruptly and totally from the film scene and that for twenty years his name was as completely erased from Soviet film history as historians are capable of erasing a name. Within the past year 'V. Nilsen' again appears in the credits of Alexandrov's first musical comedies, which may represent the 'rehabilitation' of Nilsen or of historical integrity.

* M. Bleiman, M. Bolshintsov, F. Ermler, 'Work on the Scenario,' *Iskusstvo Kino*, April-May, 1938; at the time of the change in film industry administrations, Lenfilm's executives were removed, almost to a man, largely on the evidence of their interference with *A Great Citizen*.

Less central to the fate of Soviet cinema, but of greater importance to the world where their work outside films was well known, were the arrests of Sergei Tretyakov and Isaac Babel, each of whom had contributed a share to the modern film. Konstantin Eggert was the only known director whose disappearance at this time was noticed, but various actors, careless in their views or speech, would leave and sometimes not return. A potentially great Soviet film-maker, Vsevolod Meyerhold, who had for various reasons never pursued his interesting pre-revolutionary film ideas, was arrested and later executed, for reasons that are now admitted to have been false.

In this darkest period of suspicions, informers, arrests, disappearances, some of the most lasting and hopeful Soviet films appeared—deeper than the jollities of Pyriev and Alexandrov, or the victories of *A Great Citizen*.

Long before a children's film studio was established as Soyuzdetfilm, the idea of filming Gorky's memoirs of his boyhood was discussed. After Varvara Massalitinova's unforgettable performance as Gorky's grandmother, she wrote that she had sought Gorky's approval in 1928, just after he returned to Moscow from Capri. She asked him, point blank, what he would say to her as the Grandmother, should his autobiographical books be filmed. He did not reply at first, but throughout the following conversation on literature and theatre he kept turning to her as if weighing each feature. A half hour later, just as she was leaving, he said, 'You'll do!' And he added, 'Just make your nose a little more snub.'[5]

Ten years later the idea began to be realized. The Gorky works planned by Soyuzdetfilm for three consecutive films were *Childhood*, *Among People*, and *My Universities*. Gruzdev made the adaptations, and Mark Donskoy was chosen to direct them. The trilogy was his masterpiece. All that was brightest and most hopeful in his own unsimple character responded fully to Gorky's belief in people and his anger at their waste. The three films show a young boy moving, absorbed, through a widening world of exciting encounters, each contributing to the outlook and art of the man who became Gorky. Gruzdev concluded the third film with Gorky's autobiographical anecdote, 'A Person Is Born': holding the new baby over the waves where he has washed it, Alyosha Peshkov pronounces a humanist credo that nourished the whole trilogy.

Only Donskoy's former collaborator, Vladimir Legoshin (who studied with both Kuleshov and Eisenstein) had had, in *Lone White Sail*, such success with a group of child-actors. Especially in the first two parts of the trilogy Donskoy was dependent on the co-operation of child-actors, and he has fortunately left a record of the principles he applied in this difficult task:[6]

'1 The idea of the whole film, the aim of each scene and image must be explained by the director to the child-actor in full detail, just as to an adult actor.

'2 The director should not show the child how to act, or he will imitate the director, whose basic task it is to summon the *spontaneous* from the child. He need be shown no more than a hint that he can catch and develop for himself.

'That's how I worked with Alyosha Lyarsky, who plays the rôle of the boy Gorky. For example, it was very difficult for me to get sufficient emotion for the episodes that demanded the display of a fiery temperament. Lyarsky possessed considerable but concealed inner power and it was up to me in preparing these scenes to summon memories of his own life that related to the situations of his rôle; this had the effect of developing strong emotional responses.

'3 Rehearsals with children are necessary, sometimes many rehearsals. But one must not film the child that day—or he will act without spontaneity.

'Generally in working with children it is very dangerous to over-rehearse or over-instruct them. This happened with another talented boy, Igor Smirnov, who plays the rôle of Lenka, the cripple. Igor himself longs "to be an actor", and this caused his mother to interfere by energetically rehearsing with him at home. As a result of this "preparation" the boy would come to the studio so "drilled" that before he faced the camera he was played out. Every spontaneity and freshness was lost. We almost had to "remake" Igor in bringing back his childlike self.

'4 The director must be demanding and even somewhat stern in his relations with the child-actor, allowing him none of the unnecessary "attentions" customary in studio treatment of children—over-feeding him with cakes and sweets, etc. Indulgence in this sort of sentimentalism spoils the child's relation to his work.'

1938 was not an anniversary year for Anton Chekhov, yet it was the beginning of a steady stream of Chekhov film adaptations—his vaudevilles were ready-made short film comedies, and the rich concentration of his best stories made them ideal material to expand into full-length films. Chekhov became a favourite source for the graduation films of talented student directors.* Isidor Annensky chose the farce of *The Bear* for his diploma film, and with the experienced help of Zharov and Androvskaya in its two rôles gave a human base to the vaudeville's violent humour. This first film served Chekhov better than the more trained hands that combined two Chekhov stories, *The Masque* and *Burbot*. In the following year Annensky made another Chekhov film, *The Man in a Case*, with the little-filmed Moscow Art actor, Nikolai Khmelyov. It was with an effort, but a necessary effort, that Annensky finally broke away from a dependence on Chekhov's tempting mixture of irony and humanity.

One advantage in having no German market was that it could exert no influence on the subject-matter of Soviet films. This was a large factor in the softening of anti-Fascist subjects in any film industry that would be hurt by a German boycott of its total product; the later anti-Nazi films made by American and British companies always *followed* a German severance of relations. Soviet film-makers were free to do their energetic best with these explosive subjects. Within two years they produced the three least equivocal anti-Nazi films made anywhere in the world: *Professor Mamlock*, adapted from Friedrich Wolff's play by the

* This 'tradition' continues into the present, with Samsonov's sensitive first film, *The Gadfly* (1955).

playwright with Minkin and Rappoport; *Swamp-Soldiers,* written by Yuri Olesha and directed by Macheret; and *The Oppenheims,* an adaptation of Lion Feuchtwanger's novel directed by Roshal. *Mamlock* and *The Oppenheims* had an authenticity partly explained by their German sources. *Swamp-Soldiers,* set in a concentration-camp, had the most violence and least depth of the three. All, with their hope as well as hate, were formidable attacks on an enemy that most of the film-world ignored. The extra strength of *Professor Mamlock* came from a recent arrival in the Soviet Union, Herbert Rappoport, the serious, quiet, experienced artist who had worked for many years as Pabst's assistant.

'Suppose such a scene: a person in a room is talking to a man who excitedly awaits a meeting with his brother. The brother is expected by air. The excited wait is interrupted by the ring of a telephone bell. Information is given that the aeroplane is about to land. On the screen the action changes to an aerodrome where we see the plane landing and a sudden crash that causes the death of the brother arriving. The next piece to follow portrays the waiting brother receiving the terrible news.

'Should one in the rehearsal period strive to work out separately the two pieces of the state of the waiting man, separated as they will be on the screen by the conventionalized plane crash?

'For work with the actor this would not only be unnecessary, but wrong and harmful. The only correct course is to rehearse both pieces in conjunction, thus enabling the actor to stay in the acting image without interruption, and to replace the specifically cinematic element of the portrayal of the crash by a single telephone call announcing the disaster.'

This simple example of rehearsal work, written for *Film Acting* about the end of 1933, serves to date a beginning for Pudovkin's least happy film project, *The Happiest One,* broken by its author's death and Pudovkin's own subsequent collapse. In an attempt to get both film and man going again, various writers, including Vishnevsky, tried to revise Zarkhi's scenario. Pudovkin's efforts to realize his friend's last script strangely echoed the film's subject: a Soviet mother, who learns that her son has vanished on an experimental Arctic flight, insists that her second son make another attempt at the flight; the younger man succeeds and rescues his brother. Pudovkin and Golovnya began actual filming in 1936, with an Arctic expedition, though no one, including himself, was satisfied with the patchwork working script. Once, in a revealing conversation on his way through Leningrad, he rationalized (with the help of both Engels and Freud) his difficulties: it was the conflict between his earlier emotional attitudes and present social tasks that produced, dialectically, his art.

Pudovkin's art, however, showed increasing dependence on a simply reflecting expression of extremely simple emotional situations. The experiments that had continued from *Mother* to *Deserter* were now stripped from a simplicity that needed only a small part of his artistry. Any skilled, sensitive Soviet director could have made the films that Pudovkin signed from now on; the unsatisfactory new film was the last that bore the recognizable signature of his artistic youth.

The Happiest One was so tangled in delays and troubles that it was about to be shelved, when Doller again saved Pudovkin. He joined the crew as co-director, revived the whole lapsing enterprise, recommended a return to Zarkhi's original, helped to finish the film efficiently, and it finally appeared, in July 1938, as *Victory* (the name of the experimental plane).

Now back in working habits, Pudovkin's next film, *Minin and Pozharsky*, a physically more difficult film than *Victory*, was ready within a year.* This was the first of his historical spectacles, and the first of several important Soviet films to show Poland as an aggressor. The expert scenarist, Victor Shklovsky, selected from the turbulence of the 'Time of Troubles' that embarrassing period at the beginning of the seventeenth century when Moscow was occupied by the Polish King Sigismund. Visitors to Moscow may recall the classically heroic bronze of Minin and Pozharsky in Red Square; it was the task of Shklovsky and Pudovkin to transform that bronze into a semblance of the flesh and blood that brought Russia through the crisis. As told by the film, lack of unity among the few loyal Russian princes enabled the Poles to crush every Russian uprising. Kuzma Minin, a butcher of Nizhny-Novgorod, calls upon the country to unite its money and arms. Prince Dmitri Pozharsky is elected commander-in-chief and a people's army chases the Poles from Moscow and from Russia. The lavishness of this historical reconstruction seemed richer than its ideas and film expression. It does contain scenes of frankly physical excitement, such as the scattering of the plumed, silken Polish camp and the fleeing Polish warriors with their fantastic metal wings (apparently useful only to give Pudovkin and Golovnya striking compositions); and Boris Livanov made a majestically memorable figure of Prince Pozharsky, a passionate bronze.

Two other talents brought back to practice in this period were those of Victor Turin and Nikolai Ekk. But from the nine years since the triumph of *Turksib* Turin came up, not with another such originality, but with a well-made imitation of the *Maxim* films: *Men of Baku*'s hero also developed from naïveté to underground work. Turin's normally good film reminded even his admirers of those efficient films he had made for VUFKU before *Turksib*. Ekk, after the crumbling of his *Grunya Kornakova* trilogy and his *Hamlet* project, went to work for the Kiev Studio, where his further use of colour in two Gogol films, *Fair at Sorochintsy* and *May Night*, was more effective than their lack of publicity would lead one to expect. To have made a *Turksib* or a *Road to Life* or a *Chapayev* exaggerated the subsequent demands placed on their creators.

And another man came back to work. Whatever else the removal of Shumyatsky may signify, it is at least clear that before the removal Eisenstein did not finish a film, and that afterwards he finished a film, a successful film, and was restored to his almost forgotten place at the creative head of the Soviet cinema.

'Party and Government, and Stalin personally, intervened to help Eisenstein. On the evening when *Alexander Nevsky* was first shown at the Dom Kino in November 1938, Eisenstein spoke of his deep gratitude to Comrade Stalin who, at Eisenstein's request, gave him the possibility to achieve a new film, responding sensitively, attentively.

* Before beginning *Minin*, Pudovkin planned an adaptation of *Anna Karenina*.

'. . . Eisenstein began his new work in close association with a writer whom he had met and who had given him much help. This was Pyotr Pavlenko. . . .

'The scenario of Pavlenko and Eisenstein was published in *Znamya* (No. 12, 1937). Again the old story of critical attacks, saying that the Russ of the scenario was not Russ, Novgorod was not Novgorod, the war was not thus, the scenario should not be thus, etc. etc.

'But this time the work did not collapse. Production began.'[7]

One of the typical critical attacks, an ill-timed survival of a past attitude, appeared in the March 1938 issue of *Iskusstvo Kino*: Khersonsky, in 'The Historical Theme in Cinema', examined two new scenarios, *Stepan Razin*, by Olga Preobrazhenskaya and Pravov, and *Russ*, the Pavlenko-Eisenstein treatment. *Stepan Razin* was praised, *Russ* (the original title of *Alexander Nevsky*) was witheringly dispraised. Khersonsky quoted the concluding comment by the consultants on *Russ*:

'And finally, on the style of the film. During the discussion of this question we all agreed that the film must be *simple* (but not grey and simplified), devoid of formalist refinements, hyperbole and academic dryness. A film about the victory of the people must be, to a maximum degree, persuasive in its simplicity, clarity, purposefulness. . . .'

Khersonsky waxed ironic on the (im)possibility of any Eisenstein film staying simple. He also complained about a quantity of historical and artistic errors in the scenario. Yet in their further work both Eisenstein and Pavlenko made the film even *more* simple; and some of the situations and dialogue complained of most bitterly are those most significant in the finished film. Khersonsky's complaints were blind to the fable quality of the film's idea—to show a critical situation of today through a crisis (and victory) of the past. The satisfying execution of this aim is the basis for the film's enormous success.

There are some ironies in the success of *Alexander Nevsky* and in its re-elevation of Eisenstein to the place where he belonged. Of his six completed films *Nevsky* is, in its ideas, the most superficial and the least personal of his work—though you are never in any doubt that you are watching an Eisenstein film. It is also the least directly executed of his films: though he planned every sequence and every composition with Dmitri Vasiliev, it was only with Vasiliev taking over much of the actual shooting that this large-scale film was made in an extraordinarily short time—and completed five months ahead of schedule! Eisenstein had interpreted the decree of March 23, 1938 as a challenge, to show the advantages, artistically as well as industrially, of planning, scheduling, plotting the film-to-be on grand lines and precise effects.

After a trip to Novgorod, to see if its thirteenth century buildings could be used for the film, Eisenstein wrote Vishnevsky: 'Almost nothing remains; it would be impossible to film there. There are architectural remains, but they have sunk so deeply into the earth that the proportions are ruined.' So thirteenth century Russ was built for the film, on designs originally planned by him and executed by the film's designers. When I saw the gleaming white walls of ancient

Novgorod in the finished film, I was reminded not only of the white-walled churches of *Que Viva Mexico*, but also of his irritation on one occasion when we had attended a new production of *Prince Igor*: 'Imagine assuming that the buildings then looked like the same buildings today—ruined and grey!'

Each costume, each weapon, each ornament had also passed through Eisenstein's notebook on its way to the artists in charge. The greatest technical feat of the production was the filming of the Battle on the Ice—without waiting for winter. A suitable broad flat field near the Mosfilm Studio was chosen, a substance of melted glass and alabaster, topped with a sprinkling of chalk and salt (suggested by Vasiliev), gave the illusion of ice and snow, and the wintry battle between Russians and Teutons was shot in the heat-wave of July 1938. This climax of the film was one of the sequences for which Eisenstein, not Vasiliev, worked with Tisse on each shot. Tisse was obliged to devise a filter that altered the natural summer quality of the sky to something more wintry, and the rhythm of the actual fighting was corrected by slowing down his hand-turned camera. One of the most active actors in the scene was Nikolai Okhlopkov, who played the jolly hero, Vasili Buslai; he felt that his participation was *too* efficient, and cited the incident as a negative example of film-acting:

'My first day of work on *Alexander Nevsky* was the battle with the German knights. Hundreds of participants were there, including those that I was soon to be fighting. I was seeing and meeting them for the first time. If this had been theatre I would have met them in the rehearsal period and found with them the core of the scene, established contact and broken our work down into "large, medium, and small" pieces. Here in cinema all that was impossible—and not only because of my unexpected meeting with my fellow-actors; the chief difference is that in the theatre the image grows and develops, not suddenly, but only (in the best circumstances) after three or four months of work. But here—I arrived, I was given my costume, I was made-up, they put a weapon in my hand and—be so kind as to be filmed!'[8]

The great attention to the sound-track, where all of Eisenstein's and Prokofiev's combined ingenuities aimed at bold and inescapable harmonies between picture and sound, tends to give *Alexander Nevsky* the character of opera.* It is as opera that the film has been scorned by foreign critics, but it is as a totally original film-music work that it will survive all dismissal. After the film was shown in America I sent Eisenstein the reviews, including mine; Eisenstein replied:

'I think there could be said more about the visual and sound unity and composition: in some of the sequences we've reached with Prokofiev the results I was dreaming about pretty long ago.'

This aspect of *Alexander Nevsky* is clearly the one of greatest joy and satisfaction to him. He has repeatedly referred to the 'symphonic' construction of the film, and on several occasions has written of his admiration for Prokofiev's wholehearted co-operation:

* All of Prokofiev's film music was preserved by him in non-theatrical forms; he arranged a dramatic cantata from the *Nevsky* score.

'. . . It makes no difference whether the composer writes music for the "general idea" of a sequence, or for a rough or final cutting of the sequence; or, if procedure has been organized in an opposite direction, with the director building the visual cutting to music that has already been written and recorded on soundtrack. I should like to point out that in *Alexander Nevsky* literally all these possible approaches were employed. There are sequences in which the shots were cut to a previously recorded music-track. There are sequences for which the entire piece of music was written to a final cutting of the picture. There are sequences that contain both approaches. There are even sequences that furnish material for the anecdotists. One such example occurs in the battle scene where pipes and drums are played for the victorious Russian soldiers. I couldn't find a way to explain to Prokofiev what precise effect should be "seen" in his music for this joyful moment. Seeing that we were getting nowhere, I ordered some "prop" instruments constructed, shot these being played (without sound) *visually*, and projected the results for Prokofiev—who almost immediately handed me an exact "musical equivalent" to that visual image of pipers and drummers which I had shown him.'[9]

The most closely analysed moment in the film, the moment of suspense before the attack—subjected to such extraordinary post-facto analysis by Eisenstein in *The Film Sense*—was also an instance of music following film:

'Of particular interest in this case is the fact that the music was composed to a completely finished editing of the pictorial element. The visual movement of the theme was fully grasped by the composer to the same degree that the completed musical movement was caught by the director in the subsequent scene of the attack, where the shots were matched to a previously recorded music-track.'

Though this 'congruence of the movement of the music with the movement of the visual contour—with the graphic composition of the frame' has been so minutely examined by its maker, one must constantly remind oneself that when put together in this sequence as well as in others, there were some pleasant surprises.

On February 1, 1939, Eisenstein finally received his Order of Lenin—along with Cherkasov, who played the rôle of Nevsky; also Alexandrov, Orlova, and Alexander Ivanov, who had made a modest, effective and useful film, *On the Border*. The Order of the Red Banner of Labour went to thirty-six directors, actors, cameramen, including the new chief of fictional films for the Committee, and the new head of Mosfilm. Ninety-seven others were awarded the 'Token of Honour'. Alyosha Lyarsky received the medal, 'For Labouring Excellence'. Other honours extended beyond film-circles. In the elections of June 1938 for the Supreme Soviet several film workers represented their districts. Everyone was enthusiastic about the drama-come-true election of Cherkasov—from Professor Polezhayev, Baltic Deputy of 1918, to Nikolai Cherkasov (without make-up), deputy from the Kuibyshev electoral district of Leningrad; when he arrived for the Battle on the Ice just after his election he was hurrahed by both the Russian and the 'Teuton' forces. Shengelaya was elected from a Georgian district, and the collaborators on the music and lyrics of so many film-songs, Isaac Dunayevsky and Vasili Lebedev-Kumach, represented their respective Leningrad and Moscow neighbourhoods. There were to be film-people in every following Supreme Soviet. Eisenstein, however, was content to be made a doctor of the science of art-studies. 'Professor Eisenstein' was a suitable image.

After the successful innovation, in *Lenin in October*, of showing Lenin and Stalin in dramatic rôles, the flood-gates were open. In the portrayal of Stalin, the younger actor Goldstab eventually left the field to Mikhail Gelovani, and throughout the remaining years of Stalin's life Gelovani made a career of this one rôle—and was kept constantly employed in it. He appeared in more than twenty films with little variation in performance: the sitter for the portrait liked uniformity. The Lenin portrait was a far more interesting assignment for an actor, and two of the best Soviet actors became identified with the rôle— Boris Shchukin and Maxim Strauch. Strauch's first sketch was made in Yutkevich's film of Pogodin's scenario and play, *Man with a Gun*, released the same week (November 1938) with Chiaureli's *Great Dawn*, in which Lenin was impersonated by a young Tbilisi actor named Miuffke. Strauch again played Lenin in the last of the *Maxim* trilogy, *Vyborg Side*, just before the release of *Lenin in 1918*, in which Shchukin perfected and deepened his original portrait of Lenin, giving the last performance of his life with a sureness and devotion that seemed then to put all other attempts in the shade.

Shchukin approached this rôle* as a fascinating problem—for a brave artist and a Soviet citizen. Considering the quantity of detail that went into its making, Shchukin's performance is a masterpiece of synthesis and artistic control. It never ceases to amaze me that this figure of a national leader, a revolutionist and philosopher could be shown so completely without pose of any sort. No country's hero has been served so well; think of the stiff Washingtons and Bolivars, the incredible Napoleons! Shchukin's first preparation for the rôle was in 1936, when Pogodin showed him the script of *November* (the first version of *Man with a Gun*) that Yutkevich was to direct at Lenfilm.[10] It was at Shchukin's enthusiastic suggestion that Pogodin also turn his script into a play for the Vakhtangov Theatre, which saved the idea, for by mid-1937 it became clear that *November* would have difficulties at Lenfilm. In August Shchukin accepted the rôle of Lenin for *Revolt* (the working title of *Lenin in October*) while he prepared the same rôle for the theatre in Pogodin's play. Both film and play were to open in three months, for the November celebrations of the twentieth anniversary of the Revolution. Though thousands were still alive who had seen Lenin in life, Shchukin had not, so he saturated himself in pictures, photographs, sketches, newsreels, gramophone records that preserved fragments of the living Lenin. He read all the reminiscences that touched Lenin's life, finding Gorky's brief memoir the most suggestive—and he had several talks with Krupskaya, Lenin's widow. Shchukin never enjoyed writing himself, so he left only the barest record of his intense research, but the two films tell more than any notebooks. The eighty-seven-day shooting schedule for *Lenin in October* began on August 10th

* Shchukin's previous film rôles: in Raizman's *Flyers*, and as a character modelled on Lenin's early years, in Stroyeva's *Generation of Conquerors*.

with scenes that did not require Shchukin's presence; he was absorbed into the work in September, immediately on his return from a short Crimean vacation. His personal working schedule for this period sounds physically impossible, for with his home-work on both play and film, rehearsals at the theatre and studio, and the filming, he never had more than about four hours' sleep. It soon became clear that his health was threatened, and that both jubilee play and jubilee film would have to be interrupted. Of the two, Stalin apparently chose to sacrifice the play, for the Committee on Art Affairs postponed it altogether, so that Shchukin could concentrate on the film. After the enormous success of *Lenin in October*, a sequel was prepared, with a more relaxed shooting schedule (three and a half months), for Shchukin's health was worse. Exactly six months after his appearance in *Lenin in 1918*, and while a third Lenin film was in preparation, Shchukin was dead.

Shchukin's and Strauch's Lenin rôles were created almost simultaneously in the theatre and on film. Comparisons were inevitable in this curious contest between artists of equal independence. Shchukin's Lenin was of course on fuller display in the Romm films than the briefer episodes that Strauch's Lenin played, yet Strauch's vivid miniature in Yutkevich's *Man with a Gun* grew through the years to a sureness and stature that gave a more relaxed and credible portrait. Strauch and Yutkevich often worked together on this problem; in *Yakov Sverdlov* (1940) the polishing process continued, and in their latest film together, *Stories of Lenin* (1958), Strauch's art is so quietly in command that it is almost unnoticed as art.

It is well known that the subject of Dovzhenko's next film was proposed by Stalin. Their meetings extended over a number of years; it was during the writing of *Aerograd* that they first met. Mosfilm's bureaucrats were making obstacles for the *Aerograd* script; Dovzhenko wrote directly for advice to Stalin and was given an appointment twenty-two hours later, at which he read his scenario to Stalin, Voroshilov, Molotov and Kirov. The *Aerograd* difficulties were straightened out and production started briskly with the expedition to Siberia. At the February 1935 session of the Central Committee, at which the film-makers received their decorations, Stalin remarked, while pinning the Order of Lenin on Dovzhenko, 'Now you must give us a Ukrainian *Chapayev*', and briefly proposed that Dovzhenko look into the Civil War activity of Shchors as a film subject. Dovzhenko naturally agreed and the press carried considerable publicity on Stalin's suggestion. While *Aerograd* was still in production Dovzhenko was again summoned (as usual, at night) to the Kremlin. After asking him how the work was going, Stalin came to the point:

'The reason I wanted to see you is this. When I spoke to you about Shchors last time, I was merely making a suggestion. I simply thought of what you might do in the Ukraine. But neither my words nor the articles in the press place any obligations upon you. You have a free choice in the matter. If you want to do *Shchors*—go ahead and do it but if you have other plans, then keep to them by all means. Don't think that you are bound to anything. I called you in to tell you this.'[11]

Work on *Shchors* began before the release of *Aerograd* and its production was to
be a long, troubled one. Never again, except in making his war-time documentary
films, was Dovzhenko to experience a concentrated, brief creative excitement.
And *Shchors* taught him the new difficulties of executing a suggestion from Stalin.
In the three years before its release, Dovzhenko had to submit every decision
and every episode to a seemingly endless series of people 'who knew what
Stalin wanted'. There were more midnight interviews, some bitter, with the
Leader himself, who was beginning to show the signs of megalomania and
infallibility that gave a nightmare colour to his last years. Dovzhenko later told
friends about one frightening arrival in Stalin's office, when he refused to speak
to Dovzhenko, and Beria accused him of joining a nationalist conspiracy. For the
old ghosts of Ukrainian nationalism rose around the dramatized figure of Nikolai
Shchors. His own early death protected him from accusations of complicity,
but many of his comrades' names were now taboo in the purest political circles.
Most of his comrades in the finished film were inventions by Dovzhenko, who
was actually happier with an invention like his emotional Bozhenko (drawn,
again, from Dovzhenko's grandfather) than with the morally god-like figure of
Shchors, whose every word and gesture had to be approved by microscopic
censorship. Knowing these circumstances it is amazing—and a testimony of
Dovzhenko's art—that the figure of Shchors has as much life as it has. Its casting was a serious problem. After the film had been in production for several
months, Dovzhenko's nervousness about the actor chosen for the rôle finally
forced him to replace the actor with another, Yevgeni Samoilov, and re-shoot
the months of work. The scenario took eleven months, the filming twenty. In
Dovzhenko's words it seemed 'a lifetime'. During production a delegation of
British trade-unionists visited the Kiev studio:

'. . . the Film Trust built for him at the expense of the state a complete studio
block to his own layout, he having expressed his dislike of the existing studios.
Last winter he began shooting, for his script involves scenes in all seasons of the
year, and he has had at his disposal thousands of troops from the Red Army
and all the equipment he has asked for . . . when it is finished, he plans to begin
another on a subject which he has already chosen—*Taras Bulba*, from the novel
of sixteenth century Ukraine by Gogol.[12]

Shchors lives as a film, despite everything, possibly because the autobiographical
source of all Dovzhenko's films is frankest here. He had taken part in many of the
military and political actions shown in the film. He knew the real-life models
of every personage in it (no matter under what name)—and there is, of course,
much of himself in the person of Shchors, a firm, determined intellectual who
has pledged his being and talents to the new social order. As in all his best work,
Shchors leaves in the memory burning images of death and of passionate life.
To move from the pitiless ferocity of the opening to the tragic dirge of the close
—both set in the same shattered fields—gives the film a wide form that can absorb
any amount of speechifying. But all the rhetoric of the film is outweighed by
moving pictures—riderless horses, smoking ruins of destroyed homes and lives,
a boisterous wedding procession that jingles through a bombardment, cavalry

through snowy meadows and icy avenues, military bands at the disposal of any victor, hand to hand struggle, riderless horses—pictures that pour across the screen. That always perceptive critic, Shklovsky, wrote of *Shchors* that, 'just as Eisenstein in *Alexander Nevsky* infinitely deepened the screen, so has Dovzhenko broadened it'.[13] And another remark of Shklovsky's fits this and all other films by the great Ukrainian, 'It makes you forget to think how it was done.'

Stalin's original commission was surpassed, for there is nothing here akin to *Chapayev*. Dovzhenko's genius could take him more deeply into human motives than could be attempted by the Vasilievs. His humour was both more exuberant and more mordant. *Shchors* contains such a gallery of portraits of the many-faced enemy as no one but a fearless poet would risk—beyond realism. Contemporary criticism complained of this as exaggeration, but history has transmuted this complaint into admiration. Once again the foremost Communist in Soviet films had demonstrated the true magnitude of a political artist's responsibilities.

The reformed industry (at whose head Ivan Bolshakov replaced Dukelsky in June 1939), had put almost all its best talents to work, sometimes after years of idleness. Of all the original creators who had helped shape the modern Soviet film, the only ones not properly employed in this period were Vertov, whose later difficulties I have never understood, Kuleshov, who had been teaching in the six years since *The Great Consoler*, and Kozintsev and Trauberg; the inventors of FEX were bogged down in the commendable but tortuous task of a scenario about Karl Marx's life. Their much revised script consumed more than a year and was never filmed. This was a warning of some end: they were to make only one more film together, a film that would cause trouble.

The responsible film artist was caught between his fear of formalism and his equal fear of naturalism, and the capricious apparatus of supervision offered him no helpful solution. It defeated even its industrial purpose, for the giant wringers that every scenario had to pass through delayed production to a degree that would be incredible in a capitalist film industry. Few were sure that such delays were socially useful. Each revision of a script or film in progress meant another year of work after each complaint; the Yutkevich film that was eventually released as *Miners* consumed three years in adjusting to changing requirements.

On the diplomatic front Nazi aggression had realized a series of victories, climaxed at Munich, and made concrete in Austria, the Ruhr, the Sudetenland, and now aimed at Danzig. With German expansion edging both East and West, the Soviet Union proposed a military alliance with Britain and France. When stalled negotiations on this convinced Soviet diplomats that the Western allies continued to hope for further German expansion eastward, the Foreign Ministry offered a non-aggression pact to Germany; Von Ribbentrop came to Moscow and signed the pact with Molotov. This shock was announced to the world on August 23, 1939.

CHAPTER XVI

Semi-War

1939–1941

> It is not he who never makes a mistake who is wise.
> There are no such men nor can there be. He is wise
> who makes not very serious mistakes and knows how
> to correct them easily and quickly
>
> LENIN

The shock of the pact, no matter what its logic, was registered instantly in cinema, but negatively. All films attacking the German Government and Hitler's brand of fascism were withdrawn from Soviet distribution. Abroad, the same films were removed from circulation whenever the distributor operated on terminable lease. In those instances where *Mamlock* had been sold outright, it continued to be shown for a while, giving courage to the badly shaken anti-fascist forces, disconcerted as it became clear that the Soviet Union was determined to respect the letter of the pact.

Not only were foreign circulations of Soviet films cut voluntarily, but the public confusion produced by the pact, multiplied by maximum fear propaganda in the foreign press, resulted in a drastic lowering of foreign audiences for the films. Many theatres formerly friendly to an occasional Soviet programme withdrew their support, more dedicated theatres were compelled to revise their policies, and some foreign distributors of Soviet films went out of business altogether. One symptom of the reduced market in America was that even so important a film as *Minin and Pozharsky* was shown there without translated dialogue-titles—to minimum audiences. One effect of the world situation was to push a national tendency, already well begun in Soviet films, further in an isolationist direction.

The non-aggression pact purchased a respite, to prepare for the eventual clash, but events outside the country and on its frontiers gave the next two years the bitter taste of semi-war. A week after signing the pact Germany delivered the ultimatum to Poland that brought declarations of war from Britain and France. Almost simultaneously with the German blitz on Poland, the Red Army moved in to a buffer zone, comprised of 'Western Ukraine' and 'Western Byelorussia'. This new temporary territory became the material of several films, chiefly documentary reports on conditions there; of these the only one that went beyond reporting was *Liberation*, made by Dovzhenko and Solntseva with their assistants and cameramen. Similar in spirit, though more placid, was *Bukovina—Ukrainian Earth*, made later by Solntseva with Lazar Bodik. Abram Room made a story-film of the new territory, *Wind from the East*, and Mikhail Romm planned another, *Dream*.

The Soviet Union's next protective move brought a war that was limited in space but devastating in lives and in its reaction on foreign opinion. On October 14, 1939 a memorandum was delivered to Finland protesting the strengthening by foreign (German) advisers on the Mannerheim Line that gave it a direct shelling capacity against Leningrad. Finland resisted when Soviet soldiers crossed the border on November 30th. The winter war on the Mannerheim Line consumed lives and morale that Russia could ill afford to lose, though concessions were forced from Finland that may have affected the fate of Leningrad in the later struggle. A high price was paid also in foreign reaction. Two weeks after the Red Army entered Finland the Soviet Union was expelled from the League of Nations, and for the next year and a half anti-Soviet propagandists had little opposition to their picture of Hitler and Stalin as wicked partners. The Baltic Republics of Estonia, Latvia, and Lithuania were also converted into another buffer zone. Soviet isolation was more complete than at any time since the Civil War.

It was from Leningrad, closest to the actual fighting, that the most impressive films of the period came, but it was more than a year before the Finnish War entered directly into the subject-matter of Lenfilm's programme. Immediately after the release of Part Two of *A Great Citizen*, Gerasimov's new film, *Teacher*, appeared in December 1939. His scenario for this film had won the first prize of 15,000 roubles in the 1939 scenario contest; it had dramatically drawn attention to a critical situation in the Soviet educational system. The discussion around the published scenario gave the film an importance long before its filming was completed. Disputants appeared from all quarters. Film critics, who imagined that love and humour obscured heroism, attacked it. Teachers, who found in the scenario a useful weapon against weaknesses in the educational programme, rallied to its defence with substantiating facts, details, anecdotes, problems. Out of this constructive criticism from the teaching profession (a thousand understanding collaborators!) came a complete revision of the scenario, and the changes were incorporated in the unfinished film. This seems one instance when lay criticism was not a hindrance to the film-maker, for comparison of the original script with the finished film shows a richer and more realistic result.

Lenfilm showed a film by Zarkhi and Heifitz that was no less a triumph than their *Baltic Deputy*: this was *Member of the Government* (known abroad as *The Great Beginning*), from a scenario by Katerina Vinogradskaya (author of *Fragment of an Empire*) about the tribulations of a woman devoted to the ideal of a collective farm. The centre of the film's art was the great performance of Vera Maretskaya, who had often taken small film rôles (since the mid-1920s) while maturing as an actress in the theatre. It was while she was playing a quite different rôle, Catherine in *The Taming of the Shrew*, that the directors chose her for *Member of the Government*:

'This was not my first rôle on the screen, but it proved to be the most interesting and most difficult. The difficulty lay in the fact that Alexandra is so real and contemporary a figure that the slightest false note in rendering her on the screen would be taken as a personal affront by the audience to which she is so dear. It was necessary to know her as well as I knew myself, and to do so meant to study a vast mass of materials.'[1]

In October 1940, Lenfilm released its best musical comedy,* *Musical Story*, directed by Alexander Ivanovsky and Herbert Rappoport—a film about professional and amateur musicians, written by Yevgeni Petrov and G. Munblit. The Bolshoi tenor, Sergei Lemeshev, made a satisfactory hero-chauffeur, the dispatcher-heroine was played by a popular young actress, Zoya Fyodorova, and Erast Garin played a pseudo-intellectual chauffeur, the obstacle to true love. Lenfilm also evolved the 'concert' musical—a programme of separate musical and ballet numbers. Ilya Trauberg and Dubson made *Concert Valse*, and a large group of directors made *Film-Concert 1941*.

In the first months of 1941 two smashing surprises came from Lenfilm, Kalatozov's *Valeri Chkalov* and Eisimont's *Front-Line Girl-Friends*—more familiar outside the Soviet Union as *Wings of Victory* and *The Girl from Leningrad*.

Kalatozov's return to film-making, with *Manhood* in August 1939, served not only to bring him back to personal direction, but also to introduce him to the subject of aviation, which led him to his next story, the flying career of the late Valeri Chkalov. The idea for the film came from Chkalov's co-pilot, Baidukov, and the scenario was prepared by Chirskov. The air force gave full co-operation, and the aviator Borisenko and others flew duplications of Chkalov's exploits. Chkalov himself was played by a newcomer from the theatre, Vladimir Belokurov, whom Kalatozov surrounded with veteran actors, perhaps to emphasize his hero's individuality. In addition to Stalin-Gelovani, there are portraits of Gorky and Ordjonikidze (the latter played by Mezhinsky, of *Mamlock* fame). The Americans briefly shown at Chkalov's landing, from his polar flight, at Vancouver, Washington (where the army post was under the command of General George Marshall), are the most credible and sympathetic in any Soviet film. The finished film conveys Kalatozov's excitement in the 'mere act of flying', plus his sympathy with a hero whose temperament often got him into trouble. The photography by Ginsburg of *Valeri Chkalov* is extremely modest and direct, while Kalatozov encouraged the performances to be passionately on the edge of exaggeration—and it may be in this stylistic reflection of the thematic conflict between discipline and passion that the film's power lies.

Victor Eisimont was a new, young director whose previous work was on defence films. He was given the delicate job of making the first studio film about the war with Finland.† The scenarists were young and serious, the cast was chosen from both the experienced and the young, the treatment avoided all

---

* In this same time Mosfilm's musical comedy specialists made *Favourite Daughter* (Pyriev) and *Bright Path* (Alexandrov). The latter, a socialist version of Cinderella, was later successful in the United States, where it was drastically re-cut, as *Tanya*.

† Another film on the Finnish War released on the same day: *In the Rear of the Enemy*, directed by Yevgeni Schneider for Sergei Yutkevich at Soyuzdetfilm.

sensational aspects of war without hiding its hardships—and the result was astonishingly strong, and popular everywhere it was shown. *The Girl from Leningrad* even achieved the dubious, later, wartime accolade of being remade in Hollywood (*Three Russian Girls*, directed in 1943 by Otsep).

The military movements and wars of this period restored the documentary film to its former importance. Though Vertov remained unemployed (so far as I know), the other documentary leader, Esther Shub, applied her editing talents to accumulated Spanish war footage, collaborating with Vsevolod Vishnevsky on *Spain*, released August 20, 1939 (just as Roman Karmen returned from his year of filming in China). Her next job was a collaboration with Pudovkin, *Twenty Years of Cinema*, an anniversary film that presented highlights of Soviet film history. The nearing war brought *Mannerheim Line* (April 27, 1940), a record of the hard winter's war by Vasili Byelayev (supervising a large group of newsreel cameramen), Dovzhenko's *Liberation*, with Yekelchik (the cameraman of *Shchors* and *Bogdan Khmelnitsky*) working with newsreel assistants, and *To the Danube* (August 27, 1940), made for the Central and Ukrainian Newsreel Studios by Poselsky and Kopalin. Byelayev made *Estonian Earth* in the winter of 1940-41. Almost half of the seventy-nine orders awarded to film workers in May 1940 were to the makers of newsreel and documentary films. These men and women also figured in the first Stalin Prizes of March 1941.

The largest single documentary enterprise of 1940 was chiefly peaceful— *A Day in a New World*. The idea for the film was Gorky's, the only one of his grand film projects to be realized, and posthumously. He had proposed that on a single ordinary day all documentary cameramen, at different points of the Soviet Union, should film everything they saw around them; he promised that the edited result would tell something about modern Soviet life. At a congress of newsreel cameramen early in 1940 Gorky's plan was suggested by Zeitlin and Yagling, accepted by vote, and prepared for. One hundred telegrams went out to the cameramen waiting at their posts: 'August 24th is the day.' Forty thousand feet of film were exposed that day. The Central Newsreel Studio cut this down to a first draft of 14,500 feet; the final version (released December 7th) came to seven reels (6,800 feet). Gorky's idea was a good one, worthy of a Vertov, and the result is more 'down to earth' than it might have been had Vertov had the handling of its material.

A documentary series in a new form was introduced at this time. Alexander Zguridi and his staff began their dramatically detailed films of animal life, built with the same infinite patience and ingenuity that distinguished the earlier *Secrets of Nature* series in England, and the later nature films of Arne Sucksdorff that were followed by the large-scale nature-films issued from the Walt Disney studio. Zguridi was a lawyer who in 1932 had begun to make short films of bird life and sea life. The first of Zguridi's feature-length studies were *In the Depths of the Sea* and *The Power of Life*. These careful studies continued to the present with a regularity that ignored wars and administrative change. A less important innovation that soon froze into a pattern was the short biographical film, using the surroundings and documents of the subject—whether Tchaikovsky, Mayakovsky, or Pavlov.

Mosfilm's staff of directors produced films that did less than justice to their reputations. The subject of each touched on the theme of sabotage: Barnet made *A Night in September*, Macheret made a spy story, *The Mistakes of Engineer Kochin*; Macheret did a better job with his assistance to Yuli Raizman in adapting Sholokhov's sprawling novel, *Virgin Soil Upturned*, directed by Raizman. Mosfilm's major film of this period was left unfinished; Vishnevsky's script of *First Cavalry Army* was being filmed by Dzigan on a scale to equal *We from Kronstadt*, but the subject was unlucky*—twice in the past Eisenstein had hoped to work on it, and now Dzigan was halted (without explanation) just before the film was finished.

Eisenstein's restoration to his deserved high place seemed complete when Vsevolod Vishnevsky published in June 1939 a eulogistic 39-page brochure on his life and work. In his comment to me Eisenstein does not seem to have taken the brochure very seriously, but I'm sure he was grateful for Vishnevsky's gesture. For the first time there was a printed account of his difficulties with the film administration, beginning with *Que Viva Mexico*:

'The wreckers in charge of the film industry played Eisenstein a spiteful joke. He was removed from the work [QVM] just before beginning its montage. The film was lost to the USSR. Other people in America put it together. The negative was cut to pieces—

'Everyone can understand what such a blow means to an artist. . . . It was a very heavy, hard and dark period for him, but he continued to work. He made a fresh start. He wrote an important Soviet film-comedy, *MMM*, that he wished to make with Maxim Strauch. Again the wreckers snatched this from him, and proposed other subjects to him that would have led him away from the basic line of cinema growth: they pushed unnecessary themes at him that he rejected.

'In the summer of 1935 Eisenstein made the film *Bezhin Meadow*.

'A new failure. Many factors woven into the very process of production, including the intrigues of enemies, brought this work to an unsuccessful halt. . . .

'Eisenstein continued to be active, working out plans, seeking resolutions of subjective and objective appearances—the problem always at the base of his work. He had plans to make a film about Spain, plans for a film about 1917, the creation of the Red Army. The wreckers shattered these plans. . . .

'I tell about this in such detail so that tens and hundreds and thousands of Soviet readers and spectators can see a concrete example of the crimes that enemies committed on the art front. We can only imagine what obstacles must have been placed before Eisenstein and many other masters. How many strong films, how many great works they might have realized!'

Yet the industry's waste of Eisenstein was not all in the past. After *Alexander Nevsky* another period began of projects whose frustration threw him back into the theoretical work that did not depend on administrative approval. At first this work was necessary as a refreshment, after the exhausting completion of *Nevsky*:

* Unlucky only in films, for it had been the subject and title of Vishnevsky's first play, a lasting success.

'[April 21, 1939] I've started to work on "Vol. I" of "Rezhissera" but strange as it may seem, I'm still so tired after "Nevsky"—who was a hell of a job to be made on so short a schedule—that I cannot concentrate on the work, as concentrated as I should be! . . .

'The next film will be not *so very* soon: it will probably take the whole of next summer. I'll try like hell to manage something with the book during the time the script and preparations are done.'

He was to turn often to 'Vol. I' during the next two years.

'[May 12, 1939] I'm working on a new script, this time with Fadeyev—it will be Frunze—Perekop—Wrangel. Details will follow. . . .'

On August 23, 1939 he wrote to Ivor Montagu:

'. . . everything has been changed—instead of Frunze and Perekop I'm making another film dealing with the enormous thing that is being done in Central Asia—the Fergana Canal—I'm sure you've heard about that—all the newspapers are full of it. I've been there already—that's why I was out of Moscow for about a month.

'The film will be a big machine—no "khronika" or documentary—but a big film about Uzbekistan starting with—Tamerlane on the wonderful background of Samarkand, Bokhara, Hiva etc—which are fantastically beautiful.

'It will be a great tragedy of the struggle of human beings among themselves and the hopeless struggle of humanity against deserts and sands. The hundreds of years' struggle which could become victorious only now. It is highly dramatic and very pictorial. I'm leaving for Tashkent today. Edward is already there.'

'To the very heart of the theme'—Eisenstein always insisted upon such visits in approaching a new subject, whether it was the California valley where 'Sutter's gold' was found, or the remnants of thirteenth-century Novgorod. Eisenstein and Pavlenko wrote a treatment on the spot, and the shooting script (dated August 1-2-3, 1939, Kratovo) was published in *Iskusstvo Kino*, September 1939.[2] The script has an epic structure similar to that of *Que Viva Mexico*—set in three widely separated periods: antiquity, before the Revolution, and today. Prokofiev began to work on its score, Eisenstein sketched the sets and costumes in October, actors were tested and cast—and then the whole project evaporated. 'It didn't come off, and couldn't come off—we knew too little,' said Pavlenko.[3] The preliminary footage that Tisse filmed at the Canal was edited into a short documentary film—and that, with the script and sketches, is all that is left of an extraordinary film. This hectic diplomatic and military autumn may have had something to do with the halt of *Ferghana Canal*.

The next large project (recently revealed in the examination of Eisenstein's archive) was a film about Pushkin, in March 1940. It was planned in an experimental colour method that used selected colours only when necessary, rather than the whole spectrum. The only completed creative work that Eisenstein could show at the end of this year was his production of *Die Walküre* at the Bolshoi Opera. 'Made all the schemes of settings myself and had a great fun in doing the production,' he wrote. For an artist who enjoyed hard work as much as Eisenstein did, it is a pity he was given so little to do.

In addition to his little-used responsibilities as director, and his private much-asserted capacities as theoretician, Eisenstein was usefully employed as a producer. One of the best ideas of the new film order was to place the best artists in charge of each studio's output, releasing them for their own work whenever they chose a film subject. Eisenstein was appointed artistic head of Mosfilm, Ermler of Lenfilm, Dovzhenko of the Kiev Studio, and Yutkevich of Soyuzdetfilm. As I am not certain how their production duties fitted in to their own films, I hesitate to credit Ermler with everything good that came from Lenfilm in these years, yet it is possible to trace Eisenstein's authority and taste in the surprisingly fine film made by Roshal, *The Artamanov Affair*, and the breadth of vividness of *Bogdan Khmelnitsky*, though certainly Savchenko's, had Dovzhenko's support. One memory of Eisenstein's behaviour as a producer recalls other producers encountered in other countries. A weak, amorphous scenario is being discussed:

'Do you realize what 606 and 914 mean? Why should these medicines be known by numbers, and such large ones, at that? Because they had been preceded by 605 and 913 attempts! Why is there an automobile called ZIS-101? Because there had been 100 models before it! And that's the point. Before publishing *Anna Karenina* Tolstoy wrote a trunkful of drafts! And what has this author submitted to us today? The first thing that came from his pen. . . .'[4]

Kuleshov, like Eisenstein, divided his life between film-making and film-teaching at this time and, unlike Eisenstein, had something to show in both fields. His first film after a silence of seven years was *Siberians* (released December 13, 1940), for Soyuzdetfilm—and his return to film-making may be to the credit of Yutkevich, then head of that studio. Vitenson's story of Siberian hunters centred on two eager boys. Its success was considered a testimony to Kuleshov's sound-picture scenario method, an even more precise preparation on paper than was followed in *Nevsky*. I do not know about Kuleshov's next film, a collaboration with Alexandra Khokhlova, *Incident on a Volcano* (March 22, 1941), but his lasting contribution of this year was his text-book, *Fundamentals of Film Direction*, a practical manual that could be used to teach film-making in any country at any time.

Yutkevich's own film of this period was released the day before *Siberians*. Planned as the first of a series of film-biographies of noted Bolsheviks, *Yakov Sverdlov* was a surprisingly gentle film, even in its villainies. It was adapted by Pavlenko from Levin's play, *Bolshevik*, and the actor Leonid Lyubashevsky had a long practice in the play's rôle of Sverdlov (first president of the Soviet Republic) before coming to the film, though his characterization was rather lost beside the greater skill of Strauch's Lenin, and Okhlopkov's brief but striking performance as Shalyapin. The ambitious young actor, Pavel Kadochnikov, assumed two rôles in the film, a peasant lad, and Gorky as a young man.

Protazanov's films for Soyuzdetfilm were *Seventh Grade* (released December 30, 1938) and *Salavat Yulayev* (February 21, 1941). The latter, on the revolutionary struggles of the Bashkir people, was the only historical film made by Protazanov —now ageing—since his return to Russia, but this was a period when the best

Soviet directors found it simpler to retreat into history* rather than to cope with the more tangled administrative problems involved in contemporary subjects. The Russian nationalism and patriotism of *Nevsky* or *Minin and Pozharsky* was not Protazanov's aim in *Salavat Yulayev*; its interest for him was the new colour of Central Asia, and this was to give him the material for his next and last film.

Soyuzdetfilm was temporarily associated with the most publicized Soviet film invention, a successful stereoscopic effect without the use by the spectators of any coloured glasses. The young inventor, Semyon Ivanov, had been demonstrating tests on a reduced scale since 1938, and a programme for public demonstration was completed at Soyuzdetfilm in January 1941, for use in Moscow's first stereoscopic theatre, opening in February. Eventually a studio was turned over to the exclusive use of 'Stereokino'. Ivanov was solely interested in the technical perfection of the new instrument, leaving the artistic problems of the first programme (*World of Youth*) and the later stereoscopic comedies and dramas in the hands of a merely energetic director, Alexander Andriyevsky (also responsible for the early all-talkie, *Mechanical Traitor*). Up to the present, no first-rate director has touched the new medium.

Now working at Mosfilm, Pudovkin's next scenario was by Grebner, a large-scale account of General Suvorov's last years, emphasizing that his forgotten victories over Napoleon were accomplished in spite of his sovereign, Paul I, the Tsar's trusted advisers, and his two-faced allies. The style of the finished *Suvorov* is far simpler than that of *Peter the First*, and Pudovkin and Golovnya may have had Eisenstein's support in producing its grand, unencumbered manner. The boiling centre of the film was the actor in the rôle of Suvorov. His name was also Nikolai Cherkasov (sometimes called Cherkasov-Sergeyev, to distinguish him from the Leningrad Cherkasov), and he was in his sixties before being cast in this, his first important film-rôle.† He was an actor on the verge of retirement from a Moscow theatre. He did not live long after the film's release, but his dynamic performance gives him a permanent niche in Soviet film history. His manner in the film reminds one of Pudovkin's own abrupt behaviour. The climax of production and of film was the scene of Suvorov's famous unexpected crossing of the Alps, to extricate his army from envelopment. This was filmed in the Caucasus mountains, and the transport there of crew, equipment, and enough extras to represent the Russian army, was a proud industrial accomplishment. The behaviour of the venerable Cherkasov equally excited admiration:

'Regardless of his age N. P. Cherkasov declined all "exemptions" and insisted on being filmed in the most dangerous situations. For example, Suvorov-Cherkasov, as he rides along a precipice, shows his soldiers a great snow-covered peak ahead, and shouts back to them: "Well, brothers, there's a hill for us to jump over!" In order to film this shot, some guides led a horse with difficulty along

---

* On February 8, 1940, there was a conference devoted to the problems of historical films, with addresses by Eisenstein, Shklovsky, Yutkevich and others. The proceedings of this conference were published.

† One of his earlier film rôles: in Schneiderov's adventure-film *Julbars*.

the cliff, and then rode him in the rehearsal before impatient Cherkasov was allowed to mount himself.'[5]

Bogdan Khmelnitsky had a grand scale equal to *Suvorov*'s. The cameraman, Yekelchik, wrote that precautions had to be taken to resist the lure of 'surface loveliness' in this extra-rich costume film, but the other lure of 'bigness' was evidently not guarded against, fortunately, for it is the uninhibited sweep of *Bogdan Khmelnitsky* that one remembers first—from the opening scene of endless rows of hoisted Ukrainian victims set aflame, to the contributed handfuls of earth, making a final memorial that becomes a small hill before your eyes. When Bogdan addresses the people, the hills and valleys seem covered with them, swaying like a Dovzhenko harvest to the gestures of Bogdan—played by Nikolai Mordvinov with the same bigness that Savchenko has given the whole film. This is also the biggest of the anti-Polish films, set in 1648, at the height of Ukrainian resistance to Polish power, when Ukrainians and Russians joined against it.

Next to *Bogdan* the most interesting new Ukrainian film was *A Great Life*, by Leonid Lukov, which did dare to touch the present. Protected by the praise of Alexei Stakhanov[6] the complaints about its realism were temporarily stilled, after they held up the film's release for a year, but Lukov's later attempt to film the succeeding chapters of Pavel Nilin's novel, *Man Goes to the Mountain*, brought unanswerable condemnation to Part Two of *A Great Life*. In the earlier period of Part One the only serious banning was of *The Law of Life*, a critical film from Mosfilm on Komsomol behaviour, written by Avdeyenko (author of Lukov's *I Love*) and directed by Alexander Stolper and Boris Ivanov. The noise of this banning was not equalled until the post-war ban of *A Great Life*—Part Two. No, the modern subject, treated seriously, remained dangerous to handle. In Georgia, too, there was the fascination of the far past. Chiaureli began the first part of his sixteenth-century chronicle, *Georgi Saakadze*, but I cannot judge it, having seen neither Part One, nor the sequel.

Mid-June 1941 was a quiet time in the Soviet film industry. The crew to make *Sukhe-Bator* in Mongolia left for there on June 12th. Eisenstein was released from his Mosfilm duties to prepare a film about Ivan the Terrible. And the little newsreel studio in Alma-Ata, Kazakhstan, enlarged its facilities to handle the dubbing of films.

CHAPTER XVII

Test

1941–1947

Ah, but the wise know how to learn from enemies and gain their ends.
Precaution is what saves a state, and that you'd never learn from friends,
While enemies compel you to . . .

The Birds, ARISTOPHANES

In the dawn of June 22, 1941, the German army in unprecedented strength struck across the Soviet border in a three-pronged attack—towards Leningrad (supported by the Finnish army), towards Moscow, and towards the Black Sea across the Ukraine. Border-guards had been killed and passed, and German tanks were deep into Byelorussia and the Ukraine before the country heard Molotov on the radio:

'Today at four a.m., without any claims having been presented to the Soviet Union, without a declaration of war, German troops attacked our country, attacked our borders at many points and bombed from their aircraft our cities, Zhitomir, Kiev, Sevastopol, Kaunas. . . .'

The air attacks on cities and airfields were more successfully opposed than on the ground, where the German army rolled on so triumphantly that there was a note of stern anxiety in Stalin's broadcast and filmed speech of July 3rd, 'A grave danger hangs over our country. How could it have happened that our glorious Red Army surrendered a number of our cities and districts to the Fascist armies?' His speech ended with his appeal to oppose the invasion with 'scorched earth' and guerrilla fighters. The following day, July 4th, along with the administrations of many vulnerable industries, the Cinema Committee was ordered to leave Moscow. It was to administer the film industry from Novosibirsk.

The film studios had held defence meetings immediately after Molotov's speech. Cameramen were sent to the moving front, and in the cities all the anti-fascist films shelved two years before were brought out for intense distribution, along with every patriotic film. Erskine Caldwell and Margaret Bourke-White, who happened to be visiting Moscow in June, saw Eisenstein just before the attack:

'. . . he got the reels out of a safe where they were stowed away and gave Erskine and me a private showing. "We think," he commented sagely, "that it will not be much longer before *Alexander Nevsky* will be shown in public cinema theatres again".'[1]

The first wartime issue of the weekly *Kino* (June 27th) shows the Soviet film already on a war footing. There are stirring statements from every leading film-maker. There are detailed proposals to speed production, and cut waste. There is editorial description of widening newsreel coverage of every vital move, behind and at the front, so that no Soviet citizen would lack visual information on his country's struggle. The small studios at Tashkent, Stalinabad, and Alma-Ata are alerted for production emergencies. A full programme of instructional films for civilian war activity is launched. Every studio has its air-raid drills, its blood-donors and its rifle classes. The newly available anti-fascist films are re-reviewed, and Eisenstein writes about Chaplin's *The Great Dictator*. Units are already working on short dramatic and satirical films—poster films that recall the *agitki* of the Civil War. The Soviet cinema had declared war.

On the day of the invasion film-makers in every studio had held conferences to determine how best they could help their country fight its war. Without any inter-studio conference, two of the Moscow studios and Lenfilm arrived at the same solution—short, sharply pointed films to be made quickly by any crew that could submit a good idea. Within a week eight different films of various short lengths were in production, and a whole group of three-minute cartoon-posters. The first of the shorts to be made (and finished on July 2nd) was by Eisimont, *Girl-Friends, to the Front*, with the heroines of *Girl from Leningrad*. As the first shock of attack wore away, the film industry examined its war-baby, found it worthy, and decided to foster it with an extra production care, a working plan, and an editorial committee. This latter was formed in the first week of July, and included Pudovkin, Donskoy, and Alexandrov. Their job was to organize the spontaneous short productions into regular monthly issues, *Fighting Film Albums*.* These were open to short films in any form, any style, so long as they made a useful statement about some phase of the war against fascism. They poured in, from Moscow and Leningrad, from Kiev and Odessa—farce, fantasy, comedy, tragedy. Pushkin's *Tales of Byelkin* had found a cinematic heir.

In Mosfilm the film-makers discussed the values and problems of the new form. Eisenstein led the discussion, citing the short-story methods of Robert Louis Stevenson and Ambrose Bierce as useful for study. He read a Russian translation of a Bierce Civil War story, 'The Affair at Coulter's Notch', as a suggestive model for the short story film form. *Kino* of July 18th published Pudovkin's thoughtful analysis of the new short form. At a conference at Lenfilm, chaired by Ermler, every director-writer team submitted a script for the *Albums*. It was at once evident that important new writing techniques were being evolved within the new form. With Shostakovich and other composers throwing their rich talents into songs for a fighting people to sing, and with the best painters crowding the TASS windows with posters and caricatures, and with Sholokhov and Simonov

---

* At first the series title was *Victory Will be Ours*, from the final words of Molotov's radio speech.

and Petrov* working as war-correspondents, it is not surprising to find the best film-artists devoting themselves to this useful short film form. They were creating the patriotic poetry of wartime.

Photographed in sets left over from more ambitious films,† played by volunteer actors, great and unknown, who refused payment for their work, the first compilation of shorts had a gratifying popular success when it was released on August 2nd. It opened on 'Meeting with Maxim', made by Sergei Gerasimov with Boris Chirkov in his familiar rôle of Maxim, introducing the separate parts and helping the morale of his new audience with spirited words to his old song. 'Dream in the Hand' gave a cutting caricature of Hitler (played by Pyotr Repnin). The concluding item. 'Three in a Shell-hole', was a miniature drama, though with life and death as stakes, of a Red Army soldier, a Russian nurse, and a German soldier.

The second *Album*, shown in North and South America as *This Is the Enemy*, appeared from Lenfilm on August 11th. Two of its five items were written by V. Byelayev and Mikhail Rosenberg, the latter from the team that wrote *The Girl from Leningrad*, and its director, Eisimont, made another of the items. The climactic fourth item, a bitter drama of Yugoslav hostages, was directed by Herbert Rappoport. The close was a 'gag' by Grigori Kozintsev: 'Incident at the Telegraph Office' shows a warning being sent to Hitler by Napoleon. Every month for the next year, no matter what hardships the studios endured, and no matter where the studios happened to be, a fresh *Fighting Film-Album* appeared. In November the Tbilisi Studio released an *Album* made entirely by Georgian film-makers.

The newsreel's job was the toughest of all. In the first week after invasion four crews were sent to four sectors of the long front, all headed by veteran newsmen. Newsreel cameramen covered every phase of the fight even to parachuting with paratroops and hiding with guerrilla fighters deep in the German rear. Cameramen Schneiderov and Bunimovich gave graphic and exciting accounts of their experiences. This is from Schneiderov's diary:

'It was a dark night when we flew over the German lines. My photographic supplies were to take one parachute, myself another. German searchlights probed the sky around us and Nazi anti-aircraft sent up a trail of bullets after us. I jumped and as we parachuted to the ground a group of German night-fighters attacked us. Our planes gave fight and one of our men was killed. Three of us, myself included, were wounded.

'I was worried about my camera and equipment and would not leave the spot despite the commander's suggestion. We couldn't move, for the planes still circled over us, and I worried all night about my camera. Towards morning I saw the red flag marker on our supplies and hurried to claim it. By some miracle, nothing was damaged. Guerrilla troops found us just before dawn. . . .

* Yevgeny Petrov, who had worked on various comedy scripts, including *Musical Story*, was killed in an aeroplane accident, July 1942.
† Using the sets of Pyriev's musical set in the Agricultural Exhibition, *Swineherd and Shepherd*, Medvedkin and Ilya Trauberg began an entire 'concert-film' on July 11th, released September 30th as *We Expect Your Victory*.

'Our paratroops immediately began their raiding activities and I did what I could to keep up their pace. The first thing we captured was a large baggage train destined for the Germans. There were three hundred cars filled with trench mortars, rifles, machine-guns, tommy-guns and shells. And to my delight, among all the weapons was an expensive German movie camera. I now had three cameras. . . .'

As fighter-planes were used up in defence of the cities, German bombings behind the lines grew more successful. Film projectors were installed in the big Metro stations of Moscow being used as air-raid shelters. Incendiary bombs fell on the sound-stage at Mosfilm where Pudovkin was filming a short story* for an *Album*. In Kiev, under the supervision of Dovzhenko, Lukov was filming *Alexander Parkhomenko*, about the Lugansk worker who helped rout the Germans from the Ukraine in 1919. The film of history was often interrupted by bombs of the present, Lukov reported:

'We found ourselves in the war zone. This could not fail to influence our work. The incessant air-raid alarms, the bombing and later the shelling of the city, interfered with our progress. But upon returning to the set after an air-raid, we often resumed our work with even greater enthusiasm. Many times we were obliged to make changes in our earlier plans. On the other hand, some of the situations in the script were so similar to the reality around us that we almost forgot we were recreating the events of 1919.'[2]

The men and women who made films often took up arms in defence of their cities. As the Nazis approached Kiev, many of the film-workers joined the armed forces while the main body of the studio moved east to Tashkent (where *Parkhomenko* was completed). There was no public news for months of the whereabouts of Dovzhenko. His parents stayed in occupied Kiev; his eighty-year-old father was thrown down a flight of stairs and killed, and Dovzhenko's apartment was sacked and mined. Two weeks before the war Dovzhenko had begun a play, *The Measure of Life*, and it was this that he continued to work on in his months with the army, where his job was to edit a front-line newspaper and write leaflets that Soviet planes dropped in occupied Ukrainian territory. As Dovzhenko was the Soviet film artist to have seen the most of the Civil War, so he was also the director to participate most directly in the Patriotic War.

In threatened Leningrad Lenfilm was not able to hold back from actual battle many of its young and old artists. Lola Fyodorina, the 'Chizhik' of *Girl from Leningrad*, brought her rôle to life by joining a unit of nurses at the front. Mikhail Rosenberg, one of that film's authors, joined a Komsomol detachment and was killed in action, as was my best friend from GIK days, Oleg Pavlenko. Poslavsky, the actor of *Golden Mountains* and *Peasants*, helped construct the Leningrad

---

* 'Feast at Zhirmunka', by Leonov and Shpikovsky—used in the sixth compilation, released November 24th. This was Pudovkin's first short film since *Chess Fever*, when Shpikovsky had been his co-director. Another bomb made a direct hit on the film-vault where the most valuable negatives, including *Chapayev*, were stored. It is supposed that all of *Bezhin Meadow* was also lost in the subsequent fire-fighting.

defences, day and night. As studio-workers and projectionists left their jobs for the front, women took over. Films had to be made and shown.

The Central Newsreel Studio received not only extraordinary footage from all fronts, but the news, also, of casualties. The first deaths of newsreel cameramen were reported from the Baltic front at the end of July. In a battle outside Leningrad in November, Philip Pechul put aside his camera and with hand-grenade and rifle helped his comrades to make a wedge into an enemy position, and died in the effort. Another Leningrad cameraman, Sergei Fomin, was rescued from a shelled transport vessel after spending more than an hour in the icy waters of the Gulf of Finland. In writing about Leningrad's siege, Roman Karmen mentioned that 'very soon we saw [Fomin] back on his job'. The twenty-two camera graduates from VGIK left directly for the fronts. The newsreel had acquired an importance it had never known before. It is good to see that Newsreel Seventy-seven, of front-line action in August, was edited by Vertov.

As the enemy drew near Moscow at the beginning of the first winter the Government made its decision to withdraw eastwards all Government offices unrelated to the defence of the city, all representatives of foreign governments, and all the film studios. The removal of all vital industries excepting those needed in Moscow and Leningrad at that critical moment had already taken place. Marshal Stalin remained in Moscow with a large military and civilian staff, to conduct the defence operation from what was becoming the front-line. Even his bitterest critics of the future—including people who left Moscow and some who stayed with him—have not tried to disguise their admiration of his tenacity when faced with what seemed certain defeat.

Administrative offices, embassies and correspondents were concentrated in the temporary capital of Kuibyshev, on the Volga. The film studios were evacuated from danger zones and scattered to the furthest corners of the Soviet Union. This move away from threatened Moscow was accomplished in twenty-four hours—on October 16th—but not without a degree of confusion that included even panic. The magnitude of this operation may be imagined, if at all, if one could realize the mechanics of shifting the entire organization of Twentieth Century-Fox from Beverly Hills to Minneapolis, and that of Paramount to New Orleans, while the whole U.S. Army moves in the opposite direction towards the West Coast. This is what happened when the huge studios of Mosfilm and Lenfilm were moved to Alma-Ata in the Kazakhstan Republic and Soyuzdetfilm was abruptly shifted to Stalinabad in Tadjikistan. The Kiev Studio had moved, much earlier, to Ashkhabad and Tashkent. The animated cartoon studio was evacuated to Samarkand. The stereoscope studio was closed, and Ivanov joined the communications branch of the army. The only large studio in the path of the enemy, but not yet moved, was the Tbilisi Studio, where Chiaureli continued his historical two-part film, *Georgi Saakadze*. Into all the vacated Moscow studios moved, busily, the enlarged staffs of the Central Newsreel Studio; they stayed.

The descent on only slightly prepared oriental communities and studios by an exhausted, anxious group of intellectuals and artists created a confusion equal to that on the day of departure from Moscow. There began a period of improvisation, in everything from housekeeping to set construction, that gave a healthy upset to film styles and methods that had been getting dangerously satisfied with themselves. For more than a year all Soviet films, except the splendidly organized and executed newsreel features, had a rough look that helped their directors and cameramen, as much as the new short films helped the scenarists, to revive their interest in the actual crude magic of the medium, beneath its handsome surface.

The physical and administrative tasks of the newly dumped studios were tremendous. In Alma-Ata, where the combined studios of Mosfilm and Lenfilm were to resume operations, no office workers had been brought along. In the whole community there was only one stenographer who knew Russian, a Polish refugee, and she was in constant demand by both the day and night shifts at the tiny Alma-Ata studio. When VGIK was moved into the People's House of Alma-Ata, it increased the film personnel of the community without reducing its problems. My sister-in-law, who with her husband worked as a camera team in Soyuzdetfilm, wrote from Tadjikistan:

'Stalinabad is the furthest point south on the Soviet map (that's why we are here). It is a very nice town, quiet, the lights burn at night, and once a week we get an earthquake, but an earthquake is much, much better than a bomb. . . .

'The fact that we have to start life all over again in a new place makes it all the more interesting. Working here is not easy as we are like pioneers, having to make the Studio all over again. Our studio here will be better than the one in Moscow and of course the weather is ideal for filming. . . .

'Shura and I have found a little house of two rooms with a garden and a castor-oil tree. I have decided to raise strawberries and chickens. I wake up every morning feeling how wonderful it is to be alive. One only starts to realize this when you can get up in the morning and look at mountains, and go to bed at night and *sleep until morning*.'

Films almost completed before the invasion continued to appear throughout 1941: *Masquerade*, Gerasimov's plush adaptation of Lermontov's verse tragedy, was timed for the centenary of Lermontov's death; Roshal's *Artamanov Affair* appeared in October; and Pyriev's brightest musical comedy, *Swineherd and Shepherd* (re-titled abroad *They Met in Moscow*) came in the dark days of November, as the Germans drove towards the capital.

The boast was that Hitler would address his victorious army in Red Square on November 7th, but it was Stalin who spoke to the Red Army there. The military units that marched past Lenin's tomb marched right on out to the defence of Moscow. The clearest ground view that the Germans had of Moscow in early December was across the roofs of Mosfilm, near the same Sparrow Hills from which Napoleon had first seen Moscow. On December 5th the German drive was halted and the battle on December 6th was the first decisive engagement of the war. The soldiers who went to it were accompanied by the cameramen who recorded *The Defeat of the German Armies near Moscow*—to be the most widely shown film of the war. The Soviet release of the finished film, a record of the capital's civilian defence as well as of the major battle and its aftermath of recaptured villages, was on February 18, 1942. Two months later the film reached

New York, and Elliot Paul began an English commentary for it. The adaptation of the film was shifted to Hollywood in June, where Albert Maltz completed the commentary that was recorded by Edward G. Robinson. The film was re-titled *Moscow Strikes Back*, and its American release in August and its Academy Award in the following January made it one of the most powerful propaganda weapons in an alliance that began the day after the Moscow battle, when the Japanese bombed Pearl Harbour.

It was *Moscow Strikes Back* and many later wartime adaptations of one country's documentary films into another country's language* that gave Pudovkin the idea for his formulation of 'The Global Film':

'If you agree with me that modern methods of producing a sound-film narrow the audience for it, as a complete art experience, to a single country and a single language group, then you, too, must come to the unavoidable conclusion that the problem of creating a film comprehensible to all peoples must be taken up with far more conviction and strength than we have hitherto given it. . . .

'Here I want to draw attention to one sort of film that has acquired particularly clear definition during the war,

'This is the feature-length documentary film which uses the facts of living actuality as filmed by the motion picture camera, but which unites them in montage with the aim of communicating to the spectator certain, sometimes quite general and abstract, ideas.

'Such a documentary film is not merely informational. It differs from the newsreel in the same way that an editorial or article in a newspaper differs from the news item in the next column.'

After an analysis of the pictorial means of communicating political and humanist concepts in *Prelude to War*, supervised by Frank Capra, Pudovkin states:

'Such a film is fully international, and can be fully understood anywhere. The commentator's voice may be translated into any language without disturbing the integrity of impression. The montage of visual images does not require translation. . . .

'I am convinced that this form of the documentary feature film will gain ever increasing significance in the post-war period, because . . . it can be widely used for fully and profoundly acquainting peoples with one another, and can serve to a very considerable degree in expressing universal ideas in a graphic and striking way.

'The task of the artist working in this form is to find more subtle means for artistic communication of simple propositions as well as of their profound development on the philosophic and pictorial planes.'[3]

The next major documentary film, *Siege of Leningrad*, found, in Pudovkin's term, 'more subtle means', chiefly because of the tragic ambiance that touched all that was shown, and all those who showed it to us:

* Using the original title, *The Defeat of the German Armies near Moscow*, the same film was differently adapted by Ivor Montagu for British audiences; his narration was spoken by Wilfred Pickles.

'Together with the other inhabitants, the cameramen were in the clutches of the siege. In those grim days they realized that every foot of film shot in the beleaguered city would become as a precious jewel. . . .

'It has sometimes been argued that in a documentary film where there is no plot the dramatic element must be lacking . . . [In *Siege of Leningrad*] the tragic element evolves naturally; it could not be planned—it was determined by the course of events, by life itself, and the struggle of a united body of men who barred the enemy's way to the city. The culminating point of the picture was the terrible months of the blockade. . . .

'It was hard work. The cameramen got the same scanty bread ration of the whole population. The weather was intensely cold. Shouldering their cameras they made more than six miles every day, walking along the ice-bound streets. . . . Galina Zakharova, an assistant producer, made from ten to twelve miles on foot each day, carrying her apparatus. Weary and exhausted Fedulov and Pirogov dragged their lights from one factory to another. . . .'[4]

The German film industries were also engaged on the Russian front. The entire brilliant advance on Moscow was fully covered by cameramen who had been trained in the tanks that smashed through France and in the planes that obliterated Rotterdam. But the Moscow sector was understandably neglected by the cameramen when the Germans began their withdrawal; Goebbels' explanation for the diminished coverage was that cameras were rendered useless by the December frosts. The Russian cameramen who filmed the defeat and retreat on and after December 6th were too busy to let their cameras freeze.

'While the cameraman I. Sokolnikov was filming the action of the partisan detachment in the Podmoskovsky woods, the partisans took turns at warming the equipment he wasn't using. In a captured automobile V. Yeshurin found the automatic camera that a German newsreel cameraman had left behind, still loaded with a film magazine. With this camera and its film he photographed a whole panorama of the field of battle, scattered with fascist bodies, and when the film ran out, he resumed work with his own camera.'[5]

Occupied Ukraine and the Southern front continued to send victory footage to Berlin. There was even a dash of private enterprise: the Ukraine Filmgesellschaft was formed to operate fifty theatres in occupied territory, in which German films prepared with Ukrainian sub-titles were being shown.[6] There was no talk of German-Ukrainian production, however. Film archives, also, were in operation, collecting all captured films for transfer to Berlin, presumably for study. Some German film-makers, too, found themselves in war jobs:

'Before the war there was a Berlin movie actor named Kittel. Occasionally he played minor villains in UFA films. . . . When the war began he found a new vocation; he became an executioner. He had four assistants picked up from the fringe of the Berlin film world. It was they who killed thousands of Riga's citizens. Then Kittel went to Vilna, where he was commissioned to liquidate the ghetto.'[7]

Despite the supremacy, both in quality and in attendance, of the war documentary over the fictional film, the latter continued bravely, under the extraordinary difficulties of wartime production conditions. It was not until 1942 that the first 'fictional' films about the war began to appear from the scattered studios. The first important one to have been begun, Donskoy's adaptation of *How the Steel Was Tempered*, Nikolai Ostrovsky's novel about Civil War, was not finished and released until the end of September 1942. Before that, only two stories that touched the war were distributed to Soviet audiences: *Mashenka*, a delicate and unassuming film about nurses, directed by Yuli Raizman, and *Fellow from Our Town*, directed by Stolper and Ivanov. For a year the only reflection of the war on Soviet screens was in newsreels, documentary film (or newsreels of feature length), and in the short *Album* films.

The *Albums* influenced the war features, once the new Asian studios got started. In the third collection one of the stories and its chief character, *Antosha Rybkin*, was so liked that Antosha was expanded into a feature film directed by the same director, Konstantin Yudin, at the Alma-Ata Studio. When the great humorous character of Brave Soldier Schweik, conceived by the Czech novelist Hasek, was examined by the Soyuzdetfilm directors for adaptation to this war, not only did Schweik, now an involuntary fascist soldier, find his way into the seventh collection, but a full-length comedy of his *New Adventures* was prepared by Sergei Yutkevich at Stalinabad, with Boris Tenin playing Schweik. Pudovkin put aside his plan for a sequel to *Suvorov*, and in his first months in Alma-Ata worked on the most ambitious result of the *Album* form—*The Face of Fascism* (once called *School for Villainy* and later titled *Murders Are on Their Way*), based on a series of sketches by Berthold Brecht—*Furcht und Elend des dritten Reiches*, scenes of the first years of Nazi power in Germany, beginning in 1933. When completed, however, it seemed too gentle a treatment of an enemy that the audience was now desperately protecting itself against, and it was shelved—the only completed Pudovkin film that we have not seen in any form.

Films initiated before the invasion continued to appear throughout the war, struggling through the confusion of moved studios and changed circumstances; the new background of real war altered the viewpoint of many a pre-war scenario. Donskoy's last pre-war subject, *Romantics*,[*] described by Catherine de la Roche as 'about the first school organized by Soviet pioneers for Chukchee children in the Far Eastern Arctic', appeared at the end of 1941, after Donskoy had been working for five months on his first wartime film. The more militant historical film by the Vasilievs, *Defence of Tsaritsin* (Stalingrad), acquired an even more militant tone by the time it was released in March 1942. The Ukrainian *Parkhomenko*, shifted with the Kiev studio to Tashkent in August, finally reached the screen in July 1942. The Mongolian film begun just before the invasion *His Name Is Sukhe-Bator*, directed by Zarkhi and Heifitz, appeared in October. A version of *The Prince and the Pauper*, emphasizing all of Twain's satirical intent more than his dramatic framework, was ready early in 1943. Romm's *Dream*, prepared in Moscow, was completed in Tashkent, and out by September 1943.

[*] A half-hour version, entitled *Children of the Soviet Arctic*, was shown in all British war factories at lunch-hour.

The grandest project of pre-war months was Eisenstein's script of *Ivan the Terrible*.

Put aside after the invasion for a feature-length newsreel film to be made with Quentin Reynolds (a project halted by the removal of the correspondents to Kuibyshev), both *Ivan* and Eisenstein were first moved from Moscow to Baku, and then to Alma-Ata. Here Eisenstein's attention was chiefly turned to the supervision of the reorganized studio, and the later transfer of VGIK to Alma-Ata (where his hope was finally realized that Kuleshov would be appointed head of the school), so that the actual photography of *Ivan the Terrible* was not begun until April 22, 1943, in the more hopeful atmosphere after the German surrender at Stalingrad. Meanwhile he had had the joy of seeing his first published book. Soon after the invasion he had written to me, proposing that four connected essays recently printed in *Iskusstvo Kino* be translated for American and English publication. A year later, in August 1942, *The Film Sense* appeared in New York, and I had the good luck to get the first copy to him through Grigori Irsky, just returning to the Soviet Union after purchasing American film equipment.

No assignment seemed impossible to the newsreel cameramen.* When the Germans reached the Black Sea and the fight continued out onto and under the water, this too was recorded with competence and fullness, in *Men of the Black Sea*. The whole Arctic operation that made Allied contact possible through the Barents Sea and Murmansk was covered in *69th Parallel*, an efficient film organized by Belayev and Oshurkov. On June 13, 1942, cameramen on all fronts contributed to a wartime sequel to *A Day in a New World*:

'From headquarters in Moscow, assignments for the film were sent to all parts of the Soviet Union. We asked that the camermen strive for outward effect, in preference to inner significance or film dramatizations. Everyone was told of the actual date only two days in advance. Early in the morning of the thirteenth work was begun by 240 cameramen at 140 "filming points" scattered throughout the Soviet Union. The first to begin was M. Glider, in the Far East. . . .

'The morning of the thirteenth in Moscow, with which the picture opens, was filmed by F. Provorov. . . . A. Lebedev succeeded in taking shots from a tank turret, during a battle on the North-western Front. . . . Bunimovich filmed the repulse of a German tank attack on the South-western Front. . . . M. Oshurkov filmed a submarine cruise in the Barents Sea. . . . Also noteworthy was the work of S. Fomin, who recorded an artillery bombardment of Leningrad, and D. Rymarev's and B. Mikosha's Sevastopol scenes, in the taking of which Mikosha was wounded. On that day, too, veteran cameramen P. Yermolov [a veteran of the Civil War newsreel who had photographed six Protazanov films and the Gorky trilogy] was wounded on the Kalinin Front, and I. Veinerovich in a guerrilla detachment.'[8]

A month and a half later the edited result was on the screen, as *A Day of War*, a film that told so much about the many sides of war in Russia that it was highly

---

* Later in the war, to record the fighting in Eastern Prussia at even closer range, Medvedkin requisitioned forty sergeants to learn how to operate automatic hand-cameras.

valued on Allied screens as well. Mikhail Slutsky who, with the writing help of Alexei Kapler, organized and edited the film, wrote hopefully:

'This will not be the last film of its kind. I believe the time is not far off when we will make "A Day of Victory". We also hope to produce, together with our friends abroad, a film to be called "Moscow-London-Washington", about the united anti-Hitlerite front. Such a film may become a document of the greatest historical significance, which mankind will treasure for ages to come.'

One of the war's greatest film achievements was the making of *Stalingrad*, directed by Varlamov with a crew of cameramen that changed its personnel with remarkable infrequency during the six months of the stand at Stalingrad—from the first German air-attacks on August 23, 1942, through the incredible street-to-street, house-to-house, room-to-room battles that ended in a German surrender on January 31, 1943, ten years after Hitler took power. Roman Karmen, who helped in the last days of the battle and film, does not conceal his glee:

'We filmed the surrender of Field Marshal von Paulus—a moment we had all been eagerly awaiting. In one sector on the western outskirts of Stalingrad we recorded the surrender of Lieutenant-General von Daniel, Commander of the 376th Division. The camera caught him walking down the street in full-dress, followed by a file of luggage-laden officers.'

The newsreel and documentary accomplishments of the war were so obviously distinguished that their cameramen were repeatedly rewarded and honoured. In January 1942 the Cinema Committee, just before moving back triumphantly from Novosibirsk to their old Moscow quarters, gave special commendations to thirty newsreel cameramen working at the fronts. When the Stalin Prizes for 1941 were announced in April 1942 the film list included, alongside the artists responsible for *Bogdan Khmelnitsky, Defence of Tsaritsin, Girl from Leningrad*, and *Swineherd and Shepherd*, the seventeen directors and chief cameramen of *Moscow Strikes Back* and *Day in a New World*.

And Roman Karmen was among the speakers at the Conference on American and British Cinema, organized by VOKS on August 21-22, 1942. A friendly and mutually respectful relationship among the film-makers of the three Allies, so hopefully counted on by Slutsky, was to last only three more years, only as long the Allies needed each other to win the war. Looking back, it now seems almost dream-like to read the messages of greeting to this Conference from Samuel Goldwyn, the Warner Brothers, Darryl Zanuck, David Selznick, Walt Disney, and to read the speeches of Eisenstein and Pudovkin, who were to speak so differently about the American cinema a few years later. It was Dovzhenko, recently emerging from his months with the army, who pronounced the words most consistent with both past and future:

'Film workers, do not varnish the world of today, do not put "make up" on the world in your pictures! The world is now very ill. Do not divert your art to trivial, individual matters. The cinema can and must set itself great aims. The cinema must give the answers to the sorest, sharpest contemporary problems. It must honestly help suffering mankind to find its bearings.'[9]

When the evacuated film-makers settled down to the job of dramatizing the war continuing on the now safely remote fronts, there were fresh physical obstacles. Russian journalists who visited the new Asian studios remarked some of the normal difficulties of filming war stories in these surroundings. Amasovich visited the Tashkent Studio in a 'merciless' Central Asian heat (fifty degrees above zero, Centigrade) to find Kalatozov and Gerasimov making their film about Leningrad's defence (*Invincible*) in a set of snowdrifts and a cast in winter clothing.[10] With the Ukraine occupied by German troops, Novogrudsky accompanied Igor Savchenko on a journey from Turkmenia to Siberia, seeking believable locations for use in *Partisans of the Ukrainian Steppes*.[11] To convey the hardships of a Ukrainian winter in *The Rainbow*, Donskoy and his cast had to make double use of the Stanislavsky method to forget they were in Turkestan. Pudovkin, who had never made exteriors in a studio, was forced to film the whole of Simonov's play, *Russian People*, carefully protected from the real exteriors around Alma-Ata; he could not but agree when Ivor Montagu wrote him that the result was 'airless'.

'I like natural settings in the cinema and cannot abide artificial sets. I do not like to build up a scene but to seek it out. A forest built in the studio bores me. It takes away all the fascination and joy of the game. I cannot find in it what others see. I can discover nothing in the studio.'[12]

This may have been a factor in Dovzhenko's decision to work in other media during the war, though I suspect that there were more serious conflicts behind his choice. He remained in Moscow, writing, instead of joining his studio at Ashkhabad. In 1942 a volume of his stories was published, *The Great Comradeship*, containing 'Night Before the Battle', and 'Ukraine in Flames'.[13] More of his stories appeared during the war, and in 1943 he published a novel, *Victory*, of which he said in an interview, 'I wrote it in October of last year as a result of my stay at the front. In this book I describe all that I saw with my own eyes, all that I myself experienced.' To the play he finished at the front, *Measure of Life*, he added a sequel, *Ukraine in Flames*:

'I want to express in this play the boundless sufferings and great sacrifices made by my people in the struggle against the fascist invader. . . . I shall also use this theme for a new film script, putting on the screen, for all to see, the monstrous sins of the Hitlerites, and exposing their deep-rooted hatred for man and for all that is humane. I shall try to impregnate my play and film with the noble resentment of the people, their fearlessness, hatred for the fascist enslavers, self-sacrifice and valour. Stalin will be one of the main characters in the play and script.'[14]

The film was not made, nor did he work in any studio, except the Central Newsreel Studio, for the duration. *The Fight for Our Soviet Ukraine*, directed by Yulia Solntseva and Yakov Avdeyenko, and supervised by Dovzhenko, is a documentary feature quite unlike the organized and efficient wartime documentaries from other Soviet film-makers. From its opening scenes of the rich Ukrainian crops of 1941, waiting for harvest, but reaped by bombers, this is an astonishingly *personal* film, making one believe that its 'supervisor' had controlled all of its seemingly uncontrollable elements of unstaged reality. It is obvious that the 'directors' and the twenty-four cameramen believed unitedly in Dovzhenko. Though not signed by him, except as author of its commentary, this is as much *his* film as was *Earth*; it has an equally passionate lyricism, and maintains the same high level of tension. The finished film is also an exhibit of the capacity of one powerful, determined artist to mould the most inflexible materials to his own viewpoint—it could be an inspiration to every artist who works in the documentary film.

Near the end of the war the same united group made another feature documentary, *Victory in the Ukraine and the Expulsion of the Germans from the Boundaries of the Ukrainian Soviet Earth**, with the same power and personality of its predecessor. Just as the montage of this film was being completed, Dovzhenko took part in a discussion on the American series, *Why We Fight*, in which he gave a vivid glimpse of his own documentary method:

'Once we needed shots of mud—just the sort of shot that directors usually reject and for which cameramen are growled at. When these shots of mud—in themselves saying nothing at all—were joined together in a sequence about the difficulties of the 1944 offensive on the left bank of the Ukraine, they acquired point and meaning. Now they are accompanied by a commentary on how these infinite expanses, washed in the blood of Soviet people like the fields under spring floods, saw the destiny of mankind decided, for here the military art of Nazi Germany was crushed and the liberation of Europe was assured. And instantly this vast stretch of mud begins to gleam like something precious. One does not need pathos to express deep emotion—pathos can be born not from a raised voice but from a profound and truthful assembly of materials.'[15]

These two 'documents' are the least known and least studied films of all Dovzhenko's work, though with great significance for both his career and for this period of Soviet film history. He had acutely observed that the fierce, direct material of the war newsreel feature gave its makers a freedom from the wearingly bureaucratic censorship that he had experienced in *Shchors*, and that was even more minutely applied to the wartime studio film. Perhaps we have the shelving of Pudovkin's Brecht film to thank for Dovzhenko's war documentaries.

After Donskoy's *How the Steel Was Tempered*, wartime studio films appeared regularly and with increasing assurance. Though based on a Civil War novel, Donskoy's script chose only those chapters about Ukrainian resistance to the German invaders of 1918, filming them in such a way that the story's parallels with the current invasion were emphasized. [Fifteen years later, in 1957, a team of young directors again filmed Ostrovsky's novel (as *Pavel Korchagin*) with such a different aim that the two films do not seem to have a common source.] Donskoy

---

* This was exhibited abroad as *Ukraine in Flames*, but it has no relation to Dovzhenko's story, play, or film project of that title.

also gave the film a structure resembling that of the Gorky trilogy—a boy accumulates lessons in his encounters with life. Both in Donskoy's film and in 'Beacon', his contribution to the *Albums*, as in many films that followed from the studios, it was the heroism of individuals in partisan activity that furnished plot and drama—usually showing co-ordinated action of partisan detachments and regular army. Pyriev's *Secretary of the District Committee* employed such a subject, as did Savchenko's *Partisans in the Ukrainian Steppes* (based on Korneichuk's play about 1918), Ermler's *She Defends Her Country*, and Pudovkin's *In the Name of the Fatherland* (from Simonov's play)—all released in the winter of 1942 and the spring of 1943, when partisan heroism still furnished the most exciting news stories. Of these the most successful was Ermler's film, with Vera Maretskaya as 'Comrade P' (the original title of the script)—a peasant woman whose husband is killed at the front. Maretskaya, for whom the film and rôle had been written, later wrote of the preview of the completed film, at which the rest of the crew and friends had nothing to say to her:

' "What a strange thing our art must be", I thought, "I must have bungled my part—yet I felt my playing was lifelike."

'It was only the next day that I learned the cause of this silence on the part of my comrades. Just before the preview a telegram had been received announcing that my husband had been killed at the front, and my friends had decided not to show it to me on the day of the first screening. Excepting myself, everyone in the hall knew of this, as they sat watching me give an impersonation of what had actually happened to me in real life.

'Since then I have never seen this film again. . . .'[16]

For her work in Ermler's film Maretskaya was made a People's Artist. *She Defends Her Country* was one of the few Soviet films to be dubbed for English and American audiences and, in spite of a prejudice against English dubbing, this film (as *No Greater Love*) vastly increased its foreign audience with the adaptation.

One symptom of growing assurance reflected in fictional handling of the war was the development, presently, of attempts at 'light' stories of wartime, encouraged by the comedies that were often part of the *Albums*. *Actress*, directed by Ilya Trauberg, was an agreeable comedy about an evacuated musical comedy singer. Yevgeni Petrov's last script, *Air-Chauffeur*, was directed by Herbert Rappoport; in Baku Alexandrov made *One Family* (which I have not seen); and Simonov's tender love-poem, *Wait for Me*, was filmed appealingly by Stolper and Ivanov. All of these appeared in the last half of 1943; a year later there was even a musical comedy about the war! *At Six p.m. After the War*, directed by Pyriev with Ladynina and Samoilov, was the surest signal the Soviet audience had that they were winning the war, surer than any moral exhortation from the top, such as they had been hearing since the first tragic June and December. There was, in 1944, a competition for comedy scenarios, but times had changed again before the winning entries could be filmed.

Comedies, however, especially good ones, remained rare. It was more natural for fiction about war to be serious, even tragic. The last film of 1943 was *Front*, directed by the Vasilievs from Korneichuk's play—a seriously unpleasant drama of old versus young commanders. The first film of 1944 was the first dramatic film to have a value beyond the war: *The Rainbow*, Wanda Wasilewska's adaptation of her novel about occupied Ukraine, directed with all the anger that Donskoy was capable of expressing—an anger missing from his first war film. Donskoy's enemy portraits were more subtle and more powerful than in previous fictional films, possibly because he took the trouble to interview and study a number of German prisoners, both officers and soldiers. Hans Klering, who plays the German garrison commander, gives as credible a performance as the group of fine actresses: Natalia Uzhvy, Nina Alisova, Yelena Tyapkina.

The tragic heroes of this period were usually women and children. The story of the real eighteen-year-old Zoya Kosmodemyanskaya, working behind the German lines, captured, tortured, and hanged, was made into a surprisingly lyrical film by Lev Arnstam. Both *Zoya* and Eisimont's film of Leningrad children, *Once There Was a Girl*, have poetic qualities that distinguish them from all other films of the period. Even with the lessons that it teaches, *Zoya* could be called a successfully impressionist film, in performance as well as in photography.

'When Zoya is shown on her last road, at night, walking through the snow, spectators first see her bare feet and slender legs, then her whole figure in vague outline against a background of whirling snow, and then her radiant and inspired face, seeming lit from within by the flame of her thoughts and emotions.'[17]

In praising the equally touching *Once There Was a Girl*, Lev Kassil, himself a writer of children's books, has one complaint—the film's neglect of the adult characters, even though the film is dedicated to children:

'. . . one cannot help wishing that the mother (Ada Voitsik) would abandon—were it only now and then—the plaintive key she uses so invariably from the very outset of the story, or that the good Head of the Tenement House Office were not quite so unalterably and touchingly good.'[18]

Girl No. 217, on the other hand, is as hard and harsh as its subject demanded. The story, by Gabrilovich, is set in a German family that has acquired a Russian slave. Mikhail Romm makes their treatment of the slave-girl (played by Kuzmina) as much of an agony for us as it is for her. No dramatic or cinematic device for underlining villainy has been overlooked. The camera team, Volchok and Savelyova, had worked on Pudovkin's Brecht film, so that their skilful conveyance of the terrible atmosphere of the Brecht stories has also been absorbed by Romm's image of Nazi Germany. *Invasion*, adapted from Leonov's play and directed by Abram Room, suffered from the disunity of the play: one act of psychologically credible characters in a real situation, one act of fantastic satire, one act of blatant melodrama.

How gentle and harmless American films about the war must have seemed to Russian audiences! The first American film to be dubbed during the war was Henry King's *In Old Chicago*—the Chicago fire was a catastrophe that could be comprehended here. Hollywood's reflections of the war in Russia were received generously as commendable American gestures to an ally, but they must have been far less comprehensible. A dubbed version of *Mission to Moscow*, the Warner Brothers' contribution, appeared on Moscow screens in July 1943, followed a year later by *North Star*, Lillian Hellman's scenario for Samuel Goldwyn, directed by Lewis Milestone, and *Song of Russia*, Metro-Goldwyn-Mayer's musical. The Capra unit's *Battle of Russia*, compiled from Soviet newsreels and captured German newsreels, needed no excuses. A British film, Noel Coward's *In Which We Serve*, made a more serious impression than any other foreign dramatic film about the war. The best-known American film had nothing to do with the war; indeed, it wasn't even as a film that it made its Soviet fame: the Capra-Riskin comedy, *It Happened One Night*, adapted for the stage in 1942 as *New York-Miami Bus*, became the most popular play to run during the Leningrad siege. The past and present work of Chaplin was honoured repeatedly, but it is a little strange to read serious Soviet critical studies of the art of Deanna Durbin or Bing Crosby.

The Stalin Prizes for 1942, announced in March 1943, were awarded to the makers of *Georgi Saakadze* (Part One), *Mashenka*, *Secretary of the District Committee*, and the newsreel features: *Stalingrad*, *Siege of Leningrad*, *Men of the Black Sea*, and other newsreel cameramen who did distinguished work in 1942.* In September 1943 the Cinema Committee again drew attention to the industry's indebtedness to the newsreel cameramen by awards and advancements. And in the giant list of 490 film awards and new orders on April 14, 1944, the most dangerous film-work was amply recognized again. Donskoy was the only studio regisseur to receive the Order of Lenin, and all Orders of the Red Banner went to front-line cameramen.

Film makers already working in their own Asian studios received great technical help and encouragement from the evacuees (many of the wartime studio films had Asian co-directors) who, for their part, were inevitably tempted by their new exotic surroundings to draw upon them for film subjects. 'Film-concerts' were made of Uzbek, Kazakh, and Tadjik arts. Zguridi's wartime nature study was *In the Sands of Central Asia*; an equally important film in this genre was made by Zguridi's former assistant, Dolin, *The Law of the Great Love*, filming a family of foxes in the Siberian forest. (This latter film was unique among Soviet nature films in fusing delicate sensitivity with pitiless realism.) The first feature film of the evacuated studios to use their new locale was *Son of Tadjikistan*, directed by Pronin—a story of a Tadjik soldier in the Red Army, with scenes at the front and at home. Both Stroyeva and Roshal made local subjects at Alma-Ata, but the only memorable wartime piece of *exotica in situ* was made by Protazanov—*Nasreddin in Bukhara*, based on the store of folk legends around the witty and ingenious Nasreddin, protector of the poor and unhappy, a thorn in the side of every emir and clerk. Protazanov had weathered a heart attack on his way to Tashkent, but he soon came back to work on his last film, one of his best comedies, set against the beauties of ancient Uzbekistan, photographed by Dovzhenko's former cameraman, Danylo Demutski. Nasreddin was played by the expert Lev Sverdlin with a lightness of touch and movement that I had not

* These were the last wartime Stalin Prizes; those for 1943-44 were announced in February 1946.

seen since Sverdlin's days with Meyerhold. Without the athletic quality of Douglas Fairbanks, Sverdlin, with more wit, was able to rival *The Thief of Baghdad* himself. An attempt was made at a sequel to *Nasreddin*, but without Protazanov and Sverdlin it could not rise to the original's comic height.

To the home-front, protected from enemy bombers, was dedicated a series of politically important films that I am unable to judge, having seen none of them in America. In the first months of the war the scenarist Mikhail Papava lived on a collective farm in Gorky Province, and brought back to his own industry a story of wartime farmers that Boris Babochkin, in collaboration with the former designer Bosulayev, chose for his first work in film direction. *Native Fields* is better remembered for his performance in it than for its direction. Gerasimov, a native of the Urals, made a story, *The Great Earth*, or *Mainland*, about a town in the Urals that receives a factory and staff evacuated from Leningrad. Another film about the evacuation of a factory eastward was more realistic in showing the confusions and tragedies of such wholesale displacements, and had a stormy career for that reason. Kozintsev and Trauberg must have planned *Plain People* for production in Alma-Ata, for its setting is a new factory town constructed in the desert of Uzbekistan, to house the workers of a Leningrad aeroplane factory. But by the summer of 1944, when the script was ready for filming, it was possible to return to Leningrad, and *Plain People* was the first production finished after the war's end to appear from the restored Lenfilm. Ermler, who headed the other crew to return to work there, described the studio, hit by thirty-two German shells:

'All the machinery had been wrecked, and in filming we had to use old, anti-quated lighting equipment. Wednesdays were off-days for filming, as this was rehabilitation day, when everyone—directors, actors, technical staff—from studio head to commissionaire—rolled up their sleeves and gave a hand in rebuilding the wrecked studio.'[19]

Interest in the country's past had not been diminished by the war. Stalin's frequent references to Alexander Nevsky and Suvorov made everyone conscious of the historical link between Russia's history and today's Patriotic War—and encouraged film-makers to continue their search for dramatic material in the real past. When the moved studios were able to face the problem, several large historical films were begun. *Georgi Saakadze*, Part Two of Chiaureli's epic of seventeenth-century Georgia, and Bek-Nazarov's *David-Bek*, about Armenia's war of independence from Persia, came from the less disturbed Caucasian studios. When some groups of Mosfilm returned to their damaged studio (a year earlier than the return to Lenfilm), one of the first films to start was, appropriately, *Kutuzov*, about the expulsion of Napoleon from Moscow and the destruction of his army. Director Vladimir Petrov arranged for the filming of the battle of Borodino to take place on the 131st anniversary of the battle, in August 1943. Alexei Diky, after playing Field Marshal Kutuzov, went directly into the rôle of Admiral Nakhimov, in Pudovkin's film of the Crimean War, also at Mosfilm. The wish for a sequel to *Suvorov* was cancelled with the death of Cherkasov-Sergeyev; audiences would accept no one else in the rôle. A surprisingly beautiful

Lermontov, delayed by the war beyond the anniversary year, came from Soyuzdet-film, still at Stalinabad. The most awaited of the historical films was *Ivan the Terrible*.

Eisenstein's several aims in making *Ivan the Terrible* have continued and will continue to be defined and argued. The theories find no common ground and do little to resolve the many questions the film evokes. For years we had only three pieces of evidence—the released version of *Ivan*, Part One; the published script of the whole two-part (later three-part) film; and denunciations and rumours of the unreleased *Ivan*, Part Two. On this basis were formed the political interpreta-tion (Ivan IV shown as a prototype of Stalin), the psychological interpretation (explored, in detail, through Chapter XV of Marie Seton's biography of Eisen-stein), the artistic interpretation (usually the formal freezing of a too deliberate artist), and other theories that explore side-issues or private phobias. Now we have another important piece of evidence, the released version of *Ivan*, Part Two. (The sequences filmed for Part Three are, it sadly appears, now un-recoverable.) A last piece of evidence will, I hope, become generally available soon: Eisenstein's notes and drawings in preparing the entire work. Weighing these materials brings one to the conclusion that the best perspective on *Ivan the Terrible* is still that given by Eisenstein in an introductory article on his approach to the historical place and complex character of Ivan IV:

'And thus—concealing nothing, smoothing over nothing in the history of the actions of Ivan Grozny—detracting nothing from the formidably impressive romanticism of that splendid image of the past, it has been our wish to present it in all its integrity to the audience of the world. This image—fearful and wonder-ful, attracting and repelling, utterly tragic in Ivan Grozny's inner struggle along with his struggle against the enemies of his country—can be comprehensible to the man of our day.'[20]

A reading of the whole scenario, and a viewing of both parts—the only just way to experience Eisenstein's last film—shows a scrupulous execution of this large programme that he set himself. Ivan's historical 'mission' is never lost sight of, nor are the human contradictions in his motives and behaviour, along which the main dramatic line is built. The separation of the two parts by the film's critics is a fault for which they are not entirely responsible, for Eisenstein could not have foreseen how many years would pass between the appearance of Parts One and Two. Seen together at last, the majestic, ceremonial qualities of Part One, growing more passionate towards its conclusion, are transformed into the flaming bitter-ness and physical violence of Part Two. The calculated stylistic growth of the whole drama could only be guessed by the disgruntled critics of Part One, in-cluding the outraged Hollywood audience at its Academy preview. To see Part Two by itself must have been equally a shock to the private political viewers in 1946—here was the intrigue and carnage of *Hamlet*'s conclusion without the preparation and artistic justification of the first two acts, or the torture and storm of *Lear* without the introductory dramatic mask of ceremony and hypocrisy that Shakespeare spent scene by scene, stripping away. If any of the Kremlin viewers had some parallel with Stalin in mind,* or even felt the need to change the popular concept of the *Terrible,* one can imagine how personally insulting Ivan's drama appeared.

An error, possibly fatal for both the work and its creator, may have been made in the war-time decision to divide Part Two, as published, into two parts—to produce a trilogy. Several scenes planned for the original Part Two required northern exteriors (and Tisse) that could not be adapted to the studio work in Alma-Ata. (In any case, reading the published Part Two today, it is difficult to see how all its material and ideas could ever have been crowded into a film of normal length.) The resulting trilogy plan thus concluded with a Part Three of great mass movement, battle, breadth, etc., transforming the new Part Two into a purely 'interior' dramatic interlude between grander and more open sections. This doomed Part Two to a concentration on psychology and on intrigue, the most dangerous elements in any 'social' treatment of Ivan's reign.

For a project of such complex magnitude it is good to see that Eisenstein was just as intent on efficiency of schedule and budget as in the simpler *Nevsky,* regardless of the multiplied problems of filming in the Palace of Culture at Alma-Ata—possible only at night, when the munitions factories were not using the power. Within a year after its start, in April 1943, almost all of Part One was in the cutting-room, along with much of Part Two; later scenes had often been filmed out of sequence, for the benefit of the set-builders and outside demands on the actors in the cast. The photography was divided between Tisse, who took the exteriors (including the siege of Kazan, and the thrilling 'shots in depth' at the end of Part One), and Andrei Moskvin, who filmed all interiors, the larger part of the film. The colour sequences of Part Two were also filmed by Moskvin. After a generation of discreet film colour it is a new stimulation to see colour used indiscreetly, boldly, and with ideas. Like another group of instruments it heightens every purpose it is applied to, and you can almost hear Prokofiev encouraged to orchestrate for it, with the same unreal dramatic enhancement that is in the boyarina's ambitious lullaby when her exultation is suddenly supported chorally. Though the cathedral climax between the two colour passages was filmed earlier in black and white, the transitions between colour and monochrome were turned ingeniously to the film's advantage.

The tasks that Eisenstein gave to the actors caused more friction than in any of his previous experiences with trained actors, for their training had not prepared them for the heroic Elizabethan manner, the startling 'noble' style invented for *Ivan.* The staging of Shakespeare tragedy had grown increasingly realistic; the works of his more extreme contemporaries, Marlowe and Webster, impossible to play realistically, were almost unknown in the Soviet theatre (though beloved by Eisenstein); and the one Russian 'Elizabethan' drama, Pushkin's *Boris Godunov,*† was unthinkable except on a realist stage. The most resistance came from the most trained actors; up to Eisenstein's death Nikolai Cherkasov (whom I had seen

---

* Plays about Ivan ran into the same trouble, trying to resolve the new historical attitude to him with a minimum of blood-letting. † In his Pushkin project of 1940 Eisenstein had tackled the problem of *Boris*; a facsimile has been published (*Iskusstvo Kino,* Mar. 1959) of his plan to film Boris's monologue, in a style anticipating *Ivan.*

play happily in *Boris* with another realist actor, Babochkin) complained bitterly of the compositions he had been twisted into, the aching positions he had been forced to maintain.

'Carried away by his enthusiasm for pictorial composition, Eisenstein moulded expressive, monumental *mises-en-scène*, but it was often difficult to justify the content of the form he was striving to achieve. In some of his *mises-en-scène*, extremely graphic in idea and composition, an actor's strained muscles often belied his inner feelings. In such cases, the actor found it difficult indeed to mould the image demanded of him. Eisenstein insisted that his ideas be carried out. This insistence infected us. . . .

'My confidence in the film waned and my worries grew with each passing day. After watching scenes of the second part run through I criticized some episodes, but Eisenstein brushed my criticisms aside, and in the end stopped showing me edited bits altogether. In films, it is the director who has the last word.'[21]

For this style Eisenstein had no need for the shadings and delicate indications that Cherkasov had learned with such psychological 'truth'. When Michael Chekhov saw the film in America, he could not believe that his former colleague, Serafima Birman, could have accepted such a 'betrayal' of all their lessons without protest. On the other hand, younger actors—such as Ludmila Tselikovskaya (playing Ivan's bride) and Pavel Kadochnikov—enjoyed the new problems Eisenstein gave them.

'The grandeur of our subject called for monumental means of presentation. . . . This was how the style of the film was determined, a style that ran counter to many of the traditional methods to which we have grown accustomed. . . . The general custom is to try to make the historical personage "accessible", to portray him as an ordinary person sharing the ordinary, human traits of all other people— to present him "in dressing-gown and nightcap".

'But with Ivan we wanted a different tone. In him we wished chiefly to convey a sense of majesty, and this led us to adopt majestic forms. We had the actors speak in measured tones, frequently accompanied by music. . . .'[22]

The unified 'deliberate' film, especially the film that does not conceal its maker's calculation, has always been the least popular film anywhere in the world—in and out of the film industry. A *Rashomon* or a *Cobweb Castle* will always have a harder life than a *Gate of Hell*; a Murnau or a Dreyer will always suffer more than a Lubitsch or a Huston. The rare film artist who defies the spontaneous, to show that the medium can invent as well as mirror, has as much to contribute to the future of cinema as do all the great artists—including Chaplin, Dovzhenko, Fellini—who treasure the *effect* of improvisation. Since the release of *Ivan*, Part One, there has been some slight use, by Soviet and foreign film-makers, of the lessons it teaches, but full use of *Ivan*'s art apparently awaits for the future.

By 1944 the world, including that part of it controlled by the German and Japanese armies, realized that the balance of war had turned against the Axis. On March 26th Konyev's army reached the Prut River, the first return to the boundary of June 22, 1941, and went right on, into the enemy territory of Rumania. In April the Russians retook Odessa and Sevastopol, and a new Allied offensive began in Italy—it was clear that Hitler's Europe was to be invaded from the west, co-ordinating with a renewed Russian offensive in the east, and on June 6th a 'second front' was opened on the Normandy beaches; there were American and British cameramen in the first landing-craft.

A fresh confidence showed in all phases of Soviet life in the summer of 1944. As usual, in crisis as in success, the film industry had a broad organizational over-hauling. In September two important experiments were initiated. A special Theatre for Film-Actors was formed, under the direction of a committee of actors and directors; and an Artistic Council of twenty-two members was appointed by Bolshakov to plan all productions and, with duties and powers rather like those of a supreme court, to handle all questions (except purely industrial or technological ones) that could not be settled within the lower art councils at the studios. The composition of the Council was formidable: six directors—Eisenstein, Pudovkin, Romm, Alexandrov, Chiaureli, Savchenko; a cameraman—Moskvin; four writers; five actors—including Babochkin, Cherkasov, Okhlopkov; four composers—including Shostakovich; and two military consultants. The Council met every Thursday at two p.m., examined current production plans and heard all cases for the week (troubles and problems of all degrees) until three-thirty—time for the screening of a newly completed film or an unfinished problem film. The entire crew and cast of the screened film would take part in the following discussion. After a balloting on each point at issue (for example, is this change required or only recommended ?), the Council's findings were turned over directly to the film's director; Bolshakov would endorse this judgment, intervening only in an equal division of votes. If any member of the Council held out against the majority decision, not only could he file his minority opinion, but he could also have the entire question reviewed at the following week's meeting.

At the same time the two largest studios acquired new artistic supervisors: with Ermler busy with his film about a general, Sergei Vasiliev was made head of Lenfilm; Eisenstein was deep in *Ivan* and Alexandrov was appointed in his place at Mosfilm. In order to direct at Mosfilm, Yutkevich was relieved of his admini-strative duties at Soyuzdetfilm, where Savchenko took his place. Ptushko was put in charge of Soyuzmultfilm, the animation studio. An interesting appointment was that of Sergei Gerasimov, made head of the Documentary Film Studio, a post that he kept through the end of the war. A film organization of great useful-ness to the whole war effort—the studio that produced teaching films—was moved back to Moscow from Sverdlovsk. The quiet makers of instructional films, joined by most of the animated cartoon technicians, were busily employed throughout the war, keeping close on the heels of the war's progress. One can almost watch the changing character of the war in the many dozens of instructional defence film titles: 1942—*How to Fight the Enemy's Tanks*; 1943—*How to Manoeuvre Heavy Bombers*; 1944—*Driving a Packard*; 1945—*Fighting Behind the Enemy's Lines*.

With the approach of the war's end, even the most wounded communities were returning to a semblance of normal life, not without memories of their tragedies. Dovzhenko restored something of his home:

'My mother survived. When our soldiers re-entered Kiev [in November 1943], she went up to them and asked, "Haven't you seen my son, Dovzhenko?" This was repeated and came to the ears of Khrushchov and Zhukov; they told me, "Your mother goes through the streets of Kiev asking the soldiers for you." I found her in a cellar where she lived with twelve other old women, like animals, for lack of everything.

'After my apartment was cleared of mines I installed my mother there. Later she came to live with us in Moscow, where she would stand at the window looking down at the street, saying over and over, "Why are all those poor people always running, always in a hurry?" In the evening she would say, "Let's sing!" and we all sang old Ukrainian tunes. Finally she went back to Kiev. She told us, "When your father died, I told myself I would stay a widow for seven years. Five years have now passed and I don't have much longer. But don't burn me. If you do, I'll come back from the other world to trouble you. Put me in the earth. I love the earth. I want to end there.'[23]

Gerasimov's régime at the Documentary Studio brought in a new element there. Possibly inspired by Dovzhenko's work with the newsreel feature, Gerasimov assigned five important films of the last months of war to directors new to such work. Yuli Raizman was put in charge of the newsreel recording of *Towards an Armistice with Finland* (shown in December 1944), Zarkhi and Heifitz were assigned to *The Defeat of Japan,* and Yutkevich was given all the raw material to edit *Liberated France.* After Finland was passed, Raizman was given the larger responsibility of supervising the cameramen who accompanied the army to the fall of Berlin:

'I had quite a number of cameramen at my disposal and could place them at my discretion. But conditions and circumstances were constantly changing, and filming assignments also, so that it was essential that uninterrupted communication be maintained with the cameramen.

'The Front Command were of great assistance to us in this. They detailed motor-cycle despatch riders to serve our filming group: we were in constant telephone communication with the Army Political Department to which the various cameramen in the field could send in memos with details of what they had filmed. The Front Political Administration kept us posted on all troop movements.

'There was a second channel of communication with the cameramen, through the Secretary of the War Council. . . . Therefore, even when a non-stop fifty mile march was being made, we could tell, at any moment, exactly where one or another cameraman was posted, and give him new filming assignments.

'Director Shpikovsky, group chief Saakov and I had special army permits to use liaison planes, thanks to which, within an hour we could reach any sector of the front to take charge of a particular sequence.'

Raizman found that montage was as essential to the newsreel as to the studio film:

'I recall the disappointment on the faces of those who saw the screened rushes of the scenes of preparation for the decisive offensive against Berlin—I mean those of us who had not been eye-witnesses of these scenes.

'The shots did not seem very vivid—platform cars loaded with tanks, a forest road hidden beneath a huge camouflage net, sappers putting a bridge across a river, trucks fuelling up from a petrol pipeline, another column of trucks concealed in tree-branches and moving into the mist at the river-crossing just built.

'Our companions in the projection-room found this material commonplace and even boring, while it told us a great deal; for we realized the vast scope and scale that these shots indicated, and we were able to appreciate the thoroughness and precision with which the whole operation had been planned and executed.

'We were able to edit this material so that spectators would sense what we had seen, thought, and understood out there, at the front.'

The montage itself was done at great speed:

'We did *Berlin* in sixteen days. Towards the end of May material was still coming in from the laboratory. We aimed the general release for June 22nd, the day when the session of the Supreme Soviet of the USSR was to open, the fourth anniversary of the outbreak of war. And two days later, on June 24th, was to be the VE Day Parade. The film was ready on June 17th.'[24]

One of the cameramen who crossed the Polish border into Germany with the Red Army was killed in action near Breslau; a fitting memorial to Vladimir Sushinsky was a film compiled in 1946, *A Cameraman at the Front,* following his work through the war.

Germany's surrender on May 8, 1945 and Japan's in September after the atom-bombs dropped in August, brought a long, hard war to an end. It was not long before conflicts that had been submerged in the greater crisis came to the surface, domestically and internationally.

Following the Allied victory in Europe and Asia, Soviet cinema honours almost equalled the military honours conferred on the victors—some military and camera honours had been won side by side. Now films begun in war were completed and released in victory. The best of these was, again, by Donskoy—*Unconquered,* adapted from a novel by Boris Gorbatov about occupied Kiev, showing Ukrainians and Jews as fellow-victims and fellow-heroes; the actors were still intimate with the actuality of their rôles:

'The actor Dunaisky who played the old bee-keeper (and Grandpa Okhapko in *The Rainbow*) had lost his family when they were driven off to German slavery.

'The day we shot the most important scene of the film the actress Yelena Tyapkina (Fedosya in *The Rainbow*) received notification of the death of her son.

'Most of the people who worked in our film had left Kiev with the army, undergoing all the ordeals and trials of those first months of war.'[25]

Gorbatov also provided the idea for Leonid Lukov's last wartime film, a story of the Donbas miner, Lukov's favourite subject—*It Happened in the Donbas.* Boris

Barnet made an almost expressionist film for the Armenian studio, *One Night*. Just before victory, Igor Savchenko's brave attempt at a wartime colour-film appeared—*Ivan Nikulin, Russian Sailor*. Inventor Semyon Ivanov and director Andriyevsky resumed work in the autumn of 1944 at the re-opened stereoscope studio, making their first dramatic essay in the new medium of three-dimensional colour-film, *Robinson Crusoe*.

The last of the prodigious newsreel features—*Berlin*—was also the last significant documentary film for some months thereafter; the modes of attack or of poetry would seem more stimulating for the documentary form than the mode of self-congratulation, the prevailing post-victory posture of the Soviet documentary film. When victory came, the friction of physical hardship was removed too suddenly from the Soviet newsreel makers, leaving only a completely mastered technique with its attendant clichés. The next most interesting development in this field came in the winter of 1946-47, when the best documentary artists were assigned to single issues of the newsreel for January and February 1947: 1, Poselsky; 3, Kopalin; 6, Vertov; 7, Shub.

There was a brief period between victory and the creeping, engulfing cold war when people believed that wartime friendships and collaborations could continue. A comic reflection of this hope can be found in the headlines of the *Hollywood Reporter* through the summer of 1945:

'June 22nd—RUSS SEEKING U.S. FILM STARS. Soviet Representative Due Here to Ink Bob Cummings For Rôle In Eisenstein Pic [*War and Peace!*]

'August 10th—RUSSIA PLANS PRODUCTION HERE. Would Aim Films At World Market, Using Borrowed BO Names, Eisenstein [referred to as "film czar in Moscow"] Expected.'

On August 8, 1945, Yakov Protazanov died. The first Russian film director to evolve an original style—a style that contributed to the French film as well as to the Russian—worked to the end on a shooting-script, an adaptation of Ostrovsky's play, *Wolves and Sheep*. Determined to go ahead with the casting of his film, he was so ill that he had to accept Barnet's offer of help; so long as he had the choice, Protazanov worked.

When Eisenstein first proposed to me the book that became *The Film Sense*, he described further writing intended for another 'booklet':

'Am finishing (at last!) the Greco article. Am working on English version of very large article about Griffith and the history of montage through the arts. Will add to it probably a survey of the idea of the Close Up through art history. These three articles could make another little booklet . . . the completion of the articles may take some time. . . .'

Along with other news in letters and cables of the next six years, there was often some reminder of this promised work: in a cable of June 1945, '. . . am completing new book wire if interested publishing' [!]; a cable in September, '. . . just completing second volume will cable details quite soon;' in November, 'Just finishing second volume not including Griffith and Ivan contains three normal articles one enormous large appendix;' a good-humoured letter in January 1946:

'I was (and still am for about three weeks) busy like hell: just finishing to shoot and cut the second part of Ivan. This part includes two reels made in colour [the banquet before the murder of Vladimir]. Colour used in quite different a way, than it is usually done—so that it gives a big additional chapter to what is nearly ready in book form. If everything is all right here with the picture I expect to take a vacation and finish the book—three-quarters of which are ready for print. Most of the stuff is unpublished (part of it even—unwritten yet!) and is mostly concerned with the development of the principles started by "Potemkin" during these twenty years in different media (is that the way to say it?)—treatments of sound, music, colour. The way of composing extatic scenes, etc. "Ivan" in connection with "Potemkin". I will send you a detailed plan as soon as the film goes to the laboratory to be printed. . . .'

Part Two was completed under a great lift of morale; the postponed Stalin Prizes of 1943 and 1944 were announced in early February 1946: the cinema awards (first class) were to the makers of *Kutuzov*, *Ivan the Terrible* (Part One), *Zoya*, *Georgi Saakadze* (Part Two), and *The Rainbow*; prizes (second class) went to the makers of *Invasion*, *At Six p.m. after the War*, *Girl No. 217*, and *She Defends Her Country*.*

The final work on the editing of *Ivan*, Part Two, was done on the day that Part One's prize was to be celebrated. Eisenstein left the cutting-room, for the last time, at ten-thirty p.m., went directly to the dinner of celebration, and while dancing with Vera Maretskaya, at about two a.m., he collapsed on the floor with a heart attack. Five weeks later, lying in the Kremlin Hospital, he described the next few horrible moments to Brooks Atkinson:

'They told him to lie still; they told him not to move, that they would carry him to the hospital.

' "But I was temperamental", Mr Eisenstein continued, "I insisted on getting up and walking to the car unassisted."

'According to the doctors, that is when he died. . . .

' "I am dead right now", he said mischievously. "The doctors say that, according to all rules, I cannot possibly be alive. So this is a postscript for me, and it's wonderful. Now I can do anything I like. I am going to have a good time".'[26]

His 'good time' was to read the accumulation of old and new books that *Ivan* had kept him from; his cable to me of March 21st, renewed the writing promise: '. . . looking forward long reconvalescence entirely devoted writing books.' And on April 18, 1946: '. . . trying hard to recover . . . working on opus two.' At the end of May he was transferred to a sanatorium outside Moscow, and in June, to his cottage in the country. I do not know for how long the news was concealed from him that the Central Committee was extremely critical of Part Two. Unless he was allowed no papers he must have seen the attack in *Soviet-skoye Iskusstvo* (a weekly he always read), of August 16, 1946:

* In newsreel and documentary films: *Rebirth of Stalingrad*, *Towards an Armistice with Finland*, *The People's Avengers*, *In the Sands of Central Asia*, *Law of the Great Love*, and to a group of newsreel cameramen.

'The second part of *Ivan the Terrible* provides a very clear illustration of the results to which a lack of responsibility, a disdainful attitude towards the study of essential material, and a careless and arbitrary treatment of historical themes may lead.'[27]

The Vasilievs also had post-war difficulties. In an article written some years later by Sergei Vasiliev, he gave a discouraging account:

'In 1944 the brothers Vasiliev's suggestion for the production of a film devoted to the Leningrad blockade [script by Tikhonov] was rejected by the Ministry of Cinema on the grounds that after such a terrible war the people needed recreation and therefore entertainment films should be produced.

'After tedious negotiation the brothers Vasiliev were given a new, interesting and useful theme—the struggle of the Slav peoples against the fascist invaders. For this purpose the producers and the script writer Chirskov went on a long trip through the Balkan countries and collected a large amount of interesting material. On their return they found that the Ministry had changed its mind and appointed a new producer and writer for this subject.

'The Ministry suggested a new film for the brothers Vasiliev—Tchaikovsky's opera, *The Queen of Spades*. Fearing to be idle the producers agreed to make this film. Preparations for it had been completed when the theme was removed from the programme.

'Several months passed before they were given a new task. Then suddenly in 1946 the Ministry suggested that the brothers Vasiliev should make a film on the Leningrad blockade!'[28]

Georgi Vasiliev died on June 18, 1946. The obituaries did not refer to his two last wasted years.

A negative period in Soviet film history was introduced by the Central Committee's resolution of September 4, 1946—bypassing the Artistic Council—in a cleansing operation similar to those announced in theatre, literature and music. The particular target of its detailed attack was the second part of *A Great Life*, directed by Leonid Lukov. The main emphasis of the film, the resolution[29] said, was 'placed on a crude representation of all sorts of personal experiences and episodes from daily life'. The restoration of the Don Basin is depicted as 'carried out not by the use of modern advanced techniques and mechanized working procedures, but by crude physical strength, long-obsolete techniques and outmoded work methods'. The restoration 'is pictured as if the initiative of the workers not only received no support from but was opposed by state organizations'. Even the songs 'are pervaded with drunken melancholy and are alien to Soviet people'.

'*A Great Life* [the title is referred to as sounding "like a mockery of Soviet reality"] preaches backwardness, vulgarity and ignorance. The wholesale promotion to top positions of technically semi-literate workers with backward outlook and temperament, as shown by the producers, is completely unreasonable and false. The director and scenarist failed to grasp the fact that in our country it is the modern, cultured people, well acquainted with their field, and not backward and vulgar people, who are highly valued and boldly promoted, and that, now that the Soviet power has created its own intelligentsia, it is ridiculous nonsense to present as reality the promotion of backward and vulgar people to responsible positions.'

This claim is especially embarrassing in view of the resolution's next blow, the condemnation of 'a number of unsuccessful and faulty films': Eisenstein's *Ivan the Terrible*, Part Two, Pudovkin's *Admiral Nakhimov*, Kozintsev and Trauberg's *Plain People*—the considered work of four of the most widely recognized masters of the Soviet cinema, 'modern, cultured people, well acquainted with their field'.

'Pudovkin, for instance, undertook the production of a film on Nakhimov without studying the details of the matter, and distorted historical truth. The result was a film not about Nakhimov but about balls and dances with episodes from the life of Nakhimov.

'Eisenstein in the second part of *Ivan the Terrible* displayed his ignorance of historical facts by portraying the progressive army of the oprichniki as a band of degenerates similar to the American Ku Klux Klan, and Ivan, a man of strong will and character, as a man of no will and little character, something like Hamlet.'

No details were offered for the ban on *Plain People*. The only clue remaining was its criticism in *Sovietskoye Iskusstvo* of two weeks before. Though Bolshakov and his Artistic Council were held responsible for this 'frequent production of incorrect and erroneous films', he did not leave his position, recently strengthened as Minister of Cinema; the new ministry had been created in March 1946. We shall never be able to compare the condemned films (all of which were eventually released in revised versions) with approved films; but the films released in 1946 seem in perspective to stand on a lower level.

The best of them was written by Ermler and Chirskov, *The Great Turning-Point*, originally entitled *General of the Army*:

'The idea of a film about a Soviet general started in February 1942. . . . The summer campaign of 1942 upset more than one expert concept of war and the military art to say nothing of our feeble attempts!

'Gradually we became reconciled to the idea that we had undertaken the impossible and busied ourselves with other work [Ermler directed *She Defends Her Country*, Chirskov collaborated on the scenario of *Zoya*]. Then, the great finale of the battle of Stalingrad electrified the world. Stalingrad was the answer to all the questions that had troubled us. . . .

'Stalingrad supplied the event, but it was too early to produce an historically exact film about Stalingrad; insuperable difficulties confronted the artist the moment he decided to give historical names to his characters . . . [Stalingrad is not mentioned in the finished film.]

'How could we portray the drama of personal human passions through the medium of the professional conversations of generals? How could we express the invisible mental strain of the general bending over a dry map? Where was the struggle in which the fate of heroes was decided? The vision of a map, as a symbol of boredom, dogged us to the very end of our work on this film. To get away from it, we had to resort to past experience, to the tried secrets of traditional dramaturgy. We sought personal conflicts—but there were none, or they were so insignificant that they had no place in the historical drama in which our characters were involved. The idea of depicting the struggle through the alternate picturing of the Soviet and German sides was immediately rejected—there were plenty of puppets representing German officers and soldiers to be seen in other films.

'There was of course the inevitable wish to include romantic incidents by introducing women into the story, but women could not find their way into head-quarters where the main conflict was staged. . . . And we had decided to make a film about generals. In our innermost thoughts we sighed for the additional excitement of the occasional presence of a spy.'[30]

The authors went to the front, then near Kiev, to check on the accuracy of their work. In their talks with General Vatutin (later killed) and with a great number of officers and soldiers, Ermler and Chirskov came near another discouragement. 'What [Vatutin] said gave us to understand that nothing was right in the screen-play we had written. It was too naïve and was overloaded with our own imaginings.'[31]

'This experience was the high point of our work on the scenario. Now we no longer approached our material from the viewpoint of the "laws of dramaturgy" but with a sense of the material itself. . . . The really surprising thing was that front-line life revealed to us the secret of our film's genre. At the front we came to understand that we were not planning a battle film but a psychological film.'[32]

The battle-scenes for *The Great Turning-Point* were shot in the ruins of Lenin-grad, but as the authors said, the originality of their film is in its depiction of the psychological strain on generals who control thousands of lives, not only in the present battle, but in battles to come. Of all films to make drama out of military strategy, including its successors, Ermler's film has the most validity as cinema and, perhaps, as life, too. Mikhail Derzhavin, who plays General Muravyov (a composite of several generals whom the authors met) is as credible in the rôle as Filimonov in *Fragment of an Empire*, or the old people in *Counterplan*. Similar to his work on having the Filimonov character's outer aspect accepted, Ermler was not content with his Muravyov until officers on the street saluted him. [The 'historically exact' film about Stalingrad that Ermler could not make was written at this time by Nikolai Virta and issued in 1947. Petrov filmed both parts of *The Battle of Stalingrad* (1949 and 1950) in a glorified manner that had become standard practice for showing Stalin, acted here by Alexei Diky, as Supreme Commander.]

Two good-looking films of the year; Arnstam's *Glinka*, and Ptushko's fairy-tale, *The Stone Flower*, were made (partly in a Prague studio) with the captured Agfa colour process. Zguridi made his first film with actors, *White Fang*, from Jack London's novel of Alaska. The politically big film of the year was *The Vow*, a forbidding demonstration of the artistic evils inherent in the monumentally heroic, and the social danger of idolizing a living 'leader'. The effect of the film is of a few mortals on an excursion to Mount Olympus, where even the lesser gods look to Jupiter for their welfare and salvation. An independent decision not okayed by Jupiter has a tinge of crime that inevitably leads one deeper into Hades. *The Vow* made the figure of Gelovani's Stalin so much more grand and godlike that subsequent films were hard put to equal the applauded triumph of Chiaureli. Only Chiaureli and Gelovani could do it so 'well' again, in *The Fall of Berlin* (1950).

Two other films of 1946 were possibly important; I have seen neither, and I have seen little comment on either, but both were made by original, responsible artists. At Sverdlovsk Alexander Medvedkin made a film of the Kuban, called *Liberated Earth*, with a distinguished cast that would not have been assigned to an unimportant film. At Mosfilm, with Tisse as cameraman, Abram Room directed Mdivani's script on a subject that was to become an extremely delicate matter in coming years, possibly the reason why *In the Mountains of Yugoslavia* (with Bersenev playing Marshal Tito) has dropped from the histories.

Of the condemned film-makers Pudovkin was the first to go to work on correcting his errors. He dropped his attempt to show the fierce diplomatic struggles going on beneath the polite surface of court life ('balls and dances') in 1855, and concentrated on reconstructing Nakhimov's capture of Sinope and created an important new rôle, of the Turkish admiral, Osman Pasha, for Reuben Simonov. The revised version appeared in 1947, and was rewarded handsomely for its conscientiousness. Ten years later, in 1956, *Plain People* was quietly released, probably with major cuts and revisions. *A Great Life* remained banned until its revised release at the end of 1958.

For a while Eisenstein's physical condition prevented either defence or revision of his film—and at that time there was no one else brave enough either to defend or to revise it. Two days after the resolution was published I received a cable from him that may have been intended as an antidote to the bad news. After ordering some more books he added, 'am shipping you first quarter of my opus very soon'. That was the last hopeful word I received on any planned sequel to *The Film Sense*. I do not know how close to completion it was before he put it aside, along with a 'comic autobiography' that he had begun dictating in the carefree atmosphere of the hospital. Later in September there was another official slap: *Pravda* published a reprimand to Pyriev (of all people!) for permitting *Iskusstvo Kino* to publish a formalist article by Eisenstein. In the following winter Eisenstein made two careful moves, calculated to bring his *Ivan* back to life. In *Culture and Life* he published a reply to the resolution's criticism; agreeing for the most part with the condemnation, even going further in some details, there is yet one ambiguous passage that has a flavour of defence:

'We know Ivan Grozny as a man with a strong will and firm character. Does that exclude from the characterization of this tsar the possibility of the existence of certain doubts? It is difficult to think that a man who did such unheard-of and unprecedented things in his time never thought over the choice of means or never had doubts about how to act at one time or another. But could it be that these possible doubts overshadow the historical rôle of historical Ivan as it was shown in the film ? Could it be that the essence of this powerful sixteenth-century figure lies in these doubts and not in his uncompromising fight against them or the unending success of his state activity ? Is it not so that the centre of our attention is and must be Ivan the builder, Ivan the creator of a new, powerful, united Russian power, Ivan the inexorable destroyer of everything that resisted his progressive undertakings ?'[33]

Alexandrov later told Marie Seton of another move this winter. Eisenstein wrote to Stalin, asking for a discussion of the banned film, and Stalin invited him and Cherkasov to talk with him about their plans. The result was a compromise: as soon as Eisenstein was well enough to work, he should complete Part Three, incorporating the least offensive sequences from Part Two. It was just after this that he cabled me (March 14, 1947): 'Everything okay continue working Ivan.'

A month later I happened to be in Boston for the opening there of *Ivan*, Part One, when the theatre manager arranged for a telephone conversation with Eisenstein and Prokofiev at their end, and with Koussevitsky and newspaper reporters at the Boston end. The tone of the reporters already smacked of the cold war, and by the time I got to the telephone Eisenstein was on the offensive. He demanded to know why I hadn't told him I was going to Boston and what was I doing there, anyway ? I couldn't tell him that I was preparing a book to surprise him, about Herman Melville, using Eisenstein's montage lessons. He sounded healthy and busy, talking about plans for *Ivan*, but when I asked about 'Opus Two', he dismissed my inquiry rather brusquely and changed the subject. I'm glad that it didn't occur to me to ask whether he had received the 16 mm. prints that had been sent him of *Thunder Over Mexico* and *Time in the Sun*. When he wrote to Georges Sadoul on May 10, 1947, he said that two months before he had seen for the first time these efforts to make *Que Viva Mexico* without him, and that, 'Ce qu'ils en ont fait comme montage est plus que navrant.'

The Stalin Prizes for fictional films in 1945 and 1946 provided no surprises. The 1945 prizes were announced in July 1946: to the makers of *The Great Turning-Point, Guilty Though Guiltless*, Petrov's adaptation of Ostrovsky's play, and *Arshin Mal-Alan*, an Azerbaijan musical comedy. In 1946 the prizes went to the makers of *The Vow, Admiral Nakhimov, The Stone Flower, Glinka*, and *The Cruiser 'Varyag'*, the last directed by Victor Eisimont.

The return of peace-time fears and bureaucratic censorship continued its ravages into 1947, in which year the defeated films were only slightly less notable than those condemned in 1946. The most surprising denunciation was of Sergei Gerasimov's *Young Guard*. Alexander Fadeyev's novel about the Komsomol resistance organization in occupied Krasnodon had won a Stalin Prize, and appeared the most solid base for Gerasimov's interest. It had for him the special challenge of young characters (and actors) and Part One was completed before serious faults were detected in Fadeyev's novel:

'. . . it had misrepresented the withdrawal from Krasnodon during the German offensive as a rather shameful panicky stampede and portrayed the Young Guard as the product of the spontaneous enthusiasm of a handful of young people, neglecting to point out that the organization was in fact part of a great resistance network which had been woven by the more experienced hands of the Communist Party.'[34]

Part One of the film was put back into production for extensive revision, and Part Two* was made with greater attention to now obvious requirements. Yet it is difficult to believe that the style of Gerasimov's released film(s) can differ greatly from the style of his first version. Before the war Gerasimov wanted to do a film about Chekhov—'I dream of showing in this film the meaning of modesty in combination with talent, of what results it gives in human life.'[35] And this could have stood as Gerasimov's artistic credo up to that point—but something altered his direction during the war years: it may have been the handling of the beauties of *Masquerade*, it may have been his dissatisfaction with both his wartime films—*Invincible*, with Kalatozov, and *Mainland*—or some part of the reason may be sought in his decision to join the Communist Party in 1944, or in his work at the Documentary Film Studio. In any case the first film he made after the war is artistically one of the least modest films ever produced in the Soviet Union. In *Young Guard* the formerly acute observation of simple behaviour is transformed into grandiose, inflated mock heroics of popular nineteenth-century literature; Gerasimov's source, Fadeyev's excellent novel, cannot be held responsible for the film's style.

Dovzhenko's first treatment for his idea of Ivan Michurin's life was as a play— and he agreed reluctantly to turn it into a scenario and a film. One argument finally convinced him: that all the physical beauties that were an essential part of the naturalist's long, ripe life—orchards, blossoms, fruit—could never be conveyed as satisfactorily on any stage as in a Dovzhenko film. The prospect of working in colour for the first time was the final inducement, and Dovzhenko began work on what was to be his last film. An unforeseeable misfortune came during production: the theories of Michurin's most famous follower, Trofim Lysenko, became a matter for public and international discussion, and the Soviet Government backed Lysenko's position with its authority at home and harsh words abroad. A lyrical film about a stubborn scientist hero now had to pass the minute inspection (*not* by Lysenko himself) of a major political statement. The required revisions irritated Dovzhenko so much that a large part of the final version was made without him. His play, called *Life in Blossom*, was not revised. The film, released as *Michurin*, has beauties and intensities that no one but Dovzhenko could have given us—such as the remarkable sequence following the death of Michurin's wife—but the film also teaches several commonplace lessons (with Lysenko in mind) that Dovzhenko the former teacher would never have put into a work of art.

The troubled films of 1947 were less publicized than the resolution of September 4, 1946. The nature of Dovzhenko's and Gerasimov's revisions was kept a 'family affair', not broadcast outside the film industry. But the fact of trouble was clear to anyone who noted the elapsed years between a film's start and its

---

* I have seen only a condensation of both parts into a single feature-length film, somewhat longer than usual at that time.

release: *Michurin* was begun in 1946 and came to screens in 1949. As for the total banning of Yutkevich's *Light Over Russia*, the issues of the conflict can only be guessed as there was no open accusation to explain the ban. The film was based on Pogodin's popular play, *The Kremlin Chimes*, about Lenin's electrification programme. If Stalin did not approve the new player of Lenin (Nikolai Kolesnikov), the film could have been re-shot with another actor—so there must have been a more serious (and incurable) disease in the film. Yutkevich found himself in the 'band of cosmopolitans' two years later, but cosmopolitanism was not yet a crime in 1947.

There was, in 1947, an even greater gulf between the 'wrong' and the 'right' films—the latter including Alexandrov's strange comedy, *Spring*, partly filmed in Prague (with Orlova in a dual rôle and Cherkasov as a caricature of a film director), and Pyriev's *Tales of the Siberian Land*, with pretty colour and a sentimental story of a composer's inspiration. Romm's filming of Simonov's play, *The Russian Question*, was the opening gun in the barrage of anti-American films that were a sad phenomenon of the state that we called 'the cold war'. The two films that chiefly save the year from being forgotten were both simple, Donskoy's (again!) *Village Schoolteacher*, with Vera Maretskaya, and *In the Name of Life*, nearly the last film that Zarkhi and Heifitz were to make together. Two valuable teams, both at Lenfilm, split up at this time. Zarkhi and Heifitz were to part, each to make his own films. After the trouble with *Plain People*, Kozintsev and Trauberg never again worked together. In 1947 Kozintsev directed a film about the nineteenth-century surgeon, *Pirogov*, and Leonid Trauberg adapted August Jakobson's Estonian play, *Life in the Citadel*, for Herbert Rappoport. Vera Stroyeva's *Marite* was a Lithuanian Komsomolka killed during the German occupation. These last two Baltic films, together with Barnet's adventure-film, *The Scout's Secret*, were the only important Soviet films of this year to get their material from the war. The transition to peace, Bolshakov had declared in the first post-war issue of *Iskusstvo Kino*, is not merely a return to a peaceful life interrupted by war. The whole film industry had listened when he said that films must reveal the dynamics and dialectic of this new period. People were injured more than materially; of 'the millions of our Soviet people who were destroyed and mutilated, there are many who have suffered profound spiritual *trauma* and they need warm human relationships.' Work on the healing of these wounds, as well as on the restoration of ruined communities and industrial centres, was to replace the recent emphasis on war. Nineteen hundred and forty-seven, seems a year of intermission between the films of wartime actuality and the approaching films of coloured or inflated war reminiscence. It was another decade before the war could be drawn upon for realistic film works.

When hopes for a new book from Eisenstein grew remote, because (as I thought) his return to work on *Ivan* left no time for writing, I proposed to him a collection of his purely theoretical essays from among those for which I already had Russian texts, including his contribution to a new volume on Griffith. The publisher of *The Film Sense* wanted another book from him, and without further reference to the unfinished book, he enthusiastically took part in all arrangements for the substitute book. Along with the proposed contents I sent him some suggested titles, and on December 4, 1947, he cabled his approval, and his choice:

'Prefer Film Form title would add Prokofiev's biography preface and Chaplin essay will cable additions concerning Monsieur Verdoux. . . .'

A week later:

'Please withhold publishing article from Voices of October as completely out-dated would suggest instead Gordost [Pride] Iskusstvo Kino 1940. . . .'

At this time he selected from all his published work enough to fill four volumes that he proposed for French publication; these typescripts he corrected and sent to Armand Panigel. I did not hear of him again until February 11, 1948, when I heard a radio news broadcaster mention that Sergei Eisenstein had died.

His heart had failed for a final time the night before. There was some un-finished writing on his desk, on colour in films. With his death at the age of fifty ended an epoch in Soviet film history.

Postscript
1948–1958

Into a *discoverer* I have sunk
from an *inventor*

S. T. COLERIDGE

IN 1958 those dark days experienced by Soviet arts in 1947 seem much further away than a mere decade. The *mystique* of socialist realism is still a governing factor, at least in declarations and criticism, but there is a broadening recognition that it is dramatically debilitating to ignore all forces except external, material ones. Film makers are surely recovering from their fear of the extraordinary; the norm is still exalted and praised, but elements outside the simple categories are now taken seriously. Attitudes and certain images and characters under a taboo in film-making of ten years ago—such as the depiction of black-market operations or draft-dodgers in war-time films—are now open and common points of reference in films touching that same period. The mixed blessings of 'unity' as a policy in selecting script subjects are being re-examined and a distinction is finally being made between unity and uniformity, with some precautions taken against encroachments from the dangerous latter. The similar danger of making the Soviet audience passive with monotony or conformity is also recognized at both the administrative and creative levels of the industry, and some ambiguity is admitted for participation's sake. Attacks on stories that you can't whistle have almost ceased.

In the film-producing nations of greatest Soviet influence this decade has also been swift, and progress marked. In the years after victory these countries showed, proudly, a tendency to follow the lead of the Soviet cinema—and in the most conformist period of its history. This was not surprising in those countries with no more than a scattered previous experience in films (for all technical assistance was coming from Soviet factories and studios), but the tendency was equally noticeable in countries, such as Czechoslovakia, with a film tradition. The effect of this family resemblance on the parent art was to make it more cautious and guarded against change. But within the last few years the whole family of film industries has grown less narrow in its views, to the benefit of all. Now that it has absorbed Soviet film lessons, each of these countries is searching, often successfully, for its own film character. In Poland, for example, the promising young director Andrzej Wajda learned much from the work of Kozintsev and Trauberg, fused that wit and edge with the romantic realism of his immediate master, Alexander Ford, and the result, in his first film, *A Generation*, was an admirable variant, in Wajda's own style, on the theme and structure of *The Youth of Maxim*. The Czech director Jiri Weiss could, in *Wolf Trap*, produce a brilliant technical achievement with affinities also close to French and German traditions (as in Feyder's *Thérèse Raquin*); and there is an oblique but decent treatment of private fears and pressures in the Hungarian film *At Midnight*. At DEFA Studio, Wolfgang Staudte maintains a high level of creative invention. I hear encouraging accounts of Yugoslav films that I have not yet seen. We may be impatient with the seemingly slower progress towards characteristic, original works in China, a country of the greatest cinematic potentialities, but this progress can only be measured against the rare moments of interest in pre-war Chinese films to make their advance over this decade look tremendous.

In August 1948, however, the death of Andrei Zhdanov, responsible for much of the tight lacing of Soviet arts, offered no guarantee of critical peace, for at the beginning of 1949 there was a curious and disgraceful campaign—against the 'cosmopolitans'. It is alongside Konstantin Simonov's definition of cosmopolitanism—as 'the desire to undermine the roots of national pride because people without roots are easier to defeat and sell into the slavery of American imperialism'—that we must place, with astonishment, the film makers who were victims of this sweeping, poisonous attack. The first issue in 1949 of *Iskusstvo Kino* labelled a 'group of aesthetician-cosmopolitans in cinema' as including Leonid Trauberg (who had failed with his scenario on the scientist, Popov), Mikhail Bleimen (his collaboration on *A Great Citizen* was not referred to), and the critic-theoreticians Sutyrin, Otten, Kovarsky and Volkenstein. The evidence presented of their anti-patriotic behaviour was ridiculous: Trauberg had not praised *The Russian Question*, Bleiman had had an 'intolerant attitude' to Pyriev's *Tales of the Siberian Land*, and Sutyrin had been impatient with Dovzhenko's published script of *Michurin*. A 'cleansing of Soviet film-theory' was announced, menacingly. The volumes published in 1944 and 1945 on Griffith and Chaplin were quoted as damaging exhibits against Bleiman, a contributor to both, and three other contributors were implicated without being named: Eisenstein, Kozintsev, and Yutkevich; the last two careers were seriously threatened for a while; Eisenstein was protected by his death exactly a year before. Another important name, Alexei Kapler, was dropped from all his script credits, including *Lenin in October* and *Lenin in 1918*. Since Stalin's death all these wounds have healed over.

The films produced in 1949 and 1950 included a disproportionate number of films on anti-American subjects. After the Simonov-Romm *Russian Question* of 1947 nearly every Soviet film director rushed to write or direct a film on the villain, the United States. With Bolshakov frowning on continuing the Patriotic War on the screen, and the elimination of 'the German' as villain, the dramatic usefulness in these years of the American threat must have been as appealing to the film scenarist as the propaganda significance of showing the Marshall Plan and related conspiracies. Alexandrov's *Meeting on the Elbe*, Kalatozov's

Conspiracy of the Doomed, Romm's *Secret Mission*, Room's *Court of Honour*, were only the most important contributions to a stream that by now is happily merely a trickle of sub-plots and stock characters. A counter-stream rushed as logically but imprudently from the other direction, with Hollywood turning out *The Iron Curtain, The Red Menace, I Married a Communist, Red Danube, Conspirator* at the depth of the cold war; scenarists there were no doubt just as relieved to have an artificial villain to replace the Japanese and German villains taken from them. Of course, neither stream ever reached the other's source— the 'free' American screens were just as protected (by the Customs House) from anti-American films as were Soviet screens from anti-Soviet films—but there was an audience sitting in between as well as a home audience.

Gerasimov, too, fired his verbal shot in the cold war when he attended the Cultural and Scientific Conference for World Peace in New York in 1949. His characterization of the enemy's films was so clearly his description of Hollywood's films that no one could mistake him for diplomat or friend:

'Some films state that to live better, to attain happiness, one must deceive, oppress and enslave, obtain profits by hook or by crook—shoving one's fellow-creatures around, pushing others out of the way and crushing everything in the path to make one's way to happiness at any cost. . . . Irrespective of whether they deal with wages, honour, love or matrimony the decisive argument in these films is violence, firearms, shooting, murder and death. The victor triumphs, he gains the right to happiness, though this is only for the time being since he is followed by another, a stronger one, who no longer depends on a revolver or a gun, but is equipped with a bomb.'

And one of Eisenstein's last published articles was an attack on American films that one wishes had not been written, 'Purveyors of Spiritual Poison'.[1]

Looking back at this recent embarrassment one sighs with relief that some of the most bitter anti-American films did not get beyond the script stage: Dovzhenko's *Farewell, America; Guarding the Peace*, written (before cosmopolitanism) by Bleiman, Kovarsky and Ermler; *Great Heart*, by Ehrenburg and Kozintsev; Arnstam's *Warmongers; The Man from Wall Street*, by Katayev and Kalatozov. It was no crime, artistically, to have written such fierce anti-American films, even as weapons to protect the peace, but to have made so many of them, concentrating on this theme to the near-exclusion of others, this was a mistake as absurd as the quantity of films at this time expressing the 'personality cult', which was to end more abruptly than the anti-cosmopolitan and anti-American campaigns.

The death of Stalin, in 1953, and Khrushchov's temporarily secret report on him to the Twentieth Congress of the Communist Party, in February 1956, are two dates within this decade that cannot be ignored by any historian of a Soviet art. One striking aspect of Khrushchov's remarkable document is that the only art repeatedly cited as misused to enhance the Stalin idolization is the art of the cinema:

'. . . let us take, for instance, our historical and military films and some literary creations; they make us feel sick. Their true objective is the propagation of the theme of praising Stalin as a military genius. Let us recall the film *Fall of Berlin*. In it only Stalin acts, issuing orders from a hall in which there are many empty chairs. . . . And where is the Military Command? Where is the Political Bureau? Where is the Government? What are they doing, what keeps them busy? There is nothing about them in the film. Stalin acts for everybody. . . . Everything is shown to the nation in this false light. Why? In order to surround Stalin with glory, contrary to the facts and contrary to historical truth. . . .

'Stalin loved to see the film *The Unforgettable Year 1919* [1951], in which he was shown on the steps of an armoured train and where he practically vanquished the foe with his own sabre. Let Kliment Yefremovich [Voroshilov], our dear friend . . . write the truth about Stalin; after all, he knows how Stalin fought. . . .

'[Stalin] knew the country and agriculture only from films. And these films had dressed up and beautified the existing situation in agriculture. Many films so pictured collective farm life that the tables groaned beneath the weight of turkeys and geese. Evidently Stalin thought that it was actually so. . . . The last time he visited the countryside was in January 1928, when he visited Siberia in connection with grain deliveries.'

Nor was Stalin the only 'personality' to exploit the film's possibilities. When Marshal Konyev later recited the vanities and exaggerations of Marshal Zhukov, he pointed out that when a film about Stalingrad (evidently the Virta-Petrov *Battle of Stalingrad*) was made, Marshal Zhukov doctored the script to give himself an 'undeserved rôle'.

The present effect of these revelations and criticisms is twofold: not only have the large number of 'Stalin films' been revised or wholly withdrawn, but all members of the Soviet Government today are conspicuously absent from current films, except in very restrained newsreel appearances.

A new type of film, two-edged in effect, was introduced on a broad scale in the early 1950s. Following the success of filmed collections of scenes from the repertoires of the Moscow Art and Maly Theatres, it was decided to make and distribute publicly film-recordings of complete theatre productions. During 1952 and 1953 twenty-five plays were filmed in the most important theatres of Moscow, Leningrad, and Kiev. The selection from the Maly Theatre concentrated on its Ostrovsky repertoire, while the Moscow Art Theatre offered Gorky's *Lower Depths*, Sheridan's *School for Scandal*, and their dramatization of *Anna Karenina*. Most of the other theatres' productions were of Russian plays (favouring Ostrovsky), but plays by Lope de Vega and Goldoni were also recorded. Each of these uncondensed records was released in two full-length parts, and their popularity was marked. They competed on an equal footing with 'normal' new films, for the recordings were always made by experienced film directors (including Zarkhi, Solntseva, and Lukov) and film-technicians, and of course they showed some of the best actors who were already familiar on the screen; young actors, too, for the productions of the recently formed Theatre-Studio of Film-Actors were included in the recording programme. For those in Britain and America who see a more menacing competitor in television it can be pointed out that Soviet television, though widely used, has never rivalled the popularity of cinema as the Soviet theatre has. Many film energies, indeed, are devoted to preparing other purely theatre forms and works for film presentation. The most successful effort to film opera has been Stroyeva's disciplined adaptation of Musorgsky's *Boris Godunov* (1955), and the most interesting ballet-film has been Prokofiev's *Romeo and Juliet* (1955).

I have not seen Pudovkin's last work, including his contribution to *Three Encounters* (1948). I have been told that *Zhukovsky* (1950, in colour), on an early theoretician of flight, could not be distinguished from the multitude of biographical films made after the war; but that Pudovkin's last film, *The Return of Vasili Bortnikov* (1953), showed a glimmer of the old courage and power. It was based on a farm novel by Galina Nikolayeva, *Harvest*, and the fresh, contemporary material may have summoned, once more, Pudovkin's lyrical best, before his death in July 1953. His loyal assistant, Doller, died a year earlier.

Another great film-maker died in 1954, and there has been no attempt to explain the silence of Dziga Vertov's last years. No feature film since *Lullaby* (1937) had been released over his name.

And no one will see the films that Dovzhenko wished to make before his death on December 1956. Two of the films he tried to start (one an adaptation of Gogol's *Taras Bulba*, a project he had fostered since 1940)* were stopped with heart attacks that took him from the studio to the hospital. His last plan came very close to realization; he told Georges Sadoul about it:

'In my new film there will be no mountain-peaks, no cliffs, no crimes, nothing to excite the spectator. All will be simple, without big effects. . . .

'I have written a film trilogy that has for its frame and subject a Ukrainian village, my village. The first part—I have written it as a play—is set in 1930, during collectivization. The second part is an account of the fiery years of the patriotic war, of the battles between the collective farmers and Nazis. The third part comes up to our time. A great dam is built that places the village at the bottom of a new sea; the village dies under forty-five feet of waters that vitalize and impregnate the earth.

'I begin the production of this trilogy with its last part, *Poem about a Sea*. The title is perhaps too ambitious; I'd prefer *Prose about a Sea*. I have enjoyed planning my future work for the panoramic screen. . . . In 1930, I saw such a giant screen in Paris and it made a profound impression on me. The long horizontal shape suits the elements in my next film: broad and monochrome steppes, stretching waters of a sea, airplanes, the idea of great spaces. . . .'[2]

Poem about a Sea was prepared with great care. For two years before actual shooting was to begin Dovzhenko and two cameramen recorded the progress of the construction of the dam at Kakhovka. Compositions and details of the entire production were sketched by Dovzhenko, and the film's designer prepared these in a graphic continuity. Yulia Solntseva worked on all stages of the preparation; the casting was completed, and on the night before shooting was to start

---

* Scripts that survive from this period: *Opening the Antarctic* (1952, based on the 1819 notebook of Thaddeus Bellinghausen), *Into the Depths of the Cosmos* (1954, on interplanetary travel), and his beautiful script on his own childhood, *The Enchanted Desna*.

Dovzhenko's heart stopped. His widow went ahead with the prepared production, but the result is less impressive than the script[3] and sketches. A more appropriate memorial to him was the renaming of the Kiev Studio as the Dovzhenko Studio.

These deaths are irreparable losses to the world of film-making, as well as to Soviet art, and they force one to count and guard the good film-makers still at work, and to hunt for the young people who carry the responsibility for the next epoch of Soviet cinema. The films of Ermler, Kozintsev, Donskoy, Raizman, Stroyeva, Barnet, Yutkevich, Vasiliev, Arnstam and Savchenko continue to give us testimony of a Soviet film tradition energetically if not dazzlingly maintained, though often, as in Vasiliev's *Heroes of Shipka*, one admires the hands that made it rather than the minds. It is good to hear that Ermler, after a severe illness, has returned to film-making, and I hope the two films he has made since then will be shown abroad. Kozintsev's *Don Quixote* (1957) has been seen and admired widely. Donskoy's *At Great Cost* (1956) and Raizman's *Communist* (1958) are both important, emotional films. Yutkevich has shown himself a master of the spectacle (*Skanderbeg* and *Othello*) as well as the intimate drama (*Stories about Lenin*). Even Alexandrov is trying to break the increasingly stifling hold that musical comedy has had on him. The world attention given to Kalatozov's *The Cranes Are Flying* (1957) places him among the most hopeful talents in Soviet cinema today. Films from other directors of that generation—notably Romm, Pyriev, Gerasimov, Chiaureli—pursue the naturalist tradition in a leisurely, hearty assured way that does not seem to intimidate the youngest generation of film-makers. And the young are looking forward to the announced return of Okhlopkov to film-making.

This was a decade encouragingly full of *first* films. Few of these young films have had the authority of Kalatozov's *Cranes*, and some of them have been as easily forgotten as Chukhrai's pretty version of *The Forty-First* (1956), but any quantity of first films reflects favourably on thorough schooling and wise administration, as well as on the higher authorities' increasing faith in the Soviet public's capacity for judging varied points of view: that public may even be passing the 'protected' stage of its development. The decade need not be ashamed of Samsonov's tenderly handled adaptation of Chekhov's *Gadfly* (1955), of the second film use of Ostrovsky's *How the Steel was Tempered* in Naumov and Alov's virtuoso version, *Pavel Korchagin* (1956), or of the modest Georgian surprise, *Our Courtyard* (1957), directed by Revaz Chkheidze. *The House Where I Live* (1957) has been an immediate favourite with Soviet audiences for its warm, well-told story of the war years—it is only the second film by a young directorial team, Lev Kulijanov and Yakov Segel.

Since the war years the young film industries of Soviet Asia have grown immensely. It is one of the most positive results of the temporary Asian wartime shelters for the studios of Moscow, Leningrad and Kiev. Alongside *Alisher Navoi* from Tashkent and *Jambul* from Alma-Ata, whose young makers were trained at the Cinema Institute, the central studios have maintained their Asian links: Vasili Pronin's *Saltanat*, filmed in Kirghizia, was Mosfilm's surprise for 1955.

This is also a period of 're-makes', when a younger director, armed with colour, cinemascope screen, stereophonic sound and fresh attitudes, wants to treat a film of the past—even a classic such as *Mother* or *The Forty-First*—in *his* manner. The new generation includes members of the same families who made the great films of the past: Alexei Batalov has the experience of playing the same rôle in Donskoi's *Mother* that his uncle played in Pudovkin's film, and Tatyana Samoilova in *The Cranes Are Flying* communicates the same electricity as her father's in Dovzhenko's *Shchors*. Igor Savchenko's son is a promising scenarist.

The emergence of new directors in their twenties reminds us, too, that we have entered a period when subjects drawn from the first years of Soviet authority are being treated by artists who were too young (or unborn!) in those years to bring personal experiences to their imaginations. When a film about 1917 is made today by a writer, a director, a cameraman, and actors in their thirties and forties, it is inevitable that it will be more remote in impact, more a 'period' film than films about the revolution and civil war made from direct participation and observation, as in the work of Eisenstein and Dovzhenko and others of their generation. That is why I believe that the important Soviet film works of the future will be based on subjects from the present or recent past (the war of 1941-1945, for example) that will not be easily compared with the films of the 1920s.

Now, as then, and outside the Soviet Union as well as at Mosfilm and Lenfilm, the least discussable problem is the contradictions in the medium itself, an art and an industry. The sad, blank chapters in the careers of Stroheim and Flaherty have some motifs in common with the silences of Eisenstein and Dovzhenko. Though it is a discouraging notion to those workers and officials who give their lives to improving the physical circumstances of any film industry, it seems clear that the larger the 'plant', the more convenient the equipment, the more organized the distribution apparatus—the greater the danger of the film growing less individual, more uniform, and less worth everyone's effort. Throughout Soviet film history, the films were finest when they had the individuality that any industrial administration, by its nature and purpose, was bound to distrust. A consciousness of this danger is a great step forward.

A wide-screen composition by Dovzhenko for *Poem about a Sea*, sketched on his office blackboard the day before his death

THE FIRST DOCUMENTARY SERIES
FILMED IN RUSSIA

LUMIÈRE (from *Catalogue Général des Vues Cinématographiques Positives de la Collection Lumière*, published 1900).

Russie
    Couronnement du Czar
300 Les Souverains et les Invités se rendant au Sacre (escalier rouge).
301 L'Impératrice mère et la Grande-Duchesse Eugénie en carosse.
302 Czar et Czarine entrant dans l'Eglise de l'Assomption.
303 Comte de Montebello et Général de Boisdeffre se rendant au Kremlin.
304 Comtesse de Montebello.
305 Amiral Sallandrouze et Général Tournier.
306 Députations asiatiques.
    Moscow
307 Rue Tverskaia.

These first Russian films were used as evidence by Boleslas Matuszewski in a far-sighted proposal to establish a 'Dépot de Cinématographie Historique'; his publication, *Une nouvelle source de l'histoire*, is dated March 25, 1898.

The two series following are quoted from B. S. Likhachov's *Film in Russia*.

PATHÉ (the series: *Picturesque Russia*)
1	Sevastopol—military base	70 m.
2	Manoeuvres of the naval squadrons in the Black Sea	130 m.
3	Manufacture of kerosene in Baku	125 m.
4	Fishing in Astrakhan	145 m.
5	Canning fish in Astrakhan	120 m.
6	Fire in Odessa	100 m.
7	Caucasian customs	120 m.
8	Moscow flooded	90 m.
9	Picturesque Odessa	165 m.
10	Fiftieth anniversary of the Belostok Regiment	145 m.
11	Swimming in the Moscow River at 20 degrees	75 m.
12	Travelling on the Volga	105 m.
13	Scenes of Caucasian life	120 m.
14	Travels through Russia	100 m.
15	Panoramas of Yalta	140 m.
16	The mouths of the Volga	95 m.

17	Picturesque Russia	95 m.
18	Russian types	85 m.
19	Picturesque Kiev	130 m.
20	The Moscow railway system	60 m.
21	Funeral of the Grand Duke Alexei	110 m.

DRANKOV

1	Solemn funeral of Prof. Chuprov in Moscow followed by a great crowd of mourners	120 m.
2	Views of Moscow and the Kremlin	153 m.
3	The Moscow Rogues' Market	100 m.
4	Funeral of General-Adjutant Linevich . . .	140 m.
	(shortened version of same)	100 m.
5	Gala reception of the Swedish King and royal family at Revel and St Petersburg on the occasion of the nuptials of Her Highness Princess Marie with the Swedish King . .	300 m.
6	Palm Sunday in Moscow	85 m.
7	The Moscow Race-Track	100 m.
8	Figure-skating by the famous skater Panin at St Petersburg .	40 m.
9	Views of Warsaw: Main streets and skating-rink . . .	60 m.
10	New films of St Petersburg and life in the capital . .	165 m.
11	Departure of the Swedish King and royal family after the nuptials of Her Highness Princess Marie with the Swedish King	120 m.
12	Finland	150 m.
13	Meeting of our Emperor with the English King, Edward VII in Revel harbour	300 m.
	(shortened version of same)	200 m.
14	Meeting of the German Emperor, Wilhelm II with the Swedish King at Stockholm (both monarchs clearly visible) . .	120 m.
15	Panorama and views of Revel	120 m.
16	Arrival of President Fallières at Revel for the meeting with our Emperor	130 m.
17	Meeting of the French President with the Norwegian King, Haakon, in Christiania	120 m.

APPENDIX 2

MAXIM GORKY

A review of the Lumière programme at the Nizhni-Novgorod Fair, as printed in the *Nizhegorodski listok*, newspaper, July 4, 1896, and signed 'I. M. Pacatus'. Translated by Leda Swan.

Last night I was in the Kingdom of Shadows.

If you only knew how strange it is to be there. It is a world without sound, without colour. Everything there—the earth, the trees, the people, the water and the air—is dipped in monotonous grey. Grey rays of the sun across the grey sky, grey eyes in grey faces, and the leaves of the trees are ashen grey. It is not life but its shadow, it is not motion but its soundless spectre.

Here I shall try to explain myself, lest I be suspected of madness or indulgence in symbolism. I was at Aumont's and saw Lumière's cinematograph—moving photography. The extraordinary impression it creates is so unique and complex that I doubt my ability to describe it with all its nuances. However, I shall try to convey its fundamentals.

When the lights go out in the room in which Lumière's invention is shown, there suddenly appears on the screen a large grey picture, 'A Street in Paris'— shadows of a bad engraving. As you gaze at it, you see carriages, buildings and people in various poses, all frozen into immobility. All this is in grey, and the sky above is also grey—you anticipate nothing new in this all too familiar scene, for you have seen pictures of Paris streets more than once. But suddenly a strange flicker passes through the screen and the picture stirs to life. Carriages coming from somewhere in the perspective of the picture are moving straight at you, into the darkness in which you sit; somewhere from afar people appear and loom larger as they come closer to you; in the foreground children are playing with a dog, bicyclists tear along, and pedestrians cross the street picking their way among the carriages. All this moves, teems with life and, upon approaching the edge of the screen, vanishes somewhere beyond it.

And all this in strange silence where no rumble of the wheels is heard, no sound of footsteps or of speech. Nothing. Not a single note of the intricate symphony that always accompanies the movements of people. Noiselessly, the ashen-grey foliage of the trees sways in the wind, and the grey silhouettes of the people, as though condemned to eternal silence and cruelly punished by being deprived of all the colours of life, glide noiselessly along the grey ground.

Their smiles are lifeless, even though their movements are full of living energy and are so swift as to be almost imperceptible. Their laughter is soundless, although you see the muscles contracting in their grey faces. Before you a life is surging, a life deprived of words and shorn of the living spectrum of colours —the grey, the soundless, the bleak and dismal life.

It is terrifying to see, but it is the movement of shadows, only of shadows. Curses and ghosts, the evil spirits that have cast entire cities into eternal sleep, come to mind and you feel as though Merlin's vicious trick is being enacted before you. As though he had bewitched the entire street, he compressed its many-storied buildings from roof-tops to foundations to yard-like size. He dwarfed the people in corresponding proportion, robbing them of the power of speech and scraping together all the pigment of earth and sky into a monotonous grey colour.

Under this guise he shoved his grotesque creation into a niche in the dark room of a restaurant. Suddenly something clicks, everything vanishes and a train appears on the screen. It speeds straight at you—watch out! It seems as though it will plunge into the darkness in which you sit, turning you into a ripped sack full of lacerated flesh and splintered bones, and crushing into dust and into broken fragments this hall and this building, so full of women, wine, music and vice.

But this, too, is but a train of shadows.

Noiselessly, the locomotive disappears beyond the edge of the screen. The train comes to a stop, and grey figures silently emerge from the cars, soundlessly greet their friends, laugh, walk, run, bustle, and . . . are gone. And here is another picture. Three men seated at the table, playing cards. Their faces are tense, their hands move swiftly. The cupidity of the players is betrayed by the trembling fingers and by the twitching of their facial muscles. They play. . . . Suddenly, they break into laughter, and the waiter who has stopped at their table with beer, laughs too. They laugh until their sides split but not a sound is heard. It seems as if these people have died and their shadows have been condemned to play cards in silence unto eternity. Another picture. A gardener watering flowers. The light grey stream of water, issuing from a hose, breaks into a fine spray. It falls upon the flowerbeds and upon the grass blades weighted down by the water. A boy enters, steps on the hose, and stops the stream, The gardener stares into the nozzle of the hose, whereupon the boy steps back and a stream of water hits the gardener in the face. You imagine the spray will reach you, and you want to shield yourself. But on the screen the gardener has already begun to chase the rascal all over the garden and having caught him, gives him a beating. But the beating is soundless, nor can you hear the gurgle of the water as it gushes from the hose left lying on the ground.

This mute, grey life finally begins to disturb and depress you. It seems as though it carries a warning, fraught with a vague but sinister meaning that makes your heart grow faint. You are forgetting where you are. Strange imaginings invade your mind and your consciousness begins to wane and grow dim. . . .

But suddenly, alongside of you, a gay chatter and a provoking laughter of a woman is heard . . . and you remember that you are at Aumont's, Charles Aumont's. . . . But why of all places should this remarkable invention of Lumière find its way and be demonstrated here, this invention which affirms once again the energy and the curiosity of the human mind, forever striving to solve and grasp all, and . . . while on the way to the solution of the mystery of life, incidentally builds Aumont's fortune? I do not yet see the scientific importance of

Lumière's invention but, no doubt, it is there, and it could probably be applied to the general ends of science, that is, of bettering man's life and the developing of his mind. This is not to be found at Aumont's where vice alone is being encouraged and popularized. Why then at Aumont's, among the 'victims of social needs' and among the loafers who here buy their kisses? Why here, of all places, are they showing this latest achievement of science? And soon probably Lumière's invention will be perfected, but in the spirit of Aumont-Toulon and Company.

Besides those pictures I have already mentioned, is featured 'The Family Breakfast', an idyll of three. A young couple with its chubby first-born is seated at the breakfast table. The two are so much in love, and are so charming, gay and happy, and the baby is so amusing. The picture creates a fine, felicitous impression. Has this family scene a place at Aumont's?

And here is still another. Women workers, in a thick, gay and laughing crowd, rush out of the factory gates into the street. This too is out of place at Aumont's. Why remind here of the possibility of a clean, toiling life? This reminder is useless. Under the best of circumstances this picture will only painfully sting the woman who sells her kisses.

I am convinced that these pictures will soon be replaced by others of a genre more suited to the general tone of the 'Concert Parisien'. For example, they will show a picture titled: 'As She Undresses', or 'Madam at Her Bath', or 'A Woman in Stockings'. They could also depict a sordid squabble between a husband and wife and serve it to the public under the heading of 'The Blessings of Family Life'.

Yes, no doubt, this is how it will be done. The bucolic and the idyll could not possibly find their place in Russia's markets thirsting for the piquant and the extravagant. I also could suggest a few themes for development by means of a cinematograph and for the amusement of the market place. For instance: to impale a fashionable parasite upon a picket fence, as is the way of the Turks, photograph him, then show it.

It is not exactly piquant but quite edifying.

LEV TOLSTOY

A record by I. Teneromo of a conversation with Tolstoy on his eightieth birthday, August 1908.
Translated by David Bernstein (published in the *New York Times*, January 31, 1937).

'You will see that this little clicking contraption with the revolving handle will make a revolution in our life—in the life of writers. It is a direct attack on the old methods of literary art. We shall have to adapt ourselves to the shadowy screen and to the cold machine. A new form of writing will be necessary. I have thought of that and I can feel what is coming.

'But I rather like it. This swift change of scene, this blending of emotion and experience—it is much better than the heavy, long-drawn-out kind of writing to which we are accustomed. It is closer to life. In life, too, changes and transitions flash by before our eyes, and emotions of the soul are like a hurricane. The cinema has divined the mystery of motion. And that is greatness.

'When I was writing "The Living Corpse", I tore my hair and chewed my fingers because I could not give enough scenes, enough pictures, because I could not pass rapidly enough from one event to another. The accursed stage was like a halter choking the throat of the dramatist; and I had to cut the life and swing of the work according to the dimensions and requirements of the stage. I remember when I was told that some clever person had devised a scheme for a revolving stage, on which a number of scenes could be prepared in advance. I rejoiced like a child, and allowed myself to write ten scenes into my play. Even then I was afraid the play would be killed.

'But the films! They are wonderful! Drr! and a scene is ready! Drr! and we have another! We have the sea, the coast, the city, the palace—and in the palace there is tragedy (there is always tragedy in palaces, as we see in Shakespeare).

'I am seriously thinking of writing a play for the screen. I have a subject for it. It is a terrible and bloody theme. I am not afraid of bloody themes. Take Homer or the Bible, for instance. How many bloodthirsty passages there are in them—murders, wars. And yet these are the sacred books, and they ennoble and uplift the people. It is not the subject itself that is so terrible. It is the propagation of bloodshed, and the justification for it, that is really terrible! Some friends of mine returned from Kursk recently and told me a shocking incident. It is a story for the films. You couldn't write it in fiction or for the stage. But on the screen it would be good. Listen—it may turn out to be a powerful thing!'

And Leo Tolstoy related the story in detail. He was deeply agitated as he spoke. But he never developed the theme in writing. Tolstoy was always like that. When he was inspired by a story he had been thinking of, he would become excited by its possibilities. If some one happened to be near by, he would unfold the plot in all its details. Then he would forget all about it. Once the gestation was over and his brain-child born, Tolstoy would seldom bother to write about it.

Some one spoke of the domination of the films by business men interested only in profits. 'Yes, I know, I've been told about that before', Tolstoy replied. 'The films have fallen into the clutches of business men and art is weeping! But where aren't there business men?' And he proceeded to relate one of those delightful little parables for which he is famous.

'A little while ago I was standing on the banks of our pond. It was noon of a hot day, and butterflies of all colours and sizes were circling around, bathing and darting in the sunlight, fluttering among the flowers through their short— their very short—lives, for with the setting of the sun they would die.

'But there on the shore near the reeds I saw an insect with little lavender spots on its wings. It, too, was circling around. It would flutter about, obstinately, and its circles became smaller and smaller. I glanced over there. In among the reeds sat a great green toad with staring eyes on each side of his flat head, breathing quickly with his greenish-white, glistening throat. The toad did not look at the butterfly, but the butterfly kept flying over him as though she wished to be seen. What happened? The toad looked up, opened his mouth wide and—remarkable!—the butterfly flew in of her own accord! The toad snapped his jaws shut quickly, and the butterfly disappeared.

'Then I remembered that thus the insect reaches the stomach of the toad, leaves its seed there to develop and again appear on God's earth, become a larva, a chrysalis. The chrysalis becomes a caterpillar, and out of the caterpillar springs a new butterfly. And then the playing in the sun, the bathing in the light, and the creating of new life, begin all over again.

'Thus it is with the cinema. In the reeds of film art sits the toad—the business man. Above him hovers the insect—the artist. A glance, and the jaws of the business man devour the artist. But that doesn't mean destruction. It is only one of the methods of procreation, or propagating the race; in the belly of the business man is carried on the process of impregnation and the development of the seeds of the future. These seeds will come out on God's earth and will begin their beautiful, brilliant lives all over again.'*

* Madame Alexandra Tolstaya warns me that there are several aspects of this record that make it suspect as a record, but that it incorporates remarks that Tolstoy may have made, either to Teneromo or others—but not on his eightieth birthday.

VLADIMIR MAYAKOVSKY

An article 'Theatre, Cinema, Futurism', published in *Kine-Journal* July 27, 1913.

Dear Ladies and Gentlemen,

The grand break-up that we see beginning in all spheres of beauty, in the name of art of the future—the art of the futurists—does not halt, and cannot be halted, at the door of the theatre.

Hate of yesterday's art, of the neurasthenic, cultivated arts of colours, verses, footlights (and I cannot admit the validity of showing tiny bits of emotions removed from life), compels me to introduce, in demonstrating that your acknowledgement of our ideas is inevitable, not only lyrical pathos, but also precise science—research into the relations between art and life.

Scorn of the actual, as displayed by such 'art-journals' as *Apollo* and *Masks*, where muddled foreign phrases float, like greasy globs, on a grey background of senselessness, has pushed me to house my speech in a technical, a cinematographic journal.

Today, I propose two questions:

(1) Is the modern theatre an art?

(2) Can the modern theatre endure the competition of the cinema?

The City, whose machines consume thousands of horsepower, gave the first chance to satisfy the world's material demands in something like 6-7 hours of daily labour, yet the tension and strain of modern life give renewed urgency to the free play of perceptional faculties, taking the forms of art.

This explains the powerful attraction of art for the modern man.

The division of labour tends to isolate those who work with beauty—so, when, for example, an artist who refuses to describe 'the delights of drunken mistresses' goes over to a broad democratic art, then he is responsible to society for the means by which his individually necessary labour can become useful to society.

The artist, declaring the dictatorship of the eye, has the right to existence. Asserting colour, line, form, as self-sufficient powers, painting has found its true path to development. In the ways that the word, in shape and in phonetics, has determined the flourishing of poesy, the poet has the right to existence. This is the road to the eternal well-being of the poet's verse.

But shouldn't the theatre, that in our times serves only as an artificial crust over all aspects of art, enjoy a self-sufficient existence as an art in its own right?

The modern theatre has halted, and this is why: it is the product of decorative work by artists who have forgotten their freedom and their aim of an utilitarian outlook on art.

In consequence, from this point of view, the theatre can function only as an anti-cultural enslaver of art.

The other half of theatre is 'The Word'. Here also aesthetic advance depends not on the inner growth of the word itself, but on its application to the expression of moral and political ideas that are incidental to art.*

In this way the modern theatre functions only as an enslaver of the word and the poet.

This means that until our arrival the theatre as an independent art did not exist. Does history show any trace of a similar affirmation? Yes, of course!

Shakespeare's theatre did not use settings. The ignorant critic gets around this by explaining that they weren't acquainted with scenic art.

But wasn't it in that period that realistic painting experienced such a rich development? And is the Passion Play at Ober-Ammergau fettered by inscribed lines?

All these phenomena can be explained only as a forecast of the special art of the actor, where more than intonation is required to give definition to the word, and where the devised but rhythmically free movements of the human body will express the greatest inner feeling.

That will be the new, free art of the actor.

At present, attempting a photographic rendering of life, the theatre lapses into the following contradictions:

The art of the actor, in its dynamic nature, is chained to the dead background of the setting,—this absurd contradiction is abolished by the cinema which is firmly attached to the action of actuality.

The theatre moves towards its own destruction, and must hand over its heritage to the cinema. And the cinema industry, branching away from the naïve realism and artifice of Chekhov and Gorky, opens the door to a theatre of the future—linked to the art of the actor.

---

* For example: the supposed flourishing of the theatre these past 10-15 years can be understood only as a temporary social advance (*The Lower Depths*, *Peer Gynt*), for such plays of trivial ideas, living only a few hours, die in the repertoires.—V.M.

APPENDIX 5

SIXTY-FIVE YEARS OF RUSSIAN AND

SOVIET FILMS, 1907–1971

A SELECT LIST

1907

Boris Godunov. 285 metres, Drankov (unfinished)   Aug.
Fragments from Pushkin's play, as performed at the Eden summer theatre in
St Petersburg; *directed by* I. Shuvalov; *photographed by* Alexander & L. Drankov.
Cast: G. Martini (the Pretender), Z. Loranskaya, Khovansky.

1908

Cossacks of the Don (Donskiye kazaki). 135 m., Pathé Frères, Moscow 15 Feb.
Dir.: Maurice Maitre; *phot.:* Georges Meyer (Joseph Mundviller), Tapis, and
others.

Stenka Razin. 224 m., Drankov   15 Oct.
Scen.: Vasili Goncharov; *dir.:* Vladimir Romashkov; *phot.:* Alexander Drankov,
Nikolai Kozlovsky; *mus.* (for performance): Mikhail Ippolitov-Ivanov.
Cast: Yevgeni Petrov-Krayevsky.

Drama in a Gypsy Camp near Moscow (Drama v tabore podmoskovnikh
tzigan). 140m., Khanzhonkov & Hoche   20 Dec.
Dir. & phot.: V. Siversen.

1909

Song about the Merchant Kalashnikov (Pesn pro kuptsa Kalashnikova).
250 m., Khanzhonkov   2 Mar.
Scen.: (from poem by Lermontov): Vasili Goncharov; *dir.:* Goncharov,
Pavlovsky; *phot.:* V. Siversen; *des.:* V. Fester; *mus.* (for performance): Mikhail
Ippolitov-Ivanov.
Cast: Pyotr Chardynin, A. Goncharova, A. Gromov, I. Potemkin (Ivan the
Terrible).

The Happy-go-lucky Merchant (Ukhar-kupets). 260 m., Pathé Frères, Moscow
29 Sep.
Scen. & dir.: Vasili Goncharov; *phot.:* Georges Meyer (Mundviller), Tapis;
des.: M. Kozhin.
Cast: A. Slavin, Y. Goreva, G. Ardatov.

Death of Ivan the Terrible (Smert Yoanna Groznovo). 300 m., Gloria (Thiemann
& Reinhardt)   6 Oct.
Scen. & dir.: Vasili Goncharov; *phot.:* A. Serano; *des.:* Ignatev, Benes.
Cast: A. Slavin (Ivan), Y. Uvarova (Tsaritsa), S. Tarasov (Godunov), Protazanov.

1910

Peter the Great (Pyotr veliky). 590 m., Pathé Frères, Moscow   6 Jan.
Scen.: Vasili Goncharov; *dir.:* Kai Hansen, Goncharov; *phot.:* Georges Meyer
(Mundviller), Tapis; *des.:* M. Kozhin.
Cast: P. Voinov (Peter), Y. Trubetskaya (Catherine), Van Der Weyde (Sophia).

At Midnight in the Graveyard (V polnoch na kladbishche). 150 m., Khanzhonkov 30 Jan.
Scen. & dir.: Vasili Goncharov; *phot.:* Louis Forestier (?).
Life and Death of Pushkin (Zhizn i smert A. S. Pushkina). 350 m., Gaumont 21 Aug.
Scen.: Vasili Goncharov, Makarova; *dir.:* Goncharov; *phot.:* Alphonse Winkler.
Cast: V. Krivtsov (Puskhin).
Queen of Spades (Pikovaya dama). 380 m., Khanzhonkov 30 Nov.
Scen. (from story by Pushkin) *& dir.:* Pyotr Chardynin; *phot.:* Louis Forestier; *des.:* V. Fester.
Cast: P. Biryukov, A. Goncharova, A. Pozharskaya, A. Gromov.

1911
L'khaim. 375 m., Pathé Frères, Moscow 4 Jan.
Scen.: Alexander Arkatov (?); *dir.:* Maurice Maitre, Kai Hansen; *phot.:* Georges Meyer (Mundviller); *des,.:* Cheslav Sabinsky.
Cast: M. Reizen, Nikolai Vasiliev, L. Sychova, Mikhail Doronin.
Demon. 425 m., Thiemann & Reinhardt 2 Feb.
From the poem by Lermontov; *dir. & phot.:* Giovanni Vitrotti.
Cast: M. Tamarov.
Yevgeni Onegin. 270 m., Khanzhonkov 1 Mar.
Scen. (from the Tchaikovsky opera of Pushkin's poem) *& dir.:* Vasili Goncharov; *phot.:* Louis Forestier.
Cast: A. Goncharova (Tatyana), A. Gromov (Lensky), P. Biryukov (Onegin).
A Peasant Wedding (Krestyanskaya svadba). 196 m., Drankov & Cines, Moscow 11 Apr.
Scen. (from suggestion by Leo Tolstoy) *& dir.:* Tatyana Tolstaya; *phot.:* L. Drankov, Nikolai Kozlovsky; *des.:* N. Orlov.
A Living Corpse (Zhivoi trup). 600 m., Persky 27 Sep.
Scen. (from the play by Lev Tolstoy): R. Persky; *dir.:* V. Kuznetsov & Boris Chaikovsky; *phot.:* Noske.
Cast: Nikolai Vasiliev, Y. Pavlova, Maria Blumenthal-Tamarina.
The Kreutzer Sonata (Kreitzerova sonata). 570 m., Khanzhonkov 1 Oct.
Scen. (from story by Lev Tolstoy) *& dir.:* Pyotr Chardynin; *phot.:* Louis Forestier.
Cast: Chardynin, L. Varyagina, Ivan Mozhukhin.
The Prisoner's Song (Pesnya katorzhanina). 380 m., Thiemann & Reinhardt 8 Oct.
Scen. (from a popular song) *& dir.:* Yakov Protazanov; *phot.:* Giovanni Vitrotti.
Cast: N. Saltikov, Vladimir Shaternikov, M. Koroleva.
Romance with Double-Bass (Roman s kontrabasom). 240 m., Pathé Frères 16 Nov.
Scen. (from the story by Chekhov): Cheslav Sabinsky; *dir.:* Kai Hansen; *phot.:* Georges Meyer (Mundviller); *des.:* Sabinsky.
Cast: V. Gorskaya, Nikolai Vasiliev.
Prince Serebryany and the Captive Varvara (Knyaz Serebryany i plenitsa Varvara). 320 m., Prodafilm 6 Dec.
Scen. (from novel by A. Marlinsky) *& dir.:* A. Alexeyev; *phot.:* A. Bulla.
Cast: G. Glebov-Kotelnikov, A. Sokolovskaya.
Defence of Sevastopol (Oborona Sevastopolya), 2,000 m., Khanzhonkov 9 Dec.
Scen. & dir.: Vasili Goncharov, Alexander Khanzhonkov; *phot.:* Louis Forestier, Alexander Rillo; *des.:* V. Fester; *mus.* (for performance): G. Kazachenko.
Cast: A Gromov (Nakhimov), N. Semyonov, P. Biryukov, Ivan Mozhukhin.

Old Times in Kashira (Kashirskaya starina). 855 m., Thiemann & Reinhardt
13 Dec.
Scen. (from play by Averkiev); *dir.:* V. Krivtsov; *phot.:* Giovanni Vitrotti.
Cast: Y. Roshchina-Insarova, V. Maximov, A. Bestuzhev, Vladimir Shaternikov.

1912

Anfisa. 860 m., Thiemann & Reinhardt 24 Jan.
Scen.: Leonid Andreyev (from his play); *dir.:* Yakov Protazanov; *phot.:* Giovanni
Vitrotti.
Cast: Y. Roshchina-Insarova, V. Maximov, Y. Uvarova, Vladimir Shaternikov.

Workers' Quarters (Rabochaya slobodka). 620 m., Khanzhonkov 7 Apr.
Scen. (from a play by Karpov) *& dir.:* Pyotr Chardynin; *phot.:* Louis Forestier.
Cast: A. Goncharova, P. Biryukov, Ivan Mozhukhin.

The Beautiful Leukanida (Prekrasnaya Lyukanida). 230 m., Khanzhonkov 26 Apr.
Scen., dir., phot. & des.: Wladyslaw Starewicz [who followed this first animated
model film with **Happy Scenes from Animal Life** (134 m.), **Aviation Week
Among the Insects, The Cameraman's Revenge** (285 m., Oct. 27, 1912),
Christmas at the Fox's Boarding-House (174 m.), **Dragonfly and Ant**
(158 m.)].

1812. 1,300 m., Khanzhonkov & Pathé Frères, Moscow 25 Aug.
Scen. supervised by Afonsky; *dir.:* Vasili Goncharov, Kai Hansen, A. Uralsky;
phot.: Georges Meyer (Mundviller), Alexander Levitsky, Louis Forestier, Alexander Rillo; *des.:* Cheslav Sabinsky, V. Fester.
Cast: V. Seryozhinikov, P. Knorr (Napoleon).

Without Dowry (Bespridannitsa). 765 m., Pathé Frères, Moscow 16 Oct.
From play by Ostrovsky; *dir.:* Kai Hansen; *phot.:* Georges Meyer (Mundviller);
des.: Cheslav Sabinsky.
Cast: Vera Pashennaya, B. Pyasetzky, Nikolai Vasiliev, L. Sychova.

God of Vengeance (Bog mesti). 835 m., Pathé Frères, Moscow 10 Nov.
Scen.: (from play by Sholom Asch) *& dir.:* Alexander Arkatov; *phot.:* Georges
Meyer (Mundviller); *des.:* Cheslav Sabinsky.
Cast: Arko, Braginskaya, Brandesco, Kundinskaya.

Ward No. 6 (Palata No. 6). Stern & Co., & Varyag
Scen. (from story by Chekhov) *& dir.:* Boris Chaikovsky; *phot.:* Ivan Frolov.
Cast: A. Bestuzhev, N. Alexeyeva, A. Neverov.

Departure of a Grand Old Man (Ukhod velikovo startza). 800 m., Thiemann &
Reinhardt [unreleased in Russia, shown only abroad]
Scen.: I. Teneromo; *dir.:* Yakov Protazanov, Y. Thiemann; *phot.:* Georges
Meyer (Mundviller), Alexander Levitsky; *des.:* Ivan Kavaleridze.
Cast: Vladimir Shaternikov (Tolstoy), O. Petrova, M. Tamarova, Y. Thiemann.

1913

Accession of the Romanov Dynasty (Votsareniya doma Romanovikh). 940 m.,
Khanzhonkov 16 Feb.
Scen. & dir.: Vasili Goncharov, Pyotr Chardynin; *phot.:* Louis Forestier.
Cast: S. Goslavskaya, V. Stepanov, N. Semyonov, Chardynin.

Tercentenary of the Romanov Dynasty's Accession to the Throne
(Tryokhsotletiye tsarstoivaniya doma Romanovikh). 1,200 m., Drankov &
Taldykin 16 Feb.
Scen.: Yevgeni Ivanov; *dir.:* A. Uralsky, N. Larin; *phot.:* Nikolai Kozlovsky;
des.: Yevgeni Bauer, I. Nemensky.
Cast: Mikhail Chekhov, L. Sychova, Nikolai Vasiliev, S. Tarasov, Pyotr Baksheyev.

Where Is Mathilda? (Gdye Matilda ?). 800 m., Tanagra & Bioscop, Berlin 29 Apr.
Scen.: Anatoli Kamensky; *dir.:* Georg Jacobi, A. Bistritsky; *des.:* Baruch.
Cast: Konstantin Varlamov, Y. Smirnova.
Romance of a Russian Ballerina (Roman russkoi balerini). 1,300 m., Tanagra
and Bioscop, Berlin   25 May
Scen.: Nikolai Breshko-Breshkovsky; *dir.:* Georg Jacobi, A. Bistritzky; *des.:*
Baruch.
Cast: Konstantin Varlamov, Y. Smirnova, Flink.
Sorrows of Sarah (Gore Sarri). 800 m., Khanzhonkov   10 Sep.
Scen.: Volberg; *dir.:* Alexander Arkatov; *phot.:* Alexander Rillo.
Cast: T. Shornikova, A. Bibikov, P. Maximova, Ivan Mozhukhin, V. Turzhansky.
Crime and Punishment (Prestupleniye i nakazaniye). 1,250 m., Drankov &
Taldykin.   15 Sep.
Scen. (from Dostoyevsky's novel) *& dir.:* I. Vronsky; *phot.:* Nikolai Kozlovsky.
Cast: Pavel Orlenev, Vronsky, M. Nesterova, V. Zimovoy.
The Shattered Vase (Razbitaya vaza). 700 m., Thiemann & Reinhardt   17 Sep.
Scen. (from a poem by Apukhtin) *& dir.:* Yakov Protazanov; *phot.:* Alexander
Levitsky; *des.:* Cheslav Sabinsky.
Cast: V. Maximov, Varvara Yanova, Alexander Volkov.
Keys to Happiness (Klyuchi shchastya). 4,700 m. in 2 series, Thiemann & Rein-
hardt   7 & 28 Oct.
Scen.: A. Verbitskaya (from her novel) & Volberg; *dir.:* Vladimir Gardin, Yakov
Protazanov; *phot.:* Georges Meyer (Mundviller), Alexander Levitsky, Giovanni
Vitrotti (in Italy).
Cast: V. Maximov, Olga Preobrazhenskaya, M. Troyanov, Alexander Volkov,
Vladimir Shaternikov, Gardin.
Conquest of the Caucasus (Pokoreniye Kavkaza). 2,525 m., Drankov & Taldykin
8 Oct.
Scen.: S. Esadze; *dir.:* L. Chorny, Esadze; *phot.:* Nikolai Kozlovsky; *des.:* Rubo
Cast: V. Guniya, N. Eristov, D. Chavchavadze.
How Fine, How Fresh the Roses Were (Kak khoroshi, kak svezhi byli rozi).
715 m., Thiemann & Reinhardt   12 Oct.
Scen. & dir.: Yakov Protazanov; *phot.:* Alexander Levitsky; *des.:* Cheslav
Sabinsky.
Cast: M. Tamarov (Turgenev), Varvara Yanova, Y. Uvarova (Paulina Viardot),
Vladimir Shaternikov (Lev Tolstoy).
A Terrible Revenge (Strashnaya mest), 1,500 m., Khanzhonkov   26 Nov.
Scen. (from the story by Gogol), *dir., des. & phot.:* Wladyslaw Starewicz.
Cast: Ivan Mozhukhin (witch), O. Obolenskaya, V. Turzhansky, P. Knorr.
Christmas Eve (Noch peryod rozhdestvom). 1,115 m., Khanzhonkov   26 Dec.
Scen. (from Gogol's story), *dir., des. & phot.:* Wladyslaw Starewicz.
Cast: Ivan Mozhukhin (devil), Olga Obolenskaya, L. Tridenskaya, P. Lopukhin.
Drunkenness and Its Consequences (Pyanstvo i yevo posledstviya). 1,200 m.,
Khanzhonkov
Dir. & ed.: A. Dvoretsky.
Cast: Ivan Mozhukhin.

1914
Freed Bird (Volnaya ptitsa). 685 m., Star & Pathé Frères, Moscow   4 Jan.
Scen.: V. Demert; *dir.:* Yevgeni Bauer; *phot.:* K. Bauer.
Cast: N. Chernova, Demert, M. Golubkov.

Drama in the Futurists' Cabaret No. 13 (Drama v kabare futuristov No. 13).
431 m., Toporkov & Winkler   28 Jan.
Dir.: Vladimir Kasyanov; *phot.:* N. Toporkov, Alphonse Winkler.
Cast: M. Larionov, Nataliya Goncharova.

Child of the Big City (Ditya bolshovo goroda). 1,135 m., Khanzhonkov
Dir. & des.: Yevgeni Bauer; *phot.:* Boris Zavelyov.   5 Mar.
Cast: Y. Smirnova, M. Salarov, A. Bibikov, Emma Bauer, L. Tridenskaya.

Tears (Slezi). 970 m., Khanzhonkov   16 Mar.
Scen.: A. Voznesensky; *dir.:* Yevgeni Bauer; *phot.:* Boris Zavelyov; *mus.:* I. Satz.
Cast: V. Yureneva, Ivan Bersenev, A. Barov, N. Pomerantsev

Woman of Tomorrow (Zhenshchina zavtrashevo dnya). 1,075 m., Khanzhonkov
Scen.: A. Voznesensky; *dir.* Pyotr Chardynin; *phot.:* Boris Zavelyov.   28 Apr.
Cast: V. Yureneva, Ivan Mozhukhin, M. Morskaya.

The Coward (Trus). 1,500 m., Russian Ribbon.   1 May
Scen.: Alexander Kuprin (from his story); *dir.:* R. Ungern, Boris Glagolin;
phot.: A. Pechkovsky.
Cast: I. Uralov, Glagolin, Y. Timme.

Anna Karenina. 2,700 m., Russian Golden Series   7 Oct.
Scen. (from Tolstoy's novel) *& dir.:* Vladimir Gardin; *phot.:* Alexander Levitsky;
des.: Cheslav Sabinsky.
Cast: Maria Germanova, Vladimir Shaternikov, M. Tamarov, Zoya Barantsevich, Vera Kholodnaya.

Life in Death (Zhizn v smerti). 1,300 m., Khanzhonkov   24 Oct.
Scen.: Valeri Bryusov; *dir.:* Yevgeni Bauer; *phot.:* Boris Zavelyov.
Cast: Ivan Mozhukhin, I. Lashchinilina, P. Biryukov.

Chrysanthemums (Krizantemi). 1,140 m., Khanzhonkov   4 Nov.
Dir.: Pyotr Chardynin; *phot.:* Boris Zavelyov; *mus.:* Y. Bakaleinikov.
Cast: Vera Coralli, Ivan Mozhukhin, R. Reizen.

Days of Our Life (Dni nashei zhizni). 1,662 m., Russian Golden Series   11 Nov.
Scen.: Leonid Andreyev (from his play); *dir.:* Vladimir Gardin; *phot.:* Alexander
Levitsky.
Cast: M. Tamarov, B. Orlitsky, Y. Butkova, L. Sychova.

Volga and Siberia (Volga i sibir). 1,600 m., Khanzhonkov   18 Nov.
Dir.: Vasili Goncharov; *phot.:* Louis Forestier, Alexander Rillo; *mus.* (for
performance): Mikhail Ippolitov-Ivanov.
Cast: P. Lopukhin (Yermak), Pyotr Chardynin (Ivan the Terrible), P. Knorr.

Symphony of Love and Death (Simfoniya lyubvi i smerti). 1,300 m., Taldykin
Scen. (from play by Pushkin): B. Martov; *dir.:* V. Turzhansky,   26 Nov.
S. Yuriev; *phot.:* Nikolai Kozlovsky.
Cast: Alexander Geirot (Mozart), A. Michurin (Salieri), Olga Baklanova.

Slave of Passion, Slave of Vice (Raba strastei, raba poroka), 1,100 m., Creo
Dir.: M. Martov (?).   7 Dec.
Cast: Pola Negri, V. Bridzinsky, V. Shavinsky.

Daughter of Albion [and] **Illegal** (Doch Albiona. Bezzakoniye). 450 m., Russian
  Ribbon
From stories by Chekhov; *dir.:* Boris Glagolin; *phot.:* A. Pechkovsky.
Cast: K. Karatygina, Konstantin Yakovlev.

When the Strings of the Heart Sound (Kogda zvuchat struni serdtza). 1.050 m.,
Dir.: Boris Sushkevich (?).   Libken
Cast: Yevgeni Vakhtangov, Mikhail Chekhov, Olga Baklanova, Sushkevich.

Sonka the Golden Hand (Sonka zolotaya ruchka), in eight serial parts (1914-16)
Drankov & Kinolenta
Scen.: V. Garlitsky, V. Rubinov, I. Rapgof (Count Amori); *dir.:* Y. Yurevsky,
Vladimir Kasyanov, Alexander Chargonin; *phot.:* Ivan Frolov.
Cast: V. Hoffman, B. Svetlov, A. Varyagin, Chargonin.

1915

Ghosts (Privideniya). 1,200 m., Russian Golden Series   13 Jan.
Scen. (from Ibsen's play) *& dir.:* Vladimir Gardin; *phot.:* Alexander Levitsky.
Cast: Pavel Orlenev.

Ruslan i Ludmila. 1,514 m., Khanzhonkov   19 Jan.
Scen. (from poem by Pushkin), *dir., phot. & des.:* Wladyslaw Starewicz.
Cast: Ivan Mozhukhin, S. Goslavskaya, A. Bibikov, E. Pukhalsky, N. Pomer-
antsev, A. Gromov.

The Bloody East (Krovavy vostok). 1,875 m., Kinolenta   5 Feb.
Scen.: Emil Beskin; *dir.:* Alexander Arkatov; *phot.:* Ivan Frolov.
Cast: N. Chernobayeva, M. Tarov, I. Talanov.

An American Millionaire Perishes on the 'Lusitania' (Gibel amerikanskovo
milliardera na 'Lusitanii'). 900 m., Lucifer   6 Feb.
Dir.: E. Pukhalsky.
Cast: N. Saltikov (Vanderbilt).

A Nest of Noblemen (Dvoryanskoye gnezdo). 2,200 m., Russian Golden Series.
9 Feb.
From novel by Turgenev; *dir.:* Vladimir Gardin; *phot.:* Alexander Levitsky.
Cast: Olga Preobrazhenskaya, M. Tamarov, Y. Uvarova, L. Sychova, Vladimir
Shaternikov, B. Orlitsky.

Petersburg Slums (Peterburgskiye trushchobi), in four series, Yermoliev
12 Feb.-30 Aug.
Scen. (from novel by Krestovsky) *& dir.:* Vladimir Gardin, Yakov Protazanov;
phot.: Alexander Levitsky.
Cast: Olga Preobrazhenskaya, L. Sychova, Lydia Rindina, V. Maximov.

War and Peace (Voina i mir). 10 reels, in two series, Russian Golden Series
13 Feb.-14 Apr.
Scen. (from Tolstoy's novel) *& dir.:* Vladimir Gardin, Yakov Protazanov; *phot.:*
Alexander Levitsky; *des.:* Cheslav Sabinsky, Ivan Kavaleridze.
Cast: Olga Preobrazhenskaya, N. Nikolsky, N. Rumyantzev, V. Vasiliev, V.
Schilling, T. Krasovskaya, Osip Runich, A. Bestuzhev, G. Novikov, Gardin
(Napoleon).

Natasha Rostova. 1,600 m., Khanzhonkov   13 Feb.
From Tolstoy's *War and Peace*; *dir.:* Pyotr Chardynin; *des.:* V. Fester.
Cast: Vera Coralli, Vitold Polonsky, Ivan Mozhukhin, P. Lopukhin.

Brand. 1,250 m., Russian Golden Series (filmed in Norway)   19 Feb.
Scen. (from Ibsen's play) *& dir.:* Pavel Orlenev; *co-dir.:* Kai Hansen; *phot.:*
George Meyer (Mundviller); *ed.:* Vladimir Gardin (?).
Cast: Orlenev, V. Popova, G. Gnesin, Orlov.

Plebeian (Plebei). 4 reels, Russian Golden Series   4 Mar.
Scen. (from Strindberg's play, *Froken Julie*) *& dir.:* Yakov Protazanov; *phot.:*
N. Yefremov.
Cast: Olga Preobrazhenskaya, Nikolai Radin.

The Great Magaraz. (Veliky Magaraz). 1,400 m., Kinolenta   27 Mar.
Scen.: Anatoli Kamensky; *dir.:* Vyacheslav Turzhansky, Kamensky.

Cast.: Yevgeni Vakhtangov, M. Goricheva, Turzhansky (Magaraz), Olga Baklanova.

Flood (Potop). 8 reels in two series, Khanzhonkov   14 Apr.
From novel by Henryk Sienkiewicz; *dir.:* Pyotr Chardynin.
Cast: A. Virubov, Ivan Mozhukhin, Pyotr Starkovsky, A. Kheruvimov, A. Bibikov, P. Knorr, P. Lopukhin, A. Gromov, N. Nelskaya.

The Dead Man (Myortvetz). 1,050 m., Drankov   7 May
Scen.: (from play by Lemonnier) & *dir.:* Alexander Tairov.
Cast: Izvolsky, Catherine Devilliers, G. Voskresensky.

Cricket on the Hearth (Sverchok na pechi). 710 m., Russian Golden Series
20 May
Scen.: (from Dickens's story) & *dir.:* Boris Sushkevich, A. Uralsky; *phot.:* Brizzi; *des.:* Vladimir Yegorov, V. Uzunov.
Cast: Grigori Khmara, Yevgeni Vakhtangov, Mikhail Chekhov, M. Durasova, Vera Soloviova.

The Venetian Stocking (Venetziansky chulok). 602 m., Khanzhonkov   25 July
Scen.: Valentin Turkin; *dir.:* Pyotr Chardynin.
Cast: V. Glinskaya, N. Bashilov.

Wanderer Beyond the Grave (Zagrobnaya skitalitsa). 1,100 m., Taldykin, Kozlovsky & Co.   6 Aug.
Scen.: Anatoli Kamensky; *dir.:* V. Turzhansky; *phot.:* Nikolai Kozlovsky.
Cast: Olga Baklanova, Turzhansky, A. Virubov, A. Michurin.

Song of Triumphant Love (Pesn torzhestvuyushchei liubvi). 1,433 m., Khanzhonkov.   22 Aug.
Scen.: (from Turgenev's story) & *dir.:* Yevgeni Bauer; *phot.:* K. Bauer, Boris Zavelyov.
Cast: Vera Kholodnaya, Osip Runich, Vitold Polonsky.

Nikolai Stavrogin. 2,200 m., Yermoliev   1 Sep.
Scen. (from Dostoyevsky's novel, *Devils*) & *dir.:* Yakov Protazanov; *phot.:* Yevgeni Slavinsky; *des.:* Nikolai Suvorov.
Cast: Ivan Mozhukhin, Lydia Rindina, A. Ivonin, Pyotr Starkovsky, Nikolai Panov, Vera Orlova.

Yekaterina Ivanovna. 2,030 m., Russian Golden Series   15 Sep.
Scen.: Leonid Andreyev (from his play); *dir.:* A. Uralsky; *phot.:* Alexander Levitsky.
Cast: Maria Germanova, N. Massalitinov, M. Durasova, Ivan Bersenev.

Tsar Ivan Vasilyevich Grozny. 1,600 m., Sharez   20 Oct.
From the play and opera, *Pskovityanka; dir.:* A. Ivanov-Gai; *phot.:* Alphonse Winkler; *des.:* Vladimir Yegorov.
Cast: Fyodor Shalyapin, N. Saltikov, Richard Boleslawski, Boris Sushkevich.

Singed Wings (Obozhzhenniye krylya). 6 reels, Khanzhonkov   27 Oct.
From novel by Slezkin, *Olga Org; dir.:* Yevgeny Bauer; *phot.:* Boris Zavelyov.
Cast: S. Rassatov, Vera Coralli, Osip Runich, Vitold Polonsky, K. Karenin.

Love of a State Councillor (Lyubov statskovo sovietnika. 1,415 m., Khanzhonkov
10 Nov.
Scen.: Yevgeni Chirikov; *dir.:* Pyotr Chardynin; *phot.:* Boris Zavelyov.
Cast: V. Elsky, M. Kassatskaya, Vera Coralli.

The Picture of Dorian Gray (Portret Doriana Greya). 2,124 m., Russian Golden Series
1 Dec.
Scen. (from Wilde's novel) & *dir.:* Vsevolod Meyerhold; *co-dir.:* Mikhail Doronin; *phot.:* Alexander Levitsky; *des.:* Vladimir Yegorov.

Cast: Varvara Yanova (Dorian), Meyerhold (Lord Henry Wotton), G. Enriton, P. Belova, Doronin, Y. Uvarova, Alexander Volkov.

In the Claws of a Professor-Speculator (V lapakh professora-aferista). 800 m. *Dir.:* Boris Glagolin; *phot,:* A. Pechkovsky.

Cast: D. Rabrin, N. Ribnikov, Sabinina.

Inhabitant of a Desert Isle (Zhitel nyeobitayemovo ostrova). 850 m., Skobelev Committee.

Scen., dir., phot. & des.: Wladyslaw Starewicz.

Cast: A. Gromov, N. Valitzkaya, Yelena Chaika, Starewicz (faun).

1916

Miss Peasant (Barishna-krestyanka). 1,281 m., Vengerov & Gardin   4 Feb.
Scen. (from Pushkin's story) *& dir.:* Olga Preobrazhenskaya; *phot.:* A. Stanke; *des.:* Sergei Kozlovsky.

Cast: A. Miklashevskaya, N. Skryabin, S. Golovin.

Thief (Vor). 4 reels, Persky   11 Feb.
Scen. (from Notari's novel, *The Three Thieves*): Anatoli Kamensky; *dir.:* M. Bonch-Tomashevsky; *phot.:* Alexander Lemberg.

Cast.: V. Maximov, Vera Baranovskaya.

Love's Surprises Are Futile (Liubvi syurprizi tshchetniye). 400 m., Russian Golden Series   16 Feb.
From O. Henry's story, 'The Gift of the Magi'; *dir.:* Vyacheslav Viskovsky; *phot.:* Brizzi; *des.:* Vladimir Yegorov.

Cast: Mikhail Chekhov, Brodskaya, Malevich.

Queen of the Screen (Koroleva ekrana). 1,950 m., Khanzhonkov   29 Feb.
Scen.: A. Voznesensky; *dir.:* Yevgeni Bauer; *phot.:* Boris Zavelyov.

Cast: Vitold Polonsky, V. Yureneva, Grigori Khmara.

The Queen of Spades (Pikovaya dama). 2,300 m., Yermoliev   19 Apr.
Scen. (from Pushkin's story): Fyodor Otsep; *dir.:* Yakov Protazanov; *asst.:* Georgi Azagarov; *phot.:* Yevgeni Slavinsky; *des.:* Vladimir Balliuzek, S. Lilienberg, V. Pshibitnevsky.

Cast: Ivan Mozhukhin, Vera Orlova, Y. Shebuyeva.

A Life for a Life (Zhizn za zhizn). 2,175 m., Khanzhonkov   10 May
Scen. (from *Serge Panine,* by Georges Ohnet) *& dir.:* Yevgeni Bauer; *phot.:* Boris Zavelyov.

Cast: Olga Rakhmanova, Lydia Koreneva, Vera Kholodnaya, Vitold Polonsky.

In the Kingdom of Oil and Millions (V tzarstve nefti i millionov). 8 reels in two series, Filma, Baku   14 & 27 May
Scen. (from novel by Ibrahim Bek-Musabekov): A. Panova-Potemkina; *dir.:* B. Svetlov; *phot.:* Grigori Lemberg.

Cast: K. Piontkovskaya, R. Lazareva, Y. Muromsky, Y. Orlitskaya, V. Lenin.

Woman with a Dagger (Zhenshchina s kinzhalom). 1,650 m., Yermoliev 31 May
Scen: Nikolai Rimsky; *dir.:* Yakov Protazanov.

Cast: Ivan Mozhukhin, Olga Gzovskaya, Nikolai Panov, Zoya Karabanova.

The Green Spider (Zelyonyi pauk). 1,600 m., Russian Golden Series   30 Aug.
dir.: Alexander Volkov; *asst.* Yuri Zhelyabuzhsky; *phot:* Alexander Rillo; *des.:* Vladimir Yegorov.

Cast: Maria Rutz, Nikolai Tseretelli, Konstantin Khokhlov.

His Eyes (Yevo glaza). 1,500 m., Russian Golden Series   19 Sep.
Scen. (from novel by Fyodorov) *& dir.:* Vyacheslav Viskovsky; *phot.:* Alexander Rillo; *des.:* Vladimir Yegorov.

Cast: A. Rudnitsky, M. Moravskaya, Vera Soloviova.

Griffon of an Old Warrior (Grif starovo bortza). 4 reels, Khanzhonkov 28 Sep.
Scen.: Ivan Perestiani; *dir.:* Yevgeni Bauer; *phot.:* Boris Zavelyov.
Cast: Vera Coralli, Perestiani, Vladimir Strizhevsky.

On the Warsaw Highroad (Na Varshavskom trakte). 1,250 m., Skobelev Committee 4 Oct.
Scen.: V. Veronich; *dir. & phot.:* Wladyslaw Starewicz; *des.:* Boris Mikhin, Ivan Suvorov.
Cast: S. Chapelsky, Z. Valevskaya, S. Zelinsky.

Thought (Mysl). 1,185 m., Vengerov & Gardin 11 Oct.
Scen. (from story by Andreyev)*:* Vladimir Gardin; *dir.:* Gardin, Josef Soifer; *phot.:* Yevgeni Frantzisson; *des.:* V. Ilyin.
Cast: Grigori Khmara, N. Komarovskaya.

He Who Gets Slapped (Tot, kto poluchayet poshchechini). 1,500 m., Drankov 16 Oct.
Scen. (from Andreyev's play) *& dir.:* Alexander Ivanov-Gai, I. Schmidt; *phot.:* Louis Forestier; *des.:* Dmitri Kolupayev, S. Kuznetzov.
Cast: Illarion Pevtsov, Olga Baklanova, I. Vronsky, A. Nekrasov.

The Double (Dvoinik). 5 reels, Taldykin, Kozlovsky & Co. 3 Nov.
Scen.: Anatoli Kamensky; *dir.:* V. Demert; *phot.:* Nikolai Kozlovsky.
Cast: N. Chernova, Oleg Froelich (in two rôles).

The Corner (Ugolok). Yermoliev 22 Nov.
Scen. & dir.: Cheslav Sabinsky; *phot.:* Yevgeni Slavinsky.
Cast: Maria Germanova.

Sin (Grekh). 13 reels in three series, Yermoliev 20 Sep. & 24 Jan. '17
Scen.: Ivan Mozhukhin; *dir.:* Yakov Protazanov, Georgi Azagarov.
Cast: Mozhukhin, Natalia Lisenko, Pyotr Baksheyev, Vera Orlova.

1917
Death of the Gods (Smert bogov). 5 reels, Kino-tvorchestvo 6 Jan.
Scen. (from Merezhkovsky's novel) *& dir.:* Vladimir Kasyanov; *phot.:* Louis Forestier; *des.:* A. Yakimchenko, K. Yefimov & others.
Cast: Illarion Pevtsov (Julian), V. Gradov, Margerita Froman.

Public Prosecutor (Prokuror). 1,750 m., Yermoliev 20 Feb.
Dir.: Yakov Protazanov.
Cast: Ivan Mozhukhin, Vera Orlova, Natalia Lisenko.

Great Days of the Russian Revolution (Velikiye dni Rossiiskoi revolutsii s 28/II po 4/III 1917 goda). Union of Patriotic Cinematographers.
Dir.: M. Bonch-Tomashevsky, Vyacheslav Viskovsky; *phot.:* Alexander Levitsky, Samuel Bendersky, Yevgeni Slavinsky.

The Flowers Are Late (Tsveti zapozdaliye). 1,302 m., Vengerov & Gardin 19 Mar.
From a story by Chekhov; *dir.:* Boris Sushkevich; *phot.:* A. Stanke; *des.:* Sergei Kozlovsky.
Cast: Olga Baklanova, Alexander Geirot, Sushkevich, Maria Uspenskaya.

Revolutionist (Revolutsioner). 4 reels, Khanzhonkov 3 Apr.
Scen.: Ivan Perestiani; *dir.:* Yevgeni Bauer.
Cast: Perestiani, Vladimir Strizhevsky, Z. Bogdanova.

Isle of Oblivion (Ostrov zabvenya). 5 reels, Biofilm 7 Apr.
Scen.: Lev Nikulin (from a story by Poe); *dir.:* Vyacheslav Turzhansky; *phot.:* F. Verigo-Darovsky; *des.:* V. Rakovsky.
Cast: Turzhansky, Y. Chaika, V. Elsky.

Her Sacrifice (Yeyo zhertva). 5 reels, Yermoliev   8 Apr.
From Ibsen's *Doll's House*; *dir.*: Cheslav Sabinsky.
Cast: Olga Gzovskaya, Vladimir Gaidarov, Nikolai Panov.

Andrei Kozhukhov. 2,264 m., in two series, Yermoliev   19 Apr.
Scen. (from story by Stepniak-Kravchinsky) *& dir.:* Yakov Protazanov.
Cast: Ivan Mozhukhin, Georgi Azagarov, Vera Orlova, Nikolai Rimsky.

The Beilis Case (Delo Beilisa). 6 reels, Svetoten, Kiev   25 Apr.
Scen.: N. Breshko-Breshkovsky; *dir.:* Josef Soifer; *phot.:* N. Toporkov.
Cast: Y. Yakovlev (Mendel Beilis), Malkevich-Khodakovskaya, S. Kuznetsov.

The Alarm (Nabat). 7 reels, Khanzhonkov   5 May
Scen. (from novel by Werner) *& dir.:* Yevgeni Bauer; *phot.:* Boris Zavelyov;
des.: Lev Kuleshov, N. Belyi; *ed.:* Antonina Khanzhonkova, V. Popova.
Cast: Nikolai Radin, Vera Coralli, M. Narokov, V. Svoboda, Zoya Barantsevich,
Vladimir Strizhevsky, Konstantin Khokhlov, Nikolai Tseretelli.

Blood Need Not Be Spilled (Ne nado krovi). 5 reels, Yermoliev   30 May
Scen. & dir.: Yakov Protazanov.
Cast: Olga Gzovskaya, Nikolai Panov, Vladimir Gaidarov.

The Life and Death of Lieutenant Schmidt (Zhizn i smert Leitenanta
Schmidta). 5 reels, Kinolenta   5 July
Scen. & dir.: Yakov Poselsky, Alexander Razumni; *phot.:* Alphonse Winkler

Cursed Millions (Prokliatiye millioni). 8 reels, in two series, Yermoliev
From novel by Pazukhin; *dir.:* Yakov Protazanov.   1 & 9 Aug.
Cast: A. Gribunina, Nikolai Rimsky, V. Charova, Z. Valevskaya.

The King of Paris (Korol Parizha). Khanzhonkov
From Georges Ohnet's novel; *dir.:* Yevgeni Bauer; *phot.:* Boris Zavelyov;
des.: Lev Kuleshov.
Cast: Nikolai Radin, Vera Coralli, L. Koreneva, M. Boldyrev.

Tsar Nikolai II. 5 reels, Skobelev Committee   9 Oct.
Scen.: A. Voznesensky, supervised by V. Burtsev; *dir.:* A. Ivonin, Boris Mikhin;
phot.: Alexander Levitsky; *des.:* Mikhin.
Cast: Pyotr Baksheyev, Vera Orlova, N. Golosov, M. Kemper.

The Strong Man (Silnyi chelovek). 7 reels, Era   9 Oct.
Scen.: (from novel by Przybyszewski): Vitold Akhramovich; *dir.:* Vsevolod
Meyerhold; *asst.:* Akhramovich, Mikhail Doronin; *phot.:* Samuel Bendersky;
des.: Vladimir Yegorov.
Cast: Konstantin Khokhlov, Varvara Yanova, Meyerhold, M. Zhdanova, Doronin.

Satan Triumphant (Satana likuyushchii). 3,683 m., in two series, Yermoliev.
     21 Oct.
Scen.: Olga Blazhevich; *dir.:* Yakov Protazanov; *phot.:* Fyodor Burgasov.
Cast: Ivan Mozhukhin, Natalia Lisenko, P. Pavlov, A. Chabrov, Vera Orlova.

Don't Build Your Happiness on Your Wife and Child (Ne stroi s'chastya
svoyevo na zhene i rebyonke). 5 reels, Vengerov
Scen. (from Hauptmann's play, *Elga*) *& dir.:* Josef Soifer; *phot.:* A. Stanke;
des.: K. Kostin.
Cast: M. Zhdanova, Grigori Khmara, Soifer.

1918
Creation Can't Be Bought (Nye dlya deneg radivshisya). Antik   Apr.
Scen. (from Jack London's *Martin Eden)*: David Burlyuk, Vladimir Mayakovsky;
dir.: Nikandr Turkin; *phot.:* Yevgeni Slavinsky; *des.:* Burlyuk, Vladimir Yegorov.
Cast: Mayakovsky, Burlyuk, Margerita Kibalchich, L. Grinkrug, V. Kamensky.

The Young Lady and the Hooligan (Barishnya i khuligan). 885 m., Neptune May
  Scen. (from *Cuore*, by Edmond d'Amicis): Vladimir Mayakovsky; *dir. & phot.:*
  Yevgeni Slavinsky; *des.:* Vladimir Yegorov.
  Cast: Mayakovsky, A. Rebikova.

Father Sergius (Otets Sergii). 1,920 m., Yermoliev   14 May
  Scen. (from Tolstoy's story): Alexander Volkov; *dir.:* Yakov Protazanov; *phot.:*
  Fyodor Burgasov, N. Rudakov; *des.:* Vladimir Balliuzek, A. Loshakov, N.
  Vorobyov; *mus.* (for performance): Y. Bukke.
  Cast: Ivan Mozhukhin, V. Dzheneyeva, Vladimir Gaidarov (Nikolai I), Natalia
  Lisenko, Vera Orlova, Pyotr Baksheyev, Nikolai Panov.

Aziade. Khabsayev   May
  Scen. & dir.: Josef Soifer; *phot.:* A. Stanke.
  Cast: Mikhail Mordkin, Margerita Froman.

Shackled by Film (Zakovannaya filmoi). 5 reels, Neptune   June
  Scen.: Vladimir Mayakovsky; *dir.:* Nikandr Turkin.
  Cast: Mayakovsky, Lily Brik, Margerita Kibalchich, A. Rebikova.

Engineer Prite's Project (Proyekt inzhenera Praita). 4 reels, Khanzhonkov
  Scen.: B. Kuleshov; *dir. & des.:* Lev Kuleshov; *phot.:* N. Naletni.
  Cast: L. Polevoy, Boris Kuleshov, E. Komarova, Ernest Kulganin.

The Woman Who Invented Love (Zhenshchina, kotoraya izobrela liubov).
  10 reels in two series, Kharitonov.
  Dir.: Vyacheslav Viskovsky; *phot.:* V. Siversen; *des.:* Alexander Utkin.
  Cast: Vera Kholodnaya, V. Maximov, Osip Runich, I. Khudoleyev.

The Power of Darkness (Vlast tmy). 1,200 m., Yermoliev.
  Scen.: (from Tolstoy's play) *& dir.:* Cheslav Sabinsky; *phot.:* Mikhail
  Vladimirsky.
  Cast: Pyotr Baksheyev, Vera Orlova, Nikolai Panov.

Eva. 5 reels, Biofilm.
  Dir.: Ivan Perestiani.
  Cast: Zoya Karabanova, Amo Bek-Nazarov, Perestiani.

Maids of the Mountain (Devi gori). Russ.
  Scen.: Yevgeni Chirikov (from his 'Volga Legend'); *dir.:* Alexander Sanin;
  phot.: Wladyslaw Starewicz, Yuri Zheliabuzhsky; *des.:* Victor Simov; *mus.:*
  Arkhangelsky.
  Cast: Alexandrovsky (Judas), V. Podgorni (Satan), Sergei Aidarov.

A Living Corpse (Zhivoi trup). 6 reels, Kharitonov
  Scen. (from Tolstoy's play) *& dir.:* Cheslav Sabinsky; *phot.:* V. Siversen,
  Alexander Rillo; *des.:* Alexander Utkin.
  Cast: V. Maximov, Vera Kholodnaya, Osip Runich.

Bruised by the Storms of Life (Burei zhizni smyatiye). 5 reels, Merkazor
  Dir.: Josef Soifer.
  Cast: M. Zhdanova, Grigori Khmara, A. Gromov.

When Will We Dead Awaken? (Kogda my, myortviye, voskresnyom?) 6 reels,
  Literfilm
  From Ibsen's play; *dir.:* Yakov Poselsky; *phot.:* Grigori Giber; *des.:* K. Kostin,
  N. Mendelevich.
  Cast: Mikhail Doronin, S. Volkhovskaya, L. Zhukov.

Love—Hate—Death (Liubov—nenavist—smert). 7 reels, Biofilm
  Scen.: A. Smoldovsky; *dir.:* Ivan Perestiani; *phot.:* Grigori Giber; *des.:* V.
  Rakovsky.

Cast: Zoya Karabanova, Perestiani, Richard Boleslawsky.
Paradise Without Adam (Rai bez Adama). 1,200 m., Kozlovsky, Yuriev & Co.
Dir.: Vyacheslav Turzhansky; *phot.:* Nikolai Kozlovsky.
Bread (Khleb). 1,300 m., Mos-Kino-Committee
Scen.: V. Dobrovolsky (Fyodorovich); *dir.* Boris Sushkevich, Richard Boleslawski; *phot.:* N. Rudakov.
Cast: Leonid Leonidov, Olga Baklanova, Boleslawski, Yevgeni Vakhtangov.
Signal. 600 m., Mos-Kino-Committee
Scen. (from a story by Garshin): I. Vinyar; *dir.:* Alexander Arkatov; *phot.:* Edward Tisse, I. Dored.
Cast: Grabevetskaya.
Tale of Priest Pankrati (Skazka o pope Pankrate). 1,100 m., Mos-Kino-Committee 7 Nov.
Scen. (from a fable by Demyan Byedny) & *dir.:* Preobrazhensky, Alexander Arkatov; *phot.:* Alexander Levitsky.
Cast: Preobrazhensky, L. Sychova.
Underground (Podpolye). 400 m., Mos-Kino-Committee 7 Nov.
Scen.: Alexander Serafimovich, I. Vinyar; *dir.:* Vladimir Kasyanov; *phot.:* Alexander Levitsky.
Uprising (Vosstaniye). 5 reels, Mos-Kino-Committee 7 Nov.
Scen.: V. Dobrovolsky (Fyodorovich); *dir.:* Alexander Razumni, Vladimir Karin; *phot.:* Alexander Levitsky; *des.:* Vladimir Yegorov.
Congestion (Uplotneniye). 1,560 m., Petro-Kino-Committee 7 Nov.
Scen.: Anatoli Lunacharsky, Alexander Panteleyev; *dir.:* Panteleyev, D. Pashkovsky, A. Dolinov; *phot.:* Vladimir Lemke, Pyotr Novitsky.
Cast: I. Lersky, Dmitri Leshchenko.

1919
Runaway (Beglets). 413 m., Khanzhonkov & Mos-Kino-Committee 23 Feb.
Scen.: G. Nikolayev; *dir.:* Boris Chaikovsky, Alexander Anoshchenko.
Father and Son (Otetz i syn). 358 m., Khanzhonkov & Mos-Kino-Committee
Scen.: A. Rublev; *dir.:* Ivan Perestiani. 23 Feb.
Cast: Perestiani, T. Maximova.
Tovarishch Abram. 533 m., Yermoliev & Mos-Kino-Committee 23 Feb.
Scen.: Feofan Shipulinsky; *dir., phot.* & *des.:* Alexander Razumni.
Cast: Dmitri Bukhovetsky.
Daredevil (Smelchak). 1,045 m., Neptune & Mos-Kino-Committee 23 Feb.
Scen.: Anatoli Lunacharsky; *dir.:* M. Narokov, Nikandr Turkin; *phot.:* Yevgeni Slavinsky.
Cast: Narokov, Alperov.
For the Red Banner (Za krasnoye znamya). 316 m., Neptune & Mos-Kino-Committee 23 Feb.
Scen.: A. Smoldovsky; *dir.:* Vladimir Kasyanov; *phot.:* S. Zebel; *ed.:* Vladimir Gardin.
Cast: V. Ostrovsky, Oleg Froelich, V. Vasiliev, A. Kasyanov.
Children—Flowers of Life (Deti—tzveti zhizni). 1,246 m., VFKO (Science Dept.)
Scen.: Yuri Zheliabuzhsky, Nikolai Tikhonov; *dir.* & *phot.:* Zheliabuzhsky; *des.:* Sergei Kozlovsky.
Cast: V. Osvetsinsky, Anna Dmokhovskaya, A. Nelidov.
Savva. 1,000 m., Yermoliev & Mos-Kino-Committee 1 May
Scen. (from Andreyev's play) & *dir.:* Cheslav Sabinsky; *phot.:* Mikhail Vladimirsky.

The Emperor's New Clothes (Novoye platye korolya). 800 m., Russ & VFKO.
Scen. (from story by Hans Andersen), *dir. & phot.:* Yuri Zheliabuzhsky; *des:*
Sergei Kozlovsky.
Peter and Alexis (Pyotr i Alexei). Russ.
Scen. (from Merezhkovsky's play) *& dir.:* Yuri Zhelyabuzhsky.
Cast: Leonid Leonidov, N. Rybnikov.
Scared Bourgeoisie (Zapugannii burzhui). 740 m., All-Ukrainian Kino Committee.
Scen.: Lev Nikulin, Yakov Yadov; *dir.:* Mikhail Werner; *phot.:* A. Stanke.
Cast: Frank-Nikolsky, L. Tridenskaya, A. Werner, V. Gradov.
Peace to the Cottage, War to the Palace (Mir khizhinam, voina dvortzam).
Film Section of the People's Commissariat of War, Ukraine
Scen.: Lev Nikulin, Boris Leonidov; *dir.:* M. Bonch-Tomashevsky; *phot.:*
Vladimir Dobrozhansky.
The Queen's Secret (Taina korolevy). 1,800 m., Yermoliev (Moscow & Yalta) 5 Nov.
Scen. (from Elinor Glyn's *Three Weeks*) *& dir.:* Yakov Protazanov; *phot.:* N.
Rudakov; *des.:* Vladimir Balliuzek.
Cast: Ivan Mozhukhin, Natalia Lissenko, Nikolai Rimsky, I. Talanov.
The Iron Heel (Zhelaznaya pyata). Gos-Kino-School & VFKO   7 Nov.
Scen. (from Jack London's novel) *& dir.:* Vladimir Gardin; *phot.:* Alexander
Levitsky, Grigori Giber.
Cast: Leonid Leonidov, A. Shakhalov, N. Znamensky, Olga Preobrazhenskaya.
Polikushka. 6 reels, Russ (released October 1922)
Scen. (from Tolstoy's story): Valentin Turkin, Fyodor Otsep, Nikolai Efros;
dir.: Alexander Sanin; *phot.:* Yuri Zheliabuzhsky; *des.:* Sergei Kozlovsky, S.
Petrov; *mus.* (for performance): Dobrovein.
Cast: Ivan Moskvin, Vera Pashennaya, Yevgeniya Rayevskaya, V. Bulgakov,
Varvara Massalitinova.

1920
Story of Seven Who Were Hanged (Rasskaz o syemi poveshchennikh). 2,350 m.,
All-Ukrainian Kino Committee (Moscow release March 1924)
Scen. (from Andreyev's story) *& dir.:* Pyotr Chardynin, N. Saltikov; *phot.:*
Alexander Grinberg, Y. Kapitta, G. Drobin; *des.:* Nikolai Suvorov, Alexander
Utkin
Cast: Loren, Chitorin, Lorenzo, Vostorgov, Insarov.
Mother (Mat) 1,150 m , Mos-Kino-Committee   1 May
Scen. (from Gorky's novel): M. Stupina; *dir.:* Alexander Razumni; *phot.:*
Alexander Levitsky, N. Rudakov; *des.:* Vladimir Yegorov.
Cast: Vladimir Karin, L. Sychova, Ivan Bersenev.
Thieving Magpie (Soroka-vorovka). Russ & VFKO
Scen. (from a story by Herzen): Nikolai Efros; *dir.:* Alexander Sanin; *phot:*
Alexander Levitsky; *des.:* A. Arapov, Sergei Kozlovsky; *mus.* (for performance):
V. Ziring.
Cast: Olga Gzovskaya.
Jola. Russ
Scen. (from a story by Zhulavsky): Nikolai Efros; *dir.* Wladyslaw Starewicz.
Cast: Olga Gzovskaya, Vladimir Gaidarov.
Domestic-Agitator (Domovoi agitator). 1,000 m., VFKO
Scen.: I. Alexeyev (Novikov); *dir. & phot.:* Yuri Zheliabuzhsky; *des.:* Vladimir
Yegorov.
Cast: G. Burdzhalov, N. Kostromsky, Nikolai Khmelyov, N. Dobronravov.

Village in Crisis (Derevnya na perelome). 1,200 m., Slonfilm & VFKO
  Scen.: I. Alexeyev (Novikov); *dir.:* Cheslav Sabinsky; *phot.:* Alexander Rillo;
  des.: Vladimir Balliuzek.
On the Red Front (Na krasnom fronte). 700 m., Kino-Section, Moscow Soviet
  & VFKO
  Scen. & dir.: Lev Kuleshov; *phot.:* Pyotr Yermolov.
  Cast: Leonid Obolensky, Y. Reich, Alexandra Khokhlova.
In the Days of Struggle (V dni borbi). 600 m., Gos-Kino-School & VFKO
  Scen. & dir.: Ivan Perestiani; *phot.:* Nikolai Kozlovsky.
  Cast: Vsevolod Pudovkin, Andrei Gorchilin, Nina Shaternikova, N. Vishnyak,
  Feofan Shipulinsky.

1921
Sickle and Hammer (Serp i molot). 1,500 m., Gos-Kino-School & VFKO
  Scen.: Andrei Gorchilin, Feofan Shipulinsky; *dir.:* Vladimir Gardin; *asst.:*
  Vsevolod Pudovkin; *phot.:* Edward Tisse.
  Cast: Pudovkin (Andrei Krasnov), A. Gromov, Gorchilin, N. Zubova.
History of the Civil War (Istoriya grazhdanskoi voini). 13 reels, All-Russian
  Kino Committee (of Narkompros)
  Ed.: Dziga Vertov.
Arsen Georgiashvili (or **The Murder of General Gryaznov**). 1,500 m., Kino
  Section of Georgian Commissariat of Education
  Scen.: Shalvoi Dadiani, Ivan Perestiani; *dir.:* Perestiani, A. Nikidze; *phot.:*
  Alexander Digmelov; *des.:* F. Push.
  Cast: Mikhail Chiaureli (Arsen), Perestiani, N. Yachmenev (Gryaznov), N.
  Dolidze, Alisa Kikadze.
Hunger—Hunger—Hunger (Golod . . . golod . . . golod). 500 m., Gos-Kino-
  School & VFKO
  Scen. & dir.: Vladimir Gardin, Vsevolod Pudovkin; *phot.:* Eduard Tisse.
  Cast: N. Vishnyak, A. Gromov.

1922
Infinite Sorrow (Skorb beskonechnaya). 2,200 m., Sevzapkino & First Petrograd
  Collective of Screen Artists
  Scen.: A. Zorin; *dir.:* Alexander Panteleyev; *phot.:* Nikolai Kozlovsky; *des.:*
  S. Vorobyov.
  Cast: P. Kirillov, U. Krug, V. Maximov, Y. Chaika.
Film-Truth (Kino-pravda).   First issue released 21 May
  Dir.: Dziga Vertov; *asst.:* Ilya Kopalin; *phot.:* Mikhail Kaufman, I. Belyakov,
  A. Lemberg; *ed.;* Yelizaveta Svilova.
Miracle-Maker (Chudotvorets). 1,600 m., Sevzapkino & First Petrograd Collective
  of Screen Artists   22 Nov.
  Scen.: A. Zorin; *dir.:* Alexander Panteleyev; *phot.:* Nikolai Kozlovsky.
  Cast: Kirillov, Y. Tumanskaya.
In the Whirlwind of Revolution (V vikhre revolutsii). 1,750 m., VFKO
  Scen. (from an idea by Troyekurov): P. Voyevodin; *dir.:* Alexander Chargonin;
  phot.: Yuri Zhelyabuzhsky; *des.:* Vladimir Balliuzek.
  Cast: N. Vishnyak, Zoya Barantsevich.

1923
A Spectre Haunts Europe (Prizrak brodit po Yevrope). 2,630 m., VUFKU, Yalta
                                                 13 Feb.

Scen. (from Poe's 'Masque of the Red Death'): Georgi Tasin; *dir.:* Vladimir Gardin; *phot.:* Boris Zavelyov; *des.:* Vladimir Yegorov.
Cast: Zoya Barantsevich, Oleg Froelich, I. Talanov, Vasili Kovrigin.

Locksmith and Chancellor (Slesar i kantzler). 2,165 m., VUFKU
Scen. (from Lunacharsky's play): Vladimir Gardin, Vsevolod Pudovkin; *dir.:* Gardin; *asst.:* Olga Preobrazhenskaya; *phot.:* Yevgeni Slavinsky; *des.:* Vladimir Yegorov.
Cast: I. Khudoleyev, Nikolai Panov, Gardin, V. Maximov, Zoya Barantsevich, I. Talanov, N. Saltikov.

Kombrig Ivanov, 1,750 m., Proletkino [US: Beauty and the Bolshevik]   24 Oct.
Scen. (from poem by Lelevich): Volero; *dir., phot. & des.:* Alexander Razumni.
Cast: Leontiev, Olga Tretyakov, Maria Blumenthal-Tamarina, N. Belayev.

Red Imps (Krasniye diavolyata). 3,800 m., in two series, Kino Section of Georgian Commissariat of Education   30 Nov.
Scen.: Pavel Blyakhin, Ivan Perestiani; *dir.:* Perestiani; *phot.:* Alexander Digmelov; *des.:* F. Push.
Cast: Pyotr Yesikovsky, Sofia Jozeffi, Kador Ben-Selim, V. Sutyrin (Makhno).

Fight for the 'Ultimatum' Factory (Borba za 'Ultimatum'). 1,865 m., Proletkino   24 Dec.
Scene: Mikhail Boitler, Vladimir Kirshon; *dir.:* Dmitri Bassaligo; *phot.:* Vladimir Dobrozhansky; *des.:* Alexander Utkin.
Cast: Olga Tretyakova, Tsekhanskaya, M. Lenin, Vladimir Karin.

1924

Palace and Fortress (Dvorets i krepost). 3,000 m., Sevzapkino   5 Feb.
Scen. (from a novel by Olga Forsh): Forsh & Pavel Shchegolev; *dir.:* Alexander Ivanovsky; *phot.:* Ivan Frolov, V. Glass; *des.:* V. Shchuko, B. Roerich.
Cast: Y. Boronikhin, Y. Korvin-Krukovsky, K. Yakovlev, S. Shishko, Gennadi Michurin.

Elder Vasili Gryaznov (Starets Vasili Gryaznov). 2,287 m., Goskino 25 Mar.
Scen.: I. Spitzberg; *dir.:* Cheslav Sabinsky; *asst.:* Abram Room; *phot.:* Eduard Tisse; *des.:* Dmitri Kolupayev.
Cast: Pyotr Starkovsky, Y. Kaverina, Max Tereshkovich, Maria Babanova, A. Gromov.

Father Frost (Morozko). 1,500 m., Mezhrabpom-Russ   9 Apr.
Scen. (from a Russian fairy-tale), *dir. & phot.:* Yuri Zheliabuzhsky; *des.:* Victor Simov, Sergei Kozlovsky.
Cast: Klavidya Yelanskaya, Varvara Massalitinova, Vasili Toporkov, Boris Livanov.

Extraordinary Adventures of Mr West in the Land of the Bolsheviks (Neobychainiye priklucheniya Mistera Vesta v stranye bolshevikov.) 2,680 m., Goskino   27 Apr.
Scen.: Nikolai Aseyev, Vsevolod Pudovkin; *dir.:* Lev Kuleshov; *asst.:* Pudovkin, Alexandra Khokhlova, Leonid Obolensky, Sergei Komarov, Porfiri Podobed, Leo Mur; *phot.:* Alexander Levitsky; *des.:* Pudovkin.
Cast: Podobed (Mr West), Valya Lopatina, Boris Barnet (cowboy), Pudovkin (the 'Count'), Khokhlova (the 'Countess'), Pyotr Galadzhev, Komarov, Obolensky, Vladimir Fogel.

In the Pillory (U pozernovo stolba). 1,686 m., Goskinprom, Georgia   6 May
Scen. (from *Patricide*, by Kazbek) *& Dir.:* Amo Bek-Nazarov; *phot:* Sergei Zabozlayev; *des.:* Valerian Sidamon-Eristov, K. Tir.
Cast: Nata Vachnadze, Kira Andronikashvili, Akaki Vazadze.

Interplanetary Revolution (Mezhplanetnaya revolutsiya). 350 m., Animation Workshop 18 Aug.
Des.: E. Komissarenko, Y. Merkulov, N. Khodatayev; *phot.:* V. Alexeyev.

Aelita. 1,841 m., Mezhrabpom-Russ 25 Sep.
Scen. (from novel by Alexei Tolstoy): Fyodor Otsep, Alexei Faiko; *dir.:* Yakov Protazanov; *phot.:* Yuri Zhelyabuzhsky, E. Schöneman; *des.:* Sergei Kozlovsky, Alexandra Exter, Isaac Rabinovich, Victor Simov.
Cast: Valentina Kuinzhi, Nikolai Tseretelli, Konstantin Eggert, Yulia Solntseva, Yuri Zavadsky, Igor Ilinsky, Nikolai Batalov.

From Sparks—Flames (Iz iskry plamya). 9,200 m., in six parts, Proletkino
Scen. & Dir.: Dmitri Bassaligo; *phot.:* Vladimir Dobrozhansky; *des.:* Y. Ivanov-Barkov.
Cast: Olga Tretyakova, G. Levkoyev.

Kino-Eye (Kino-glaz). 1,627 m., Goskino 31 Oct.
Scen. & dir.: Dziga Vertov; *phot.:* Mikhail Kaufman; *ed.:* Yelizaveta Svilova.

Cigarette-Girl from Mosselprom (Papirosnitsa ot Mosselproma). 2,325 m., Mezhrabpom Russ 2 Dec.
Scen.: Alexei Faiko; *dir. & phot.:* Yuri Zhelyabuzhsky; *des.:* Sergei Kozlovsky, Vladimir Balliuzek.
Cast: Yulia Solntseva, Igor Ilinsky, Anna Dmokhovskaya, Nikolai Tseretelli, L. Baratov, M. Tsibulsky, Galina Kravchenko, Naum Rogozhin, N. Vishnyak, Mikhail Zharov.

Abortion (Abort). 1,714 m., Kultkino 2 Dec.
Scen.: Noah Galkin; *dir.:* Grigori Lemberg, Galkin; *phot.:* Lemberg.
Cast: Liliyeva.

Adventures of Oktyabrina (Pokhozdeniya Oktyabrini). 970 m., Sevzapkino & FEX 9 Dec.
Scen. & dir.: Grigori Kozintsev, Leonid Trauberg; *phot.:* F. Verigo-Darovsky, Ivan Frolov; *des.:* Vladimir Yegorov.
Cast: Z. Tarkhovskaya, Sergei Martinson (Poincaré).

1925
Leninist Film-truth (Leninskaya kinopravda). 755 m., Kultkino 22 Jan.
Dir.: Dziga Vertov; *phot.:* Mikhail Kaufman; *ed.:* Yelizaveta Svilova.

His Call (Yevo prizyv) [in US: Broken Chains]. 1,700 m., Mezhrabpom-Russ
17 Feb.
Scen.: Vera Eri; *dir.:* Yakov Protazanov; *phot.:* Louis Forestier; *des.:* Vladimir Yegorov.
Cast: Anatoli Ktorov, V. Popova, Maria Blumenthal-Tamarina, Ivan Koval-Samborsky.

The Death Ray (Luch smerti). 2,995 m., Goskino 16 Mar.
Scen.: Vsevolod Pudovkin; *dir.:* Lev Kuleshov; *asst.:* Pudovkin, Alexandra Khokhlova, Sergei Komarov, Leonid Obolensky; *phot.:* Alexander Levitsky; *des.:* Pudovkin, Vasili Rakhals.
Cast: Komarov, Porfiri Podobed, Vladimir Fogel, Khokhlova, Pyotr Galadzhev, Obolensky, Pudovkin.

Stepan Khalturin. 2,000 m., Sevzapkino 7 Apr.
Scen.: Pavel Shchegolev; *dir.:* Alexander Ivanovsky; *phot.:* Ivan Frolov, F. Verigo-Darovsky; *des.:* Alexander Utkin, Vladimir Yegorov.
Cast: Anotoli Morozov, Angelo Raupenas, A. Sysoyev, N. Schmidthof, Valentina Kuinzhi, Y. Boronikhin, Konstantin Khokhlov, Yelena Korchagina-Alexandrovskaya.

Strike (Stachka). 1,969 m., Goskino & Proletkult   28 Apr.
Scen.: Proletkult collective (Valeri Pletnyov, Sergei Eisenstein, I. Kravchunov-
sky, Gregori Alexandrov); *dir.:* Eisenstein; *asst.* Alexandrov, Kravchunovsky,
A. Levshin; *phot.:* Eduard Tisse, Vasili Khvatov; *des.:* Vasili Rakhals.
Cast: Alexandrov, Maxim Strauch, Mikhail Gomarov, Judith Glizer, Boris
Yurtsev, Alexander Antonov.

The Station Master (Kollezhski registrator). 2,100 m., Mezhrabpom-Russ 22 Sep.
Scen. (from Pushkin's story): Valentin Turkin; *dir.:* Yuri Zheliabuzhsky; *co-
dir.:* Ivan Moskvin; *phot.:* Zheliabuzhsky, Yevgeni Alexeyev; *des.:* Victor
Simov, I. Stepanov.
Cast: Moskvin, Vera Malinovskaya, Boris Tamarin.

Jewish Luck (Yevreiskoye schastye). 2,400 m., Goskino   12 Nov.
Scen. (from Sholom Aleichem's story) *& dir.:* Alexei Granovsky; *asst.:* Grigory
Gricher-Cherikover; *phot.:* Eduard Tisse, Vasili Khvatov, N. Strukov; *des.:*
Nathan Altman; *mus.:* Lev Pulver.
Cast: Solomon Mikhoels, Tamara Adelheim.

Chess Fever (Shakhmatnaya goryachka). 400 m., Mezhrabpom-Russ   21 Nov.
Scen.: Nikolai Shpikovsky; *dir.:* Vsevolod Pudovkin, Shpikovsky; *phot.:* Anatoli
Golovnya.
Cast: Vladimir Fogel, Anna Zemtsova, Jose Raoul Capablanca, Anatoli Ktorov,
Ivan Koval-Samborsky, Yakov Protazanov, Yuri Raizman, Mikhail Zharov.

Ninth of January (Devyatoye Yanvarya). 2,720 m., Sevzapkino   2 Dec.
Scen.: Pavel Shchegolev; *dir.:* Vyacheslav Viskovsky; *phot.:* Andrei Moskvin,
A. Kuhn, A. Dolmatov; *des.:* Alexander Utkin.
Cast: Yevgeni Boronikhin (Gapon), Alexei Bogdanovsky, Nikolai Simonov.

Battleship Potemkin (Bronenosets 'Potyomkin'). 1,740 m., Goskino
Scen. ('1905'): Nina Agadzhanova-Shutko; *dir.:* Sergei Eisenstein; *asst.:* Grigori
Alexandrov (with Alexander Antonov, Mikhail Gomarov, A. Levshin, Maxim
Strauch); *phot.:* Eduard Tisse; *des.:* Vasili Rakhals; *sub-titles:* Nikolai Aseyev;
mus. (for performance, abroad): Edmund Meisel.
Cast: Antonov, Alexandrov, Vladimir Barsky, Levshin, Gomarov, Strauch.

1926

The Bear's Wedding (Medvezhya svadba). 2,296 m., Mezhrabpom-Russ 25 Jan.
Scen. (from Merimée's story, 'Lokis'): Georgi Grebner, Anatoli Lunacharsky;
dir.: Vladimir Gardin, Konstantin Eggert; *asst.:* Yuli Raizman; *phot.:* Pyotr
Yermolov, Eduard Tisse; *des.:* Vladimir Yegorov.
Cast: Eggert, Vera Malinovskaya, Natalya Rosenel, Yuri Zavadsky, A. Geirot.

Death Bay (Bukhta smerti). 2,284 m., Goskino   5 Feb.
Scen. (from story by Alexei Novikov-Priboy): Boris Leonidov; *dir.:* Abram
Room; *phot.:* Yevgeni Slavinsky; *des.:* Vasili Rakhals, Dmitri Kolupayev; *sub-
titles:* Victor Shklovsky.
Cast: V. Yaroslavtsev, N. Saltikov, Kartashova, L. Yurenev, Nikolai Okhlopkov.

The Devil's Wheel (Chyortovo koleso). 2,650 m., Lenihgradkino   Mar.
Scen. (from a story by Kaverin): Andrei Piotrovsky; *dir.:* Grigori Kozintsev,
Leonid Trauberg; *phot.:* Andrei Moskvin; *des.:* Yevgeni Enei.
Cast: Ludmila Semyonova, N. Foregger, Pyotr Sobolevsky, Sergei Gerasimov,
Emil Gal.

The Cloak (Shinel). 1,921 m., Leningradkino   10 May
Scen. (from two Gogol stories): Yuri Tinyanov; *dir.:* Grigori Kozintsev, Leonid
Trauberg; *phot.:* Andrei Moskvin, Yevgeni Mikhailov; *des.:* Yevgeni Enei.
Cast: Andrei Kostrichkin, Sergei Gerasimov, Anna Zheimo.

Stride, Soviet! (Shagai, Soviet). 1,650 m., Goskino (Kultkino). 23 July
Scen. & dir.: Dziga Vertov; *phot.:* I. Belyakov; *ed.:* Yelizaveta Svilova.

Children of Storm (Deti buri). 1,547 m., Leningradkino 17 Aug.
Scen. & dir.: Eduard Johanson, Friedrich Ermler; *phot.:* Naum Aptekman.
Cast: Yakov Gudkin, Valeri Solovtsov, Mili Taut-Korso, Veronika Buzhinskaya.

The Three Million Case (Protsess o tryokh millyonakh). 1,931 m., Mezhrabpom-
Russ 23 Aug.
Scen.: (from Umberto Notari's novel, *The Three Thieves*): Oleg Leonidov, Yakov
Protazanov; *dir.:* Protazanov; *asst.:* Yuli Raizman; *phot.:* Pyotr Yermolov;
des.: Isaac Rabinovich.
Cast: Igor Ilinsky, Mikhail Klimov, Anatoli Ktorov, Olga Zhizneva.

Traitor (Predatel). 2,100 m., Goskino 27 Sep.
Scen.: Lev Nikulin, Victor Shklovsky; *dir.:* Abram Room; *asst.:* Sergei Yut-
kevich; *phot.:* Yevgeni Slavinsky; *des.:* Vasili Rakhals, Yutkevich.
Cast: Nikolai Panov, P. Korizno, David Gutman, Nikolai Okhlopkov, Naum
Rogozhin.

Namus. 2,300 m., Goskinprom, Georgia & Armenkino 4 Oct.
Scen. (from novel by A. Shirvanzade) *& dir.:* Amo Bek-Nazarov; *phot.:* Sergei
Zabozlayev; *des.:* M. Surgunov.
Cast: S. Abelian, O. Maisurian, A. Khachanian, A. Avetisian, G. Narsesian.

Mother (Mat). 1,800 m., Mezhrabpom-Russ 11 Oct.
Scen. (from Gorky's novel): Nathan Zarkhi; *dir.:* Vsevolod Pudovkin; *asst.:*
Mikhail Doller, V. Strauss; *phot.:* Anatoli Golovnya; *des.:* Sergei Kozlovsky.
Cast: Vera Baranovskaya, Nikolai Batalov, A. Chistyakov, Ivan Koval-
Samborsky.

Miss Mend. 5,100 m., in 3 series, Mezhrabpom-Russ Oct.
Scen. (from novel by Marietta Shaginyan): B. Sakhnovsky, Fyodor Otsep,
Boris Barnet; *dir.:* Barnet, Otsep; *phot.:* Yevgeni Alexeyev; *des.:* Vladimir
Yegorov.
Cast: Natalia Glan, Igor Ilinsky, Vladimir Fogel, Barnet, Sergei Komarov.

Wings of a Serf (Krylya kholopa). 2,136 m., Sovkino (Moscow) 16 Nov.
Scen.: Konstantin Schildkret, Victor Shklovsky, Yuri Tarich; *dir.:* Tarich;
co-dir.: Leonid Leonidov; *asst.:* Ivan Pyriev, V. Korsh; *phot:* Mikhail Vladimirsky; *des.:* Vladimir Yegorov; *ed.:* Esther Shub.
Cast: Leonidov (Ivan IV), I. Klyukvin, Nikolai Prozorovsky, Korsh, S. Askarova.

Mechanics of the Brain (Mekhanikha golovnovo mozga). 1,850 m., Mezhrab-
pom-Russ 20 Nov.
Scen. & dir.: Vsevolod Pudovkin; *phot.:* Anatoli Golovnya; *consultants:* L.
Voskresenky, D. Fursikov.

By the Law (Po zakonu). 1,673 m., Goskino 3 Dec.
Scen. (from Jack London's story, 'The Unexpected'): Victor Shklovsky, Lev
Kuleshov; *dir.:* Kuleshov; *phot.:* Konstantin Kuznetsov; *des.:* Isaac Makhlis.
Cast: Alexandra Khokhlova, Sergei Komarov, Vladimir Fogel, Pyotr Galadzhev,
Porfiri Podobed.

Katka's Reinette Apples (Katka—bumazhnyr anyot). 2,084 m., Sovkino (Lenin-
grad) 25 Dec.
Scen.: M. Borisoglebsky, Boris Leonidov; *dir.:* Eduard Johanson, Friedrich
Ermler; *asst.:* Robert Maiman; *phot.:* Yevgeni Mikhailov, Andrei Moskvin;
des: Yevgeni Enei.
Cast: Veronica Buzhinskaya, B. Chernova, Valeri Solovtsov, Yakov Gudkin.

A Sixth of the World (Shestaya chast mira). 1,767 m., Goskino (Kultkino)
31 Dec.
Dir.: Dziga Vertov; *asst.:* Mikhail Kaufman; *phot.:* Kaufman, I. Belyakov, Samuel Bendersky, P. Zotov, N. Konstantinov, A. Lemberg, N. Strukov, Yakov Tolchan.

1927
Decembrists (Dekabristi). 2,100 m., Leningradkino
8 Feb.
Scen.: Pavel Shchegolev, Alexander Ivanovsky; *dir.:* Ivanovsky; *phot.:* Ivan Frolov; *des.:* Anatoli Arapov.
Cast: S. Shishko, Gennadi Michurin, Boris Tamarin, V. Maximov (Alexander I), Y. Boronikhin (Nikolai I).
The Forty-First (Sorok pervyi). 1,885 m., Mezhrabpom-Russ
1 Mar.
Scen.: Boris Lavrenyov (from his story), Boris Leonidov; *dir.:* Yakov Protazanov; *asst.:* Yuli Raizman; *phot.:* Pyotr Yermolov; *des.:* Sergei Kozlovsky.
Cast: Ada Voitsik, Ivan Koval-Samborsky, I. Strauch.
Fall of the Romanov Dynasty (Padeniye dinasti Romanovikh). 1,700 m., Sovkino
Scen. & ed.: Esther Shub.
11 Mar.
[Bed and Sofa] (Tretya Meshchanskaya). 2,025 m., Sovkino (Moscow) 15 Mar.
Scen.: Victor Shklovsky, Abram Room; *dir.:* Room; *asst.:* Sergei Yutkevich; *phot.:* Grigori Giber; *des.:* Vasili Rakhals, Yutkevich.
Cast: Nikolai Batalov, Ludmila Semyonova, Vladimir Fogel.
Mitya. 1,997 m., VUFKU
5 Apr.
Scen.: Nikolai Erdman; *dir.:* Nikolai Okhlopkov; *phot.:* Marius Goldt; *des.:* Heinrich Weisenherz.
Cast: Okhlopkov, Sergei Minin.
Mabul. 2,700 m., Proletkino & Sovkino
11 Apr.
Scen. (from novel by Sholom Aleichem): D. Rudensky, V. Popova-Khanzhonkova; *dir.:* Yevgeni Ivanov-Barkov; *phot.:* Alphonse Winkler, A. Solodkov, G. Yegyazarov; *des.:* R. Falk, Dmitri Kolupayev.
Cast (from the Habima Theatre Collective)*:* A. Dzyubina, Chechik-Efrati, Benno Schneider, I. Vinyar-Kagur.
Giulli. 2,060 m., Goskinprom-Georgia
16 Apr.
Scen.: Nikolai Shengelaya, L. Push, Mikhail Kalatozov; *dir.:* Push, Shengelaya; *phot.:* Kalatozov; *des.:* Valerian Sidamon-Eristov.
Cast: Nata Vachnadze, M. Vardeshvili.
Girl with the Hat-Box (Devushka s korobkoi). 1,650 m., Mezhrabpom-Russ
19 Apr.
Scen.: Valentin Turkin, V. Shershenevich; *dir.:* Boris Barnet; *phot.:* Boris Frantsisson, B. Filshin; *des.:* Sergei Kozlovsky.
Cast: Anna Sten, Ivan Koval-Samborsky, Vladimir Fogel, Serafima Birman, Pavel Pol.
The Club of the Big Deed (S.V.D.). 2,100 m., Sovkino (Leningrad) 23 Aug.
Scen.: Yuri Tinyanov, Yuri Oxman; *dir.:* Grigori Kozintsev, Leonid Trauberg; *phot.:* Andrei Moskvin; *des.:* Yevgeni Enei.
Cast: Pyotr Sobolevsky, Sergei Gerasimov, Sophie Magarill, Andrei Kostrichkin.
Your Acquaintance (Vasha znakomaya). 1,800 m., Sovkino (Moscow) 25 Oct.
Scen. (from story by Alexander Kurs)*:* Kurs, V. Ashmarin, Lev Kuleshov; *dir.:* Kuleshov; *phot.:* Konstantin Kuznetsov; *des.:* Vasili Rakhals, Alexander Rodchenko.
Cast: Alexandra Khokhlova, B. Ferdinandov, Vasilchikov, A. Chekulayeva.

The Great Road (Veliky put). 2,350 m., Sovkino (Moscow) 6 Nov.
Scen. & ed.: Esther Shub.

Two Days (Dva dnya). 1,724 m., VUFKU 7 Nov.
Scen.: Solomon Lazurin; *dir.:* Grigori Stabovoi; *phot.:* Danylo Demutsky; *des.:* Heinrich Weisenherz.
Cast: Ivan Zamychkovsky, Sergei Minin, Y. Gekebush.

Moscow in October (Moskva v Oktyabre). 2,100 m., Mezhrabpom-Russ 8 Nov.
Scen.: Oleg Leonidov; *dir.:* Boris Barnet; *phot.:* Boris Frantsisson, Konstantin Kuznetsov, Yakov Tolchan; *des.:* Alexander Rodchenko.

The End of St Petersburg (Konyets Sankt-Peterburga). 2,500 m., Mezhrabpom-
Russ 13 Dec.
Scen.: Nathan Zarkhi; *dir.* Vsevolod Pudovkin; *co-dir.:* Mikhail Doller; *asst.:* A. Gendelstein, A. Ledashov, Alexander Feinzimmer, V. Strauss; *phot.:* Anatoli Golovnya; *des.:* Sergei Kozlovsky.
Cast: A. Chistyakov, Vera Baranovskaya, Ivan Chuvelyov, V. Obolensky.

Women of Ryazan (Babi ryazanskye). 1,845 m., Sovkino 13 Dec.
Scen.: Olga Vishnevskaya, Boris Altschuler; *dir.:* Olga Preobrazhenskaya; *co-dir.:* Ivan Pravov; *phot.:* Konstantin Kuznetsov; *des.:* Dmitri Kolupayev.
Cast: Kuzma Yastrebetsky, G. Bobynin, Yelena Maximova, Emma Tsessar-skaya, R. Puzhnaya.

Moscow (Moskva). 1,749 m., Kultkino
Scen. & dir.: Mikhail Kaufman, Ilya Kopalin; *phot.:* N. Byelyakov, P. Zotov.

Kira Kiralina. 2,369 m., VUFKU
Scen. (from novel by Panait Istrati): N. Plessky, Y. Valerskaya; *dir.:* Boris Glagolin; *phot.:* Nikolai Farkash; *des.:* R. Sharfenberg.
Cast: Valerskaya, Rubini, Krestinsky, Akitov.

1928

Three Friends and an Invention (Dva druga, model i podruga). 1,815 m.,
Sovkino 20 Jan.
Scen.: Alexei Popov, M. Karostin; *dir.:* Popov; *phot.:* Alexander Grinberg, G. Troyansky; *des.* Victor Aden.
Cast: S. Lavrentyev, S. Yablokov, Olga Tretyakova, Popov.

Parisian Cobbler (Parizhsky sapozhnik). 2,065 m., Sovkino (Leningrad) 7 Feb.
Scen.: N. Nikitin, Boris Leonidov; *dir.:* Friedrich Ermler; *phot. & des.:* Yevgeni Mikhailov, G. Bushtuyev.
Cast: Veronica Buzhinskaya, Fyodor Nikitin, Valeri Solovtsov, Yakov Gudkin, Varvara Myasnikova.

The Sold Appetite (Prodannyi appetit). 1,992 m., VUFKU 5 Mar.
Scen. (from a story by Paul Lafargue): Anatoli Marienhof, Nikolai Erdman; *dir.:* Nikolai Okhlopkov; *phot.:* Josif Rona; *des.:* Heinrich Weisenherz, B. Erdman.
Cast: Ambrose Buchma, M. Tsibulsky, Marie Doucemetier.

October. 2,800 m., Sovkino (Moscow & Leningrad) 14 Mar.
Scen. & dir.: Sergei Eisenstein, Grigori Alexandrov; *asst.:* Maxim Strauch, Mikhail Gomarov, Ilya Trauberg; *phot.:* Eduard Tisse; *phot.-asst.:* Vladimir Nilsen, Vladimir Popov; *des.:* Vasili Kovrigin; *mus.* (for performance, abroad): Edmund Meisel.
Cast: Nikandrov (Lenin), N. Popov (Kerensky).

The House in the Snow-Drifts (Dom v sugrobakh). 1,757 m., Sovkino (Leningrad) 23 Mar.

Scen. (from Zamyatin's story, 'The Cave'): *dir.:* Friedrich Ermler; *phot.:* Yevgeni Mikhailov, G. Bushtuyev; *des.:* Yevgeni Enei.
Cast: Valeri Solovtsov, Fyodor Nikitin, Yakov Gudkin.

Zvenigora. 1,799 m., VUFKU　　　　　　　　　　　　　　　　　13 Apr.
Scen.: Mikhail Johansen, Yuri Yurtik; *dir.:* Alexander Dovzhenko; *phot.:* Boris Zavelyov; *des.:* Vasili Krichevsky.
Cast: Semyon Svashenko, Mikola Nademsky, Alexander Podorozhny.

A Shanghai Document (Shanghaisky dokument). 1,700 m., Soyuzkino　1 May
Dir.: Yakov Blyokh; *phot.:* V. Stepanov.

The Eleventh [Year] (Odinnadtsati). 1,600 m., VUFKU　　　　　15 May
Scen. & dir.: Dziga Vertov; *phot.:* Mikhail Kaufman; *ed.:* Yelizaveta Svilova.

Lace (Kruzheva). 2,100 m., Sovkino　　　　　　　　　　　　　　1 Jun.
Scen. (from a story by M. Kolosov): Sergei Yutkevich, Yuri Gromov, Vladimir Legoshin; *dir.:* Yutkevich; *phot.:* Yevgeni Schneider; *des.:* Victor Aden.
Cast: Nina Shaternikova, Boris Poslavsky, K. Gradopolov, Boris Tenin.

House on Trubnaya Square (Dom na Trubnoi). 1,757 m., Mezhrabpom-Russ
　　　　　　　　　　　　　　　　　　　　　　　　　　　　　　4 Sep.
Scen.: B. Zorich, Anatoli Marienhof, V. Shershenevich, Victor Shklovsky, Nikolai Erdman; *dir.:* Boris Barnet; *phot.:* Yevgeni Alexeyev; *des.:* Sergei Kozlovsky.
Cast: Vera Maretskaya, Vladimir Fogel, Anna Sudakevich, Yelena Tyapkina, Sergei Komarov.

The White Eagle (Byelyi orel). 1,850 m., Mezhrabpomfilm.　　　9 Oct.
Scen. (from Andreyev's story, 'The Governor'): Oleg Leonidov, Y. Urinov, Yakov Protazanov; *dir.:* Protazanov; *phot.:* Pyotr Yermolov, B. Filshin; *des.:* Isaac Rabinovich.
Cast: Vasili Kachalov, Vsevolod Meyerhold, Anna Sten, Ivan Chuvelyov.

Eliso. 2,300 m., Goskinprom-Georgia　　　　　　　　　　　　23 Oct.
Scen. (from material by Kazbegi): Oleg Leonidov, Sergei Tretyakov, Nikolai Shengelaya; *dir.:* Shengelaya; *phot.:* Vladimir Kereselidze; *des.:* D. Shavaradnadze.
Cast: I. Mamporiya, Kira Andronikashvili, Kokta Karalashvili.

The Heir to Jenghis-Khan (Potomok Chingis-khan). 3,092 m., Mezhrabpomfilm
　　　　　　　　　　　　　　　　　　　　　　　　　　　　　10 Nov.
Scen. (from a story by I. Novokshonov): Osip Brik; *dir.:* Vsevolod Pudovkin; *asst.:* A. Ledashev, L. Bronstein; *phot.:* Anatoli Golovnya; *des.:* Sergei Kozlovsky, M. Aaronson.
Cast: Valeri Inkizhinov, A. Dedintsev, Anna Sudakevich, V. Tsoppi, Boris Barnet.

The Russia of Nikolai II and Lev Tolstoy (Rossiya Nikolaya II i Lev Tolstoy).
　1,700 m., Sovkino (Moscow)　　　　　　　　　　　　　　　　10 Nov.
Scen. & ed.: Esther Shub.

Katorga [Penal Servitude]. 1,960 m., Gosvoyenkino　　　　　27 Nov.
Scen.: Sergei Yermolinsky; *dir.* Yuli Raizman; *asst.:* Alexander Feinzimmer; *phot.:* Leonid Kosmatov; *des.:* Vasili Komardenkov.
Cast: Vladimir Popov, P. Tamm, Andrei Zhilinsky, Boris Lifanov　Mikhail Yanshin, Vladimir Taskin.

1929
Man with Movie Camera (Chelovek s kinoapparatom). 1,830 m., VUFKU　8 Jan.
Scen. & dir.: Dziga Vertov; *asst. ed.:* Yelizaveta Svilova; *phot.:* Mikhail Kaufman.

Arsenal. 1,820 m., VUFKU 25 Feb.
Scen. & dir.: Alexander Dovzhenko; *asst.:* Lazar Bodik, A. Kapler; *phot.:* Danylo Demutsky; *des.:* Isaac Shpinel, Vladimir Muller; *mus.* (for performance)*:* Igor Belza.
Cast: Semyon Svashenko, Mikola Nademsky, Ambrose Buchma, Pyotr Masokha.

The New Babylon (Novyi Vavilon). 2,200 m., Sovkino (Leningrad) 16 Mar.
Scen. & dir.: Grigori Kozintsev, Leonid Trauberg; *asst.:* Sergei Gerasimov; *phot.:* Andrei Moskvin, Yevgeni Mikhailov; *des.:* Yevgeni Enei; *mus.* (for performance)*:* Dmitri Shostakovich.
Cast: Yelena Kuzmina, Pyotr Sobolevsky, D. Gutman, Sophie Magarill, Gerasimov, Andrei Kostrichkin.

A Living Corpse (Zhivoi trup), 2,233 m., Mezhrabpomfilm & Prometheus (Berlin) 26 Mar.
Scen. (from Tolstoy's play)*:* B. Gusman, Anatoli Marienhof; *dir.:* Fyodor Otsep; *asst.:* A. Gendelstein, L. Bronstein; *phot.:* Anatoli Golovnya; *des.:* Victor Simov, Sergei Kozlovsky.
Cast: Vsevolod Pudovkin, Maria Jacobini, Gustav Diessl, Nata Vachnadze, S. Uralsky, Vera Maretskaya, Boris Barnet.

Saba. 2,100 m., Goskinprom-Georgia. 20 May
Scen. (from idea by G. Arustanov)*:* A. Aravsky, S. Alkhazishvili; *dir.:* Mikhail Chiaureli; *phot.:* A. Polikevich; *des.:* L. Gudiashvili, D. Kakabidze.
Cast: Sandro Djaliashvili, Veriko Andjaparidze, Eka Chavchavadze.

Ranks and People (Chiny i liudi). 1,770 m., Mezhrabpomfilm 1 Oct.
Scen. (from three stories by Chekhov)*:* Oleg Leonidov, Yakov Protazanov; *dir.:* Protazanov; *co-dir.:* Mikhail Doller; *phot.:* Konstantin Kuznetsov; *des.:* Vladimir Yegorov.
Cast: Ivan Moskvin, Mikhail Tarkhanov, Vladimir Yershov, Maria Strelkova, V. Popov.

Turksib. 1,666 m., Vostok-kino 15 Oct.
Scen. & dir.: Victor Turin (with scen. assistance by Alexander Macheret, Victor Shklovsky, Y. Aron); *phot.:* Yevgeni Slavinsky, Boris Frantzisson.

The Black Sail (Chyorni parus). 1,952 m., Sovkino (Leningrad) 15 Oct.
Scen.: K. Feldman, G. Zelondzhev-Shipov; *dir.:* Sergei Yutkevich; *asst.:* Boris Poslavsky; *phot.:* Z. Martov; *des.:* Yevgeni Enei.
Cast: Nina Shaternikova, Poslavsky.

Fragment of an Empire (Oblomok imperii). 2,203 m., Sovkino (Leningrad) 28 Oct.
Scen.: Katerina Vinogradskaya, Friedrich Ermler; *dir.:* Ermler; *phot.:* Yevgeni Schneider, G. Bushtuyev; *des.:* Yevgeni Enei; *mus.* (for performance)*:* V. Deshevov.
Cast: Fyodor Nikitin, Yakov Gudkin, Ludmila Semyonova, Valeri Solovtsov, Vyacheslav Viskovsky.

Old and New (Staroye i novoye). 2,469 m., Sovkino (Moscow) 7 Nov.
Scen. & dir.: Sergei Eisenstein, Grigori Alexandrov; *phot.:* Eduard Tisse; *asst.:* V. Popov; *des.:* A. Burov, Vasili Kovrigin, Vasili Rakhals.
Cast: Marfa Lapkina, Vasya Buzenkov, Kostya Vasiliev.

Post (Pochta). 550 m., Sovkino (Leningrad) 25 Nov.
Scen.: Samuel Marshak (from his children's book); *dir. & des.:* M. Tsekhanovsky; *asst.:* I. Druzhinin.

Blue Express (Goluboi ekspress [China Express]). 1,700 m., Sovkino (Leningrad) 20 Dec.

Scen.: L. Ierikhonov, Ilya Trauberg; *dir.:* Trauberg; *phot.:* B. Khrennikov, Yuri Stilianudis; *des.:* Boris Dubrovsky-Eshke, Moisei Levin.
Cast: Sun Bo-yang, Chou Hsi-fan, Chang Kai, Sergei Minin.

Neurasthenia (Bolniye nervy). 1,635 m., Sovkino
Scen.: Noah Galkin, L. Sukharebsky; *dir.:* Galkin; *phot.:* Alexander Ginsburg; *des.:* Nikolai Akimov.
Cast: Sergei Minin, Y. Yegorova.

1930

Transport of Fire (Transport ognya). 2,106 m., Sovkino (Leningrad)   13 Jan.
Scen.: Alexander Zarkhi, Josif Heifitz; Alexander Ivanov; *dir.:* Ivanov; *phot.:* Alexander Ginsburg; *des.* Boris Dubrovsky-Eshke.
Cast: Xenia Klyaro, Gleb Kuznetsov, N. Michurin.

Plan of Great Works (Plan velikikh rabot). 6 reels, Soyuzkino (Leningrad)   6 Mar.
Scen.: Vladimir Legoshin; *dir.:* Abram Room; *phot.:* F. Zandberg, V. Solodovnikov; *mus.:* A. Avraamov, N. Malakhovsky, G. Rimsky-Korsakov, N. Timofeyev.

The Ghost That Will Not Return (Privideniye, kotoroye ne vozvrashchayetsya). 2,330 m., Sovkino (Moscow).   15 Mar.
Scen. (from a story by Barbusse)*:* Valentin Turkin; *dir.:* Abram Room; *phot.:* Dmitri Feldman; *des.:* Victor Aden.
Cast: B. Ferdinandov, Olga Zhizneva, Maxim Strauch.

Earth (Zemlya). 1,704 m., VUFKU   8 Apr.
Scen. & dir.: Alexander Dovzhenko; *phot.:* Danylo Demutsky; *des.:* Vasili Krichevsky; *mus.* (for performance)*:* L. Revutsky.
Cast: Semyon Svashenko, Stepan Shkurat, Mikola Nademsky, Yelena Maximova, Pyotr Masokha.

Holiday of St Jorgen (Prazdnik svyatovo Iorgena). 2,290 m., Mezhrabpomfilm   25 Aug.
Scen. (from novel by Harald Bergstedt) *& dir.:* Yakov Protazanov; *phot.:* Pyotr Yermolov; *des.:* Sergei Kozlovsky, Vladimir Balliuzek, Anatoli Arapov.
Cast: Anatoli Ktorov, Igor Ilinsky, Mikhail Klimov, Maria Strelkova, I. Arkadin.

The Earth Thirsts (Zemlya zhazhdyot). 1,816 m., Vostok-kino   26 Oct.
Scen.: Sergei Yermolinsky; *dir.:* Yuli Raizman; *phot.:* Leonid Kosmatov, F. Timofeyev; *mus.:* Reinhold Glier, S. Ryauzov, V. Sokolov (for sound version, 1931).
Cast: Kira Andronikova, D. Konsovsky, N. Sanov.

Today (Sevodnya). 2,000 m., Soyuzkino (Moscow)   2 Nov.
Scen.: Esther Shub, M. Zeitlin; *dir.:* Shub; *phot.:* Yuri Stilianudis, Stepanov.

Perekop. 2,200 m., Ukrainfilm   3 Nov.
Scen.: Mokin, Trachtenberg; *dir.:* Ivan Kavaleridze; *phot.:* N. Topchi; *des.:* G. Dovzhenko.
Cast: O. Pidlisna, M. Astafiev, V. Kravchenko, Semyón Shagaida.

Cities and Years (Goroda i godi). 1,800 m., Soyuzkino (Leningrad)   11 Dec.
Scen. (from Fedin's novel): Nathan Zarkhi, Yevgeny Chervyakov; *dir.:* Chervyakov; *phot.:* Svyatoslav Belayev, Alexander Sigayev; *des.:* Semyon Menken;' *mus.* (for performance)*:* Dmitri Astradantsev.
Cast: Bernhard Goetzke, Ivan Chuvelyov, Sophie Magarill, Andrei Kostrichkin.

Salt for Svanetia (Sol Svanetii). 1,500 m., Goskinprom-Georgia
Scen. (from idea by Sergei Tretyakov) *& dir.:* Mikhail Kalatozov; *phot.:* Kalatozov, M. Gegelashvili.

Way of the Enthusiasts (Put entuziastov). 1,993 m., Sovkino [not released]
Scen.: Nikolai Okhlopkov, G. Pavlyuchenko; *dir.:* Okhlopkov; *asst.:* Alexander
Medvedkin; *phot.:* Mikhail Vladimirsky, Yakov Tolchan, Mikhail Gindin;
des.: V. Komardenko.
Cast: N. Sibiryakov, V. Maslatsov, V. Panasyuk.

1931

Symphony of the Donbas (Entuziazm). 2,600 m., Ukrainfilm   2 Apr.
Scen. & dir.: Dziga Vertov; *phot.:* Zeitlin; *mus.:* N. Timofeyev.
A Pass to Life [Road to Life] (Putyovka v zhizn). 3,300 m., Mezhrabpomfilm
                                                                  1 June
Scen.: Nikolai Ekk, Alexander Stolper, R. Yanushkevich; *dir.:* Ekk; *phot.:*
Vasili Pronin; *mus.:* Y. Stolyar; *des.:* I. Stepanov, A. Yevmenenko.
Cast: I. Kyrla, Nikolai Batalov, Mikhail Zharov.
The Quiet Don (Tikhii Don). 2,160 m., Soyuzkino (Moscow)   14 Sep.
Scen. (from Sholokhov's novel) *& dir.:* Olga Preobrazhenskaya, Ivan Pravov;
phot.: Dmitri Feldman, B. Epstein; *des.:* Dmitri Kolupayev.
Cast: N. Podgorny, Andrei Abrikosov, Yelena Maximova, Emma Tsesarskaya.
Alone (Odna). 2,200 m., Soyuzkino (Leningrad)   10 Oct.
Scen. & dir.: Grigori Kozintsev, Leonid Trauberg; *phot.:* Andrei Moskvin;
des.: Yevgeni Enei; *mus.:* Dmitri Shostakovich; *sound dir.:* Leo Arnstam.
Cast: Yelena Kuzmina, Pyotr Sobolevsky, Sergei Gerasimov.
Tommy. 1,730 m., Mezhrabpomfilm   1 Nov.
Scen. (from Ivanov's play, *Armoured Train* 14-69) *& dir.:* Yakov Protazanov;
phot.: Konstantin Kuznetsov; *des.:* Vladimir Yegorov; *mus.:* A. Shenshin.
Golden Mountains (Zlatye gori). 3,585 m., Soyuzkino (Leningrad)   6 Nov.
Scen.: A. Mikhailovsky, V. Nedobrovo, Sergei Yutkevich, Leo Arnstam; *dir.:*
Yutkevich; *phot.:* I. Martov, Wulf Rappoport, A. Val; *des.:* Nikolai Suvorov;
mus.: Dmitri Shostakovich.
Cast: Boris Poslavsky, B. Fedosyev, I. Strauch, Boris Tenin, N. Michurin.
Anush. 2,216 m., Armenkino   13 Nov.
Scen. (from a poem by Ovanes Tumanian) *& dir.:* Ivan Perestiani; *phot.:*
A. Cui, K. Rodendorff; *des.:* Yevgeni Lanceret, Martiros Sarian.
Cast: N. Arzumanian, L. Aristagesian, L. Isaakian.
Out of the Way! (Khabarda!) 1,700 m., Goskinprom-Georgia   13 Dec.
Scen. & dir.: Mikhail Chiaureli; *phot.:* A. Polikevich; *des.:* L. Gudiashvili.
Cast: S. Zarichev, P. Chkoniya, S. Asatiani, O. Vachnadze.

1932

The House of the Dead (Myortvyi dom). 2,500 m., Mezhrabpomfilm   10 Apr.
Scen. (from Dostoyevsky's novel)*:* Victor Shklovsky, V. Fyodorov; *dir.:*
Fyodorov; *phot.:* Vasili Pronin; *des.:* Vladimir Yegorov; *mus.:* V. Kryukov.
Cast: Nikolai Khmelyov (Dostoyevsky).
Nail in the Boot   [not released]
Scen.: A. Bezimensky; *dir.:* Mikhail Kalatozov.
Cast: Akaki Khorava.
Men and Jobs [Jobs and Men] (Dela i lyudi). 2,800 m., Soyuzkino (Moscow) 9 Oct.
Scen. & dir.: Alexander Macheret; *asst.* Mikhail Romm; *phot.:* Alexander
Galperin; *des.:* Alexander Utkin; *mus.:* Visarion Shebalin, S. Germanov,
Nikolai Kryukov.
Cast: Nikolai Okhlopkov, Victor Stanitsin, Alexander Geirot.

Ivan. 2,800 m., Ukrainfilm 6 Nov.
Scen. & dir.: Alexander Dovzhenko; *phot.:* Danylo Demutsky, Yuri Yekelchik, Mikhail Glider; *des.:* Yuri Khomaza; *mus.:* Igor Belza, Yuli Meitus, Boris Lyatoshinsky.
Cast: Pyotr Masokha, Stepan Shkurat, Semyon Shagaida.
Counterplan (Vstrechnyi). 3,170 m., Rosfilm (Leningrad) 7 Nov.
Scen.: Leo Arnstam, D. Del, Friedrich Ermler, Sergei Yutkevich; *dir.:* Ermler, Yutkevich; *co-dir.:* Arnstam; *asst.:* Boris Poslavsky, G. Kazansky, Victor Eisimont; *phot.:* I. Martov, Alexander Ginsburg, Wulf Rappoport; *des.:* Boris Dubrovsky-Eshke, N. Pavlov, A. Ushin; *mus.:* Dmitri Shostakovich.
Cast: Vladimir Gardin, Maria Blumenthal-Tamarina, T. Guretskaya, Andrei Abrikosov, Boris Tenin, Poslavsky.
A Simple Case (Prostoi sluchai). 2,633 m., Mezhrabpomfilm 3 Dec.
Scen.: Alexander Rzheshevsky; *dir.:* Vsevolod Pudovkin; *co-dir.* Mikhail Doller; *phot.:* G. Kabalov, G. Bobrov; *des.:* Sergei Kozlovsky.
Cast: A. Baturin, Yevgeniya Rogulina, Alexander Chistyakov, A. Byelov.
A Song about Heroes (Pesn o geroyakh). 1,500 m., Mezhrabpomfilm
Scen.: Joris Ivens, I. Sklyut; *dir.:* Ivens; *asst.:* H. P. J. Marshall; *phot.:* Alexander Shelenkov; *mus.:* Hanns Eisler.

1933
Twenty-Six Commissars (Dvadtsat shest komissarov). 3,000 m., Azerfilm, Baku 19 Feb.
Scen.: Alexander Rzheshevsky; *dir.:* Nikolai Shengelaya; *co-dir.:* S. Kevorkov; *phot.:* Yevgeni Schneider; *des.:* Victor Aden.
Cast: Vladimir Gardin, Igor Savchenko, K. Gasanov.
Outskirts [US.: **Patriots**] (Okraina). 2,700 m., Mezhrabpomfilm 25 Mar.
Scen.: Konstantin Finn (from his story), Boris Barnet; *dir.:* Barnet; *phot:* M. Kirillov, M. Spiridonov; *des.:* Sergei Kozlovsky; *mus.:* Sergei Vasilenko.
Cast.: Yelena Kuzmina, Nikolai Bogolyubov, Mikhail Zharov, A. Chistyakov, Sergei Komarov, Hans Klering, Nikolai Kryuchkov.
Deserter. 2,661 m., Mezhrabpomfilm 19 Sep.
Scen.: Nina Agadzhanova, M. Krasnostavsky, A. Lazebnikov; *dir.:* Vsevolod Pudovkin; *asst.:* N. Kochetov, Erna Ruttmann, B. Sveshnikov; *phot.:* Anatoli Golovnya, Yuli Fogelman; *des.:* Sergei Kozlovsky; *mus.:* Yuri Shaporin.
Cast: Boris Livanov, Tamara Makarova, Vasili Kovrigin, Judith Glizer, A. Chistyakov.
The Great Consoler (Velikii uteshitel). 2,693 m., Mezhrabpomfilm 17 Nov.
Scen. (based on O. Henry motifs): Alexander Kurs, Lev Kuleshov; *dir. & des.:* Kuleshov; *phot.:* Konstantin Kuznetsov; *mus.:* Z. Feldman.
Cast.: I. Novoseltsev, Konstantin Khokhlov (O. Henry), Galina Kravchenko, Andrei Fait, Vasili Kovrigin, Wayland Rudd, Alexandra Khokhlova.
Torn Shoes (Rvanyi bashmaki). 2,577 m., Mezhrabpomfilm 17 Dec.
Scen. & dir.: Margarita Barskaya; *phot.:* G. Bobrov, Sergei Gevorkian; *des.:* Vladimir Yegorov; *mus.:* Visarion Shebalin.

1934
Petersburg Night (Peterburgskaya noch). 2,926 m., Soyuzfilm (Moscow) 19 Feb.
Scen. (from Dostoyevsky's stories, 'White Nights' and 'Netochka Nezvanova'): Serafina Roshal, Vera Stroyeva; *dir.:* Grigori Roshal, Stroyeva; *phot.:* Dmitri Feldman; *des.:* Isaac Shpinel, P. Beitner; *mus.:* Dmitri Kabalevsky.

Cast: Boris Dobronravov, Anatoli Goryunov, Xenia Tarasova, Lev Fenin, Lubov Orlova.

Lieutenant Kizhe [US: The Tsar Wants to Sleep] (Poruchik Kizhe). 2,370 m., Belgoskino   7 Mar.
Scen.: Yuri Tinyanov (from his story); *dir.* Alexander Feinzimmer; *phot.:* Abram Kaltsati; *des.:* P. Snopkov, K. Kartashov; *mus.:* Sergei Prokofiev.
Cast: Mikhail Yanshin (Paul I), Erast Garin, Sophie Magarill.

Thunderstorm (Groza). 2,607 m., Soyuzfilm (Leningrad)   25 Mar.
Scen. (from Ostrovsky's play) & *dir.:* Vladimir Petrov; *phot.:* Vyacheslav Gardanov; *des.:* Nikolai Suvorov; *mus.:* Vladimir Shcherbachov.
Cast: Alla Tarasova, Ivan Chuvelov, Mikhail Tarkhanov, Varvara Massalitinova, I. Zarubina, Mikhail Zharov.

Accordion (Garmon). 1,800 m., Mezhrabpomfilm   26 June
Scen.: A. Zharov, Igor Savchenko; *dir.:* Savchenko; *co-dir.:* Yevgeni Schneider; *phot.:* Schneider, Yuli Fogelman; *des.:* V. Khmelyova; *mus.:* Sergei Pototsky.
Cast: P. Savin, Zoya Fyodorova, Savchenko.

Tale of Tsar Duranda (Skazka o Durandaye). 1,000 m., Mezhrabpomfilm
                                                                        13 Sep.
Scen.: Alexander Kurs; *dir.* & *des.:* V. Vano [Ivanov], V. Brumberg, Z. Brumberg; *mus.:* Anatoli Alexandrov.

Boule de Suif (Pyshka). 1,893 m., Mosfilm   15 Sep.
Scen. (from Maupassant's story) & *dir.:* Mikhail Romm; *phot.:* Boris Volchok; *des.:* Isaac Shpinel, P. Beitner.
Cast: Galina Sergeyeva, Anatoli Goryunov, Andrei Fait, Faina Ranevskaya.

Song about Happiness (Pesnya o s'chastye). 2,400 m., Vostokfilm   1 Oct.
Scen.: G. Kholmsky; *dir.:* Mark Donskoy, Vladimir Legoshin; *phot.:* N. Ushakov; *des.:* Semyon Menken; *mus.:* G. Lobachev; *supervision:* Sergei Yutkevich.
Cast: Yanina Zheimo, Boris Tenin, Vladimir Gardin.

Revolt of the Fishermen (Vostaniye rybakov). 2,670 m., Mezhrabpomfilm
                                                                         5 Oct.
Scen. (from Anna Seghers' novel); Georgy Grebner; *dir.:* Erwin Piscator; *phot.:* Pyotr Yermolov, M. Kirillov; *des.:* Vladimir Kaplunovsky; *mus.:* F. Sabo, V. Ferre, N. Chemberzhi.
Cast: Alexei Diky, Emma Tsesarskaya, Vera Yanukova.

The Last Masquerade (Posledni maskarad). 2,700 m., Goskinprom-Georgia
                                                                        25 Oct.
Scen. & *dir.:* Mikhail Chiaureli; *phot.:* A. Polikevich; *des.:* Valerian Sidamon-Eristov; *mus.:* G. Kiladze.
Cast: Sandro Djaliashvili, D. Tzerodze, Mikhail Gelovani, Nata Vachnadze.

Three Songs of Lenin (Tri pesni o Leninye). 1,873 m., Mezhrabpomfilm 1 Nov.
Scen. & *dir.:* Dziga Vertov; *phot.:* Surensky, Mark Magidson, Bentsion Monastirsky; *mus.:* Yuri Shaporin.

Chapayev. 2,600 m., Lenfilm   7 Nov.
Scen. (on material by Dmitry Furmanov and A. Furmanova) & *dir.:* Sergei & Georgy Vasiliev; *phot.:* Alexander Sigayev, A. Xenofontov; *des.:* I. Makhlis; *mus.:* Gavril Popov.
Cast: Boris Babochkin, B. Blinov, Leonid Kmit, Varvara Myasnikova, Illarion Pevtsov, Stepan Shkurat, Boris Chirkov.

Jolly Fellows [Jazz Comedy] (Vesyolye rebyata). 2,577 m., Mosfilm   25 Dec.
Scen.: Grigori Alexandrov, V. Mass, Nikolai Erdman; *dir.:* Alexandrov; *phot.:* Vladimir Nilsen; *des.:* Alexander Utkin; *mus.:* Isaac Dunayevsky.
Cast: Leonid Utyosov, Lubov Orlova, Maria Strelkova, Yelena Tyapkina.

1935
The Youth of Maxim (Yunost Maksima). 2,678 m., Lenfilm   27 Jan.
Scen. & dir.: Grigori Kozintsev, Leonid Trauberg; *phot.:* Andrei Moskvin; *des.:* Yevgeny Enei; *mus.:* Dmitri Shostakovich.
Cast: Boris Chirkov, Stepan Kayukov, Valentina Kibardina, Mikhail Tarkhanov.
Snatchers (Styazhateli). 1,819 m., Mosfilm   2 Mar.
Scen. & dir.: Alexander Medvedkin; *phot.:* G. Troyansky; *des.:* Alexander Utkin.
Cast: P. Zinoviev, Yelena Yegorova, V. Uspensky.
A New Gulliver (Novyi Gulliver). 2,200 m., Mosfilm   25 Mar.
Scen. (on Swift's theme)*:* Grigori Roshal, Alexander Ptushko; *dir.:* Ptushko; *phot.:* N. Renkov; *des.:* Y. Schwetz, Sara Mokil; *mus.:* Lev Schwartz.
Peasants (Krestyaniye). 3,100 m., Lenfilm   7 Apr.
Scen.: Mikhail Bolshintsov, V. Portnov, Friedrich Ermler; *dir.:* Ermler; *phot.:* Alexander Ginsburg; *des.:* Nikolai Suvorov; *mus.:* Venedict Pushkov.
Cast: Nikolai Bogolyubov, A. Petrov, Yelena Yunger, Boris Poslavsky, Vladimir Gardin, Yelena Korchagina-Alexandrovskaya.
Flyers (Lyotchiki). 2,200 m., Mosfilm   25 Apr.
Scen.: Alexander Macheret, Yuri Olesha; *dir.:* Yuli Raizman; *co-dir.:* G. Levkoyev; *phot.:* Leonid Kosmatov; *des.:* G. Grivtsov; *mus.:* Nikolai Kryukov.
Cast: Boris Shchukin, Y. Melnikova, A. Chistyakov, Ivan Koval-Samborsky.
Pepo. 2,338 m., Armenkino   15 June
Scen. (from Sundukian's play) *& dir.:* Amo Bek-Nazarov; *phot.:* Dmitri Feldman; *des.:* Valerian Sidamon-Eristov, S. Safarian; *mus.:* Aram Khachaturian.
Cast: Grachya Nersesian, Asmik, Tatyana Makhmurian, David Malian, Avet Avetisian.
Aerograd. 2,296 m., Mosfilm & Ukrainfilm [US.: Frontier]   6 Nov.
Scen. & dir.: Alexander Dovzhenko; *asst.:* Yulia Solntseva, S. Kevorkov; *phot.:* Eduard Tisse, Mikhail Gindin; *des.:* Alexander Utkin, V. Panteleyev; *mus.:* Dmitri Kabalevsky.
Cast: Semyon Shagaida, Stepan Shkurat, Boris Dobronravov, Sergei Stolyarov.

1936
Girl-Friends (Podrugi). 2,611 m., Lenfilm   19 Feb.
Scen. & dir.: Leo Arnstam; *co-dir. & des.:* Moisei Levin; *phot.:* Wulf Rappoport, A. Shafran; *mus.:* Dmitri Shostakovich; *supervision:* Sergei Yutkevich.
Cast: Yanina Zheimo, Zoya Fyodorova, I. Zarubina, B. Blinov, Boris Babochkin.
The Bold Seven (Semero smelykh). 2,531 m., Lenfilm   4 Mar.
Scen.: Yuri German, Sergei Yutkevich; *dir.:* Gerasimov; *co-dir. & des.:* A. Bosulayev; *phot.:* V. Velichko; *des.:* V. Semyonov; *mus.:* Venedict Pushkov.
Cast: Nikolai Bogolyubov, Tamara Makarova, I. Novoseltsev, Oleg Zhakov, Pyotr Aleinikov.
We from Kronstadt (My iz Kronstadt). 2,655 m., Mosfilm   20 Mar.
Scen.: Vsevolod Vishnevsky; *dir.:* Yefim Dzigan; *co-dir.:* G. Berezko; *phot.:* N. Naumov-Strazh; *des.:* Vladimir Yegorov; *mus.:* Nikolai Kryukov.
Cast: Vasili Zaichikov, Grigori Bushuyev, Oleg Zhakov, Raisa Yesipova, P. Kirillov.

By the Bluest of Seas (U samovo sinevo morya). Azerkino & Mezhrabpomfilm
20 Apr.
Scen.: K. Mintz; *dir.:* Boris Barnet; *co-dir.:* S. Mardanov; *phot.:* M. Kirillov,
M. Mustafayev; *des.:* Victor Aden, Sergei Kozlovsky; *mus.:* Sergei Pototsky.
Cast: Lev Sverdlin, Nikolai Kryuchkov, Yelena Kuzmina.

I Love (Ya lyublyu). Ukrainfilm.   9 May
Scen.: Alexander Avdeyenko (from his novel); *dir.:* Leonid Lukov. *phot.:* I.
Shekker; *des.:* Mauritz Umansky; *mus.:* Shishov.
Cast: Vladimir Gardin, Ivan Chuvelyov, Alexander Chistyakov, Gulya Koroleva,
Natalia Uzhvi.

Grunya Kornakova [Nightingale, Little Nightingale]. Mezhrabpomfilm. 11 June
Scen. & dir.: Nikolai Ekk; *colour-phot.:* Fyodor Provorov; *des.:* I. Stepanov;
mus.: Y. Stolyar.
Cast: Valentina Ivashova, Yelena Maximova, V. Atalov, A. Korsakov.

Son of Mongolia (Syn Mongolii). Lenfilm   17 July
Scen.: B. Lapin, Lev Slavin, Z. Khatzrevin; *dir.:* Ilya Trauberg; *co-dir.:* R.
Suslovich; *phot.:* M. Kaplan, V. Levitin, E. Shtirtskober; *des.:* I. Vuskovich;
mus.: Isaac Rabinovich, E. Grikurov.

Seekers of Happiness (Iskateli s'chastya). Sovietskaya Byelorus   25 Sep.
Scen.: Johann Zeltzer, G. Kobets; *dir.:* V. Korsh-Sablin; *co-dir.:* I. Shapiro;
phot.: B. Ryabov, K. Pogodin; *des.:* V. Pokrovsky; *mus.:* Isaac Dunayevsky.
Cast: Maria Blumenthal-Tamarina, Veniamin Zuskin.

Generation of Conquerors (Pokoleniye pobeditelei). 3,004 m., Mosfilm   5 Nov.
Scen. (from an idea by Arosev)*:* Serafina Roshal, Vera Stroyeva; *dir.:* Stroyeva;
phot.: Leonid Kosmatov, N. Vlasov; *des.:* Isaac Shpinel, A. Zharenkov; *mus.:*
Nikolai Kryukov.
Cast: Boris Shchukin, Nikolai Khmelyov, Xenia Tarasova, Vera Maretskaya,
Nikolai Plotnikov.

1937
Without Dowry (Bespridannitsa). 2,392 m., Mezhrabpomfilm   26 Jan.
Scen. (from Ostrovsky's play)*:* Vladimir Schweitzer, Yakov Protazanov; *dir.:*
Protazanov; *phot.:* Mark Magidson; *des.:* Anatoli Arapov, S. Kuznetsov.
Cast: Nina Alisova, Mikhail Klimov, Anatoli Ktorov, Boris Tenin, Olga Pizhova.

The Last Night (Poslednaya noch). 2,700 m., Mosfilm   2 Feb
Scen.: Yevgeni Gabrilovich, Yuli Raizman; [1] *dir.:* Raizman; *co-dir.:* Dmitri
Vasiliev; *phot.:* Dmitri Feldman; *des.:* Alexander Utkin; *ed.:* G. Shirokov;
mus.: A. Veprik.
Cast: I. Peltser, M. Yarotskaya, Nikolai Dorokhin, A. Konsovsky.

Baltic Deputy (Deputat Baltiki). 2,628 m., Lenfilm   27 Mar.
Scen.: D. Del, Alexander Zarkhi, Leonid Rakhmanov, Josif Heifits; *dir.:* Zarkhi,
Heifits; *phot.:* M. Kaplan; *des.:* Nikolai Suvorov, V. Kalyagin; *mus.:* N. Timo-
feyev.
Cast: Nikolai Cherkasov, M. Domasheva, Boris Livanov, Oleg Zhakov, A.
Melnikov.

The Thirteen (Trinadtsat). 2,355 m., Mosfilm   8 May
Scen.: I. Prut, Mikhail Romm; *dir.:* Romm; *phot.:* Boris Volchok; *des.:* Vladimir
Yegorov, M. Karyakin, A. Nikulin; *mus.:* Anatoli Alexandrov.
Cast: I. Novoseltsev, Yelena Kuzmina, A. Chistyakov, Andrei Fait, Pyotr Masokha.

Arsen 2,579 m., Goskinprom-Georgia   20 May
Scen.: A. Shanshiashvili (from his play), Mikhail Chiaureli; *dir.:* Chiaureli;

phot.: Alexander Digmelov; *des.*: I. Gamrekeli, T. Abakeliya; *mus.*: G. Kiladze. *Cast:* Spartak Bagashvili, Nata Vachnadze, B. Gamrekeli, N. Chkheidze, Ivan Perestiani.

The Return of Maxim (Vozvrashcheniye Maksima). 3,082 m., Lenfilm   23 May
Scen.: Grigori Kozintsev, Lev Slavin, Leonid Trauberg; *dir.*: Kozintsev, Trauberg; *phot.*: Andrei Moskvin; *des.*: Yevgeni Enei; *mus.*: Dmitri Shostakovich.
Cast: Boris Chirkov, Valentina Kibardina, Alexander Zrazhevsky, A. Kuznetsov, Mikhail Zharov, Vasili Vanin, A. Chistyakov.

Peter the First (Pyotr I): Part One. 2,815 m., Lenfilm   31 Aug.
Scen.: Alexei Tolstoy, Vladimir Petrov; *dir.*: Petrov; *phot.*: Vyacheslav Gardanov, Vladimir Yakovlev; *des.*: Nikolai Suvorov; *mus.*: Vladimir Shcherbachov.
Cast: Nikolai Simonov, Alla Tarasova, Nikolai Cherkasov, Mikhail Zharov, Mikhail Tarkhanov, I. Zarubina.

Lenin in October (Lenin v Oktyabre). 3,034 m., Mosfilm   7 Nov.
Scen.: Alexei Kapler; *dir.*: Mikhail Romm; *co-dir.*: Dmitri Vasiliev; *phot.*: Boris Volchok; *des.*: Boris Dubrovsky-Eshke; *mus.*: Anatoli Alexandrov.
Cast: Boris Shchukin, Nikolai Okhlopkov, Vasili Vanin, I. Golshtab (Stalin).

Lone White Sail (Byeleyet parus odinoky). 2,371 m., Soyuzdetfilm   25 Nov.
Scen.: Valentin Katayev (from his novel); *dir.*: Vladimir Legoshin; *phot.*: Bentsion Monastirsky, G. Garibian; *des.*: Vladimir Kaplunovsky, S. Kuznetsov; *mus.*: M. Rauchberger.
Cast: Igor But, Boris Runge, A. Melnikov, I. Peltser, A. Chekayevsky.

1938

Volochayevsk Days (Volochayevskiye dni). 3,066 m., Lenfilm   20 Jan.
Scen. & dir.: Sergei & Georgi Vasiliev; *phot.*: Alexander Sigayev, Apollinari Dudko; *des.*: Y. Rivosh, I. Zablotsky; *mus.*: Dmitri Shostakovich.
Cast: Nikolai Dorokhin, Varvara Myasnikova, Lev Sverdlin, B. Blinov, Boris Chirkov.

A Great Citizen (Veliki grazhdanin): Part One. Lenfilm   13 Feb.
Scen.: Mikhail Bleiman, Mikhail Bolshintsov, Friedrich Ermler; *dir.*: Ermler; *phot.*: Arkadi Kaltsati; *des.*: Nikolai Suvorov, A. Wechsler, Semyon Menken; *mus.*: Dmitri Shostakovich.
Cast: Nikolai Bogolyubov, Ivan Bersenev, Oleg Zhakov, Alexander Zrazhevsky.

The Rich Bride (Bogataya nevesta). 2,675 m., Ukrainfilm   2 Mar.
Scen.: Yevgeni Pomeshchikov; *dir.*: Ivan Pyriev; *phot.*: Vladimir Okulich; *des.*: M. Simashkevich; *mus.*: Isaac Dunayevsky.
Cast: Marina Ladynina, Anna Dmokhovskaya, B. Bezgin, Ivan Lyubeznov.

Volga-Volga. 2,867 m., Mosfilm   24 Apr.
Scen. & dir.: Grigori Alexandrov; *phot.*: B. Petrov; *des.*: G. Grivtsov, M. Karyakin, K. Yefimov; *mus.*: Isaac Dunayevsky.
Cast: Lyubov Orlova, Igor Ilinsky, V. Volodin.

Komsomolsk. 2,954 m., Lenfilm   1 May
Scen.: Z. Markina, M. Vitukhnovsky, Sergei Gerasimov; *dir.*: Gerasimov; *phot.*: Alexander Ginsburg; *des.*: V. Semyonov; *mus.*: Venedict Pushkov.
Cast: I. Novoseltsev, Tamara Makarova, Nikolai Kryuchkov, S. Krylov.

Childhood of Gorky (Detstvo Gorkovo). 2,753 m., Soyuzdetfilm   18 June
Scen. (from Gorky's memoirs): I. Gruzdev, Mark Donskoy; *dir.*: Donskoy; *phot.*: Pyotr Yermolov; *des.*: I. Stepanov; *mus.*: Lev Schwartz.
Cast: Alexei Lyarsky, Varvara Massalitinova, M. Troyanovsky, Daniel Sagal.

The Bear (Medved). 1,236 m., Belgoskino   11 July
Scen. (from a Chekhov vaudeville) & *dir.:* Isidor Annensky; *phot.:* Y. Shapiro; *des.:* L. Putiyevskaya; *mus.:* V. Zhelobinsky.
Cast: Mikhail Zharov, Olga Androvskaya, I. Peltser.

Victory (Pobeda). 2,325 m., Mezhrabpomfilm & Mosfilm   15 July
Scen.: Nathan Zarkhi (revised by Vsevolod Vishnevsky); *dir.:* Vsevolod Pudovkin, Mikhail Doller; *phot.:* Anatoli Golovnya; *asst. phot.:* Sergei Urusevsky; *des.:* V. Ivanov, V. Kamsky; *mus.:* Yuri Shaporin.
Cast: V. Solovyov, A. Zubov, Yelena Korchagina-Alexandrovskaya.

Professor Mamlock. 2,867 m., Lenfilm   5 Sep.
Scen.: Friedrich Wolff (from his play), Adolf Minkin, Herbert Rappoport; *dir.:* Minkin, Rappoport; *phot.:* G. Filatov; *des.:* P. Betaki; *mus.:* Y. Kochurov, N. Timofeyev.
Cast: Sergei Mezhinsky, Oleg Zhakov, Nina Shaternikova, Vasili Merkuriev.

The Man with a Gun (Chelovek s ruzhyom). 2,800 m., Lenfilm   1 Nov.
Scen.: Nikolai Pogodin; *dir.:* Sergei Yutkevich; *co-dir.:* P. Armand, M. Itina; *phot.:* I. Martov, G. Maximov; *des.:* Alexander Black; *mus.:* Dmitri Shostakovich.
Cast: Boris Tenin, Maxim Strauch (Lenin), Zoya Fyodorova, Vladimir Lukin, Mark Bernes.

Alexander Nevsky. 3,044 m., Mosfilm   1 Dec.
Scen.: Pyotr Pavlenko, Sergei Eisenstein; *dir.:* Eisenstein, Dmitri Vasiliev; *phot.:* Eduard Tisse; *des.:* Isaac Shpinel, N. Soloviov, K. Yeliseyev; *mus.:* Sergei Prokofiev.
Cast: Nikolai Cherkasov, Nikolai Okhlopkov, Andrei Abrikosov, Valentina Ivashova, Dmitri Orlov, Vladimir Yershov, Varvara Massalitinova.

1939
The Oppenheim Family (Semya Oppenheim). 2,823 m., Mosfilm   5 Jan.
Scen. (from Feuchtwanger's novel): Serafima Roshal; *dir.:* Grigori Roshal; *phot.:* Leonid Kosmatov; *des.:* Isaac Shpinel; *mus.:* Nikolai Kryukov.
Cast: Vladimir Balashov, Josif Tolchanov, Ada Voitsik, Nikolai Plotnikov, Solomon Mikhoels.

Amangeldi. Lenfilm   25 Jan.
Scen.: Vsevolod Ivanov, Gabit Musrepov; *dir.* & *des.:* Moisei Levin.
Cast: Umurzakov, Shara Zhandarbekova.

The Vyborg Side (Vyborgskaya storona). 3,276 m., Lenfilm   2 Feb.
Scen. & *dir.:* Grigori Kozintsev, Leonid Trauberg; *phot.:* Andrei Moskvin, G. Filatov; *des.:* V. Vlasov; *mus.:* Dmitri Shostakovich.
Cast: Boris Chirkov, Valentina Kibardina, Natalia Uzhvi, Mikhail Zharov, A. Chistyakov, Yuri Tolubeyev, Maxim Strauch (Lenin), Mikhail Gelovani (Stalin).

Peter the First (Piotr Pervyi): Part Two. 3,423 m., Lenfilm   7 Mar.
Scen.: Alexei Tolstoy, Vasili Petrov, N. Leshchenko; *dir.:* Petrov; *co-dir.:* S. Bartenev; *phot.:* Vladimir Yakovlev; *des.:* Nikolai Suvorov, V. Kalyagin; *mus.:* Vladimir Shcherbachov.
Cast: Nikolai Simonov, Alla Tarasova, Nikolai Cherkasov, Mikhail Zharov, Mikhail Tarkhanov, I. Zarubina.

Among People (V lyudyakh) [In the World]. 2,730 m., Soyuzdetfilm   31 Mar.
Scen. (from Gorky's memoirs): I. Gruzdev; *dir.:* Mark Donskoy; *phot.:* Pyotr Yermolov; *des.:* I. Stepanov; *mus:* Lev Schwartz.
Cast: Alexei Lyarsky, Varvara Massalitinova, Mikhail Troyanovsky.

Lenin in 1918 (Lenin v 1918 godu). 3,677 m., Mosfilm 7 Apr.
Scen.: Alexei Kapler, Tatiana Zlatogorova; *dir.:* Mikhail Romm; *phot.:* Boris Volchok; *des.:* Boris Dubrovsky-Eshke, V. Ivanov; *mus.:* Nikolai Kryukov.
Cast: Boris Shchukin, Mikhail Gelovani, Nikolai Cherkasov (Gorky), Nikolai Bogolyubov (Voroshilov), Nikolai Okhlopkov, Vasili Vanin.

Shchors. 3,850 m., Kiev Studio 1 May
Scen. & dir.: Alexander Dovzhenko; *co-dir.:* Yulia Solntseva; *asst.* Lazar Bodik; *phot.:* Yuri Yekelchik; *des.:* Mauritz Umansky; *mus.:* Dmitri Kabalevsky.
Cast: Yevgeni Samoilov, Ivan Skuratov, Hans Klering.

The Man in the Case (Chelovek v futlyare). 3,608 m., Sovietskaya Belorus 25 May
Scen. (from Chekhov's story) *& dir.:* Isidor Annensky; *phot.:* Y. Shapiro; *des.:* L. Putiyevskaya; *mus.:* A. Golubentsov.
Cast: Nikolai Khinelyov, Mikhail Zharov, Olga Androvskaya, Vladimir Gardin.

Tractor-Drivers (Traktoristi). 3,200 m., Mosfilm & Kiev Studio 3 July
Scen.: Yevgeni Pomeshchikov; *dir.:* Ivan Pyriev; *phot.:* Alexander Galperin; *des.:* Vladimir Kaplunovsky; *mus.:* brothers Pokrass.
Cast: Marina Ladynina, Nikolai Kryuchkov, Boris Andreyev, Pyotr Aleinikov, Stepan Kayukov.

Spain (Ispaniya) 20 July
Scen.: Vsevolod Vishnevsky; *dir. & ed.:* Esther Shub.

Riders (Vsadniki) [US. title: Guerrilla Brigade]. 2,592 m., Kiev Studio 29 July
Scen.: V. Pavlovsky; *dir.:* Igor Savchenko; *co-dir.:* A. Golovanov; *phot.:* Vladimir Okulich; *des.:* M. Simashkevich; *mus.:* Sergei Pototsky.
Cast: Lev Sverdlin, Pyotr Masokha, Stepan Shkurat, Yelena Kuzmina, Leonid Kmit.

A Night in September (Noch v Sentyabre). 2,916 m., Mosfilm 16 Oct.
Scen.: I. Chekin; *dir.:* Boris Barnet; *phot.:* N. Naumov-Strazh; *des.:* Vladimir Balliuzek.
Cast: E. Abkhaidze (Ordjonikidze), Nikolai Kryuchkov, Daniel Sagal, Zoya Fyodorova.

Minin i Pozharsky. 3,647 m., Mosfilm 3 Nov.
Scen.: Victor Shklovsky; *dir.:* Vsevolod Pudovkin, Mikhail Doller; *phot.:* Anatoli Golovnya, Tamara Lobova; *des.:* Alexander Utkin, K. Yefimov; *mus.:* Yuri Shaporin.
Cast: Boris Livanov, Alexander Khanov, Boris Chirkov, Lev Sverdlin, Anatoli Goryunov.

A Great Citizen (Velikii grazhdanin): Part Two. 3,640 m., Lenfilm 27 Nov.
Scen.: Mikhail Bleiman, Mikhail Bolshintsov, Friedrich Ermler; *dir.:* Ermler; *phot.:* Arkadi Kaltsati; *des.:* Semyon Menken.
Cast: Nikolai Bogolyubov, Oleg Zhakov, Ivan Bersenev, Boris Poslavsky, Yuri Tolubeyev.

Teacher (Uchitel). 2,909 m., Lenfilm 10 Dec.
Scen. & dir.: Sergei Gerasimov; *phot.:* Vladimir Yakovlev; *des.:* V. Semyonov; *mus.:* Venedict Pushkov.
Cast: Boris Chirkov, Tamara Makarova, P. Volkov, L. Shabalina.

1940
A Great Life (Bolshaya zhizn): Part One. 2,677 m., Kiev Studio 4 Feb.
Scen.: Pavel Nilin (from his novel); *dir.:* Leonid Lukov; *phot.:* I. Shekker; *des.:* S. Zaritsky; *mus.:* Nikita Bogoslovsky.

Cast: I. Peltzer, Boris Andreyev, Pyotr Aleinikov, I. Novoseltsov, Stepan Kayukov, Pyotr Masokha.

Member of the Government (Chlen pravitelstva). 2,912 m., Lenfilm [US.: Great Beginning] 8 Mar.
    Scen.: Katerina Vinogradskaya; *dir.:* Alexander Zarkhi, Josif Heifits; *phot.:* Alexander Ginsburg; *des.:* O. Pchelnikova, V. Kalyagin; *mus.:* N. Timofeyev.
    Cast: Vera Maretskaya, Vasili Vanin, P. Nazarov, Vasili Merkuriev.

My Universities (Moi universiteti.)2,813 m., Soyuzdetfilm 27 Mar.
    Scen. (from Gorky's memoirs): I. Gruzdev, Mark Donskoy, *dir.:* Donskoy; *phot.:* Pyotr Yermolov; *des.:* I. Stepanov; *mus.:* Lev Schwartz.
    Cast: Y. Valbert, Stepan Kayukov, Nikolai Dorokhin, Lev Sverdlin.

The Mannerheim Line (Liniya Mannerheim). 27 Apr.
    Dir.: Vasili Belayev; *phot.:* Vladimir Yeshurin, Solomon Kogan, Georgi Simonov, Sergei Fomin, Philip Pechul.

Virgin Soil Upturned (Podnyataya tzelina). 3,236 m., Mosfilm 5 May
    Scen.: Mikhail Sholokhov (from his novel), Sergei Yermolinsky; *dir.:* Yuli Raizman; *phot.:* Leonid Kosmatov; *des.:* Vladimir Yegorov, M. Tiunov, V. Kamsky; *mus.:* Yuri Sviridov.
    Cast: Boris Dobronravov, M. Bolduman, S. Blinnikov, G. Belov, A. Khokhlov.

Liberation (Osvobozhdeniye). 1,720 m., Kiev Studio 25 Aug.
    Dir.: Alexander Dovzhenko; *co-dir.:* Yulia Solntseva; *asst.:* Lazar Bodik; *phot.:* Yuri Yekelchik, G. Alexandrov, Y. Tamarsky, Nikolai Bykov; *mus.:* Liatoshinsky.

A Musical Story (Muzikalnaya istoriya). 2,284 m., Lenfilm 24 Sep.
    Scen.: Yevgeni Petrov, G. Munblit; *dir.:* Alexander Ivanovsky, Herbert Rappaport; *phot.:* Abram Kaltsati, M. Rotinov; *des.:* S. Mandel.
    Cast: Zoya Fyodorova, Sergei Lemeshev, Nikolai Konovalov, Erast Garin.

Brother of a Hero (Brat geroya). 8 reels, Soyuzdetfilm 7 Nov.
    Scen.: Lev Kassil (from his story); *dir.:* Mark Donskoy; *phot.:* I. Malov; *des.:* N. Valerianov; *mus.:* A. Lepin.
    Cast: Nikolai Kryuchkov, L. Mirsky, L. Dranovskaya.

A Day in a New World (Den novovo mira). Central Newsreel Studio 7 Dec.

Yakov Sverdlov. 3,604 m., Soyuzdetfilm 12 Dec.
    Scen (from the play by B. Levin & Pyotr Pavlenko): D. Dell, Sergei Yutkevich, M. Itina; *dir.:* Yutkevich; *co-dir:* Itina; *phot.:* I. Martov; *des.:* Vladimir Kaplunovsky, G. Rozhalin.
    Cast: Leonid Lyubashevsky, Pavel Kadochnikov (Gorky & Lenka), Nikolai Kryuchkov, Nikolai Okhlopkov (Shalyapin).

1941

Suvorov. 2,948 m., Mosfilm 23 Jan.
    Scen.: Georgi Grebner, H. Ravich; *dir.:* Vsevolod Pudovkin, Mikhail Doller; *phot.:* Anatoli Golovnya, Tamara Lobova; *des.:* Vladimir Yegorov, K. Yefimov; *mus.:* Yuri Shaporin.
    Cast: Nikolai Cherkasov-Sergeyev, A. Yachnitsky (Paul I), Alexander Khanov, Vsevolod Aksyonov, Mikhail Astangov.

Salavat Yulayev. 2,098 m., Soyuzdetfilm 21 Feb.
    Scen.: S. Zlobin, G. Spevak; *dir.:* Yakov Protazanov; *phot.:* Alexander Shelenkov; *des.:* V. Ladyagin, S. Kuznetsov, S. Voronikov; *mus.:* Aram Khachaturian.
    Cast: Arslan Muboryakov, M. Bolduman (Pugachov), Nikolai Kryuchkov.

Valeri Chkalov. 2,783 m., Lenfilm [US. title: Wings of Victory] 12 Mar.
    Scen.: Georgi Baidukov, D. Tarasov, Boris Chirskov; *dir.:* Mikhail Kalatozov;

phot.: Alexander Ginsburg; *des.:* Alexander Black; *mus.:* Venedict Pushkov. *Cast:* Vladimir Belokurov, Vasili Vanin, Xenia Tarasova.

Bogdan Khmelnitsky. 3,118 m., Kiev Studio   7 Apr.
Scen.: Alexander Korneichuk; *dir.:* Igor Savchenko; *phot.:* Yuri Yekelchik; *des.:* Y. Rivosh, Y. Mayer, M. Solokha, V. Korolev; *mus.:* Sergei Pototsky.
Cast: Nikolai Mordvinov, Boris Andreyev, Mikhail Zharov.

Front-Line Girl Friends (Frontoviye podrugi). 2,592 m., Lenfilm [US.: **Girl from Leningrad**]   19 May
Scen.: Sergei Mikhailov, Mikhail Rosenberg; *dir.:* Victor Eisimont; *phot.:* Wulf Rapoport; *des.:* F. Bernstam; *mus.:* Visarion Shebalin.
Cast: Zoya Fyodorova, Boris Blinov, Andrei Abrikosov, Yuri Tolubeyev, Oleg Zhakov.

Kino-Concert 1941 [GB.: **Russian Salad**]. Lenfilm   16 June
Dir.: I. Menaker, Adolf Minkin, Herbert Rappoport, Sergei Timoshenko, M. Tsekhanovsky, M. Shapiro.

Masquerade. 2,739 m., Lenfilm   16 Sep.
Scen. (from Lermontov's play) *& dir.:* Sergei Gerasimov; *phot.:* Vyacheslav Gardanov; *des.:* Semyon Menken; *mus.:* Venedict Pushkov.
Cast: Nikolai Mordvinov, Tamara Makarova, Sophie Magarill, Gerasimov.

The Artamanov Affair (Delo Artamonovikh). 2,643 m., Mosfilm   8 Oct.
Scen. (from Gorky's novel): Sergei Yermolinsky; *dir.:* Grigori Roshal; *phot.:* Leonid Kosmatov; *des.:* Vladimir Yegorov, S. Vishnevetskaya; *mus.:* Marian Koval.
Cast: S. Romodanov, A. Smirnov, Mikhail Derzhavin, Vera Maretskaya, Vladimir Balashov.

Swineherd and Shepherd (Svinyarka i pastukh). 2,470 m., Mosfilm [US.: **They Met in Moscow**]   7 Nov.
Scen.: Victor Gusev; *dir.:* Ivan Pyriev; *phot.:* Valentin Pavlov; *des.:* A. Berger; *mus.:* Tikhon Khrennikov.
Cast: Marina Ladynina, V. Zeldin, Nikolai Kryuchkov.

Fighting Film Albums:
1 Meeting with Maxim. *Dir.:* Sergie Gerasimov; *cast:* Boris Chirkov; *typo.:* Sergei Gerasimov.
   Dream in the Hand. *Scen.:* Boris Laskin, Leonid Lench; *dir.:* Y. Nekrasov; *phot.:* Yuli Fogelman; *cast:* Pyotr Repnin (Hitler), Vladimir Kantsel (Napoleon).
   Three in a Shell-hole. *Scene:* Leonid Leonov; *dir.:* I. Mutanov, Alexei Olenin; *phot.:* N. Naumov-Strazh; *mus.:* Nikolai Kryukov; *cast:* N. Petropavlovskaya, M. Yandulsky, A. Gehr.
2 Meeting. *Scen.:* Vasili Belayev, Mikhail Rosenberg; *dir.:* V. Feinberg.
   One of Many. *Scen.:* Yuri German, I. Zeltzer, A. Stein; *dir.:* Victor Eisimont.
   At the Old Nurse's. *Scen.:* Vasili Belayev, Mikhail Rosenberg; *dir.:* Yevgeni Cherviakov.
   A Hundred for One. *Scen.:* Y. Riss, V. Voyevodin; *dir.:* Herbert Rappoport.
   Incident at the Telegraph Office. *Dir.:* Grigori Kozintsev.
3 English Anti-Aircraft
   Manhood. *Scen.:* I. Bondin; *dir.:* Boris Barnet; *phot.:* K. Wenz; *Cast:* V. Shishkin.
   Antosha Rybkin. *Scen.:* A. Schiffers; *dir.:* Konstantin Yudin; *cast:* Boris Chirkov.
4 The British Fleet
   Patriot. *Scen.:* Yevgeni Pomeshchikov, Nikolai Rozhkov; *dir.:* Vasili Pronin.
   Order Carried Out. *Scen.:* G. Fish, Konstantin Isayev; *dir.:* Y. Aron.

5 London Will Not Surrender
Our Moscow. *Scen.:* Alexei Kapler; *dir.:* Mikhail Slutsky.
6 Women of the Air Force [WAAF]
Feast at Zhirmunka. *Scen.:* Leonid Leonov, Nikolai Shpikovsky; *dir.:* Vsevolod
Pudovkin, Mikhail Doller; *phot.:* Anatoli Golovnya, Tamara Lobova; *des.* Boris
Dubrovsky-Eshke; *mus.:* Nikolai Kryukov; *cast:* P. Geraga, V. Uralsky,
A. Zuyeva, A. Danilova.
War Songs. Sung by Nikolai Kryuchkov.
7 Schweik in the Concentration-Camp. *Scen.:* Yevgeni Pomeshchikov, Nikolai
Rozhkov; *dir.:* Sergei Yutkevich; *phot.:* I. Martov, Georgi Garibian; *des.:*
Sergei Kozlovsky; *cast:* Vladimir Kantsel, Erast Garin, Nikolai Okhlopkov.
Exactly at Seven. *Scen.:* A. Sazonov; *dir.:* A. Gendelstein, A. Rau.
Elixir of Courage. *Scen.:* Nikolai Erdman, M. Volpin; *dir.:* Sergei Yutkevich;
cast: Erast Garin.
Depot for Catastrophes. *Scen.:* D. Yeremin, I. Manevich; *dir.:* R. Perelstein,
L. Altsev.
The Most Valiant. *Scen. & dir.:* Klimenti Mintz; *cast:* Sergei Martinson
(Hitler), Ivan Liubeznov.
A Real Patriot. *Scen.:* Klimenti Mintz, M. Vitukhnovsky; *dir.:* Mintz.
The White Raven. *Scen.* (from story by Lev Nikulin)*:* A. Sazonov; *dir.:* Sergei
Yutkevich; *cast:* Nikolai Okhlopkov.

1942
Defeat of the German Armies near Moscow (Razgrom nemetzkikh voisk pod
Moskvoi). 18 Feb.
Dir.: Leonid Varlamov, Ilya Kopalin; *phot.:* Fyodor Bunimovich, G. Bobrov,
P. Kasatkin, A. Krylov, A. Lebedev, M. Schneiderov, Alexander Elbert, Roman
Karmen, V. Soloviov, Boris Sher, I. Belyakov, Victor Statland, Boris Makaseyev,
Maria Sukhova, V. Frolenko, I. Sokolnikov, Vladimir Yeshurin.
Defence of Tsaritsin (Oborona Tsaritsina). 2,880 m., Lenfilm 29 Mar.
Scen. & dir.: Sergei & Georgi Vasiliev; *phot.:* Apollinari Dudko, S. Ivanov,
Alexander Sigayev; *des.:* P. Yakimov; *mus.:* Nikolai Kryukov.
Cast: Mikhail Gelovani (Stalin), Nikolai Bogoliubov (Voroshilov), Mikhail Zharov.
Mashenka. 2,097 m., Mosfilm 31 Mar.
Scen.: Yevgeni Gabrilovich; *dir.:* Yuli Raizman; *co-dir.:* Dmitri Vasiliev; *phot.:*
Yevgeni Andrikanis; *des.:* Isaac Shpinel, M. Tiunov.
Cast: Valentina Karavayeva, Mikhail Kuznetsov, Vera Altaiskaya.
Murderers Are on Their Way (Ubitzi vykhodyat na dorogu). 7 reels, Combined
Studio Unreleased
Scen. (from plays by Brecht)*:* E. Bolshintsov, Vsevolod Pudovkin; *dir.:* Pudovkin,
Yuri Tarich; *phot.:* Boris Volchok, E. Zavelyova; *des.:* A. Berger; *mus.:* Nikolai
Kryukov.
Cast: Pyotr Sobolevsky, V. Kulakov, A. Antonov, Oleg Zhakov, B. Blinov, Ada
Voitsik, Sophie Magarill, Olga Zhizneva.
Leningrad in Combat (Leningrad v borbe). 7 reels, Leningrad Studio 9 Jul.
Dir.: Roman Karmen, N. Komarevtsev, Valeri Solovtsov, Y. Uchitel; *phot.:*
A. Bogorov, Anatoli Pogoreli, V. Stradin, Uchitel, K. Stankevich, Sergei Fomin,
B. Dementiev, L. Isaacson, E. Leibovich, G. Trofimov, G. Shuliatin, G. Simonov,
Yakov Slavin, Boris Sher, O. Ivanov, N. Golod, David Edelson, Vladimir
Sumkin, Pavel Lamprecht, Anatoli Bistrov, Philip Pechul, Karmen, N. Gladkov,
P. Pall, V. Maximovich, F. Ovsiannikov.

Georgi Saakadze: Part One. 2,517 m., Tbilisi Studio [Part Two, 2,531 m., 1943]
14 Sep.
Scen.: Anna Antonovskaya (from her novel), Boris Chorni; *dir.:* Mikhail Chiaureli; *phot.:* Alexander Digmelov; *des.:* M. Gotziridze, R. Mirzashvili; *mus.:* Andrei Balanchivadze.
Cast: Akaki Khorava, S. Gambashidze, Veriko Anjaparidze, A. Vasadze.

How the Steel was Tempered (Kak zakalyalas stal). 2,529 m., Kiev &
Ashkhabad Studios 28 Sep.
Scen. (from Nikolai Ostrovsky's novel) & *dir.:* Mark Donskoy; *phot.:* Bentsion Monastirsky; *des.:* M. Salokha; *mus.:* Lev. Schwartz.
Cast: V. Perest-Petrenko, Daniel Sagal, I. Fedotova.

His Name is Sukhe-Bator (Yevo zovut Sukhe-Bator). 11 reels, Tashkent Studio
12 Oct.
Scen.: B. Lapin, Z. Khatsrevin; *dir.:* Alexander Zarkhi, Josif Heifits; *phot.:* Alexander Ginsburg; *des.* A. Bosulayev; *mus.:* V. Arapov, Venedict Puskhov.
Cast: Lev Sverdlin, Nikolai Cherkasov, Maxim Strauch (Lenin), S. Goldstab.

Day of War (Den voini). 8 reels, Central Newsreel Studio 22 Oct.
Dir.: Mikhail Slutsky; *commentary:* Alexei Kapler; *phot.:* 240 cameramen.

Secretary of the District Committee (Sekretar raikom). 2,460 m., Combined
Studio 30 Nov.
Scen.: I. Prut; *dir.:* Ivan Pyriev; *phot.:* Valentin Pavlov; *des.:* Alexander Utkin, M. Krotkin; *mus.:* B. Volsky.
Cast: Vasili Vanin, Marina Ladynina, Mikhail Zharov, Mikhail Astangov.

Fighting Film Albums:
8 Night Over Belgrade. *Scen.:* I. Skylut; *dir.:* Leonid Lukov; *cast:* T. Okunevskaya, O. Abdulov, I. Novoseltsov, Pyotr Aleinikov.
Three in a Tank. *Scen.:* Vsevolod Ivanov; *dir.:* N. Sadkovich; *cast:* Mark Bernes, Pyotr Aleinikov, Boris Andreyev.
9 Block 14. *Scen.:* Solomon Lazurin; *dir.:* Igor Savchenko.
Blue Crags. *Scen.:* L. Smirnova, S. Gergel; *dir.:* Vladimir Braun.
Beacon. *Scen.:* N. Severov; *dir.:* Mark Donskoy.
10 A Priceless Head. *Scen.:* B. Petker, G. Rublev; *dir.:* Boris Barnet; *cast:* Nikolai Cherkasov-Sergeyev.
Young Wine. *Scen.:* Konstantin Isayev; *dir.:* Y. Aron.
11 Spider. *Scen.:* M. Berestinsky; *dir.:* Ilya Trauberg, I. Zemgano; *cast:* Maxim Strauch, N. Volkov.
The 102nd Kilometre. *Scen.:* B. Fayans; *dir.:* Vladimir Braun; *cast:* Ivan Pereverzev, I. Bobrov.
Career of Lieut. Gopp. *Scen.:* Boris Laskin, I. Sklyut; *dir.:* N. Sadkovich; *cast:* Sergei Martinson, O. Abdulov, E. Geller.
12 Vanka. *Scen.:* S. Polotzky, M. Tevelev; *dir.:* Herbert Rappoport; *cast:* Yanina Zheimo, Nikolai Cherkasov-Sergeyev.
Son of a Fighter. *Scen.:* Sergei Mikhailov, I. Prut; *dir.:* Vera Stroyeva.

1943
Stalingrad. 7 reels, Central Newsreel Studio 10 Mar.
Dir.: Leonid Varlamov; *phot.:* Boris Vakar, A. Kazakov, V. Orliankin, A. Sofin, G. Ostrovsky, A. Krichevsky, D. Ibragimov, Nikolai Vikhirev, Y. Mukhin, M. Golbrikh, I. Goldstein, M. Poselsky, V. Shadronov, I. Katzman, Ivan Malov.

In the Sands of Central Asia (V peskakh Srednei Azii). 1,286 m., Kiev-Tech-
Film 6 May

Scen. & dir.: Alexander Zguridi; *phot.:* G. Troyansky, V. Asmus.

She Defends Her Country (Ona zashchishchayet rodinu). 2,189 m., Combined Studio   20 May
Scen.: Mikhail Bleiman, I. Bondin; *dir.:* Friedrich Ermler; *co-dir.:* K. Gakkel; *phot.:* Wulf Rapoport; *des.:* Nikolai Suvorov; *mus.:* Gavril Popov.
Cast: Vera Maretskaya, L. Smirnova, Pyotr Aleinikov, Nikolai Bogolyubov.

Lermontov. 9 reels, Soyuzdetfilm & Stalinabad Studio   6 July
Scen.: Konstantin Paustovsky; *dir.:* A. Gendelstein; *phot.:* Alexander Shelenkov, Mark Magidson; *des.:* Konstantin Yefimov; *mus.:* Sergei Prokofiev.
Cast: A. Konsovsky, Nina Shaternikova, A. Rayevsky, P. Springfeld.

In the Name of the Fatherland (Vo imya rodini). 2,626 m., Combined Studio
                                                                              20 July
Scen.: Konstantin Simonov (from his play, *Russian People*); *dir.:* Vsevolod Pudovkin, Dmitri Vasiliev; *phot.:* Boris Volchok, E. Zavelyova; *des.:* A. Wechsler.
Cast: Nikolai Kryuchkov, Mikhail Zharov, V. Gribkov, Olga Zhizneva, Pyotr Aleinikov.

Nasreddin in Bukhara (Nasreddin v Bukhare). 2,399 m., Tashkent Studio 2 Aug.
Scen.: Leonid Soloviov, V. Vitkovich; *dir.:* Yakov Protazanov; *phot.:* Danylo Demutsky; *des.:* Varshan Yeremian; *mus.:* M. Ashrafi, B. Arapov.
Cast: Lev Sverdlin, K. Mikhailov, E. Geller, Vasili Zaichikov, Stepan Kayukov.

The People's Avengers (Narodniye mstiteli). 6 reels, Central Newsreel Studio
                                                                              19 Aug.
Dir.: Vasili Belayev; *phot.:* Nikolai Bykov, Victor Muromtzev, Semyon Shkolnikov, I. Veinerovich, Mikhail Glider, B. Dementiev, G. Donets, L. Isaacson, A. Kairov, Boris Makaseyev, Maria Sukhova, B. Eberg, N. Mestechkin.

The Fight for Our Soviet Ukraine (Bitva za nashu Sovietskayu Ukrainu). 7 reels, Central and Ukrainian Newsreel Studios.   25 Oct.
Dir.: Yulia Solntseva, Y. Avdeyenko, under supervision of Alexander Dovzhenko; *phot.:* Boris Vakar, V. Orliankin, P. Kasatkin, A. Sofin, Victor Statland, V. Frolenko, Vsevolod Afanasyev, K. Bogdan, Nikolai Bykov, Mikhail Glider, M. Bolbrikh, I. Goldstein, Ivan Zaporozhsky, Mordukh Kapkin, I. Katzman, I. Komarov, Yuli Kun, Gregori Mogilevsky, B. Rogachevsky, S. Semyonov, V. Smorodin, Sergei Urusevsky, A. Frolov, S. Sheinin.

Wait for Me (Zhdi menya). 2,479 m., Combined Studio   1 Nov.
Scen.: Konstantin Simonov (from his poem); *dir.:* Alexander Stolper, Boris Ivanov; *phot.:* S. Rubashkin; *des.:* A. Berger, V. Kamsky; *mus.:* Nikolai Kryukov, Y. Biryukov.
Cast: B. Blinov, V. Serova, Lev Sverdlin, Mikhail Nazvanov.

New Adventures of Schweik (Noviye pokhozdeniya Shveika). 8 reels, Soyuzdetfilm and Stalinabad Studios   22 Nov.
Scen.: Yevgeni Pomeshchikov, Nikolai Kozhkov; *dir.:* Sergei Yutkevich; *phot.:* Mark Magidson; *des.:* Sergei Kozlovsky; *mus.:* A. Lepin.
Cast: Boris Tenin, Sergei Martinson, Faina Ranevskaya, N. Nikotina, P. Springfeld.

1944

The Rainbow (Raduga). 2,634 m., Kiev & Ashkhabad Studios   24 Jan.
Scen.: Wanda Wasilewska (from her novel); *dir.:* Mark Donskoy; *phot.:* Bentsion Monastirsky; *des.:* V. Khmelyova; *mus.:* Lev Schwartz.
Cast: Natalia Uzhvi, Nina Alisova, Yelena Tyapkina, A. Dunaisky, Hans Klering.

David-Bek. 2,594 m., Erevan Studio　　　　　　　　　　　14 Feb.
Scen.: Amo Bek-Nazarov, Y. Dukor, S. Arutinian, Vsevolod Solovyov; *dir.:* Bek-Nazarov; *co-dir.:* A. Martirosian, Dukor; *phot.:* Dmitri Feldman (interiors), Garush Bek-Nazarov (exteriors); *des.:* M. M. Arutchian; *mus.:* A. Satian.
Cast: Grachya Nersesian, David Malian, Yevgeni Samoilov, Avet Avetisian.

Kutuzov. 3,100 m., Mosfilm　　　　　　　　　　　　　　15 Mar.
Scen.: Vsevolod Solovyov; *dir.:* Vladimir Petrov; *phot.:* Mikhail Gindin; *des.:* Vladimir Yegorov; *mus.:* Yuri Shaporin.
Cast: Alexei Diki, Nikolai Okhlopkov (Barclay de Tolly), S. Zakariadze (Bagration), Sergei Mezhinsky (Napoleon).

Moscow Sky (Nebo Moskvy). 2,400 m., Mosfilm　　　　　　1 June
Scen. (from play by Mdivani): Mikhail Bleiman, Mikhail Bolshintsov; *dir.:* Yuli Raizman; *2nd dir.:* G. Levkoyev; *phot.:* Yevgeni Andrikanis; *des.:* Nikolai Suvorov, A. Weisfeld.
Cast: Pyotr Aleinikov, Nina Mazayeva, Nikolai Bogulyubov, Pyotr Sobolevsky.

Jubilee. 1,093 m., Mosfilm　　　　　　　　　　　　　　14 July
Scen. (from vaudeville by Chekhov) *& dir.:* Vladimir Petrov; *phot.:* Vladimir Yakovlev, N. Brusilovskaya; *des.:* Vladimir Yegorov, N. Galustian; *mus.:* Nikolai Kryukov.
Cast: Victor Stanitsin, Olga Androvskaya, Vasili Toporkov, A. Zuyeva.

Wedding (Svadba). 7 reels, Tbilisi Studio　　　　　　　　14 July
Scen. (from vaudeville by Chekhov) *& dir.:* Isidor Annensky; *phot.:* Yuri Yekelchik; *des.:* S. Mandel; *mus.:* V. Zhelobinsky.
Cast: Alexei Gribov, Faina Ranevskaya, Erast Garin, Mikhail Yanshin, Sergei Martinson, Vera Maretskaya, Nikolai Plotnikov, Lev Sverdlin.

Zoya. 2,601 m., Soyuzdetfilm　　　　　　　　　　　　　22 Sep.
Scen.: Leo Arnstam, Boris Chirskov; *dir.:* Arnstam; *co-dir.:* I. Frez, V. Sukhobokov; *phot.:* Alexander Shelenkov; *des.:* Urbetis; *mus.:* Dmitri Shostakovich.
Cast: Galina Vodyanitskaya, Katya Skvortsova, Xenia Tarasova, Boris Poslavsky.

At 6 p.m. After the War (V shest chasov vechera posle voiny). 2,772 m., Mosfilm
　　　　　　　　　　　　　　　　　　　　　　　　　　　Nov.
Scen.: Victor Gusev, Nikolai Rozhkov; *dir.:* Ivan Pyriev; *phot.:* Valentin Pavlov; *des.:* Alexander Utkin, B. Chebotarev; *mus.:* Tikhon Khrennikov.
Cast: Marina Ladynina, Yevgeni Samoilov, Ivan Lyubeznov.

Once There was a Girl (Zhila-byla devochka). 2,016 m., Soyuzdetfilm　Dec.
Scen.: Vladimir Nedobrovo; *dir.:* Victor Eisimont; *phot.:* Georgi Garibian; *des.:* I. Bakhmetev; *mus.:* Venedict Pushkov.
Cast: Ada Voitsik, N. Korn, Vera Altaiskaya, A. Kirillova, (children:) Nina Ivanova, Natasha Zashchipina.

Girl No. 217 (Chelovek No. 217). 2,776 m., Mosfilm & Tashkent Studio　Dec.
Scen.: Yevgeni Gabrilovich, Mikhail Romm; *dir.:* Romm; *phot.:* Boris Volchok, E. Zavelyova; *mus.:* Aram Khachaturian.
Cast: Yelena Kuzmina, Anna Lisyanskaya, Vasili Zaichikov.

Ivan the Terrible (Ivan Grozny): Part One. 2,745 m., Combined Studio　30 Dec.
Scen. & dir.: Sergei Eisenstein; *asst.:* B. Sveshnikov, L. Indenbom; *phot.:* Eduard Tisse (exteriors), Andrei Moskvin (interiors); *des.:* Isaac Shpinel, L. Naumova; *mus.:* Sergei Prokofiev.
Cast: Nikolai Cherkasov, Ludmila Tselikovskaya, Serafima Birman, Pavel Kadochnikov, Mikhail Nazvanov, Andrei Abrikosov, Mikhail Zharov, Ambrosi Buchma, Vsevolod Pudovkin.

1945

Invasion (Nashestviye). 2,745 m., Combined Studio, Alma-Ata　　　　Feb.
Scen. (from play by Leonid Leonov)*:* Boris Chirskov; *dir.:* Abram Room; *co-dir.:* Oleg Zhakov; *phot.:* S. Ivanov; *des.:* L. Milchin, L. Schildknecht; *mus.:* Y. Biryukov.
Cast: Zhakov, Olga Zhizneva, Vasili Vanin, V. Gremin.

Duel (Poyedinok). 9 reels, Soyuzdetfilm　　　　Mar.
Scen.: Tur Brothers, Lev Sheinin; *dir.:* Vladimir Legoshin; *phot.:* Sergei Urusevsky; *des.:* I. Pashkevich, S. Sletov; *mus.:* Klimenti Korchmarev.
Cast: A Tutishkin, Sergei Lukyanov, N. Malishevsky, Alexei Gribov, Vladimir Belokurov.

Law of the Great Love (Zakon velikoi lyubvi). 5 reels, Mosvoyentekhfilm　Mar.
Scen.: S. Skitev; *dir.:* Boris Dolin; *phot.:* G. Kabalov.

Ivan Nikulin, Russian Sailor (Ivan Nikulin—russkoi matros). 11 reels, Mosfilm Apr.
Scen.: Leonid Solovyov (after his story); *dir.:* Igor Savchenko; *co-dir.:* Yevgeni Schneider, A. Davidson; *colour-phot.:* Fyodor Provorov; *des.:* K. Yuon, M. Samorodsky; *mus.:* Seregei Pototsky.
Cast: Ivan Pereverzev, Boris Chirkov, Stepan Kayukov, Erast Garin, Zoya Fyodorova.

Victory in the Ukraine and the Expulsion of the Germans from the Boundaries of the Ukrainian Soviet Earth (Pobeda na Pravoberezhnoi Ukraine i izgnaniye nemetsikh zakhvatchikov za predeli ukrainskikh sovietskikh zemel). 7 reels, Central Newsreel & Kiev Studios　　　　May ?
Dir.: Alexander Dovzhenko, Yulia Solntseva; *asst.-dir.:* F. Fillipov; *phot.:* Boris Vakar, Nikolai Vikhirev, V. Voitenko, I. Goldstein, Victor Dobronitsky, D. Ibragimov, I. Katzman, Alexander Kovalchuk, Yuli Kun, K. Kutub-Zade, A. Lapti, Gregori Mogilevsky, V. Orliankin, N. Rusanov, Alexei Syomin, A. Sofin, N. Topchi, D. Sholomovich, V. Shtatland, S. Gurov, M. Oshurkov.

One Night (Odnazhdi noch). 6 reels, Erevan Studio　　　　June
Scen.: Fyodor Knorr (from his story and play); *dir.:* Boris Barnet; *phot.:* Stepan Gevorkian; *des.:* Safarian, Yerzekian, Arutian.
Cast: Irina Radchenko, Boris Andreyev, Barnet.

Berlin. 9 reels, Central Newsreel Studio　　　　June
Dir.: Yuli Raizman, Yelizaveta Svilova; *asst.:* Nikolai Shpikovsky; *phot.:* Leon Saakov, M. Oshurkov, A. & Y. Alexeyev, I. Aarons, Nikolai Vikhirev, K. Ventz, G. Giber, G. Golubov, B. Dementiev, L. Dultsev, G. Yepifanov, D. Ibragimov, Roman Karmen, I. Komarov, N. Kiselev, A. Levitan, F. Leontovich, V. Lizerson, Y. Mukhin, L. Mazrukho, Ivan Panov, M. Poselsky, S. Semyonov, V. Soloviov, A. Sofin, G. Senatov, V. Simkhovich, B. Sokolov, V. Tomberg, V. Frolenko, M. Schneiderov, G. Alexandrov, M. Arabov, A. Bogorov, K. Brovin, P Gorbenko, G Ostrovsky, A. Pogereli, S. Sheinin, Nikolai Bikov.

It Happened in the Donbas (Eto bylo v Donbase). Soyuzdetfilm　　　　July
Scen. (from material by Boris Gorbatov)*:* Gorbatov, Mikhail Bleiman, Sergei Antonov; *dir.:* Leonid Lukov; *phot.:* Alexander Ginsburg; *des.:* Mauritz Umansky; *mus.:* Nikita Bogoslovsky.
Cast: Tatyana Okunevskaya (in two rôles), Boris Poslavsky, Ivan Pereverzev, Yelena Tyapkina, Vera Altaiskaya.

Days and Nights (Dni i nochi). 11 reels, Mosfilm　　　　Sep.
Scen.: Konstantin Simonov (from his novel); *dir.:* Alexander Stolper; *phot.:* Yevgeni Andrikanis; *des.:* Mauritz Umansky, S. Voronkov; *mus.:* Nikolai Kryukov.

Cast: Vladimir Soloviov, Daniel Sagal, Alla Lisyanskaya, Lev Sverdlin, Mikhail Derzhavin.

Unconquered (Nepokorenniye). 2,590 m., Kiev Studio   Oct.
Scen. (from novel by Boris Gorbatov): Gorbatov, Mark Donskoy, L. Barn, G. Grakov; *dir.:* Donskoy; *phot.:* Bentsion Monastirsky; *des.:* Mauritz Umansky; *mus.:* Lev Schwartz.
Cast: Ambrose Buchma, Lydia Kartashova, Venyamin Zuskin, Daniel Sagal, Yelena Tyapkina.

Guilty Though Guiltless (Bez vini vinovatiye). 2,696 m., Mosfilm   Oct.
Scen. (from play by Ostrovsky) & *dir.:* Vladimir Petrov; *phot.:* Vladimir Yakovlev; *des.:* Vladimir Yegorov; *mus.:* Nikolai Kryukov.
Cast: Alla Tarasova, Victor Stanitsin, Boris Livanov, Alexei Gribov, Vladimir Druzhnikov.

Arshin Mal-Alan. 2,629 m., Baku Studio   Oct.
Scen. (from musical comedy by Uzeir Gadjibekov): Sabir Rakhman; *dir.:* Rza Takhmasib, Nikolai Leshchenko; *phot.:* A. Atakishiev, M. Dadashev; *des.:* Y. Schwetz; *mus.:* Gadjibekov.
Cast: Rashid Beibutov, Leila Djavanshirova, Husein Zade, Minover Kalantarly.

Plain People (Prostiye lyudi). 2,147 m., Lenfilm (released in August 1956)
Scen. & *dir.:* Grigori Kozintsev, Leonid Trauberg; *phot.:* Andrei Moskvin, Anatoli Nazarov; *des.:* Yevgeni Enei, D. Vinitsky; *mus.:* Dmitri Shostakovich.
Cast: Yuri Tolubeyev, Boris Zhukovsky, Yelena Korchagina-Alexandrovskaya.

1946

The Great Turning-Point (Veliki perelom). 11 reels, Lenfilm   Jan.
Scen.: Boris Chirskov; *dir.:* Friedrich Ermler; *phot.:* Abram Kaltsati; *des.:* Nikolai Suvorov; *mus.:* Gavril Popov.
Cast: Mikhail Derzhavin, P. Andriyevsky, Andrei Abrikosov, Alexander Zrazhevsky, Mark Bernes.

Glinka   Feb.
Scen. & *dir.:* Leo Arnstam; *phot.:* Alexander Shelenkov, Chen Yu-lan; *des.:* Vladimir Kaplunovsky; *musical supervision:* Vissarion Shebalin.
Cast: Boris Chirkov, V. Serova, Vasili Merkuriev, Boris Livanov (Nikolai I).

Ivan the Terrible: Part Two (Ivan Grozny). Mosfilm (released in Sept. 1958)
Scen. & *dir.:* Sergei Eisenstein; *phot.:* Andrei Moskvin; *des.:* Isaac Shpinel; *mus.:* Sergei Prokofiev.
Cast: Nikolai Cherkasov, Serafima Birman, Pavel Kadochnikov, Andrei Abrikosov, Mikhail Zharov, Ambrose Buchma.

The Stone Flower (Kamenni tsvetok). 2,380 m., Mosfilm   May
Scen.: Pavel Bazhov (from his Urals stories), Ivan Keller; *dir.:* Alexander Ptushko; *colour-phot.:* Fyodor Provorov; *des.:* M. Bogdanov, G. Myasnikov; *mus.:* Lev Schwartz.
Cast: Vladimir Druzhnikov, Yelena Derevshchivova, Tamara Makarova, Mikhail Troyanovsky.

Liberated Earth (Osvobozhdennaya zemlya). Sverdlovsk Studio   July
Scen.: Zinaida Markina, Dmitri Tarasov; *dir.:* Alexander Medvedkin; *des.:* Victor Krylov, Yevgeni Vladimirov; *mus.:* Semyon Pototsky
Cast: Emma Tsesarskaya, Vasili Vanin, Alexander Khvilya, Vera Altaiskaya.

The Vow (Klyatva). 14 reels, Tbilisi Studio   July
Scen.: Pyotr Pavlenko, Mikhail Chiaureli; *dir.:* Chiaureli; *phot.:* Leonid Kosmatov; *des.:* L. Mamaladze; *mus.:* Andrei Balanchivadze.

Cast: Mikhail Gelovani (Stalin), Sophia Giatsintova, Nikolai Bogolyubov, Alexei Gribov, Tamara Makarova, Nikolai Plotnikov.
A Great Life: Part Two (Bolshaya zhizn). 9 reels (released December 1958).
Scen.: Pavel Nilin (from his novel); *dir.:* Leonid Lukov; *phot.:* M. Kirilov; *des.:* F. Boguslavsky; *mus.:* Sergei Pototsky (score revised by N. Bogoslovsky).
Cast: Boris Andreyev, Pyotr Aleinikov, I. Peltser, Stepan Kayukov.
In the Mountains of Yugoslavia. Mosfilm   Nov.
Scen.: Georgi Mdivani; *dir.:* Abram Room; *phot.:* Edward Tisse; *mus.:* Yuri Biryukov.
Cast: Nikolai Mordvinov, Ivan Bersenev (Tito), Olga Zhizneva.
Admiral Nakhimov. 2,541 m., Mosfilm   Dec.
Scen.: Igor Lukovsky; *dir.:* Vsevolod Pudovkin; *phot.:* Anatoli Golovnya, Tamara Lobova; *des.:* Vladimir Yegorov, A. Weisfeld, M. Yuferov; *mus.:* Nikolai Kryukov.
Cast: Alexei Diki, Yevgeni Samoilov, Reuben Simonov, Pudovkin (Prince Menshikov).
Robinson Crusoe: Part One. Stereokino Studio
Scen. (from Defoe's novel): Fyodor Knorre, Alexander Andriyevsky, Sergei Yermolinsky; *dir.:* Andriyevsky; *stereo-colour-phot.:* D. Surensky; *mus.:* Lev Schwartz.
Cast: Pavel Kadochnikov, Y. Lyubimov (Friday).

1947
In the Name of Life (Vo imya zhizni). 2,767 m., Lenfilm   Mar.
Scen.: Yevgeni Gabrilovich, Alexander Zarkhi, Josif Heifitz; *dir.:* Zarkhi & Heifitz; *phot.:* Vyacheslav Gardanov; *des.:* Nikolai Suvorov; *mus.:* Venedict Pushkov.
Cast: Victor Kokryakov, Mikhail Kuznetsov, Oleg Zhakov, Katya Lepanova.
Tales of the Siberian Land (Skazaniye o zemlye Sibirskoi). 3,146 m., Mosfilm
Scen.: Yevgeni Pomeshchikov, Nikolai Rozhkov; *dir.:* Ivan Pyriev; *colour-phot.:* Valentin Pavlov; *des.:* A. Berger, B. Chebotarev, K. Urbetis; *mus.:* Nikolai Kryukov.
Cast: Vladimir Druzhnikov, Marina Ladynina, Boris Andreyev.
A Village Schoolteacher (Selskaya uchitelnitsa). 2,882 m., Soyuzdetfilm
Scen.: Maria Smirnova; *dir.:* Mark Donskoy; *phot.:* Sergei Urusevsky; *des.:* D. Vinitsky, P. Pashkevich; *mus.:* Lev Schwartz.
Cast: Vera Maretskaya, Daniel Sagal, P. Olenev.
Alisher Navoi. 2,717 m., Tashkent Studio
Scen.: A. Speshnev, I. Sultanov, S. Uigun, Victor Shklovsky; *dir.:* Kamil Yarmatov; *phot.:* M. Krasniansky; *des.:* Varshan Yeremian; *mus.:* Reinhold Gliere, T. Sadykov.
Cast: Razak Khamrayev, Asad Ismatov.
Life in the Citadel (Zhizn v tsitadel). 2,472 m., Lenfilm
Scen. (from the play by August Jakobson): Leonid Trauberg; *dir.:* Herbert Rappoport; *phot.:* S. Ivanov; *des.:* Yevgeni Enei, L. Schildknecht, I. Ivanov; *mus.:* E. Kapp.
Cast: Hugo Laur, Lea Laats, Lembet Reyal, Boris Dobronravov.
Pirogov. 10 reels, Lenfilm
Scen.: Yuri German; *dir.:* Grigori Kozintsev; *phot.:* Andrei Moskvin, Anatoli Nazarov; *des.:* Yevgeni Enei, S. Malkin; *mus.:* Dmitri Shostakovich.
Cast: Konstantin Skorobogatov, Nikolai Cherkasov, V. Chestnokov, Alexei Diki.
The Scout's Exploit (Podvig razvedchika). 2,505 m., Kiev Studio   Sept.
Scen.: Mikhail Bleiman, Konstantin Isayev, Isidor Maklyarsky; *dir.:* Boris

Barnet; *phot.:* Danylo Demutsky; *des.:* Mauritz Umansky; *mus.:* D. Klebanov, O. Sandler.
Cast: Pavel Kadochnikov, Sergei Martinson, Barnet, Ambrose Buchma.

Michurin. 2,830 m., Mosfilm (revised and released in 1948)
Scen. & dir.: Alexander Dovzhenko; *colour-phot.:* Leonid Kosmatov, Yuli Kun; *des.:* M. Bogdanov, G. Myasnikov; *mus.:* Dmitri Shostakovich.
Cast: G. Belov, A. Vasilieva, F. Grigoriev.

Young Guard (Molodaya gvardiya), in 2 parts, 2,761 m. and 2,368 m., Soyuzdet-
film (revised and released in 1948)
Scen. (from the novel by Alexander Fadeyev) *& dir.:* Sergei Gerasimov; *phot.:* Wulf Rapoport; *des.:* I. Stepanov; *must.:* Dmitri Shostakovich.
Cast: V. Ivanov, Sergei Gurzo, Inna Makarova, Tamara Makarova, V. Khokhryakov.

Light Over Russia (Svet nad Rossiei) unreleased
Scen.: Nikolai Pogodin (from his play, *Kremlin Chimes*); *dir.:* Sergei Yutkevich.
Cast: Nikolai Kolesnikov (Lenin), Mikhail Gelovani (Stalin), Venyamin Zuskin, Nikolai Okhlopkov, Nikolai Kryuchkov.

Marite. 10 reels, Mosfilm
Scen.: Fyodor Knorre; *dis.:* Vera Stroyeva; *phot.:* Yevgeni Andrikanis, G. Pyshkova; *des.:* A. Parkhomenko, V. Kamsky; *mus.:* V. Dvarionas.
Cast: T. Lennikova, N. Lautsius, N. Chapligin.

1948

The Russian Question (Russkii vopros). 9 reels, Mosfilm
Scen. (from the play by Konstantin Simonov) *& dir.:* Mikhail Romm; *phot.:* Boris Volchok; *des.:* Semyon Mandel; *mus.:* Aram Khachaturian.
Cast: Vsevolod Aksyonov, Boris Tenin, Mikhail Astangov, Mikhail Nazvanov, Yelena Kuzmina, Boris Poslavsky.

Story of a Real Man (Povest o nastoyashchem cheloveke). 10 reels, Mosfilm
Scen. (from novel by Boris Polevoyi): Maria Smirnova; *dir.:* Alexander Stolper; *phot.:* Mark Magidson; *des.:* Isaac Shpinel; *mus.:* Nikolai Kryukov.
Cast: Pavel Kadochnikov, Nikolai Okhlopkov, Vasili Merkuriev.

The Distant Bride (Dalyokaya nevesta). 10 reels, Ashkhabad Studio
Scen.: Yevgeni Pomeshchikov, Nikolai Rozhkov, Victor Shklovsky; *dir.:* Y. Ivanov-Barkov; *phot.:* A. Bulinsky; *des.:* V. Khmelyova; *mus.:* K. Korchmarev.
Cast: A. Karliev, V. Neshchiplenko, M. Shafigulina.

Three Encounters (Tri vstrechi). 2,276 m., Mosfilm
Scen.: Sergei Yermolinsky, Nikolai Pogodin, Mikhail Bleiman; *dir.:* Sergei Yutkevich, Vsevolod Pudovkin, Alexander Ptushko; *colour-phot.:* Fyodor Provorov, I. Gelein, Abram Kaltsati, Yevgeni Andrikanis; *des.:* G. Myasnikov, G. Turilev; *mus.:* Nikolai Kryukov.
Cast: Tamara Makarova, Boris Chirkov, Nikolai Kryuchkov, Mikhail Derzhavin.

1949

Academician Ivan Pavlov. 11 reels, Lenfilm
Scen.: Mikhail Papava; *dir.:* Grigori Roshal; *phot.:* Vyacheslav Gardanov, Mark Magid; *des.:* Yevgeni Enei, A. Wechsler; *mus.:* Dmitri Kabalevsky.
Cast: A. Borisov, Nina Alisova, V. Chestnokov, Nikolai Plotnikov.

Rainis. 11 reels, Riga Studio
Scen.: F. Rokpelnis, V. Kreps; *dir.:* Yuli Raizman; *phot.:* Alexander Shelenkov, Chen Yu-lan; *des.:* G. Likums; *mus.:* A. Skulte.
Cast: Y. Grantin, M. Kletniyetse, A. Filipson.

Meeting on the Elbe (Vstrecha na Elbe). 11 reels, Mosfilm
Scen.: Tur brothers, L. Sheinin; *dir.:* Grigori Alexandrov; *phot.:* Edward Tisse; *des.:* Alexander Utkin; *mus.:* Dmitri Shostakovich.
Cast: Boris Andreyev, Mikhail Nazvanov, Lubov Orlova, V. Davydov.
Alitet Leaves for the Hills (Alitet ukhodit v gory). 10 reels, Gorky Studio
Scen.: T. Semushkin (from his novel); *dir.:* Mark Donskoy; *phot.:* Sergei Urusevsky; *des.:* D. Vinitsky, P. Pashkevich; *mus.:* Lev Schwartz.
Cast: Lev Sverdlin, Andrei Abrikosov, Boris Tenin.
The Fall of Berlin: Parts One, Two (Padeniye Berlina). 9, 8 reels, Mosfilm
Scen.: Pyotr Pavlenko, Mikhail Chiaureli; *dir.:* Chiaureli; *colour-phot.:* Leonid Kosmatov; *des.:* Vladimir Kaplunovsky, A. Parkhomenko; *mus.:* Dmitri Shostakovich.
Cast: Mikhail Gelovani (Stalin), Boris Andreyev, Oleg Froelich (Roosevelt), Victor Stanitsin(Churchill), V. Savelyov (Hitler).

1950
Battle of Stalingrad: Parts One, Two (Stalingradskaya bitva). 10, 10 reels, Mosfilm
Scen.: Nikolai Virta; *dir.:* Vladimir Petrov; *phot.:* Yuri Yekelchik; *des.:* L. Mamaladze; *mus.:* Aram Khachaturian.
Cast: Alexei Diki (Stalin), Yuri Shumsky (Vasilevsky), Boris Livanov (Rokossovsky), Nikolai Simonov (Chuikov), Nikolai Plotnikov.
Conspiracy of the Doomed (Zagovor obrechyonnikh). 11 reels, Mosfilm
Scen.: Nikolai Virta; *dir.:* Mikhail Kalatozov; *colour-phot.:* Mark Magidson; *des.:* Isaac Shpinel; *mus.:* Vissarion Shebalin.
Cast: L. Skopina, Pavel Kadochnikov, Vladimir Druzhnikov, Vsevolod Aksyonov, A. Vertinsky, Oleg Zhakov, Maxim Strauch.

1951
Przhevalsky. 11 reels, Mosfilm
Scen.: A. Speshnev, V. Schweitzer; *dir.:* Sergei Yutkevich; *colour-phot.:* Yevgeni Andrikanis, F. Firsov; *des.:* M. Bogdanov, G. Myasnikov; *mus.:* Yuri Sviridov.
Cast: S. Panov, V. Larionov, Boris Tenin, Sergei Martinson.
Taras Shevchenko. 11 reels, Kiev Studio
Scen. & dir.: Igor Savchenko; *colour-phot.:* Abram Kaltsati, Danylo Demutsky; *des.:* L. Shengelaya, B. Nemechek, M. Solokha; *mus.:* Boris Lyatoshinsky
Cast: Sergei Bondarchuk, Natalia Uzhvi, Yevgeni Samoilov, Alexei Konsovsky

1952
The Unforgettable Year 1919 (Nezabyvayemyi 1919 god). 11 reels, Mosfilm
Scen.: Vsevolod Vishnevsky (from his play), Mikhail Chiaureli, A. Filimonov; *dir.:* Chiaureli; *colour-phot.:* Leonid Kosmatov, V. Nikolayev; *des.:* Vladimir Kaplunovsky; *mus.:* Dmitri Shostakovich.
Cast: I. Molchanov (Lenin), Mikhail Gelovani, Boris Andreyev, M. Kovaleva, Yevgeni Samoilov, Sergei Lukyanov, Victor Stanitsin (Churchill), V. Koltsov (Lloyd George), Gnat Yura (Clemenceau), L. Korsakov (Wilson).
Glinka. (Kompozitor Glinka). 11 reels, Mosfilm
Scen.: Pyotr Pavlenko, N. Treneva, Grigori Alexandrov; *dir.:* Alexandrov; *colour-phot.:* Edward Tisse; *des.:* Alexander Utkin.
Cast: B. Smirnov, Lubov Orlova, Mikhail Nazvanov (Nikolai I), Svyatoslav Richter (Liszt).

Jambul. 10 reels, Alma-Ata Studio
Scen.: Nikolai Pogodin, A. Tazhibayev; *dir.:* Yefim Dzigan; *colour-phot.:* N. Bolshakov, I. Gelein; *des.:* Vladimir Yegorov, Yevgeni Enei, I. Kaplan; *mus.:* Nikolai Kryukov, M. Tulebayev.
Cast: Shaken Aimanov, K. Djandarbekov.
Revizor. 13 reels, Mosfilm
Scen. (from Gogol's play) & *dir.:* Vladimir Petrov; *colour-phot.:* Yuri Yekelchik; *des.:* Vladimir Kaplunovsky; *mus.:* N. Timofeyev.
Cast: I. Gorbachev, Alexei Gribov, Yuri Tolubeyev, Erast Garin.

1953
The Return of Vasili Bortnikov. 11 reels, Mosfilm May
Scen.: Galina Nikolayeva (from her novel, *Harvest*), Yevgeni Gabrilovich; *dir.:* Vsevolod Pudovkin; *colour-phot.:* Sergei Urusevsky; *des.:* A. Freidin, B. Chebotarev; *mus.:* K. Molchanov.
Cast: Sergei Lukyanov, Natalia Medvedeva, N. Timofeyev, V. Sanayev.
Admiral Ushakov. 11 reels, Mosfilm
Scen.: Alexander Stein; *dir.:* Mikhail Romm; *colour-phot.:* Alexander Shelenkov, Chen Yu-lan; *des.:* A. Parkhomenko, L. Shengelaya, A. Weisfeld; *mus.:* Aram Khachaturian.
Cast: Ivan Pereverzev, Boris Livanov (Potemkin), Olga Zhizneva (Catherine II).

1954
The Great Warrior Skanderbeg (Veliki voin Albanii Skanderbeg). Mosfilm & Albanian Film Studio Feb.
Scen.: Mikhail Papava; *dir.:* Sergei Yutkevich; *colour-phot:* Yevgeni Andrikanis; *des.:* Isaac Shpinel; *mus.:* I. Sviridov, Chesk Zadeja.
Cast: Akaki Khorava, Veriko Andjaparidze, Oleg Zhakov, B. Imami, Boris Tenin.
True Friends (Verniye druzya). Mosfilm June
Scen.: Alexander Galich, Konstantin Isayev; *dir.:* Mikhail Kalatozov; *colour-phot.:* Mark Magidson; *des.:* A. Parkhomenko; *mus.:* Tikhon Khrennikov.
Cast: Vasili Merkuriev, Boris Chirkov, A. Borisov.
The Big Family (Bolshaya semya).
Scen.: V. Kochetov, S. Kara; *dir.:* Josif Heifitz; *phot.:* S. Ivanov; *des.:* V. Volin, V. Savostin; *mus.:* Venedict Pushkov.
Cast: Sergei Lukyanov, Boris Andreyev, Alexei Batalov.
Restless Youth (Trevozhnaya Molodost). 10 reels, Kiev Studios
Scen.: V. Belayev (from his trilogy *The Old Fortress*, Mikhail Bleiman; *dir.:* A. Alov, Vladimir Naumov; *phot.:* A Pishchikov; *des.:* V. Agranov; *mus.:* Y. Shurovsky
Cast: A Susnin, M. Krasnat, T. Loginova, Nikolai Kryuchkov

1955
Romeo and Juliet. 2,545 m., Mosfilm Mar.
Scen. (from ballet by Sergei Prokofiev) & *dir.:* Leo Arnstam, L. Lavrovsky; *colour-phot.:* Alexander Shelenkov, Chen Yu-lan; *des.:* A. Parkhomenko, Peter Williams, K. Yefimov; *mus.:* Prokofiev.
Cast: Galina Ulanova, Yuri Zhdanov, A. Yermolayev, Sergei Koren.
The Gadfly (Poprigunya) 9 reels, Mosfilm June
Scen. (from Chekhov's story) & *dir.:* Samson Samsonov; *colour-phot.:* F. Dobronravov, V. Monakhov; *des.:* L. Chibisov, Y. Volchanetsky; *mus.:* Nikolai Kryukov; *supervision:* Mikhail Romm, Sergei Yutkevich.
Cast: Sergei Bondarchuk, Ludmila Tselikovskaya, Vladimir Druzhnikov.

Boris Godunov. 3,038 m., Mosfilm Oct.
Scen. (from the Pushkin-Musorgsky opera)*:* N. Golovanov, Vera Stroyeva; *dir.:* Stroyeva; *colour-phot.:* V. Nikolayev; *des.:* P. Kiselev, Y. Serganov; *mus.:* Musorgsky.
Cast: A. Pirogov, G. Nelepp, M. Mikhailov.
Unfinished Story (Neokonchennaya povest). 2,712 m., Lenfilm Oct.
Scen.: Kilsayev; *dir.:* Friedrich Ermler; *phot.:* Anatoli Nazarov; *des.:* I. Kaplan.
Cast: Yelina Bystritskaya, Sergei Bondarchuk, Yevgeni Samoilov, Sophia Giatsintova.
Saltanat. Mosfilm Dec.
Scen.: Rosa Budantseva; *dir.:* Vasili Pronin; *colour-phot.:* A. Egina, V. Masevich; *des.:* Y. Chernayev, I. Novoderezhkin; *mus.:* Aram Khachaturian.
Cast: Baken Kidikeyeva, Muratbek Riskulov.
Princess Mary (Knyazhna Meri). 10 reels, Gorki Studio
Scen.: (from story by Lermontov) *& dir.:* Isidor Annensky; *colour-phot.:* M. Kirillov; *des.:* A. Dikhtar; *mus.:* Lev. Schwartz.
Cast: K. Sanova, A. Verbitsky, Mikhail Astangov, K. Yelenskaya
Magdana's Donkey (Lurdzha Magdany). 7 reels, Georgia Films
Scen.: K. Gogodze (from story by Gabashvili); *dir.:* T. Abuladze, Revaz Chkheidze; *phot.:* L. Sukhov, Alexander Digmelov; *des.:* I Sumbatishvili; *mus.:* A Keresilidze.
Cast: D. Tserodze, Akaki Vasadze.

1956
Mother (Mat). 10 reels, Kiev Studio Feb.
Scen. (from Gorky's novel)*:* N. Kovarsky, Mark Donskoy; *dir.:* Donskoy; *colour-phot.:* A. Mishurin; *des.:* V. Agranov; *mus.:* Lev Schwartz.
Cast: Vera Maretskaya, Alexei Batalov.
Othello. 11 reels, Mosfilm Feb.
Scen. (from Shakespeare's play) *& dir.:* Sergei Yutkevich; *colour-phot:* Yevgeni Andrikanis; *des.:* A. Weisfeld, V. Dorrer, M. Karyakin; *mus.:* Aram Khachaturian.
Cast.: Sergei Bondarchuk, Irina Skobtseva, Andrei Popov, Vladimir Soshalsky.
The First Echelon (Pervi eshelon). 11 reels, Mosfilm Mar.
Scen. & dir.: Mikhail Kalatozov; *colour-phot.:* Yuri Yekelchik, Sergei Urusevsky; *des.:* M. Bogdanov, G. Myasnikov; *mus.:* Dmitri Shostakovich.
Cast: V. Sanayev, S. Romodanov, N. Annenkov, O. Yefremov, Isolda Izvitskaya.
The Forty-First (Sorok pervyi). 10 reels, Mosfilm Oct.
Scen. (from Lavrenev's story)*:* G. Koltunov; *dir.:* Grigori Chukhrai; *colour-phot.:* Sergei Urusevsky; *des.:* V. Kamsky, K. Stepanov; *mus.:* Nikolai Kryukov.
Cast: Isolda Izvitskaya, Oleg Strizhenov, Nikolai Kryuchkov.
Prologue. 12 reels, Mosfilm Dec.
Scen.: Alexander Stein; *dir.:* Yefim Dzigan; *wide-screen colour-phot.:* Valentin Pavlov, B. Petrov; *des.:* P. Kiselev, Y. Serganov; *mus.:* Nikolai Kryukov.
Cast: Nikolai Plotnikov (Lenin), Marina Pastukhova (Krupskaya), Pavel Kadochnikov (Gorky).

1957
Carnival Night (Karnavalnaya noch). 8 reels, Mosfilm Jan.
Scen.: B. Laskin, V. Polyakov; *dir.:* Eldar Ryazanov; *colour-phot.:* Abram Kaltsati; *des.:* K. Yefimov, O. Grosse; *mus.:* A. Lepin.
Cast: Igor Ilinsky, Ludmila Gurchenko, Yuri Belov, Olga Vlasova.

Pavel Korchagin. 10 reels, Kiev Studio Feb.
  Scen. (from Nikolai Ostrovsky's novel): Konstantin Isayev; *dir.:* A. Alov,
  Vladimir Naumov; *colour-phot.:* I. Minkovetsky, S. Shakhbazian; *des.:* V.
  Agranov; *mus.:* Y. Shchurovsky.
  Cast: V. Lanovoy, E. Lezhdei, T. Stradina.
Don Quixote. 11 reels, Lenfilm Apr.
  Scen. (from Cervantes' novel): Yevgeni Schwartz; *dir.:* Grigori Kozintsev;
  wide-screen colour-phot.: Andrei Moskvin, Apollinari Dudko; *des.:* Yevgeni
  Enei; *mus.:* Kar-Karayev.
  Cast: Nikolai Cherkasov, Yuri Tolubeyev, Serafima Birman.
At Great Cost (Dorogoi tsenoi). Dovzhenko Studio, Kiev
  Scen. (*from works by Kotsubinsky*): Irina Donskaya; *dir.:* Mark Donskoy;
  colour-phot.: N. Topchi; *des.:* N. Reznik; *mus.:* Lev Schwartz.
  Cast: Vera Donskaya, Yuri Dedovich.
Our Courtyard (Nash dvor). 9 reels, Georgia Films Aug.
  Scen.: Georgi Mdivani; *dir.:* Revaz Chkheidze; *phot.:* G. Chelidze; *des.:* G.
  Gigauri, K. Khutsishvili; *mus.:* L. Kereselidze.
  Cast: Georgi Shengelaya, Leila Abashidze, Sophia Chiaureli.
The Cranes Are Flying (Letyat zhuravli). 10 reels, Mosfilm Nov.
  Scen.: Victor Rosov (from his play); *dir.:* Mikhail Kalatozov; *phot.:* Sergei
  Urusevsky; *des.:* Y. Svidetelev; *mus.:* M. Weinberg.
  Cast: Tatyana Samoilova, Alexei Batalov, Vasili Merkuriev.
The Quiet Don (Tikhi Don): Parts I, II, III. 11, 12, 12 reels, Gorky Studio
  Scen. (from Sholokhov's novel) *& dir.:* Sergei Gerasimov; *colour-phot.:* Wulf
  Rapoport; *des.:* Boris Dulenkov; *mus.:* Yuri Levitin.
  Cast: Daniel Ilchenko, Pyotr Glebov, Yelina Bystritskaya, Zinaida Kirienko.

1958
The Communist (Kommunist). 3045 m., Mosfilm Jan.
  Scen.: Yevgeni Gabrilovich; *dir.:* Yuli Raizman; *colour-phot.:* Alexander Shelen-
  kov, Chen Yu-lan; *des.:* M. Bogdanov, G. Myasnikov; *mus.:* Rodion Shchedrin.
  Cast: Yevgeni Urbansky, Sophia Pavlova, Yevgeni Shutov, Sergei Yakovlev.
Stories about Lenin (Rasskazi o Lenine). 3147 m., Mosfilm Apr.
  Scen.: Mikhail Volpin, Nikolai Erdman, Yevgeni Gabrilovich; *dir.:* Sergei Yut-
  kevich; *phot.:* Yevgeni Andrikanis, (*colour*) Andrei Moskvin; *des.:* A. Berger,
  P. Kiselev; *music* of Rachmaninov and Taneyev.
  Cast: Maxim Strauch (Lenin), Marina Pastukhova (Krupskaya), A. Lisyanskaya,
  Vsevolod Sanayev.
My Dear Fellow! (Dorogoi moi chelovek!). 2958 m., Lenfilm Oct.
  Scen.: Yuri German (from his novel), Josef Heifitz; *dir.:* Heifitz; *colour-phot.:*
  M. Magid, L. Sokolovsky; *des.:* B. Manevich, I. Kaplan; *mus.:* V. Pushkov.
  Cast: Alexei Batalov, Inna Makarova, P. Konstantinov.
Poem of a Sea (Poema o morye). 3020 m., Mosfilm Nov.
  Scen.: Alexander Dovzhenko; *dir.:* Yulia Solntseva; *colour-phot.:* Gavril Yegia-
  zarov; *des.:* A. Borisov, I. Plastinkin; *mus.:* Gavril Popov.
  Cast: Boris Livanov, Boris Andreyev, M. Romanov, Zinaida Kirienko.
The First Day (Pervi dyen). 2498 m., Lenfilm Nov.
  Scen.: Konstantin Isayev; *dir.:* Friedrich Ermler; *colour-phot.:* Anatoli Nazarov;
  des.: Yevgeni Enei; *mus.:* O. Karavaichuk.
  Cast: Olga Petrenko, Eduard Bredun, G. Yuchenkov (Lenin).
In the October Days (V dni Oktyabrya). 3269 m., Lenfilm Nov.

Scen.: Sergei Vasiliev, Nikolai Otten; *dir.:* Vasiliev; *colour-phot.:* Apollinari Dudko; *des.:* Alexander Black; *mus.:* Boris Chaikovsky.
Cast: V. Chestnokov (Lenin), V. Brener (Krupskaya), A. Kobaladze (Stalin), A. Fyodorinov (John Reed), Galina Vodyanitskaya (Louise Bryant).

1959
Two Fyodors (Dva Fyodora). 2442 m., Odessa Studio   Jan.
Scen.: Valeri Savchenko; *dir.:* Marlen Khutsiyev; *phot.:* Poytr Todorovsky; *des.:* O. Grosse; *mus.:* Yuli Meitus.
Cast: Vasili Shukshin, Kolya Chursin, Tamara Syomina.
Destiny of a Man (Sudba cheloveka). 2807 m., Mosfilm   Apr.
Scen.: (from a story by Sholokhov): Yuri Lukin, Fyodor Shakhmagonov; *dir.:* Sergei Bondarchuk; *phot.:* Vladimir Monakhov; *des.:* I. Novoderezhkin, S. Voronov; *mus.:* Venyamin Basner.
Cast: Bondarchuk, Zinaida Kirienko, Pavlik Boriskin.
My Father's House (Otchii dom). 2729 m., Gorky Studio   Apr.
Scen.: Budimir Metalnikov; *dir.:* Lev Kulidjanov; *phot.:* Pyotr Katayev; *des.:* M. Gorelik, S. Serebrenikov; *mus.:* Yu. Biryukov.
Cast: V. Kuznetsova, Valentin Zubkov, Noyabrina Mordyukova, Pyotr Aleinikov.
The Incorrigibles (Nepoddayushchiyosya). 2198 m., Mosfilm   June
Scen.: Tatyana Sytina; *dir.:* Yuri Chulyukin; *phot.:* Konstantin Brovin; *des.:* I. Shreter; *mus.:* A. Spadavekkia, K. Molchanov; *artistic supervision:* Yuli Raizman.
Cast: Nadezhda Rumyantseva, Yuri Belov, Yuri Nikulin.
Foma Gordeyev. 2728 m., Gorky Studio   Nov.
Scen.: (from novel by Gorky): B. Byalik, Mark Donskoy; *dir.:* Donskoy; *phot.:* Margarita Pilikhina; *des.:* P. Pashkevich; *mus.:* Lev Schwartz.
Cast: Sergei Lukyanov, G. Yepifantsev.
Khovanshchina. 3324 m., Mosfilm   Nov.
Scen.: (from opera by Musorgsky): Anna Abramova, Dmitri Shostakovich; *dir.:* Vera Stroyeva; *colour-phot.:* Victor Dombrovsky; *des.:* Alexander Borisov; *music editor and orchestration:* Shostakovich.
Cast: A. Krivchyonya, A. Grigoriev, Ye. Kibkalo, Mark Reizen, K. Leonova.
Ballad of a Soldier (Ballada o soldatye). 2452 m., Mosfilm   Dec.
Scen.: Valentin Yezhov, Grigori Chukhrai; *dir.:* Chukhrai; *phot.:* Vladimir Nikolayev, Era Savelyova; *des.:* B. Nemechyok; *mus.:* Mikhail Ziv.
Cast: Vladimir Ivashov, Zhanna Prokhorenko, Antonina Maximova, Nikolai Kryuchkov, Yevgeni Urbansky.

1960
Lady with the Little Dog (Dama s sobachkoi). 2450 m., Lenfilm   Jan.
Scen.: (from story by Chekhov) & *dir.:* Josef Heifitz; *phot.:* Andrei Moskvin, Dmitri Meskhiyev; *des.:* B. Manevich, I. Kaplan; *mus.:* N. Simonyan.
Cast: Iya Savvina, Alexei Batalov.
Reason vs. Insanity (Razum protiv bezumiya). 5 reels, Central Documentary Studio
Scen.: B. Leontiev, Alexander Medvedkin; *dir.:* Medvedkin.
The Letter That Wasn't Sent (Neotpravlennoye pismo). 2668 m.,
Mosfilm   June
Scen.: (from story by Valeri Osipov): Grigori Koltunov, Osipov, Victor Rozov; *dir.:* Mikhail Kalatozov; *phot.:* Sergei Urusevsky; *des.:* D. Vinitsky; *mus.:* N. Kryukov.

Cast: Innokenti Smoktunovsky, Tatyana Samoilova, Boris Livanov, Yevgeni Urbansky.

Living Heroes (Zhiviye geroi). 2193 m., Lithuanian Studio   Nov.
Four stories, with four scenarists and four directors.

Resurrection (Voskreseniye). 2760 m. (I),
    2970 m. (II), Mosfilm   Nov. (I), March 62 (II)
    Scen.: (from Tolstoy's novel): Yevgeni Gabrilovich; *dir.:* Moisei Schweitzer; *phot.:* Era Savelyova; *des.:* D. Vinitsky; *mus.:* G. Sviridov.
    Cast: Tamara Syomina, Yevgeni Matveyev.

1961

Story of Flaming Years (Povest plamennikh let). 2928 m., Mosfilm   Feb.
    Scen.: Alexander Dovzhenko; *dir.:* Yulia Solntseva; *colour-phot.:* (wide-screen): Fyodor Provorov, Alexei Temerin; *des.:* Alexander Borisov; *mus.:* Gavril Popov.
    Cast: Boris Andreyev, Sergei Lukyanov, Vasili Merkuriyev.

Five Days—Five Nights (Pyat dnei—pyat nochei). 2895 m., Mosfilm &
    DEFA   Feb.
    Scen.: Lev Arnstam, V. Ebeling; *dir.:* Arnstam; *colour-phot.:* Alexander Shelenkov, Chen Yu-lan; *des.:* A. Parkhomenko, G. Nitzshke; *mus.:* Dmitri Shostakovich.
    Cast: Vsevolod Safonov, G. Knaup, Vsevolod Sanayev, Anna Burger.

Farewell, Doves! (Proshchaite, golubi!). 2645 m., Yalta Studio   March
    Scen. & dir.: Yakov Segel; *phot.:* Vadim Ilyenko; *des.:* L. Georgiev, V. Levental; *mus.:* M. Fradkin.
    Cast: Lyosha Loktev, Svetlana Savelova, Valentina Telegina, Sergei Plotnikov.

Clear Sky (Chistoye nebo). 3016 m., Mosfilm   May
    Scen.: Daniil Khrabrovitsky; *dir.:* Grigori Chukhrai; *colour-phot.:* Sergei Poluyanov; *des.:* B. Nemechek; *mus.:* Mikhail Ziv.
    Cast: N. Drobyshyova, Yevgeni Urbansky, Vitali Konyaev, Georgi Kulikov.

Peace to Those Who Enter (Mir vkhodyashchemu). 2451 m., Mosfilm   Sep.
    Scen.: Leonid Zorin, Alexander Alov, Vladimir Naumov; *dir.:* Alov, Naumov; *phot.:* Anatoli Kuznetsov; *des.:* Ye. Chernayev; *mus.:* Nikolai Karetnikov.
    Cast: Victor Avdyushko, Alexander Demyanenko, L. Shaporenko, Nikolai Grinko.

1962

And What If It's Love? (A yesli eto lyubov?). 2799 m., Mosfilm   March
    Scen.: Josif Olshansky, Nikolai Rudnev, Yuli Raizman; *dir.:* Raizman; *phot.:* Alexander Kharitonov; *des.:* N. Novoderezhkin, S. Voronov; *mus.:* Rodion Shchedrin.
    Cast: Zhanna Prokhorenko, Igor Pushkarev, Anna Nazarova, N. Fedosova.

When Trees Grow Tall (Kogda derevya byli bolshimi). 2609 m., Gorky Studio
    March
    Scen.: Nikolai Figurovsky; *dir.:* Lev Kulidjanov; *phot.:* Valeri Ginzburg; *des.:* Pyotr Galadjev; *mus.:* L. Afanasyev.
    Cast: Inna Gulaya, Yuri Nikulin, Leonid Kuravlyov, Vasili Shukshin.

Ivan's Childhood (Ivanovo detstvo). 2638 m., Mosfilm   May
    Scen.: Vladimir Bogomolov (from his story), Mikhail Papava; *dir.:* Andrei Tarkovsky; *phot.:* Vadim Yusov; *des.:* Ye. Chernayev; *mus.:* Vyacheslav Ovchinnikov.
    Cast: Kolya Burlayev, Valentin Zubkov, Nikolai Grinko.

The Girls (Devchata). 2676 m., Mosfilm   March
Scen.: Boris Bedny; *dir.:* Yuri Chulyukin; *phot.:* Timofei Lebeshov; *des.:*
I. Shreter; *mus.:* A. Pakhmutova; *artistic supervision:* Yuli Raizman.
Cast: Nadezhda Rumyantseva, Nikolai Rybnikov, Inna Makarova, Nina Men-
shikova.
The Bath (Banya). 1458 m., Soyuzmultfilm   Aug.
Scen.: (from play by Mayakovsky) *& Dir.:* Sergei Yutkevich, Anatoli Karano-
vich; *colour-phot.:* (and wide-screen): Mikhail Kamenetsky; *des.:* (animation):
Felix Zbarsky; *mus.:* Rodion Shchedrin.

1963
Introduction (Vstupleniye). 2761 m., Mosfilm   May
Scen.: Vera Panova (from two of her stories); *dir.:* Industrii Talankin; *phot.:*
Valeri Vladimirov, Vladimir Minayev; *des.:* S. Ushakov; *mus.:* A. Shnitke.
Cast: Borya Tokarev, Nina Urgant, Natasha Bogunova, Victor Avdyushko.
Heat (Znoi). 2309 m., Kirghizfilm   June
Scen.: (from a story by Chinghiz Aitmatov): Josif Olshansky; *dir.:* Larissa
Shepitko; *phot.:* Yuri Sokol, Vladimir Arkhangelsky; *des.:* A. Makarov; *mus.:*
R. Lyodenev.
Cast: Bolot Shamshiyev, Nurmukhan Zhanturin, Klara Yusupzhanova, K.
Dosumbayev.
The Living and the Dead (Zhiviye i myortviye). I, 10 reels; II, 10 reels,
Mosfilm
Scen.: (from novel by Konstantin Simonov) *& Dir.:* Alexander Stolper; *phot.:*
Nikolai Olonovsky; *des.:* S. Volkov.
Cast: K. Lavrov, Anatoli Papanov, Alexei Glazyrin, Oleg Yefremov.
White Caravan (Byelyi karavan). 9 reels, Gruzia-film
Scen.: Merab Eliozishvili; *dir.:* Eldar Shengelaya, Tamaz Meliava; *phot.:* Georgi
Kalatozishvili, Leonid Kalashnikov; *des.:* Dmitri Takaishvili, Christopher
Lebanidze; *mus.:* I. Gedzhadze.
Cast: Spartak Bagashvili, A. Shengelaya, G. Kikodze, Eliozishvili.
I Am Cuba (Ya Kuba). Mosfilm
Scen.: Yevgeni Yevtushenko, Enrico Barnet; *dir.:* Mikhail Kalatozov; *phot.:*
Sergei Urusevsky.

1964
Silence (Tishina). I, 10 reels; II, 10 reels, Mosfilm
Scen.: Yuri Bondarev (from his novel), Vladimir Basov; *dir.:* Basov; *phot.:*
Timofei Lebeshyov; *des.:* G. Turylev; *mus.:* Venyamin Basner.
Cast: Vitali Konyaev, Georgi Martynyuk, Vladimir Yemelyanov.
Hamlet I, 8 reels; II, 8 reels, Lenfilm
Scen.: (from Shakespeare) *& Dir.:* Grigori Kozintsev; *phot.:* Jonas Gricius; *des.:*
Yevgeni Enei, G. Kropachyov, S. Virsaladze; *mus.:* Dmitri Shostakovich.
Cast: Innokenti Smoktunovsky, Mikhail Nazvanov, E. Radzinya, Yuri Tolube-
yev, Anastasia Vertinskaya.
There's a Certain Fellow (Zhivyot takoi paren). 10 reels, Gorky Studio
Scen. & dir.: Vasili Shukshin; *phot.:* Valeri Ginzburg; *des.:* A. Vagichev; *mus.:*
P. Chekalov.
Cast: Leonid Kuravlyov, L. Alexandrova, L. Burkova.
I'm Twenty (Mnye dvadtsat let [or, Lenin's Sentries]) 18 reels, Gorky Studio
Scen.: Marlen Khutsiyev, Gennadi Shpalikov; *dir.:* Khutsiyev; *phot.:* Margarita

Pilikhina; *des.:* I. Zakharova; *mus.:* N. Sidelnikov.
Cast: V. Popov, Nikolai Gubenko, Stanislav Lyubshin, Marianna Vertinskaya.
Chairman (Predsedatel). I, 10 reels; II, 8 reels, Mosfilm
Scen.: Yuri Nagibin; *dir.:* Alexei Saltykov; *phot.:* Vladimir Nikolayev; *des.:*
S. Ushakov; *mus.:* A. Kholminov.
Cast: Mikhail Ulyanov, Ivan Lapikov, Noyabrina Mordyukova.
Shadows of Forgotten Ancestors (Teni zabytykh predkov). 10 reels,
Dovzhenko Studio
Scen.: Sergei Paradjanov, Ivan Chendei (from works by Kotsyubinsky): *dir.:*
Paradjanov; *colour-phot.:* Yuri Ilyenko; *des.:* M. Rakovsky, G. Yakutovich; *mus.:*
M. Skorik.
Cast: Ivan Mikolaichuk, Larisa Kadochnikova, Spartak Bagashvili, Nikolai
Grinko.
Father of a Soldier (Otets soldata). 9 reels, Gruzia-film
Scen.: Suliko Zhgenti; *dir.:* Rezo Chkheidze; *phot.:* Lev Sukhov, Arkhil Fili-
pashvili; *des.:* Z. Medzmariashvili, N. Kazbegi; *mus.:* S. Tsintsadze.
Cast: Sergo Zakariadze, V. Privaltsev, A. Nazarov.

1965
Someone's Ringing — Open the Door (Zvonyat, otkroitye dver). 8 reels,
Mosfilm
Scen.: Alexander Volodin; *dir.:* Alexander Mitta; *phot.:* A. Panasyuk; *des.:*
P. Kiselev; *mus.:* Venyamin Basner.
Cast.: Roland Bykov, Lena Proklova, Vladimir Belokurov, Sergei Nikolenko,
Ilya Savvina.
Lenin in Poland (Lenin v Polshe). 10 reels, Mosfilm
Scen.: Yevgeni Gabrilovich, Sergei Yutkevich; *dir.:* Yutkevich; *phot.:* Jan Lias-
kowski; *des.:* Jan Grandys; *mus.:* Adam Waliachinski.
Cast: Maxim Strauch, A. Lisyanskaya, A. Pavlychyova.
Loyalty (Vernost).
Scen.: Bulat Okudjava, Pyotr Todorovsky; *dir.:* Todorovsky.
Operation 'Y'. 9 reels, Mosfilm
Scen.: Yakov Kostyukovsky, Moris Slobodskoy, Leonid Gadai; *dir.:* Gadai;
phot.: Konstantin Brovin; *des.:* A. Berger; *mus.:* A. Zatsepin.
Cast: Alexander Demyanenko, Alexander Smirnov, Mikhail Pugovkin, Vladimir
Basov.
The First Teacher (Pervyi uchitel). 10 reels, Kirghizfilm & Mosfilm
Scen.: Chingiz Aitmatov (from his story), Boris Dobrodeyev, Andrei Koncha-
lovsky; *dir.:* Konchalovsky; *phot.:* Georgi Rerberg; *des.:* M. Romadin; *mus.:*
Vyacheslav Ovchinnikov.
Cast: Bolot Beishenaliyev, Natalya Arinbasarova, Darkul Kuyukova.
Ordinary Fascism (Obyknovennyi fashizm). I, 7 reels; II, 7 reels, Mosfilm
Scen.: Mikhail Romm, Maya Turovskaya, Yuri Khanyutin; *dir. & edit.:* Romm;
commentary written and spoken by Romm.

1966
Watch Out—Automobiles (Beregis avtomobilya). 9 reels, Mosfilm
Scen.: Emmanuel Braginsky, Eldar Ryazanov (from their story); *dir.:* Ryazanov;
phot.: A. Mukasei, V. Nakhabtsiyev; *des.:* B. Nemechyok, L. Semyonov; *mus.:*
A. Petrov.
Cast: Innokenti Smoktunovsky, Oleg Yefremov, L. Dobrzhanskaya, O. Aroseva.

Sky of Our Childhood. Kirghiz-film
Scen. & dir.: Tolomush Okeyev; *phot.:* Kadyrzhan Kydyraliyev.
Andrei Rublyov. Mosfilm [released 1972]
Scen.: Andrei Tarkovsky, Andrei Konchalovsky; *dir.:* Tarkovsky; *phot.:* Vadim
Kusov; *des.:* Yevgeni Chernayev; *mus.:* Vyacheslav Ovchinnikov.
Cast: Anatoli Solonytsin, Ivan Lapikov, Nikolai Grinko, Nikolai Sergeyev,
Roland Bykov, Bolot Beishenaliyev.
War and Peace (Voina i mir). I, 16 reels; II, 12 reels; III, 10 reels; IV, 10 reels,
Mosfilm
Scen.: (from Tolstoy's novel): Sergei Bondarchuk, Vasili Solovyov; *dir.:* Bondar-
chuk; *colour-phot.:* (wide-screen): Alexander Shelenkov, Chen Yu-lan, Anatoli
Petritsky; *des.:* M. Bogdanov, G. Myasnikov; *mus.:* Vyacheslav Ovchinnikov.
Cast: Ludmilla Savelyova, Bondarchuk, Vyacheslav Tikhonov, Victor Stanitsin,
Oleg Tabakov, Anatoli Ktorov, Anastasia Vertinskaya, Irina Skobtseva, Vasili
Lanovoi.
The White, White Cranes. Uzbek film
Scen.: Odelsha Agishev; *dir.:* Ali Khamrayev.

1967
Your Contemporary (Tvoi sovremyonnik). I, 6 reels; II, 9 reels, Mosfilm
Scen.: Yevgeni Gabrilovich, Yuli Raizman; *dir.:* Raizman, *phot.:* Naum Ardash-
nikov; *des.:* G. Turliyev.
Cast: I. Vladimirov, Nikolai Plotnikov, Antonina Maximova.
Triangle (Trivgolnik). Armenfilm
Dir.: Genrikh Malyan.
Cast: Armen Jigarkhanyan, Frunze Mkrtchan.
Katerina Izmailova.
Scen.: (from opera by Shostakovich, based on story by Leskov) *& dir.:* Mikhail
Shapiro.
Cast: Galina Vishnevskaya.
Prayer (Molba). Gruzia-film
Scen.: Tengiz Abuladze, Anzor Salukvadze; *dir.:* Abuladze; *phot.:* Alexander
Antipenko.

1968
Anna Karenina. I, 2620 m.; II, 2361 m., Mosfilm
Scen.: (from Tolstoy's novel): Vasili Katanyan, Alexander Zarkhi; *dir.:* Zarkhi;
colour-phot.: (wide-screen): Leonid Kalashnikov; *des.:* A. Borisov, Yu. Kladi-
enko; *mus.:* Rodion Shchedrin.
Cast: Tatyana Samoilova, Nikolai Tritsenko, Anastasia Vertinskaya, Vasili
Lanovoi, Iya Savvina, Maya Plisetskaya.
Sixth of July (Shestoye Iyulya). 11 reels, Mosfilm
Scen.: Mikhail Shatrov; *dir.:* Yuli Karasik; *phot.:* (wide-screen): Mikhail Suslov;
des.: B. Blank; *mus.:* A. Shnitke.
Cast: Yuri Kayurov, Alla Demidova, Vladimir Tatosov, Vasili Lanovoi.
Sayat Nova. Armenfilm
Scen. & dir.: Sergei Paradjanov.
Wings (Krylya). Mosfilm
Scen.: Valentin Yezhov, Nataliya Ryantseva; *dir.:* Larisa Shepitko; *phot.:* (wide-
screen): Igor Slabnevich; *des.:* Ivan Plastinkin; *mus.:* P. Ledyonev.
Cast: Maya Bulgakova, P. Krymov, Zhanna Bolotova, Nikolai Grabbe.

Falling Leaves (Listopad). Gruzia-Film (Russian title: Spring Will Come Soon)
Scen.: Otar Ioseliani, T. Maglaperadze, Otar Abesadze; *dir.:* Ioseliani.
No Ford Through the Flames, (V ognye broda nyet). Lenfilm
Scen.: Yevgeni Gabrilovich, Gleb Panfilov; *dir.:* Panfilov.
Cast: Inna Churikova.

1969

A Nest of Gentlefolk. 3040 m., Mosfilm
Scen.: (from novel by Turgenev): Valentin Yezhov, Andrei Konchalovsky; *dir.:*
Konchalovsky; *colour-phot.:* Georgi Rerberg; *mus.:* Vyacheslav Ovchinnikov.
Cast: Leonid Kulagin, Beata Tyszkiewicz, Irina Kupchenko, Nikolai Gubenko.
Belorussian Station (Belorussky vokzal). 10 reels, Mosfilm
Scen.: Vadim Trunin; *dir.:* Andrei Smirnov; *phot.:* Pavel Lebeshyov; *des.:*
V. Korovin.
Cast: Anatoli Papanov, Yevgeni Leonov, Vsevolod Safonov, Alexei Glazyrin.
The Beginning (Nachalo). 2495 m., Lenfilm
Scen.: Yevgeni Gabrilovich, Gleb Panfilov; *dir.:* Panfilov; *phot.:* Dmitri Dolynin;
des.: M. Gankhman-Sverdlov; *mus.:* Vadim Bibergan.
Cast: Inna Churikova, Leonid Kuravlyov, Mikhail Kononov, Valentina Telichkina.

1970

Crime and Punishment, (Prestupleniye i nakazaniye). I, 3074 m.; II, 2981 m.,
Gorky Studio
Scen.: (from novel by Dostoyevsky): Nikolai Figurovsky, Lev Kulidjanov; *dir.:*
Kulidjanov; *phot.:* Vyacheslav Shumsky; *des.:* P. Pashkevich; *mus.:* Mikhail Ziv.
Cast: Georgi Taratorkin, Innokenti Smoktunovsky, Tatyana Bedova, Yefim
Kopelyan, Maya Bulgakova, Viktoria Fyodorova.
The Golden Gate (Zolotiye vorota). 8 reels, Mosfilm
Scen.: Yuliya Solntseva, Valeri Karen; *dir.:* Solntseva; *phot.:* Georgi Rerberg;
des.: A. Boim; *mus.:* Vyacheslav Ovchinnikov.
Cast: R. Tkachuk, Nikolai Grinko, Valentina Telichkina, Nikolai Gubenko.
By the Lake. I, 2782 m.; II; 2252 m., Gorky Studio
Scen. & dir.: Sergei Gerasimov; *phot.:* (wide-screen): Vladimir Rappoport,
Vladimir Arkhangelsky; *mus.:* Ilya Katayev.
Cast: Natalya Belokhvostikova, Oleg Zhakov, Vasili Shukshin, Valentina Telichkina.

1971

Flight (Beg). I, 3236 m.; II, 3478 m., Mosfilm
Scen.: (based on works by Mikhail Bulgakov) *& dir.:* Alexander Alov, Vladimir
Naumov; *colour-phot.:* (wide-screen): Levan Paatashvili; *des.:* A. Parkhomenko;
mus.: Nikolai Karetnikov.
Cast: Ludmilla Savelyova, Alexei Batalov, Mikhail Ulyanov, Vladislav Dvorzhetsky, Yevgeni Yevstigneyev, Oleg Yefremov.
There Was a Singing Blackbird. Gruzia-film (Russian title: Day After Day)
Scen.: Otar Ioseliani, D. Eristavi, A. Krapichashvili, O. Mekhrishvili; *dir.:*
Ioseliani; *phot.:* Abesalom Maisuradze; *mus.:* T. Bakradze.
Cast: Gela Kandelaki.
King Lear I, 7 reels; II, 7 reels, Lenfilm
Scen.: (from Shakespeare's play) *& dir.:* Grigori Kozintsev; *phot.:* (wide-screen):

Jonas Gricius; *des.:* Yevgeni Enei, V. Ulitko, S. Virsaladze; *mus.:* Dmitri Shosta-kovich.
Cast: Yuri Jarvet, Elza Radzinya, Galina Volchok, Valentina Shendrikova, Donatas Banionis, Oleg Dal, Regimantas Adomaitis, Eduard Merzin.

Daughter-in-Law (Nevestka). Turkmenfilm
Scen.: Khodjakuli & Khodjadura Narliyev; *dir.:* Khodjakuli Narliyev.

Uncle Vanya (Dyadya Vanya). 10 reels, Mosfilm
Scen.: (from Chekhov's play) & *dir.:* Andrei Konchalovsky; *colour-phot.:* Georgi Rerberg, Ye. Guslinsky; *des.:* N. Dvigubsky; *mus.:* A. Shnitke.
Cast: Innokenti Smoktunovsky, Sergei Bondarchuk, Irina Kupchenko.

Memory (Pamyat). Mosfilm
Scen. & dir.: Grigori Chukhrai; *phot.:* B. Brozhovsky, O. Zguridi; *mus.:* Mikhail Ziv.

IMAGE + SOUND

Enthusiasm (1931), by Dziga Vertov.

Road to Life (1931), directed by Nikolai Ekk. On the right, Ivan Kyrla, the Chuvash boy chosen for the rôle of Mustapha.

Golden Mountains (1931), scenario by Mikhailovsky, Nedobrovo, Yutkevich and Arnstam; directed by Sergei Yutkevich. In photo at right, the Georgian director Nikolai Shengelaya as an oil-worker.

Above: Men & Jobs (1932), written and directed by Alexander Macheret. With Nikolai Okhlopkov.

Below: The Great Consoler (1933), by Lev Kuleshov. With Alexandra Khokhlova and Andrei Fait.

Okraina (Outskirts), 1933, written by Konstantin Finn, directed by Boris Barnet. *Below:* Nikolai Bogolyubov and Alexander Chistyakov.

Above: Deserter (1933), directed by Pudovkin.
Left: Counterplan (1932), directed by Friedrich Ermler and Sergei Yutkevich. Boris Poslavsky plays a traitorous engineer.

Two solo sequences in Dovzhenko films: *left*, Stepan Shkurat as the samurai in *Aerograd* (1935); *below*, as the 'idler' in *Ivan* (1932).

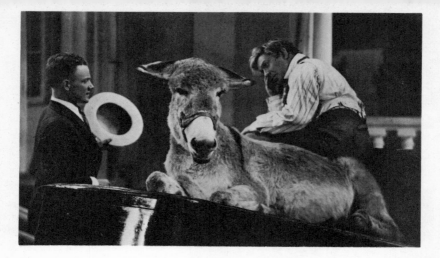

Above: Jolly Fellows (1934, Jazz Comedy), written by Alexandrov, Mass and Erdman; directed by Grigori Alexandrov. At right, Leonid Utyosov. *Right: Accordion* (1934), directed by Igor Savchenko and Yevgeni Schneider. Savchenko plays the young kulak leader.

Ostrovsky's *Groza* (1934, Thunderstorm), adapted and directed by
Vladimir Petrov. *Above:* Ivan Chuvelov (foreground, center) in the
brothel. *Opposite:* Irina Zarubina
and Varvara Massalitinova.

Above: Three Songs About Lenin (1934), by Vertov.

Below: Spain (1939), a compilation film by Esther Schub.

Tragedy and comedy in *The Youth of Maxim* (1934), written and directed by Grigori Kozintsev and Leonid Trauberg. *At the right*, Boris Chirkov as Maxim entering prison.

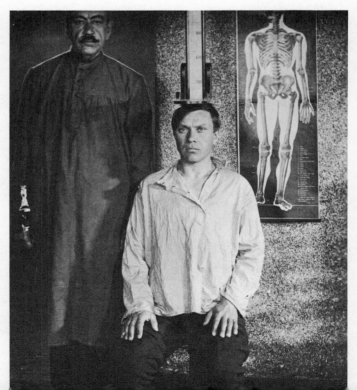

Above: A New Gulliver (1935), adapted from Swift by Grigori Roshal and Alexander Ptushko.

Below: Boule de Suif (1934), a silent adaptation of Maupassant's story by Mikhail Romm.

Chapayev (1934), written and directed by Sergei and Georgi Vasiliev. *Above*, Varvara Myasnikova and Leonid Kmit.

Georgi Vasiliev playing a rôle in a discarded episode of *Chapayev*. Found by Darya Shpirkan for her film on the Vasilievs.

Above: Revolt of the Fishermen (1934), from the novel by Anna Seghers, directed by Erwin Piscator. *Below: The Bold Seven* (1936), a scenario by Yuri German and Sergei Gerasimov, directed by Gerasimov. In the surf, Pyotr Aleinikov.

Snatchers (1934), a silent satire written and directed by Alexander Medvedkin. Pyotr Zinoviev as the peasant Khmir.

Girl-Friends (1936), written and directed by Leo Arnstam. *Above*, a design by Moisei Levin for the scene below.

Maretskaya in *Generation of Conquerors* (1936), directed by Vera Stroyeva.

Maretskaya as Sokolova in *Member of the Government* (1940), written by Katerina Vinogradskaya, directed by Alexander Zarkhi and Josif Heifits.

SOLOMON MIKHOELS
(1890–1948)

Mikhoels as Nathan's father in *The Return of Nathan Becker* (1932), written by Peretz Markisch; directed by Boris Shpis. *Below:* Mikhoels in *The Oppenheim Family* (1938), adapted from the novel by Lion Feuchtwanger, directed by Grigori Roshal.

BORIS
SHCHUKIN
(1894–1939)

Above: Shchukin (standing) in *Flyers* (1935), written by Alexander Macheret and Yuri Olesha; directed by Yuli Raisman. The kneeling actor is Ivan Koval-Samborsky.

Below: Shchukin as Lenin in *Lenin in October* (1937), written by Alexei Kapler and directed by Mikhail Romm. *At left,* Nikolai Okhlopkov.

Above: The Man with a Gun (1938), a play by Nikolai Pogodin, filmed by Sergei Yutkevich. *Below:* Nikolai Cherkasov as the *Baltic Deputy* (1937), directed by Zarkhi and Heifits.

Eisenstein's lost *Bezhin Meadow* (1935–37). The role of Pavlik Morozov was played by Victor Kartashov.

Childhood of Gorky (1938), the first of a film trilogy; scenario by Ilya Gruzdev, directed by Mark Donskoy. *Above*, Alexei Lyarsky, Mikhail Troyanovsky, Varvara Massalitinova. *Below:* Donskoy directing *Brother of a Hero* (1940), written by Lev Kassil.

Above: The unprogrammed sword-dance at the wedding in Dovzhenko's *Shchors* (1939).

Below: Rescuing a sailor from the Potemkin mutiny, in *Lone White Sail* (1937), adapted by Valentin Katayev from his novel; directed by Vladimir Legoshin.

THE GEORGIAN FILMS
OF MIKHAIL CHIAURELI

Above: The Last Masquerade (1934).

Below: Arsen (1937), with Nata Vachnadze.

Above: His Name is Sukhe-Bator (1942), directed by Zarkhi and Heifits. With Lev Sverdlin as the Mongolian leader.

Below: Pepo (Armenkino, 1935), by Amo Bek-Nazarov.

Alexander Nevsky (1938), written by Pyotr Pavlenko and Sergei Eisenstein. *Above:* Filming "The Battle on the Ice" near the Mosfilm Studio. *Below:* Naum Rogozhin as the black-robed monk.

A Great Citizen, Part I (1938), written by Bleiman, Bolshintsov and Ermler; directed by Friedrich Ermler. *Above*, Ivan Bersenev and Nikolai Bogolyubov (as Kirov). *Peter the First*, Part II (1939), written by Alexei Tolstoy; directed by Vladimir Petrov. *Below*, Nikolai Simonov and Nikolai Cherkasov as father and son.

Above: Suvorov (1940), directed by Pudovkin and Doller; Cherkasov-Sergeyev in the rôle of Suvorov. *Below: Bogdan Khmelnitsky* (1941), written by Alexander Korneichuk and directed by Igor Savchenko.

FIGHTING FILM ALBUMS, 1941

Above: From *Album* 6: 'Feast at Zhirmunka,' written by Leonov and Shpikovsky, directed by Pudovkin. *Below:* From *Album* 2: 'Incident at the Telegraph Office' (Napoleon wires a warning to Hitler), directed by Grigori Kozintsev.

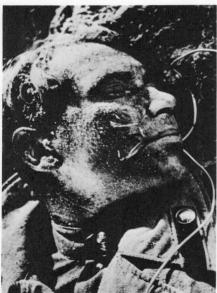

Above: Lermontov (1943), written by Konstantin Paustovsky; directed by Albert Gendelstein. With Alexei Konsovsky as Lermontov. *Left:* Mark Bernes in *The Great Turning-Point* (1945), scenario by Boris Chirskov, directed by Friedrich Ermler.

Above: The House Where I Live
(1957), written and directed by
Lev Kulijanov and Yakov Segel.
Right: Tatyana Samoilova in
The Cranes Are Flying (1951),
directed by Kalatozov from a
play by Victor Rozov.

FRIEDRICH ERMLER
(1898–1967)

Above: The filming of *Peasants* (1935);
Ermler is standing in front of the camera.
Right: The filming of *Before the Judgment-
Seat of History* (1965), with the returned
émigré, Vasili Shulgin.

SOURCES

Introduction.
1 'Thirty Years of Soviet Cinema and the Tradition of Russian Culture,' *Iskusstvo Kino*, May 1949; translated by S. Davis in *Anglo-Soviet Journal*, Summer 1950.
2 *Film Chronicle*, December 1945.

Chapter I: The Illusions 1896-1907.
Epigraph: *Narodnaya Volya*, No.11-12 (October), 1885.
1 17 [o.s.5] May 1896.
2 May 30, 1896, printed in *Iskusstvo Kino*, March 1957.
3 *Harpers Weekly*, 1896, p. 706; see also Tolstoy's story 'Khodinka' and Gorky's *Bystander* for their descriptions of this day. An objective, detailed account: *The Tsar's Coronation* [by Aylmer Maude] (London 1896).
4 Under his real name of A. Peshkov and as I. M. Pacatus. These forgotten essays were discovered by Venyamin Vishnevsky and reprinted in *Iskusstvo Kino*, August 1936. The one quoted was translated by Leonard Mins for *New Theatre and Film* (New York), March 1937. The complete text of the other is in the appendix. Supplementary Gorky documents were published by Vishnevsky in *Iskusstvo Kino*, No. 1, 1951
5-6 Félix Mesguich, *Tours de manivelle* (Paris 1933).
7 B. S. Likhachov, *Film in Russia* (Leningrad 1927).
8 *Memoirs of James Whishaw* (Methuen & Co., London 1935).
9 Mesguich, op. cit.
10 Isadora Duncan, *My Life* (Victor Gollancz, London 1928).
11 Mavor, *An Economic History of Russia* (J. M. Dent & Sons, London 1914).
12 Vsevolod Chaikovsky, *Infant Years of the Russian Cinema* (Leningrad 1928).
13 Mirsky, *Russia, A Social History* (Cresset, London 1931).
14 Likhachov, op. cit.

Chapter II: The Costume Business 1908-1911.
Epigraph: *North American Review*, March 1905; Twain's piece is dated February 2, 1905.
1 Hans von Eckardt, *Russia* (Jonathan Cape, London 1932).
2 V. F. Dobrovolsky, under the *nom-de-plume* of 'Jeremiah', in *Ciné-Phono*, January 1911; quoted by V. Vishnevsky in *Iskusstvo Kino*, November 1937.
3 *Ciné-Journal*, II, No. 54, in an amusing article by Georges Dureau, 'Histoire d'un Ballon Allemand d'un Appareil Cinématographique et de la Police Russe.' Messter also gives a detailed account in his memoirs, *Mein Weg mit dem Film* (Berlin 1936), p. 125.
4 Alexandra Tolstaya, *The Tragedy of Tolstoy* (G. Allen & Unwin, London 1933).

5 Ibid. In Sophia Tolstaya's diary of 1910, published in *The Final Struggle*, this visit is recorded: 'After nine in the evening he went with the whole group to a cinema in Arbat Street. He had never seen one before.'

6 An item in *Russkoye Slovo*, January 9, 1910. On the following day Drankov wrote this sly letter to Sophia Andreyevna: 'I take no responsibility for the diffuse paragraph in *Russkoye Slovo*, for I had no idea that the couple of words I said to a friend working on the paper would be transformed into such an article. I am once more convinced that your remarks about newspapers are the holy truth.' This and subsequent Drankov letters were found in the Tolstoy archives by V. Vishnevsky and published in 'The Legend of L. N. Tolstoy's Film-Scenario', *Iskusstvo Kino*, November 1940.

7 This and the following three documents are cited by Vishnevsky, op. cit.

8 *The Final Struggle*, translated by Aylmer Maude (G. Allen & Unwin, London 1936).

9 Alexandra Tolstaya, op. cit.

10 *The Final Struggle*.

11 See *Meyerhold*, by Nikolai Volkov (Leningrad 1929), Vol. II, pp. 162-163.

12 Nemirovich-Danchenko, *My Life in the Russian Theatre*, translated by John Cournos (Geoffrey Bles, London 1937).

13 *Russkoye Slovo*, September 15, 1911.

14 Stephen Graham, *Changing Russia* (John Lane, London 1913).

15 August 12, 1911.

16 Full details of the production and promotion of *The Defence of Sevastopol* can be found in Khanzhonkov's memoirs: *The First Years of Russian Cinematography* (Moscow 1937).

Chapter III: Enter—Author and Stockholder 1912-1913.

Epigraph: *The Letters of Sacco and Vanzetti* (Constable & Co., London 1929).

1 In '*Left-Wing*' *Communism*, written in 1920; published in English in the Marxist-Leninist Library by the Co-operative Publishing Society of Foreign Workers in the USSR (Moscow 1935).

2 Masaryk, *The Spirit of Russia* (G. Allen & Unwin, London 1919), p. 198.

3 *The Bookman* (New York), January 1911.

4 Artsibashev, in *Drama* (New York), 1916.

5 *Theatre* (New York), May 1912.

6 Alexander Kaun, *Leonid Andreyev* (B. W. Huebsch, New York 1924), p. 119.

7 'The Booth', by Vsevolod Meyerhold; translated by Alexander Bakshy, in *Drama*, August 1917.

8 The financial history of *1812* can be found in Khanzhonkov, op. cit., pp. 60-63.

9 Chaikovsky, op. cit.

10 An autobiographical foreword to a projected, unpublished volume of his scenarios; first published in Mayakovsky, *Kino* (Moscow 1940).

11 Robert Florey, *Pola Negri* (Paris 1926).

12 Chekhov, *Path of an Actor*.

13 Khanzhonkov, op. cit.

14 The following citations are quoted from *Pre-October* '*Pravda*' *on Art and Literature*, edited by S. Breitburg (Moscow 1937).

15 Ibid., pp. 258-260; originally printed in *Za Pravdu*, November 3, 1913.

16 Ibid., pp. 261-266; originally printed in *Proletarskaya Pravda*, January 12, 1914.

Chapter IV: A Crumbling Empire 1914-1917.

Epigraph: *The Letters of Tsar Nicholas and Empress Marie* . . . edited by Edward J. Bing (I. Nicholson & Watson, London 1937).

1 Their opinions can be found in Meyerhold's magazine, *Love of Three Oranges*, No. 3; Ozarovsky was cinema's champion, Volkonsky its enemy.

2 W. Mansell Merry, *Two Months in Russia, July-September*, 1914 (B. H. Blackwell, Oxford 1916).

3 Khanzhonkov, op. cit.

4 Shalyapin, *Man and Mask* (Victor Gollancz, London 1932).

5 Kaun, op. cit.

6 Rothay Reynolds, *My Slav Friends* (Mills & Boon, London 1916).

7 Linda Arvidson Griffith, *When the Movies Were Young* (New York 1925), p. 76.

8 Interview with Yuri Zhelyabuzhsky, Andreyeva's son, in Ilya Weisfeld, 'Gorky and Cinema,' *Iskusstvo Kino*, March 1958.

9 Conversations with Stanislavsky on this and later occasions are recorded in Aleinikov, *Paths of the Soviet Cinema and the Moscow Art Theatre* (Moscow 1947).

10 Lev Nikulin, *Fyodor Shalyapin* (Moscow 1954), pp. 126-7.

11 After Mozhukhin's death *Pour Vous* (February 1, 1939) printed his memoirs, written before his departure to America in 1926.

12 Stephen Graham, *Russia in* 1916 (Cassell & Co., London 1917).

13 Volkov, op. cit.

14 Ibid.

15 Quoted by Lev Nikulin, in *Sovietskoye Kino*, November-December 1934.

16 R. H. Bruce Lockhart, *Memoirs of a British Agent* (Putnam, London and New York 1932).

17 Ibid.

18 Alfred Knox, *With the Russian Army*, 1914-1917 (Hutchinson & Co., London 1921).

19 *The History of the Civil War in the USSR.* (Lawrence & Wishart, London 1937).

20 David Francis, *Russia from the American Embassy* (C. Scribner's Sons., New York 1921). Among other items on war-time Russian trade, the most illuminating are *How to Do Business with Russia; Hints and Advice to Business Men Dealing with Russia*, by C. E. W. Petersson (published in February 1917!) and 'Russia's Future Needs for Capital', by S. McRoberts, Vice-President of the National City Bank, in *Russia, Then and Now*.

21 C. F. Coxwell, *Through Russia in War-Time* (T. Fisher Unwin, London 1917).

22 Graham, op. cit.

23 Arthur Ruhl, *White Nights* (C. Scribner's Sons, New York 1917).

24 *The Soul of Russia*, edited by Winifred Stevens (London 1916).

25 *The History of the Civil War in the USSR.*

26 *Fall of the Tsarist Régime.*

27 Ibid.

28 Quoted by Terry Ramsaye in *Million and One Nights* (Simon & Schuster, New York 1926), Vol. II, p. 766.

An Interlude 1916.

1 *The Letters of the Tsar to the Tsaritsa* 1914-17, translated by A. L. Hynes from the official edition of the Romanov correspondence (John Lane, London 1929).

Chapter V: From February to October 1917.
Epigraph: *Three Sisters*, translated by Constance Garnett.
1 Khanzhonkov, op. cit.
2 James L. Houghteling, *A Diary of the Russian Revolution* (Dodd, Mead & Co., New York 1918).
3 A. Ilyin-Genevsky, *From the February Revolution to the October Revolution* 1917 (Modern Books, London 1931).
4 Capt. Donald C. Thompson, *From Czar to Kaiser, the Betrayal of Russia* (Doubleday, Page & Co., New York 1918); this is a picture book with imaginative captions that give some idea of what the sub-titles in *Blood-Stained Russia* must have been. Another of his illustrated publications is *Donald Thompson in Russia* (New York 1918).
5 A letter from Moscow, published in the New York *Evening Post*, May 5, 1917.
6 V. Rosolovskaya, *Russian Cinematography in* 1917 (Moscow 1937). All the material in this chapter relating to trade unions has been drawn from Rosolovskaya's excellent study.
7 Gardin, 'First Years of the Soviet Cinema', *Sovietskoye Kino*, November-December 1934. This is amplified in Gardin's *Reminiscences* (1949).
8 'Beecroft's Enlightening Views', printed in *Wid's Year Book*, 1919.
9 *Brachnaya gazeta*, 37, 1917, quoted by Vishnevsky in *Sovietskoye Kino*, 1-2, 1933.
10 *The History of the Civil War in the USSR*.
11 Boltyansky, 'Kino and the February Revolution', *Sovietskoye Kino*, No. 2, 1927.
12 Vishnevsky, 'The First May Day Film', *Kino* [gazeta], May 1, 1936.
13 Lockhart, op. cit., pp. 185-7.
14 Quoted in Rosolovskaya, op. cit., p. 55.
15 Ibid.
16 Rheta Childe Dorr, *Inside the Russian Revolution* (Macmillan, New York 1917).
17 Shalyapin, op. cit.
18 *Vestnik Kinematografiya*, No. 127, 1917.

Chapter VI: Moscow—Odessa—Paris 1917-1920.
Epigraph: Krylov, 'The Fable of the Gadfly and the Ant', translated by Maurice Baring.
1 Christian Brinton, 'Idols of the Russian Masses', *Cosmopolitan Magazine* (New York), April 1906.
2 Khanzhonkov, op. cit.
3 See Jean Xydias, *L'Intervention Française en Russie*, 1918-19 (Paris 1927).
4 According to Oliver Sayler, in *The Russian Theatre under the Revolution* (Boston 1920).
5 Nikolai V. Tcharykov, *Glimpses of High Politics* (G. Allen & Unwin, London 1931).
6 Mozhukhin, op. cit.
7 C. Claflin Davis, 'The Refugee Situation in Constantinople', in *Constantinople Today* (New York 1922).
8 Ibid.
9 A detailed account of Mosjoukine's French career is given by Jean Arroy in *Ivan Mosjoukine* (Paris 1927).
10 *Cinéa* (Paris), June 10, 1921.
11 Bardèche and Brasillach, *The History of the Film*, translated by Iris Barry (G. Allen & Unwin, London 1938).

Chapter VII: Peace—Bread—Land 1917-1920.

Epigraph: Franklin.

1 'I Myself', translated by Herbert Marshall in *Mayakovsky and His Poetry* (Pilot Press, London 1945).

2 Alexander Kaun, *Soviet Poets and Poetry* (University of California Press, Berkeley, 1943), p. 29.

3 The texts of this and the following document have been taken from *L'art dans la Russie nouvelle: Le cinéma*, by René Marchand and Pyotr Weinstein (Paris 1927).

3a Edgar Sisson, *One Hundred Red Days* (Yale University Press, 1931), pp. 180-2.

3b Bernard Pares, *My Russian Memoirs* (Jonathan Cape, London 1931), p. 484.

4 Joseph Noulens, *Mon Ambassade en Russie* (Paris 1933), vol. II, pp. 197-8.

4a Document in Marchand and Weinstein, op. cit.

4b Preface to Marchand and Weinstein, op. cit.

5 Document in Marchand and Weinstein, op. cit.

5a Gardin, op. cit.

6 The details on the Cibrario case are taken from the record, USSR versus National City Bank of New York, in the New York Supreme Court.

7 Mayakovsky, *Kino* (Moscow 1940).

8 *Russkoye Golos* (New York), July 24 & 31, 1938.

8a In the newspaper, *Kino*, April 11, 1937.

8b *Iskusstvo Kino*, May 1956.

9 *Iskusstvo Kino*, October 1937. Pyotr Novitsky has described his filming of Lenin during the parade on Khodinka Plain later that day, with a group of cameramen under Mikhail Koltsov's supervision. The footage taken in Red Square and at Khodinka was shown in all Moscow film-theatres on the same night.

10 These synopses are taken from an essay by N. Yezuitov, in *Iskusstvo Kino*, May 1940.

11 Vladimir Nilsen, *The Cinema as a Graphic Art*, translated by Stephen Garry (Newnes, London 1937), pp. 187-8.

12 Lansbury, *What I Saw in Russia* (Leonard Parsons, London 1920).

13 Ransome, *Six Weeks in Russia in 1919* (G. Allen & Unwin, London 1919).

14 *The Bullitt Mission to Russia* (New York 1919), p. 59.

15 Isaac McBride, *"Barbarous Soviet Russia"* (T. Seltzer, New York 1920), p. 100. Mr McBride's information came, apparently, from Maxim Gorky, but he observed a use of film in a government lying-in hospital: 'Moving pictures were shown daily, portraying to the mothers the best methods of bathing, dressing, and caring for their infants, and these were supplemented with lectures.' (p. 116).

16 Henry Noel Brailsford, *The Russian Workers' Republic* (G. Allen & Unwin, London 1921), p. 14.

17 Quoted in Huntly Carter, *The New Theatre and Cinema of Soviet Russia* (Chapman & Dodd, London 1924), pp. 247-8.

18 Quoted by Venyamin Vishnevsky, in *Iskusstvo Kino*, June 1938.

19 Vishnevsky, 'Alexander Blok and Cinema', *Iskusstvo Kino*, September 1936.

20 McBride, op. cit., pp. 99-100.

21 Jacob H. Rubin, *Moscow Mirage* (Geoffrey Bles, London 1934), pp. 135-6.

22 'At Grips with Bolshevists', reviewed in *The Bioscope*, March 11, 1920.

23 Kaun, op. cit., p. 115.

24 Ibid.

25 Kuleshov, 'Our First Experiences', *Sovietskoye Kino*, November-December 1934.

26 This and the two following citations are from an interview with Jeanne Gauzner, published in 'Soviet Films and the People Who Make Them' (ca. 1943).
27 Yezuitov, op. cit.
28 *The Moving Picture World*, February 21, 1920.
29 George Creel, *How We Advertised America* (Harper & Bros., New York 1920).
30 Igor Schwezoff, *Russian Somersault* (Hodder & Stoughton, London 1936), p. 116.
31 H. G. Wells, *Russia in the Shadows* (Hodder & Stoughton, London 1921), p. 119.
32 Sergei Eisenstein, 'Through Theatre to Cinema' in *Film Form* (New York & London 1949).

Chapter VIII: Reconstruction 1921-1923.
Epigraph: Lenin's speech of October 17, 1921, translated by J. Fineberg (*Selected Works*, Vol. 9, p. 274).
 1 'The Kinema in Soviet Russia', *Kinematograph Weekly*, July 28, 1921.
 1a 'Kinema Culture in Soviet Russia', *Kinematograph Weekly*, September 22, 1921.
 1b Walter Duranty's Foreword to Hammer, *The Quest of the Romanoff Treasure* (W. F. Payson, New York 1932).
 2 Hammer, op. cit., pp. 56-7.
 3 In a conversation with Armand Hammer, the first of the NEP concessionaires, Ibid., p. 64.
 4 Marguerite E. Harrison, *Marooned in Moscow* (George H. Doran Co., New York 1921), p. 168.
 5 Kuleshov, 'Twenty Years', *Iskusstvo Kino*, March 1940.
 6 From a statement in the *ARA Bulletin*, September 1923, p. 13.
 7 Kuleshov, 'Our First Experiences', *Sovietskoye Kino*, November-December 1934.
 8 Kuleshov, 'Twenty Years', *Iskusstvo Kino*, March 1940.
 9 From a letter written by Lunacharsky to Boltyansky, at the latter's request, on January 9, 1925.
10 'Kino-Pravda', *Sovietskoye Kino*, November-December 1934.
11 New York *Times*, June 4, 1922.
12 In *Art of the Cinema* (Moscow 1929); this particular experiment was first announced in print in *Kino-Phot*, No. 3, 1922.
13 Eisenstein, 'My First Film', *Sovietsky Ekran*, No. 50, 1928.
14 Carter, op. cit., pp. 246-7.

Chapter IX: The Youth of an Art 1924-1925.
Epigraph: Lamb to Robert Lloyd, November 18, 1802.
 1 Kuleshov, 'From "West" to "Canary",' *Sovietsky Ekran*, March 12, 1929.
 2 Alexander Wicksteed, *Life Under the Soviets* (John Lane, London 1928).
 3 Kuleshov, op. cit.
 4 Pudovkin, *Film Technique*, translated by Ivor Montagu (first pub. Gollancz, London 1929).
 5 *Film Technique* combines Pudovkin's two handbooks, 'Film Director and Film Material', and 'Film Scenario and Its Theory'.
 6 Eisenstein, 'Through Theatre to Cinema'.
 7 In a report published in *Britain and the Soviets* (Martin Lawrence, London 1936).
 8 Tretyakov, *Our Cinema: Cinema Is an International Language* (VOKS, Moscow 1928).
 9 Alexander Belenson, *Cinema Today* (Moscow 1925).

10 Brik, in *Sovietskoye Kino*, No. 2, 1926.

11 Quoted in Belenson, op. cit.

12 Yuri Tinyanov, in *Sovietsky Ekran*, No. 14, 1929.

13 Eisenstein analysed his theatrical career in 'Through Theatre to Cinema'.

14 Babette Deutsch, 'The Russian Theatre Today', *Theatre Arts Monthly*, August 1925.

15 Eisenstein, 'Through Theatre to Cinema'.

16 In *Kino* [gazeta], May 24, 1940; quoted in *The Film Sense* (New York 1942), p. 80.

17 *Sight and Sound*, Autumn 1956.

17a *New Statesman*, October 11, 1958.

18 Ernestine Evans, 'The Soviet Idea in the "Kino",' *Asia* (New York), August 1926.

19 Paxton Hibben, 'The Movies in Russia', *The Nation* (New York), November 11, 1925.

20 Samuel Northrup Harper, *Civic Training in Soviet Russia* (University of Chicago Press 1929), pp. 327-8.

21 In an essay contributed to the memorial volume edited by M. N. Aleinikov, *Yakov Protazanov* (Moscow 1948).

22 Ernestine Evans, op. cit.

23 Yuri Zhelyabuzhsky, 'School of Realistic Craftsmanship', *Iskusstvo Kino*, No. 10, 1938. See also, Zhelyabuzhsky, in *Iskusstvo Kino*, No. 2, 1937, and Pudovkin's criticism, in *Film Technique*, pp. 114-15.

24 Wicksteed, op. cit., p. 115. See also Eisenstein, *Film Form*, pp. 251-2.

25 Victor Seroff, *Dmitri Shostakovich* (Knopf, New York 1943).

26 In *Information Bulletin*, USSR Embassy in Washington, No. 86, July 18, 1942.

Chapter X: Theory into Practice 1925-1926.

Epigraph: *Never to Die: The Egyptians in Their Own Words*, edited by Josephine Mayer and Tom Prideaux (Viking Press, New York 1938).

1 In *Eisenstein: Potemkin* (Moscow 1926), a brochure containing three essays, by Shklovsky, Kuleshov, and Tisse.

2 Posthumously published in *Iskusstvo Kino*, No. 4, 1950; translated as 'The Birth of a Film', in *The Hudson Review*, Summer 1951.

3 'The Birth of a Film' describes the discovery of this 'actor'.

4 Alexandrov, 'From the Memories of a Regisseur-Assistant', *Iskusstvo Kino*, December 1955.

5 Solski, 'The End of Sergei Eisenstein', *Commentary* (New York), March 1949.

6 The most detailed account of the effect of *Potemkin* on Berlin audiences is given in Feuchtwanger's novel *Success*. At the beginning of Book IV the former Bavarian Minister of Justice goes sceptically to the theatre to see the film ('Battle Cruiser Orlov') that so much fuss is being made about, and finds himself unwillingly drawn into the action, finally identifying himself with the mutineers. The Berlin success of *Potemkin* is often partially ascribed to the accompanying score, composed by Edmund Meisel.

7 Mayakovsky's speech at the Sovkino discussion, October 15, 1927, printed in Mayakovsky, *Kino* (Moscow 1940).

8 Lunacharsky's contribution to *The Soviet Film Confronted by Society*, edited by K. Maltsev (Moscow 1928); he went on to say: 'Previous to this the very good

film by Eisenstein, *Strike*, experienced a similar neglect, even in worker neighbourhoods. The excellent *Mother*, by Pudovkin, a genuine chef d'oeuvre of Russian cinema, had a very bleak reception in Moscow, and only in a few provinces was the film kept in circulation because, if I'm not mistaken, it didn't show a loss.'

9 'The Structure of the Film', *Iskusstvo Kino*, June 1939; translated in *Film Form*.
10 Paxton Hibben, op. cit.
11 From Vertov's contribution to a collection, *Paths of Art* (Proletkult, Moscow 1925).
12 Vladimir Nedobrovo, *FEX* (Leningrad 1928).
13 Quoted in ibid.
14 S. Froelich, *Art of a Film-Director*, on S. A. Gerasimov (Moscow 1954).
15 An address to a 1933 Leningrad conference of cameramen, quoted in Nilsen, op. cit.
16 Harper, op. cit., p. 328.
17 Voitsik, 'How Protazanov Taught Me', in the *Protazanov* memorial volume (1948).
18 One of these problems, recording the movement of a sea-lion, is fully described in *Film Technique*, pp. 83-4.
19 Interview with Jeanne Gauzner.
20 A document of Zarkhi's desperate attempt to re-cast the whole story in terms of *The Father* was found in the Mezhrabpom archive; his draft outline was published in *Iskusstvo Kino*, No. 3, 1936.
21 Actually, *Mechanics of the Brain* was not completed and released until after the release of *Mother*, in the autumn of 1926.
22 The lectures published as *Film Acting*, translated by Ivor Montagu (Newnes, London 1935).
23 Aleinikov, op. cit.
24 Nilsen, op. cit. See illustrations for a still of this shot.
25 N. Yezuitov, *Pudovkin, Creative Paths* (Moscow 1937).
26 *Sovietsky Ekran*, August 31, 1926.
27 Golovnya, 'Fundamentals of Camera Work', *Sovietsky Ekran*, November 1, 1927.
28 *Film Technique* ('Film Direction and Film Material'), p. 64; Hanns Sachs verified this power in his analysis of three seemingly casual gestures, in *Potemkin*, *Mother*, and Lubitsch's *Three Women* (*Close Up*, November 1928).
29 Golovnya, 'Vsevolod Pudovkin While Filming', *Iskusstvo Kino*, August 1953.
30 First in Germany, then England in Ivor Montagu's translation as *Film Technique* (1929). A 'Memorial Edition' (Vision Press, London 1958) combines the English texts of *Film Technique* and Pudovkin's later book, *Film Acting*.
31 *Film Technique*, from the introduction to the German edition, p. xvii.
31a *The New Yorker*, October 19, 1957.
32 *Rewind* (Moscow 1927).
33 Bryher, *Film Problems of Soviet Russia* (Pool. Territet 1929).
34 Tretyakov, op. cit.
35 Printed in *Kino-Front*, April 15, 1927.
36 Okhlopkov as interviewed by A. Kruk, in *Sovietsky Ekran*, November 20, 1928.
37 A speech at the All-Union Creative Conference of Film-Workers, 1935; translated in the VOKS publication, *Soviet Cinema* (1936).
38 In *Zvenigora* (Kiev 1928), a brochure about the film; translated by Alex Chorny.
39 Tretyakov, 'China on the Screen', *Sovietskoye Kino*, No. 5-6, 1927.

40 Freeman, *An American Testament* (Victor Gollancz, London 1938); see also *Voices of October* (Vanguard, New York 1930).

Chapter XI: Anniversary Year 1927.

Epigraph: T. S. Eliot's introduction to *Savonarola*, by Charlotte Eliot (R. Cobden Sanderson, London 1926).

1 Shub, 'Road from the Past', *Sovietskoye Kino*, November–December 1934.
2 Her last job as editor for someone else's film was on *The Skotinins*, directed by Roshal and released two months before the *Romanov* film.
3 Capt. Von Hahn-Jagielski and Georges Meyer (Mundviller) had served as official cameramen to the Imperial Court.
4 In an interview with V. Pfeffer, *Sovietsky Ekran*, November 1, 1927.
5 Shub, 'Road from the Past'.
6 There is a posthumously published selection from this quantity of Pudovkin's writings: *Izbrannyiye Statyi* (Moscow 1955).
7 In a letter to VUFKU, September 29, 1926, published in Mayakovsky, *Kino*, edited by A. V. Fevralsky (Moscow 1940); Fevralsky's detailed introduction was first published in *Iskusstvo Kino*, May 1936. All the following information and documents on Mayakovsky's work for films are taken from this volume.
7a This scenario, discovered after both of Fevralsky's editions, was published in *Iskusstvo Kino*, No. 5, 1955.
8 In *Novy Lef*, No. 2, 1927.
8a *Benia Krik*, translated by Ivor Montagu and Sergei Nolbandov (Collet's, London 1935).
9 Wicksteed, op. cit.
10 *Sovietskoye Kino*, No. 6-7, 1926.
11 In *Film Problems of Soviet Russia*, where she gives a detailed synopsis of the story (pp. 85-90).
12 *Soviet Cinema*, by Thorold Dickinson and Catherine de la Roche (Falcon Press, London 1948); this also provides an excellent reel-by-reel summary of *October* as released.
13 Tisse, in *Sovietsky Ekran*, No. 50, 1926.
14 Nilsen, op. cit.
15 Golovnya, 'Fundamentals of Camera Work', *Sovietsky Ekran*, November 1, 1927.
16 An afterword to *Japanese Cinema*, by N. Kaufman (Moscow 1929), translated as 'The Cinematographic Principle and the Ideogram;' see *Film Form*.
17 'Mass Movies', *The Nation* (New York), November 9, 1927; written by Louis Fischer on the basis of conversations with Eisenstein.
18 Told to Ivor Montagu, quoted in the memorial brochure, *Eisenstein 1898-1948* (London).
19 Lev Shatov, in *Novy Zritel*, November 8, 1927.
20 Tretyakov, *Our Cinema*.
21 *Kino* (Leningrad), November 7, 1927.
22 *Kino* [gazeta], December 20, 1927.
23 Paul Babitsky, in *The Soviet Film Industry* (Praeger, New York 1955).
24 Nikolai Lebedev, *An Outline History of Cinema in the USSR* (Moscow 1947). He gives no source for this quotation of Eisenstein's vulnerable words.
25 *The Nation* (New York), June 27, 1928. These are the same two examples of 'intellectual cinema' cited by Eisenstein in his article on 'A Dialectic Approach to Film Form', dated April 1929 (see *Film Form*).

26 Autobiographical sketch of 1935.
27 Dovzhenko, 'About My Film', in *Zvenigora* (Kiev 1928).
28 Eisenstein, 'Birth of a Master', *Iskusstvo Kino*, No. 1-2, 1940. The full text of this article, in another translation, appears in Eisenstein, *Notes of a Film Director* (Moscow 1958).
29 Published in *Iskusstvo Kino*, May 1958.

Chapter XII: The Cost of Virtuosity 1928-1930.

Epigraph: *The Autobiography of Lincoln Steffens* (G. G. Harrap & Co., London 1931).
 1 *Paths of the Cinema*, the proceedings of the conference as edited by B. S. Olkhovi (Moscow 1929); following quotations also from this record.
 2 Bryher, op. cit., p. 16.
 3 Interview with Jeanne Gauzner.
 4 Inkizhinov, 'Bair and I', *Sovietsky Ekran*, August 14, 1928.
 5 Yezuitov, op. cit.
 6 *Sovietsky Ekran*, February 28, 1928.
 7 'Methods of Montage' (Autumn 1929), in *Film Form*.
 8 A. Kraszna-Krausz, 'The First Russian Soundfilms', *Close Up*, December 1931.
 9 'A Dialectic Approach to Film Form' (Autumn 1929), in *Film Form*.
10 Autobiographical sketch of 1935.
11 O. Borisov, 'Film in Work', *Kino* (Kiev), No. 10, 1928.
12 Published in the collection, *Book of Scenarios* (Moscow 1935).
13 An interview translated in *Experimental Cinema*, No. 5, 1934.
14 *National Board of Review Magazine* (New York), November 1929.
15 Barbusse, *One Looks at Russia*, translated by Warre B. Wells (J. M. Dent & Sons, London 1931).
16 *Sovietsky Ekran*, September 10, 1929.
17 *Sovietsky Ekran*, July 3, 1928; caricatures by Getmansky.
18 An interview with E. Hellmund-Waldow, *Close Up*, July 1928.
19 *Partisan Review* (New York), August-September 1938, p. 70.
20 In the collection, *Face of the Soviet Film Actor* (Moscow 1935).
21 *Sovietsky Ekran*, August 28, 1928.
22 In Valentin Turkin, 'Lessons of "Turksib"', *Sovietsky Ekran*, June 11, 1929.
23 *Kino* [gazeta], October 23, 1928; details on Shub's Tolstoy film are taken from her article, 'How I Worked on the Film, "Russia of Nikolai II and Tolstoy"', *Sovietsky Ekran*, October 2, 1928.
24 Translated in *Film Writing Forms*, by Lewis Jacobs (New York 1934).
25 *Sovietsky Ekran*, December 11, 1926.
26 *Sovietsky Ekran*, January 25, 1929.
27 Pera Attasheva, 'Heroine of "General"', *Sovietsky Ekran*, February 5, 1929.
28 'The Filmic Fourth Dimension' (August 27, 1929), in *Film Form*.
29 'Methods of Montage', written in London in the autumn of 1929 to supplement the foregoing (see *Film Form*).
30 Ibid.
31 *The Film Sense*.
32 Eisenstein and Alexandrov, 'Twelfth', *Sovietsky Ekran*, November 6, 1928.
33 Alexandrov, 'Great Friend of Soviet Cinema', *Iskusstvo Kino*, December 1939. If Eisenstein made a record of this interview it has not yet been published.
34 Barbusse, op. cit.

35 There are also fragmentary film-records of Kachalov performances in plays. Meyerhold's two pre-revolutionary films have not been preserved.

36 *Close Up*, November 1930.

37 The last reel only, in *Sovietsky Ekran*, January 1, 1929.

38 An obituary article on Dovzhenko, *Sight and Sound*, Summer 1957.

39 Ibid.

40 'Dickens, Griffith, and the Film Today' (1944), in *Film Form*.

Chapter XIII: Industrial Revolution 1930-1933.

Epigraph: Mark Twain, *Life on the Mississippi*, Chap. XXVII.

1 First published in the Leningrad journal, *Zhizn Iskusstvo*, August 5, 1928. The English translation quoted appears in Eisenstein's *Film Form*.

2 Pudovkin's appreciation of Rzheshevsky's originality ('The Creative Work of the Writer in Films') appeared in *Na literaturnom postu*, No. 5-6, 1930, and was translated as 'Scenario and Direction', in *Experimental Cinema*, February 1931.

3 *Proletarskoye Kino*, January 1932; translated in *Film Technique*.

4 Bourke-White, *Eyes on Russia* (Simon & Schuster, New York 1931).

5 These details, along with subsequent matter on the first Soviet sound-films, are taken from Nikolai Lebedev's chapter on this period, published in two versions (1955 and 1956). Another work used for this period was *History of Soviet Film Art of the Sound Period* (Moscow 1946), a valuable compilation by I. V. Sokolov of professional accounts and contemporary criticism.

6 In *Soviet Cinema* (London 1948).

7 *Proletarskoye Kino*, March 1932. This dossier of praise included comments by René Clair and Moholy-Nagy.

8 *Soviet Cinema* (London 1948). In one sequence Ekk also used some of Pudovkin's slow-motion suggestions.

9 In a speech of July 12, 1931, published in *Proletarskoye Kino*, No. 9, 1931.

10 Macheret, ' "Men and Jobs", In Lieu of Preface to the Film,' *Proletarskoye Kino*, No. 13-14, 1932.

11 Nikolai Lebedev, 'Historical-Revolutionary Films', in *Outlines of the History of Soviet Cinema* (Moscow 1956).

12 Autobiography dated December 1939, published in *Iskusstvo Kino*, May 1958.

13 Translated in special supplement to *Sight and Sound*, November 1947.

14 Quoted in *Sovietskoye Kino*, No. 5-6, 1933.

14a See Tretyakov, *Svanetia* (Moscow, 1928).

15 *Film Produktion der UdSSR 1931-2;* this catalogue names the cameraman as Gegelashvili, who must have been Kalatozov's camera-assistant.

16 Harry Alan Potamkin, 'The New Kino', *Close Up*, March 1931.

17 Nos. 5 and 9-10, 1932.

18 *Soviet Cinema* (London 1948).

19 'Rhythmic Problems in My First Sound Film', in appendix to English edition of *Film Technique*.

20 'Asynchronism as a Principle of Sound Film;' this and the previously cited appendix to *Film Technique* were written for that purpose while Pudovkin was completing *Deserter*.

21 *Film Acting;* his earlier description of this sequence appeared in the appendix to *Film Technique*.

22 Introducing V. Rosolovskaya's analytical article in *Sovietskoye Kino*, No. 11, 1933.

23 Pudovkin, *Film Acting* (Newnes, London, 1937).

Chapter XIV: Witnessed Years 1934-1937.
Epigraph: Yevgeni Vakhtangov, *Notebooks*, April 1922.
1 *Literaturnaya gazeta*, November 18, 1934; translated by Leon Rutman, *New Theatre*, January 1935.
1a *Film Acting*.
2 Alexandrov, in interview, *Moscow Daily News*, May 18, 1935.
3 The scenario was published in *Iskusstvo Kino*, December 1936; the discussion of it in the issue of April 1937.
4 *Moscow Daily News*, March 6, 1936.
5 Boris Babochkin, in *Face of the Soviet Film Actor* (Moscow 1935); a partial English translation in *Soviet Cinema* (Moscow 1935).
6 Ibid.
7 Translated by Ivor Montagu as 'Film Form, 1935—New Problems', in *Life and Letters Today*, September-December 1935.
8 The translation here of Dovzhenko's speech is from that used by Marie Seton in her biography, *Sergei M. Eisenstein* (Bodley Head, London 1952).
9 Also described, from another point of view, by Marie Seton, op. cit.
10 Published in *For a Great Film Art* (Moscow 1935); the translation quoted here is that of Marie Seton, op. cit.
11 Kozintsev, 'Extracts from a Book about the Film-Actor', *Iskusstvo Kino*, January 1938.
12 Ibid.
13 L. Trauberg's report at the creative conference (*For a Great Film Art*, Moscow 1935).
14 Kozintsev, op. cit.
15 Terry Ramsaye, 'Soviet Propaganda Aided by New York Press Acclaim', *Motion Picture Herald*, November 17, 1934.
16 Schneiderov, in an interview with A. Amasovich, *Moscow Daily News*, May 9, 1935.
17 Ermler, in an interview with Amasovich, *Moscow Daily News*, April 10, 1935.
18 Fragments from Medvedkin's 'literary scenario' were published in *Sovietskoye Kino*, No. 11, 1933.
19 *Moscow Daily News*, November 22, 1935.
20 The years of collaboration have been amply documented in print: Vishnevsky's *We from Kronstadt* (Moscow 1936); Vishnevsky and Dzigan, 'How We Made the Film', in *Pravda*, March 3, 1936; extracts from Vishnevsky's letters to Dzigan, in *Iskusstvo Kino*, June 1954.
21 Vishnevsky to Dzigan, October 21, 1934; *Iskusstvo Kino*, June 1954.
22 Cherkasov, *Notes of a Soviet Actor* (Foreign Languages Publishing House, Moscow, n.d.).
23 First published in *Sovietskoye Iskusstvo*, April 17, 1937; reprinted, with slight alterations, in the pamphlet, *About the Film 'Bezhin Meadow' of Eisenstein* (Moscow 1937); a complete English translation in *International Literature*, No. 8, 1937, reprinted in Marie Seton, op. cit.
24 Shumyatsky, in *Soviet Cinema*, edited by Arosev (Moscow 1935).

Chapter XV: Full Capacity 1938-1939.
Epigraph: Goethe, *Wilhelm Meister's Apprenticeship*, translated by R. Dillon Boylan (Bohn, London 1855).
1 *Pravda*, March 24, 1938.

2 Ibid.; quotations is from summary published by the United States Department of Commerce (March 1939).

3 In Lenfilm's weekly, *Cadre*, February 5, 1936.

4 *Iskusstvo Kino*, September 1939.

5 Massalitinova, 'How I Worked in the Film, *Childhood of Gorky*', *Iskusstvo Kino*, July 1938.

6 In a discussion of *The Childhood of Gorky*, on October 17, 1938; the stenographic report was published in the anthology, *Film-Direction* (Moscow 1939).

7 Vsevolod Vishnevsky, *Eisenstein* (Moscow 1939).

8 Okhlopkov, 'Work on the Image', *Iskusstvo Kino*, August 1939.

9 *The Film Sense:* see also Eisenstein's preface to Nestyev's biography, *Prokofiev* (New York 1946).

10 Details on Shchukin's portrayal of Lenin are taken from N. Lebedev, 'Shchukin's Work on Lenin's Image', *Iskusstvo Kino*, February 1941 (incorporated in Lebedev, *Shchukin Film-Actor*, Moscow 1944). In *Man on the Screen* (Moscow 1947) Sergei Yutkevich published extracts from his diary relating to *November*.

11 Dovzhenko, 'Teacher and Friend of the Artist', *Izvestia*, November 5, 1936; reprinted in *Iskusstvo Kino*, October 1937.

12 'The Film in USSR—1937', *The Cine-Technician*, August-September 1937.

13 *Kino* [gazeta], May 5, 1939.

Chapter XVI: Semi-War 1939-1941.

Epigraph: Lenin, *Left-Wing Communism*, Ch. IV, footnote (*Selected Works*, Vol. 2, Pt. 2, p. 357).

1 *Pravda*, November 7, 1940; translated by William Mann as 'The Path to Art', *Soviet Russia Today*, May 1941.

2 The first 145 shots of this script are translated in an appendix to *The Film Sense*.

3 *Literaturnaya gazeta*, July 19, 1951.

4 Weisfeld, 'Birth of an Idea' (on some of Eisenstein's unrealized scripts), *Iskusstvo Kino*, January 1958.

5 Pudovkin, 'The Russian Army Crosses the Alps', *Izvestia*, October 5, 1940.

6 In *The Coal Industry*, November 16, 1940, quoted in Sokolov's anthology of criticism.

Chapter XVII: Test 1941-1947.

Epigraph: Aristophanes, *The Birds*, translated by Gilbert Murray (G. Allen & Unwin, London 1950).

1 Bourke-White, *Shooting the Russian War* (Simon & Schuster, New York 1942).

2 'Filming the Patriotic War', *Information Bulletin*, USSR Embassy in Washington, August 4, 1942.

3 *Cinema Chronicle*, June 1945; translated in *Hollywood Quarterly*, July 1947.

4 Roman Karmen, 'Film Chroniclers of Leningrad', *VOKS Bulletin*, No. 7-8, 1942.

5 V. Smirnov, *Documentary Films of the Great Patriotic War* (Moscow 1947).

6 *Hollywood Reporter*, July 1, 1942.

7 Ralph Parker, in New York *Times*, April 15, 1944.

8 Mikhail Slutsky, in *Information Bulletin*, USSR Embassy in Washington, October 31, 1942.

9 *Information Bulletin*, September 3, 1942.

10 *Moscow News*, July 20, 1942.

11 *American Cinematographer*, August 1944; article written two years previously.
12 Pudovkin, 'My Conception of Nakhimov', *Cinema Chronicle*, September 1944.
13 English translations of his stories appeared in *Soviet Short Stories* 1944 (London): 'Mother Stoyan', and 'The Night Before the Battle'.
14 In an interview with Venyamin Vishnevsky, *Information Bulletin*, November 12, 1942.
15 *Cinema Chronicle*, May 1945.
16 Vera Maretskaya, 'Remembrances on V-Day', *Cinema Chronicle*, May 1945.
17 *Cinema Chronicle*, August 1944.
18 *International Literature*, November 1944.
19 *Cinema Chronicle*, January 1946.
20 'Ivan Grozny', *VOKS Bulletin*, No, 7-8, 1942.
21 Cherkasov, op. cit.
22 Eisenstein, 'How We Filmed *Ivan the Terrible*', *Cinema Chronicle*, February 1945 (translated from *Izvestia*, February 4, 1945).
23 In one of Dovzhenko's last interviews, in September 1956, with Georges Sadoul, *Les lettres françaises*, 6-12 December 1956.
24 Raizman, 'How We Made the Film *Berlin*', *Cinema Chronicle*, July 1945.
25 Donskoy, 'My Work on the Film *Unvanquished*', *Cinema Chronicle*, October 1945.
26 New York *Times*, March 11, 1946.
27 An editorial, 'Increase the Sense of Responsibility Amongst Film Experts;' I quote the translation made by the British Films Officer in Moscow.
28 Vasiliev's article, 'Improve the Supervision of Film Studios;' the quoted summary was prepared by the British Films Officer in Moscow.
29 Translated in Babitsky and Rimberg, *The Soviet Film Industry* (New York 1955).
30 Ermler and Chirskov, in *Soviet Literature*, April-May 1946.
31 In an interview with Zinaida Ginsburg, *Cinema Chronicle*, January 1946.
32 Ermler and Chirskov, op. cit.
33 *Kultura i zhizn*, October 20, 1946; I quote the translation used in Marie Seton's biography.
34 Alexander Werth, 'Art as Soviet Artillery', *The Nation* (New York), February 14, 1948.
35 S. Froelich, op. cit.

Postscript 1948-1958.

Epigraph: Coleridge, *Notebooks*, ed. by Kathleen Coburn (Pantheon Books, New York 1957), No. 950.
1 *Kultura i zhizn*, July 31, 1947, translated in *Sight and Sound*, Autumn 1947.
2 *Les lettres françaises*, December 6-12, 1956.
3 Dovzhenko's script is translated in *Soviet Literature*, 6, 1957.

INDEX